ADVANCED NATIONAL CERTIFICATE MATHEMATICS

VOLUME I

THE TECHNICAL COLLEGE SERIES

General Editor
E. G. STERLAND,
M.A., B.Sc. (Eng.), C.Eng., M.I.Mech.E., A.F.R.Ae.S.
Principal of the Bristol Aeroplane Technical College

OTHER BOOKS OF INTEREST

Engineering Metallurgy
(in two volumes)

R. A. HIGGINS, B.Sc., F.I.M.

Higher National Certificate Workshop Technology

T. NUTTALL, A.M.I.Mech.E., A.M.I.P.

An Introduction to Advanced Electrical Engineering

C. JONES, B.Sc., C.Eng., M.I.E.E., A.M.Brit.I.R.E.

Principles of Engineering Production

A. J. LISSAMAN, C.Eng., A.M.I.Mech.E., M.I.Prod.E.
S. J. MARTIN, C.Eng., M.I.Mech.E., A.M.I.Prod.E.

Engineering Thermodynamics

G. THURLOW, B.Sc.(Eng.), C.Eng., A.M.I.Mech.E.
A. B. LEE, B.Sc.(Eng.), C.Eng., A.M.I.Mech.E.

An Introduction to Servomechanism

F. L. WESTWATER, O.B.E., M.A.(Edin.), M.A.(Cantab.), C.Eng., M.I.E.E.
W. A. WADDELL, B.Sc., C.Eng., M.I.E.E.

ADVANCED NATIONAL CERTIFICATE MATHEMATICS

J. PEDOE

M.A. (Cantab.), B.Sc. (Lond.), F.S.S.

Formerly Senior Lecturer, the College of Technology, Leicester

VOLUME ONE

THE ENGLISH UNIVERSITIES PRESS LTD

SAINT PAUL'S HOUSE WARWICK LANE

LONDON, E.C.4

"They were taught their elementary mathematics exactly as though they were to proceed in later years to take their degrees as high wranglers. Of course, most of them collapsed at the first stage.... anyhow, as they soon forgot it all it did not seem to matter."

A. N. Whitehead

Essays in Science and Philosophy

First Edition 1951
Second Impression (with corrections) 1954
Third Impression 1955
Fourth Impression 1957
Fifth Impression 1958
Sixth Impression (with corrections) 1961
Seventh Impression 1964
Second Edition 1965
Second Impression 1968

S.B.N. 340 04506 X

Printed and Bound in Great Britain for the English Universities Press, Limited, by Richard Clay (The Chaucer Press), Ltd., Bungay, Suffolk

GENERAL EDITOR'S FOREWORD

The last twenty years have seen far-reaching changes in technical education, changes whose objectives have been to meet the ever increasing demands of technology. A new pattern of technical education is now emerging as a result of a series of Government committees and white papers. Initially, attention was directed perhaps more intensely to the education of technologists resulting in the expansion of the universities, a greater emphasis on the teaching of science in schools and the establishment of the Colleges of Advanced Technology.

The training of technologists has hitherto fallen into two broad categories: university courses and National Certificate courses arranged on a part-time day release basis for apprentices in industry. These part-time courses have become the route through which the majority of professional engineers have received their training. It is, however, unlikely that this state of affairs will continue in the future. The professional Institutions have rightly raised their entrance requirements to a level which the part-time day release student will find extremely difficult to achieve; at the same time the greatly increased facilities for full-time and sandwich courses will provide much more satisfactory educational system for those wishing to attain professional status.

Latterly, more attention has been given to the better training of technicians, craftsmen and operatives. The Government white paper "Better Opportunities in Technical Education" seeks to establish a new pattern for technical college courses at these levels. The very high failure rate in Ordinary and Higher National Certificate courses which has caused such concern in recent years is, it is hoped, to be avoided by the introduction of the new General Course. This is designed as a diagnostic course to determine whether a student is best suited to continue with an Ordinary National Certificate course, a craft or operative course, or a technician course. The City and Guilds of London Institute are making radical changes in their existing courses, and designing new technician courses to fulfil these objectives.

The Technical College Series of books covers the General Course in Engineering, National Certificate, Higher National Certificate, Degree and the very wide field of technician courses. Many of the books in the series are now standard works, having stood the test of time over a long period of years. Such books are reviewed from time to time and new editions published to keep them up to date, both in respect of new technological developments and changing examination requirements. New works are constantly being added to the list as new courses are arranged and new techniques developed. The publishers are fully aware of the part that well-written up-to-date text-books can play in supplementing teaching, and it is their intention that the Technical College Series shall continue to make a substantial contribution to the development of technical education.

E. G. Sterland

FROM PREFACE TO FIRST EDITION

THE standard of Mathematics required in the Higher National Certificate and the various degrees in Engineering is being steadily raised since, without a good mathematical background, the student will not be able to cope with his present-day lectures on engineering subjects. This book has been written to meet this requirement, and is intended as a help to the student studying for the A.1 examination of the Higher National Certificate or for an examination such as Part I of the B.Sc.(Eng.) examination of London University.

As an aid to the student (and at the risk of boring his lecturer) a certain amount of repetition has been included. There are a large number of worked examples illustrating the text, followed by a set of exercises on the text. The book contains some twelve hundred exercises with answers, and the student should do a large proportion of them. A set of miscellaneous examples for both Higher National and Degree students is given at the end.

The author as an undergraduate at one university often heard distant noises and was told that they were caused by the engineers at their Mathematics—baying at the lecturer and his subject. It is believed that the standard of work in this book may safely be taught to engineers without causing despair to the teacher or taught.

In the proof stage as Professor of Mathematical Physics at the Royal Military College of Science, Sir Graham Sutton, C.B.E., D.Sc., F.R.S., Director-General, Meteorological Office, read the book and made a large number of suggestions. Most of these were gladly and gratefully adopted but here and there the author's obstinacy prevailed, and this probably accounts for any shortcomings that exist in the book.

The author's debt to the publishers is immense. They have taken an infinite amount of trouble with his wishes and the text and produced a book with never (or hardly ever) an error.

Various authorities have given permission for their examination questions to be produced, and the author wishes to express his thanks to them. London University (denoted by L.U.), the Union of Lancashire and Cheshire Institutes (U.L.C.I.), and the Cambridge University Press for the Qualifying Examination in Mechanical Tripos (Q.E.).

Notice of errors or suggestions will be gratefully acknowledged.

J. P.

Leicester.

PREFACE TO SECOND EDITION

In this second edition a number of changes have been made. Chapter I on the use of Naperian logarithms has been omitted, but some of its exercises have been transferred to the miscellaneous set at the end of the book. Chapters 2, 3, 4 have now become Chapters 3, 1, 2 respectively in this new edition. A new Chapter 4 on functions and continuity has been added. Chapter 9 now uses the straight line equation and its properties to introduce the elements of Linear Programming. The chapter on differential equations has been enlarged. Here and there the text has been expanded and given a less elementary outlook. At the end of the book are three new chapters on probability and statistics. A large number of new exercises have been added. The additions are so many that the book can almost be regarded as a new one. It is hoped that it retains whatever usefulness to the student it originally possessed.

J. P.

Leicester, 1965.

CONTENTS

LIST OF FORMULAE

Differential and Integral Calculus (Standard Forms only)

Function.	*Derivative.*	*Integral.*
x^n.	nx^{n-1} (all n).	$x^{n+1}/(n+1)$ $(n \neq -1)$.
x^{-1}.	$-x^{-2}$	$\log \lvert x \rvert$.

Circular Functions

$\sin ax$.	$a \cos ax$.	$-\dfrac{1}{a} \cos ax$.
$\cos ax$.	$-a \sin ax$.	$\dfrac{1}{a} \sin ax$.
$\tan ax$.	$a \sec^2 ax$.	$-\dfrac{1}{a} \log \lvert \cos ax \rvert$.
$\sin^{-1}(x/a)$.	$1/\sqrt{(a^2 - x^2)}$.	
$\cos^{-1}(x/a)$.	$-1/\sqrt{(a^2 - x^2)}$.	
$\tan^{-1}(x/a)$.	$a/(a^2 + x^2)$.	
$1/\sqrt{(a^2 - x^2)}$.		$\sin^{-1}(x/a)$.
$1/(a^2 + x^2)$.		$\dfrac{1}{a} \tan^{-1}(x/a)$.

Exponential, Logarithmic and Hyperbolic Functions

$1/x$.	$-x^{-2}$.	$\log \lvert x \rvert$.
e^{ax}.	ae^{ax}.	$\dfrac{1}{a} e^{ax}$.
$\log(ax + b)$.	$a/(ax + b)$.	
$\operatorname{sh} ax$.	$a \operatorname{ch} ax$.	$\dfrac{1}{a} \operatorname{ch} ax$.
$\operatorname{ch} ax$.	$a \operatorname{sh} ax$.	$\dfrac{1}{a} \operatorname{sh} ax$.
$\operatorname{th} ax$.	$a \operatorname{sech}^2 ax$.	$\dfrac{1}{a} \log \operatorname{ch} ax$.
$\operatorname{sh}^{-1}(x/a)$.	$1/\sqrt{(x^2 + a^2)}$.	
$\operatorname{ch}^{-1}(x/a)$.	$1/\sqrt{(x^2 - a^2)}$.	
$\operatorname{th}^{-1}(x/a)$.	$a/(a^2 - x^2)$.	
$1/\sqrt{(x^2 + a^2)}$.		$\operatorname{sh}^{-1}(x/a)$.
$1/\sqrt{(x^2 - a^2)}$.		$\operatorname{ch}^{-1}(x/a)$.
$1/(a^2 - x^2)$.		$\dfrac{1}{a} \operatorname{th}^{-1}(x/a)$.

Integration by Parts

$$\int u \frac{dv}{dx}\, dx = uv - \int \frac{du}{dx}\, v\, dx.$$

(1) (2) (1)(2) (1) (2)

The Addition Formulae

$$\sin (A \pm B) = \sin A \cos B \pm \cos A \sin B.$$
$$\cos (A \pm B) = \cos A \cos B \mp \sin A \sin B.$$
$$\sin C + \sin D = 2 \sin \tfrac{1}{2}(C + D) \cos \tfrac{1}{2}(C - D).$$
$$\sin C - \sin D = 2 \cos \tfrac{1}{2}(C + D) \sin \tfrac{1}{2}(C - D).$$
$$\cos C + \cos D = 2 \cos \tfrac{1}{2}(C + D) \cos \tfrac{1}{2}(C - D).$$
$$\cos C - \cos D = 2 \sin \tfrac{1}{2}(C + D) \sin \tfrac{1}{2}(D - C).$$

The Circular and Hyperbolic Functions

If $i \equiv \sqrt{(-1)}$

$\sin x = \frac{1}{2i} (e^{ix} - e^{-ix}).$ $\cos x = \frac{1}{2}(e^{ix} + e^{-ix}).$

$\text{sh}\, x = \frac{1}{2}(e^{x} - e^{-x}).$ $\text{sh}^{-1} (x/a) = \log \{[x + \sqrt{(x^2 + a^2)}]/a\}.$

$\text{ch}\, x = \frac{1}{2}(e^{x} + e^{-x}).$ $\text{ch}^{-1} (x/a) = \log \{[x + \sqrt{(x^2 - a^2)}]/a\}.$

$\text{th}\, x = \text{sh}\, x/\text{ch}\, x.$

$\text{ch}^2 x - \text{sh}^2 x = 1.$ $\text{th}^{-1} (x/a) = \frac{1}{2} \log (a + x)/(a - x).$

$\sin ix = i\, \text{sh}\, x.$ $\cos ix = \text{ch}\, x.$

$\tan ix = i\, \text{th}\, x.$

$\text{sh}\, iz = i \sin z.$ $\text{ch}\, iz = \cos z.$

$\tan iz = i \tan z.$

Expansions in Series

$$\exp (x) = e^x = 1 + x + \frac{x^2}{2!} + \frac{x^3}{3!} + \ldots \frac{x^n}{n!} + \ldots \text{ (all values of } x).$$

$$\log (1 + x) = x - \frac{x^2}{2} + \frac{x^3}{3} - \frac{x^4}{4} \ldots \quad (-1 < x \leqslant +1).$$

$$(1 + x)^n = 1 + nx + \frac{n(n-1)}{1 . 2} x^2 + \frac{n(n-1)(n-2)}{1 . 2 . 3} x^3 + \ldots$$

($|x| < 1$ but all values of x if n is a positive integer).

$$\sin x = x - \frac{x^3}{3!} + \frac{x^5}{5!} - \ldots \text{ (all values of } x).$$

$$\cos x = 1 - \frac{x^2}{2!} + \frac{x^4}{4!} - \ldots \text{ (all values of } x).$$

Maclaurin's Theorem

$$f(x) = f(0) + xf'(0) + \frac{x^2}{2!} f''(0) + \ldots + \frac{x^n}{n!} f^{(n)}(0) + \ldots$$

Taylor's Theorem

$$f(x + h) = f(x) + hf'(x) + \frac{h^2}{2!} f''(x) + \ldots + \frac{h^n}{n!} f^{(n)}(x) + \ldots$$

Moments of Inertia

Body.	*Axis.*	*M.I.*
Thin rod (l).	(1) At end, perp. length.	$Ml^2/3$.
	(2) At centre, perp. length.	$Ml^2/12$.
Circular disc (radius a).	(1) Any diameter.	$Ma^2/4$.
	(2) At centre, perp. plane.	$Ma^2/2$.
Sphere (radius a).	Any diameter.	$2Ma^2/5$.
Rectangular area ($a \times b$).	(1) At centre, parallel side b.	$Ma^2/12$ or $ba^3/12$.
	(2) At centre, perp. plane.	$M(a^2 + b^2)/12$.

Simpson's Three-term Rule

$$\int_a^b f(x)\,dx = \frac{(b-a)}{6}\left\{f(a) + 4f\left(\frac{a+b}{2}\right) + f(b)\right\}.$$

Statistics

$$\begin{aligned}\sigma^2 &= \frac{1}{n}\sum_1^n (x_r - \bar{x})^2 \\ &= \frac{1}{n}\left\{\Sigma(X^2) - \frac{(\Sigma X)^2}{n}\right\} \qquad (X = x - A). \\ &= S^2 - (\bar{x} - A)^2.\end{aligned}$$

MATHEMATICAL CONSTANTS

$\pi = 3{\cdot}14159$ $\qquad \sqrt{\pi} = 1{\cdot}77245$

$\dfrac{1}{\pi} = 0{\cdot}31831$ $\qquad \pi^2 = 9{\cdot}86960$

$e = 2{\cdot}71828$

1 radian $= \dfrac{180}{\pi}$ degrees $= 57{\cdot}296°$ (correct to 3 decimals) or
$57°\ 17'\ 45''$ (correct to nearest second)

$1° = \dfrac{\pi}{180}$ radian $= 0{\cdot}017453$

$\log_{10} N = \log_e N \times \log_{10} e$ $\qquad \log_e 10 = 2{\cdot}30259$

$\log_{10} \pi = 0{\cdot}49715$ $\qquad \log_a N = 1/\log_N a$

$\log_{10} e = 0{\cdot}43429$

MATHEMATICAL SYMBOLS

Lt. $\equiv$ lim. $\equiv$ limit of.

$e^x \equiv \exp(x)$.

$\simeq$ **denotes** is approximately equal to.

$\neq$,, is not equal to.

$>$,, is greater than.

$<$,, is less than.

$\geqslant$,, is greater than or equal to.

$n!$,, $n(n-1)(n-2) \ldots 3 . 2 . 1$.

CHAPTER 1

ALGEBRA (REVISION)

1.1. The Quadratic Equation

Given $$ax^2 + bx + c = 0,$$

we can solve by factorization, in simple cases, or always by using the formula

$$x = \frac{-b \pm \sqrt{b^2 - 4ac}}{2a} \qquad (b^2 \geqslant 4ac)$$

or

$$\frac{-b \pm i\sqrt{4ac - b^2}}{2a} \qquad (b^2 < 4ac,\ i \equiv \sqrt{-1}).$$

Example 1. Solve $e^{2x} - 5e^x - 6 = 0.$
This is

$$\begin{aligned} &(e^x)^2 - 5e^x - 6 = 0\\ &(e^x - 6)(e^x + 1) = 0,\\ \therefore\quad &e^x = 6 \text{ or } -1. \end{aligned}$$

e^x is always positive so that the value -1 is inadmissible.

$$\begin{aligned} \therefore\quad &e^x = 6,\\ &x \log_e e = \log_e 6,\\ &x = \log_e 6 = \underline{1{\cdot}7918.} \end{aligned}$$

Example 2. Find x from the equation

$$9 \cosh x + 23 \sinh x + 54 = 0.$$

Substitute in terms of e^x.

$$\begin{aligned} &9\left(\frac{e^x + e^{-x}}{2}\right) + 23\left(\frac{e^x - e^{-x}}{2}\right) + 54 = 0,\\ \therefore\quad &16e^x - 7e^{-x} + 54 = 0,\\ &16(e^x)^2 + 54e^x - 7 = 0,\\ &(8e^x - 1)(2e^x + 7) = 0,\\ \therefore\quad &e^x = \tfrac{1}{8} \text{ or } -\tfrac{7}{2} \text{ (inadmissible)},\\ &x = \log \tfrac{1}{8} = \underline{-2{\cdot}0795.} \end{aligned}$$

EXERCISE 1

Solve the following equations:

1. $6e^{2x} - 7e^x + 2 = 0.$
2. $8e^x + 15e^{-x} = 22.$
3. $4 \cosh x + 8 \sinh x + 1 = 0.$
4. $6\sqrt{x} = 5x^{-\frac{1}{2}} - 13.$
5. $x^2 - x + 3 = 0.$
6. If $Z = \sqrt{\left\{R^2 + \left(\omega L - \frac{1}{\omega C}\right)^2\right\}}$ obtain a quadratic equation in ω, and hence solve the equation for ω.

1.2. Approximate Solution of Algebraic Equations

When an algebraic equation is of a higher degree than the second it is often advantageous to solve approximately in the following manner.

Example 3. Find approximately the positive root of

$$2x^3 + x - 8 = 0.$$

If we call this equation $f(x) = 0$, then with

$$\begin{aligned} x &= 0 & f(0) &= 0 + 0 - 8 = -8 \\ &= 1 & f(1) &= 2 + 1 - 8 = -5 \\ &= 2 & f(2) &= 16 + 2 - 8 = +10. \end{aligned}$$

If we were drawing a graph of the function $y = 2x^3 + x - 8$, then for $x = 1$ the y ordinate is -5, whilst for $x = 2$ the y ordinate is $+10$. When we join these points to form the graph, the join cuts the x axis and so gives a root of $2x^3 + x - 8 = 0$. The change in sign from -5 to $+10$ shows therefore, without the need for a graph, that a root lies between $x = 1$ and 2. We will try to get a closer approximation:

$$f(1{\cdot}5) = 2(1{\cdot}5)^3 + (1{\cdot}5) - 8 = +0{\cdot}25.$$

The change in sign is now between $x = 1$ and $1{\cdot}5$ so that the root lies in this interval and is probably nearer to $1{\cdot}5$ than to 1, since $f(1{\cdot}5)$ is so much smaller than $f(1)$ in actual magnitude.

Let $x = 1{\cdot}5 + \delta$, where δ is small, be the exact root of the equation. The root satisfies the equation, therefore,

$$2(1{\cdot}5 + \delta)^3 + (1{\cdot}5 + \delta) - 8 = 0 \qquad \ldots\ldots\ldots \quad (1)$$

We will assume that δ, which is less than $\frac{1}{2}$, is so small that δ^2 and higher powers can be neglected. Expanding to this order of δ approximation

$$2(1{\cdot}5)^3 + 6(1{\cdot}5)^2\delta + 1{\cdot}5 + \delta - 8 = 0$$

$$\therefore \quad \delta = \frac{-0{\cdot}25}{14{\cdot}5} = -0{\cdot}02.$$

$\therefore$ the root is $1{\cdot}5 - 0{\cdot}02 = \underline{1{\cdot}48}$ approx.

If we repeat this using $1{\cdot}48 + \delta_1$ as the root where δ_1 is small

$$\begin{aligned} &2(1{\cdot}48)^3 + 6(1{\cdot}48)^2\delta_1 + 1{\cdot}48 + \delta_1 - 8 = 0, \\ \therefore \quad &\delta_1 = 0{\cdot}0364/14{\cdot}1424 = 0{\cdot}003 \\ &\text{the root is } 1{\cdot}48 + 0{\cdot}003 = \underline{1{\cdot}483} \text{ approx.} \end{aligned}$$

If the result is required correct to 3 decimal places it is now necessary to check that the figure in this place is correct. If the root is $1{\cdot}483 + \delta_2$

$$2(1{\cdot}483 + \delta_2)^3 + (1{\cdot}483 + \delta_2) - 8 = 0.$$

Proceeding as above

$$\delta_2 = \frac{-0{\cdot}00609}{14{\cdot}1957} = -0{\cdot}00043$$

Since this does not affect the third decimal, the root is $1{\cdot}483$ correct to 3 decimal places.

EXERCISE 2

1. Find correct to two decimal places the root of $x^3 - 9x - 14 = 0$ that lies between 0 and 4.

2. Find the root lying between 1 and 2 of $x^3 + 5x - 11 = 0$ correct to two decimal places.

3. Find the two real roots of $x^4 - 12x - 5 = 0$ correct to two decimal places.

4. A sphere of radius 1 is divided by a plane into two parts whose volumes are in the ratio 1 : 2. Show that x, the distance of the plane from the centre, is a root of $3x^3 - 9x + 2 = 0$ and find x correct to two decimal places.

1.3. The Binomial Theorem

By long division we find:

$$\frac{1}{1-x} = 1 + x + x^2 + x^3 + \ldots$$

Similarly,

$$\frac{1}{(1+3x)^2} = \frac{1}{1+6x+9x^2} = 1 - 6x + 27x^2 + \ldots$$

These can be written:

$$(1-x)^{-1} = 1 + (-1)(-x) + \frac{(-1)(-1-1)}{1.2}(-x)^2 + \frac{(-1)(-1-1)(-1-2)}{1.2.3}(-x)^3 + \ldots$$

and

$$(1+3x)^{-2} = 1 + (-2)(3x) + \frac{(-2)(-2-1)}{1.2}(3x)^2 + \ldots$$

These are examples of the Binomial Theorem, which gives the expansion of $(1 + x)^n$ in a series of terms in ascending powers of x as

$$(1+x)^n = 1 + nx + \frac{n(n-1)}{1.2}x^2 + \frac{n(n-1)(n-2)}{1.2.3}x^3 + \ldots$$

The $(r + 1)$th term is

$$\frac{n(n-1)(n-2)\ldots(n-r+1)}{1.2.3\ldots r}x^r.$$

If n is a positive whole number this expansion consists of $n + 1$ terms and is true for all values of x.

If n is not a positive integer the expansion never terminates and is permissible only when the value of x is such that

$$-1 < x < +1, \text{ i.e., } |x| < 1.$$

The student should use the above theorem to obtain

$$(1-x)^{-\frac{1}{2}} = 1 + \frac{1}{2}x + \frac{1.3}{2.4}x^2 + \frac{1.3.5}{2.4.6}x^3 + \ldots$$

$$(1+x)^{-1} = 1 - x + x^2 - x^3 \ldots$$

$$(1-x)^{-2} = 1 + 2x + 3x^2 + 4x^3 + \ldots$$

If in the second of these, $(1 + x)^{-1}$, we put $x = 1$ the left-hand side becomes $\frac{1}{2}$, whilst the right-hand side is

$$1 - 1 + 1 - 1 \ldots$$

the sum of which is 0 or + 1 according to whether we take an even or odd number of terms. Neither of these answers is $\frac{1}{2}$, the left-hand side. This absurdity arises because we have put $x = 1$, whilst the expansion is true, *i.e.* the two sides equal, only for $|x| < 1$.

Example 4. Find $\sqrt[3]{(997)}$ correct to six decimal places.

By the Binomial Theorem we can find the value required to any degree of accuracy, whereas with say four-figure tables we would have a four-figure answer only, with the fourth figure of doubtful accuracy.

$$997 = 1000 - 3 = 1000(1 - 0{\cdot}003),$$

$$\therefore \quad (997)^{\frac{1}{3}} = 10(1 - 0{\cdot}003)^{\frac{1}{3}}.$$

(*a*) We have arranged 997 to give a perfect cube and an x $(= -0{\cdot}003)$ such that $|x| < 1$.

(*b*) Since the result is required to six decimal places we should work to eight places, but as the expansion is multiplied by 10 we will work to nine places.

$$(1 - 0{\cdot}003)^{\frac{1}{3}} = 1 + \tfrac{1}{3}(-0{\cdot}003) + \frac{\frac{1}{3}(\frac{1}{3} - 1)}{1\,.\,2}(-0{\cdot}003)^2$$
$$+ \frac{\frac{1}{3}(\frac{1}{3} - 1)(\frac{1}{3} - 2)}{1\,.\,2\,.\,3}(-0{\cdot}003)^3 + \ldots$$
$$= 1 - \tfrac{1}{3}(0{\cdot}003) - \tfrac{1}{9}(0{\cdot}003)^2 - \tfrac{5}{81}(0{\cdot}003)^3 \ldots$$
$$= u_1 - u_2 - u_3 - u_4 \ldots$$

Negative.	*Positive.*
$u_2 = 0{\cdot}001\ 000\ 000$	$u_1 = 1{\cdot}000\ 000\ 000$
$u_3 = 0{\cdot}000\ 001\ 000$	
$u_4 = 0{\cdot}000\ 000\ 002$	$0{\cdot}001\ 001\ 002$
$0{\cdot}001\ 001\ 002$	$0{\cdot}998\ 998\ 998$

The fifth term, u_5, will obviously not affect the ninth decimal place and can be ignored with all the following terms.

$$\therefore \quad \sqrt[3]{997} = 10 \times 0{\cdot}998\ 998\ 998$$
$$= 9{\cdot}989\ 989\ 98$$
$$= \underline{9{\cdot}989\ 990} \quad \text{to six decimal places.}$$

Example 5. Expand $\dfrac{1}{(4 + 3x)^3}$ to three terms, (*a*) in ascending powers of x, (*b*) in descending powers of x, and say for what range of values of x each expansion is valid.

(*a*)
$$\frac{1}{(4 + 3x)^3} = \frac{1}{4^3\left(1 + \dfrac{3x}{4}\right)^3} = \frac{1}{64}\left(1 + \frac{3x}{4}\right)^{-3}.$$

If now
$$\left|\frac{3x}{4}\right| < 1, \text{ i.e., } |x| < \frac{4}{3},$$
we can continue

$$= \frac{1}{64}\left\{1 + (-3)\left(\frac{3x}{4}\right) + \frac{(-3)(-3-1)}{1\,.\,2}\left(\frac{3x}{4}\right)^2 + \ldots\right\}$$
$$= \underline{\frac{1}{64}\left\{1 - \frac{9x}{4} + \frac{27}{8}x^2\right\}} \quad \text{to three terms.}$$

(*b*)
$$(4 + 3x)^3 = (3x)^3\left\{\frac{4}{3x} + 1\right\}^3,$$
$$\therefore \quad \frac{1}{(4 + 3x)^3} = \frac{1}{27x^3}\left\{1 + \frac{4}{3x}\right\}^{-3}.$$

If $$\left|\frac{4}{3x}\right| < 1,\ i.e.,\ \frac{4}{3}\left|\frac{1}{x}\right| < 1 \text{ or } \frac{4}{3} < |x|,$$

we can continue with

$$\frac{1}{27x^3}\left\{1+(-3)\left(\frac{4}{3x}\right)+\frac{(-3)(-3-1)}{1 . 2}\left(\frac{4}{3x}\right)^2+\ldots\right\}$$

$$=\frac{1}{27x^3}\left\{1-\frac{4}{x}+\frac{32}{3x^2}\right\} \text{ to three terms.}$$

Example 6. Find the limit as n tends to infinity of

$$\left(1+\frac{1}{n}\right)^n.$$

We have to find

$$\lim_{n \to \infty}\left(1+\frac{1}{n}\right)^n.$$

This may appear to be 1 raised to an infinite power which will give 1. If, however, we expand

$$\left(1+\frac{1}{n}\right)^n = 1+n\left(\frac{1}{n}\right)+\frac{n(n-1)}{1 . 2}\left(\frac{1}{n}\right)^2+\frac{n(n-1)(n-2)}{1 . 2 . 3}\left(\frac{1}{n}\right)^3+\ldots$$

The R.H.S. can be written

$$1+1+\frac{1\left(1-\frac{1}{n}\right)}{1 . 2}+\frac{1\left(1-\frac{1}{n}\right)\left(1-\frac{2}{n}\right)}{1 . 2 . 3}+\ldots$$

If we now let n tend to infinity and note that

$$\frac{1}{n}, \frac{2}{n}, \frac{3}{n} \ldots$$

all tend to zero we have as the limit

$$1+1+\frac{1}{2!}+\frac{1}{3!}+\ldots\frac{1}{r!}+\ldots$$

The sum of this infinite series is 2·718281828459 ... which is denoted by e. (Like π, e has a non-terminating and non-recurring decimal part.)

Since the above is an infinite series of positive terms, the sum of these could increase steadily to give an infinite sum. It would be a serious error in such a case to stop after adding together the first few terms and quote the result as an approximation to the correct value. However, we easily see that the sum of this infinite series is bounded above by the number 3 for the sum is less than

$$1+1+\frac{1}{2}+\frac{1}{2^2}+\frac{1}{2^3}+\ldots$$

since

$$\frac{1}{3!}=\frac{1}{2 . 3}<\frac{1}{2 . 2}$$

$$\frac{1}{4!}=\frac{1}{2 . 3 . 4}<\frac{1}{2 . 2 . 2}$$

and similarly for each successive term.

This new infinite series is, after the first term, an infinite geometrical progression whose sum is 2. We have then proved that the infinite series denoted by e has a sum less than 3. It must then increase steadily (towards the value given).

This question of convergency will be dealt with later. It can be shown that for *all* values of x

$$e^x = 1 + x + \frac{x^2}{2!} + \frac{x^3}{3!} + \ldots + \frac{x^n}{n!} + \ldots$$

1.4. If x is so small that the terms in x^2 and higher powers may be neglected, then we have as an important approximation from the Binomial Theorem

$$(1 + x)^n \simeq 1 + nx$$

for all values of n.

Example 7. If x is small find an approximate value for

$$\frac{\sqrt[4]{1 + \frac{3}{5}x} + \left(1 - \frac{3x}{4}\right)^{-2}}{\sqrt[3]{1 + 2x} + \left(1 - \frac{x}{2}\right)^{-5}}.$$

Using the above approximation

$$\left(1 + \frac{3x}{5}\right)^{\frac{1}{4}} \simeq 1 + \frac{1}{4}\left(\frac{3x}{5}\right) = 1 + \frac{3x}{20},$$

$$\left(1 - \frac{3x}{4}\right)^{-2} \simeq 1 + (-2)\left(-\frac{3x}{4}\right) = 1 + \frac{3x}{2},$$

$$(1 + 2x)^{\frac{1}{3}} \simeq 1 + \frac{1}{3}(2x) = 1 + \frac{2}{3}x,$$

$$\left(1 - \frac{x}{2}\right)^{-5} \simeq 1 + (-5)\left(-\frac{x}{2}\right) = 1 + \frac{5x}{2}.$$

$$\therefore \quad \text{expression} = \frac{\left(1 + \frac{3x}{20}\right) + \left(1 + \frac{3x}{2}\right)}{\left(1 + \frac{2x}{3}\right) + \left(1 + \frac{5x}{2}\right)} = \frac{2 + \frac{33x}{20}}{2 + \frac{19x}{6}}.$$

$$= \frac{2 + \frac{33x}{20}}{2\left(1 + \frac{19x}{12}\right)} = \frac{1}{2}\left(2 + \frac{33x}{20}\right)\left(1 + \frac{19x}{12}\right)^{-1}$$

$$\simeq \frac{1}{2}\left(2 + \frac{33x}{20}\right)\left(1 - \frac{19x}{12}\right)$$

(ignore x^2 as above)

$$\simeq \frac{1}{2}\left(2 + \frac{33x}{20} - \frac{19x}{6}\right)$$

$$= 1 - \frac{91x}{120}.$$

Example 8. In a certain engine the cylinder axis does not pass through the axis of the crankshaft but is offset by a small distance d. Show that the length of the stroke L is given by

$$L = \sqrt{(l + r)^2 - d^2} - \sqrt{(l - r)^2 - d^2},$$

where l = length of connecting-rod,
r = length of crank.

Show that an approximate value for L is given by

$$L = 2r\left[1 + \tfrac{1}{2}\frac{d^2}{l^2 - r^2}\right].$$

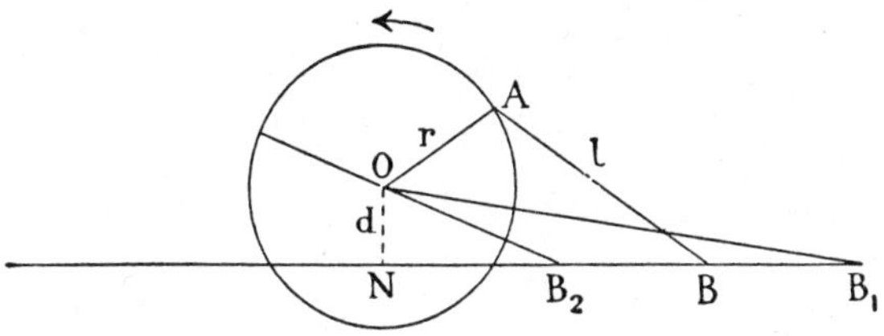

FIG. 1

As A moves round the circle the crosshead B moves between B_1 and B_2. If N is the perpendicular from the centre O upon the cylinder axis

$$\begin{aligned} L = B_2B_1 &= NB_1 - NB_2 \\ &= \sqrt{(l+r)^2 - d^2} - \sqrt{(l-r)^2 - d^2} \\ &= (l+r)\left\{1 - \left(\frac{d}{l+r}\right)^2\right\}^{\frac{1}{2}} - (l-r)\left\{1 - \left(\frac{d}{l-r}\right)^2\right\}^{\frac{1}{2}} \\ &= (l+r)\left\{1 - \tfrac{1}{2}\left(\frac{d}{l+r}\right)^2\right\} - (l-r)\left\{1 - \tfrac{1}{2}\left(\frac{d}{l-r}\right)^2\right\} \text{ approx.} \\ &= (l+r) - (l-r) - \tfrac{1}{2}\frac{d^2}{l+r} + \tfrac{1}{2}\frac{d^2}{l-r} \\ &= 2r + \frac{d^2r}{l^2 - r^2} = 2r\left\{1 + \tfrac{1}{2}\frac{d^2}{l^2 - r^2}\right\}. \end{aligned}$$

EXERCISE 3

In each of Examples 1–3 prove the given equality and expand each to four terms to obtain an approximate value for the given surd.

1. $\sqrt[3]{1001} = 10(1 + 0{\cdot}001)^{\frac{1}{3}}$.
2. $\sqrt[3]{5} = \frac{5}{3}(1 + 0{\cdot}08)^{\frac{1}{3}}$.
3. $\sqrt[5]{3} = \frac{5}{4}(1 - 0{\cdot}01696)^{\frac{1}{5}}$.
4. Expand $1/(3 + 2x)^2$ to three terms: (i) in ascending powers of x, (ii) in descending powers of x, and in each case state for what range of values of x the expansion is valid.
5. If x is small show $\sqrt{1 + x} = 1 + \frac{1}{2}x - \frac{1}{8}x^2$ approx.
6. If x is large show $\sqrt[3]{x^3 + 1} = x + \dfrac{1}{3x^2} - \dfrac{1}{9x^5}$ approx.
7. If x is small show that approximately
$$\frac{(1 - 2x)^{-\frac{1}{2}} - (1 + 2x)^{\frac{1}{2}}}{(1 - x)^{-\frac{1}{2}} - (1 + x)^{\frac{1}{2}}} = 4 + 2x.$$
8. Expand to four terms $(1 + x)^{\frac{3}{2}}$.

9. Expand to three terms $(2 + 3x)^{-4}$. For what values of x is this expansion valid?

10. If x is small so that only first powers of x need be retained find an approximate value for

$$\frac{\sqrt[3]{8 + 3x} - \sqrt[5]{1 - x}}{(1 + 5x)^{\frac{3}{5}} + \left(4 + \frac{x}{2}\right)^{\frac{1}{2}}}.$$

11. A book on hydraulics states

$$C^2 = \frac{2gz}{1 - \left(\frac{d}{d + z}\right)^2}, \quad \therefore \quad C \simeq \sqrt{gd}.$$

Obtain this value for C if it is known that z/d is small.

12. The time T in seconds for a complete oscillation of a pendulum is $T = 2\pi\sqrt{(l/32)}$. If the length l ft. increases by x in. show that the increase in time of an oscillation is

$$\frac{T}{24}\left(\frac{x}{l} - \frac{x^2}{48l^2}\right) \text{ sec.}$$ [Q.E.]

13. The energy E stored in a flywheel is given by the formula $E = Ka^5n^2$, where K is a constant, a and n are the radius and the number of revolutions per minute respectively. Find approximately the percentage increase in E when: (i) a is increased by 2 per cent. and n by 1 per cent., (ii) a is increased by 2 per cent. and n is decreased by 1 per cent.

14. A formula for the central deflection of a beam under certain conditions is

$$d = \frac{Wl^3}{48EI},$$

where $I = \dfrac{ab^3}{12}$ and E is constant.

If in measuring the quantities l is 5 per cent. too small, a is 3 per cent. too large, b is 1 per cent. too small, find the percentage error in the calculated value of d.

15. Show that if x, y and z are so small that their squares and higher powers may be neglected, then

$$\frac{(1 + x)^a(1 + y)^b}{(1 + z)^c} = 1 + ax + by - cz.$$

The deflection at the centre of a circular plate supported at the edge and uniformly loaded is proportional to wd^4/t^3, where w is the weight of the load, d the diameter of the plate and t its thickness. Find the percentage increase in the deflection if the weight w is increased by 3 per cent. the diameter d is increased by $2\frac{1}{2}$ per cent. and the thickness is increased by 4 per cent.

16. A wheel of diameter a rolls over a flat horizontal surface and strikes an electrical contact which projects a distance h vertically above the surface. If a small error δh is made in measuring h show that the resulting error in the calculated horizontal distance between the centre of the wheel and the contact at the instant of striking is $\frac{1}{2}\sqrt{a/h}\,.\,\delta h$. Assume h small compared to a. [Q.E.]

17. If $|x| < 1$ find the coefficient of x^n in the expansion in ascending powers of x of

$$\frac{a + bx + cx^2}{(1 - x)^3}.$$

Determine a, b, c so that this expansion reduces to

$$\sum_{n=1}^{\infty} n^2 x^n.$$

Show that

$$\sum_{n=1}^{\infty} \frac{n^2}{2^n} = 6.$$

CHAPTER 2

PARTIAL FRACTIONS

2.1. Single First-degree Factors

The student will know that for such an expression as

$$\frac{3x + 2}{(x - 2)(x + 5)}$$

we assume as partial fractions

$$\frac{A}{x - 2} + \frac{B}{x + 5}$$

where A and B are constants to be determined. Although in the following the triple sign for identity is often written as the double sign for equality, we should put

$$\frac{3x + 2}{(x - 2)(x + 5)} \equiv \frac{A}{x - 2} + \frac{B}{x + 5} \quad . \quad . \quad . \quad (1)$$

If we multiply by $(x - 2)$ we have

$$\frac{3x + 2}{(x + 5)} \equiv A + \frac{B(x - 2)}{x + 5}.$$

An identity is true for all values of x; put $x = 2$.

$$\frac{3(2) + 2}{2 + 5} \equiv A \qquad \therefore \quad A = \frac{8}{7}.$$

Similarly, if we had multiplied by $x + 5$ and then put $x = -5$, we would have

$$\frac{3(-5) + 2}{-5 - 2} \equiv B \qquad \therefore \quad B = \frac{13}{7}.$$

It is clear that the above method for finding A and B is equivalent to the following: in the expression (1) on the L.H.S. ignore or "cover up" the factor $x - 2$. Put $x = 2$ in the rest of the expression to find A, the numerator of the partial fraction for the factor $x - 2$. Similarly for the factor $x + 5$ to find B.

Example 1. Find the partial fractions for

$$\frac{x^2 + 2x + 6}{(x - 1)(x + 3)(x - 5)}.$$

If they are

$$\frac{A}{x-1}+\frac{B}{x+3}+\frac{C}{x-5}$$

then

$$A=\frac{1^2+2(1)+6}{(\quad)(1+3)(1-5)}=-\frac{9}{16}.$$

$$B=\frac{(-3)^2+2(-3)+6}{(-3-1)(\quad)(-3-5)}=\frac{9}{32}.$$

$$C=\frac{5^2+2(5)+6}{(5-1)(5+3)(\quad)}=\frac{41}{32}.$$

$\therefore$ the expression equals $\underline{-\dfrac{9}{16(x-1)}+\dfrac{9}{32(x+3)}+\dfrac{41}{32(x-5)}}.$

2.2. Before attempting to find the partial fractions of any fraction we must ensure that the numerator is of *lower* degree than the denominator.

For

$$\frac{x^3+x+6}{(x-2)(x-4)}$$

we must first divide until the remainder is less than the second degree since the denominator is of the second degree.

By long division, the expression is

$$x+6+\frac{29x-42}{x^2-6x+8}$$

and we now find the P.F. for the fractional part as

$$\frac{A}{x-2}+\frac{B}{x-4}=\frac{-8}{x-2}+\frac{37}{x-4}.$$

$$\therefore\quad \frac{x^3+x+6}{(x-2)(x-4)}=x+6-\frac{8}{x-2}+\frac{37}{x-4}.$$

2.3. Repeated First-degree Factors

When one of the first-degree factors is repeated we must still assume constants as numerators of each of the fractions composing the P.F. corresponding to the repeated factor.

Example 2. Put $\dfrac{1}{(x-2)(x+1)^3}$ into partial fractions.

This should be assumed identical with

$$\frac{A}{x-2}+\frac{B}{x+1}+\frac{C}{(x+1)^2}+\frac{D}{(x+1)^3}.$$

Since we can still multiply both sides by $x-2$ and then put $x=2$ we still obtain A by the " cover-up " method. However, if we multiply both sides by $(x+1)^3$ then *each* fraction on the R.H.S. will contain a power of $x+1$ in its numerator except the last fraction with D. When we put $x=-1$ all vanish except D, giving the value of D. Therefore with a repeated factor the " cover-up " method gives the coefficient of the *highest* power of the factor covered up.

With the above example

$$\frac{1}{(x-2)(x+1)^3}\equiv\frac{A}{x-2}+\frac{B}{x+1}+\frac{C}{(x+1)^2}+\frac{D}{(x+1)^3}$$

$$\equiv\frac{1}{27(x-2)}+\frac{B}{x+1}+\frac{C}{(x+1)^2}-\frac{1}{3(x+1)^3},$$

A and D being found by the cover-up method.

Now multiplying, we have

$$1 \equiv \tfrac{1}{27}(x+1)^3 + B(x-2)(x+1)^2 + C(x-2)(x+1) - \tfrac{1}{3}(x-2).$$

Equating the coefficient of x^3 on each side

$$0 = \tfrac{1}{27} + B \qquad \therefore \quad B = -\tfrac{1}{27}.$$

Equating the constant terms

$$1 = \tfrac{1}{27} - 2B - 2C + \tfrac{2}{3}$$
$$\therefore \quad 2C = \tfrac{1}{27} + \tfrac{2}{3} + \tfrac{2}{27} - 1$$
$$\therefore \quad C = -\tfrac{1}{9}.$$

$\therefore$ expression is

$$\frac{1}{27(x-2)} - \frac{1}{27(x+1)} - \frac{1}{9(x+1)^2} - \frac{1}{3(x+1)^3}.$$

2.4. Second-degree Factors

Any second-degree expression in x can be factorized into two first-degree factors, but if the factors would contain surds or imaginary numbers, then it is usual to leave the expression in the second-degree form. In this case we must assume a *first-degree* expression for the corresponding numerator.

Example 3. Put into P.F.

$$\frac{x^2+3x+2}{(x-1)(x-2)(x^2+x+5)}.$$

Here we assume as the P.F.

$$\frac{A}{x-1} + \frac{B}{x-2} + \frac{Cx+D}{x^2+x+5} = -\frac{6}{7(x-1)} + \frac{12}{11(x-2)} + \frac{Cx+D}{x^2+x+5},$$

A and B being found by the cover-up method.

Multiplying up:

$$x^2+3x+2 \equiv -\tfrac{6}{7}(x-2)(x^2+x+5) + \tfrac{12}{11}(x-1)(x^2+x+5)$$
$$+ (Cx+D)(x-1)(x-2).$$

Equating the coefficients of x^3 on either side in this identity,

$$0 = -\tfrac{6}{7} + \tfrac{12}{11} + C \qquad \therefore \quad C = -\tfrac{18}{77}.$$

Equating the constant terms,

$$2 = \tfrac{60}{7} - \tfrac{60}{11} + 2D \qquad \therefore \quad D = -\tfrac{43}{77}.$$

The P.F. are therefore

$$-\frac{6}{7(x-1)} + \frac{12}{11(x-2)} - \frac{18x+43}{77(x^2+x+5)}.$$

2.5. Expansion in Series

Partial fractions are used for two main purposes: (1) as a preliminary step to integrating any expression that we have put into partial fractions. This will be dealt with later. (2) As a preliminary to expanding any such expression in a series of powers of x. We will now deal with this.

Example 4. Expand in a series of ascending powers of x the expression

$$\frac{1}{(2x+3)(x^2+1)}.$$

We assume:

$$\frac{1}{(2x+3)(x^2+1)} \equiv \frac{A}{2x+3} + \frac{Bx+C}{x^2+1}$$

$$\equiv \frac{4}{13(2x+3)} + \frac{Bx+C}{x^2+1},$$

$$\therefore \quad 1 \equiv \tfrac{4}{13}(x^2+1) + (Bx+C)(2x+3).$$

Coefficient of x^2:

$$0 = \tfrac{4}{13} + 2B \qquad \therefore \quad B = -\tfrac{2}{13}.$$

Constant term:

$$1 = \tfrac{4}{13} + 3C \qquad \therefore \quad C = \tfrac{3}{13}.$$

$\therefore$ expression

$$= \frac{4}{13(2x+3)} - \tfrac{1}{13}\frac{2x-3}{(x^2+1)}$$

$$= \tfrac{4}{39}\frac{1}{\left(1+\frac{2x}{3}\right)} - \tfrac{1}{13}\frac{2x-3}{(1+x^2)}$$

$$= \tfrac{4}{39}\left(1+\frac{2x}{3}\right)^{-1} - \tfrac{1}{13}(2x-3)(1+x^2)^{-1}.$$

If now $\left|\frac{2x}{3}\right| < 1$, *i.e.*, $|x| < \frac{3}{2}$, the first fraction can be expanded in ascending powers of x.

If $|x^2| < 1$, *i.e.*, $|x| < 1$, the second fraction can be so expanded.

$|x| < 1$ satisfies these two requirements, *so in this case* we can expand and obtain

$$\tfrac{4}{39}\left(1 - \frac{2x}{3} + \left(\frac{2x}{3}\right)^2 - \left(\frac{2x}{3}\right)^3 \ldots\right) - \tfrac{1}{13}(2x-3)(1 - x^2 + x^4 - x^6 \ldots)$$

$$= \tfrac{4}{39}\left(1 - \frac{2x}{3} + \frac{4}{9}x^2 - \frac{8}{27}x^3 \ldots\right) + \tfrac{1}{13}(3 - 2x - 3x^2 + 2x^3 \ldots)$$

$$= \tfrac{13}{39} - \tfrac{26}{117}x - \tfrac{65}{351}x^2 \ldots$$

EXERCISE 4

Put into partial fractions:

1. $\dfrac{2x+5}{(x+3)(x+2)}$.
2. $\dfrac{4x-17}{(x-2)(x-5)}$.
3. $\dfrac{x^2+2x+5}{(x^2+2x-2)(x+1)}$.
4. $\dfrac{x^2-2x+3}{(x-1)(x^2-x-1)}$.
5. $\dfrac{4-x}{(x-3)^2}$.
6. $\dfrac{(x+2)^2}{(x-3)^2(x+5)}$.
7. $\dfrac{x-3}{(x-1)^2(x^2+2)}$.
8. Find the coefficient of x^7 in the expansion in ascending powers of x of $\dfrac{1+5x}{1+x-2x^2}$.

   For what value of x is this expansion valid?
9. Find the coefficient of x^5 in the expansion of

$$\frac{9+8x+x^2}{(3+2x)(2-x^2)}.$$

10. Given that

$$\int \frac{dx}{x+p} = \log (x+p) + \text{const.},$$

show that

$$\int \frac{dx}{x^2 - a^2} = \frac{1}{2a} \log \left(\frac{x-a}{x+a}\right) + C.$$

11. Given that

$$\int \frac{dx}{x^2 + a^2} = \frac{1}{a} \tan^{-1} \left(\frac{x}{a}\right) + C, \text{ and } \int \frac{2x dx}{x^2+4} = \log (x^2+4) + D,$$

find

$$\int \frac{dx}{(x-3)(x^2+4)}.$$

12. Put $\dfrac{x+1}{(x-2)(x+5)}$ into partial fractions, and hence differentiate this expression five times.

13. Express in three partial fractions

$$(1+5x)/(1-x)(2-x-x^2).$$

Show that when expanded in ascending powers of x the series is

$$\tfrac{1}{2} + 3\tfrac{1}{4}x + 4\tfrac{7}{8}x^2 + \ldots$$

and find the terms in x^3 and x^4.

14. Express $(3 + 2x^2 + x^3)/(2 + x^2)(1 - x)^2$ in partial fractions and show that when expanded in ascending powers of x the coefficient of x^{2n} is

$$4n + 1 - (-\tfrac{1}{2})^{n+1}.$$

15. To sum the finite series

$$\frac{1}{1.2} + \frac{1}{2.3} + \frac{1}{3.4} + \ldots + \frac{1}{(n-1)n}$$

put the last term and hence all the others into partial fractions. Show that the sum of n terms is

$$1 - \frac{1}{n}.$$

Deduce that the infinite series has a sum of unity.

16. Find the sum to n terms of the series

$$\frac{1}{1.2.4} + \frac{1}{2.3.5} + \frac{1}{3.4.6} + \frac{1}{4.5.7} + \ldots$$

and deduce that the sum to infinity of the series is 7/36.

CHAPTER 3

TRIGONOMETRY (REVISION)

3.1. The Addition Formulae

From the sine formula, page xiv, with $B = A$, we have

$$\sin 2A = 2 \sin A \cos A.$$

Another form is $\left(\text{if } A = \frac{C}{2}\right)$

$$\sin C = 2 \sin \frac{C}{2} \cos \frac{C}{2}.$$

Also

$$\begin{aligned} \cos 2A &= \cos^2 A - \sin^2 A \\ &= 2 \cos^2 A - 1 \\ &= 1 - 2 \sin^2 A. \end{aligned}$$

If $A = \frac{C}{2}$, these become respectively:

$$\cos^2 \frac{C}{2} - \sin^2 \frac{C}{2}, \; 2 \cos^2 \frac{C}{2} - 1, \; 1 - 2 \sin^2 \frac{C}{2}.$$

By writing 3A as 2A + A and using the above formulae the student should show:

$$\begin{aligned} \sin 3A &= 3 \sin A - 4 \sin^3 A, \\ \cos 3A &= 4 \cos^3 A - 3 \cos A. \end{aligned}$$

Example 1. Prove that:

$$\frac{\sin 2A}{1 + \cos 2A} = \tan A.$$

$$\begin{aligned} \sin 2A &= 2 \sin A \cos A, \\ 1 + \cos 2A &= 1 + 2 \cos^2 A - 1 = 2 \cos^2 A. \\ \therefore \quad \text{L.H.S.} &= \frac{2 \sin A \cos A}{2 \cos^2 A} = \tan A. \end{aligned}$$

EXERCISE 5

Prove:

1. $\sin 2A/(1 - \cos 2A) = \cot A$.
2. $(1 - \cos 2A)/(1 + \cos 2A) = \tan^2 A$.
3. (*a*) $\operatorname{cosec} 2A + \cot 2A = \cot A$.
   (*b*) $\sin (36 + A) - \sin (36 - A) - \sin (72 + A) + \sin (72 - A) = \sin A$.

(c) $\dfrac{\sin 5A + \sin A}{\sin 3A - \sin A} = 1 + 2\cos 2A.$

(d) $\dfrac{\cos 4A + \sin 6A}{\cos 5A + \sin 5A} = \dfrac{\cos 2A + \sin 4A}{\cos 3A + \sin 3A}.$

4. Find cos 3A when cos A $= \frac{1}{3}$.
5. Find sin 3A when sin A $= \frac{1}{4}$.
6. Using the formulae for sin 3A and cos 3A show that:

$$\tan 3A = \frac{3\tan A - \tan^3 A}{1 - 3\tan^2 A}.$$

7. Use the formula for sin 3A to find $\sin^3 A$. Hence find

$$\int_0^{\pi/2} \sin^3 A dA \text{ and } \int_0^{\pi/3} \sin^3 A dA.$$

8. Repeat the above for cos 3A to find

$$\int_0^{\pi/2} \cos^3 A dA \text{ and } \int_0^{\pi/4} \cos^3 A dA.$$

9. Show that:

$$\cos 5\theta = 16\cos^5\theta - 20\cos^3\theta + 5\cos\theta.$$

Integrate both sides between the limits 0 and $\pi/4$ and using Example 8, find

$$\int_0^{\pi/4} \cos^5 \theta d\theta.$$

10. The following occur in an electrical problem. Show that:

(a) $\cos x + \cos\left(x + \frac{2\pi}{3}\right) + \cos\left(x + \frac{4\pi}{3}\right) = 0;$

(b) $$\cos\frac{2\pi x}{a}\cos\omega t + \cos\left(\frac{2\pi x}{a} + \frac{2\pi}{3}\right)\cos\left(\omega t + \frac{2\pi}{3}\right)$$
$$+ \cos\left(\frac{2\pi x}{a} + \frac{4\pi}{3}\right)\cos\left(\omega t + \frac{4\pi}{3}\right)$$
$$= \frac{3}{2}\cos\left(\frac{2\pi x}{a} - \omega t\right).$$

11. If $e = E_m \sin \omega t$ and $i = I_m \sin(\omega t - \alpha)$ find the maximum and minimum values of the power $p = ei$ as the time t varies. (Use max. $(\cos x) = +1$ and min. $(\cos x) = -1$.)

3.2. The Form $a \cos\theta + b \sin\theta$

$a\cos\theta + b\sin\theta$ can be written

$$\sqrt{a^2 + b^2}\left\{\frac{a}{\sqrt{a^2+b^2}}\cos\theta + \frac{b}{\sqrt{a^2+b^2}}\sin\theta\right\}.$$

In the bracket we now have two numbers,

$$\frac{a}{\sqrt{a^2+b^2}} \text{ and } \frac{b}{\sqrt{a^2+b^2}},$$

the sum of whose squares is 1. We can therefore choose one to be the sine of an angle and the other the cosine of the same angle.

Example 2. Put $3\cos\theta - 4\sin\theta$ into: (1) a sine form; (2) a cosine form.

(1) $3\cos\theta - 4\sin\theta$

$$= \sqrt{3^2+4^2}\,\{\tfrac{3}{5}\cos\theta - \tfrac{4}{5}\sin\theta\}.$$

The expression in the bracket can be put into the form

$$\sin A\cos\theta - \cos A\sin\theta \equiv \sin(A-\theta).$$

For this we need

$$\sin A = \tfrac{3}{5} \text{ and } \cos A = \tfrac{4}{5}.$$

However, it is usual to obtain an expression with $+\theta$ and not $-\theta$. We therefore need

$$\sin A\cos\theta + \cos A\sin\theta \equiv \sin(\theta + A).$$

For this

$$\sin A = \tfrac{3}{5} \text{ and } \cos A = -\tfrac{4}{5}.$$

A is therefore an angle in the second quadrant, the only quadrant where the sine is positive and the cosine negative. The tables give $\sin^{-1}(\tfrac{3}{5}) = 36^\circ 52'$, and since we need the supplement of this, the required angle is $180 - 36^\circ 52' = 143^\circ 8'$.

$$\therefore\quad 3\cos\theta - 4\sin\theta = \underline{5\sin(\theta + 143^\circ 8')}.$$

(2) As a cosine form

$$\tfrac{3}{5}\cos\theta - \tfrac{4}{5}\sin\theta$$

is $\cos A\cos\theta - \sin A\sin\theta \equiv \cos(\theta + A)$,

where $\cos A = \tfrac{3}{5},\ \sin A = \tfrac{4}{5}. \quad \therefore A = 53^\circ 8'.$

$$\therefore\quad 3\cos\theta - 4\sin\theta = \underline{5\cos(\theta + 53^\circ 8')}.$$

If we had chosen

$$\cos A\cos\theta + \sin A\sin\theta \equiv \cos(\theta - A),$$

then $\cos A = \tfrac{3}{5},\ \sin A = -\tfrac{4}{5}. \quad \therefore A = -53^\circ 8' \text{ or } 360^\circ - 53^\circ 8'.$

Each of these values will give the same result as first obtained: $\cos(\theta + 53^\circ 8')$.

Note that in (1) and (2) we choose the smallest angle for A that will satisfy the conditions, but any other such angle, *e.g.*, $360^\circ - 53^\circ 8'$ in (2) will do.

EXERCISE 6

Express:

1. $5\cos x + 2\sin x$ as a cosine form.
2. $\sqrt{3}\sin x - \cos x$ as a sine form.
3. $\sin x - \sqrt{3}\cos x$ as a cosine form.
4. Express $6\sin 2\pi ft - 3\cos 2\pi ft$ in the form $A\sin(2\pi ft - \alpha)$ giving α in radians.
5. A voltage v is given by

$$v = 100 + 2{\cdot}4\sin 2\pi ft + 3{\cdot}9\cos 2\pi ft - 1{\cdot}2\sin 4\pi ft + 0{\cdot}9\cos 4\pi ft.$$

Express this as

$$A_0 + A_1 \sin(2\pi ft + \alpha_1) + A_2 \sin(4\pi ft + \alpha_2),$$

finding A_0, A_1, A_2, α_1, α_2.

6. A voltage v is given by

$$v = I_m\left\{R \sin \omega t + \left(\omega L - \frac{1}{\omega C}\right) \cos \omega t\right\}.$$

Express this as $ZI_m \sin(\omega t + \alpha)$, giving Z and α.

7. Assuming that E, I, R and X are constants, put

$$(E \cos \theta + RI)^2 + (E \sin \theta + XI)^2$$

into the form

$$A + B \sin(\theta + \alpha),$$

and hence show that the maximum and minimum values are

$$(E \pm I\sqrt{R^2 + X^2})^2.$$ [U.L.C.I.]

8. The moment acting on a flywheel rotating subject to fluid resistance is given by

$$M = f\alpha + I\frac{d\alpha}{dt}.$$

If $f = 200$, $I = 5000$, $\alpha = 20 + 0{\cdot}1 \sin 12t$, show that

$$M = 4000 + 6000 \sin(12t + 1{\cdot}57).$$

9. Given that $y = a \cos^2 x + b \sin^2 x + c \sin 2x$ where a, b and c are constants show that the maximum and minimum values of y are given by

$$\tfrac{1}{2}(a + b) \pm \tfrac{1}{2}\{(a - b)^2 + 4c^2\}^{\frac{1}{2}}$$

3.3. Inverse Circular Functions

It is useful to be able to deal with these functions to the extent shown in this section.

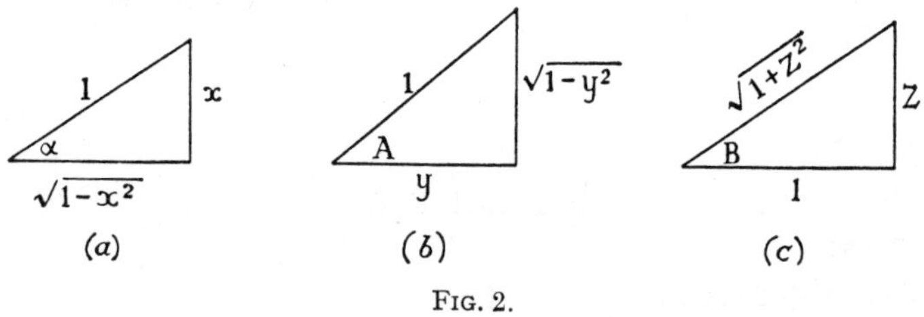

FIG. 2.

(a) Given $\sin^{-1} x = \alpha$, we can at once obtain the other ratios. If Fig. 2 (a) shows the angle α with its sine as x, then clearly

$$\alpha = \sin^{-1} x = \cos^{-1} \sqrt{1 - x^2} = \tan^{-1}(x/\sqrt{1 - x^2})$$
$$= \operatorname{cosec}^{-1} 1/x = \sec^{-1}(1/\sqrt{1 - x^2}) = \cot^{-1}(\sqrt{1 - x^2}/x),$$

all these expressions being equal and stating the same fact.

(*b*) Similarly, given $\cos^{-1} y = A$ we have, Fig. 2 (*b*),

$$A = \cos^{-1} y = \sin^{-1} \sqrt{1 - y^2} = \tan^{-1} (\sqrt{1 - y^2}/y), \text{ etc.}$$

(*c*) Given $\tan^{-1} z = B$ we have, Fig. 2 (*c*),

$$B = \tan^{-1} z = \sin^{-1} (z/\sqrt{1 + z^2}) = \cos^{-1} (1/\sqrt{1 + z^2}), \text{ etc.}$$

These formulae should not be remembered but recalled by means of a right-angled triangle with sides marked appropriately.

3.4. Addition of Inverse Circular Functions

To find $\sin^{-1} x + \sin^{-1} y$.

For a given x and y we can enter the sine tables inversely and so find the angles required, subject to a small error at each entry. Nevertheless, the following theoretical formulae are often useful.

Let $\sin^{-1} x = A$, so that $x = \sin A$ and $\sqrt{1 - x^2} = \cos A$.

Let $\sin^{-1} y = B$, so that $y = \sin B$ and $\sqrt{1 - y^2} = \cos B$.

$$\therefore \quad \sin (A + B) = \sin A \cos B + \cos A \sin B$$

$$= x\sqrt{1 - y^2} + y\sqrt{1 - x^2}.$$

$$\therefore \quad A + B, \text{ i.e., } \sin^{-1} x + \sin^{-1} y = \sin^{-1} \{x\sqrt{1 - y^2} + y\sqrt{1 - x^2}\}.$$

By finding $\tan A$ in terms of x and $\tan B$ in terms of y we could have added these angles in terms of an inverse tangent and similarly for an inverse cosine.

Similarly,

$$\cos^{-1} x + \cos^{-1} y = \cos^{-1} \{xy - \sqrt{1 - x^2} \cdot \sqrt{1 - y^2}\},$$

$$\tan^{-1} x + \tan^{-1} y = \tan^{-1} \left\{\frac{x + y}{1 - xy}\right\}.$$

Example 3. Prove

$$\tan^{-1} (\tfrac{2}{11}) + 2 \tan^{-1} (\tfrac{1}{7}) = \tan^{-1} (\tfrac{1}{2}).$$

$$2 \tan^{-1} (\tfrac{1}{7}) = \tan^{-1} \left(\frac{\frac{1}{7} + \frac{1}{7}}{1 - \frac{1}{7} \cdot \frac{1}{7}}\right) = \tan^{-1} (\tfrac{7}{24})$$

and

$$\tan^{-1} (\tfrac{7}{24}) + \tan^{-1} (\tfrac{2}{11}) = \tan^{-1} \left(\frac{\frac{7}{24} + \frac{2}{11}}{1 - \frac{7}{24} \cdot \frac{2}{11}}\right) = \tan^{-1} (\tfrac{1}{2}).$$

EXERCISE 7

Prove, without using tables, that:

1. $\cos^{-1} (\frac{16}{65}) - \cos^{-1} (\frac{12}{13}) = \sin^{-1} (\frac{4}{5})$.
2. $\sin^{-1} (\frac{4}{5}) + \cos^{-1} (\frac{12}{13}) = \tan^{-1} (\frac{63}{16})$.
3. $2 \sin^{-1} (\frac{3}{5}) = \sin^{-1} (\frac{24}{25})$.
4. $2 \tan^{-1} (x) = \tan^{-1} \left(\dfrac{2x}{1 - x^2}\right)$.

5. Prove

(*a*) $\tan^{-1}(\frac{1}{2}) + \tan^{-1}(\frac{1}{5}) + \tan^{-1}(\frac{1}{8}) = \frac{\pi}{4}$.

(*b*) $4\tan^{-1}(\frac{1}{5}) - \tan^{-1}(\frac{1}{239}) = \frac{\pi}{4}$.

Also given that

$$\tan^{-1}(x) = x - \frac{x^3}{3} + \frac{x^5}{5} - \frac{x^7}{7} + \ldots$$

use this formula to find $\pi/4$, and hence π correct to three decimal places. (This is Machin's formula for π.)

6. Differentiate:

(*a*) $2\tan^{-1} x$ and $\tan^{-1}\left(\frac{2x}{1-x^2}\right)$.

(*b*) $2\sin^{-1} x$ and $\sin^{-1}(2x\sqrt{1-x^2})$.

(*c*) $2\cos^{-1} x$ and $\cos^{-1}(2x^2 - 1)$.

and explain why the results are the same in each case.

7. If A, B, C, D are acute angles such that

$$\tan A = \tfrac{1}{8},\ \tan B = \tfrac{4}{7},\ \tan C = \tfrac{2}{9},\ \tan D = \tfrac{6}{7}$$

prove, without using tables, that

$$A + B + C + D = \frac{\pi}{2}.$$

CHAPTER 4

FUNCTIONS. LIMITS. CONTINUITY

4.1. Functions

Generally a function is a relation between two sets of numbers such as

x (hr.) . . .	0	1	2	3	4
y (gm.) . . .	1	0·90	0·82	0·74	0·67

giving in this case the weight at hourly intervals of an initial weight of 1 gm. of a disintegrating substance. If we want the values of y for other than the given values of x we must have the rule or formula by which y is calculated when x is given. Here it is

$$y = \exp(-0{\cdot}1x) \qquad (x \geqslant 0)$$

This states that we may put $x = 0$ or any positive number to obtain the corresponding value of y. As x increases without limit y decreases to zero, *i.e.*, as $x \to +\infty$, $y \to 0$. These values are limits to which the variables tend but never can attain.

For each value of x there is only one value of y, and since the above can be written as

$$x = -10 \log y \qquad (1 \geqslant y > 0)$$

for each y, there is only one x, so that we have a 1 : 1 relation. Such a relation when it exists simplifies matters considerably.

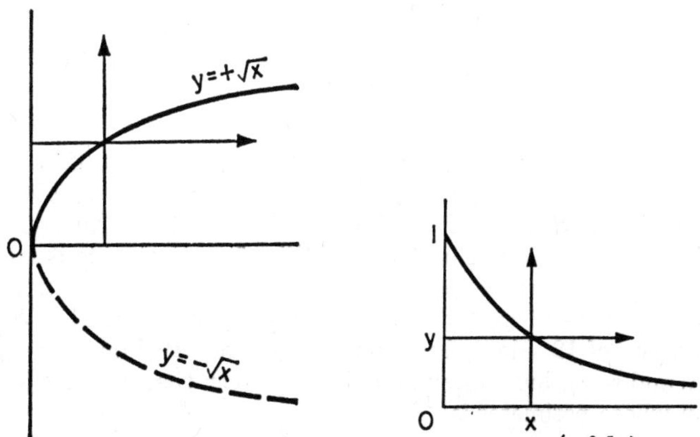

$y^2 = x$. $y = \exp(-0{\cdot}1x)$.

Fig. 3.

In the case $y^2 = x$ for each y there is only one x, but for each x there are two values of y given by $y = \pm\sqrt{x}$. If we take the upper branch only $y = +\sqrt{x}$, we now have a 1 : 1 relation for the purposes of integration. The figures illustrate how a line parallel to one axis cuts the curve in only one point giving the correspond x (or y).

The student will note that a function may need a combination of formulae to express its values. Thus, we could have

$$y = +\sqrt{(1-x)} \qquad (x \leqslant 0)$$

$$y = \cos x \qquad \left(0 < x < \frac{\pi}{2}\right)$$

$$y = 3 \qquad \left(x \geqslant \frac{\pi}{2}\right)$$

For each x there is only one y as *given*. We are still free to observe that there is a break in the gradient at $x = 0$ and $\pi/2$. Also at $x = \pi/2$ there is a jump in the value.

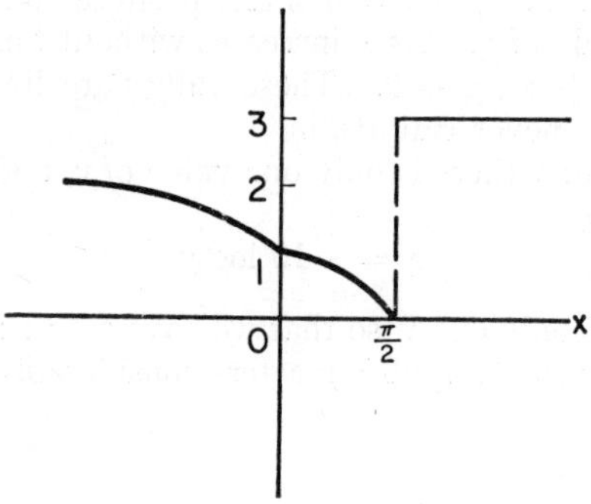

FIG. 4.

4.2. There are graphs which have no functional representation. There are functions which cannot be graphed at all, since the gradient does not exist for any value of x. For example, consider an equilateral triangle with each side of unit length (Fig. 5). Each side is trisected and an equilateral triangle erected on the centre third, external to the figure. The base of each of these triangles is now erased. We now have a figure of 12 sides. The above is now repeated on each of these 12 sides and so on indefinitely. It is easily seen that we have finally a polygon whose perimeter is

$$3 + 1 + (\tfrac{4}{3}) + (\tfrac{4}{3})^2 + (\tfrac{4}{3})^3 + \ldots$$

and so is infinite in length. However, the area enclosed is finite and is seen to be

$$\tfrac{8}{5}\text{ (area of basic triangle).}$$

Also it can be shown that the gradient at any point on this perimeter becomes indeterminate as the number of sides tends to infinity.

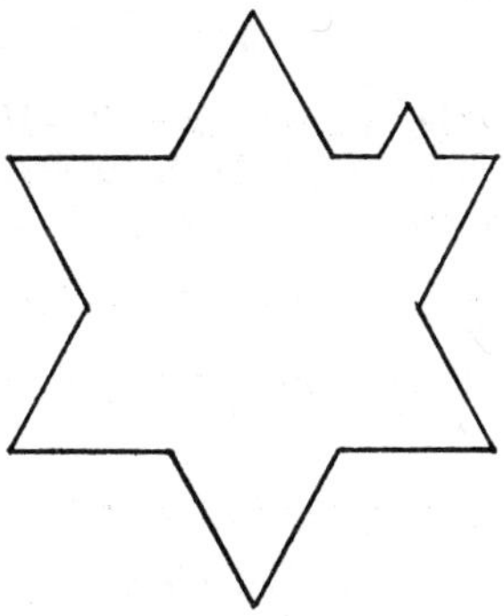

FIG. 5.

We will deal only with simple functions which give simple graphs. Even with these, *e.g.*, the case of $y = 1/x$ integration up to or across the point $x = 0$ needs a special investigation and may be meaningless.

Further development requires a study of limits and of continuity.

EXERCISE 8A

1. Give a sketch of:

(*a*) $y^2 = x$; (*b*) $y = -\sqrt{(-x)}$;
(*c*) $y = +x \ (x \geqslant 0),\ y = -x \ (x \leqslant 0)$.

2. Sketch the function

$$\begin{aligned} y &= 0 && (-\infty < x < -1) \\ &= 1 + x && (-1 \leqslant x \leqslant 0) \\ &= 1 - x && (0 \leqslant x \leqslant 1) \\ &= 0 && (1 < x < +\infty) \end{aligned}$$

3. Draw the graph of

$$y = |x| \qquad (-1 \leqslant x \leqslant 1)$$

4. Sketch: (*a*) $y = x - 1$; (*b*) $y = |x - 1|$.
5. If $[x]$ denotes the integer nearest to x which is less than or equal

to x, *i.e.*, $[1\cdot62] = 1$, $[-1\cdot62] = -2$, sketch (*a*) $y = [x]$, (*b*) $y = x + [x]$, (*c*) $y = |x| + [x]$, in each case for $-3 \leqslant x \leqslant 3$.

6. Sketch the " saw-tooth " function

$$y = x - [x] - \tfrac{1}{2}.$$

4.3. Limits

A simple relation such as

$$y = 1/x \qquad (x \neq 0)$$

defines y for all x except the one value $x = 0$. If x decreases to zero by positive values, *e.g.*, $x = 0\cdot1, 0\cdot01, 0\cdot001, 0\cdot0001, \ldots$, the value of y is always positive and increases without limit, *i.e.*,

$$y \to +\infty \text{ as } x \to +0.$$

If, however, x increases to zero through negative values the values of y tend to $-\infty$, *i.e.*,

$$y \to -\infty \text{ as } x \to -0.$$

Thus, there is no unique " limit " of $1/x$ at $x = 0$. From a graphical point of view the y axis, *i.e.*, the line $x = 0$, is an asymptote separating the two branches of the curve. Since $x = 1/y$, the x axis is also an asymptote.

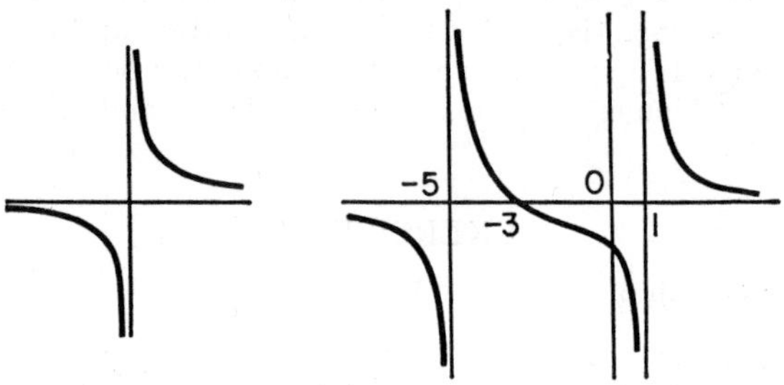

FIG. 6.

A more general case is

$$y = \frac{x+3}{(x-1)(x+5)}$$

which is defined for all values of x except $x = 1$ and -5. Again there is no unique limit of y for these values as shown by the graph, where $x = 1$ and -5 are vertical asymptotes.

4.4. We have seen that s_n, the sum of n terms of the series

$$\frac{1}{1.2} + \frac{1}{2.3} + \frac{1}{3.4} + \ldots$$

is given by

$$s_n = 1 - \frac{1}{n}.$$

As n increases, *i.e.*, we add on more terms, the sum approaches 1. This value is never reached, but we can choose n so that s_n is as near as we please to 1. In such a case it is said that 1 is the **limit** of s_n as n tends to infinity. In symbols

$$s_n \to 1 \text{ as } n \to \infty$$

or

$$\lim_{n\to\infty} s_n = \lim_{n\to\infty} \left(1 - \frac{1}{n}\right) = 1.$$

This uses the obvious limit

$$\lim_{n\to\infty} \left(\frac{1}{n}\right) = 0.$$

Example 1. Find: (i) $\lim\limits_{n\to\infty} \dfrac{3n^2 - 7n - 10{,}000}{2n^2 + n - 4}$; (ii) $\lim\limits_{n\to\infty} \dfrac{\sin n}{n}$.

(i) The expression can be written

$$\frac{\left(3 - \frac{7}{n} - \frac{10{,}000}{n^2}\right)}{\left(2 + \frac{1}{n} - \frac{4}{n^2}\right)}$$

Since $$\lim. \left(\frac{7}{n}\right) = 7 \lim. \left(\frac{1}{n}\right) = 0.$$

$$\lim. \left(\frac{10{,}000}{n^2}\right) = 10{,}000 \lim. \left(\frac{1}{n^2}\right) = 0$$

and similarly for any such ratio with a constant, however large, in the numerator. The required limit is $\frac{3}{2}$.

(ii) As $n \to \infty$, $\sin n$ does not tend to a definite value but being a sine function is always between $+1$ and -1, end values included.

Since $$-1 \leqslant \sin n \leqslant +1$$

or $$0 \leqslant |\sin n| \leqslant 1$$

it follows that

$$0 \leqslant \frac{|\sin n|}{n} \leqslant \frac{1}{n}$$

for any value of n, a positive number. In the limit $1/n = 0$, and since $|\sin n|/n$ is thus hemmed in between two zero values, the equality signs must hold and the limit is zero.

EXERCISE 8B

Show that:

1. $\lim\limits_{n\to\infty} \dfrac{3n}{2n+1} = \frac{3}{2}$.

2. $\lim\limits_{n\to\infty} \dfrac{4}{5n-1} = 0$.

3. $\lim\limits_{n\to\infty} \dfrac{3n^2 + 2n + 7}{n^3 - n + 2} = 0$.

4. $\lim\limits_{n\to\infty} \dfrac{1 + 2 + 3 + \ldots + n}{n^2} = \frac{1}{2}$.

4.5. The Limit Definition

We will now consider the limit approached by a function as the independent variable x approaches a given finite value. Often the answer is obvious, *e.g.*, substitution gives

$$\lim_{x\to 2} (x^2 + 1) = 5$$

but in important cases such as

$$\lim_{x\to 1} \frac{(x^3 - 1)}{(x - 1)}$$

where substitution gives the indeterminate form 0/0 further examination is needed. [The student will note that differentiation from first principles always involves the evaluation of such a form.]

In the above so long as x is not equal to 1 we may cancel the factor $x - 1$ and obtain

$$\frac{(x^3 - 1)}{(x - 1)} = x^2 + x + 1.$$

For $x = 0{\cdot}999$ either expression gives the value $2{\cdot}997001$, and as x *increases* towards 1 the value of either expression increases towards

$$(x^2 + x + 1)_{x=1} = 3.$$

Similarly, when $x = 1{\cdot}00001$ the value of either expression is $3{\cdot}0000300001$ and as x *decreases* to 1 the expression decreases to the value 3.

Using an obvious notation

$$\lim_{x\to 1+0} \left(\frac{x^3 - 1}{x - 1}\right) = 3 = \lim_{x\to 1-0} \left(\frac{x^3 - 1}{x - 1}\right)$$

or, since they are the same,

$$\lim_{x\to 1} \left(\frac{x^3 - 1}{x - 1}\right) = 3.$$

This leads to the following considerations. Suppose that $f(x)$, a given expression in x, tends to the value A as x tends to a. We must specify what we mean by " tends to ". This means that if you require $f(x)$ to be within a certain range of A, then I can state that this will always be so if x is within a certain range of a. We can state this in exact symbolic form.

Let ϵ be a very small positive number which you choose, and you require

$$A - \epsilon < f(x) < A + \epsilon \quad . \quad . \quad . \quad . \quad . \quad (1)$$

I will then find another positive number η such that the above will always be true whenever

$$a - \eta < x < a + \eta \quad . \quad . \quad . \quad . \quad . \quad (2)$$

Now from (1),

$$A - \epsilon < f(x)$$

we obtain

$$A - f(x) < \epsilon \quad . \quad . \quad . \quad . \quad . \quad . \quad . \quad (3)$$

From the other half

$$f(x) < A + \epsilon$$

we obtain

$$f(x) - A < \epsilon \quad . \quad . \quad . \quad . \quad . \quad . \quad . \quad (4)$$

(3), (4) can be put together as

$$|f(x) - A| < \epsilon$$

Similarly, (2) can be expressed as

$$|x - a| < \eta.$$

We now have the definition:

> A function $f(x)$ tends to the limit A as x tends to the value a if when given ϵ a positive number, however small, another positive number η can be found such that
>
> $$|f(x) - A| < \epsilon$$
>
> whenever
>
> $$|x - a| < \eta.$$

Graphically the figure shows $y = f(x)$, in which $y = A$ when $x = a$. The band of dotted lines shows levels $A \pm \epsilon$ which enclose that part of the curve for which $f(x)$ lies between the values $A \pm \epsilon$. The corresponding boundary values of x are p and q. If we choose η less than both $a - q$ and $p - a$, then clearly

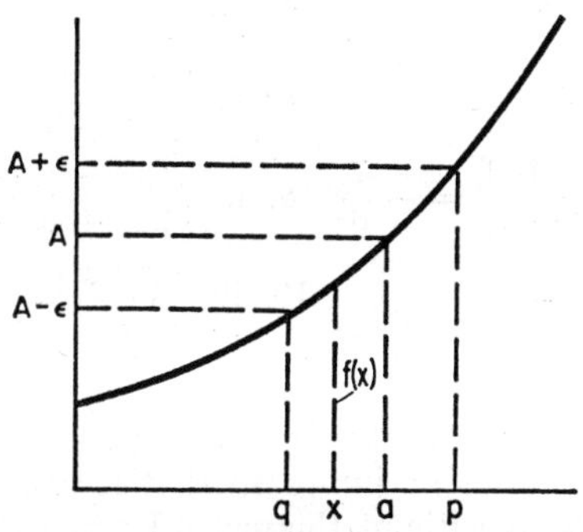

FIG. 7.

$$|f(x) - A| < \epsilon$$

whenever

$$|x - a| < \eta.$$

If the curve represents $y = (x^3 - 1)/(x - 1)$, which is $x^2 + x + 1$ everywhere except at $x = 1$, and the value of a is 1, then only the one point on the curve, $(a, A) = (1, 3)$, is missing and every other point on the curve, however near to this, is as calculated from the equation and shown on the graph. We have filled in this one point by the limit and if we choose to define the function as

$$\begin{aligned} y &= (x^3 - 1)/(x - 1) & (x \neq 1) \\ &= 3 & (x = 1) \end{aligned}$$

the curve is now continuous at $x = 1$ (as defined later) and for all other values of x.

Example 2. Evaluate the following:

(a) $\lim\limits_{x \to 3} \dfrac{2x + 3}{x - 4}$. (b) $\lim\limits_{x \to \infty} \dfrac{2 + x}{3 - 7x}$. (c) $\lim\limits_{x \to 2} \dfrac{2x^2 - 3x - 2}{x^2 + x - 6}$.

(a) $\lim\limits_{x \to 3} \dfrac{2x + 3}{x - 4} = \dfrac{6 + 3}{3 - 4} = -9$. (b) $\lim\limits_{x \to \infty} \dfrac{2 + x}{3 - 7x} = \lim\limits_{x \to \infty} \dfrac{2/x + 1}{3/x - 7} = -\dfrac{1}{7}$.

(c) $f(x) = \dfrac{2x^2 - 3x - 2}{x^2 + x - 6} = \dfrac{(2x + 1)(x - 2)}{(x + 3)(x - 2)} = \dfrac{2x + 1}{x + 3}$ $(x \neq 2)$

$$\therefore \lim_{x \to 2} f(x) = \lim_{x \to 2} \frac{2x + 1}{x + 3} = 1.$$

EXERCISE 8C

Show that:

1. $\lim\limits_{x \to 1} \dfrac{3x + 2}{2x - 1} = 5$.
2. $\lim\limits_{x \to 0} \dfrac{x + 3}{x - 2} = -\dfrac{3}{2}$.
3. $\lim\limits_{x \to \infty} \dfrac{\sqrt{(5x - 4)}}{x + 2} = 0$.
4. $\lim\limits_{x \to 0} \dfrac{\sqrt{(1 + x)} - \sqrt{(1 - x)}}{4x} = \dfrac{1}{4}$.
5. $\lim\limits_{x \to 2} \dfrac{x^2 - 4}{x - 2} = 4$.
6. $\lim\limits_{x \to -3} \dfrac{x^3 + 27}{x + 3} = 27$.
7. $\lim\limits_{x \to -1} \dfrac{(x + 1)(2x + 9)}{(x + 1)(x - 7)} = -\dfrac{7}{8}$.
8. $\lim\limits_{x \to \frac{1}{2}} \dfrac{6x^2 - x - 1}{2x^2 + 5x - 3} = \dfrac{5}{7}$.
9. $\lim\limits_{x \to 0} x \sin\left(\dfrac{1}{x}\right) = 0$.
10. $\lim\limits_{x \to \infty} \dfrac{\cos x}{x} = 0$.

4.6. Continuity

We naturally think of a continuous curve as one without any breaks, *i.e.*, missing points, gaps or jumps so that it can be described by a pencil moving along it without the pencil leaving the curve even at a single point. The discontinuity may occur at just one point, so we will consider continuity as the property of each point, say the point $x = a$.

From the consideration of limits we see that the curve will be continuous at $x = a$ if

$$f(a - 0) = f(a) = f(a + 0)$$

or more concisely

$$\lim_{x \to a} f(x) = f(a).$$

This involves:

(*a*) $f(x)$ must be defined at $x = a$ and in the neighbourhood of $x = a$.

(*b*) whether we move along the curve from below or above $x = a$, we get to the same point $\{a, f(a)\}$ on the curve.

Since limits are involved, we can state the above in a fashion corresponding to 4.5. $f(x)$ is continuous at $x = a$ if given any positive number ϵ, however small, there is a corresponding number η such that

$$|f(x) - f(a)| < \epsilon$$

whenever

$$|x - a| < \eta.$$

Since we are always concerned with the neighbourhood of a, put $x = a + h$ and the above is now

$$|f(a + h) - f(a)| < \epsilon$$

for all h such that $|h| < \eta$.

There are functions whose graphs are as shown. Here

$$\lim_{x \to a - 0} f(x) = A_1, \quad \lim_{x \to a + 0} f(x) = A_2$$

or

$$f(a - 0) = A_1, \quad f(a + 0) = A_2,$$

but $f(a)$ is yet another value.

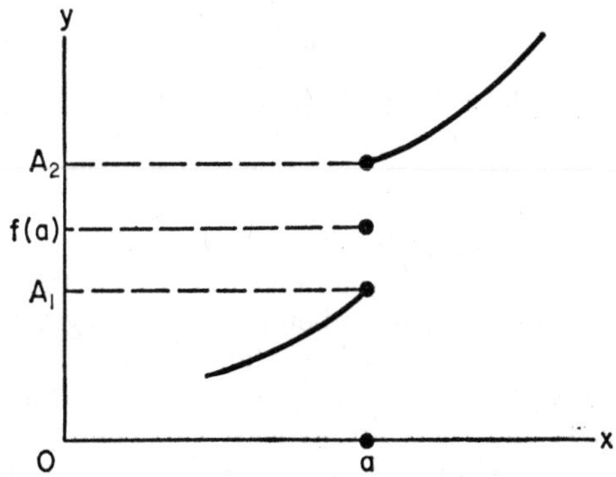

FIG. 8.

This occurs, *e.g.* in certain Fourier series, where $f(a)$ would be the mean of A_1 and A_2.

EXERCISE 8D

1. State the points at which the following functions are discontinuous:

(*a*) $1/(x+3)$; (*b*) $(x+2)/(x^2-9)$; (*c*) $\cos x/(x-1)$; (*d*) $(3x+7)/(1-\sin x)$.

2. Given that

(*a*) $|\sin \frac{1}{2}h| < |\frac{1}{2}h|$, (*b*) $|\cos(a+\frac{1}{2}h)| \leqslant 1$,

prove that $\sin x$ is continuous at any point $x = a$ by considering

$$|\sin(a+h) - \sin a|.$$

4.7. Continuous Functions

We will develop some of the properties of continuous functions. A function $f(x)$ is continuous in the open interval $a < x < b$ if it

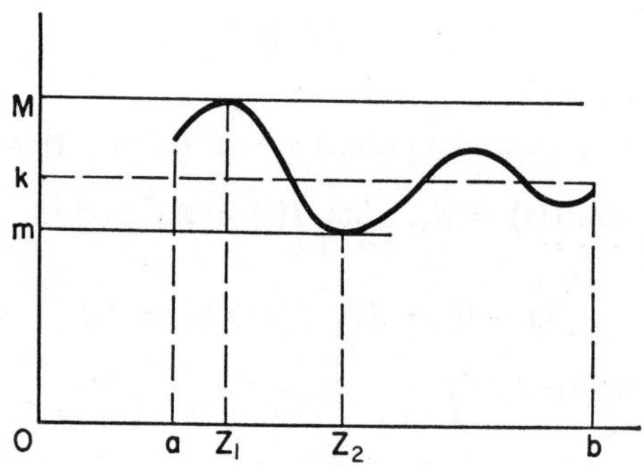

FIG. 9.

is continuous at all x in this interval. If further, for the end points,

$$\lim_{x \to a+0} f(x) = f(a), \qquad \lim_{x \to b-0} f(x) = f(b)$$

the function is continuous in the closed interval $a \leqslant x \leqslant b$.

If $y = f(x)$ is continuous in the range $a \leqslant x \leqslant b$, then it is bounded in this range and also attains its bounds. The diagram illustrates all that we shall require for this important property. There are two numbers M and m such that in (a, b) no values of $f(x)$ are greater than M or less than m and there are at least two points z_1 and z_2 where $f(z_1) = M$ and $f(z_2) = m$. M, m are called the upper and lower bounds respectively.

Also $f(x)$ takes every value between M and m at least once, *i.e.*, if $m < k < M$ there will be at least one point z such that

$$f(z) = k.$$

Example 3. The function $y = (x^2 - 2x + 1)/(x^2 + 2x + 2)$ never becomes infinite or discontinuous because of the vanishing of its denominator which is $(x + 1)^2 + 1$, and so never vanishes. The function then is clearly continuous, and since

$$y = \frac{(1 - 2/x + 1/x^2)}{(1 + 2/x + 2/x^2)},$$

$y \to 1$ as $x \to \infty$ and y will not then become infinite with x.

Since $dy/dx = 2(x - 1)(2x + 3)/(x^2 + 2x + 2)^2$ the turning points are $x = 1$ and $x = -\frac{3}{2}$, and we can show in the usual way that $x = 1$ gives a minimum value $y = 0$ whilst $x = -\frac{3}{2}$ gives a maximum value $y = 5$.

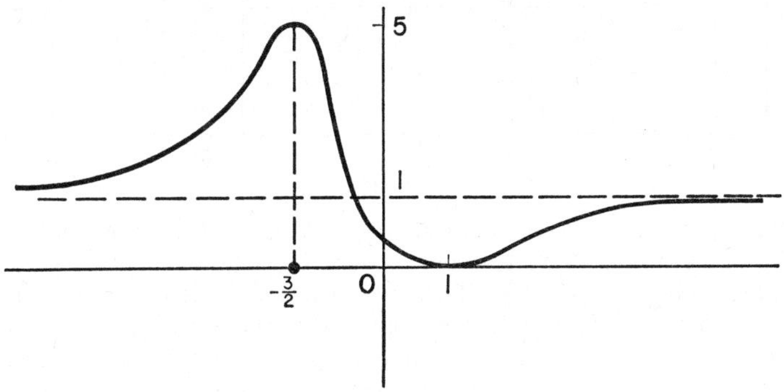

FIG. 10.

The upper bound is $M = 5$ and the lower bound $m = 0$. If we require the function to have a value k, from

$$k = \frac{(x^2 - 2x + 1)}{(x^2 + 2x + 2)}$$

we get
$$x^2(1 - k) - 2x(1 + k) + (1 - 2k) = 0.$$

Since the " $b^2 - 4ac$ " of this is $4k(5 - k)$, we verify that the function can take any value between its bounds 0 and 5 both inclusive.

4.8. Rolle's Theorem

This fundamental theorem depends on the previous work on continuity.

If (*a*) $f(x)$ is continuous in the closed interval $a \leqslant x \leqslant b$, (*b*) $f'(x)$

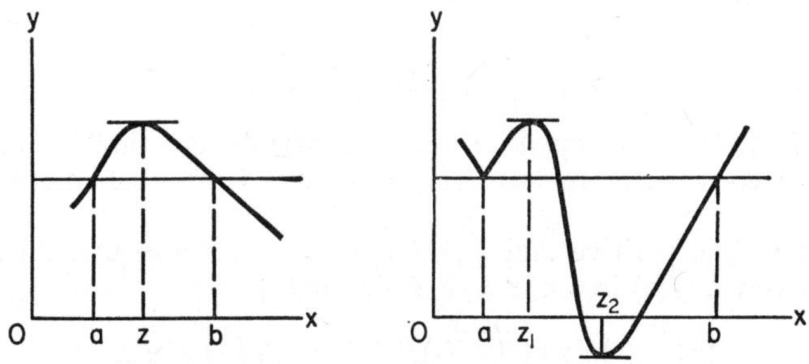

FIG. 11.

exists in the open interval $a < x < b$, (*c*) $f(a) = f(b)$, then there is at least one value z in the open interval $a < z < b$ such that $f'(z) = 0$.

Geometrically the result is obvious. The first figure in Fig. 11 shows that a *continuous* curve with a definite tangent at every point *between* a and b must have at least one tangent parallel to the x axis at inter-

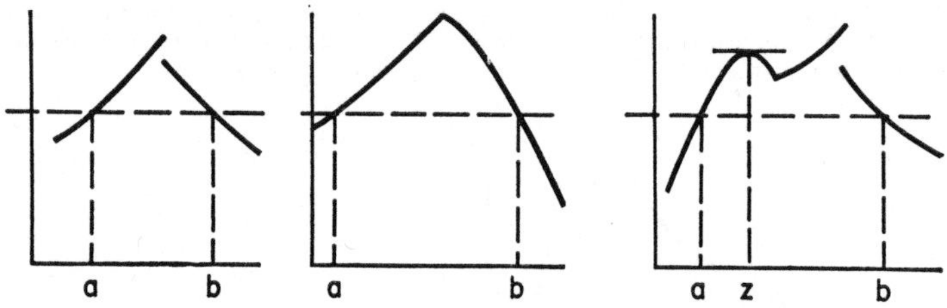

FIG. 12.

mediate points. The second figure shows that the theorem is not upset if the tangent, *i.e.*, $f'(x)$, does not exist at one or both boundary points a and b. The figures in Fig. 12 show that when $f(x)$ is not continuous or $f'(x)$ does not exist at an intermediate point there need not be a point z such that $f'(z) = 0$. The last figure shows that we can still have a point z such that $f'(z) = 0$, even when both the Rolle's conditions (*a*) and (*b*) above are not fulfilled. Therefore these conditions are sufficient but not necessary to ensure at least one point z where $f'(z) = 0$.

EXERCISE 8E

1. Show by a rough sketch that each of the following functions satisfies Rolle's theorem in the interval given. In each case find the point z where $f'(z) = 0$.

(*a*) $y = (x + 3)(x - 4)$ $\qquad -3 \leqslant x \leqslant 4$

(*b*) $y = x^2(x - 2)$ $\qquad 0 \leqslant x \leqslant 2$

(*c*) $y = (x - a)(b - x)^2$ $\qquad a \leqslant x \leqslant b$

2. If a, b are consecutive roots of a polynomial $f(x) = 0$, show that

$$f(x) = (x - a)^m(x - b)^n g(x)$$

where m, n are the powers to which these roots occur and $g(x)$ has the same sign for $a \leqslant x \leqslant b$. Verify that

$$f'(x) = (x - a)^{m-1}\,(x - b)^{n-1}\,h(x),$$

where $h(a)$, $h(b)$ have opposite signs. Hence deduce that in between any two consecutive roots of $f(x) = 0$ there is at least one root of $f'(x) = 0$.

3. If $g(x)$ is positive and m, M are the lower and upper bounds respectively of $f(x)$ in $a \leqslant x \leqslant b$, show that

$$m\int_a^b g(x)\,dx \leqslant \int_a^b f(x)g(x)\,dx \leqslant M\int_a^b g(x)\,dx.$$

(The equality sign allows for the possibility of $f(x)$ being a constant so that $m = M$.) Use this to prove that

(*a*) $$0 < \int_0^{\pi/2} x \sin^2 x \, dx < \frac{\pi^2}{8}$$

(*b*) $$\frac{\pi}{8} < \int_0^{1/\sqrt{2}} \frac{dx}{\sqrt{(1 - x^4)}} < \frac{\pi}{4}.$$

In (*b*) note that $1 - x^4 = (1 - x^2)(1 + x^2)$.

4.9. The Mean Value Theorems

Geometrically it is evident that for a curve $y = f(x)$, such as that drawn which satisfies the **Rolle's** conditions there is at least one point

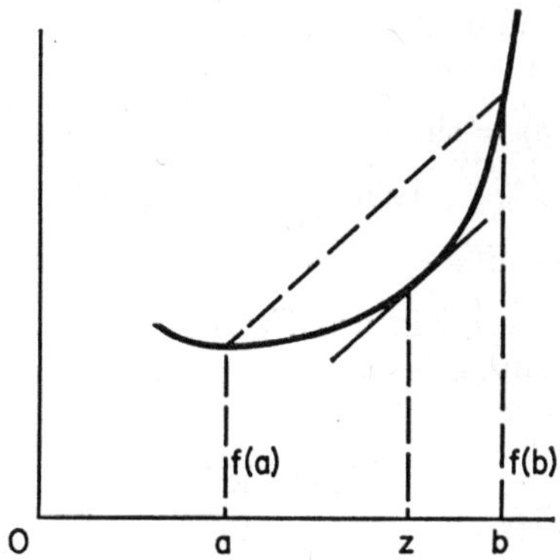

FIG. 13.

z in the open interval (a, b) such that the tangent is parallel to the chord, *i.e.*,

$$\frac{f(b) - f(a)}{b - a} = f'(z)$$

If we put $b = a + h$ so that since z is in between it may be written as $a + \theta h$ $(0 < \theta < 1)$ the above becomes

$$f(a + h) = f(a) + hf'(a + \theta h)$$

and is the **First Mean Value** theorem.

Owing to the condition $0 < \theta < 1$ this can be used to establish a number of inequalities.

Example 4. If $f(x) = \log x$ so that for $a > 0$, $a + h > 0$ the above gives the equation

$$\log (a + h) = \log a + \frac{h}{a + \theta h}$$

solve for θ:

$$\theta = \frac{1}{\log\left(1 + \frac{h}{a}\right)} - \frac{a}{h}.$$

Put $u = h/a$. Since $a + h > 0$ and $h \neq 0$, $u > -1$ and since $u \neq 0$ we now have

$$\theta = \frac{1}{\log (1 + u)} - \frac{1}{u}.$$

Since $0 < \theta < 1$

$$\frac{1}{u} < \frac{1}{\log (1 + u)} < 1 + \frac{1}{u}$$

or

$$\frac{u}{1 + u} < \log (1 + u) < u.$$

If $f(x)$ and $f'(x)$ are both continuous in $a \leqslant x \leqslant b$ and $f''(x)$ exists in the open interval $a < x < b$ we can prove the **Second Mean Value** theorem,

$$f(a + h) = f(a) + hf'(a) + \tfrac{1}{2}h^2 f''(a + \theta h)$$

where $b = a + h$ and $0 < \theta < 1$.

As an illustration

$$\sin (a + h) = \sin a + h \cos a + \tfrac{1}{2}h^2[- \sin (a + \theta h)]$$

Since

$$| \sin (a + \theta h) | \leqslant |$$

$$| \sin (a + h) - \sin a - h \cos a | = \tfrac{1}{2}h^2 \, | \sin (a + \theta h) | \leqslant \tfrac{1}{2}h^2$$

giving limits to the error incurred when $\sin a + h \cos a$ is used as an approximation to $\sin (a + h)$.

EXERCISE 9

1. Find θ when the First Mean Value theorem is applied for the interval $a \leqslant x \leqslant a + h$ to:

(*a*) x^2;
(*b*) x^3, verify that $\theta \to \frac{1}{2}$ as $h \to 0$;
(*c*) e^x, deduce from this an inequality involving h only.

2. If a is a good approximation to a root of $f(x) = 0$ and $a + h$ is the exact value so that $f(a + h) = 0$ where h is small, show that generally $a - f(a)/f'(a)$ is a better value of the root. (Newton's method for the solution of equations, see Chapter 6.)

3. Given that 1·5 is a root of $x^4 + 5x - 15 = 0$, use Newton's method repeatedly to show that 1·6206 is a better approximation.

4. Show that for $h > 0$

$$1 + \frac{h}{2\sqrt{(1 + h)}} < \sqrt{(1 + h)} < 1 + \frac{h}{2}.$$

5. Find:

(*a*) $\lim\limits_{h \to 0} [\sin (x + h) + \sin (x - h) - 2 \sin x]/h^2$;
(*b*) $\lim\limits_{h \to 0} [\log (x + h) + \log (x - h) - 2 \log x]/h^2$.

6. Assume that, as an approximation, the curve $y = f(x)$ is represented in the interval (a, b) by $y = g(x)$, a line joining the points $[a, f(a)]$, $[b, f(b)]$. Define:

$$\phi(x) = g(x) - f(x),$$

i.e., $\phi(x)$ is the length of ordinate at the point x in (a, b) intercepted between the line and the curve. Apply Rolle's theorem to this to prove the First Mean Value theorem.

7. Define in the interval (a, b):

$$\phi(x) = f(b) - f(x) - \left(\frac{b - x}{b - a}\right)\{f(b) - f(a)\}$$

show that $\phi(a) = 0 = \phi(b)$ and that $\phi(x)$ and its derivative satisfy Rolle's theorem given that the same is true for $f(x)$. Deduce the First Mean Value theorem.

8. Define:

$$\phi(x) = f(b) - f(x) - (b - x)f'(x) - \left(\frac{b - x}{b - a}\right)^2 \{f(b) - f(a) - (b - a)f'(a)\},$$

where we suppose that $f(x)$ and $f'(x)$ are both continuous in $a \leqslant x \leqslant b$ and that $f''(x)$ exists in the open interval (a, b).

Show that $\phi(x)$ satisfies the conditions for Rolle's theorem and deduce the Second Mean Value theorem.

9. A is the point $(a, 0)$ and the ordinate meets the curve $y = f(x)$ at P. B is the point $(a + h, 0)$ and the ordinate meets the curve at Q. The tangent to the curve at P meets BQ at T. Show that

$$\text{TQ} = \tfrac{1}{2}h^2 f''(a + \theta h).$$

10. By taking $a = 0$, $h = x$ in the Mean Value theorem show that

$$e^x = 1 + x + \frac{x^2}{2} e^{\theta h}$$
$$> 1 + x$$

11. Show that:

$$\log (1 + x) > x - \frac{x^2}{2} \qquad (x > 0)$$
$$< x - \frac{x^2}{2} \qquad (-1 < x < 0)$$

12. If $a_1 + h$ is a root of $f(x) = 0$ and a_1 a good approximation so that h is small, show that the next approximation to a_1 is

$$a_2 = a_1 - f(a_1)/f'(a_1)$$

If a_3 is the next approximation to a_2, show that

$$\begin{aligned} a_3 - a_2 &= -\tfrac{1}{2}h^2 f''(a_1 + \theta h)/f'(a_1 + h) \\ &\simeq -\tfrac{1}{2}h^2 f''(a_1)/f'(a_1) \\ &= -\{f(a_1)\}^2 f''(a_1)/2\{f'(a_1)\}^3. \end{aligned}$$

Solve $x + \sin x = 1{\cdot}5$ correct to 4 decimal places.

Show that beginning with $x = 1$ successive approximations are 0·7783, 0·7897. At this stage show that the error is about $2{\cdot}7 \times 10^{-5}$, so that $a_3 = 0{\cdot}7897$ is correct to 4 decimal places.

13. Solve $x^2 + \log_e x = 10$ correct to 3 decimal places. [Begin with $a_1 = 3$, obtain a_2 to 3 decimal places and check that a_3 differs from a_2 by an amount that does not affect the final decimal in a_2.]

14. $x^3 - 4x + 2 = 0$ has a root near $x = 2$. Find this root correct to 3 decimal places.

CHAPTER 5

DIFFERENTIATION (REVISION)

5.1. The Meaning of a Differential Coefficient

Suppose A is the point (x, y) on the curve $y = f(x)$ and B is a near point $(x + \Delta x, y + \Delta y)$ also on the curve. Then the gradient of the line AB is given by

$$\frac{\Delta y}{\Delta x} = \frac{f(x + \Delta x) - f(x)}{\Delta x}.$$

As B closes up to A, *i.e.*, $\Delta x \to 0$, the join AB tends to become the tangent at A to the given curve. Finally, the join is the actual tan-

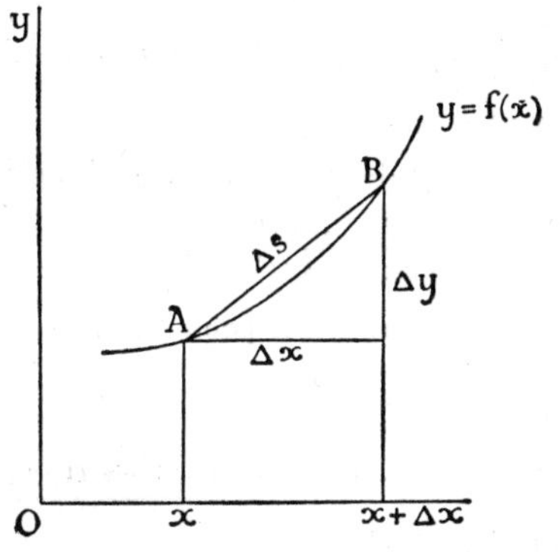

FIG. 14.

gent at A. To show that we have arrived at this limiting value we denote the left-hand side of the above equation by dy/dx. The right-hand side must be evaluated to give this required gradient of the tangent to the curve $y = f(x)$ at the general point (x, y) on the curve.

$$\therefore \frac{dy}{dx} = \lim_{\Delta x \to 0} \frac{f(x + \Delta x) - f(x)}{\Delta x}.$$

Since $\Delta x \to 0$, it is necessary that the numerator should also tend to zero or the ratio will tend to infinity. This requires that

$$\lim_{\Delta x \to 0} [f(x + \Delta x) - f(x)] = 0$$

or

$$\lim_{\Delta x \to 0} f(x + \Delta x) = \lim_{\Delta x \to 0} f(x) = f(x)$$

showing that $f(x)$ must be continuous at the point x. This is then a necessary condition for a function to have a derivative at a given point. However, it is not also a sufficient condition, *i.e.*, a function may be continuous at a point and yet not have a derivative there.

A continuous curve with a kink at one point would not have a derivative at this point. There could be two limits for the derivative, one left-hand and the other right-hand as found when, at the point x, $x + \Delta x \to x - 0$ or $x + 0$.

The function

$$y = x \sin\left(\frac{1}{x}\right) \qquad x \neq 0$$
$$= 0 \qquad x = 0$$

is also continuous at the origin and yet with no derivative there.

In the following $u, v, w, \ldots, f(x)$ will always stand for differentiable functions, *i.e.*, the derivatives can be found for a general value x.

5.2. *We will assume the following results.*

If $$y = ax^n$$

$$\frac{dy}{dx} = anx^{n-1} \text{ for all values of } n.$$

5.3. Differentiation of a Sum

If $$y = u + v + w + \ldots, \text{ all functions of } x,$$

$$\frac{dy}{dx} = \frac{du}{dx} + \frac{dv}{dx} + \frac{dw}{dx} + \ldots$$

Example 1. Find the gradient at the point (1, 2) on the curve

$$y = x^3 + 3x^2 - x - 1.$$

$$\frac{dy}{dx} = 3x^2 + 6x - 1$$

$$= 3 \,.\, 1^2 + 6 \,.\, 1 - 1 = \underline{8 \text{ at the point } (1, 2).}$$

5.4. Differentiation of a Product

If $$y = uv,$$

$$\frac{dy}{dx} = u\frac{dv}{dx} + v\frac{du}{dx}.$$

Example 2. Find the gradient at the point (1, 6) on the curve

$$y = (x^3 + 1)(x^2 + 2).$$

$$\frac{dy}{dx} = (x^3 + 1)2x + (x^2 + 2)3x^2$$

$$= \underline{13 \text{ at the point } (1, 6).}$$

5.5. Differentiation of a Quotient

If $$y = \frac{u}{v},$$

$$\frac{dy}{dx} = \frac{v\dfrac{du}{dx} - u\dfrac{dv}{dx}}{v^2}.$$

Example 3. Find the gradient at the point (1, 1) on the curve

$$y = \frac{(x^2 + 4x + 1)}{(x^2 + 2x + 3)}.$$

$$\frac{dy}{dx} = \frac{(x^2 + 2x + 3)(2x + 4) - (x^2 + 4x + 1)(2x + 2)}{(x^2 + 2x + 3)^2}$$

$$= \frac{36 - 24}{36} = \frac{1}{3} \text{ at } (1, 1).$$

5.6. Differentiation of an Implicit Function of *x*

Without the use of the notation of partial differentiation a general formula for this method cannot be given. An example will best illustrate the method.

Example 4. Find the gradient at the point (x, y) on the curve

$$x^3 + y^3 = 3axy.$$

Differentiate this as it stands.

$$3x^2 + 3y^2\frac{dy}{dx} = 3a\left(x\frac{dy}{dx} + y \cdot 1\right)$$

$$\frac{dy}{dx}(3y^2 - 3ax) = 3ay - 3x^2$$

$$\therefore \quad \frac{dy}{dx} = \frac{ay - x^2}{y^2 - ax}.$$

EXERCISE 10

Differentiate:

1. $(2x + 3)(x^2 - 1)$.
2. $\frac{1}{2\sqrt{x}} - \frac{4}{x^4}$.
3. $\frac{7}{1 + x^2}$.
4. $\frac{x}{\sqrt{x^2 + x + 1}}$.
5. $(a^2 - x^2)^{\frac{3}{4}}$.

Find the gradient at the point (x_1, y_1) of each of the curves:

6. $y = (3x^2 + x + 1)^4$.
7. $y = \frac{1}{\sqrt{a^2 - x^2}}$.
8. $ax^2 + 2hxy + by^2 = 1$.
9. $y(x - 1) = 3 - x^2$.
10. If $xy = ax^3 + b$, prove that $x^2\frac{d^2y}{dx^2} = 2y$.
11. If $xy = ax^2 + \frac{c}{x}$, prove that $x^2\frac{d^2y}{dx^2} + 2\left(x\frac{dy}{dx} - y\right) = 0$.
12. Find the equation of the tangent to the curve $y = \frac{(x^2 + x + 2)}{(x^2 - x + 2)}$ at the point (1, 2).
13. If $pv^s = c$, where s and c are constant and h is given by $h = \frac{1}{\gamma - 1}\left\{v\frac{dp}{dv} + \gamma p\right\}$, show that

$$h = \frac{\gamma - s}{\gamma - 1}p.$$

5.7. Differentiation of log x and e^{ax}

(*a*) We will show the importance of the number denoted by e in mathematics. Its importance is at once clear if we differentiate the logarithm of a number to any other base than e.

Let

$$y = \log_a x$$

where a is any positive number.

If now x increases by Δx, then $y = \log_a x$, being a continuous function of x, will increase by Δy where Δy tends to zero with Δx.

$$\therefore \quad y + \Delta y = \log_a (x + \Delta x).$$

Subtract:

$$\Delta y = \log_a (x + \Delta x) - \log_a x$$

$$= \log_a \left(1 + \frac{\Delta x}{x}\right).$$

$$\therefore \quad \frac{\Delta y}{\Delta x} = \frac{\log_a \left(1 + \frac{\Delta x}{x}\right)}{\Delta x}.$$

To reproduce the $\frac{\Delta x}{x}$ inside the logarithm we will write this as

$$\frac{\Delta y}{\Delta x} = \frac{1}{x} \cdot \frac{\log_a \left(1 + \frac{\Delta x}{x}\right)}{\frac{\Delta x}{x}}$$

$$= \frac{1}{x} \cdot \log_a \left(1 + \frac{\Delta x}{x}\right)^{\frac{x}{\Delta x}}.$$

For convenience we will put $\frac{\Delta x}{x} = \frac{1}{n}$ so that as Δx tends to zero, n tends to infinity. x is, of course, a given fixed point.

$$\therefore \quad \frac{\Delta y}{\Delta x} = \frac{1}{x} \log_a \left(1 + \frac{1}{n}\right)^n.$$

Proceeding to the limit as Δx tends to zero

$$\frac{dy}{dx} = \frac{1}{x} \lim_{n \to \infty} \log_a \left(1 + \frac{1}{n}\right)^n.$$

We have shown that

$$\lim_{n \to \infty} \left(1 + \frac{1}{n}\right)^n = 2{\cdot}71828 \ldots$$

$$\therefore \quad \frac{dy}{dx} = \frac{1}{x} \log_a (2{\cdot}71828 \ldots).$$

This shows that the differential coefficient of $\log_a x$ will be the simple answer $\frac{1}{x}$ multiplied by an awkward constant. If, however, we choose $a = 2{\cdot}718\ldots$, the number which is always denoted by e, the awkward factor becomes unity.

For this reason we always work with logarithms to this base e in calculus. Log x will mean $\log_e x$ unless any other base is mentioned.

We now have that if

$$y = \log_e x,$$
$$\frac{dy}{dx} = \frac{1}{x},$$

whilst if a is any other base and

$$y = \log_a x$$
$$= \log_e x \times \log_a e,$$

then
$$\frac{dy}{dx} = \frac{1}{x}\log_a e.$$

(*b*) If
$$y = e^x$$
$$\log_e y = x \log_e e = x.$$

Differentiate with respect to y:

$$\frac{1}{y} = \frac{dx}{dy},$$
$$\therefore \quad \frac{dy}{dx} = y = e^x.$$

We thus obtain the astonishing result that e^x reproduces itself when differentiated.

If $y = e^{ax}$, put $z = ax$ so that $\frac{dz}{dx} = a$,

$$\therefore \quad y = e^z$$
$$\frac{dy}{dz} = e^z.$$

We require
$$\frac{dy}{dx} = \frac{dy}{dz}\cdot\frac{dz}{dx}$$
$$= e^z . a$$
$$= \underline{ae^{ax}}.$$

Similarly, if
$$y = e^{f(x)},$$
$$\frac{dy}{dx} = \underline{e^{f(x)} . f'(x)}. \qquad \left[f'(x) \equiv \frac{df(x)}{dx}\right].$$

(*c*) If $y = \log f(x)$, put $f(x) = z$ so that $f'(x) = \frac{dz}{dx}$,

$$\therefore \quad y = \log z$$
$$\frac{dy}{dz} = \frac{1}{z}.$$

We require

$$\frac{dy}{dx} = \frac{dy}{dz} \cdot \frac{dz}{dx}$$

$$= \frac{1}{z} \cdot f'(x)$$

$$= \frac{f'(x)}{f(x)}.$$

E.g., in $y = \log \sin 3x$, $f(x) = \sin 3x$, $f'(x) = 3 \cos 3x$,

$$\therefore \quad \frac{dy}{dx} = \frac{3 \cos 3x}{\sin 3x}.$$

5.8. Differentiation of the Circular Functions

The following differential coefficients have previously been obtained:

$$\frac{d}{d\theta}(\sin a\theta) = a \cos a\theta. \qquad \frac{d}{d\theta}(\operatorname{cosec} a\theta) = -a \operatorname{cosec} a\theta \,.\, \cot a\theta.$$

$$\frac{d}{d\theta}(\cos a\theta) = -a \sin a\theta. \qquad \frac{d}{d\theta}(\sec a\theta) = a \sec a\theta \,.\, \tan a\theta.$$

$$\frac{d}{d\theta}(\tan a\theta) = a \sec^2 a\theta. \qquad \frac{d}{d\theta}(\cot a\theta) = -a \operatorname{cosec}^2 a\theta.$$

Example 5. If $s = a \sin \omega t$, where a and ω are constants, prove that

$$\frac{ds}{dt} = \pm \omega\sqrt{a^2 - s^2}, \quad \frac{d^2s}{dt^2} = -\omega^2 s.$$

Since $\quad s = a \sin \omega t$

$$\therefore \quad \frac{ds}{dt} = a\omega \cos \omega t \quad \dots\dots\dots \quad (1)$$

$$= a\omega(\pm\sqrt{1 - \sin^2 \omega t})$$

$$= \pm a\omega\sqrt{1 - s^2/a^2} = \pm \omega\sqrt{a^2 - s^2}.$$

Differentiate (1):

$$\frac{d^2s}{dt^2} = a\omega(-\omega \sin \omega t)$$

$$= -\omega^2(a \sin \omega t) = -\omega^2 s.$$

Example 6. The figure represents a vertical fence AB $2\frac{1}{4}$ ft. in front of a vertical wall CD. Find the length of the shortest ladder LM which, resting on the horizontal ground AX, will reach over the fence to the wall. The fence AB is $5\frac{1}{3}$ ft. high.

If the dotted line represents a position of the ladder, then a line drawn parallel to it but touching the top of the fence B is obviously shorter. The minimum length must therefore be provided by a ladder touching the fence at B. If LM ($= y$) denotes this length when it makes $\angle\theta$ with the horizontal,

$$y = \text{LB} + \text{BM}$$

$$= 5\tfrac{1}{3} \operatorname{cosec} \theta + 2\tfrac{1}{4} \sec \theta,$$

$$\therefore \quad \frac{dy}{d\theta} = -\tfrac{16}{3} \operatorname{cosec} \theta \,.\, \cot \theta + \tfrac{9}{4} \sec \theta \,.\, \tan \theta.$$

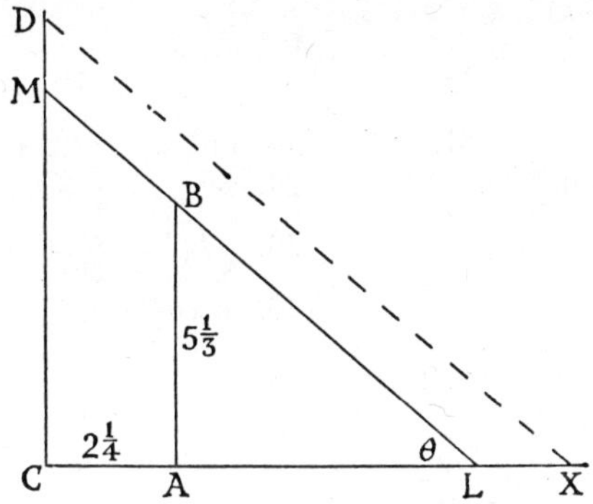

FIG. 15.

The turning values of y are given by solving $\frac{dy}{d\theta} = 0$.

$$-\frac{16}{3}\frac{\cos\theta}{\sin^2\theta} + \frac{9}{4}\frac{\sin\theta}{\cos^2\theta} = 0,$$

$$\tan^3\theta = \tfrac{64}{27}, \quad \tan\theta = \tfrac{4}{3}.$$

Again, if we denote $\sin\theta$ by s and $\cos\theta$ by c,

$$\frac{d^2y}{d\theta^2} = \frac{16}{3}\frac{(1+c^2)}{s^3} + \frac{9}{4}\frac{(1+s^2)}{c^3},$$

which is obviously positive when positive values are substituted—as obtained from the above value of $\tan\theta$. $\therefore$ the above value of θ gives a minimum length.

Since $\tan\theta = \tfrac{4}{3}$, $\operatorname{cosec}\theta = \tfrac{5}{4}$ and $\sec\theta = \tfrac{5}{3}$.

$$\begin{aligned}\therefore\quad y\text{ (min.)} &= 5\tfrac{1}{3}\operatorname{cosec}\theta + 2\tfrac{1}{4}\sec\theta \\ &= \tfrac{16}{3}\times\tfrac{5}{4} + \tfrac{9}{4}\times\tfrac{5}{3} \\ &= \underline{10\text{ ft. }5\text{ in.}}\end{aligned}$$

EXERCISE 11

Differentiate:

1. $3\sin 2x$.
2. $p\cos(ax+b)$.
3. $\sin(-x)$.
4. $\tan\left(\frac{\pi}{4} - \frac{x}{2}\right)$.
5. $\sin^2 x + \cos^2 x$.
6. $x\sin 2x$.
7. $4\tan 2x$.
8. $\cot(ax+b)$.
9. $\frac{\cos 2x}{x^2}$.
10. $\sin 2x\cos x$.
11. $\frac{(1+\tan x)}{(1-\tan x)}$.
12. $\frac{\tan x}{(1+\sec x)}$.
13. $\tan x\sin 2x$.
14. If $y = \operatorname{cosec} x + \cot x$, prove that $\frac{d^2y}{dx^2} + y\frac{dy}{dx} = 0$.
15. If $y = \sec x$, prove that $\frac{d^2y}{dx^2} = y(2y^2 - 1)$.

Differentiate:

16. $3\cos(1-4x)$.

17. $\sin^2(3x)$. 18. $\left(\sin\frac{x}{3}\right)^{\frac{1}{2}}$. 19. $\sqrt{\cos 2x}$.

20. $\sec^2(3x)$. 21. $\sec^2(x)-\tan^2(x)$. 22. $\tan^3(2x)$.

23. $3\tan x+\tan^3(x)$. 24. $\sec^3(x)-3\sec x$.

25. $\frac{\cos^2(x)}{x^2}$. 26. $\sqrt{\left(\frac{1-\sin x}{1+\sin x}\right)}$.

27. $x+\cot x$. 28. $x^2\cos^2(x)$.

Find the equation of the tangent to:

29. $y=\sin x$ at $(\pi/6, \frac{1}{2})$.

30. $y=(\sin x)/x$ at $(\pi, 0)$.

31. $y=\tan^2 x$ at $(\pi/4, 1)$.

32. If $y=\frac{(1+\sin x)}{\cos x}$ show $\frac{d^2y}{dx^2}=\frac{\cos x}{(1-\sin x)^2}$.

33. If $y^2=\sec 2x$, show $\frac{d^2y}{dx^2}=3y^5-y$.

Differentiate:

34. $5e^{4x}$. 35. $7e^{-2x}$. 36. xe^{2x}.

37. e^{x^2}. 38. $e^{2x}\sin 4x$. 39. $\frac{x^2}{e^{4x}}$.

40. If $y=ae^{px}+be^{-px}$, show $\frac{d^2y}{dx^2}=p^2y$.

41. If $y=e^x\sin x$ show $\frac{d^4y}{dx^4}=-4y$.

42. Find m if $y=e^{mx}$ satisfies $\frac{d^2y}{dx^2}-5\frac{dy}{dx}+6y=0$.

Differentiate:

43. $\log x^2$. 44. $\log(x^2+2x+3)$. 45. $\log\cos 4x$.

46. $\log(e^{x^2})$. 47. $x^2\log x$. 48. $\frac{\log 2x}{x}$.

49. $\log(x+\sqrt{x^2+a^2})$. 50. $\log(x+\sqrt{x^2-a^2})$.

51. $(\log x)^4$. 52. $\log(\log x)$.

53. Show that the minimum value of $x^2e^{1/x}$ is 1·85.

54. In a submarine cable the distance to which a signal travels varies directly as $d^2\log_e\left(\frac{D}{d}\right)$, where d is the diameter of the core and D that of the covering. For a given D show that maximum distance is obtained when $d=De^{-\frac{1}{2}}$.

5.9. Maxima and Minima

Example 6, as solved above, should serve to remind the student of the following practical rules for solving problems on " maxima and minima", "turning values" or "stationary values" of a function:

(1) Obtain an expression for the value y, whose turning values are required in terms of *one variable* x only. To do this we often have to use the given data or the geometry of the figure. We will then have $y = f(x)$.

(2) Solve the equation $\frac{dy}{dx} = 0$ and if $x = a$ is a root,

(3) Substitute $x = a$ in $\frac{d^2y}{dx^2}$. If the result is positive, then $x = a$ gives a minimum value; if negative a maximum value. Each root of $\frac{dy}{dx} = 0$ must be tested in this way.

(4) We will deal later with the case when $\frac{d^2y}{dx^2} = 0$ for $x = a$.

Example 7. We will solve Example 6 using a different variable. Let AL $= x$,

$$\therefore \quad \text{BL} = \sqrt{x^2 + (5\tfrac{1}{3})^2} = \tfrac{1}{3}\sqrt{9x^2 + 256}.$$

We need MB in terms of x.

$$\frac{\text{MB}}{2\frac{1}{4}} = \frac{\text{BL}}{x},$$

$$\text{MB} = \frac{2\frac{1}{4}}{x} \cdot \text{BL} = \frac{3}{4x}\sqrt{9x^2 + 256},$$

$$\therefore \quad y = \text{BL} + \text{MB}$$

$$= \frac{1}{3}\sqrt{9x^2 + 256} + \frac{3}{4x}\sqrt{9x^2 + 256}$$

$$= \left(\frac{3}{4x} + \frac{1}{3}\right)\sqrt{9x^2 + 256},$$

$$\frac{dy}{dx} = \frac{9 + 4x}{12x} \cdot \frac{1}{2} \cdot \frac{18x}{\sqrt{9x^2 + 256}} - \sqrt{9x^2 + 256}\left(\frac{3}{4x^2}\right).$$

$$= \frac{3}{4}\,\frac{4x^3 - 256}{x^2\sqrt{9x^2 + 256}},$$

the turning values are given by $4x^3 - 256 = 0$,

$$\therefore \quad x = 4.$$

This will give the same value for y (min.) as before. The student may differentiate the above expression for $\frac{dy}{dx}$ again and show that $x = 4$ makes $\frac{d^2y}{dx^2}$ positive. Otherwise he may note that the above value is clearly a minimum, since the maximum values are infinite. These occur when the point L is far away to the right and when the point L is against the foot of the fence at A so that M is infinitely high up the wall.

Example 8. The total surface of a right circular cone is given as A. Show that the volume will be a maximum when the semi-vertical angle is $\tan^{-1}\left(\frac{1}{2\sqrt{2}}\right)$.

$$V = \tfrac{1}{3}\pi r^2 h$$

This expression for V contains two variables. The given data will be used to eliminate one of them.

Given $\quad$ A = curved surface + base surface

$$= \pi l r + \pi r^2,$$

$$\therefore \quad \frac{A}{\pi} = r\sqrt{h^2 + r^2} + r^2.$$

It is easy to find h^2 from this equation, so we will use it to substitute in V for the value of h.

$$\frac{9V^2}{\pi^2} = r^4h^2$$

$$= r^4\left[\frac{1}{r^2}\left(\frac{A}{\pi} - r^2\right)^2 - r^2\right],$$

$$\therefore \quad 9V^2 = A^2r^2 - 2\pi Ar^4.$$

If V is a maximum so is $9V^2$.

$$\frac{d}{dr}(9V^2) = 2A^2r - 8\pi Ar^3,$$

$$\frac{d^2}{dr^2}(9V^2) = 2A^2 - 24\pi Ar^2.$$

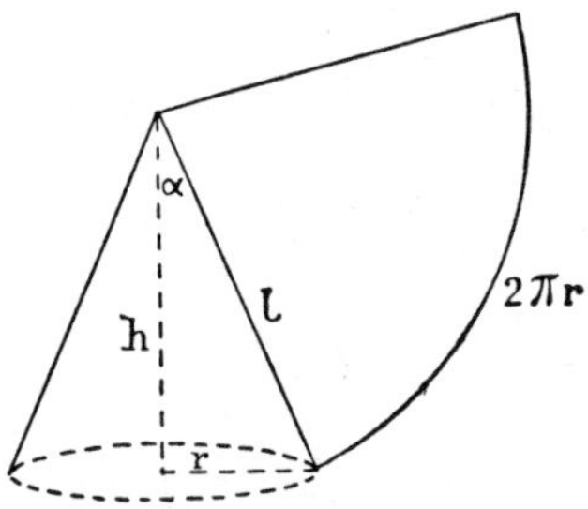

FIG. 16.

The stationary values are given by

$$2A^2r - 8\pi Ar^3 = 0,$$

$$\therefore \quad r = 0 \text{ or } \tfrac{1}{2}\sqrt{A/\pi}.$$

$r = 0$ makes the second differential coefficient +ve and gives a minimum, whilst $r = \frac{1}{2}\sqrt{A/\pi}$ makes it −ve, and therefore gives a maximum value to V. When $r = \frac{1}{2}\sqrt{A/\pi}$, $l = \frac{3}{2}\sqrt{A/\pi}$ and $h = \sqrt{2}\sqrt{A/\pi}$,

$$\therefore \quad \tan\alpha = \frac{r}{h} = \frac{1}{2\sqrt{2}}.$$

The student should endeavour to solve this problem by substituting for r and h in terms of α.

This gives:

$$A = \frac{\pi h^2 \sin\alpha}{(1 - \sin\alpha)}$$

$$V = \frac{1}{3}\frac{A^{\frac{3}{2}}}{\pi^{\frac{1}{2}}}\left[\frac{\sin\alpha\,(1 - \sin\alpha)}{(1 + \sin\alpha)^2}\right]^{\frac{1}{2}}.$$

EXERCISE 12

1. Show that $y = x^2 - 3x + 1$ has a minimum value only, and $y = 4 - 7x - x^2$ a maximum only.

2. Show that $y = ax^2 + bx + c$ has a maximum or minimum only, depending on the sign of a, maximum if a is negative and minimum if a is positive.

3. Prove that $y = (2 - x)/(x - 1)$ has no turning value.

4. Find the values of x for which the following functions have turning values. In each case state whether the value of x gives a maximum or minimum value.

(a) $y = x + 1 + \frac{1}{x}$, (b) $y = \frac{x(x-1)}{x-2}$, (c) $y = x^2(x - 2)$.

In each of these cases the student should, if possible, give a rough sketch of the curve to illustrate his results.

5. A length of wire is to be cut into two parts, a square being formed of one part and a circle of the other. Find the ratio of these parts if the sum of the areas of the square and circle is to be a minimum.

6*. Through the point A(a, b) in the first quadrant a straight line is drawn cutting the axes Ox, Oy on the positive side of the origin O at B, C respectively. Find:

(i) the minimum value of the area OBC;
(ii) the minimum value of OB + OC.

7. The intensity of illumination produced by a lamp A at a point P varies directly as the candle-power of the lamp and inversely as the square of the distance AP. Two lamps of candle-power 27 and 8 respectively are placed 30 ft. apart. Write down an expression for the total intensity of illumination at a point between them distant x from one of them, and hence find the value of x for minimum intensity.

8. The torque T ton ft. on the crankshaft of an engine is given by

$$T = 8 + 3 \sin 2\theta - 4 \cos 2\theta.$$

Find the values of θ between 0° and 180° for which T is a maximum or minimum and find the corresponding values of T.

9. A man at a point A on a road wishes to reach a point B, whose shortest distance from the road is BC, which is a miles. The man can walk u miles per hour on the road, and v miles per hour when off it, crossing a field to B, where u is greater than v. If the distance AC is b miles, find how far from A the man must leave the road to reach B in the minimum time.

10. The efficiency e of a screw jack is given by $e = \frac{\tan \alpha}{\tan (\alpha + A)}$, where α is an acute angle and A is constant. Prove that for maximum efficiency $\alpha = \frac{\pi}{4} - \frac{A}{2}$ and e (maximum) $= \frac{(1 - \sin A)}{(1 + \sin A)}$.

11. A cylindrical tin can has a close-fitting lid which is bent at the perimeter to overlap the curved surface of the can by 1 in. The total area of metal used in the construction is 16π sq. in.

Prove that if the base radius of the can is r in., then the volume, V cu. in., of the can is given by

$$V = \pi(8r - r^2 - r^3),$$

and find the dimensions of the can for maximum volume. [L.U.]

12. Two voltages E_S and E_R are connected by the equation

$$E_S^2 = (E_R \cos \phi + RI)^2 + (E_R \sin \phi + XI)^2$$

where on the right-hand side ϕ is the only variable. Show that the maximum and minimum values of E_S are

$$E_R \pm I\sqrt{(R^2 + X^2)}.$$

13. Find the maximum and minimum values of $8 \sin x - \tan x$.

14. A steel plant can produce x tons of low-grade steel and y tons of high-grade steel per day where $y = \frac{(6 - 2x)}{(4 - x)}$. If the price of low-grade steel is one-half that of high-grade steel find how much low-grade steel per day should be produced for maximum total revenue.

15. Show that $y = x + \frac{1}{x}$ has one minimum and one maximum value and that the minimum value is greater than the maximum value. Give a sketch of the function to illustrate this.

16. A cricket field is rectangular with a semicircular area at two opposite ends, the diameter of each of these areas being equal to the width of the field. The total perimeter of this field is to be a running-track of $\frac{1}{4}$ mile length. Find the dimensions of the rectangle for it to have a maximum area.

17. Show that $\frac{x}{(1 + x \tan x)}$ will be a maximum when $x = \cos x$. Check that $x = 0{\cdot}739$ is an approximate root of this equation.

18. The velocity of flow of water in a channel with a given slope is directly proportional to the square root of the ratio of the area of cross-section of the water to the wetted perimeter. Show that with a rectangular channel for a given area of cross-section of stream the maximum discharge per second will be obtained by making the breadth equal to twice the depth.

19. A dish is made in the form of an inverted cone. Determine the vertical angle of the cone which will give the maximum volume in the dish if: (i) the slant height is specified, (ii) the area of the curved surface is specified. [Q.E.]

20. An isosceles triangle of vertical angle 2θ is inscribed in a circle of radius a. Show that the area of the triangle is $4a^2 \sin \theta \cos^3 \theta$, and hence that the area is a maximum when the triangle is equilateral. [L.U.]

21. Under certain conditions the work done per cu. ft. of steam is given by

$$\omega = 144p_1(1 + \log r) - 144p_3 r,$$

where p_1, p_3 are given constants. Show that ω is a maximum when $r = \frac{p_1}{p_3}$.

22. The torque T exerted by an induction motor is given by

$$T = \frac{ARs}{R^2 + X^2s^2},$$

s being the only variable on the right-hand side. Show that when T is a maximum its value is $\frac{A}{2X}$.

23. The weight of gas which will flow through an orifice from pressure p_1 to pressure p_0 is proportional to

$$x^{1/\gamma}\sqrt{(1 - x^{(\gamma-1)/\gamma})},$$

where γ (>1) is a constant. Show that the maximum value of this expression occurs when $x = \left(\frac{2}{\gamma + 1}\right)^{\gamma/(\gamma-1)}$.

24. The strain energy u in the case of a beam of length l clamped at one end, supported at the other and carrying a uniformly distributed load w per unit length, is given by

$$u = \frac{1}{2EI}\int_0^l x^2\left(\frac{wx}{2} - R\right)^2 dx,$$

where R is the reaction at the support. Evaluate u and then, regarding u as a function of R, find the value of R for which u is a minimum. Find also the minimum value of the strain energy.

25. The speed V m.p.h. of a car travelling from rest is given by

$$V = 6x^{\frac{1}{2}} - \tfrac{1}{6}x^{\frac{3}{2}}$$

where x ml. is the distance travelled from the start. Petrol is used at a rate of

$$(16 + 5V)/1152 \text{ gall. per ml.}$$

where the speed is V m.p.h. Find the amount of petrol used in the first 16 miles.

Prove that over this distance the maximum rate of consumption of petrol is

$$(2 + 5\sqrt{3})/144 \text{ gall. per ml.}$$

26. A rectangular box on a square base has a tightly fitting lid with a rim 1 in. deep. It is made of sheet metal to have a volume of 1 cu. ft. Show that the area of metal used will be a minimum when the side x ft. of the square base is a root of the equation

$$12x^3 + x^2 - 12 = 0.$$

Show that $x = 0{\cdot}98$ ft. is a root correct to 2 decimal places.

CHAPTER 6

FURTHER DIFFERENTIATION

6.1. The Stage-by-stage Method

This chapter is intended to revise and extend the student's knowledge of differentiation. The basic formula used is

$$\frac{dy}{dx} = \frac{dy}{dz} \cdot \frac{dz}{dx}$$

Example 1. $y = \sin(2 - 3x^2)$.

Put $2 - 3x^2 = z$ so that $-6x = \frac{dz}{dx}$.

We now have $y = \sin z,$

$$\therefore \quad \frac{dy}{dz} = \cos z.$$

But we require

$$\begin{aligned} \frac{dy}{dx} &= \frac{dy}{dz} \cdot \frac{dz}{dx} \\ &= \cos z \,.\, (-6x) \\ &= \underline{-6x \cos(2 - 3x^2)}. \end{aligned}$$

After some practice in the above method the student should not need to make the substitution but should use the following " stage-by-stage " method:

(*a*) d.c. of $\sin(2 - 3x^2) = \cos(2 - 3x^2)$;

(*b*) now " go inside " the bracket to the next function which here is $2 - 3x^2$.

$$\text{d.c. of } (2 - 3x^2) = -6x.$$

We have now differentiated with respect to the variable concerned, x, and so have finished the succession of stages. The required result is the product of the successive stages. Here

$$\begin{aligned} \frac{dy}{dx} &= \cos(2 - 3x^2) \times (-6x) \\ &= -6x \cos(2 - 3x^2). \end{aligned}$$

Example 2. $y = \tan^3 x = \{\tan x\}^3$.

Put $z = \tan x$ so that $\frac{dz}{dx} = \sec^2 x$.

Now $y = z^3,$

$$\frac{dy}{dz} = 3z^2,$$

$$\begin{aligned} \therefore \quad \frac{dy}{dx} &= \frac{dy}{dz} \cdot \frac{dz}{dx} \\ &= 3z^2 \,.\, \sec^2 x \\ &= \underline{3 \tan^2 x \,.\, \sec^2 x}. \end{aligned}$$

By the above method of stages we would have:

(a) d.c. of $\{\tan x\}^3 = 3\{\tan x\}^2$;
(b) d.c. of $\tan (x) = \sec^2 x$;
(c) d.c. of $(x) = 1$.

$$\therefore \quad \frac{dy}{dx} = 3 \tan^2 x \,.\, \sec^2 x \,.\, 1.$$

Example 3. $y = \log \cos (1 - x^2)$.

(a) d.c. of $\log \{\cos (1 - x^2)\} = \dfrac{1}{\cos (1 - x^2)}$;
(b) d.c. of $\cos (1 - x^2) = - \sin (1 - x^2)$;
(c) d.c. of $(1 - x^2) = - 2x$.

$$\therefore \quad \frac{dy}{dx} = \frac{1}{\cos (1 - x^2)} \times - \sin (1 - x^2) \times - 2x$$
$$= \underline{2x \tan (1 - x^2)}.$$

Example 4. $y = e^{\cos 2x}$.

(a) d.c. of $e^{\cos 2x} = e^{\cos 2x}$;
(b) d.c. of $\cos (2x) = - \sin (2x)$;
(c) d.c. of $2x = 2$.

$$\therefore \quad \frac{dy}{dx} = e^{\cos 2x} \times - \sin 2x \times 2 \quad \ldots\ldots \quad (1)$$
$$= \underline{- 2 \sin (2x) e^{\cos 2x}}.$$

With practice the student should be able to write down the successive stages side by side as in (1).

Example 5. $y = \sinh^3 (\sqrt{1 - x}) = \{\text{sh} \sqrt{1 - x}\}^3$.

$$\frac{dy}{dx} = 3\{\text{sh} \sqrt{1 - x}\}^2 \times \text{ch} \sqrt{1 - x} \times \frac{1}{2} \frac{1}{\sqrt{1 - x}} \times - 1.$$
$$= \underline{- \frac{3}{2} \frac{\text{sh}^2 \sqrt{1 - x} \,.\, \text{ch} \sqrt{1 - x}}{\sqrt{1 - x}}}.$$

EXERCISE 13

Differentiate:

1. $(x^2 + 3x - 4)^5$.
2. $1/(4 - x^3)^2$.
3. $\sqrt{1 - x^2}$.
4. $5 \cos 4x$.
5. $7 \tan (1 - x^2)$.
6. $2 \sin (x^2 - 1)$.
7. $3 \log (\tan 2x)$.
8. $x^2 e^{5x}$.
9. $3 \text{ sh } 4x$.
10. $2 \text{ ch } (1 - x^2)$.
11. $e^{\sin 3x}$.
12. $7e^{x^2}$.
13. $x\sqrt{9 - x^2}$.
14. $x/\sqrt{9 - x^2}$.
15. $\sqrt{(x^2 + 2)}/x$.
16. $\sin^2 (2 - 3x)$.
17. $\cos^n \left(\dfrac{x}{2}\right)$.
18. $\tan \sqrt{x}$.
19. $\dfrac{1 + \cos^2 2x}{1 - \cos^2 2x}$.
20. $\sqrt{\left(\dfrac{1 + x^2}{1 - x^2}\right)}$.
21. $\dfrac{\text{sh } 2x}{\text{ch } 4x}$.
22. $\log (x + \sqrt{x^2 - 1})$.
23. $\log (x + \sqrt{x^2 + a^2})$.
24. $5 \text{ cosec}^2 (2 - 3x)$.
25. $7 \sec^2 (5x)$.
26. $3 \cot^2 (4x)$.

6.2. Logarithmic Differentiation

It is sometimes helpful to take logarithms to base e of both sides of an equation before differentiating.

Note that

$$\frac{d}{dx}(\log_e y) = \frac{1}{y}\frac{dy}{dx}.$$

(*a*) Where the index varies.

Example 6.

$$\begin{aligned} y &= e^{\cos 2x}, \\ \therefore \quad \log_e y &= \log_e (e^{\cos 2x}) \\ &= \cos 2x. \end{aligned}$$

Now differentiate both sides of this equation.

$$\begin{aligned} \frac{1}{y}\frac{dy}{dx} &= -2 \sin 2x, \\ \therefore \quad \frac{dy}{dx} &= -2y \sin 2x \\ &= \underline{-2e^{\cos 2x} \sin 2x.} \end{aligned}$$

Example 7.

$$\begin{aligned} y &= x^x, \\ \log_e y &= x \log_e x, \\ \therefore \quad \frac{1}{y}\frac{dy}{dx} &= x \cdot \frac{1}{x} + \log x \,.\, 1 \\ &= 1 + \log x, \\ \frac{dy}{dx} &= y(1 + \log x) \\ &= \underline{x^x(1 + \log x).} \end{aligned}$$

(*b*) Where the function to be differentiated is a product of other functions.

Example 8.

$$\begin{aligned} y &= (2x + 3)^2(1 - 4x^2)^3, \\ \log y &= \log (2x + 3)^2 + \log (1 - 4x^2)^3 \\ &= 2 \log (2x + 3) + 3 \log (1 - 4x^2), \\ \therefore \quad \frac{1}{y}\frac{dy}{dx} &= 2 \cdot \frac{2}{2x + 3} + 3 \cdot \frac{-8x}{1 - 4x^2}. \\ \frac{dy}{dx} &= (2x + 3)^2(1 - 4x^2)^3\left\{\frac{4}{2x + 3} - \frac{24x}{1 - 4x^2}\right\}. \end{aligned}$$

Example 9.

$$\begin{aligned} y &= e^{2x}\frac{\cos 3x}{\tan 4x}, \\ \log y &= 2x + \log \cos 3x - \log \tan 4x, \\ \therefore \quad \frac{1}{y}\frac{dy}{dx} &= 2 + \frac{-3 \sin 3x}{\cos 3x} - \frac{1}{\tan 4x} \cdot 4 \sec^2 4x, \\ \frac{dy}{dx} &= y\{2 - 3 \tan 3x - 4 \operatorname{cosec} 4x \sec 4x\}. \end{aligned}$$

6.3. Differentials

In the previous work we have regarded $\frac{dy}{dx}$ as the limit of $\frac{\Delta y}{\Delta x}$ as $\Delta x \to 0$ and dy or dx alone had no meaning. It will now be shown that we can justify using these separately.

Consider that you have never before seen the symbols dy or dx and we will use Dy or $f'(x)$ to denote the derivative of $y = f(x)$ at the point $P(x, y)$ on the curve. If now x increases by Δx (not necessarily a small

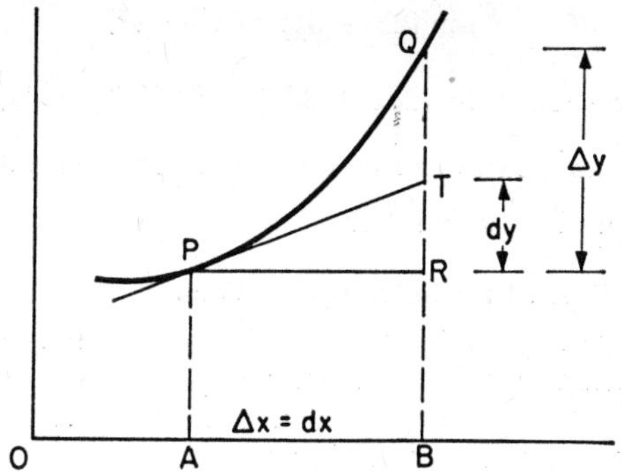

FIG. 17.

quantity) where $\Delta x = AB = PR$ whilst RT is the change in y needed to move to the tangent at P, then

$$RT = Dy\,.\,\Delta x$$

We define this to be represented by dy so that

$$dy = Dy\,.\,\Delta x \quad . \quad . \quad . \quad . \quad . \quad . \quad . \quad . \qquad (1)$$

and dy is called the differential of y corresponding to the increment Δx. Similarly, dx is called the differential of x. We have a meaning for dy defined by (1); we can find a meaning for dx, for if $y = x$, (1) shows that

$$dx = 1\,.\,\Delta x$$

(1) is now

$$dy = Dy\,.\,dx \quad . \quad . \quad . \quad . \quad . \quad . \quad . \quad . \qquad (2)$$

so that

$$dy/dx = Dy = \frac{d}{dx}(y) = f'(x),$$

where dy and dx are two separate entities whose ratio is $f'(x)$.

Finally if

$$y = f(x)$$

we may write

$$dy = f'(x)dx$$

when convenient. Here $f'(x)$ is the coefficient of dx, which is the reason for $\frac{dy}{dx}$ or $f'(x)$ being called the differential coefficient.

As further examples note:

(*a*) if

$$x^2y + y^2 = 3,$$

then

$$x^2dy + y2xdx + 2ydy = 0,$$

from which, if required, the ratio $\frac{dy}{dx}$ can be obtained.

(*b*) if $$\sin(2x + 3y) = x^2 + y^3,$$
then
$$\cos(2x + 3y)[2dx + 3dy] = 2xdx + 3y^2dy,$$
from which $\frac{dy}{dx}$ as a ratio can be obtained. Differentials will be used later. (Chapters 18, 19 and 24.)

6.4. Newton's Method for Solving Equations

In 1.2 we solved approximately equations of the type $x^3 + 3x + 2 = 0$. We will now consider a method which applies equally well to another type such as $1 + \log_e r = \frac{1}{2}r$ which cannot be solved by the first method. (Note exercise 9, nos. 2 and 12.)

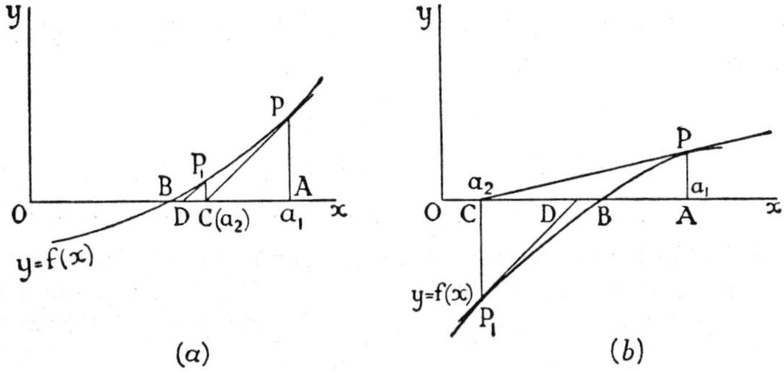

FIG. 18.

To solve $f(x) = 0$. Let $y = f(x)$ cross the x axis at B so that OB is a root. We guess (or find by trial) that $OA = a_1$ is near to the root. A method is then needed of moving from our first value a_1 to a nearer approximation to the exact root OB. At the point $P(a_1, f(a_1))$ on the curve whose x co-ordinate is a_1 draw the tangent to meet the x axis at C. The figure 18 (*a*) suggests that C is nearer to B than is A, so that if we can find OC we will have a nearer approximation to the root than $OA = a_1$.

Now:
$$\frac{PA}{CA} = \tan PCA = \text{the gradient at P}$$
$$= f'(a_1) \qquad \left[\frac{df(x)}{dx}\right]_{x=a_1} \equiv f'(a_1),$$
$$\therefore \quad CA = \frac{PA}{f'(a_1)} = \frac{f(a_1)}{f'(a_1)}.$$

$\therefore$ if $a_1(= OA)$ is a first approximation to the root OB and $a_2(= OC)$ is the second, since
$$OC = OA - CA,$$

$$\therefore a_2 = a_1 - \frac{f(a_1)}{f'(a_1)} \quad . \quad . \quad . \quad . \quad . \quad . \quad (1)$$

and is often a better approximation to the root.

(1) Note that there is no need to draw the graph $y = f(x)$. The graph merely illustrates the process. (In practice, having found a_1, we apply (1) to find a_2.)

(2) Having found a_2, we can regard this as an approximation to the root, and at P_1 on the curve we draw the tangent to meet the x axis at D, where if

$$OD = a_3$$

$$a_3 = a_2 - \frac{f(a_2)}{f'(a_2)}$$

and is often a still better approximation to the root than a_1 or a_2. This process can be repeated until the required degree of accuracy is obtained.

Example 10. Solve $f(x) = (x + 3)(2x - 3) = 0$.

We have chosen a simple equation with known roots to illustrate the method, and will find the root $x = 1{\cdot}5$ by Newton's method.

$$f(x) = 2x^2 + 3x - 9 \quad \text{and} \quad f'(x) = 4x + 3,$$

when
$$x = 0 \qquad f(0) = -9$$
$$x = 1 \qquad f(1) = 2 + 3 - 9 = -4$$
$$x = 2 \qquad f(2) = 8 + 6 - 9 = +5,$$

$\therefore$ there is a root between $x = 1$ and 2.

If we choose $x = 2$ as the first approximation, the second is given by

$$a_2 = 2 - \frac{f(2)}{f'(2)} = 2 - \left(\frac{2x^2 + 3x - 9}{4x + 3}\right)_{x=2}$$
$$= 2 - \frac{5}{11} = 1{\cdot}5,$$

correct to one decimal place, and this is the exact root. If we had chosen $x = 1$ as the first approximation

$$a_2 = 1 - \left(\frac{2x^2 + 3x - 9}{4x + 3}\right)_{x=1} = 1 - \frac{-4}{7} = 1{\cdot}6,$$

correct to one decimal place.

For the next approximation

$$a_3 = 1{\cdot}6 - \left(\frac{2x^2 + 3x - 9}{4x + 3}\right)_{x=1{\cdot}6} = 1{\cdot}6 - \frac{0{\cdot}92}{9{\cdot}4} = \underline{1{\cdot}50},$$

correct to two decimal places.

6.5. In the above example we have found that a root lies between $x = 1$ and 2, but so far have no indication which value to choose for the first approximation. Fig. 18(*b*) shows that a_2 obtained after one application of Newton's method may be worse than a_1 as an approximation to OB. If, however, we had chosen OC as a first approximation, a point on the other side of B, the tangent to the curve at P_1 would certainly meet the x axis nearer to B than is C.

Comparing the two figures 18(*a*) and (*b*), we find the reason for this. In 18(*a*), $f''(x)$ is positive and we have chosen as a first approximation a_1 where $f(a_1)$ is also positive. In 18(*b*), $f''(x)$ is negative, but we have chosen a_1 where $f(a_1)$ is positive. If we choose a_2 say where $f(a_2)$ is negative, then the difficulty vanishes. From this we deduce the rule: Find a root in an interval $x = a, b$. This means that $f(a)$ and $f(b)$ are of opposite signs. Then choose that value a or b which makes $f(x)$ of the same sign as $f''(x)$. Thus in Example 10 $f''(x) = +4$, so we would choose $x = 2$ as a_1 since $f(2)$ is positive. This rule will give us a sequence $a_1, a_2, a_3 \ldots$ steadily approaching the root.

Since we refer to the sign of $f''(x)$ it is clear that $f''(x)$ must not change sign in the interval a, b. If it should, then we must find a smaller interval in which it does not change sign and apply the rule to that interval.

Example 11. Find the negative root of $3x^3 - 4x + 5 = 0$.

If
$$f(x) = 3x^3 - 4x + 5,$$
$$f(0) = +5,$$
$$f(-1) = +6,$$
$$f(-2) = -11,$$
$\therefore$ a root lies between -1 and -2.

Also $f'(x) = 9x^2 - 4$, $f''(x) = 18x$ and is negative throughout the range -1 to -2. By the above rule we should choose -2 as a_1 since $f(-2)$ is negative. If, however, we choose -1 as a_1 we find

$$a_2 = -1 - \left(\frac{3x^3 - 4x + 5}{9x^2 - 4}\right)_{-1}$$
$$= -1 - 1{\cdot}2 = -2{\cdot}2,$$

giving a value for a_2 outside the range in which we know the root to lie.

If we obey the rule and choose $a_1 = -2$,

$$a_2 = -2 - \left(\frac{3x^3 - 4x + 5}{9x^2 - 4}\right)_{-2}$$
$$= -2 + \tfrac{11}{32} = -1{\cdot}7,$$

which will do as a second approximation.

$$a_3 = -1{\cdot}7 - \left(\frac{3x^3 - 4x + 5}{9x^2 - 4}\right)_{-1\cdot7}$$
$$= -1{\cdot}7 - \left(-\frac{2{\cdot}939}{22{\cdot}01}\right)$$
$$= -1{\cdot}57.$$

Finally,
$$a_4 = -1{\cdot}57 + \frac{0{\cdot}3297}{18{\cdot}1841}$$
$$= -1{\cdot}57 + 0{\cdot}01814$$
$$= \underline{-1{\cdot}55},$$

correct to two decimals.

Example 12. A is a point on the circumference of a circle and chords AB and AC divide the area of the circle into three equal parts. Show that the angle BAC is a root of the equation

$$x + \sin x - \frac{\pi}{3} = 0.$$

Find this angle correct to three decimal places.

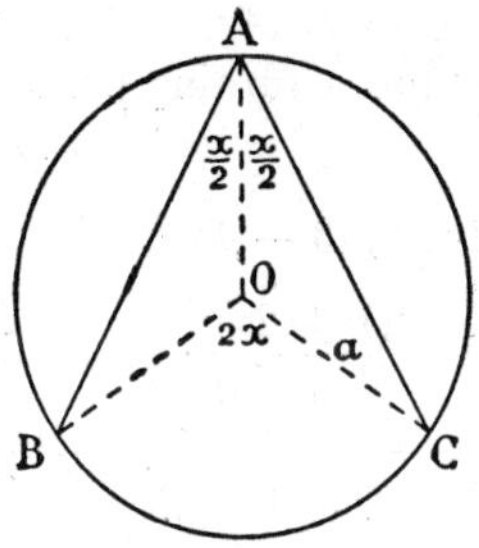

FIG. 19.

Let $\angle BAO = \angle CAO = \frac{1}{2}x$ (radians).
Area $BACB = \frac{1}{3}\pi a^2$
and $\angle AOB = \angle AOC = \pi - x.$

Therefore, since $\triangle BOA + \triangle COA + \text{sector } BOC = \frac{1}{3}\pi a^2,$

$$\tfrac{1}{2}a^2 \sin x + \tfrac{1}{2}a^2 \sin x + \tfrac{1}{2}a^2(2x) = \tfrac{1}{3}\pi a^2,$$

$$\therefore \quad \sin x + x - \frac{\pi}{3} = 0.$$

Let

$$f(x) = \sin x + x - \frac{\pi}{3},$$

$$\therefore \quad f'(x) = \cos x + 1,$$

$$f''(x) = -\sin x,$$

$$f(0) = -\tfrac{1}{3}\pi = -1{\cdot}05,$$

$$f(1) = \sin 1 + 1 - \tfrac{1}{3}\pi$$

$$= 0{\cdot}84 + 1 - 1{\cdot}05 = +0{\cdot}79,$$

$\therefore$ there is a root between $x = 0$ and 1.

$$f(0{\cdot}5) = \sin(0{\cdot}5) + 0{\cdot}5 - \tfrac{1}{3}\pi$$

$$= 0{\cdot}48 + 0{\cdot}5 - 1{\cdot}05 = -0{\cdot}07.$$

The root therefore lies between 0·5 and 1, and as $f''(x)$ is negative over this range we must choose $x = 0{\cdot}5$ as a_1, since $f(0{\cdot}5)$ is negative.

$$\therefore \quad a_2 = 0{\cdot}5 - \left(\frac{\sin x + x - \pi/3}{\cos x + 1}\right)_{0\cdot5}$$

$$= 0{\cdot}5 - \frac{-0{\cdot}06777}{1{\cdot}8776}.$$

$$= 0{\cdot}536.$$

To check the last decimal we find

$$a_3 = 0{\cdot}536 - \frac{-0{\cdot}00041}{1{\cdot}859}$$

$$= \underline{0{\cdot}536},$$

correct to three decimals.

EXERCISE 14A

Differentiate:

1. $(2x + 3)(x - 1)(4 + x^2)$.
2. $\dfrac{(x^2 + 6x - 5)^3}{(x^2 + 2)^4}$.
3. $5e^{2x} \sin 3x \cos 4x$.
4. $e^{ax} \cos bx$.
5. 10^x.
6. ae^{bx}.
7. e^{x^2}.
8. a^{ax+b}.
9. $(\cos x)^x$.
10. $x^x + x^{3/x}$.
11. $x^3 a^x + x^{\sin^{-1} x}$.
12. Show that $y = x^{1/x}$ has a turning point at $x = e$.

Differentiate:

13. $(2 - 3x)^3$.
14. $\sqrt{(3 - 4x)^5}$.
15. $\left(x - \dfrac{1}{x}\right)^2$.
16. $\sqrt{\left(x - \dfrac{1}{x}\right)}$.
17. $\dfrac{(1 + 2x)^3}{(1 + 3x)^2}$.
18. $\sqrt{\left(\dfrac{1 - x}{1 + x}\right)}$.
19. $\sqrt{\left(\dfrac{a^2 + x^2}{a^2 - x^2}\right)}$.
20. $\dfrac{x}{\sqrt{(a^2 + x^2)}}$.
21. $(1 + x)^4(1 - x)^3$.
22. $\sqrt{\left(\dfrac{a^2 - x^2}{a^2 + x^2}\right)}$.
23. $\left(\dfrac{a + x}{a - x}\right)^n$.
24. $\dfrac{\sqrt{a + x} + \sqrt{a - x}}{\sqrt{a + x} - \sqrt{a - x}}$.
25. $(1 + x^n)^n + (1 - x^n)^n$.
26. If $y = (x - 2)^{-1}$ show that $\dfrac{d^2y}{dx^2} = 2(x - 2)^{-3}$.
27. If $y = \dfrac{3x}{(x + 1)(x - 2)}$ show that

$$\frac{d^2y}{dx^2} = \frac{2}{(x + 1)^3} + \frac{4}{(x - 2)^3}.$$

28. Find the smaller positive root of $x^3 - 3x + 1 = 0$ correct to three decimal places.

29. Find the root which lies between 1 and 2 of the equation $x^3 + 5x - 11 = 0$, correct to two decimal places.

30. Find the root of the equation $\tan x = x$ which is near to 4·5 radians, correct to two decimal places.

31. Solve correct to two decimal places: (*a*) $1 + \log_e r = 0{\cdot}5r$. (*b*) $\dfrac{1}{r}(1 + \log_e r) = 0{\cdot}792$ (in each case $r > 1$).

32. Find the smallest positive root of the equation $\sin x = \dfrac{1}{2x}$, to two decimal places.

33. An acute angle ϕ (degrees) is such that

$$\phi \cos 2\phi - 28{\cdot}65 \sin 2\phi + 45 = 0.$$

Show that the value of ϕ lies between 50 and 60 degrees and by a graphical method or otherwise find this value correct to 1 decimal place. [U.L.C.I.]

34. Solve the equation $x^x = 10$, correct to three decimal places. [Take logarithms to base 10, and let $f(x) = \dfrac{1}{x} - \log_{10} x$.]

35. By drawing the graphs of $y = x^3$ and $y = x^2 - 2x + 3$, or otherwise, show that the equation $x^3 - x^2 + 2x - 3 = 0$ has only one real root and find it correct to three decimal places.

36. We are asked to solve the equation $x^3 - 10x^2 + 40x - 35 = 0$ and find the positive root between 1 and 2 correct to three decimal places. Show that the substitution $x = y + \frac{10}{3}$ reduces the equation to one without the term in x^2. Solve this simpler cubic and hence obtain the required result.

37. Show graphically that the equation $x - \frac{1}{2}\pi = \sin x$ has only one root and find it correct to three decimal places.

38. Solve correct to two decimals:

(a) $2{\cdot}42x^3 - 3{\cdot}15 \log_e x - 20{\cdot}5 = 0$;
(b) $e^x - e^{-x} + 0{\cdot}4x - 10 = 0$.

In (b) it is simpler to put $e^x - e^{-x} = 2 \operatorname{sh} x$.

39. It can be shown that $\cos(\frac{1}{7}\pi)$ is a root of

$$8x^3 - 4x^2 - 4x + 1 = 0.$$

Solve the equation to verify this value as far as the tables allow for the value of $\cos(\frac{1}{7}\pi)$.

40. Show graphically that $e^x = 1 + 2x$ has only one root other than $x = 0$ and find its value correct to three decimal places.

41. Solve graphically $\sin \frac{1}{4}(2x - 3) = 2x - x^2$, showing that it has two real roots, one positive and the other negative. Find the approximate values from the graph and then find the positive root correct to three decimals. [L.U.]

42. Show that the equation $x = e^{-x}$ has one and only one real root, and find it correct to three decimals. [L.U.]

43. A semicircle is bounded by its diameter. From one end of this diameter a line is drawn across the semicircle to bisect the area. If this line makes α radians with the diameter show that

$$2\alpha + \sin 2\alpha = \frac{\pi}{2}.$$

Find α correct to three decimal places.

44. To find the height of a certain vertical column which will sag under its own weight requires the solution of the equation

$$\frac{x^3}{12960} - \frac{x^2}{180} + \frac{x}{6} - 1 = 0.$$

Show that there is a root between 7 and 8 and find it correct to one decimal place.

45. A template is to be made in the shape of the area enclosed by the curves $y = 4 \cos x$ and $y = x^2$. Solve the equation $4 \cos x = x^2$, and hence find the area enclosed correct to three decimal places.

46. Show that $e^x = x^3 + 1$ has a root between $x = 1$ and 2. Show

that if Newton's method is to be used $x = 1$ will not do as a first approximation and find the root correct to two decimal places.

6.6. The Sign of the Derivative

It is clear that if for $y = f(x)$, dy/dx is positive at a point $x = a$, then the curve is increasing through $x = a$, *i.e.*, near to $x = a$ we have

$$f(x) < f(a) \quad \text{for} \quad x < a$$

and

$$f(x) > f(a) \quad \text{for} \quad x > a.$$

Similarly, if dy/dx is negative at $x = a$, the curve is decreasing through $x = a$ and

$$f(x) > f(a) \quad \text{for} \quad x < a$$

and

$$f(x) < f(a) \quad \text{for} \quad x > a.$$

This simple fact can be applied to prove some important inequalities.

Example 13. Prove that

$$\log(1 + x) > x - \tfrac{1}{2}x^2 \quad \text{for} \quad x > 0.$$

Let

$$y = \log(1 + x) - x + \tfrac{1}{2}x^2,$$

then for $x = 0$, $y = 0$, so that the curve passes through 0.

also,

$$\frac{dy}{dx} = \frac{1}{1 + x} - 1 + x = \frac{x^2}{1 + x},$$

which is clearly positive for all values of $x > 0$. The curve is then steadily increasing from the value zero at $x = 0$. It follows that for $x > 0$

$$\log(1 + x) - x + \tfrac{1}{2}x^2 > 0$$

or

$$\log(1 + x) > x - \tfrac{1}{2}x^2$$

The student should prove similarly, for $x > 0$,

(*a*) $x > \sin x > x - \frac{1}{6}x^3$
(*b*) $1 - \frac{1}{2}x^2 < \cos x < 1 - \frac{1}{2}x^2 + \frac{1}{24}x^4$

EXERCISE 14B

1. If $f(x) = x \sin x - \frac{1}{2}\sin^2 x$ find $f'(x)$. Hence prove that for $0 < x < \frac{1}{2}\pi$

$$0 < f(x) < \tfrac{1}{2}(\pi - 1).$$

2. Differentiate

(*a*) $$x - \frac{3\sin x}{2 + \cos x}$$

(*b*) $$2\sin x + \tan x - 3x.$$

Use the results to show that if $0 < x < \frac{1}{2}\pi$

$$\frac{3\sin x}{2 + \cos x} < x < \tfrac{2}{3}\sin x + \tfrac{1}{3}\tan x$$

CHAPTER 7

THE DIFFERENTIATION OF INVERSE CIRCULAR FUNCTIONS

7.1. The Function $\sin^{-1} x$

The student should convince himself that the graph shown is $y = \sin^{-1} x$. It is the graph $y = \sin x$ rotated through $+90°$ and then turned over about the y axis. There are an infinite number of angles whose sine is x so that $\sin^{-1} x$ is a " many valued " function.

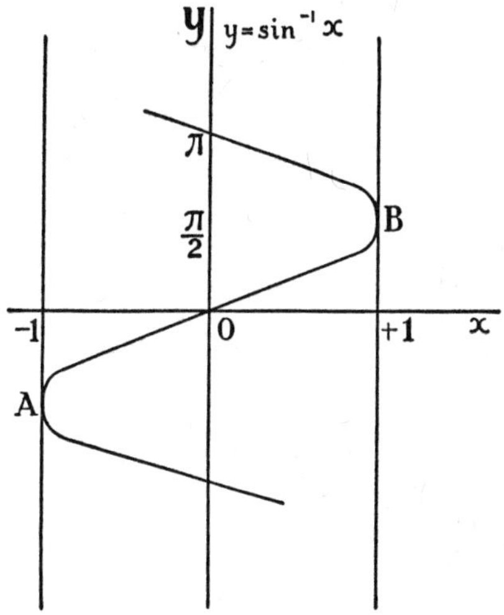

FIG. 20.

In calculus this would cause inconvenience so we simplify matters by defining $\sin^{-1} x$ as that angle which lies between $-\frac{\pi}{2}$ and $+\frac{\pi}{2}$. This range of values covers every possible case that can occur and yet restricts us to only one possible angle when a value x is given.

On the graph this definition confines us to the portion AB over which the gradient is positive.

7.2. To Differentiate $y = \sin^{-1} x$

If $$y = \sin^{-1} x,$$
then $$\sin y = x,$$

$$\therefore \quad \cos y \frac{dy}{dx} = 1$$

$$\frac{dy}{dx} = \frac{1}{\cos y} = \pm \frac{1}{\sqrt{1 - \sin^2 y}}.$$

$$= + \frac{1}{\sqrt{1 - \sin^2 y}} = + \frac{1}{\sqrt{1 - x^2}}.$$

since the gradient is positive over AB (Fig. 20).
This is the form used for differentiation, but for purposes of integration we must generalize this.

If
$$y = \sin^{-1}\left(\frac{x}{a}\right) \qquad (a > |x|)$$

$$\frac{dy}{dx} = \frac{1}{\sqrt{1 - \left(\frac{x}{a}\right)^2}} \times \frac{1}{a} = \frac{1}{\sqrt{a^2 - x^2}}.$$

$a > |x|$ is inserted here to remind the student that an inverse sine numerically greater than 1 has no meaning. The square root of $(a^2 - x^2)$ in the derivative emphasizes the same warning, since this requires $a^2 - x^2 > 0$ or $(a - x)(a + x) > 0$, *i.e.*, x must lie between $+a$ and $-a$ or $a > |x|$.

7.3. The Function $\cos^{-1} x$

For the same reasons as above we define $\cos^{-1} x$ as that angle which lies between 0 and π. We cannot use the range $-\frac{\pi}{2}$ to $+\frac{\pi}{2}$ as above, for throughout this range the cosine of an angle is always positive so that, for example, $\cos^{-1}(-\frac{1}{2})$ would have no meaning.

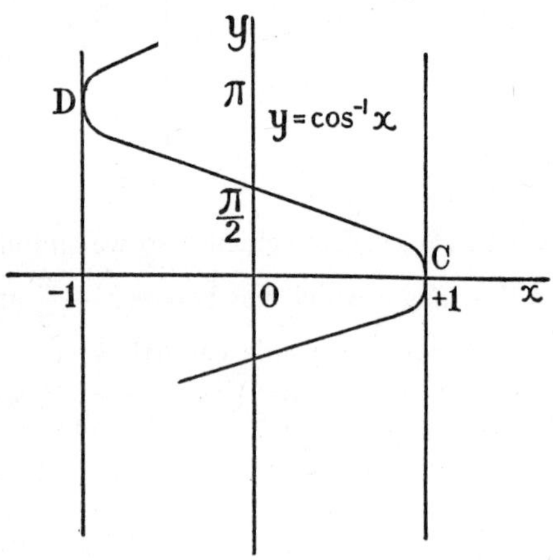

FIG. 21.

This range 0 to π confines us to the portion CD of the graph over which the gradient is negative.

7.4. To Differentiate $y = \cos^{-1} x$

The student should obtain the result by using the same method as for $\sin^{-1} x$. An alternative proof is:

$$\cos^{-1} x + \sin^{-1} x = \frac{\pi}{2}.$$

Differentiate:

$$\frac{d}{dx}[\cos^{-1} x] + \frac{1}{\sqrt{1-x^2}} = 0,$$

$$\therefore \quad \frac{d}{dx}[\cos^{-1} x] = -\frac{1}{\sqrt{1-x^2}}.$$

7.5. The Function $\tan^{-1} x$

The graph shown is $\tan^{-1} x$. By definition $\tan^{-1} x$ is defined as that angle which lies between $-\frac{\pi}{2}$ and $+\frac{\pi}{2}$.

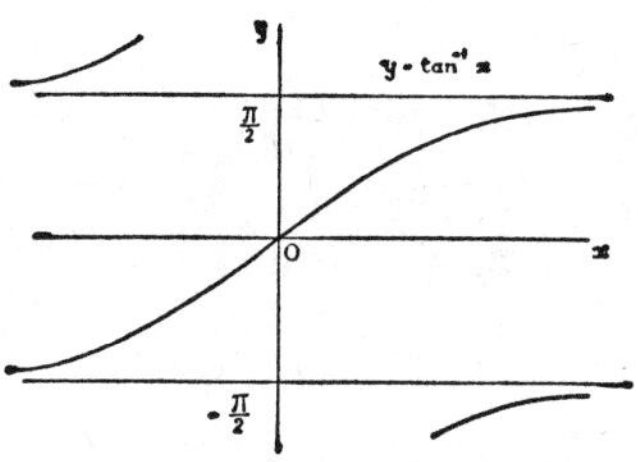

FIG. 22.

7.6. To Differentiate $y = \tan^{-1} x$

If

$$y = \tan^{-1} x$$

$$\tan y = x,$$

$$\therefore \quad \sec^2 y \frac{dy}{dx} = 1.$$

$$\therefore \quad \frac{dy}{dx} = \frac{1}{\sec^2 y} = \frac{1}{1+\tan^2 y}$$

$$= \frac{1}{1+x^2}.$$

This is the form to be used in differentiation, but for purposes of integration we must generalize. If

$$y = \tan^{-1}\left(\frac{x}{a}\right), \quad \frac{dy}{dx} = \frac{1}{1+\left(\frac{x}{a}\right)^2} \times \frac{1}{a} = \frac{a}{a^2+x^2}.$$

Example 1. Differentiate $y = \sin^{-1}\{\sqrt{1 - x^2}\}$.

$$\frac{dy}{dx} = \frac{1}{\sqrt{1 - \{\sqrt{1 - x^2}\}^2}} \times \frac{1}{2}\frac{1}{\sqrt{1 - x^2}} \times - 2x$$

$$= -\frac{1}{\sqrt{1 - x^2}}.$$

Example 2. Differentiate $y = \tan^{-1}\left(\frac{2x}{1 - x^2}\right)$.

$$\frac{dy}{dx} = \frac{1}{1 + \left(\frac{2x}{1 - x^2}\right)^2} \times \frac{(1 - x^2)2 - 2x(-2x)}{(1 - x^2)^2}$$

$$= \frac{(1 - x^2)^2}{(1 + x^2)^2} \times \frac{2(1 + x^2)}{(1 - x^2)^2} = \frac{2}{1 + x^2}.$$

Note that we regard the whole of the expression $\frac{2x}{(1 - x^2)}$ as the "x" of our formula and differentiate according to the rule for $\tan^{-1}(x)$. This gives

$$\frac{1}{1 + \left(\frac{2x}{1 - x^2}\right)^2}.$$

We then proceed according to the stage-by-stage method.

EXERCISE 15

Differentiate:

1. $\sin^{-1}\left(\frac{x}{3a}\right)$.
2. $\tan^{-1}\left(\frac{2x}{a}\right)$.
3. $\sin^{-1}\left(\frac{2x - 1}{4}\right)$.
4. $\tan^{-1}(1 - 3x)$.
5. $\sin^{-1}(1 - 3x^2)$.
6. $\sin^{-1}\sqrt{x}$.
7. $\cos^{-1}(mx)$.
8. $\sin^{-1}(\sin x)$.
9. $\tan^{-1}(\tan 2x)$.
10. $(1 + x^2)\tan^{-1} x$.
11. $\cos^{-1}\left\{\frac{1 - x^2}{1 + x^2}\right\}$.
12. $\sqrt{1 - x^2}\sin^{-1} x$.
13. $\tan^{-1}\left(\frac{\sin^2 x}{1 - \cos x}\right)$.
14. $\sin^{-1}(\sqrt{\sin x})$.
15. Prove that the d.c. of $\cos^{-1}\left\{\frac{b + a\cos x}{a + b\cos x}\right\}$ is $\frac{\sqrt{a^2 - b^2}}{(a + b\cos x)}$.
16. If $y = (\sin^{-1} x)^2$, show that $(1 - x^2)\frac{d^2y}{dx^2} - x\frac{dy}{dx} - 2 = 0$.
17. For $x > 0$ prove that $x - \frac{1}{3}x^3 < \tan^{-1}x < x - \frac{1}{3}x^3 + \frac{1}{5}x^5$.
18. If $y = \sqrt{(ax - x^2)} - a\tan^{-1}\sqrt{\left\{\frac{a - x}{x}\right\}}$

prove that

$$x\left(\frac{dy}{dx}\right)^2 = a - x.$$

19. Show that

$$\int_0^{\frac{1}{2}} \frac{dx}{\sqrt{(1 - x^2)}} = \frac{\pi}{6}.$$

Use Simpson's three-term rule to evaluate this integral and hence show that $\pi = 3{\cdot}143$ approximately.

20. Since $$1 - x^2 = (1 - x)(1 + x)$$

and $$\sqrt{\frac{2}{3}} \leqslant \frac{1}{\sqrt{(1 + x)}} \leqslant 1 \qquad (0 \leqslant x \leqslant \tfrac{1}{2})$$

show, using the result of number 19 above, that

$$0{\cdot}478 < \frac{\pi}{6} < 0{\cdot}586.$$

CHAPTER 8

CO-ORDINATE GEOMETRY
THE STRAIGHT LINE

8.1. The earliest knowledge of Geometry that we have is from the writings of an ancient Egyptian priest Ahmes, entitled Directions for Knowing all Dark Things. Later came the development in Greece with Euclid as its chief product. This has led to Pure Geometry, in which every problem is solved in a special manner. In this book we are concerned only with Co-ordinate, Algebraic or Cartesian Geometry named after its inventor Descartes. This method develops a general plan of attack applicable to problems in geometry.

8.2. Use of Co-ordinates

We will revise some of the elementary uses.

(a) *Distance between two points* (Fig. 23(a)).

If (x_1, y_1) and (x_2, y_2) are the two points and d the distance between them,

$$d = \sqrt{\{(x_1 - x_2)^2 + (y_1 - y_2)^2\}}.$$

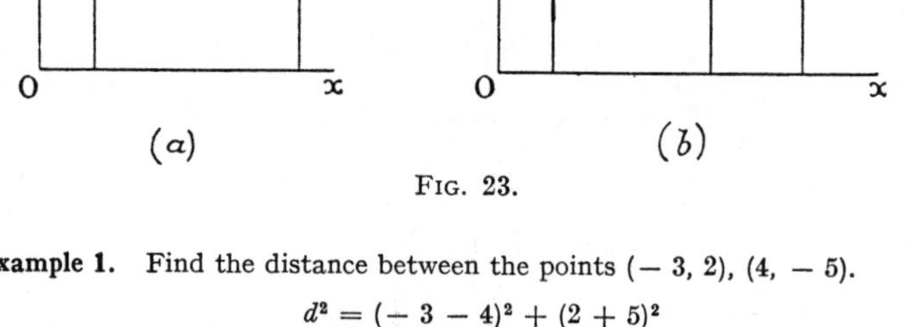

FIG. 23.

Example 1. Find the distance between the points (– 3, 2), (4, – 5).

$$d^2 = (-3 - 4)^2 + (2 + 5)^2$$
$$= 98,$$
$$\therefore \quad \underline{d = 7\sqrt{2}.}$$

Example 2. Show that the points (1, – 1), (– 1, 1), ($-\sqrt{3}$, $-\sqrt{3}$) form the vertices of an equilateral triangle.

If we call these points in the order given P, Q, R, then

$$PQ^2 = (1 + 1)^2 + (-1 - 1)^2 = 8,$$
$$QR^2 = (-1 + \sqrt{3})^2 + (1 + \sqrt{3})^2 = 8,$$
$$PR^2 = (1 + \sqrt{3})^2 + (-1 + \sqrt{3})^2 = 8.$$

∴ the three sides are equal and the triangle is equilateral.

(b) *Point dividing a line in a given ratio* (Fig. 23(*b*)).

To find the co-ordinates of the point B $(\bar{x}, \bar{y})$ which divides the join $A(x_1, y_1)$ to $C(x_2, y_2)$ in the ratio $m : n$.

We are given

$$\frac{AB}{BC} = \frac{m}{n}.$$

Suppose AC makes angle θ with the x axis.

From the figure

$$AB \cos \theta = \bar{x} - x_1,$$
$$BC \cos \theta = x_2 - \bar{x}.$$
$$\therefore \quad \frac{AB \cos \theta}{BC \cos \theta} = \frac{\bar{x} - x_1}{x_2 - \bar{x}}.$$

But

$$\frac{AB}{BC} = \frac{m}{n}.$$
$$\therefore \quad \frac{\bar{x} - x_1}{x_2 - \bar{x}} = \frac{m}{n},$$
$$\therefore \quad \bar{x} = \frac{mx_2 + nx_1}{m + n}$$

Similarly,

$$\frac{AB \sin \theta}{BC \sin \theta} = \frac{\bar{y} - y_1}{y_2 - \bar{y}} = \frac{m}{n}.$$
$$\therefore \quad \bar{y} = \frac{my_2 + ny_1}{m + n}.$$

Note that m, which corresponds to the segment AB, multiplies the co-ordinate of C, while n, which refers to BC, multiplies the co-ordinate of A.

If $m = n$, we find that the co-ordinates of the mid point are

$$\frac{x_1 + x_2}{2}, \ \frac{y_1 + y_2}{2}.$$

Example 3. Find the mid point of the join of $(-1, -2)$ to $(-7, 8)$. Find also the co-ordinates of the point dividing this join in the ratio 1 : 2.

For the mid point $(\bar{x}, \bar{y})$,

$$\bar{x} = \frac{(-1) + (-7)}{2} = -4,$$

$$\bar{y} = \frac{(-2) + (8)}{2} = 3.$$

For the other point (x, y),

$$x = \frac{1(-7) + 2(-1)}{1 + 2} = -3,$$

$$y = \frac{1(8) + 2(-2)}{1 + 2} = \frac{4}{3}.$$

The student should use the method of Example 1 above and check that the distance of $(-3, \frac{4}{3})$ from $(-1, -2)$ is one-half its distance from $(-7, 8)$.

(c) *External division*

In the above it was assumed that the point B divided AC *internally* in the ratio $m : n$. This means that the point B is between A and C. If AC is divided *externally* by B, then B lies outside AC. The student should repeat the above method, and using the same diagram with B and C interchanged he will find

$$\bar{x} = \frac{nx_1 - mx_2}{n - m}, \quad \bar{y} = \frac{ny_1 - my_2}{n - m}.$$

Note that if the given ratio is 4 : 3, then B lies on AC produced, whilst if the ratio is 3 : 4, then B is on CA produced and to the left of A. The formula takes care of this.

Summary. In each case we have the formula

$$\bar{x} = \frac{nx_1 + mx_2}{n + m}, \quad \bar{y} = \frac{ny_1 + my_2}{n + m},$$

but if the join of (x_1, y_1) to (x_2, y_2) is to be divided *externally*, then we must change the sign of *one* of the numbers m or n.

Example 4. Find the point which divides the join of $(-2, -4)$ to $(-1, -7)$ in the ratio 4 : 3 (*a*) internally, (*b*) externally.

(*a*)

$$\bar{x} = \frac{4(-1) + 3(-2)}{4 + 3} = -\frac{10}{7},$$

$$\bar{y} = \frac{4(-7) + 3(-4)}{4 + 3} = -\frac{40}{7}.$$

(*b*)

$$\bar{x} = \frac{4(-1) - 3(-2)}{4 - 3} = 2,$$

$$\bar{y} = \frac{4(-7) - 3(-4)}{4 - 3} = -16.$$

8.3. Locus. Equation to a Locus

When a point moves so as always to satisfy certain conditions the path it traces out is called its *locus*. Thus a point which moves so as always to be 3 units from the origin of co-ordinates will describe as locus a circle radius 3 and centre at the origin.

One purpose of co-ordinate geometry is to obtain the connection between the x and y of a point which describes a given locus. Such a connection is called the *equation to the locus*. This equation holds for no other points on the paper except those on the locus.

8.4. The Straight Line

A straight line is the locus of a point which moves so that the gradient at every point is the same.

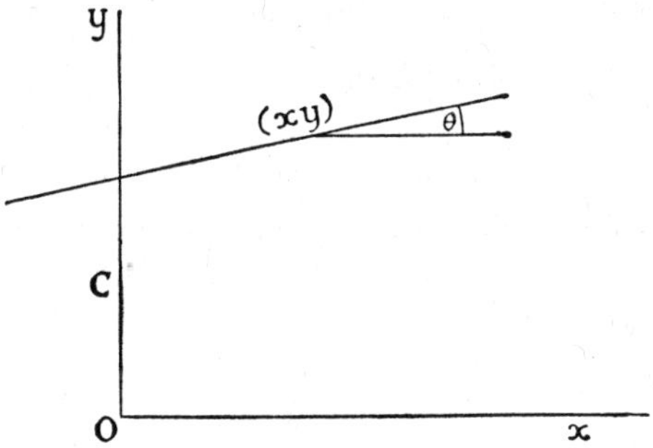

FIG. 24.

If $\tan \theta = m$, then at any point (x, y) on the line

$$\frac{dy}{dx} = m$$

Integrate this:

$$y = mx + c \quad . \quad . \quad . \quad . \quad . \quad (1)$$

where c is the constant of integration. This is the relation between every x and its y on the line or the "equation" to the line, showing that the equation to a line is a first-degree equation. If we put $x = 0$ in (1) we find $y = c$, showing that $(0, c)$ is a point on the line, *i.e.*, the line intercepts c on the y axis, giving a meaning to the constant c.

Example 5. Write down the equations of the following lines: (1) $m = 3$, $c = -2$; (2) the line makes 60° with the positive x axis and intercepts 3 on the y axis; (3) the line makes 150° with the x axis, and the intercept on the y axis is -4.

(1) $$y = mx + c$$
$$= \underline{3x - 2.}$$

(2) $$y = x \,.\, \tan 60 + 3$$
$$= \underline{x\sqrt{3} + 3.}$$

(3) $$y = x \,.\, \tan 150 - 4$$
$$= \underline{-\frac{1}{\sqrt{3}}x - 4.}$$

The student should draw rough sketches to show each of the above lines lying across the axes.

8.5. The above work shows that only two relations are needed to fix a line, *e.g.*, m and c. Also a straight line is fixed by two points. Yet the general equation of the first degree $ax + by + c = 0$ contains three unknown constants. However, it can be written

$$y = -\frac{a}{b}x - \frac{c}{b} \quad . \quad . \quad . \quad . \quad . \quad . \quad . \quad (1)$$

so that only the ratios $\frac{a}{b}, \frac{c}{b}$ matter, and there are only two of these.

If we differentiate this relation we find

$$\frac{dy}{dx} = -\frac{a}{b},$$

a constant, so that a first-degree equation represents a straight line, since it gives a constant gradient at any point (x, y) on it.

By writing the general equation in the form (1) we can at once see its gradient $\left(-\frac{a}{b}\right)$ and its intercept on the y axis $\left(-\frac{c}{b}\right)$.

8.6. Line Through a Given Point

If the line $y = mx + c$ passes through a given point (x_1, y_1), then the values (x_1, y_1) satisfy the given equation.

$\therefore$ from $\quad y = mx + c$

we obtain $\quad y_1 = mx_1 + c$

Subtract: $\quad y - y_1 = m(x - x_1) \quad . \quad . \quad . \quad . \quad . \quad . \quad (2)$

giving the important equation of a line restricted to pass through a given point (x_1, y_1). Note that m can still be given any value, showing that the line may have any direction.

If we choose the line to be horizontal then $m = 0$ and we obtain

$$y - y_1 = 0$$

as the equation of a line parallel to the x axis and always y_1 distant from it.

If we choose the line to be vertical, then $m = \tan 90°$ and is infinite. We deal with infinity by using the fact that 1/(infinity) is zero. We write equation (2)

$$\frac{y - y_1}{m} = x - x_1.$$

Now when m is infinite the left-hand side is zero and we obtain

$$x - x_1 = 0$$

as the equation to a line parallel to the y axis and distant x_1 from it.

Example 6. Find the equation of a line which passes through the point (1, − 2) and (1) makes 45° with the x axis, (2) is horizontal, (3) is vertical, (4) also passes through the point (4, 5).

Any line through (1, − 2) is

$$y + 2 = m(x - 1).$$

(1) If this line makes 45° with the x axis, $m = \tan 45 = 1$,

$\therefore$ equation is $y + 2 = 1(x - 1)$ or $\underline{y = x - 3}$.

(2) If the line is horizontal, equation is

$$\underline{y + 2 = 0}.$$

(3) If the line is vertical, equation is

$$x - 1 = 0.$$

(4) So far the line is

$$y + 2 = m(x - 1).$$

If it passes through (4, 5)

$$5 + 2 = m(4 - 1) \qquad \therefore\ m = \tfrac{7}{3}.$$

$\therefore$ equation is

$$y + 2 = \tfrac{7}{3}(x - 1) \quad \text{or} \quad 3y = 7x - 13.$$

8.7. Line Through Two Given Points

If the points are (x_1, y_1) and (x_2, y_2), then a line through (x_1, y_1) is

$$y - y_1 = m(x - x_1).$$

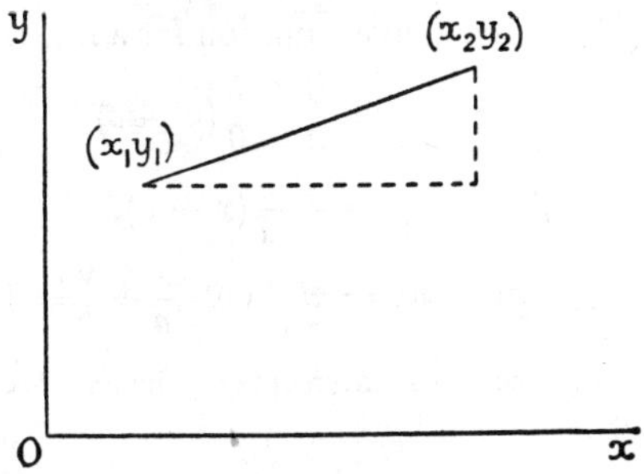

FIG. 25.

But the figure shows that m is fixed by the condition that the line also passes through the second point. In fact

$$m = \frac{y_2 - y_1}{x_2 - x_1},$$

$\therefore$ the equation is

$$y - y_1 = \frac{y_2 - y_1}{x_2 - x_1}(x - x_1).$$

Note that having put y_2 first in the numerator of the expression for m we must also put x_2 first in the denominator.

Example 7. Find the equation of the line passing through (– 3, 2) and (4, – 5).

Equation is

$$y - 2 = \frac{2 - (-5)}{-3 - 4}(x + 3)$$

$$= -1(x + 3),$$

$$\therefore\ y + x + 1 = 0.$$

Or using the other point (4, – 5).

$$y + 5 = \frac{2 - (-5)}{-3 - 4}(x - 4)$$

$$= -(x - 4),$$

$$\therefore\ y + x + 1 = 0.$$

8.8. The Intercept Form

Suppose it is given that the line makes intercepts a, b on the x and y axes respectively. This means that it passes through the points

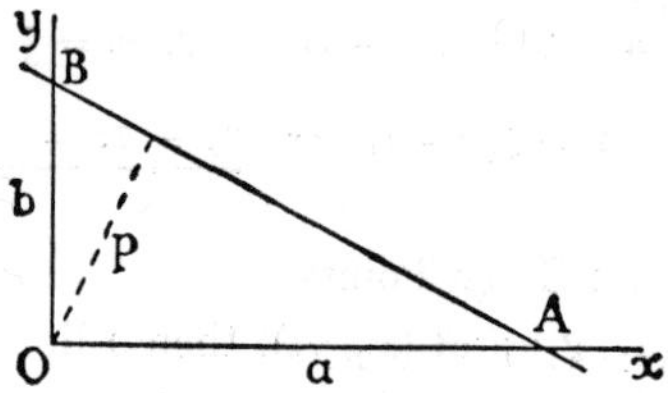

FIG. 26.

$(a, 0)$ and $(0, b)$. Using the above equation for a line through two points

$$y - 0 = \frac{0 - b}{a - 0}(x - a)$$
$$= -\frac{b}{a}(x - a),$$
$$\therefore \quad ay + bx = ab \quad \text{or} \quad \frac{x}{a} + \frac{y}{b} = 1.$$

Example 8. Find the line whose intercepts on the axes are: (1) 2, 3; (2) -2, -3; (3) 2, -3.

(1) Equation is

$$\frac{x}{2} + \frac{y}{3} = 1.$$

(2) Equation is

$$\frac{x}{-2} + \frac{y}{-3} = 1 \quad \text{or} \quad \frac{x}{2} + \frac{y}{3} + 1 = 0.$$

(3) Equation is

$$\frac{x}{2} + \frac{y}{-3} = 1 \quad \text{or} \quad \frac{x}{2} - \frac{y}{3} = 1.$$

Note that any line

$$ax + by + c = 0$$

can be written

$$-\frac{ax}{c} - \frac{by}{c} = 1 \quad \text{or} \quad \frac{x}{\frac{-c}{a}} + \frac{y}{\frac{-c}{b}} = 1.$$

showing its intercepts on the axes. A quicker way is to put $x = 0$, $y = 0$ successively in the given equation.

8.9. The Distance of the Origin from a Line $ax + by + c = 0$

Place $y = 0$ in the given line equation and find (Fig. 27)

$$\text{OA} = -\frac{c}{a}.$$

Similarly,

$$\text{OB} = -\frac{c}{b}.$$

$$\therefore \quad \text{AB} = \sqrt{\frac{c^2}{a^2} + \frac{c^2}{b^2}} = \frac{c}{ab}\sqrt{b^2 + a^2}.$$

If p is the perp. distance of O from the line

$$\tfrac{1}{2} . p . AB = \tfrac{1}{2} . OA . OB = \text{area AOB},$$

$$p \cdot \frac{c}{ab}\sqrt{a^2 + b^2} = \left(-\frac{c}{a}\right)\left(-\frac{c}{b}\right),$$

$$\therefore \quad p = \frac{c}{\sqrt{a^2 + b^2}}.$$

8.10. The Distance of a Point (x_1, y_1) from a Line $ax + by + c = 0$

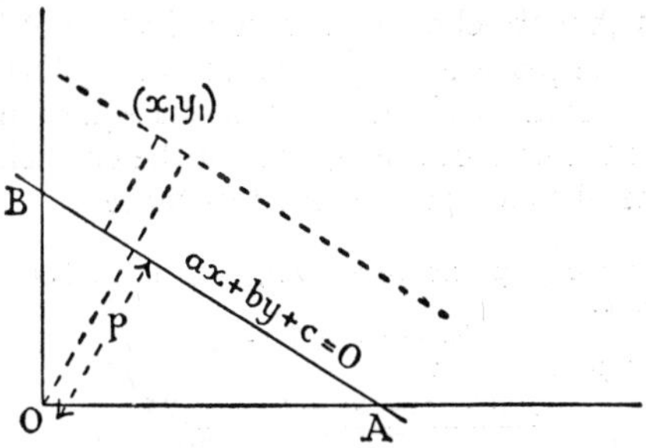

FIG. 27.

A parallel line to the given line is

$$ax + by + K = 0.$$

If this passes through (x_1, y_1)

$$ax_1 + by_1 + K = 0.$$

$$\therefore \quad a(x - x_1) + b(y - y_1) = 0$$

is the line through (x_1, y_1) parallel to the given line, and this can be written

$$ax + by - (ax_1 + by_1) = 0.$$

By the above, the perp. distance of O from this line is

$$\frac{-(ax_1 + by_1)}{\sqrt{a^2 + b^2}}.$$

But the perp. distance of O from $ax + by + c = 0$ is

$$\frac{c}{\sqrt{a^2 + b^2}}.$$

$\therefore$ the distance between these lines, which is the perp. distance of (x_1, y_1) from the given line, is

$$\frac{-(ax_1 + by_1)}{\sqrt{a^2 + b^2}} - \frac{c}{\sqrt{a^2 + b^2}}.$$

$$= -\frac{(ax_1 + by_1 + c)}{\sqrt{a^2 + b^2}}.$$

If, however, (x_1, y_1) was on the other side of the line we would have taken

$$\frac{c}{\sqrt{a^2+b^2}} - \frac{-(ax_1+by_1)}{\sqrt{a^2+b^2}}.$$

$$= \frac{(ax_1+by_1+c)}{\sqrt{a^2+b^2}}.$$

We therefore take as the perp. distance

$$\frac{ax_1+by_1+c}{\pm\sqrt{a^2+b^2}},$$

where this means that we choose the positive value of the result.

Rule. To find the perpendicular distance of a point from a line we substitute the co-ordinates of the point in the equation and divide by the square root of the sum of the squares of the coefficients of x and y. The positive value of this is the required distance.

Example 9. Find the perp. distance of $(2, -3)$ from $3x = 4y - 7$.

We write the line as

$$3x - 4y + 7 = 0,$$

$\therefore$ by the rule, perp. distance is

$$\frac{3(2) - 4(-3) + 7}{\pm\sqrt{3^2+4^2}} = \pm\frac{25}{5}.$$

$\therefore$ perp. distance is 5.

Example 10. Find the area of the triangle whose vertices are $(-3, 2)$, $(1, 4)$ and $(2, -5)$.

If we denote these points by A, B, C respectively

$$AB^2 = (-3-1)^2 + (2-4)^2$$
$$= 20,$$
$$\therefore \quad AB = \sqrt{20}.$$

The equation to AB is

$$y - 2 = \frac{2-4}{-3-1}(x+3) \quad \text{or} \quad 2y - x - 7 = 0.$$

Perp. distance of C $(2, -5)$ from this line is

$$\frac{2(-5) - (2) - 7}{\pm\sqrt{2^2+1^2}} = \frac{19}{\sqrt{5}}.$$

$$\therefore \quad \text{area ABC} = \tfrac{1}{2}\cdot\text{base}\cdot\text{height}$$
$$= \tfrac{1}{2}\times\sqrt{20}\times\frac{19}{\sqrt{5}}$$
$$= 19 \text{ square units.}$$

Example 11. Find the perpendicular distance of the point of intersection of the lines $2x - 3y + 4 = 0$, $x - 4y + 7 = 0$ from a line drawn through $(2, 3)$ parallel to $2x + 3y + 4 = 0$.

The lines $2x - 3y + 4 = 0$, $x - 4y + 7 = 0$ meet at $(1, 2)$.

Any line through $(2, 3)$ is $y - 3 = m(x - 2)$.

If this line is to be parallel to $2x + 3y + 4 = 0$ we must have $m = -\frac{2}{3}$.

$\therefore$ required parallel line is

$$y - 3 = -\tfrac{2}{3}(x-2) \quad \text{or} \quad 3y + 2x - 13 = 0.$$

Perp. distance of $(1, 2)$ from this line is

$$\frac{3(2) + 2(1) - 13}{\pm\sqrt{3^2+2^2}} = \frac{5}{\sqrt{13}}.$$

8.11. The Angle between Two Straight Lines

Let the two lines be of gradients m and m_1 respectively so that $\tan\theta = m$ and $\tan\theta_1 = m_1$.

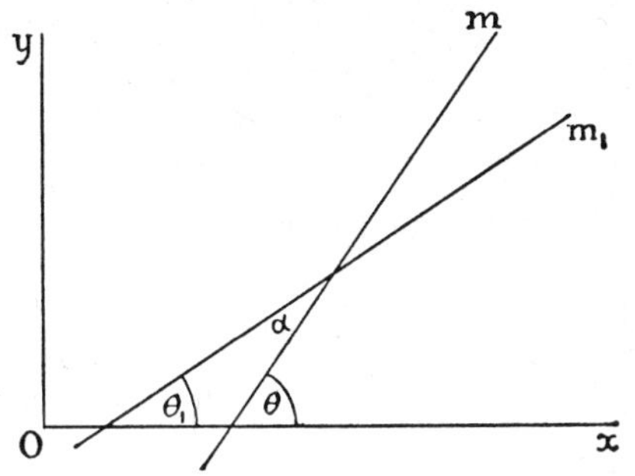

FIG. 28.

Then if α is the required angle

$$\alpha = \theta - \theta_1,$$
$$\tan\alpha = \tan(\theta - \theta_1)$$
$$= \frac{\tan\theta - \tan\theta_1}{1 + \tan\theta \,.\, \tan\theta_1} = \frac{m - m_1}{1 + mm_1}.$$
$$\therefore \quad \alpha = \tan^{-1}\left(\frac{m - m_1}{1 + mm_1}\right).$$

Example 12. Find the angle between

$$x - y + 1 = 0 \quad \text{and} \quad x + 4y + 1 = 0.$$

From the first $m = 1$. The second gives $m_1 = -\frac{1}{4}$.

$$\tan\alpha = \frac{1 - (-\frac{1}{4})}{1 + (1)(-\frac{1}{4})} = \frac{5}{3},$$
$$\therefore \quad \alpha = \tan^{-1}(\tfrac{5}{3}) = \underline{59^\circ\, 2'}.$$

Note 1. If the lines are parallel $\alpha = 0$, *i.e.*, $m = m_1$ as is obvious, since two parallel lines have the same gradient.

Note 2. If the lines are perpendicular $\alpha = 90^\circ$ and $\tan\alpha$ is infinite. This means that the denominator $1 + mm_1$ in the formula is zero so that

$$1 + mm_1 = 0$$
$$\therefore m_1 = -\frac{1}{m}.$$

This is an important result, and can be expressed in the following rule: To find the gradient of a line perpendicular to a given line, *invert* the given gradient and *change its sign.*

Example 13. Find the line through (2, 3) perpendicular to $2x + 7y - 1 = 0$.
The gradient of the given line is $-\frac{2}{7}$,
∴ the gradient of the perp. line is $\frac{7}{2}$,
∴ the required equation is

$$y - 3 = \tfrac{7}{2}(x - 2) \quad \text{or} \quad \underline{2y - 7x + 8 = 0}.$$

Example 14. Show that the points (1, 4), (− 4, −1), (2, 1) are the vertices of a right-angled triangle.

If these points as given are denoted by A, B, C, then a rough sketch on paper shows that the right angle, if any, is at C.

$$\text{Gradient of BC} = \frac{1-(-1)}{2-(-4)} = \frac{1}{3} = m.$$

$$\text{Gradient of AC} = \frac{4-1}{1-2} = -3 = m_1.$$

$\therefore$ $mm_1 = \frac{1}{3} \times -3 = -1,$

$\therefore$ BC and AC are perpendicular.

8.12. Condition for Perpendicularity

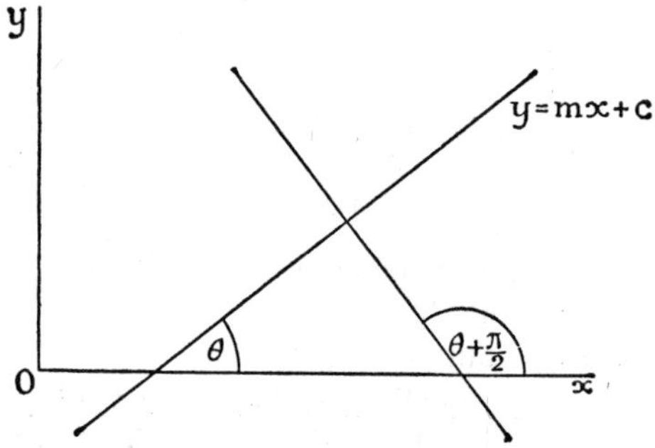

FIG. 29.

This condition is so important that we will give a separate proof. If $y = mx + c$ makes an angle θ with the positive x axis so that

$$\tan\theta = m,$$

then a perpendicular line makes an angle $\left(\theta + \frac{\pi}{2}\right)$ with the positive x axis.

Now

$$\tan\left(\theta + \frac{\pi}{2}\right) = -\cot\theta$$

$$= -\frac{1}{\tan\theta} = -\frac{1}{m},$$

$\therefore$ the gradient of the perpendicular line is $-\dfrac{1}{m}$.

EXERCISE 16

1. Find the distance between the points:

(i) (0, 0), (3, − 4); (ii) (− 1, 2), (3, − 1);
(iii) (a, b), $(a, -b)$; (iv) (− 3, − 6), (− 14, − 8).

2. Prove that the points (5, 5), (7, 3), (− 1, − 3) are the vertices of an isosceles triangle and find the length of the base.

3. A triangle ABC has as its vertices the points $(-2, -2)$, $(-3, 2)$, $(5, 4)$ which are A, B, C respectively. By finding the lengths of the sides AB, BC, CA, show that angle ABC is a right angle.

4. Prove that the distance between the points $(a \cos A, a \sin A)$ and $(a \cos B, a \sin B)$ is $2a \sin \dfrac{A - B}{2}$.

5. Prove that the distance between the points $(at^2, 2at)$ and $\left(\dfrac{a}{t^2}, -\dfrac{2a}{t}\right)$ is $a\left(t + \dfrac{1}{t}\right)^2$.

6. Find the co-ordinates of the points which divide the join of $(2, 1)$ to $(-1, 5)$ into five equal parts.

7. Find the co-ordinates of the points which divide internally and externally in the ratio $3 : 2$ the line joining the points $(-2, 3)$, $(1, -2)$.

8. Given the following data find the equations to the lines:

(i) $m = 2$, $c = -4$;
(ii) gradient $= \frac{4}{3}$, y intercept $= \frac{1}{2}$;
(iii) gradient $= -\frac{1}{4}$, y intercept $= -2$;
(iv) inclination to x axis $= 45°$, y intercept $= -3$;
(v) inclination to x axis $= 170°$, y intercept $= 4$.

9. In each of the following cases find the gradient and y intercept. Find also the x intercept.

(i) $2y = 3x - 4$; (ii) $3x + 4y + 7 = 0$; (iii) $4x = 2y + 1$.

10. Find the equations of the straight lines determined by the following data:

(i) of gradient $\frac{3}{4}$ and through the point $(-2, -4)$;
(ii) of gradient $-\frac{2}{7}$ and through $(3, -1)$;
(iii) through the point $(-1, 2)$ and inclined at 60° to the x axis;
(iv) through the point $(2, -3)$ and inclined at 135° to the x axis;
(v) of gradient 1 and through the origin;
(vi) of gradient $\tan \alpha$ through the point $(a \cos \alpha, a \sin \alpha)$.

11. Write down the equations of the lines:

(i) through $(1, 2)$ and parallel to the x axis;
(ii) through $(-2, -4)$ and parallel to the y axis.

12. Find the equations of the lines joining the following pairs of points:

(i) $(0, 0)$, $(1, -1)$;
(ii) (a, b), (b, a);
(iii) $(-1, -2)$, $(2, 4)$;
(iv) $(1, 3)$, $(-1, 3)$;
(v) $(ct, c/t)$, $(2ct, c/2t)$;
(vi) $(\frac{1}{2}, \frac{3}{2})$, $(\frac{3}{2}, -\frac{1}{2})$.

13. Write down the equations of the lines which make the following intercepts on the x and y axes respectively:

(i) 1, 1; (ii) -1, 1; (iii) 2, -3; (iv) -3, -4.

14. Show that the points $(1, -1)$, $(7, 3)$, $(3, 5)$, $(-3, 1)$, are the vertices of a parallelogram.

15. Find the lengths of the perpendiculars on to the lines in the following cases. From:

(i) $(0, -1)$ on $3x - 4y + 1 = 0$;
(ii) $(2, 3)$ on $x + 4y = 7$;
(iii) (a, b) on $x - y = 0$;
(iv) $(2, 3)$ on $3x - y - 3 = 0$.

What do you deduce in the last case?

16. Find the angles between the following pairs of lines:

(i) $3x - y = 0$ and $4x - 5y + 20 = 0$;
(ii) $x + y = 0$ and $2x - 3y + 5 = 0$:
(iii) $x - y + 1 = 0$ and $x + 4y + 1 = 0$;
(iv) $\frac{x}{3} + \frac{y}{4} = 1$ and $\frac{x}{4} - \frac{y}{3} = 1$.

17. Find the equations of the following lines:

(i) Through $(-2, -3)$ perpendicular to $\frac{x}{2} - \frac{y}{3} = 1$;
(ii) Through $(0, 0)$ perpendicular to $3x - 4y - 1 = 0$;
(iii) Through $(2, -1)$ perpendicular to $x + 2y + 1 = 0$.

18. Prove that the points $(4, 1)$, $(1, 6)$, $(-4, 3)$, $(-1, -2)$ are the vertices of a square.

19. A, B, C are the points $(-3, 2)$, $(1, -5)$, $(5, 3)$. Find the gradients of AB, BC and tan ABC.

20. Find the distance between the two parallel lines $3x + 4y + 7 = 0$ and $6x + 8y + 1 = 0$. [Find the length of the perpendicular from the origin upon each.]

21. Repeat the above problem for the lines $3x + 4y + 7 = 0$ and $6x + 8y - 1 = 0$. [A rough sketch of the lines in each problem will help.]

22. Find the coordinates of the centroid and the equations of the medians of the triangle whose vertices are the points $(5, 8)$, $(-2, 0)$, and $(9, -2)$.

23. Find the area of the parallelogram formed by the two straight lines $y = 2x + 3$ and $x = 3y + 1$ and the lines parallel to them through the point $(6, 5)$. Find also the equation of the diagonal that passes through the given point.

CHAPTER 9

LOCUS PROBLEMS

9.1. We require to find the equation of a curve or locus traced out by a point moving under certain conditions. The method of procedure is best illustrated by examples.

Example 1. A variable straight line cuts the axes at P and Q so that OP + OQ is constant. Find the locus of the mid point of PQ.

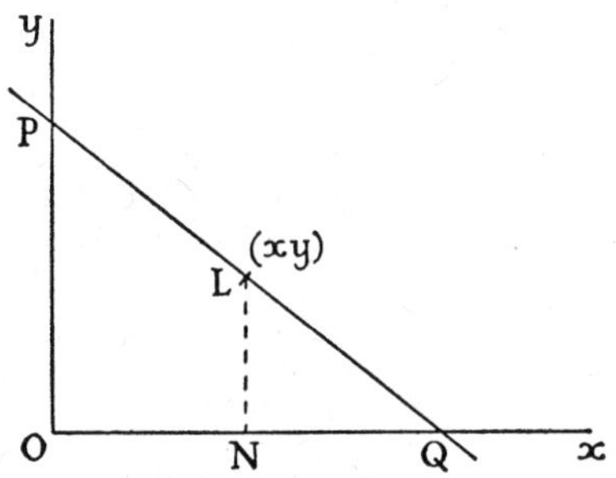

FIG. 30.

Let L ≡ (x, y) be the mid point of any line of this system of lines drawn so that OP + OQ = C (a constant).

$$\therefore \quad OQ = 2ON = 2x$$
$$OP = 2NL = 2y,$$

but

$$OP + OQ = C,$$
$$\therefore \quad \underline{2y + 2x = C},$$

giving the connection between x and y required. Since the equation is of the first degree the required locus is a straight line.

9.2. The student should note the above procedure. We call the point (x, y) in any one position and then use the geometrical data to obtain any other required values in terms of x and y. We then state the given condition OP + OQ = C algebraically and so get the locus.

Example 2. A point moves so that its distance from the given line

$$ax + by + c = 0$$

is always equal to 3 units. Find its locus.

If we call the point (x, y) we may get confused with the x, y used in the line equation. Let the point be (X, Y) in any position. The perpendicular distance from the line is

$$\frac{aX + bY + c}{\pm\sqrt{a^2 + b^2}}$$

and we require this to be 3 units,

$$\therefore \quad \frac{aX + bY + c}{\pm \sqrt{a^2 + b^2}} = 3.$$

$$\therefore \quad aX + bY + c \pm 3\sqrt{a^2 + b^2} = 0.$$

This shows that (X, Y) satisfies the equation

$$\underline{ax + by + c \pm 3\sqrt{a^2 + b^2} = 0,}$$

which is the required locus. As is obvious, the locus is two lines parallel to the given line and 3 units from it. The lines are on either side of the given line $ax + by + c = 0$.

Example 3. Two pins are pushed upright into a board 4 units apart. A piece of thin string has an end tied to each pin so that ten units lies freely between.

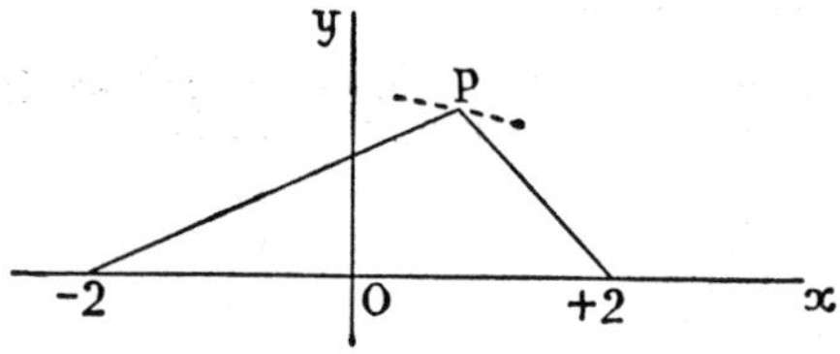

FIG. 31.

A pencil point keeps the string taut and moves over the board. Find the equation to the curve traced out by the pencil.

In this case the axes are not given, so we will choose them to make the problem as simple as possible. Choose the mid point of the pins as origin, the x axis through the pins and the y axis through the origin perpendicular to the x axis as shown. The pins then become the points (2, 0), (– 2, 0). Call these A and B respectively.

If in any position of the pencil P its co-ordinates are (x, y)

$$PA + PB = 10,$$

$$\therefore \quad \sqrt{(x-2)^2 + y^2} + \sqrt{(x+2)^2 + y^2} = 10.$$

This is the required locus, but we must simplify the equation as far as possible in order to get a recognizable equation.

We have

$$\begin{aligned} \sqrt{(x+2)^2 + y^2} &= 10 - \sqrt{(x-2)^2 + y^2}, \\ \therefore \quad (x+2)^2 + y^2 &= 100 - 20\sqrt{(x-2)^2 + y^2} + (x-2)^2 + y^2 \\ 8x - 100 &= -20\sqrt{(x-2)^2 + y^2} \\ 25 - 2x &= 5\sqrt{(x-2)^2 + y^2}, \\ 625 - 100x + 4x^2 &= 25\{(x-2)^2 + y^2\} \\ \underline{21x^2 + 25y^2} &\underline{= 525.} \end{aligned}$$

Later, the student will know this as the equation of an ellipse.

9.3. The student's attention is again called to the method of procedure. (i) The axes of co-ordinates are given or else must be chosen at the start, and we choose them to simplify the steps required to solve the problem. (ii) We suppose the co-ordinates of the point to be (x, y) in any one of its positions and express all other variables (lengths, etc.) in terms of x and y. If to call the point (x, y) would lead to confusion we may call it (X, Y), (α, β), (h, k) or anything else that is convenient. (iii) When all unknowns are expressed in terms of these values of x and y (or X, Y, etc.) we express by means of an equation the given fact that fixes the locus. (iv) This is the required equation, but it should be simplified if possible. If we have used say (h, k) as the variable point we change the result into (x, y) the conventional variables.

Example 4. Find the equation of the locus of a point which moves so that it is always equidistant from a fixed point and a fixed line.

Let A be the fixed point and BC the given fixed line. Draw AO perpendicular to BC. Take as axes OA for the x axis and OB for the y axis.

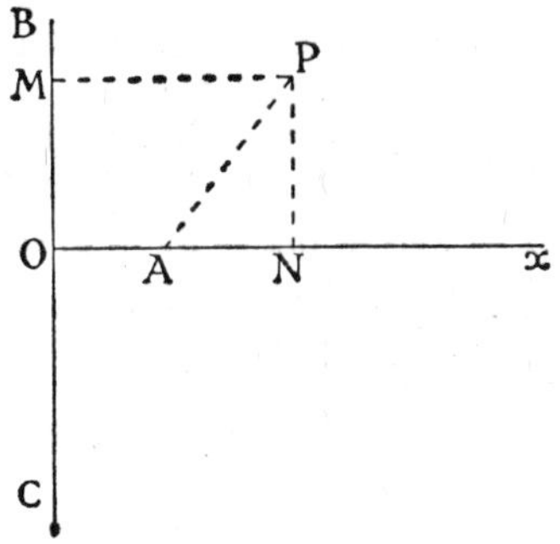

FIG. 32.

OA is a fixed length, so we must give it a magnitude. Let OA $= a$.

In any one position of the moving point P, let (x, y) be its co-ordinates so that PN $\perp$ to Ox is y whilst PM $\perp$ Oy is x.

We are given

$$PA = PM,$$

$$\therefore \quad \sqrt{(x-a)^2 + y^2} = x.$$

Square: $$(x-a)^2 + y^2 = x^2$$

or $$\underline{y^2 = 2a(x - \tfrac{1}{2}a).}$$

Later the student will know this as the equation to a parabola.

EXERCISE 17A

1. Find the equations of the loci of a point P which moves so that:

   (i) it is equidistant from the axes;
   (ii) the sum of its distances from the axes is 4;
   (iii) the sum of the squares of its distances from the axes is 16;
   (iv) the ratio distance from y axis : distance from x axis $= 4 : 3$.

2. A point moves so that it is equidistant from the points (1, 2) and (– 3, 4). Find its locus.

3. P, Q are the points (– 8, 0), (– 2, 0); a point A(x, y) moves so that PA $=$ 2QA. Show that

$$x^2 + y^2 = 16.$$

4. A, B are two fixed points. A point P moves so that $PA^2 + PB^2$ is always equal to a fixed quantity k^2. Find the locus of P. [Choose A, B as $\pm a, 0$.]

5. Show that the locus of a point, the sum of the squares of whose distances from the lines

$$x + 2y - 1 = 0,\ 2x - y + 3 - 0$$

is 2, has as its equation

$$x^2 + y^2 + 2x - 2y = 0.$$

6. A, B are the points (1, 2), (– 2, 3). A point P moves so that $PA^2 - PB^2 = 5$. Show that the locus of P is a straight line and find the ratio in which this line divides AB.

7. Show that the locus of a point which is equidistant from the point (– 1, 2) and the line $2x - y + 1 = 0$ has as its equation

$$(x + 2y)^2 + 6(x - 3y + 4) = 0.$$

8. A, B, C are the points (1, 2), (2, – 3), (– 2, 3). A point P moves so that $PA^2 + PB^2 = 2PC^2$. Find the locus of P.

9.4. Algebraic geometry can also be used to obtain relations between magnitudes shown on a diagram.

Example 5. From a point $C \equiv (a, b)$ perpendiculars CA and CB are drawn to the axes of x and y respectively. D is the mid point of OA and E of BC. Show that BD and AE trisect OC.

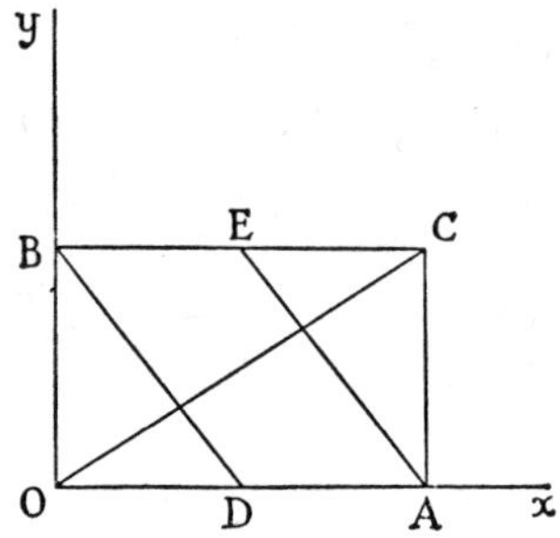

FIG. 33.

The point of trisection of OC near O has as its co-ordinates

$$x = \frac{1.a + 2.0}{1 + 2} = \frac{a}{3}$$

$$y = \frac{1.b + 2.0}{1 + 2} = \frac{b}{3}.$$

Since $OD = \frac{a}{2}$ and $OB = b$ equation to BD is

$$\frac{x}{a/2} + \frac{y}{b} = 1$$

or

$$\frac{2x}{a} + \frac{y}{b} = 1,$$

which is clearly satisfied by the point $\left(\frac{a}{3}, \frac{b}{3}\right)$ obtained above, showing that OC and BD meet in a point of trisection.

The other point of trisection of OC is

$$x = \frac{2 \cdot a + 1 \cdot 0}{2+1} = \frac{2a}{3}, \quad y = \frac{2 \cdot b + 1 \cdot 0}{2+1} = \frac{2b}{3}.$$

Now A is the point $(a, 0)$, E is the point $(a/2, b)$,

$\therefore$ equation to AE is

$$y - 0 = \frac{b - 0}{\frac{a}{2} - a}(x - a)$$

or

$$y = -\frac{2b}{a}(x - a),$$

and this line is satisfied by $\left(\frac{2a}{3}, \frac{2b}{3}\right)$ showing that AE meets OC in the other point of trisection.

Example 6. A straight line cuts the axes at P and Q, but always passes through the point (3, 3). Show that in any position of the line

$$\frac{1}{\text{OP}} + \frac{1}{\text{OQ}} = \frac{1}{3}.$$

Any line through (3, 3) is

$$y - 3 = m(x - 3).$$

Put $y = 0$ in this and find OP

$$0 - 3 = m(\text{OP} - 3),$$
$$\text{OP} = 3 - \frac{3}{m} = \frac{3(m-1)}{m}.$$

Put $x = 0$ in the equation and find OQ.

$$\text{OQ} - 3 = m(0 - 3),$$
$$\text{OQ} = 3(1 - m).$$

$$\therefore \quad \frac{1}{\text{OP}} + \frac{1}{\text{OQ}} = \frac{m}{3(m-1)} - \frac{1}{3(m-1)} = \frac{1}{3}.$$

EXERCISE 17B

1. OACB is a rectangle. If E is the mid point of BC, find where AE crosses the y axis. Find where OC and AE meet. [A is $(a, 0)$ and B is $(0, b)$.]

2. P, Q are points on the x and y axes respectively such that PQ always passes through the point (5, 3). Show that

$$5\text{OQ} + 3\text{OP} = \text{OP} \cdot \text{OQ}.$$

3. OACB is a square. A point P is taken on AB. Prove that PM + PN is constant where PM is perpendicular to OB and PN to OA.

4. A square ABCD is set with the corners A and B on OX and OY respectively so that OA $= a$ and OB $= b$. If CD is turned away from O, find where OC and OD cut AB.

5. Two straight lines perpendicular to one another are drawn cutting the axes at A, B and L, M respectively. Prove that OA . OL and OB . OM are numerically equal.

6. ABCD is a square, F is the mid point of AD and E is taken on AC so that AE : EC = 1 : 2. Prove that DE is perpendicular to FC.

7. CAB is a right-angled triangle. A line perpendicular to the hypotenuse AB meets CB at Q and CA at P. Prove BP perpendicular to AQ.

8. Find the co-ordinates of the foot of the perpendicular from the origin to the line $\frac{x}{a} + \frac{y}{b} = 1$.

If the line cuts the axes at A and B and if D is the foot of the perpendicular from O to AB, find OD, AD and BD in length, and hence prove that $OD^2 = AD \,.\, DB$.

9. From the vertex B of an isosceles triangle ABC a perpendicular BD is drawn to the base. DE is drawn perpendicular to AB, and B is joined to F, the mid point of DE. Prove BF perpendicular to CE.

10. A variable triangle ABC has A on the x axis, B on the y axis and C on the line $y = x$. The sides AB, AC always pass through the points (2, 1) and (3, 2) respectively. Show that BC always passes through the point (4, 3).

11. (*a*) Show that

$$\frac{3x + 4y - 2}{\sqrt{(3^2 + 4^2)}} = \pm \frac{5x + 12y - 7}{\sqrt{(5^2 + 12^2)}}$$

gives the locus of a point (x, y) which moves so that its distance from the line $3x + 4y - 2 = 0$ is equal to its distance from the line $5x + 12y - 7 = 0$. Hence find the equations of the two bisectors of the angle between the lines. Check that these two bisectors are perpendicular.

(*b*) Find the bisectors of the angle between the lines

$$8x + y = 7,\ 4x - 7y = 11.$$

12. Show that if k is an as yet unknown constant the equation

$$2x - 3y + 7 + k(3x + y - 9) = 0$$

is a straight line which passes through the point of intersection of the two lines

$$2x - 3y + 7 = 0,\ 3x + y - 9 = 0.$$

Hence find the line which passes through the point of intersection of these two lines and respectively:

(*a*) is parallel to the y axis;
(*b*) is perpendicular to the line $x + y + 2 = 0$;
(*c*) passes also through the point (1, 2).

13. A triangle is formed by the lines

$$5y - 2x + 8 = 0,\quad 2x + 4y + 7 = 0,\quad x + y - 2 = 0.$$

Find the line through each vertex perpendicular to the opposite side (without solving for the vertices). Hence show that the altitudes of a triangle are concurrent, *i.e.*, the point of intersection of any two lies on the third. Give an accurate sketch.

9.5. The Sign of $ax + by + c$

The line $ax + by + c = 0$ of infinite extent divides the xy plane into two infinite half planes, one each side of the line. The points (x_r, y_r) in each half plane all have one feature in common. When substituted in $ax + by + c$ they give an expression

$$ax_r + by_r + c$$

which, whatever its magnitude, always has the same sign. The points in the other half plane all give an expression of the opposite sign. All points on the line give, of course, a value of zero.

When the line does not pass through the origin we have an easy way of determining this sign. Substitute the coordinates of the origin (0, 0) in the expression and find its sign. Then all points on the origin side of the line will give the same sign and all points on the non-origin side will give the sign opposite to this.

Example 7. Consider the line $2x = 8 - 4y$ and the points (0, 0), $(1, \frac{1}{2})$, (2, 0). Also the points (0, 4), (2, 6), (5, 1). A rough sketch shows that the first set of points is on the origin side of the line and the second set on the other side.

With the linear expression written on one side as

$$2x + 4y - 8$$

substitution gives

(0, 0)	$0 + 0 - 8 = -8$
$(1, \frac{1}{2})$	$2 + 2 - 8 = -4$
(2, 0)	$4 + 0 - 8 = -4$

and all are negative in sign, the sign caused by (0, 0). But for

(0, 4)	$0 + 16 - 8 = +8$
(2, 6)	$4 + 24 - 8 = +20$
(5, 1)	$10 + 4 - 8 = +6$

all the values are positive.

When the line passes through the origin a trial with any point not on the line will determine the sign for all points on the same side of the line.

9.6. Linear Inequalities

We will now find the set of points which satisfy an inequality such as

$$350 \leqslant 3x + 5y$$

or

$$350 - 3x - 5y \leqslant 0 \quad . \quad . \quad . \quad . \quad . \quad . \quad . \quad (1)$$

Since (0, 0) causes the expression to take a positive value, +350, whereas we require the value to be less than or equal to zero, the set of points which satisfy the inequality constitute the half plane on the *non-origin* side of the line $350 - 3x - 5y = 0$.

Similarly, for $$2x + 4y \leqslant 8$$

or $$2x + 4y - 8 \leqslant 0 \quad . \quad . \quad . \quad . \quad . \quad . \quad . \qquad (2)$$

(0, 0) gives this a negative value, -8, in accordance with the inequality, so the set of points required is the half plane on the origin side of the line $2x + 4y - 8 = 0$. In the diagram on which this line has been

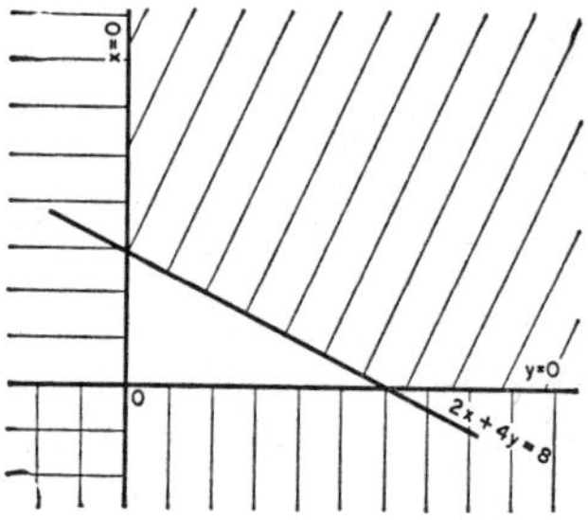

FIG. 34.

drawn the first quadrant area in which the points required do not lie has been shaded out to show that points in this region are excluded by (2).

Suppose, further, that, as is usual in practical applications, x, y are outputs and so essentially positive values or at least zero. We now have further inequalities restricting the values, *i.e.*

$$x \geqslant 0, y \geqslant 0.$$

These effectively restrict the point (x, y) to the first quadrant, so the other quadrants have been ruled out. Finally, we find that we are left with the set of points on or inside the triangle shown whose boundaries are $2x + 4y - 8 = 0$, $x = 0$, $y = 0$, and such a set of points satisfies the simultaneous inequalities

$$2x + 4y - 8 \leqslant 0,$$
$$x, y \geqslant 0.$$

EXERCISE 18A

Draw the boundaries of the inequalities given to obtain the area containing the set of points which are solutions of the systems of simultaneous inequalities. Note that in each case we have a convex polygon as the boundary. (A polygon is a closed figure bounded by three or more lines. By " convex " is meant that if any two points are inside the boundary so is every point on the line segment joining them.)

1. $x + 3y \leqslant 9,$
$x \geqslant 0, y \geqslant 0.$

2. $x + 3y \leqslant 9,$
$x \leqslant 4, x, y \geqslant 0.$

3. $x + 2y \leqslant 8,$
$x \leqslant 4, y \leqslant 3,$
$x, y \geqslant 0.$

4. $x + 4y \leqslant 24,$
$3x + y \leqslant 21,$
$x + y \leqslant 9,$
$x, y \geqslant 0.$

5. $2x/3 + y/4 \leqslant 5,$
$x/3 + 3y/4 \leqslant 5,$
$x \leqslant 7, y \leqslant 6,$
$x, y \geqslant 0.$

6. In number 4 above show that the vertices of the polygon are (0, 0), (0, 6), (4, 5), (6, 3), (7, 0).

7. Show that in number 5 above the vertices of the polygon are (0, 0), (0, 6), (3/2, 6), (6, 4), (7, 4/3), (7, 0).

8. A convex polygon has the points (−1, 0), (3, 4), (0, −3) and (1, 6) as vertices. Show the system of inequalities which defines this convex polygon is given by

$$y - 3x - 3 \leqslant 0, \qquad y + x - 7 \leqslant 0,$$
$$y + 3x + 3 \geqslant 0, \qquad 3y - 7x + 9 \geqslant 0.$$

9. A convex polygon has the vertices (0, 1), (0, 3), (2, 4), (4, 2), (3, 0), (1, 0) in order taken clockwise. Show that the system of inequalities which defines the set of points within or on this polygon is

$$x \geqslant 0, y \geqslant 0, \qquad x + y \geqslant 1, \qquad x - 2y + 6 \geqslant 0,$$
$$y + x - 6 \leqslant 0, \qquad y - 2x + 6 \geqslant 0.$$

10. We will soon require to find the optimum value (maximum or minimum) of a linear expression such as $x + 2y$, where we are restricted to values (x, y), the set of points on or inside a convex polygon such as those above. Find the value of this expression at each of the vertices given in number 6 above. Try one or two points inside the polygon such as (6, 1) or (3, 2) and show that optimum values appear to occur at the vertices.

11. Draw the lines so as to enclose the set of points satisfying the inequalities $4x + 8y \geqslant 32$, $7x + 2y \geqslant 14$, $3x/2 + 5y \geqslant 15$, $3x/2 + 5y \leqslant 18$, $x, y \geqslant 0$. Show that (2, 3) is the vertex that gives a minimum value, 18, to the function $z = 3x + 4y$.

9.7. Optimum Value of $ax + by + c$

We will now prove the theorem that a linear function $ax + by + c$ to be evaluated over a set of points (x, y) on or enclosed by a convex polygon will take its maximum (or minimum) value at a vertex, *i.e.*, the optimum values occur at the vertices.

Suppose that the value of $ax + by + c$ is found for each vertex (x, y) shown (Fig. 35) and the maximum of these values is at A. If P is any point inside join AP to meet another side CD at Q. The x of Q is between the x's of C and D. Hence for some value of t between 0 and 1 (see page 67)

$$x_Q = t \,.\, x_C + (1 - t) \,.\, x_D$$

Using the a, b, c from $ax + by + c$, this gives

$$ax_Q = t \,.\, ax_C + (1 - t)ax_D$$

also
$$by_Q = t \,.\, by_C + (1 - t)by_D$$
$$c = t \,.\, c + (1 - t)c$$

add: $(ax + by + c)_Q = t(ax + by + c)_C + (1 - t)(ax + by + c)_D$

showing that the value of $ax + by + c$ at Q is between the values it takes at C and D respectively. Hence it is less than that at A. Similarly, the value at P is between the values at A and Q and hence less than that at A. The same method shows that the minimum vertex value is also the minimum value for the whole set of points.

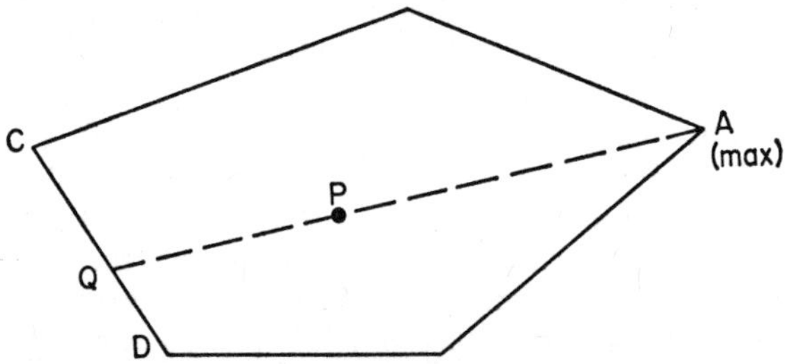

FIG. 35.

Should two points, say A and C, give the same optimum value, it is still true that this value occurs at a vertex, but in this case there are an infinite number of solutions, every point on the join AC.

9.8. Linear Programming

We are now in a position to solve the simpler problems in which a linear expression in two variables is to be made a maximum or minimum subject to linear restrictions on the variables.

Example 8. A firm can make two kinds of components A and B. Each A requires 3 oz. of copper and 1 oz. of zinc. Each B requires 1 oz. of copper and 4 oz. of zinc. There are only 21 oz. of copper and 24 oz. of zinc available. Each type of component takes 1 hour to make and there are only 9 hours available. The profit is £2 on each A and £5 on each B. Find the number of each of A and B to be made so as to make a maximum profit.

Suppose x of A and y of B are made.

(1) We have $\quad x \geqslant 0,\ y \geqslant 0.$

(2) By the copper restriction $\quad 3x + y \leqslant 21.$

(3) By the zinc restriction $\quad x + 4y \leqslant 24.$

(4) By the time restriction $\quad x + y \leqslant 9.$

(5) We have to maximize the profit £z where $\quad z = 2x + 5y.$

The polygon of possible values given by (1)–(4) is as shown. It has already been obtained in number 4 of the previous exercises. The vertices are as given in

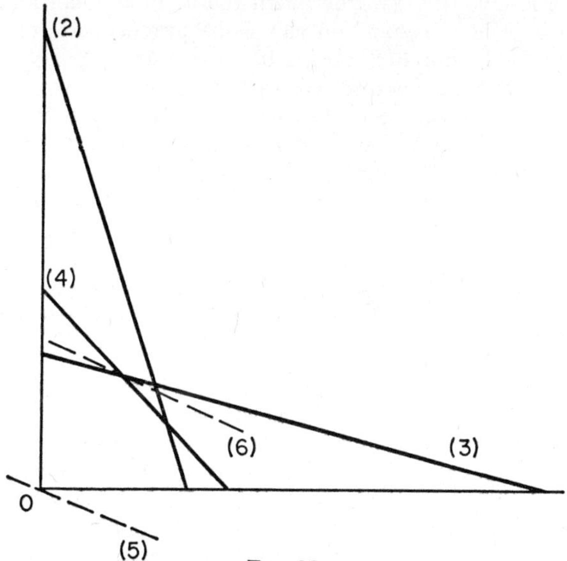

FIG. 36.

(2) $3x + y = 21$ (3) $x + 4y = 24$ (4) $x + y = 9$
(5) $2x + 5y = 0$ (6) $z = 2x + 5y$ a maximum at A

number 6: (0, 0), (0, 6), (4, 5), (6, 3), (7, 0). If we try each of these in turn we obtain for z the values 0, 30, 33, 27, 14. The maximum is then £33 obtained at the vertex (4, 5) so that 4 of A and 5 of B should be made.

(Instead of evaluating $2x + 5y$ at each vertex it is sometimes easier to draw $2x + 5y = 0$, *i.e.*, the line through the origin. Then imagine it moved parallel to itself across the first quadrant until as (6) it passes through the last vertex available. This is the one at which the maximum value will occur, and the others need not be evaluated.)

EXERCISE 18B

1. Find the maximum value of $z = x + 2y$ subject to the inequalities

$$x, y \geqslant 0$$
$$x + y - 7 \leqslant 0$$
$$y - x + 5 \geqslant 0$$
$$3y - 2x - 6 \leqslant 0$$

(Draw the polygon bounded by the lines and note from the slope of $x + 2y = C$, which vertex it passes through last as it moves away from the origin.)

2. Find the minimum of $z = 2y + x$

subject to
$$x, y \geqslant 0$$
$$5x - 2y \leqslant 3$$
$$x + y \geqslant 1$$
$$-3x + y \leqslant 3$$
$$3x + 3y \leqslant 20$$

3. For a fête you are provided with 100 lb. of almonds and 50 lb. of raisins to be sold mixed. You can make up two sorts of mixtures: (*a*) 60% almonds and 40% raisins to be sold at 2*s*. per lb.; (*b*) 80% almonds and 20% raisins to be sold at 3*s*. per lb. How many pounds of each mixture should be made, assuming all will be sold, to obtain a maximum return for the fête? What is the maximum return?

4. A firm makes two types of cloth X and Y. The material required per yard of each, the amount available and the profit made are as shown.

	X	Y	Amount available
Material needed	3 oz.	2 oz.	800 oz. of C yarn
(per yard made):	12 oz.	5 oz.	3000 oz. of D yarn
	2 oz.	7 oz.	1500 oz. of E yarn
Profit per yard	4*s*.	3*s*.	

Find how many yards of each should be made in order to make a maximum profit and how much of each is left unused.

[Assume $100x$ yd. of X and $100y$ yd. of Y are made.]

5. A firm makes two kinds of articles, A and B, on which the profits are £0·4 and £0·3 respectively per article. Each A takes twice as long to make as a B and if only A's were made a total of 500 per day could be attained. Both use the same amount of raw material, and enough of this is held per day to make a total of 800 articles. Owing to other facilities being in short supply, no more than 400 of A or 700 of B can be made. Find how many of each should be made for maximum profit.

6. An area coal board has two depots and supplies two markets. The first depot has a stock of 100 tons, whilst the second has 80 tons. The first market requires 70 tons and the second 90 tons. What amounts should be sent from each depot to each market so as to minimize the total delivery cost? The following schedule gives the cost of delivery in shillings per ton:

	Market	
	1st	2nd
Depot 1st	6	10
2nd	9	12

7. A firm makes 3 types of components A, B and C which are alternatives, so that it is estimated that the combined sales will never exceed 500. The firm decides to make at least 200 of A, at least 100 of B, but at most 150 of C, which is the most expensive. If the profit is £0·3 on each A, £0·4 on each B and £1 on each C, find how many of each should be made for maximum profit. It is assumed that 500 total are made and sold. [Suppose that x of A, y of B and $500 - x - y$ of C are made so that $150 \geqslant 500 - x - y \geqslant 0$.]

8. Two products A and B must be processed by three machines M_1, M_2 and M_3 one after the other, but the order does not matter.

The time each article of the products requires per machine is given, *e.g.*, each of A requires 5 minutes on machine M_2. It is assumed that no time is lost in waiting or moving between machines. The time available per machine is also given.

		M_1	M_2	M_3
Processing time (minutes)	A	10	5	7
	B	8	13	10
Machine time available (hours)		160	130	120

If A yields a profit of £40 per 100 and B of £50 per 100, what quantity of each should be made so as to produce the maximum profit?

How much idle time is there per machine?

9. A coal merchant has two depots D_1 and D_2 with stocks of 30 and 15 tons of coal respectively. He requires to supply three customers C_1, C_2 and C_3 with 20, 15 and 10 tons respectively. The distances in miles between the various customers and depots are as shown

	C_1	C_2	C_3
D_1	7	4	1
D_2	3	2	1

If the cost of sending coal is a fixed amount per ton-mile, find the cheapest way of fulfilling the orders and the cost.

10. A nutritionist wishes to provide a diet of two kinds of food X and Y so that the total vitamin content will be at least as shown below to be required. The vitamin content of a lb. of each food is as given. Also X costs 5*s.* per lb. whilst Y is 7*s.* per lb. Find the minimum cost of a suitable mixture.

	Vitamin units			
	A	*B*	*C*	*D*
Minimum required	12	10	7	9
X contains per lb.	1	1	1	2
Y contains per lb.	3	2	1	1

CHAPTER 10

THE CIRCLE

10.1. The Equation of a Circle

A circle is the locus of a point which moves so as always to be at a fixed distance from a given point. Let the fixed point be (x_1, y_1) and

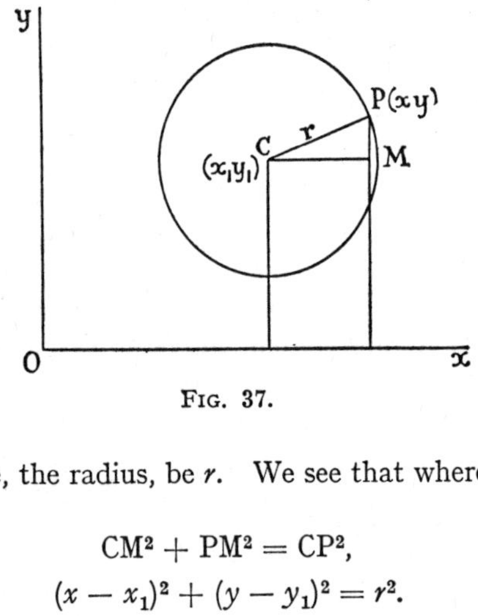

FIG. 37.

the fixed distance, the radius, be r. We see that wherever P is on the locus

$$CM^2 + PM^2 = CP^2,$$

i.e.,

$$(x - x_1)^2 + (y - y_1)^2 = r^2.$$

This equation has the following characteristics:

(1) it is of the second degree;
(2) the coefficients of x^2 and y^2 are equal;
(3) there is no term in xy.

We will now show that any equation with these characteristics is a circle. It is usual to adopt as the " standard " equation

$$x^2 + y^2 + 2gx + 2fy + c = 0.$$

This can be written

$$(x + g)^2 - g^2 + (y + f)^2 - f^2 + c = 0$$

or

$$(x + g)^2 + (y + f)^2 = g^2 + f^2 - c.$$

Therefore this standard equation represents a circle with centre $(-g, -f)$ and radius $\sqrt{g^2 + f^2 - c}$.

Example 1. Write down the equation of a circle whose centre is (1, – 2) and radius 4.

Equation is

$$(x - 1)^2 + (y + 2)^2 = 4^2,$$

which could be written as

$$\underline{x^2 + y^2 - 2x + 4y = 11.}$$

Example 2. Find the centre and radius of

$$x^2 + y^2 + 2x + 4y + 1 = 0.$$

This is

$$(x + 1)^2 - 1^2 + (y + 2)^2 - 2^2 + 1 = 0$$

or

$$(x + 1)^2 + (y + 2)^2 = 4,$$

$$\therefore \quad \underline{\text{centre is } (-1, -2) \text{ and radius} = 2.}$$

Note that we write all the terms in x^2 and x as a square in x and adjust for the term added by subtracting it from the square.

Thus $\qquad x^2 + 2x = (x + 1)^2 - 1^2.$

Similarly, $\qquad y^2 + 4y = (y + 2)^2 - 2^2.$

EXERCISE 19

1. Find the locus of a point which moves at a distance of 3 units from the point (2, – 1).
2. A circle has its centre at (3, 4) and radius r. Find r if the circle is to pass through the origin.
3. Find the centres and radii of the following circles:
   (i) $x^2 + y^2 - 6x - 8y = 0$;
   (ii) $x^2 + y^2 - 2x - 6y + 6 = 0$;
   (iii) $2x^2 + 2y^2 - 4x - 12y + 12 = 0$;
   (iv) $6x^2 + 6y^2 - 16x + 20y = 15$.

10.2. Tangent and Normal at any Point of a Circle

Definition: A *normal* at any point on a curve is the line through the point perpendicular to the tangent at the point. In the case of a circle all normals are radii and pass through the centre.

Let the equation be

$$x^2 + y^2 + 2gx + 2fy + c = 0.$$

Differentiating:

$$2x + 2y\frac{dy}{dx} + 2g + 2f\frac{dy}{dx} = 0,$$

$$\therefore \quad \frac{dy}{dx} = -\frac{(x + g)}{y + f}$$

$$= -\frac{(x_1 + g)}{(y_1 + f)} \quad \text{at } (x_1, y_1).$$

$\therefore$ the tangent at (x_1, y_1) is

$$y - y_1 = -\frac{(x_1 + g)}{(y_1 + f)}(x - x_1),$$

and the normal is

$$y - y_1 = \frac{(y_1 + f)}{(x_1 + g)}(x - x_1).$$

Example 3. Find the equations of the tangent and normal at the point $(2, -5)$ on $x^2 + y^2 - 7x - 9y - 60 = 0$ and verify that the normal passes through the centre of the circle.

Differentiate the given equation:

$$2x + 2y\frac{dy}{dx} - 7 - 9\frac{dy}{dx} = 0,$$

$$\therefore \quad \frac{dy}{dx} = \frac{7 - 2x}{2y - 9} = \frac{3}{-19} \text{ at } (2, -5).$$

$\therefore$ tangent is $\quad y + 5 = -\frac{3}{19}(x - 2)$

or $\quad 3x + 19y + 89 = 0;$

normal is $\quad y + 5 = \frac{19}{3}(x - 2)$

or $\quad 3y - 19x + 53 = 0.$

The equation to the circle may be written

$$(x - \tfrac{7}{2})^2 + (y - \tfrac{9}{2})^2 = \tfrac{370}{4},$$

and the centre $(\frac{7}{2}, \frac{9}{2})$ clearly lies on the normal.

10.3. The Length of the Tangent from a Point to a Circle

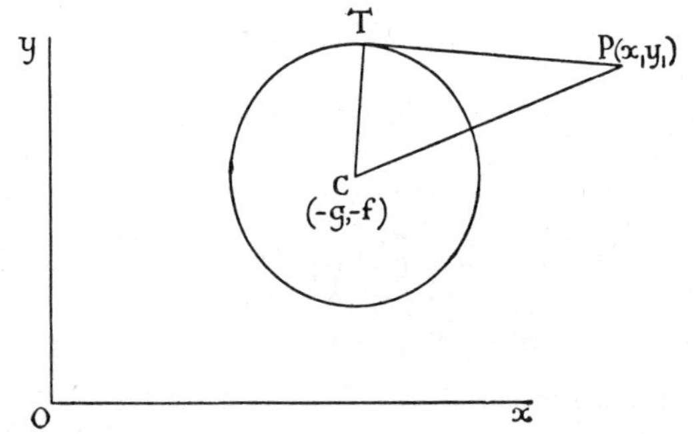

FIG. 38.

Let the given circle, centre C, be

$$x^2 + y^2 + 2gx + 2fy + c = 0$$

or

$$(x + g)^2 + (y + f)^2 = g^2 + f^2 - c,$$

and the given point

$$P = (x_1, y_1).$$

If PT is the tangent

$$\begin{aligned} PT^2 &= PC^2 - CT^2 \\ &= (x_1 + g)^2 + (y_1 + f)^2 - (g^2 + f^2 - c) \\ &= x_1^2 + y_1^2 + 2gx_1 + 2fy_1 + c. \end{aligned}$$

Rule: Arrange the equation of the circle to have the coefficients of x^2 and y^2 unity. Substitute the co-ordinates of the point (x_1, y_1) in the equation. This gives the square of the length of the tangent.

NOTE: If the point (x_1, y_1) is outside the circle we will get a positive quantity by the above substitution. If the point is on the circle we will, of course, get zero. If, however, the point is inside the circle the tangents are " imaginary " and we will get a negative quantity for PT^2 showing algebraically that PT is imaginary.

Example 4. Find the length of the tangent from the point (10, 3) to the circle

$$2x^2 + 2y^2 - 4x + 8y - 2 = 0.$$

We write the equation

$$x^2 + y^2 - 2x + 4y - 1 = 0.$$

Substitute:

$$\begin{aligned} PT^2 &= 100 + 9 - 20 + 12 - 1 \\ &= 100, \\ \therefore \quad PT &= 10. \end{aligned}$$

Example 5. Find the length of the tangent from (2, 1) to the circle

$$x^2 + y^2 - 2x + 4y - 12 = 0.$$

Here

$$\begin{aligned} PT^2 &= 4 + 1 - 4 + 4 - 12. \\ &= -7. \end{aligned}$$

$\therefore$ PT is imaginary and the point (2, 1) lies inside the given circle.

10.4. Miscellaneous Examples

Example 6. Show that $8x + 5y - 34 = 0$ is a tangent to the circle

$$x^2 + y^2 + 10x + 6y - 55 = 0.$$

Method 1. Since $8x + 5y - 34 = 0$,

$$x = \frac{(34 - 5y)}{8}.$$

Substitute in the equation of the circle

$$\left(\frac{34 - 5y}{8}\right)^2 + y^2 + \frac{10(34 - 5y)}{8} + 6y - 55 = 0,$$

$$89y^2 - 356y + 356 = 0,$$

$$y^2 - 4y + 4 = 0$$

or

$$(y - 2)^2 = 0.$$

$\therefore$ the line meets the circle in two coincident points and is therefore a tangent.

Method 2. The circle can be written

$$(x + 5)^2 + (y + 3)^2 = 89,$$

$\therefore$ the centre is $-5, -3$ and radius $= \sqrt{89}$.

Now the perpendicular from $(-5, -3)$ on to $8x + 5y - 34 = 0$ is of length

$$\frac{8(-5) + 5(-3) - 34}{\pm\sqrt{8^2 + 5^2}} = \sqrt{89}.$$

$\therefore$ the distance of the line from the centre equals a radius and the line is a tangent.

Example 7. Find the equation of the circle through the points (0, 0), (2, −1), (− 2, − 2).

Method 1. Let the equation be

$$x^2 + y^2 + 2gx + 2fy + c = 0.$$

Since the above points lie on it

$$\begin{aligned} c &= 0, \\ 4g - 2f + c &= -5, \\ -4g - 4f + c &= -8; \\ \therefore \quad g = -\tfrac{1}{6},\ f &= \tfrac{13}{6},\ c = 0. \end{aligned}$$

$\therefore$ equation is

$$x^2 + y^2 - 2 \cdot \tfrac{1}{6}x + 2 \cdot \tfrac{13}{6}y = 0$$

or

$$3x^2 + 3y^2 - x + 13y = 0.$$

Method 2. If the points in the order given are A, B, C, then the mid point of AB is $(1, -\tfrac{1}{2})$ and its gradient is $-\tfrac{1}{2}$.

$\therefore$ the line through this mid point perpendicular to AB is

$$y + \tfrac{1}{2} = 2(x - 1)$$

or

$$2y - 4x + 5 = 0.$$

The line through the mid point of AC, perpendicular to it is

$$y + 1 = -1\,(x + 1)$$

or

$$y + x + 2 = 0.$$

Solving these two equations, we find

$$x = \tfrac{1}{6},\ y = -\tfrac{13}{6},$$

which being the intersection of the perpendicular bisectors of chords of the circle is the centre.

The distance of this centre from any point on the circumference is the radius. We choose, of course, the easiest point to work with, the point (0, 0).

$$\therefore\quad r^2 = (\tfrac{1}{6})^2 + (\tfrac{13}{6})^2$$

$$= \tfrac{170}{36}, \qquad\qquad r = \tfrac{1}{6}\sqrt{170}.$$

equation to circle is

$$\underline{(x - \tfrac{1}{6})^2 + (y + \tfrac{13}{6})^2 = \tfrac{170}{36}}.$$

EXERCISE 20

1. Find the points A, B where the line $y = 2x + 1$ cuts the circle $x^2 + y^2 = 34$. Find the tangents at A and B and C the point where these tangents meet. Verify that OC is perpendicular to AB.

2. The line $y = x + 1$ cuts $x^2 + y^2 = 6$ in the points A and B. Perpendiculars AM, BN are drawn to meet the x axis in M and N. Prove that OM . ON = 2·5.

3. Find the equation of the circle through the points:

   (*a*) (6, 0), (– 4, 0), (0, 8); (*b*) (3, 1), (2, 2), (4, 4).

4. Prove that the four points (– 1, – 4), (5, 2), (7, 0), (1, – 6) all lie on a circle.

5. Prove that two tangents can be drawn from the point (3, 3) to the circle $x^2 + y^2 = 4$ and find their gradients.

6. A variable line of constant length a cuts the axes at A and B. Find the locus of the mid point of AB.

7. AB is a fixed straight line 4 units long. P is a variable point which moves so that $PA^2 + PB^2 = AB^2$. Find its locus.

8. Find the equation of the tangent at:

   (i) the point (3, 4) on $x^2 + y^2 = 25$;
   (ii) the point (1, – 7) on $x^2 + y^2 = 50$;
   (iii) the point (– 2, 5) on $x^2 + y^2 + 3x - 8y + 17 = 0$;
   (iv) the point (– 1, 6) on $x^2 + y^2 + 8x + 10y = 89$.

9. Find the length of the tangent from the point to the circle in each of the following cases:

   (i) point (3, 4), circle $x^2 + y^2 + 8x + 5y + 2 = 0$;
   (ii) point (– 2, 6), circle $x^2 + y^2 - 4x + 7y - 5 = 0$;
   (iii) point (5, – 2), circle $3x^2 + 3y^2 + 27x - 6y + 12 = 0$.

10. Test whether the point given is within or without the given circle:

   (i) point (5, 8), circle $x^2 + y^2 + 6x + 4y = 4$;
   (ii) point (6, – 1), circle $4x^2 + 4y^2 - 20x + 18y + 6 = 0$,
   (iii) point (– 4, 3), circle $x^2 + y^2 + 10x - 5y - 12 = 0$.

10.5. Further Examples and Loci

Example 8. Show that the tangent to $x^2 + y^2 = a^2$ at the point (x_1, y_1) may be written as $xx_1 + yy_1 = a^2$.

From
$$x^2 + y^2 = a^2$$
$$2x + 2y\frac{dy}{dx} = 0,$$
$$\therefore \quad \frac{dy}{dx} = -\frac{x}{y} = -\frac{x_1}{y_1} \text{ at } (x_1, y_1),$$

$\therefore$ tangent is
$$y - y_1 = -\frac{x_1}{y_1}(x - x_1).$$

This is
$$yy_1 + xx_1 = y_1^2 + x_1^2.$$

But since (x_1, y_1) lies on the circle
$$x_1^2 + y_1^2 = a^2,$$

$\therefore$ tangent becomes
$$yy_1 + xx_1 = a^2.$$

This simple form is important and should be known.

Example 9. The tangent to $x^2 + y^2 = 9$ at a point P on the circle meets the x axis at L and the y axis at M. Prove that
$$\frac{1}{OL^2} + \frac{1}{OM^2} = \frac{1}{9}.$$

Let $P \equiv (x_1, y_1)$, $\therefore$ the tangent is
$$xx_1 + yy_1 = 9.$$
$$\therefore \quad L \text{ is } \left(\frac{9}{x_1}, 0\right), \quad M \text{ is } \left(0, \frac{9}{y_1}\right).$$
$$\therefore \quad \frac{1}{OL^2} + \frac{1}{OM^2} = \frac{x_1^2}{81} + \frac{y_1^2}{81} = \frac{x_1^2 + y_1^2}{81} = \frac{1}{9},$$

since $x_1^2 + y_1^2 = 9$.

Example 10. A circle is drawn with its centre A on the x axis. Any point B on it is joined to O, the origin. Find the locus of C, the mid point of OB.

Let C in any one position be (X, Y),
$$\therefore \quad B \text{ is } (2X, 2Y).$$

But B lies on the circle whose equation is of the form
$$(x - a)^2 + y^2 = r^2.$$

The co-ordinates of B satisfy this,
$$\therefore \quad (2X - a)^2 + (2Y)^2 = r^2$$

or
$$\left(X - \frac{a}{2}\right)^2 + Y^2 = \left(\frac{r}{2}\right)^2.$$

$\therefore$ (X, Y) describes the circle
$$\left(x - \frac{a}{2}\right)^2 + y^2 = \left(\frac{r}{2}\right)^2.$$

EXERCISE 21

1. L and M are the points $(\pm 2, 0)$. N is a point on LM, and P is a point such that PN is perpendicular to LM. If P moves so that $PN^2 = LN \,.\, NM$, find the locus of P.

2. A circle has its centre at O, but its radius varies. If this circle cuts the axes in the first quadrant at L and M, find the locus of the mid point of LM.

3. A square ABCD is inscribed in a circle. If L is any point on the circumference prove that $LA^2 + LB^2 + LC^2 + LD^2$ is twice the square on the diameter of the circle.

4. PQ is a diameter of a circle. Tangents are drawn to the circle at P and Q to meet any other variable tangent at L and M. Prove that LM subtends 90° at the centre of the circle. [Choose axes so that P, Q are the points $(\pm a, 0)$ where $2a$ is the diameter.]

5. The line $2x + 3y = 6$ meets the circle $x^2 + y^2 = 25$ at the points P and Q. Find where the tangents at P and Q meet.

6. The tangent to $x^2 + y^2 = a^2$ at a point (x_1, y_1) meets the axes at L and M. Prove that the area of the triangle LOM is $a^4/2x_1y_1$.

7. Find the co-ordinates of the point of intersection of the tangents to the circle $x^2 + y^2 - 12x + 4y - 10 = 0$ at the points (7, 5) and (1, 3). What is the angle between these tangents?

8. (*a*) Find the points of intersection of the lines

$$x + y = 5, \quad x + 3y + 4 = 0, \quad x - 2y + 1 = 0$$

and the circle through these 3 points, *i.e.*, the equation of the circumcircle of the triangle.

(*b*) Show that the curve whose equation is

$$(x + y - 5)(x + 3y + 4) + A(x - 2y + 1)(x + 3y + 4) + B(x + y - 5)(x - 2y + 1) = 0$$

passes through the vertices of the triangle in (*a*). Find the values of A and B if this curve is to represent a circle, *i.e.*, the coefficients of x^2 and y^2 are equal and the coefficient of xy is zero. Hence find the equation of this circle and check the result obtained in (*a*).

9. (*a*) If three lines are represented by

$$L_1 = 0, \quad L_2 = 0, \quad L_3 = 0$$

write down the equation of the second-degree curve through their three points of intersection.

(*b*) If the three lines are

$$2y + x = 1, \quad y + 3x = 8, \quad 3y - x = 4,$$

find the equation of the circumcircle of this triangle.

10. Find the equations of the chords of the circle

$$x^2 + y^2 - 2x - 4y - 20 = 0$$

which have length $4\sqrt{5}$ and gradient 1/2.

11. Prove that the reflection of the x axis in the line $y = mx + c$ is the line $(1 - m^2)y = 2(mx + c)$.

Prove that the circles

$$x^2 + y^2 - 2x - 4y + 1 = 0, \quad 4x^2 + 4y^2 + 4x - 8y + 1 = 0$$

touch the x axis and intersect in real points. Show also that the equation of their other common tangent is $5y = 12(x + 2)$.

CHAPTER 11

PARAMETRIC REPRESENTATION. ELIMINATION

11.1. Parametric Equations

The figure shows that any point P on a circle of radius a and centre at the origin can be represented by the co-ordinates

$$x = a \cos \theta, \ y = a \sin \theta.$$

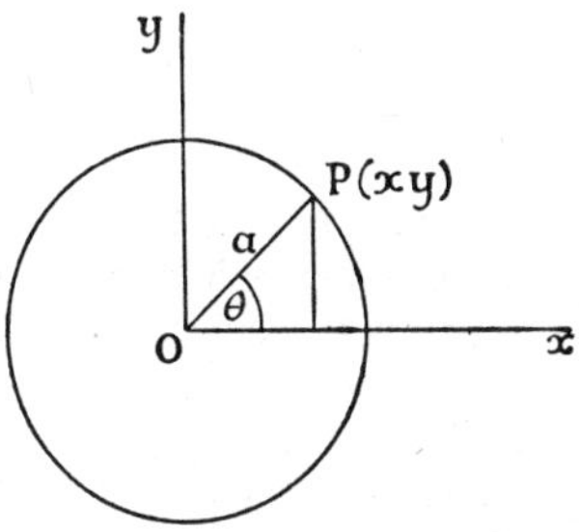

FIG. 39.

As θ increases from 0 to 2π we obtain every point on the circle. Any value of θ outside this range gives one of the points over again.

We therefore have two methods of representing the points on a circle. We can say: let (x_1, y_1) be a point on the circle of radius a so that $x_1^2 + y_1^2 = a^2$. Or we can say: let the co-ordinates of any point be

$$x = a \cos \theta, \ y = a \sin \theta.$$

Both methods are used, but the second method often simplifies work greatly in algebraic geometry and calculus. The student will note that if we attempt to express that the point $(a \cos \theta, a \sin \theta)$ lies on the circle we obtain

$$a^2 \cos^2 \theta + a^2 \sin^2 \theta = a^2$$

or

$$\cos^2 \theta + \sin^2 \theta = 1,$$

which is already known. In fact, the curve on which the point lies is implicitly represented in the equations $x = a \cos \theta$, $y = a \sin \theta$, and we seldom need to refer back to the (x, y) equation. This is the great advantage of *parametric representation.*

When x and y are both represented in terms of the same variable, θ (say), this third variable θ is called a *parameter.* The equations expressing x and y in terms of the parameter are called *parametric equations.*

11.2. Curve Sketching from Parametric Equations

Suppose we are faced with the parametric equations

$$x = t^2,\ y = 2t.$$

Since no restrictive values are placed on t, we would suppose that t may have any value. We could therefore draw up a table as follows:

t . .	-4	-3	-2	-1	0	1	2	3	4
$x = t^2$ . .	16	9	4	1	0	1	4	9	16
$y = 2t$.	-8	-6	-4	-2	0	2	4	6	8

A plot of the pairs of values (x, y) on paper will soon give an idea of the shape of the curve.

EXERCISE 22

In each of the following obtain a table of values similar to the above. Plot the points and verify the shape given:

1. $x = 10 \cos \theta$, $y = 10 \sin \theta$, letting θ increase from 0 to 180° by 30° intervals, and then letting θ decrease from 0 to $-$ 180° by 30° intervals. The join of the points is a circle, radius 10 units.
2. Repeat the above for $x = 10 \cos \theta$, $y = 5 \sin \theta$. The join will be an ellipse.
3. Let t vary from -4 to $+4$ for $x = 1 - t$, $y = t$. The join will be the line $x + y - 1 = 0$.

11.3. Differentiation in Parameters

When x and y are given in terms of θ we have

$$\frac{dy}{dx} = \frac{dy}{d\theta}\cdot\frac{d\theta}{dx} = \frac{dy}{d\theta}\bigg/\frac{dx}{d\theta}. \qquad \frac{d^2y}{dx^2} = \frac{d}{dx}\left(\frac{dy}{dx}\right) = \frac{d}{d\theta}\left(\frac{dy}{d\theta}\bigg/\frac{dx}{d\theta}\right)\cdot\frac{d\theta}{dx}.$$

Example 1. Find dy/dx and d^2y/dx^2 at the point θ on the curve

$$x = a \cos^3 \theta,\ y = a \sin^3 \theta.$$

In this case

$$\frac{dx}{d\theta} = a\,.\,3 \cos^2 \theta(-\sin \theta),$$

$$\frac{dy}{d\theta} = a\,.\,3 \sin^2 \theta \cos \theta;$$

$$\therefore\ \frac{dy}{dx} = \frac{dy}{d\theta}\bigg/\frac{dx}{d\theta} = \frac{3a \sin^2 \theta \cos \theta}{-3a \cos^2 \theta \sin \theta} = \underline{-\tan \theta.}$$

$$\frac{d^2y}{dx^2} = \frac{d}{d\theta}(-\tan \theta)/-3a \cos^2 \theta \sin \theta = \underline{1/3a \cos^4 \theta \sin \theta.}$$

Example 2. Find the equation to the tangent and normal at the point t on the curve $x = t^2$, $y = 2t$.

$$\frac{dx}{dt} = 2t,\ \frac{dy}{dt} = 2,$$

$$\therefore\ \frac{dy}{dx} = \frac{2}{2t} = \frac{1}{t}.$$

$\therefore$ tangent is

$$\underline{y - 2t = \frac{1}{t}(x - t^2);}$$

normal is

$$\underline{y - 2t = -t(x - t^2).}$$

If we put $t = 1$ in these equations, then since $x = t^2 = 1$, $y = 2t = 2$ we have found the tangent and normal at the point (1, 2), and they are respectively,

$$y - 2 = 1(x - 1),$$
$$y - 2 = -1(x - 1).$$

Example 3. The tangent to $x^2 + y^2 = a^2$ at a point P on the circle meets the axes at L and M respectively. Prove that

$$\frac{1}{OL^2} + \frac{1}{OM^2} = \frac{1}{a^2}.$$

From the equation

$$x^2 + y^2 = a^2$$

we have

$$2x + 2y\frac{dy}{dx} = 0,$$

$$\frac{dy}{dx} = -\frac{x}{y}$$

$$= -\frac{a\cos\theta}{a\sin\theta}$$

if we consider the point $(a\cos\theta, a\sin\theta)$ on the circle as P.

$\therefore$ equation of tangent at the point is

$$y - a\sin\theta = -\frac{a\cos\theta}{a\sin\theta}(x - a\cos\theta)$$

or

$$x\cos\theta + y\sin\theta = a(\sin^2\theta + \cos^2\theta)$$
$$= a.$$

Put $y = 0$ in this and find $\quad OL = \dfrac{a}{\cos\theta}$

$x = 0$ " " $\quad OM = \dfrac{a}{\sin\theta}.$

$$\therefore \quad \frac{1}{OL^2} + \frac{1}{OM^2} = \frac{\cos^2\theta}{a^2} + \frac{\sin^2\theta}{a^2} = \frac{1}{a^2}.$$

Compare Example 9 of the previous chapter, and note that here it was not necessary to say at the end that $x_1^2 + y_1^2 = a^2$.

EXERCISE 23

In examples 1–5 find $\dfrac{dy}{dx}$ in terms of the parameter.

1. $x = t^2 + t$, $y = t^3 - t^2$.
2. $x = 2t + 1$, $y = 2t(t - 1)$.
3. $x = e^t\cos t$, $y = e^t\sin t$.
4. $x = a\tan\theta$, $y = b\sec\theta$.
5. $x = a\log t$, $y = \dfrac{a}{2}\left(t + \dfrac{1}{t}\right)$.

In examples 6–9 find the equations of the tangent and normal at the general point t or θ.

6. $x = at^2$, $y = 2at$.
7. $x = a\sin\theta$, $y = b\cos\theta$.

8. $x = \dfrac{3at}{(1 + t^3)}$, $y = \dfrac{3at^2}{(1 + t^3)}$.

9. $x = 2 \sin \theta$, $y = \cos 2\theta$.

10. A certain locus is given by

$$x = 6 \cos \theta - \cos 3\theta, \quad y = 6 \sin \theta - \sin 3\theta.$$

Show that the tangent at the point $\theta = \dfrac{\pi}{4}$ is $y + 3x = 13\sqrt{2}$.

11. Find the equations of the tangent and normal at the point $\theta = \dfrac{\pi}{3}$ on the curve $x = a(\theta - \sin \theta)$, $y = a(1 - \cos \theta)$.

12. The tangent at the point t on the curve $x = ct$, $y = \dfrac{c}{t}$ meets the axes at L and M. Prove that LM is bisected at the point of contact with the curve and that the area of the triangle OLM is constant.

13. An epicycloid is given by the equations

$$x = 2 \cos \theta - \cos 2\theta \text{ and } y = 2 \sin \theta - \sin 2\theta.$$

Determine the inclination to the axis of x of the tangent to the epicycloid at the point for which $\theta = \dfrac{\pi}{6}$. [U.L.C.I.]

14. Show that for the curve

$$x = a \cos^3 t, \; y = a \sin^3 t$$

the tangent at t is

$$x \sin t + y \cos t = a \sin t \cos t.$$

15. (*a*) A curve is given by

$$x = a(2 \cos \theta + \cos 2\theta), \; y = a(2 \sin \theta - \sin 2\theta),$$

show that the normal at θ is

$$x \cos \frac{\theta}{2} - y \sin \frac{\theta}{2} = 3a \cos \frac{3\theta}{2}.$$

(*b*) If $x = \cos 2\theta + 2\theta \sin 2\theta$, $y = \sin 2\theta - 2\theta \cos 2\theta$, show that

$$(dx/d\theta)^2 + (dy/d\theta)^2 = 16\theta^2.$$

16. The tangent at the point θ on $x = a \cos \theta$, $y = a \sin^2 \theta$ meets the axes Ox, Oy, forming a triangle. Show that the minimum area possible is $a^2\, 4\sqrt{3}/9$.

17. If $x = at^2$, $y = at^3$, show that

$$\frac{d^2y}{dx^2} = \frac{3}{4at}.$$

18. If $x = 2a \cos t + a \cos 2t$, $y = 2a \sin t - a \sin 2t$, show that

$$\frac{d^2y}{dx^2} = 1/8a \cos^3 \left(\frac{t}{2}\right) \sin \left(\frac{3t}{2}\right).$$

19. If $x = a \sin 2\theta(1 + \cos 2\theta)$, $y = a \cos 2\theta(1 - \cos 2\theta)$ and the radius of curvature is given by

$$\rho = \frac{[1 + (dy/dx)^2]^{\frac{3}{2}}}{d^2y/dx^2},$$

show that at the general point θ, $\rho = 4a \cos 3\theta$.

20. If $x = a(\cos \theta + \theta \sin \theta)$, $y = b(\sin \theta - \theta \cos \theta)$, show that

$$\frac{d^2y}{dx^2} = \frac{b \sec^3 \theta}{a^2\theta}.$$

21. If $x = a(1 - \cos \theta)$, $y = a \sin \theta$, show that

$$\frac{dy}{dx} = \cot \theta \qquad \frac{d^2y}{dx^2} = -\frac{\operatorname{cosec}^3 \theta}{a}.$$

22. If $x = f(t)$, $y = g(t)$, show that

$$\frac{dy}{dx} = \frac{g'(t)}{f'(t)},$$

$$\frac{d^2y}{dx^2} = \frac{(f'g'' - g'f'')}{(f')^3}.$$

Apply this to question No. 19 above to obtain the result given.

11.4. Elimination

The student faced with a pair of equations such as $x = at^2$, $y = 2at$ may require the (x, y) equation which they represent. To obtain this we must " eliminate " the variable t from the two equations.

Example 4. Eliminate θ between

$$a \cos \theta + b \sin \theta = c,$$
$$A \cos \theta + B \sin \theta = C.$$

Solve for $\cos \theta$ and $\sin \theta$ and obtain

$$\cos \theta = \frac{bC - Bc}{bA - Ba},$$

$$\sin \theta = \frac{Ac - aC}{bA - Ba}.$$

Since $\cos^2 \theta + \sin^2 \theta = 1$, we will square and add

$$1 = \left(\frac{bC - Bc}{bA - Ba}\right)^2 + \left(\frac{Ac - aC}{bA - Ba}\right)^2.$$

or $$(bA - Ba)^2 = (bC - Bc)^2 + (Ac - aC)^2.$$

Example 5. Eliminate t between

$$x = a \log t, \quad y = \frac{a}{2}\left(t + \frac{1}{t}\right).$$

From the first we have

$$\frac{x}{a} = \log_e t,$$

$$\therefore \quad t = e^{x/a}.$$

Substitution for t in the other equation gives

$$y = \frac{a}{2}(e^{x/a} + e^{-x/a})$$

or

$$y = a \cosh\left(\frac{x}{a}\right).$$

There is no standard method of elimination. Each problem must be treated on its own. The following exercises refer to curves that usually occur.

EXERCISE 24

In each of the following exercises eliminate the parameter t or θ to obtain the (x, y) equation of the curve represented by the parametric equations:

1. $x = at^2,\ y = 2at.$
2. $x = ct,\ y = \dfrac{c}{t}.$
3. $x = a\cos\theta,\ y = b\sin\theta.$
4. $x = 2\sin\theta,\ y = \cos 2\theta.$
5. $x = 2t + 1,\ y = 2t(t - 1).$
6. $x = a\tan\theta,\ y = b\sec\theta.$
7. $x = \dfrac{3at}{(1 + t^3)},\ y = \dfrac{3at^2}{(1 + t^3)}.$
8. $x = a\cos^3\theta,\ y = a\sin^3\theta.$
9. $x = 3\cos\theta + \cos 3\theta,\ y = 3\sin\theta - \sin 3\theta.$
10. $x = a\cot^2\theta,\ y = 2a\tan\theta.$
11. $x = a + r\cos\theta,\ y = b + r\sin\theta.$
12. $x = \dfrac{a}{2}\left(t + \dfrac{1}{t}\right),\ y = \dfrac{b}{2}\left(t - \dfrac{1}{t}\right).$
13. A curve is given by

$$x = 3at^2 + 2a, \quad y = -2at^3.$$

Show that the eliminant of t is

$$4(x - 2a)^3 = 27ay^2.$$

Show that the tangent to the curve at the point "t" is also a normal to the parabola $y^2 = 4ax$ at the point $(at^2, 2at)$.

CHAPTER 12

SOME USEFUL CURVES

12.1. In this chapter we will consider some curves which are represented in parameters and of frequent occurrence.

12.2. The Cycloid

When a circle rolls on a straight line any point fixed on its circumference describes a cycloid.

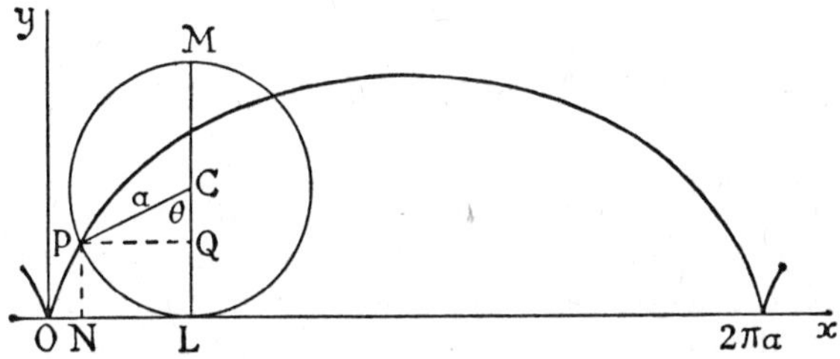

FIG. 40.

The circle of radius a has rolled along a line taken as the x axis Ox. We will find the equation to the curve described by any point P on its circumference.

Choose the origin O at the point where P was on the x axis and suppose CP the radius to P has turned through an angle θ as the circle has rolled along to its present position where L is its point of contact with the x axis.

Since the circle has rolled

$$\text{OL} = \text{arc PL} = a\theta.$$

$\therefore$ if P be (x, y)

$$\begin{aligned} x &= \text{ON} \\ &= \text{OL} - \text{NL} \\ &= a\theta - a\sin\theta \\ &= a(\theta - \sin\theta) \end{aligned}$$

and

$$\begin{aligned} y &= \text{PN} \\ &= \text{CL} - a\cos\theta \\ &= a(1 - \cos\theta). \end{aligned}$$

These are the parametric equations to the curve described by P, θ being the parameter. As θ increases from 0 to 2π one complete arc of the curve is described.

The Cartesian equation of the curve can be obtained by eliminating θ between the equations for x and y and is

$$x = a \cos^{-1}\left(\frac{a-y}{a}\right) - \sqrt{2ay - y^2}.$$

This equation is awkward to work with, whereas the parametric equations will be found to give any required result in a simple and often neat manner.

Thus

$$\frac{dy}{dx} = \frac{dy}{d\theta}\bigg/\frac{dx}{d\theta} = \frac{a \sin \theta}{a(1 - \cos \theta)}$$

$$= \frac{a \,.\, 2 \sin \frac{\theta}{2} \cos \frac{\theta}{2}}{a \,.\, 2 \sin^2 \frac{\theta}{2}}$$

$$= \cot \frac{\theta}{2}.$$

But if LM is the diameter, $\angle PML = \frac{\theta}{2}$, since $\angle PCL = \theta$,

$$\therefore \quad \tan MPQ = \tan\left(\frac{\pi}{2} - \frac{\theta}{2}\right) = \cot \frac{\theta}{2}.$$

$\therefore$ MP makes the required angle with PQ, the horizontal through P, so that PM is the tangent to the curve at P. This is otherwise evident, for since L is the instantaneous centre of the rolling circle P is moving perpendicular to PL and therefore towards M, since $\angle MPL = 90°$, the angle in a semicircle. But P is instantaneously moving along the tangent at P, therefore PM is that tangent, also PL is the normal.

12.3. The Epicycloid

The curve traced out by a point fixed on the circumference of a circle which rolls on the *outside* circumference of a fixed circle is called an epicycloid.

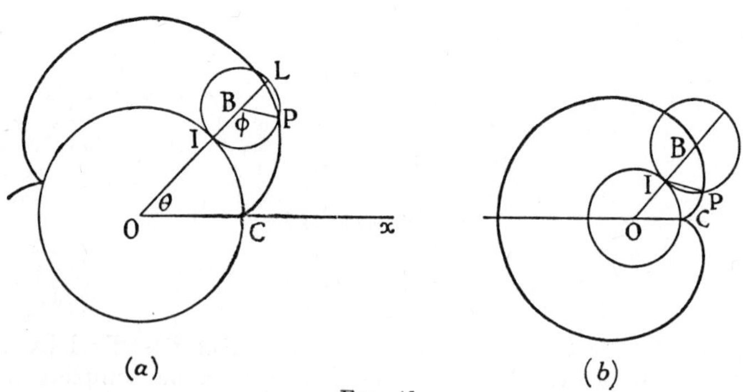

FIG. 41.

Let P in the figure (Fig. 41(*a*)) be the tracing point whose coordinates (x, y) are required, C being its starting point. If O is the centre of the fixed circle choose OC as the x axis with O as origin. Let a, b be the radii of the fixed and rolling circles, θ the angle the join of centres OB has turned through from its initial position along OC and ϕ the angle BP has turned through.

Since the circle rolls

$$\text{arc PI} = \text{arc IC},$$
$$\therefore \quad b\phi = a\theta.$$

Projecting OB and BP on to OC,

$$\begin{aligned} x &= (a + b)\cos\theta + b\cos(\pi - \overline{\theta + \phi}) \\ &= (a + b)\cos\theta - b\cos(\theta + \phi) \\ &= (a + b)\cos\theta - b\cos\left(\frac{a + b}{b}\theta\right). \end{aligned}$$

Similarly,

$$\begin{aligned} y &= (a + b)\sin\theta - b\sin(\pi - \overline{\theta + \phi}) \\ &= (a + b)\sin\theta - b\sin(\theta + \phi) \\ &= (a + b)\sin\theta - b\sin\left(\frac{a + b}{b}\theta\right). \end{aligned}$$

These are the parametric equations to the curve described by P. As θ increases from 0 to 2π the rolling circle moves once round the fixed circle. The point P will return to C after one or more complete revolutions if the ratio $b : a$ is not a surd such as $\sqrt{3}$ or some other incommensurable number.

12.4. The Cardioid (Fig. 41 (*b*))

When $b = a$, or the radii of the fixed and rolling circles are equal, the above equations become

$$x = 2a\cos\theta - a\cos 2\theta,$$
$$y = 2a\sin\theta - a\sin 2\theta.$$

This equation is more easily dealt with in polar form. If PC $= r$, then

$$r^2 = (x - a)^2 + y^2,$$
$$\therefore \quad \frac{r^2}{a^2} = (2\cos\theta - 2\cos^2\theta)^2 + (2\sin\theta - \sin 2\theta)^2,$$

and this reduces to

$$r^2 = 4a^2(1 - \cos\theta)^2,$$
$$\therefore \quad r = 2a(1 - \cos\theta) \quad . \quad . \quad . \quad . \quad . \quad . \quad . \quad . \quad (1)$$

Since $a = b$, $\angle$IBP $= \angle$IOC, and therefore CP is parallel to OB. This shows that the angle PC makes with the x axis is also θ. Equation (1) is therefore the polar equation in r, θ of the curve, the pole being at C. It is a heart-shaped curve with the cusp at C.

12.5. The Hypocycloid

The curve traced out by a point fixed on the circumference of a circle which rolls on the *inside* circumference of a fixed circle is called a hypocycloid.

The parametric equations for P(x, y) can be obtained in much the same way as for the epicycloid. Noting that the radius b is now subtracted instead of added to the radius a, we can obtain the equations by changing the sign of b in the equations of 12.3. These become

$$x = (a - b)\cos\theta + b\cos\left(\frac{a-b}{b}\theta\right),$$

$$y = (a - b)\sin\theta - b\sin\left(\frac{a-b}{b}\theta\right),$$

where, as before, θ is the angle turned through by the join of centres.

12.6. Particular Cases of the Hypocycloid

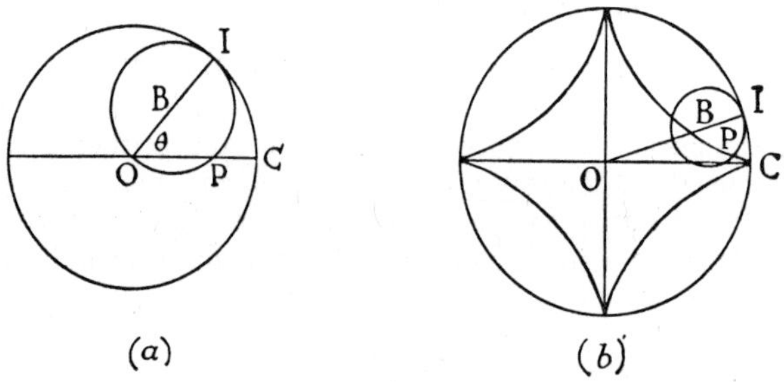

FIG. 42.

(1) When $a = 2b$ the above equations become

$$x = b\cos\theta + b\cos\theta = 2b\cos\theta,$$
$$y = b\sin\theta - b\sin\theta = 0,$$

showing that P describes a straight line, the x axis or diameter through C of the fixed circle (Fig. 42(a)).

(2) When $a = 4b$ the above equations become

$$x = \frac{3a}{4}\cos\theta + \frac{a}{4}\cos 3\theta$$

$$= \frac{a}{4}\{3\cos\theta + 4\cos^3\theta - 3\cos\theta\}$$

$$= a\cos^3\theta,$$

$$y = \frac{3a}{4}\sin\theta - \frac{a}{4}\sin 3\theta$$

$$= \frac{a}{4}\{3\sin\theta - (3\sin\theta - 4\sin^3\theta)\}$$

$$= a\sin^3\theta.$$

From these we have

$$\left(\frac{x}{a}\right)^{\frac{2}{3}} = \cos^2 \theta, \quad \left(\frac{y}{a}\right)^{\frac{2}{3}} = \sin^2 \theta,$$

$$\therefore \quad \left(\frac{x}{a}\right)^{\frac{2}{3}} + \left(\frac{y}{a}\right)^{\frac{2}{3}} = 1,$$

giving the Cartesian equation. This curve is a four-cusped hypocycloid often called the astroid (Fig. 42 (*b*)).

12.7. The Angle at which Two Curves Cut

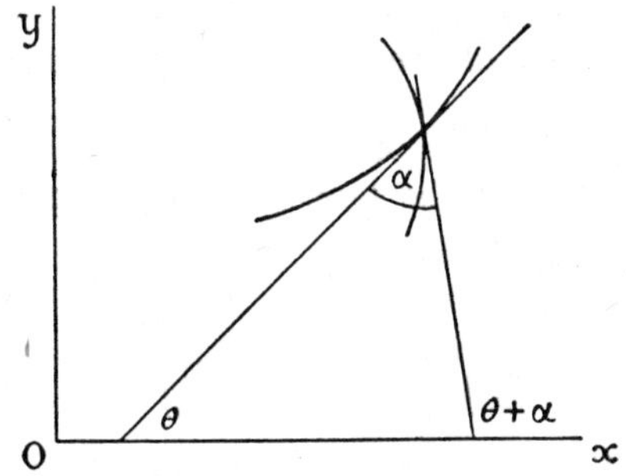

FIG. 43.

By the angle between two lines we mean the acute angle between them. At a point where two curves cut, each curve may be represented by its tangent at the point. Therefore by the angle at which two curves cut we mean the angle between the tangents to the two curves at their point (or points) of intersection. If the curves cut more than once we will generally obtain a different angle at each point.

Example 1. Find the angle in the first quadrant at which the curves $y^2 = 4x$ and $xy = 2$ cut.

Where the curves cut

$$y^2 = 4 \cdot \frac{2}{y},$$

$$y^3 = 8, \quad \therefore \quad \left.\begin{array}{l} y = 2 \\ x = 1 \end{array}\right\} \text{for the point of intersection.}$$

In the first quadrant

$$y = 2x^{\frac{1}{2}},$$

$$\therefore \quad \frac{dy}{dx} = \frac{1}{x^{\frac{1}{2}}} = 1 \text{ at } (1, 2),$$

also

$$y = \frac{2}{x},$$

$$\therefore \quad \frac{dy}{dx} = -\frac{2}{x^2} = -2 \text{ at } (1, 2).$$

The angle between the curves is

$$\tan^{-1}\left(\frac{-2-1}{1+(-2)(1)}\right) = \tan^{-1}(3)$$
$$= \underline{71{\cdot}6^\circ}.$$

If we had taken

$$\tan^{-1}\left(\frac{1-(-2)}{1+(-2)1}\right) = \tan^{-1}(-3) = 180^\circ - 71{\cdot}6^\circ$$

we could regard this as the obtuse angle between the tangents.

EXERCISE 25

1. Find the value of $\frac{dy}{dx}$ in an epicycloid. Deduce that in Fig. 41(*a*) PL is the tangent and PI the normal at P.

2. Find the equation of the tangent to the epicycloid in which $a = 2b$ at the point where $\theta = \frac{\pi}{4}$.

3. Find the equation of the tangent to the hypocycloid in which $a = 3b$ at the point where $\theta = \frac{\pi}{3}$.

4. Given that

$$\left(\frac{ds}{d\theta}\right)^2 = \left(\frac{dx}{d\theta}\right)^2 + \left(\frac{dy}{d\theta}\right)^2,$$

where s is the length of curve traced out in turning through angle θ, find $\frac{ds}{d\theta}$ for the epicycloid and deduce the length of the curve traced out in one revolution of the rolling circle.

5. P is any point on the curve $y = x^3$, PN is the ordinate and O the origin. If the tangent at P cuts ON in Q, show that OQ = 2QN, and find the ratio of the areas of the two portions of the triangle OPQ into which it is divided by the curve. [L.U.]

6. Find the equations of the tangent and normal at the point (at, at^n) to the curve $a^{n-1}y = x^n$.

If the tangent at any point P of the curve meets the axis in Q, and M is the foot of the perpendicular from P to the same axis, show that the arc of the curve divides the area of the triangle PMQ in a ratio independent of the position of P. [L.U.]

7. Find the angles at which the following curves cut:

(*a*) $x^2 + 5y^2 = 25$ and $x^2 - 4y^2 = 16$;
(*b*) $y = x^2$ and $x^3 - xy - 2y + 4x + 6 = 0$;
(*c*) $xy = 1$ and $x^2 - 2y^2 = 1$;
(*d*) $x^2 + y^2 = 144$ and $y^2 = 10x$.

8. Prove that the tangent to $x^3 + 2xy^2 - y^3 = 17$ at (2, 3) cuts OY at an angle of about 5° 42′.

9. Show that $36x + 45y = 14a$ cuts $x^3 + y^3 = ax^2$ at right angles at $(\frac{1}{9}a, \frac{2}{9}a)$.

CHAPTER 13

THE PARABOLA

13.1. Conic Sections

The student has probably drawn the types of curve which can be obtained by cutting sections through a right circular double cone. When the cutting plane is perpendicular to the axis of the cone the *conic section* obtained is a circle. When the cutting plane passes through the vertex of the cone and cuts the cone, two lines are obtained. In addition to these special cases there are three other kinds of sections called a parabola, an ellipse and a hyperbola.

13.2. Definition of a Conic Section

It is not our purpose to obtain properties of the parabola, ellipse and hyperbola by regarding them as sections of a cone. It is much easier to deal with them as loci generated by the following law: the locus of a point P which moves so that its distance from a fixed point S is a constant quantity e multiplied by its distance PM from a fixed straight line, *i.e.*, SP $= e$PM. (Fig. 44).

The fixed point S is called the *focus*.

The constant quantity e is called the *eccentricity* and always denoted by e.

The fixed straight line is called the *directrix*.

The locus is called:

an *ellipse*	when the eccentricity e is		*less than* 1;
a *parabola*	,,	,,	*equal to* 1;
a *hyperbola*	,,	,,	*greater than* 1.

13.3. Before considering the curves separately we will point out an obvious difference between them depending on the value of e.

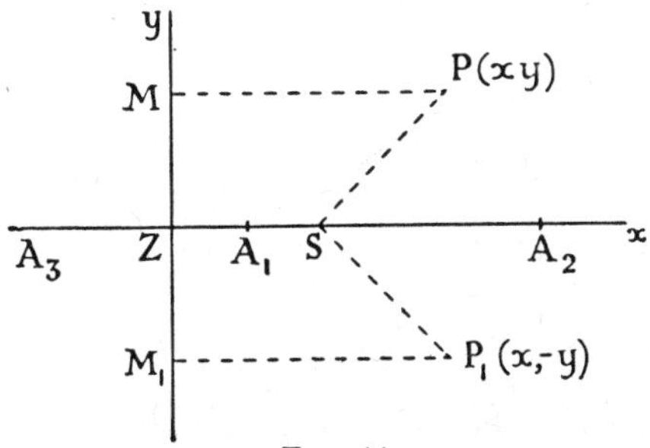

FIG. 44.

Let S be the focus and MM_1 the given directrix. Draw SZ perpendicular to MM_1 and produce in both directions. This line is called the *axis* of the conic, since for every point $P(x, y)$ above it there is in every case another point $P_1(x, -y)$ also on the locus and below this line, being the image of P in the axis.

(1) When $e = 1$ we can find a point A_1 on the axis between S and Z so that $SA_1 = A_1Z$. By definition this point A_1 is on the parabola that can be drawn with S as focus and MM_1 as directrix. Clearly there is no other point A_2 or A_3 on the axis such that $SA_2 = ZA_2$ or $SA_3 = ZA_3$. Therefore a parabola meets its axis in only one point.

(2) When $e < 1$ we can find a point A_1 between S and Z such that for $e = \frac{1}{2}$ (say) $SA_1 = \frac{1}{2}A_1Z$, giving a point on an ellipse focus S, directrix MM_1 and $e = \frac{1}{2}$. In this case there is another point A_2 such that $SA_2 = \frac{1}{2}ZA_2$, and this point is clearly on ZS produced. Therefore an ellipse meets its axis in two points both on the same side of the directrix.

(3) When $e > 1$ we can similarly show that a hyperbola meets its axis in two points, but the second point A_3 is on the other side of the directrix to A_1 the first point.

13.4. The Standard Equation to a Parabola

Let the given fixed point, the focus, be S and the directrix the line ZM. Draw SZ perpendicular to ZM and bisect SZ at O. The point O is on the locus and is called the vertex of the parabola. Take axes as shown with OS as the x axis, O being the origin.

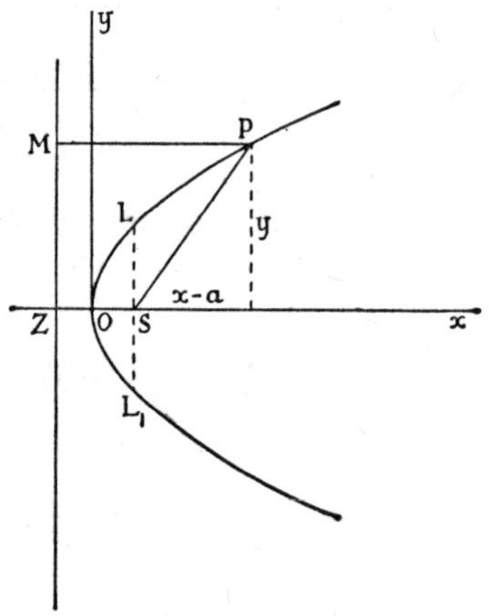

FIG. 45.

Let the given distance SZ be $2a$ so that S is the point $(a, 0)$ and ZM the line $x = -a$. If $P(x, y)$ is any point on the locus $SP = PM$, where PM is the perpendicular upon the directrix,

$$\therefore \qquad SP^2 = PM^2,$$

i.e.,
$$(x - a)^2 + y^2 = (x + a)^2.$$

This reduces to

$$y^2 = 4ax,$$

which is the standard equation.

13.5. To Trace $y^2 = 4ax$

(1) y^2 is positive; therefore, since a is a positive length x must be positive so that $4ax$ is positive. Therefore the curve lies on the positive side of the origin only.

(2) When $x = 0$, $y = 0$ and when $y = 0$, $x = 0$, so that the curve meets the axes at O only.

(3) Since $y = \pm 2\sqrt{ax}$, for every value of x there are two values of y equal and opposite, *i.e.*, the curve is symmetrical about the x axis.

(4) From $y^2 = 4ax$, $y = 2\sqrt{ax}$ for the top half.

$$\therefore \quad \frac{dy}{dx} = \sqrt{\frac{a}{x}},$$
$$= \infty \text{ at } x = 0.$$

$\therefore$ the curve is vertical at O and so touches the y axis there.

(5) As x increases so does y, and therefore the curve opens out to the right. But the gradient steadily decreases as x increases.

The curve is as shown.

13.6. The Latus Rectum

The double ordinate LSL_1 drawn through the focus is called the latus rectum and SL, one half of it, the semi-latus rectum.

Since OS $= a$, $\therefore$ from $y^2 = 4ax$, $SL^2 = 4a \cdot a$.

$\therefore$ SL $= 2a$ and the latus rectum is $4a$.

13.7. The Tangent and Normal

From
$$y^2 = 4ax$$
$$2y\frac{dy}{dx} = 4a,$$
$$\frac{dy}{dx} = \frac{2a}{y}.$$

$\therefore$ the equation of the tangent at (x_1, y_1) is

$$y - y_1 = \frac{2a}{y_1}(x - x_1)$$

or
$$yy_1 = y_1^2 + 2ax - 2ax_1.$$

But $y_1^2 = 4ax_1$, since (x_1, y_1) is on the curve,

$$\therefore \quad yy_1 = 4ax_1 + 2ax - 2ax_1$$

or
$$yy_1 = 2a(x + x_1) \qquad \ldots\ldots \quad (1)$$

The normal is

$$y - y_1 = -\frac{y_1}{2a}(x - x_1) \quad . \quad . \quad . \quad . \quad . \quad (2)$$

Example 1. Find the tangent and normal at the point (1, 3) on $y^2 = 9x$. Compare with $y^2 = 4ax$ and we find $4a = 9$ or $a = \frac{9}{4}$.

$\therefore$ Tangent is

$$y . 3 = 2 \cdot \tfrac{9}{4}(x + 1)$$

or

$$\underline{6y = 9(x + 1).}$$

Normal is

$$y - 3 = -\frac{3}{2 \times \frac{9}{4}}(x - 1).$$

or

$$\underline{3y + 2x - 11 = 0.}$$

Example 2. Find the equations of the tangents to $y^2 = 9x$ which pass through the point (4, 10).

The tangent at (x_1, y_1) is

$$yy_1 = \tfrac{9}{2}(x + x_1).$$

If this passes through (4, 10)

$$10y_1 = \tfrac{9}{2}(4 + x_1)$$

also

$$y_1^2 = 9x_1.$$

Substitute for x_1 in the first equation from the second and obtain

$$y_1^2 - 20y_1 + 36 = 0,$$
$$(y_1 - 18)(y_1 - 2) = 0;$$
$$\therefore \quad y_1 = 18 \text{ and } 2,$$
$$x_1 = 36 \text{ and } \tfrac{4}{9}.$$

The two tangents are

$$y . 18 = \tfrac{9}{2}(x + 36)$$

or

$$\underline{4y = x + 36}$$

and

$$y . 2 = \tfrac{9}{2}(x + \tfrac{4}{9}).$$

or

$$\underline{4y = 9x + 4.}$$

In each example above the student may prefer to differentiate $y^2 = 9x$ and work from first principles instead of quoting equations (1) and (2).

13.8. An Important Property

PM is the perpendicular from any point $P(x_1, y_1)$ on to the directrix ZM.

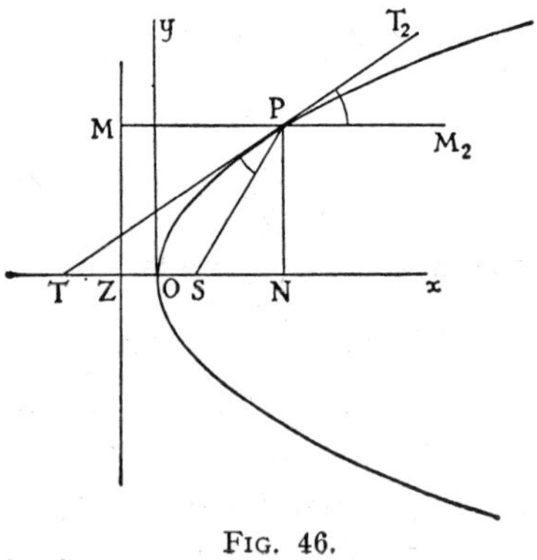

FIG. 46.

We have
$$SP = PM \quad \text{by definition}$$
$$= ZN$$
$$= a + x_1 \quad \ldots\ldots \quad (1)$$

Since the tangent at P is
$$yy_1 = 2a(x + x_1),$$
when $y = 0$
$$0 = 2a(OT + x_1),$$
$$\therefore \quad OT = - x_1.$$

Regarding magnitudes only
$$TO = x_1,$$
$$\therefore \quad TO + OS = x_1 + a = SP \text{ by } (1),$$
$$\therefore \quad TS = SP.$$

$\therefore$ the ΔTSP is isosceles and
$$\angle PTS = \angle SPT,$$
but
$$\angle PTS = \angle T_2PM_2,$$
$$\therefore \quad \angle SPT = \angle T_2PM_2.$$

This means that if a ray of light starting from S meets the curve, a parabolic mirror, at P the incident ray is SP and the reflected ray is PM_2, since the laws of reflection require the angles of incidence and reflection to be equal.

P is any point on the curve, and so the property holds for every point. Thus every ray of light from say an electric bulb at S would be reflected by the parabolic mirror parallel to the axis of the curve. Conversely, every ray of light from say the sun striking the mirror would form a parallel set of rays and so be reflected to pass through S. It is this consideration that gave the name focus to S (focus ≡ Latin for fireplace).

Motor-car headlamps and searchlights are made to use this property, a portion of the reflecting mirror often being a paraboloid of revolution.

13.9. Condition for Tangency

To find the condition that the line $y = mx + c$ should touch the parabola $y^2 = 4ax$.

Where the line meets the curve,
$$(mx + c)^2 = 4ax,$$
$$\therefore \quad m^2x^2 + 2(mc - 2a)x + c^2 = 0,$$
a quadratic equation in x showing that in general the line meets the curve in two distinct points real or imaginary.

If the line is a tangent the roots are equal since a tangent meets the curve in two coincident points.
$$\therefore \quad 4(mc - 2a)^2 = 4m^2c^2,$$
this reduces to
$$mc = a.$$

We can therefore substitute for c in $y = mx + c$ and say that

$$y = mx + a/m$$

is *always* a tangent to $y^2 = 4ax$ for all values of m.

Example 3. Prove that $y = 2x + 2$ touches $y^2 = 16x$.
Compare $y^2 = 16x$ with $y^2 = 4ax$ and note that $a = 4$,

$$\therefore \quad y = mx + \frac{4}{m} \text{ is always a tangent to } y^2 = 16x.$$

Choose $m = 2$ and we find that $y = 2x + 2$ is a tangent.
The student should note the general method:
Where $y = 2x + 2$ cuts $y^2 = 16x$,

$$(2x + 2)^2 = 16x,$$

$$\therefore \quad x^2 - 2x + 1 = 0,$$

i.e.,

$$(x - 1)^2 = 0.$$

The two values of x are equal, and therefore the line is a tangent.

Example 4. Find the tangents common to $x^2 + y^2 = 8$ and $y^2 = 16x$.

Any tangent to $y^2 = 16x$ is $y = mx + \dfrac{4}{m}$.

Where this meets $x^2 + y^2 = 8$

$$x^2 + \left(mx + \frac{4}{m}\right)^2 = 8,$$

$$x^2(1 + m^2) + 8x + 8\left(\frac{2}{m^2} - 1\right) = 0.$$

For tangency the roots of this are equal,

$$\therefore \quad 64 = 4(1 + m^2) \times 8\left(\frac{2}{m^2} - 1\right).$$

$$m^4 + m^2 - 2 = 0,$$

$$(m^2 + 2)(m^2 - 1) = 0,$$

$$m^2 = 1 \text{ and } -2 \text{ (inadmissible)},$$

$$m = \pm 1.$$

$\therefore$ there are only two real tangents common to both curves:

$y = x + 4 \qquad (m = 1),$

$y = -x - 4 \qquad (m = -1).$

EXERCISE 26

Write down the equations to the tangent and normal:

1. At the point (6, 6) on $y^2 = 6x$.
2. At the ends of the latus rectum on $y^2 = 3x$.
3. Find the tangent to $y^2 = 2x$ which is parallel to the line $y = x + 3$. Find also the point of contact.
4. Find the tangents to $y^2 = 9x$ which pass through the point (4, 10).
5. Find the area enclosed by the parabola $y = 5x - x^2$ and the x axis. Prove that the line $y = x$ divides this area into two parts whose areas are in the ratio 64 to 61. [L.U.]

13.10. Parametric Representation

In the case of the parabola

$$y^2 = 4ax$$

if we " guess " $x = at^2$, then we obtain a perfect square for y^2,

$$y^2 = 4a \cdot at^2,$$
$$\therefore \quad y = \pm 2at.$$

We can therefore use the parametric co-ordinates

$$x = at^2, \quad y = 2at$$

to denote any point t on the parabola where t may take all positive and negative values.

Example 5. Find the equations of the tangent and normal at the point t on $y^2 = 4ax$.

$$x = at^2, \qquad y = 2at,$$
$$\frac{dx}{dt} = 2at, \quad \frac{dy}{dt} = 2a,$$
$$\frac{dy}{dx} = \frac{2a}{2at} = \frac{1}{t}.$$

Tangent is

$$y - 2at = \frac{1}{t}(x - at^2).$$

or $\underline{ty = x + at^2}$ . . . . (1)

normal is

$$y - 2at = -t(x - at^2)$$

or $\underline{y + tx = 2at + at^3}$ . . . . (2)

Example 6. Find the locus of intersection of perpendicular tangents to the parabola.

The tangent at t is

$$ty = x + at^2 \quad . . . . (1)$$

The tangent at T is

$$Ty = x + aT^2.$$

If these two are perpendicular

$$\frac{1}{t} \times \frac{1}{T} = -1,$$
$$T = -\frac{1}{t}.$$

$\therefore$ the perp. tangent is

$$-\frac{1}{t}y = x + \frac{a}{t^2}$$

or $-ty = t^2x + a$ . . . . (2)

We need to find the locus of intersection of (1) and (2) as t varies.

Add these equations

$$0 = x(1 + t^2) + a(t^2 + 1)$$
$$= (x + a)(1 + t^2),$$
$$\therefore \quad x + a = 0.$$

$\therefore$ whatever the value of y may be the x co-ordinate is $-a$ and the tangents intersect upon the directrix.

EXERCISE 27

1. If PN is the ordinate at any point on $y^2 = 4ax$ and the normal at P meets the x axis at G, show that NG is a constant.

2. Show that the perpendicular from the focus upon any tangent to $y^2 = 4ax$ meets the tangent on the y axis.

3. The tangent at any point P on $y^2 = 4ax$ meets the lines $x = a$, $x = -a$ at R and Q respectively. If S is the focus show that SR = SQ.

4. The tangent at any point P on $y^2 = 4ax$ meets the directrix at a point R. Show that PR subtends 90° at the focus.

5. P and Q are two points on the parabola such that OP and OQ are perpendicular. Show that PQ cuts the x axis in a fixed point.

6. The circle $x^2 + y^2 = 5a^2$ and the parabola $y^2 = 4ax$ cut at L and M. Show that the line LM passes through the focus S.

7. Find the equation of the common tangent to $y^2 = 4ax$ and $2x^2 = ay$.

8. P is the point t on $y^2 = 4ax$ and Q is the point T. Show that the line PQ is

$$y = \frac{2}{t + T}x + \frac{2atT}{t + T}.$$

9. If the line PQ in Question 8 passes through the focus S show that $T = -\frac{1}{t}$.

10. Using the data from Question 9 show that the tangents at the ends of a focal chord of the parabola intersect at right angles on the directrix.

11. If one end of a focal chord is the point t show that the length of the chord is

$$a\left(t + \frac{1}{t}\right)^2.$$

12. From the focus of a parabola a line is drawn parallel to the tangent at P $(at^2, 2at)$ to meet the line $y = 2at$ in Q. Prove that as P moves on the curve the locus of Q is $y^2 = 2a(x - a)$.

13.11. The Parabola $y = ax^2 + bx + c$

The equation $y = ax^2 + bx + c$ often occurs in, for example, bending-moment and shearing-force problems, and is worth separate consideration.

We may write it, by completing the square,

$$y = a\left(x + \frac{b}{2a}\right)^2 - \frac{b^2}{4a} + c,$$

$$\therefore\ y + \frac{b^2 - 4ac}{4a} = a\left(x + \frac{b}{2a}\right)^2.$$

If we put $y + \frac{b^2 - 4ac}{4a} = Y$ and $x + \frac{b}{2a} = X$, *i.e.*, we transfer the origin to the point $\left(\frac{-b}{2a}, -\frac{(b^2 - 4ac)}{4a}\right)$, (see 15.2) the equation becomes

$$Y = aX^2,$$

which is a parabola with its axis along the Y axis. Knowing this we may use a quicker method to find the vertex and so obtain a rough sketch of the curve. Since

$$y = ax^2 + bx + c,$$

$$\frac{dy}{dx} = 2ax + b \quad \text{and} \quad \frac{d^2y}{dx^2} = 2a.$$

$\therefore$ if a is positive the curve has a minimum, and lies entirely above its vertex, whilst if a is negative the curve has a maximum only at the vertex and lies entirely below it. The position of the vertex is obtained by finding the maximum or minimum, *i.e.*,

$$\frac{dy}{dx} = 0 \text{ giving } 2ax + b = 0. \qquad \therefore \quad x = -\frac{b}{2a}.$$

and the corresponding y is $\dfrac{-(b^2 - 4ac)}{4a}$.

Example 7. For a shearing-force diagram we require to sketch

$$S_1 = 24x - 2x^2 \quad \text{for } 0 \leqslant x \leqslant 5$$
$$S_2 = 60 + 12x - 2x^2 \quad \text{for } 5 \leqslant x \leqslant 9$$
$$S_3 = 240 - 8x - 2x^2 \quad \text{for } 9 \leqslant x \leqslant 12$$

With the usual axes, measuring S upwards:

(1) $x = 0$, $S_1 = 0$; $x = 5$, $S_1 = 70$.

$$\frac{dS_1}{dx} = 24 - 4x, \quad \therefore x = 6 \text{ and } S_1 = 72 \text{ for the vertex.}$$

From these three points we can draw a sketch of the curve, drawing it only between $x = 0$ and 5.

(2) $x = 5$, $S_2 = 70$; $x = 9$, $S_2 = 6$.

$$\frac{dS_2}{dx} = 12 - 4x, \quad \therefore x = 3 \text{ and } S_2 = 78 \text{ for the vertex.}$$

We can now draw the curve between $x = 5$ and 9.

(3) $x = 9$, $S_3 = 6$; $x = 12$, $S_3 = -144$.

$$\frac{dS_3}{dx} = -8 - 4x, \quad \therefore x = -2 \text{ and } S_3 = 248 \text{ for the vertex.}$$

In this case the vertex is not very helpful, and it would help to find S_3 for $x = 10$ and 11. The curve could then be drawn between $x = 9$ and 12.

13.12. Chains Hanging in Parabolic Curves

A chain hanging between two points assumes the shape of a curve called the catenary.

If, however, the sag is small so that the weight of any portion may be assumed proportional to its horizontal span, we will show that the curve is a parabola.

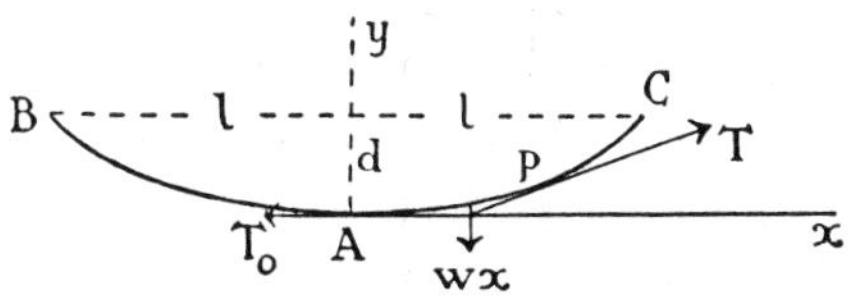

FIG. 47.

Suppose a chain or telephone wire hangs from the two fixed points B and C. Choose axes as shown through the lowest point A of the wire and consider the equilibrium of the part AP, where P is the point (x, y).

The forces acting on AP are: T_0 the horizontal tension at A, T the tension at P, which acts along the tangent to the curve at P, and the weight of the chain, which is wx if w is the weight per unit horizontal span. This weight wx acts at the mid point of AQ according to the above assumption where PQ is the ordinate at P.

Taking moments about P for the portion of wire AP, we have

$$T_0 y = wx \cdot \frac{x}{2},$$

$$\therefore \quad y = \frac{w}{2T_0} x^2 \quad \dots \dots \quad (1)$$

$\therefore$ the chain hangs in a parabola with the axis vertical. If we take moments about C for the forces acting on AC, then since the centre of gravity of the portion AC is $\frac{l}{2}$ from C, we have

$$T_0 \,.\, d = wl \cdot \frac{l}{2},$$

$$\therefore \quad T_0 = \frac{wl^2}{2d} \quad \dots \dots \quad (2)$$

$\therefore$ equation (1) can be written

$$y = \frac{d}{l^2} x^2 \quad \dots \dots \quad (3)$$

an equation not requiring the horizontal tension T_0 or the weight w.

In the case of a suspension bridge where a cable carries a horizontal roadway, the horizontal load per foot is constant so that the cable, by the above, would hang in a parabola.

Example 8. In hilly country two masts are 600 ft. apart with a difference in their heights of 100 ft. If the wire they support has a weight of 0·2 lb./ft., and the tension is 500 lb. wt., find the sag and position of the vertex of the parabola.

In practice, even when the sag is not small, the assumption that the wire hangs in a parabola provides a quick solution which is a good approximation.

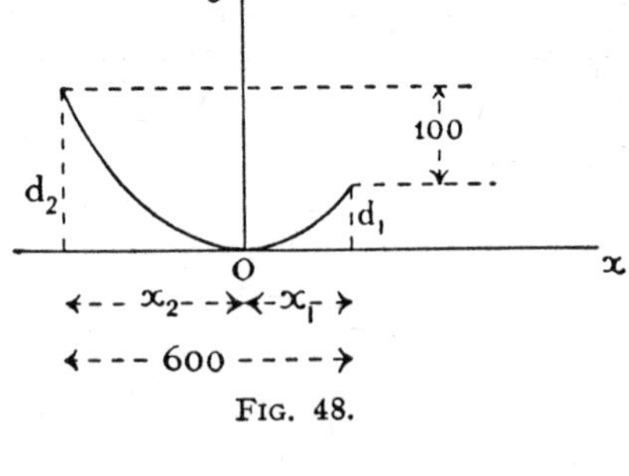

FIG. 48.

Assume there is a point between the masts where the wire is horizontal, and choose axes through this point as usual (Fig. 48).

By equation (1)

$$d_2 = \frac{w}{2T_0}x_2^2,$$

$$d_1 = \frac{w}{2T_0}x_1^2.$$

$$d_2 - d_1 = \frac{w}{2T_0}(x_2^2 - x_1^2)$$

$$= \frac{w}{2T_0}(x_2 - x_1)(x_2 + x_1).$$

But $d_2 - d_1 = 100$, whilst $x_2 + x_1 = 600$,

$$\therefore \quad 100 = \frac{w}{2T_0} \cdot 600 \cdot (x_2 - x_1),$$

$$x_2 - x_1 = \frac{2 \times 100 \times T_0}{w \times 600}$$

$$= \frac{2 \times 100 \times 500}{0{\cdot}2 \times 600} = 833 \text{ ft.}$$

But $$x_2 + x_1 = 600 \text{ ft.}$$

$$\therefore \quad x_2 = 717 \text{ ft.}, x_1 = -116 \text{ ft.}$$

The negative value for x_1 shows that the vertex of the parabola lies on the other side of the lower mast.

Also

$$d_1 = \frac{wx_1^2}{2T_0} = \frac{0{\cdot}2 \times 116^2}{2 \times 500} = 2{\cdot}7 \text{ ft.}$$

$\therefore$ the vertex of the parabola would be 2·7 ft. below the top of the lower mast. Between the masts the lowest point of the wire is the top of the lower mast.

EXERCISE 28

1. A telegraph wire has a span of 75 yd. and a sag of 1 ft. If the wire weighs 400 lb. per mile show that the tension in the wire is about 480 lb. wt.

2. Two masts for a high-tension line are of equal height and 400 ft. apart. If the tension is to be 490 lb. wt. find the sag, assuming that the wire, which weighs 0·2145 lb./ft., hangs in a parabolic curve.

3. Across a river there is an overhead line, the top of the supporting towers being 150 and 300 ft. above the water level. The horizontal distance between the towers is 1000 ft., the maximum tension in the wire is 4200 lb. wt. and its weight is 0·6 lb./ft. Find the height of the wire above the water-level at the mid point between the towers.

4. Two masts are 650 ft. apart, their tops having a difference in height of 16 ft. If the weight of the wire is 0·2 lb./ft. and the tension is 480 lb. wt., find the position of the vertex of the parabola.

5. A uniform beam, weight 2 lb./ft. and 10 ft. long, is supported at each end and carries a load of 30 lb. 4 ft. from one end. With this end as origin obtain (if you can) the equations for the bending moment

$$M_1 = 28x - x^2 \qquad 0 \leqslant x \leqslant 4,$$
$$M_2 = 120 - 2x - x^2 \qquad 4 \leqslant x \leqslant 10,$$

and give a sketch of M against x, *i.e.*, draw the B.M. diagram.

6. A beam of length 20 ft. and weight w lb./ft. is supported at two points each a distance a ft. from the centre. By symmetry we need only consider the B.M. for the left and central sections of the beam. Obtain (if you can)

$$M_1 = \tfrac{1}{2}wx^2 \qquad 0 \leqslant x \leqslant 10 - a,$$
$$M_2 = \tfrac{1}{2}w[x^2 - 20x + 200 - 20a] \qquad 10 - a \leqslant x \leqslant 10 + a.$$

Draw the B.M. diagram for the two cases: (i) $10 > 2a$ when M_2 is always positive; (ii) $10 < 2a$ when M_2 becomes negative.

7. Draw the B.M. diagram for the following:

$$M_1 = \tfrac{1}{2}wx^2 \qquad 0 < x < 10,$$
$$M_2 = \tfrac{1}{2}w(x^2 - 20x + 200) \qquad 10 < x < 15,$$
$$M_3 = \tfrac{1}{2}w(x - 10)^2 \qquad 15 < x < 20,$$
$$M_4 = \tfrac{1}{2}w(30 - x)^2 \qquad 20 < x < 30.$$

In this case there is an externally applied couple at the centre of the beam and hence a discontinuity in the B.M. diagram.

8. Draw the B.M. diagram for the following:

$$M = \tfrac{1}{2}x^2 + 2x \qquad 0 \leqslant x \leqslant 3,$$
$$\tfrac{1}{2}x^2 + 4x - 6 \qquad 3 \leqslant x \leqslant 6,$$
$$\tfrac{1}{2}x^2 - 18x + 126 \qquad 6 \leqslant x \leqslant 8,$$
$$\tfrac{1}{2}x^2 - 17x + 118 \qquad 8 \leqslant x \leqslant 9,$$
$$\tfrac{1}{2}x^2 - 13x + 82 \qquad 9 \leqslant x \leqslant 10,$$
$$\tfrac{1}{2}x^2 - 12x + 72 \qquad 10 \leqslant x \leqslant 13.$$

CHAPTER 14

THE ELLIPSE

(Eccentricity $e < 1$.)

14.1. The Standard Equation

The equation to an ellipse is most easily obtained by regarding it as the projection of a circle. Thus if the ordinates of a circle are shortened in a fixed ratio the resulting curve will be an ellipse.

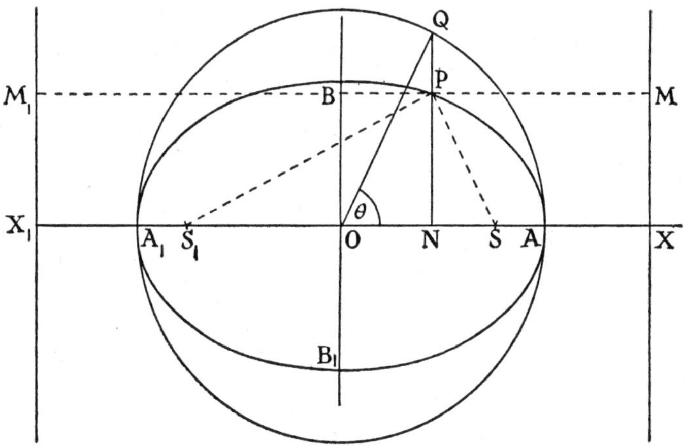

FIG. 49.

Let AA_1 be the diameter of a circle of radius a with centre at O, and QN any ordinate where Q is (X, Y).

The equation to the circle is

$$x^2 + y^2 = a^2.$$

Since Q (X, Y) is on this

$$X^2 + Y^2 = a^2 \qquad \ldots \ldots \quad (1)$$

Let P be a point on QN such that $\frac{PN}{QN} = \frac{b}{a}$, where b is less than a.

The co-ordinates of P(x, y) are

$$x = X, \quad y = \frac{b}{a}Y.$$

Substitute for X, Y in (1)

$$x^2 + \frac{a^2y^2}{b^2} = a^2$$

or

$$\frac{x^2}{a^2} + \frac{y^2}{b^2} = 1$$

giving the locus of P as Q describes its locus. $AA_1 = 2a$ is called the major axis, and $BB_1 = 2b$, the minor axis of the ellipse.

14.2. The Focal Distances of a Point

With B as centre and radius a cut AA_1 at S and S_1. OS is less than OA, let it be ae, where e is a positive constant less than 1. Then from triangle BOS

$$b^2 = a^2 - a^2e^2 \quad \ldots \quad (1)$$

also

$$\begin{aligned} QN^2 &= OQ^2 - ON^2 \\ &= a^2 - x^2, \\ \therefore \quad PN^2 &= \frac{b^2}{a^2}(a^2 - x^2) = (1 - e^2)(a^2 - x^2). \\ SP^2 &= PN^2 + (OS - ON)^2 \\ &= (1 - e^2)(a^2 - x^2) + (ae - x)^2 \\ &= a^2 - 2aex + e^2x^2, \\ SP &= a - ex \quad \ldots \quad (2) \end{aligned}$$

Similarly,

$$S_1P = a + ex \quad \ldots \quad (3)$$

$$\therefore \quad SP + S_1P = 2a.$$

An ellipse could also be defined therefore as the locus of a point P which moves so that the sum of its distances from two fixed points is constant. This property gives the usual mechanical method for describing an ellipse by using a thread of constant length fastened to two fixed pins.

14.3. The Focus and Directrix Definition

Through the points $X(a/e, 0)$ and $X_1(-a/e, 0)$ draw lines perpendicular to the x axis. These lines are called the *directrices*. From P draw perpendiculars PM, PM_1 to these lines.

Now $\quad PM = OX - ON = a/e - x,$

but $\quad SP = a - ex, \quad$ (14.2 (2))

$$\therefore \quad SP = ePM.$$

Thus the ellipse can also be defined by the focus–directrix property. The eccentricity e introduced by the equation $b^2 = a^2(1 - e^2)$ (see 14.2 (1)) then finds its real meaning.

Also $\quad PM_1 = OX_1 + ON = a/e + x,$

but $\quad S_1P = a + ex,$

$$\therefore \quad S_1P = ePM_1.$$

This shows that the ellipse has two foci S, S_1, each with its corresponding directrix.

Example 1. Find the eccentricity and position of the foci of the ellipse

$$3x^2 + 4y^2 = 12.$$

This equation is

$$\frac{x^2}{4} + \frac{y^2}{3} = 1,$$

$$\therefore \quad a^2 = 4,\ b^2 = 3 = a^2(1 - e^2) = 4(1 - e^2),$$

$$e = \tfrac{1}{2}.$$

$$OS = ae = 2 \times \tfrac{1}{2} = 1,$$

The foci are $(\pm 1, 0)$.

EXERCISE 29

1. Prove that $y = 2x + 5$ touches the ellipse $\frac{x^2}{4} + \frac{y^2}{9} = 1$.

2. An ellipse has its foci at the points $(\pm 2, 0)$, and its eccentricity is $\frac{1}{2}$. Find its equation.

3. Find the co-ordinates of the foci of:

$$(a)\ \frac{x^2}{4} + \frac{y^2}{1} = 1, \qquad (b)\ 4x^2 + 10y^2 = 1.$$

4. Find the equation to an ellipse given in the standard form if it passes through the points (2, 2) and (3, 1).

14.4. The Tangent and Normal at any Point (x_1, y_1)

From

$$\frac{x^2}{a^2} + \frac{y^2}{b^2} = 1$$

we have by differentiation

$$\frac{2x}{a^2} + \frac{2y}{b^2} \cdot \frac{dy}{dx} = 0,$$

$$\therefore \quad \frac{dy}{dx} = -\frac{b^2x}{a^2y}$$

$$= -\frac{b^2x_1}{a^2y_1} \text{ at } (x_1, y_1).$$

$\therefore$ The tangent at (x_1, y_1) is

$$y - y_1 = -\frac{b^2x_1}{a^2y_1}(x - x_1)$$

or

$$\frac{xx_1}{a^2} + \frac{yy_1}{b^2} = \frac{x_1^2}{a^2} + \frac{y_1^2}{b^2}.$$

But since the point (x_1, y_1) is on the curve

$$\frac{x_1^2}{a^2} + \frac{y_1^2}{b^2} = 1,$$

$\therefore$ the equation of the tangent can be written

$$\frac{xx_1}{a^2} + \frac{yy_1}{b^2} = 1 \quad \ldots\ldots\ldots \quad (1)$$

The equation to the normal is

$$y - y_1 = \frac{a^2 y_1}{b^2 x_1}(x - x_1) \quad . \quad . \quad . \quad . \quad . \quad (2)$$

which does not simplify.

Example 2. Find the tangent and normal at P(3, 4) to the ellipse

$$\frac{x^2}{18} + \frac{y^2}{32} = 1.$$

If the tangent meets the x axis at T, and N is the foot of the ordinate at P show that ON . OT = 18.

We can either differentiate the given equation to find $\frac{dy}{dx}$ or else quote the formulae:

$$\frac{xx_1}{a^2} + \frac{yy_1}{b^2} = 1 \quad \text{becomes} \quad \frac{x \cdot 3}{18} + \frac{y \cdot 4}{32} = 1.$$

$\therefore$ Tangent is $\underline{4x + 3y = 24.}$

Normal is $$y - 4 = \frac{18 \times 4}{32 \times 3}(x - 3)$$

or $$\underline{3x - 4y + 7 = 0.}$$

Put $y = 0$ in the equation of the tangent and we find OT = 6. ON = 3, the x co-ordinate of P.

$$\therefore \quad \text{ON . OT} = 3 \times 6 = 18.$$

14.5. The Eccentric Angle (Fig. 49)

From the method of obtaining an ellipse (see 14.1) we can derive a parametric representation. In terms of the angle θ which QO makes with the positive x axis

$$\text{ON} = \text{X} = a \cos \theta, \qquad \text{QN} = \text{Y} = a \sin \theta,$$

$\therefore$ for the point P

$$\text{ON} = x = a \cos \theta, \qquad \text{PN} = y = \frac{b}{a}\text{Y} = \frac{b}{a} \cdot a \sin \theta$$
$$= b \sin \theta.$$

We therefore find that $(a \cos \theta, b \sin \theta)$ may be used to denote any point on the ellipse. This point is called the point θ, and θ the eccentric angle of the point. Note that $\angle$POX is not θ, which is not represented on the ellipse, but is obtained from the circle.

14.6. Tangent and Normal

From

$$x = a \cos \theta \qquad y = b \sin \theta,$$
$$\frac{dx}{d\theta} = -a \sin \theta \qquad \frac{dy}{d\theta} = b \cos \theta.$$
$$\therefore \quad \frac{dy}{dx} = -\frac{b \cos \theta}{a \sin \theta}.$$

The tangent at θ is

$$y - b \sin \theta = -\frac{b \cos \theta}{a \sin \theta}(x - a \cos \theta)$$

or $$\frac{x}{a}\cos\theta + \frac{y}{b}\sin\theta = 1 \qquad . \quad . \quad . \quad . \quad . \quad . \qquad (1)$$

The normal at θ is

$$y - b\sin\theta = \frac{a\sin\theta}{b\cos\theta}(x - a\cos\theta)$$

or $$\frac{ax}{\cos\theta} - \frac{by}{\sin\theta} = a^2 - b^2 \quad . \quad . \quad . \quad . \quad . \quad . \quad . \quad . \qquad (2)$$

Example 3. Find the eccentric angle at (4, 3) on $\frac{x^2}{32} + \frac{y^2}{18} = 1$.

Since $\quad x = a\cos\theta, \qquad y = b\sin\theta,$

$$4 = \sqrt{32}\cos\theta, \qquad 3 = \sqrt{18}\sin\theta,$$

$$\therefore \quad \cos\theta = \frac{1}{\sqrt{2}}, \qquad \sin\theta = \frac{1}{\sqrt{2}}.$$

$$\therefore \quad \underline{\theta = \frac{\pi}{4}.}$$

Example 4. Two points move round an ellipse in such a way that their eccentric angles differ by a constant α. Find the locus of the point of intersection of the tangents at these points.

If one point is θ, the other point is $\theta + \alpha$.

∴ the tangents are

$$\frac{x}{a}\cos\theta + \frac{y}{b}\sin\theta = 1,$$

$$\frac{x}{a}\cos(\theta + \alpha) + \frac{y}{b}\sin(\theta + \alpha) = 1.$$

Solving for the point of intersection (x, y), we find

$$x = a\,\frac{\cos(\theta + \alpha/2)}{\cos(\alpha/2)}, \qquad y = b\,\frac{\sin(\theta + \alpha/2)}{\sin(\alpha/2)}.$$

In order to find the locus of (x, y) as θ varies we must " eliminate " θ between these equations. Whenever we have the sine and cosine of the angle to be eliminated we use the property

$$\sin^2\theta + \cos^2\theta = 1.$$

In this case we have the sine and cosine of $\theta + \alpha/2$. We therefore write the equations

$$\frac{x\cos(\alpha/2)}{a} = \cos(\theta + \alpha/2),$$

$$\frac{y\sin(\alpha/2)}{b} = \sin(\theta + \alpha/2),$$

$$\therefore \quad \left(\frac{x\cos(\alpha/2)}{a}\right)^2 + \left(\frac{y\sin(\alpha/2)}{b}\right)^2 = \cos^2(\theta + \alpha/2) + \sin^2(\theta + \alpha/2) = 1.$$

The locus is therefore

$$\frac{x^2}{(a\sec(\alpha/2))^2} + \frac{y^2}{(b\operatorname{cosec}(\alpha/2))^2} = 1,$$

an ellipse with longer axes than the original.

Example 5. ABCD is the section of a cube of side l. The intensities of the stress (*i.e.*, the force per unit area perpendicular to the face) are p and q on opposite faces. Find the stress on an interface of which LN is the trace (Fig. 50).

Total force on face LM $= p \times \text{area} = pl^2\tan\theta,$

MN $= q \times \text{area} = ql^2.$

If the resultant stress on LN is R at $\angle\phi$ to MN, and r is the intensity of stress

$$R = r \times \text{area of LN} = rl^2\sec\theta.$$

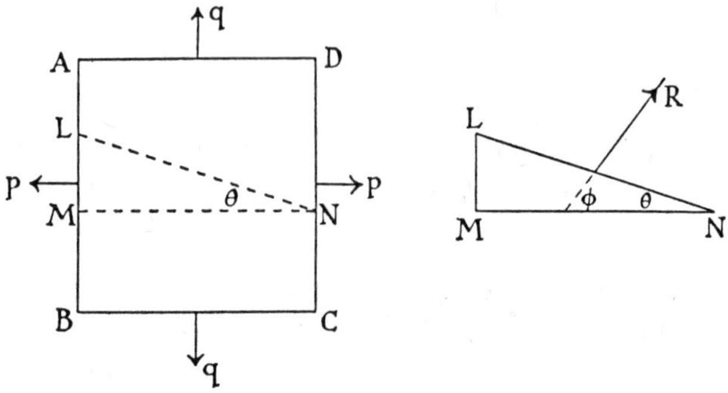

FIG. 50.

Since the wedge LMN is in equilibrium

$$pl^2 \tan\theta = R\cos\phi = rl^2 \sec\theta\cos\phi,$$

$$\therefore \quad p\sin\theta = r\cos\phi \quad \ldots \quad (1)$$

Also

$$ql^2 = R\sin\phi = rl^2\sec\theta\sin\phi,$$

$$\therefore \quad q\cos\theta = r\sin\phi \quad \ldots \quad (2)$$

Square and add:

$$p^2\sin^2\theta + q^2\cos^2\theta = r^2(\cos^2\phi + \sin^2\phi) = r^2 \quad \ldots \quad (3)$$

giving the intensity of stress on the section LN.

Divide (1) by (2): $\dfrac{p}{q}\tan\theta = \cot\phi \quad \ldots \quad (4)$

giving the direction of R, the resultant stress on LN.

Now suppose an ellipse is drawn (see Fig. 49) with axes q instead of a, p instead of b. If the point P (x, y) on this is the point θ

$$x = q\cos\theta,\ y = p\sin\theta,$$

$$\therefore \quad OP^2 = q^2\cos^2\theta + p^2\sin^2\theta$$

$$= r^2 \qquad \text{by (3).}$$

Also

$$\tan POx = \frac{p\sin\theta}{q\cos\theta} = \frac{p}{q}\tan\theta$$

$$= \cot\phi \qquad \text{by (4).}$$

$$\therefore \quad \frac{\pi}{2} - POx = \phi.$$

These equations give a geometrical method of finding r and ϕ to a sufficient degree of accuracy by measurement from an ellipse drawn to scale with q and p as the axes. This ellipse is called the ellipse of stress.

EXERCISE 30

In the following the equation to any ellipse mentioned in an exercise is to be taken as $\dfrac{x^2}{a^2} + \dfrac{y^2}{b^2} = 1$ unless otherwise directed.

1. The tangent at any point P on the ellipse cuts OX at T and PN is the ordinate at P. Show that ON . OT $= a^2$.

2. Prove that the normal at an end of the latus rectum meets the major axis AA_1 at a distance ae^3 from the centre O.

3. Prove that the line joining the points of eccentric angle α, β on the ellipse has as its equation

$$\frac{x}{a}\cos\frac{\alpha+\beta}{2}+\frac{y}{b}\sin\frac{\alpha+\beta}{2}=\cos\frac{\alpha-\beta}{2}.$$

4. Show that the tangents at the points of eccentric angle α, β on the ellipse meet at the point

$$a\frac{\cos[(\alpha+\beta)/2]}{\cos[(\alpha-\beta)/2]},\quad b\frac{\sin[(\alpha+\beta)/2]}{\cos[(\alpha-\beta)/2]}.$$

5. Using the result of Exercise 4 prove that tangents at the points whose eccentric angles are α, $\alpha+\pi/2$ meet on the ellipse

$$\frac{x^2}{a^2}+\frac{y^2}{b^2}=2.$$

6. Find a^2 and b^2 if the ellipse touches the lines $x+y=4$ and $x+2y-7=0$.

7. Show that the distance of the point θ $(a\cos\theta,\ b\sin\theta)$ from the focus $(ae, 0)$ is $a(1-e\cos\theta)$ and from $(-ae, 0)$ is $a(1+e\cos\theta)$.

8. From the foci of the ellipse perpendiculars are dropped upon any tangent to the curve. Prove that the product of the lengths of these is b^2, the square on the semi minor axis.

9. Prove that the tangents at the ends of each latus rectum of the ellipse form a quadrilateral of area $2a^2/e$.

10. R is the mid point of AB, a variable chord of the ellipse. If O is the centre show that the product of the gradients of AB and OR is constant.

11. The chord joining the variable points θ, ϕ on the ellipse subtends 90° at the point $(a, 0)$. Show that

$$\tan\frac{\theta}{2}\tan\frac{\phi}{2}=-\frac{b^2}{a^2}.$$

12. P is a variable point on the ellipse with focus S. Show that the locus of the mid point of SP is an ellipse with centre mid way between the origin and S.

13. The tangent at P, a point on the ellipse, meets the directrix at T. Show that PT subtends 90° at the focus nearest the directrix.

14. The outline of a lamina has the form of the ellipse

$$16x^2+25y^2=400,$$

the unit of length on the axes of x and y being 1 in. The lamina is cut along the straight line $4x+5y=28$, which joins two points P and Q on the outline. Determine the co-ordinates of P and Q and the length of the cut. [U.L.C.I.]

15. The line $2x+5y=14$ cuts the ellipse

$$\frac{x^2}{25}+\frac{y^2}{4}=1$$

at the two points P and Q. Find the co-ordinates of P and Q. If O is the centre of the ellipse deduce the size of the angle POQ. [U.L.C.I.]

16. If an area S lies on a slope making angle α with the horizontal its projection on the horizontal ground has as its area S $\cos \alpha$. Imagine a circle of radius a lying on the slope projected into an ellipse in this way, with major axis $2a$ and minor axis $2b$ and deduce that its area is πab.

17. Find the volume generated when the ellipse rotates completely: (*a*) round the x axis, (*b*) round the y axis.

18. The area of the parabola $y^2 = 121x$ between the curve, the x axis and the ordinate at $x = 9$ is equal to the area of the ellipse

$$\frac{x^2}{a^2} + \frac{y^2}{49} = 1.$$

Find a, the semi major axis. [I.U.]

19. A rod of fixed length slides with its ends on two fixed perpendicular lines. Show that any fixed point on the rod describes an ellipse. [U.L.C.I.]

20. A tensile stress of 4 tons/in.^{2} acts on a plane. The perpendicular (tensile) stress is 2·5 tons/in.^{2}. Apply a graphical method to find the stress on a plane inclined (i) at 30° to the above plane, (ii) at 40°.

21. Find the values of c if the straight line $y + x = c$ is a tangent to the ellipse $x^2 + 3y^2 = 12$. Find also the eccentric angle of the point of contact of the tangent corresponding to each value of c.

22. A′ is the point $(-a, 0)$, A is the point $(a, 0)$ on the ellipse $x^2/a^2 + y^2/b^2 = 1$ whilst P is any point on the ellipse and in the first quadrant. The tangent to the curve at P meets the y axis at Q and the line $x = a$ at T. The chord A′P meets the y axis at M and when produced meets the line $x = a$ at R. Prove that: (*a*) AT = TR; (*b*) $OQ^2 - MQ^2 = b^2$.

23. The tangent and normal to the ellipse $x^2/a^2 + y^2/b^2 = 1$ at the point P($a \cos \theta$, $b \sin \theta$) meet the axis of x in T and G respectively. O is the centre of the ellipse and Y the foot of the perpendicular from O to the tangent at P. Prove that: (*a*) OG . OT $= a^2 - b^2$; (*b*) OY . GP $= b^2$.

CHAPTER 15

CHANGE OF AXES

15.1. It is often necessary to transfer to another point as a " new " origin of co-ordinates. Also we often simplify the equation of a given locus by referring it to new axes which are the original axes rotated through a given angle.

15.2. Change of Origin

Suppose P is the point (x, y) and we require to find the co-ordinates of P if another point $O_1(a, b)$ is chosen as the new origin.

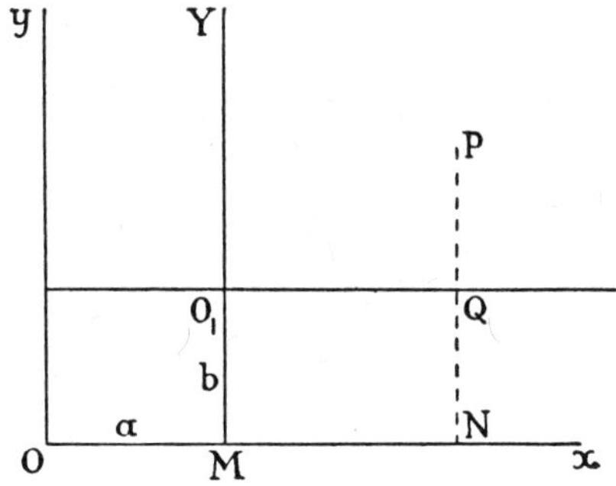

FIG. 51.

If (X, Y) are the new co-ordinates of P, then since

$$ON = MN + OM,$$
$$\therefore \quad x = X + a.$$

Also

$$PN = PQ + QN,$$
$$\therefore \quad y = Y + b.$$

$\therefore$ if we make the above substitutions for x and y in any given equation we will obtain an equation giving the locus referred to (a, b) as origin.

Example 1. Transfer the origin to the point (3, − 1) for the equation

$$y^2 + 2y - 4x + 13 = 0$$

and hence identify the curve.

We must place $x = X + 3$, $y = Y - 1$ in the given equation and obtain

$$(Y - 1)^2 + 2(Y - 1) - 4(X + 3) + 13 = 0.$$

This reduces to

$$Y^2 = 4X.$$

$\therefore$ the given equation is a parabola, but its vertex is at (3, − 1) instead of (0, 0) in the original system of axes.

15.3. Rotation of Axes

Suppose the origin remains at O but we wish to refer to new axes which make angle θ with the given axes. Let P be the point (x, y) whose co-ordinates are X, Y referred to the new axes.

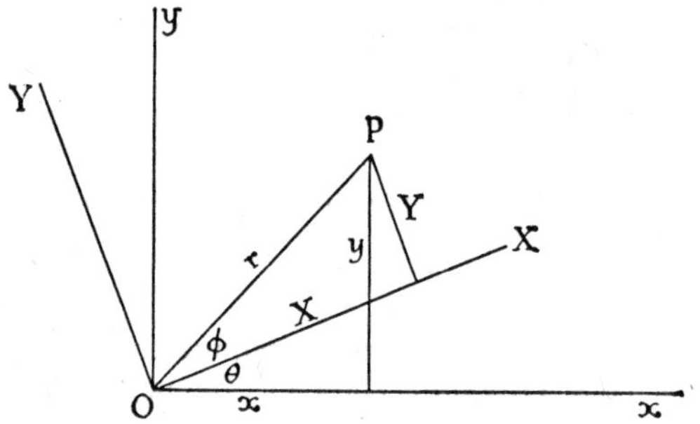

FIG. 52.

If $OP = r$ and $\angle POX = \phi$,

then
$$\begin{aligned} x &= r\cos(\theta + \phi) \\ &= r\{\cos\theta\cos\phi - \sin\theta\sin\phi\} \\ &= (r\cos\phi)\cos\theta - (r\sin\phi)\sin\theta, \\ \therefore\quad x &= X\cos\theta - Y\sin\theta. \end{aligned}$$

Similarly,
$$\begin{aligned} y &= r\sin(\theta + \phi) \\ &= (r\cos\phi)\sin\theta + (r\sin\phi)\cos\theta, \\ \therefore\quad y &= X\sin\theta + Y\cos\theta. \end{aligned}$$

$\therefore$ if we make these substitutions for x and y in any given equation, the result will be the given locus referred to the new (rotated) axes.

Example 2. Rotate the axes through $-45°$ for the curve
$$13x^2 + 10xy + 13y^2 = 72.$$

We must put
$$\begin{aligned} x &= X\cos(-45) - Y\sin(-45) \\ &= X\cos 45 + Y\sin 45 = \frac{(X + Y)}{\sqrt{2}}. \\ y &= X\sin(-45) + Y\cos(-45) \\ &= -X\sin 45 + Y\cos 45 = \frac{(-X + Y)}{\sqrt{2}}. \end{aligned}$$

The equation becomes
$$13\left(\frac{X + Y}{\sqrt{2}}\right)^2 + 10\left(\frac{X + Y}{\sqrt{2}}\right)\left(\frac{-X + Y}{\sqrt{2}}\right) + 13\left(\frac{-X + Y}{\sqrt{2}}\right)^2 = 72.$$

This reduces to
$$16X^2 + 36Y^2 = 144.$$

or
$$\frac{X^2}{9} + \frac{Y^2}{4} = 1.$$

The original equation is therefore an ellipse, but since it was referred to coordinate axes which made 45° with the " natural " axes of symmetry, the resulting equation is not easily recognizable.

Example 3. Through what angle must the axes be rotated in order that

$$ax^2 + 2hxy + by^2 = 1$$

may become an equation without the xy term?

If the axes are rotated through angle θ, the equation becomes

$$a(X\cos\theta - Y\sin\theta)^2 + 2h(X\cos\theta - Y\sin\theta)(X\sin\theta + Y\cos\theta) + b(X\sin\theta + Y\cos\theta)^2 = 1.$$

The coefficient of XY in this equation is

$$-2a\cos\theta\sin\theta + 2h(\cos^2\theta - \sin^2\theta) + 2b\sin\theta\cos\theta,$$

or

$$\sin 2\theta(b - a) + 2h\cos 2\theta.$$

If this is to be zero

$$\tan 2\theta = \frac{2h}{a - b}.$$

This will be used later in finding principal axes of inertia.

EXERCISE 31

1. The origin is changed to the point (—1, 3). Find the new coordinates of the points (1, 2), (0, 3), (—1, — 4).

2. The origin is changed to the point (1, 2). Find the new equation of the lines: (i) $2x + 4y - 7 = 0$; (ii) $x + 4y - 9 = 0$.

3. Transform the equation

$$2x^2 - 3xy - 2y^2 + 2x + 11y - 13 = 0$$

by changing the origin to the point (1, 2) and then rotating the axes through the acute angle whose tangent is 3.

4. On rotating the axes through an angle θ the line

$$2x + y - 3 = 0$$

becomes

$$x + 2y - 3 = 0.$$

Show that

$$\tan\theta = -\tfrac{3}{4}.$$

5. Transform the origin to the point (2, 3) and then rotate the axes through an angle θ in the equation

$$x^2 + y^2 - 4x - 6y + 9 = 0.$$

Explain why the result is independent of θ.

6. For the equation

$$11x^2 + 4xy + 14y^2 - 4x - 28y - 16 = 0$$

transform the origin to the point (0, 1) and then rotate the axes through an angle $\tan^{-1}(2)$.

CHAPTER 16

THE HYPERBOLA

(Eccentricity $e > 1$.)

16.1. The Standard Equation

Let S be the fixed point (focus) and LM the directrix or fixed straight

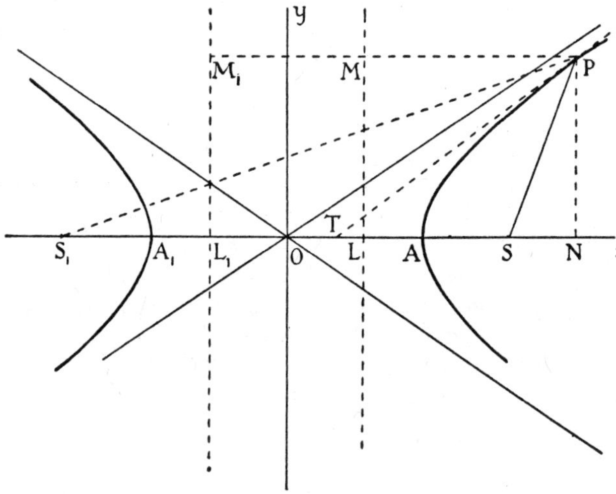

FIG. 53.

line. We require to find the locus of a point P which moves so that SP $= e$PM where $e > 1$.

Draw SL perp. to LM.

There will be points A on SL and A_1 on SL produced such that SA $= e$AL and $SA_1 = eLA_1$. These points will be on the curve.

Bisect AA_1 at O and choose O as the origin with OL as the x axis and the y axis through O perpendicular to Ox.

Mark L_1 where $A_1L_1 = AL$, so that O is also the mid point of L_1L.

Now $$SA = eAL,$$
$$SA_1 = eLA_1,$$
add: $$SA + SA_1 = e(AL + LA_1).$$

But $SA + SA_1 = 2OS$, and if we call $OA = a$, then

$$AL + LA_1 = 2a,$$
$$\therefore \quad 2OS = 2ea \quad \ldots \ldots \quad (1)$$

subtract:

$$SA_1 - SA = e(LA_1 - AL),$$
$$\therefore \quad 2a = e(LA_1 - A_1L_1)$$
$$= e \,.\, 2OL \quad \ldots \ldots \quad (2)$$

(1) shows that S is the point $(ae, 0)$;

(2) shows that the directrix is the line $x = \dfrac{a}{e}$.

$\therefore$ if P is the point (x, y) on the hyperbola,

$$SP^2 = e^2PM^2,$$
$$\therefore \quad (x - ae)^2 + y^2 = e^2\left(x - \frac{a}{e}\right)^2$$

or

$$x^2(e^2 - 1) - y^2 = a^2(e^2 - 1).$$
$$\therefore \quad \frac{x^2}{a^2} - \frac{y^2}{a^2(e^2 - 1)} = 1.$$

If we put $b^2 = a^2(e^2 - 1)$ for short, then b^2 is a real positive quantity, since $e^2 > 1$, and we have as the standard equation to the hyperbola

$$\frac{x^2}{a^2} - \frac{y^2}{b^2} = 1.$$

As with the ellipse, $2a$ is called the major axis of the curve.

16.2. To Trace the Hyperbola

(1) When $y = 0$, $x = \pm a$.

(2) When $x = 0$, $y^2 = -b^2$ $\therefore$ the curve does not cut the y axis in real points.

(3) $y = \pm \dfrac{b}{a}\sqrt{x^2 - a^2}$, $\therefore$ the curve is symmetrical about the x axis and for real values of y we must have $x^2 > a^2$, so that x cannot lie between $\pm a$.

(4) $x = \pm \dfrac{a}{b}\sqrt{b^2 + y^2}$, $\therefore$ the curve is symmetrical with respect to the y axis and y can have any value, x increasing with y.

(5) The equation of the curve can be written

$$y = \pm \frac{bx}{a}\sqrt{1 - \frac{a^2}{x^2}} \quad \ldots \ldots \quad (1)$$

$\therefore$ as x tends to infinity the curve tends to become

$$y = \pm \frac{bx}{a},$$

since $\dfrac{a^2}{x^2}$ becomes negligible.

$\therefore$ the lines $y = \pm \frac{bx}{a}$ are asymptotes to the curve (see 17.6). Also in equation (1) the square root is less than unity for all values of x, so that y for the curve always lies between the values

$$y = \pm \frac{bx}{a}.$$

$\therefore$ the curve approaches the asymptotes as shown.

(6) From the symmetrical nature of the curve it is clear that a second focus exists at $(-ae, 0)$ with a corresponding directrix

$$x = -\frac{a}{e}.$$

The curve is as shown, O, as with the ellipse, being the *centre.*

Example 1. Find the eccentricity, position of the foci and latus rectum for the hyperbola

$$\frac{x^2}{9} - \frac{y^2}{4} = 1.$$

Since

$$b^2 = a^2(e^2 - 1),$$
$$4 = 9(e^2 - 1),$$
$$e = \sqrt{\tfrac{13}{9}} = \tfrac{1}{3}\sqrt{13}.$$
$$\therefore \quad \text{OS} = ae = 3 \times \tfrac{1}{3}\sqrt{13} = \sqrt{13},$$

the foci are $(\pm\sqrt{13}, 0)$.

To find the length of the semi latus rectum—the ordinate erected at S to meet the curve—put $x = \sqrt{13}$ in the equation to the curve,

$$\frac{13}{9} - \frac{y^2}{4} = 1,$$
$$\therefore \quad y = \pm \frac{4}{3}.$$

The latus rectum is

$$2 \times \frac{4}{3} = \frac{8}{3}.$$

16.3. The Tangent and Normal at any Point (x_1, y_1)

The work is exactly similar to that for the ellipse.

Tangent: $$\frac{xx_1}{a^2} - \frac{yy_1}{b^2} = 1.$$

Normal: $$y - y_1 = -\frac{a^2y_1}{b^2x_1}(x - x_1).$$

Example 2. P is any point on the hyperbola $\frac{x^2}{a^2} - \frac{y^2}{b^2} = 1$, and the normal at P cuts Ox at Q. PN is the ordinate at P, and NP produced meets the asymptote in the first quadrant at P_1. Prove that P_1Q is perpendicular to this asymptote.

If P is (x_1, y_1) the normal is

$$y - y_1 = -\frac{a^2y_1}{b^2x_1}(x - x_1).$$

Put $y = 0$ in this equation and find that

$$OQ = x_1\left(1 + \frac{b^2}{a^2}\right).$$

N is the point $(x_1, 0)$,

$\therefore$ where NP meets $\quad y = \frac{b}{a}x,$

$$NP_1 = \frac{b}{a}x_1.$$

$\therefore$ P_1 is the point $\left(x_1, \frac{b}{a}x_1\right)$.

$\therefore$ the gradient of P_1Q is

$$\frac{\frac{bx_1}{a} - 0}{x_1 - x_1\left(1 + \frac{b^2}{a^2}\right)} = -\frac{a}{b}.$$

Since the gradient of the asymptote is $\frac{b}{a}$, P_1Q is perp. to it.

16.4. Some Properties of the Hyperbola (Fig. 53)

(1) Let P be any point on the curve, PM, PM_1 perpendiculars on the two directrices.

Then

$$\begin{aligned} S_1P - SP &= eM_1P - eMP \\ &= eM_1M \\ &= e \cdot 2\frac{a}{e} \\ &= 2a. \end{aligned}$$

$\therefore$ the difference of the focal distances of any point on a hyperbola is equal to $2a$, a constant.

[Range finding in its early days was based upon this property, S and S_1 being observation posts and P the enemy gun whose position was required.]

(2) If P is the point (x_1, y_1), the tangent is

$$\frac{xx_1}{a^2} - \frac{yy_1}{b^2} = 1.$$

$\therefore$ if this cuts the x axis at T, place $y = 0$ in this and find

$$OT = \frac{a^2}{x_1}.$$

$$\therefore \quad TS = OS - OT = ae - \frac{a^2}{x_1} = \frac{a}{x_1}(ex_1 - a)$$

also

$$S_1T = OS_1 + OT = ae + \frac{a^2}{x_1} = \frac{a}{x_1}(ex_1 + a).$$

$$\therefore \quad \frac{TS}{S_1T} = \frac{ex_1 - a}{ex_1 + a}.$$

But $$\mathrm{SP} = e\mathrm{PM} = e(\mathrm{ON} - \mathrm{OL}) = e\left(x_1 - \frac{a}{e}\right) = ex_1 - a,$$

$$\mathrm{S_1P} = e\mathrm{PM_1} = e(\mathrm{ON} + \mathrm{OL}) = e\left(x_1 + \frac{a}{e}\right) = ex_1 + a,$$

$$\therefore \quad \frac{\mathrm{TS}}{\mathrm{S_1T}} = \frac{\mathrm{SP}}{\mathrm{S_1P}}.$$

$\therefore$ the tangent bisects the angle between the focal distances. The normal at P then must bisect the exterior angle between S_1P and SP. This corresponds to the ellipse where, however, the interior angle between the focal distances is bisected by the normal and the exterior angle by the tangent.

16.5. A Parametric Representation

If we put $x = a \sec \theta$ in the equation of the hyperbola we find

$$\frac{y^2}{b^2} = \frac{x^2}{a^2} - 1 = \sec^2 \theta - 1 = \tan^2 \theta,$$

$$\therefore \quad y = \pm\, b \tan \theta.$$

$\therefore$ $x = a \sec \theta$, $y = b \tan \theta$ can be used to represent any point on the curve.

The student should obtain:

equation of tangent at the point θ,

$$\frac{x}{a} \sec \theta - \frac{y}{b} \tan \theta = 1,$$

equation of normal at the point θ,

$$\frac{ax}{\sec \theta} + \frac{by}{\tan \theta} = a^2 + b^2.$$

Example 3. S and S_1 are the foci of $\frac{x^2}{a^2} - \frac{y^2}{b^2} = 1$, and SY, S_1Y_1 are the perpendiculars upon the tangent at any point P. Prove that $SY \cdot S_1Y_1 = b^2$.

If P is the point $(a \sec \theta, b \tan \theta)$ the tangent at P is

$$\frac{x}{a} \sec \theta - \frac{y}{b} \tan \theta = 1.$$

The perpendicular upon this from $(ae, 0)$ is SY, where

$$\mathrm{SY} = \frac{(ae)\dfrac{\sec \theta}{a} - 1}{\pm\sqrt{\dfrac{\sec^2 \theta}{a^2} + \dfrac{\tan^2 \theta}{b^2}}}.$$

Similarly,
$$\mathrm{S_1Y_1} = \frac{(-\,ae)\dfrac{\sec \theta}{a} - 1}{\pm\sqrt{\dfrac{\sec^2 \theta}{a^2} + \dfrac{\tan^2 \theta}{b^2}}},$$

$$\therefore \quad \mathrm{SY} \cdot \mathrm{S_1Y_1} = \pm \frac{(e \sec \theta - 1)(e \sec \theta + 1)}{\dfrac{\sec^2 \theta}{a^2} + \dfrac{\sec^2 \theta - 1}{a^2(e^2 - 1)}}$$

$$= \frac{a^2(e^2 - 1)(e^2 \sec^2 \theta - 1)}{\sec^2 \theta(e^2 - 1) + \sec^2 \theta - 1}$$

$$= a^2(e^2 - 1) = b^2.$$

16.6. The Rectangular Hyperbola

If the asymptotes of the hyperbola are at right angles the hyperbola is called a rectangular hyperbola.

The asymptotes are

$$y = \frac{b}{a}x \quad \text{and} \quad y = -\frac{b}{a}x.$$

If these are perpendicular

$$-\frac{b}{a} \times \frac{b}{a} = -1,$$

$$\therefore \quad b = a.$$

$\therefore$ the equation $\dfrac{x^2}{a^2} - \dfrac{y^2}{b^2} = 1$

becomes $x^2 - y^2 = a^2$

with asymptotes $y = \pm x.$

Also, since $b^2 = a^2(e^2 - 1),$

we have $a^2 = a^2(e^2 - 1), \quad \therefore \quad e = \sqrt{2}.$

The foci are $(\pm ae, 0)$ which are therefore $(\pm a\sqrt{2}, 0)$.

16.7. The Standard Equation for a Rectangular Hyperbola

We get a very convenient form for the equation if we choose the

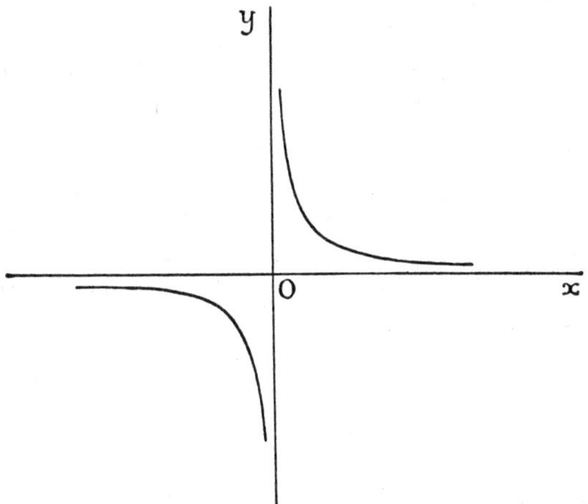

FIG. 54.

perpendicular asymptotes as axes of co-ordinates. To do this we must rotate the axes through $-45°$.

$\therefore$ we must substitute in $x^2 - y^2 = a^2$

$$x = \text{X} \cos(-45) - \text{Y} \sin(-45)$$
$$= (\text{X} + \text{Y})/\sqrt{2},$$
$$y = \text{X} \sin(-45) + \text{Y} \cos(-45)$$
$$= (-\text{X} + \text{Y})/\sqrt{2}.$$

The equation becomes

$$(\text{X} + \text{Y})^2 - (-\text{X} + \text{Y})^2 = 2a^2,$$
$$\therefore \quad \text{XY} = \tfrac{1}{2}a^2.$$

We may therefore take the equation

$$xy = c^2$$

to represent a rectangular hyperbola referred to its asymptotes as axes. Since c^2 is positive, x and y must be of the same sign, and therefore the curve lies in the first and third quadrants as shown.

16.8. Parametric Notation

The curve $xy = c^2$ can obviously be represented by

$$x = ct, \quad y = c/t$$

called the point "t" on the curve.

The student should obtain:

equation of tangent at "t"

$$x + t^2y = 2ct,$$

equation of normal at "t"

$$t^3x - ty = c(t^4 - 1),$$

equation of the join of the points t_1 and t_2

$$x + yt_1t_2 = c(t_1 + t_2).$$

Example 4. NP is the ordinate of the point P on $xy = c^2$. The tangent at P meets the y axis at M, and the line through M parallel to the x axis meets the curve at Q. Show that NQ is the tangent at Q.

If P is the point t, the tangent at t is

$$x + t^2y = 2ct.$$

Put $x = 0$ in this and find

$$\text{OM} = \frac{2c}{t}.$$

Put $y = \dfrac{2c}{t}$ in $xy = c^2$ and find

$$x = \frac{ct}{2}.$$

$\therefore$ Q is $\left(\dfrac{ct}{2}, \dfrac{2c}{t}\right)$, *i.e.*, the point $\dfrac{t}{2}$.

$\therefore$ the tangent at Q is $\quad x + \dfrac{t^2}{4}y = ct.$

But the join QN is the join of

$$\left(\frac{ct}{2}, \frac{2c}{t}\right) \quad \text{and} \quad (ct, 0),$$

which is

$$y - 0 = \frac{\frac{2c}{t} - 0}{\frac{ct}{2} - ct}(x - ct)$$

or

$$x + \frac{t^2}{4}y = ct.$$

$\therefore$ QN is the tangent at Q.

EXERCISE 32

1. P is any point on $\frac{x^2}{a^2} - \frac{y^2}{b^2} = 1$, and the tangent at P cuts Ox at T. PN is perpendicular to Ox. Prove ON . OT $= a^2$.

2. The tangent at any point P on the hyperbola $\frac{x^2}{a^2} - \frac{y^2}{b^2} = 1$ cuts the asymptotes at Q, Q_1. Prove that P is the mid point of QQ_1.

3. Find the foci and eccentricity of the following hyperbolas:

(*a*) $\frac{x^2}{4} - \frac{y^2}{9} = 1.$ (*b*) $\frac{x^2}{9} - \frac{y^2}{7} = 1.$

(*c*) $x^2 - 9y^2 = 4.$ (*d*) $9x^2 - 16y^2 = 36.$

4. Find the equations of the tangent and normal at $(4, 3\sqrt{3})$ to the hyperbola $\frac{x^2}{4} - \frac{y^2}{9} = 1.$

5. Prove that the equation of the straight line joining the points θ, ϕ on $\frac{x^2}{a^2} - \frac{y^2}{b^2} = 1$ is

$$\frac{x}{a}\cos\frac{\theta - \phi}{2} - \frac{y}{b}\sin\frac{\theta + \phi}{2} = \cos\frac{\theta + \phi}{2}.$$

Deduce from this the equation of the tangent at the point θ.

6. Show that $x - 2y + 1 = 0$ is a tangent to the curve $x^2 - 6y^2 = 3$ and find the point of contact.

7. Find the equations of the tangents to $2x^2 - 3y^2 = 6$ which are parallel to the line $x + y - 2 = 0$.

8. Show that the tangents at the points t_1 and t_2 on $xy = c^2$ meet at the point

$$\frac{2ct_1t_2}{t_1 + t_2}, \frac{2c}{t_1 + t_2}.$$

9. P, Q are the points t_1, t_2 on $xy = c^2$; TP, TQ are the tangents. Show that the line joining the origin to T bisects the chord PQ.

10. The hyperbolas $\frac{x^2}{8} - \frac{y^2}{4} = 1$ and $\frac{y^2}{8} - \frac{x^2}{4} = 1$ have four common tangents. Find their equations.

11. Any tangent to $y^2 = 4ax$ meets the hyperbola $xy = c^2$ at L and M. Find the locus of the middle point of LM.

12. N is the foot of the perpendicular from the origin O on to the normal at any point on $xy = c^2$. Find the locus of N.

13. Sound travels at 1100 ft./sec. If two stations S, S_1 are 2200 ft. apart, what is the locus of a gun the report of which is heard at S 1 sec. earlier that at S_1? If the gun is a long way off find the angle which its direction makes with SS_1.

14. The portion of the curve $xy = 8$ between the ordinates at $x = 2$ and 8 rotates round the x axis. Find the volume generated. If this portion rotates round the y axis find the volume generated.

15. The point P on the hyperbola $xy = c^2$ is such that the tangent to the hyperbola at P passes through the focus of the parabola $y^2 = 4ax$. Find the co-ordinates of P in terms of a and c.

If P also lies on the parabola, prove that $a^4 = 2c^4$ and calculate the acute angle between the tangents to the two curves at P.

16. Find the equation of the chord joining $(ct_1, c/t_1)$ and $(ct_2, c/t_2)$ on $xy = c^2$. P, Q are two points on a rectangular hyperbola which subtend a right angle at a third point R on the hyperbola. Prove that the tangent at R is perpendicular to PQ.

17. If O is the origin and P (x_1y_1) any point on the curve $x^2 - y^2 = 4$, prove that the tangent at P makes the same angle with the x axis that OP makes with the y axis. If this tangent meets the lines $y = x$, $y = -x$ at the points Q, R respectively, find the area of the triangle QOR.

18. Find the equations of the tangent and normal to the curve $y^2 = x^3$ at the point (4, 8). If they meet the axis of x in T and T′ respectively, prove that $TT' = 26\frac{2}{3}$.

19. At the point P, on the curve $y = x^4$, whose x value is a, the tangent is drawn to meet the x axis at T and the y axis at R. Show that the area of the triangle ORT is nine times that of the triangle TNP, where N is the foot of the perpendicular from P onto the x axis and O is the origin.

CHAPTER 17

CURVE SKETCHING

17.1. It is very useful to know the shape of the graph of any function with which we are dealing. This chapter will deal with the usual types of curves that occur in connection with areas, volumes, centres of gravity, etc.

17.2. Curves of the type $y^m = x^n$

Consider $y^2 = x$ (Fig. 55(*a*)).

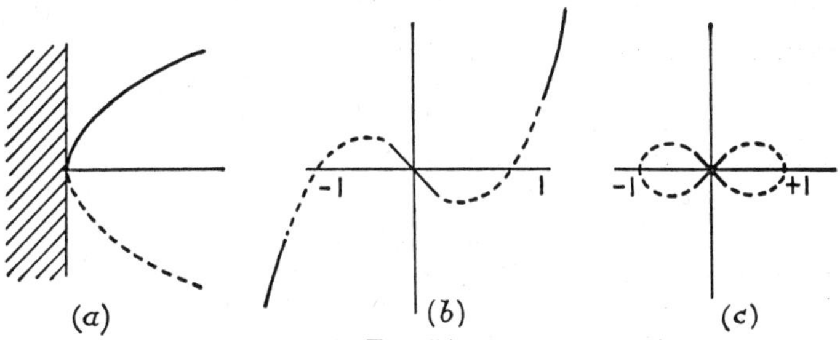

FIG. 55.

(1) x must be +ve since y^2 is +ve, $\therefore$ shade out the part of the paper for which x is −ve.

(2) $y = \pm\sqrt{x}$, $\therefore$ for every value of x there will be two of y, equal and opposite, *i.e.*, the curve is symmetrical with regard to the x axis.

(3) When $y = 0$, $x = 0$, $\therefore$ curve passes through O.

(4) When $x = 0, y = 0$, again we get O. In (3) and (4) we are finding where the curve cuts the axes. These points are often easy to obtain and very helpful.

(5) Keep to $y = +\sqrt{x}$, $\therefore \dfrac{dy}{dx} = \dfrac{1}{2\sqrt{x}}$.

$\therefore$ at O the gradient is infinite or the curve touches the y axis. Also as x increases the gradient decreases steadily.

(6) As x increases so does y.

The curve is as shown. The upper half is drawn according to the above data, and the lower half is its image in the x axis.

EXERCISE 33A

Using the above method sketch the graphs of:

1. $y^2 = x^3$. 2. $y^2 = -x$. 3. $y = x^3$. 4. $y^3 = x^4$. 5. $y = -x^2$.

17.3. The Shape of a Curve for x large and near the Origin

Consider $y = x^3 - x$ (Fig. 55(*b*)).

(1) Near O where x is very small, x^3 is so small compared to x that it may be neglected. Therefore the shape near O is $y = -x$.

(2) When x is very large the effect of x on x^3 is so small that for x large the curve is nearly $y = x^3$. These two curves are shown in the graph in full line and suggest that the rest of the curve is the dotted part shown as joining them up.

From the above we deduce the rule: If a curve is given by the equation $y = f(x)$ or $y^2 = f(x)$ the shape for x large is given by y or $y^2 =$ the term of highest degree in x. If the curve passes through O, the shape near O is given by y or $y^2 =$ the term of lowest degree in x.

Example 1. $y^2 = x^2 - x^4$ (Fig. 55(*c*)).
This passes through O,
$\therefore$ for x small $\qquad y^2 = x^2$
or $\qquad y = \pm x$
giving the shape near O.
Also $\qquad y^2 = -x^4$ when x is large.
$\therefore \quad y = \pm\sqrt{-x^4}$,
$\therefore$ there is no shape for x large.
We also note that $y = 0$ when $x = \pm 1$.

EXERCISE 33B

In each case sketch the shape near O and for x large.

1. $y = x + x^4$. 2. $y = x - 2x^2 + x^3$.
3. $y^2 = x^2 + x^3$. 4. $y^3 = x^2(x - 1)$.
5. In examples 1 and 2, find some data concerning each curve, *e.g.*, where it cuts the axes, and hence complete the graph.

17.4. To Sketch $y = x^2 + x^3$ (Fig. 56(*a*)).

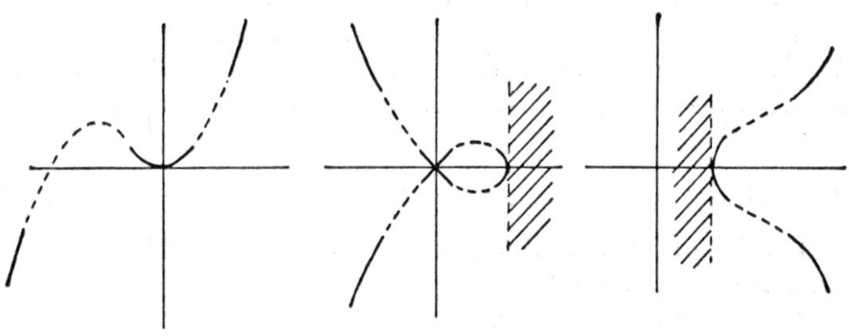

(*a*) (*b*) (*c*)

FIG. 56.

$$y = x^2(1 + x)$$

(1) When $x = 0$, $y = 0$; $\therefore$ curve passes through O.
(2) When $y = 0$, $x = 0, 0, -1$.

(3) Shape near O, $y = x^2$.

(4) Shape for x large, $y = x^3$.

This data gives the parts of the curve shown in full, and the curve consists of these full lines joined together. The student should check that the curve has a maximum between 0 and -1.

EXERCISE 34

Sketch the curves:

1. $y = x(1 - x^2)$.
2. $y = (x + 3)(x - 2)(x - 5)$.
3. $y = 15 + 12x - 3x^2$.
4. $y = x^2(3 - x)$.
5. $y = (1 + x)^2(2 - x)$.
6. $y = (1 - x^2)(1 - 4x)$.

17.5. Curves with Loops

Consider $y^2 = x^2(12 - x)$ (Fig. 56(*b*)).

(1) $y = \pm x\sqrt{12 - x}$, $\therefore$ symmetry with respect to x axis.

(2) Also x cannot be greater than 12.

(3) When $x = 0$, $y = 0$.

(4) When $y = 0$, $x = 0, 0, 12$.

(5) Shape near O, $y = \pm x\sqrt{12}$.

(6) Shape for x large, $y^2 = -x^3$.

This is sufficient to obtain the graph shown. If the student is still doubtful we can settle the shape at $x = 12$ by transferring to that point as a new origin.

Put $$x = X + 12.$$

$$\therefore \quad y^2 = -(X + 12)^2X.$$

Shape at the new origin is $y^2 = -144X$ as shown.

Example 2. Consider $y^2 = x^2 - x^4$ (Fig. 55(*c*)).
This was considered in Example 1.

(1) Shape at O, $y = \pm x$.

(2) No shape for x large.

Also

(3) $y = \pm x\sqrt{(1 - x)(1 + x)}$; $\therefore$ when $y = 0$, $x = 0, 1, -1$.

(4) y is imaginary if x does not lie between -1 and $+1$, for the square root will be of a negative quantity.

(5) Transfer to $x = +1$ as a new origin and show that shape there is $y^2 = -2X$. Similarly, shape at $x = -1$ is $y^2 = 2X$.

(6) Curve is symmetrical with respect to the x axis.

(7) Curve is also symmetrical with respect to the y axis. This is shown by the equation, which contains even powers of x only so that if (x, y) satisfies the equation $(-x, y)$ also does so.

(8) The curve must be as shown. The student should obtain the maxima and minima values of the functions so as to get the exact proportions of the loops—if required.

Example 3. Consider $y^2 = x^2(x - 2)$ (Fig. 56(*c*)).

(1) When $x = 0$, $y = 0$.

(2) When $y = 0$, $x = 0, 0, 2$.

(3) $y = \pm x\sqrt{x - 2}$, $\therefore$ symmetry with regard to x axis.

(4) Shape near O, $y^2 = -2x^2$; $\therefore$ no shape at O, although (0, 0) is on the curve. O is here an " isolated " point.

(5) From (3) we see that x is +ve and greater than 2 for real y, so that the curve exists only for $x \geqslant 2$.

(6) Shape for x large: $y^2 = x^3$.

(7) Transfer to (2, 0) as a new origin and obtain $y^2 = (X + 2)^2X$, $\therefore$ shape at new origin is $y^2 = 4X$.

(8) $\therefore$ curve is as shown.

EXERCISE 35

Sketch the following curves:

1. $y^2 = x(x - 2)^2$.
2. $y^2 = x^2(3 - x)$.
3. $y^2 = x^2(4 - x^2)$.
4. $y^2 = x^2(x^2 - 9)$.
5. $y^2 = x(3 - x)^2$.
6. $y^2 = x^3(1 - x)^2$.
7. $y^2 = x(x - 4)(x - 3)$.
8. $y^2 = (x - 1)(x - 2)(x - 3)$.

17.6. Curves with Asymptotes

Consider the graph of $xy = 1$.

(1) $y = \frac{1}{x}$ so that as x increases the distance of the point (x, y) from the x axis decreases steadily.

(2) $\frac{dy}{dx} = -\frac{1}{x^2}$ so that when x is very large the curve has almost zero gradient.

(3) Combining (1) and (2) we see that " at infinity ", *i.e.*, when the point considered has increased its distance from the origin beyond any finite limit, the curve will touch the x axis, since its distance from it will be zero and its gradient will also be zero. Note that this will never actually occur, but it tends to become more and more so as x increases. We sum this up in short by saying that " at infinity " the curve touches the x axis.

Definition of an Asymptote

(1) An asymptote is defined as a line which is a tangent to a curve at an infinite distance from the origin.

(2) An equivalent definition is: a line whose distance from a point on the curve tends to zero as the point on the curve moves to an infinite distance from the origin.

17.7. Asymptotes Parallel to the Axes

In this chapter we shall be concerned only with curves which have asymptotes parallel to the axes of co-ordinates. There is a simple rule for obtaining these.

Rule: Equate to zero the coefficients of the highest powers of x and y respectively in the equation concerned. This will give the asymptotes —if they exist.

Example 4. $xy = 1$ (Fig. 54).

y is the highest power of y, and its coefficient is x, $\therefore x = 0$, *i.e.*, the y axis is an asymptote.

Similarly, $y = 0$ is an asymptote.

Example 5. $y = x/(1 + x^2)$ or $y(1 + x^2) - x = 0$.

The coefficient of y is $1 + x^2 = 0$ whose solution gives imaginary roots. $\therefore$ there are no asymptotes parallel to the y axis.

The coefficient of x^2 is y, $\therefore y = 0$ is an asymptote.

EXERCISE 36

Write down the asymptotes parallel to the axes in the following curves:

1. $x^2y^2 - x^2y - xy^2 + 3x + 2y + 4 = 0$.
2. $y^2(x^2 - a^2) = x$.
3. $xy^3 + x^3y = a^4$.
4. Show that the asymptotes of $x^2y^2 = a^2(x^2 + y^2)$ form the sides of a square.
5. Sketch $y = (x^2 - 3x + 4)/(x - 3)$. Find its maximum and minimum and deduce from the graph that the function has no values between -1 and 7.

17.8. Points of Inflexion

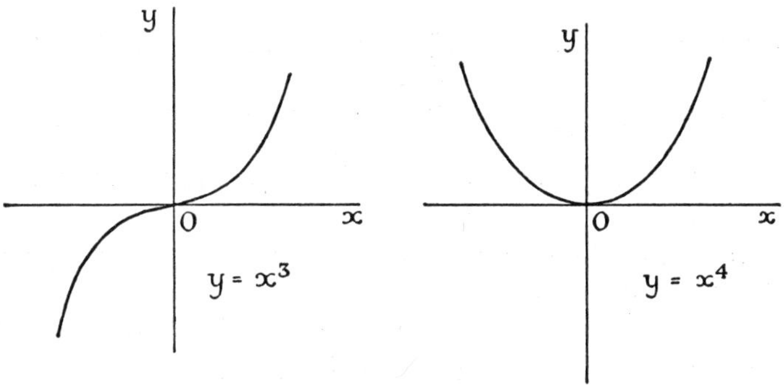

FIG. 57.

Let us test $y = x^3$ for stationary values.

$$\frac{dy}{dx} = 3x^2$$

$\therefore$ stationary values are given by

$$3x^2 = 0 \text{ or } x = 0.$$

Also
$$\frac{d^2y}{dx^2} = 6x = 0, \text{ when } x = 0.$$

$\therefore$ the value is neither positive nor negative, and we cannot decide whether the point $x = 0$ is a maximum or minimum value.

If we test $y = x^4$ in the same way

$$\frac{dy}{dx} = 4x^3,$$

$\therefore$ $x = 0$ is a possible stationary value and $\frac{d^2y}{dx^2} = 12x^2 = 0$ when $x = 0$. Yet the graphs show that $y = x^3$ has no turning point at $x = 0$, whilst $y = x^4$ has a minimum there. There is an important difference between the two graphs which provides a means of distinguishing between the two cases.

(1) $y = x^3$. To the left of the origin $\frac{dy}{dx}$ is positive and decreasing to zero as we approach O along the curve. Therefore $\frac{d^2y}{dx^2}$ is negative. As we leave O along the curve proceeding to the right, $\frac{dy}{dx}$ is positive and increasing so that $\frac{d^2y}{dx^2}$ is positive. Therefore there is *a change in sign of* $\frac{d^2y}{dx^2}$ in passing through the point that is being examined for a stationary value.

(2) $y = x^4$. To the left of O $\frac{dy}{dx}$ is negative and increasing to zero as we approach O. Therefore $\frac{d^2y}{dx^2}$ is positive to the left of O. As we leave O to the right $\frac{dy}{dx}$ is positive and increasing, so that $\frac{d^2y}{dx^2}$ is positive. Therefore there is *no change in sign of* $\frac{d^2y}{dx^2}$ in passing through the point that is being examined.

(3) Note that $y = x^3$ crosses its tangent, the x axis, at the point O, whilst $y = x^4$ does not.

Definition. A point of inflexion is a point where the curve crosses its tangent. At such a point $\frac{d^2y}{dx^2}$ is zero and has opposite signs on either side of the point.

Example 6. Test the equation for points of inflexion (Fig. 58(*a*)).

$$y = (x - 2)^2(x - 7)$$

$$\frac{dy}{dx} = (x - 2)^2 . 1 + (x - 7) . 2(x - 2)$$

$$= 3x^2 - 22x + 32.$$

$$\frac{d^2y}{dx^2} = 6x - 22.$$

$\therefore$ a possible point of inflexion is given by

$$6x - 22 = 0 \quad \text{or} \quad x = \tfrac{11}{3}.$$

Since $$\frac{d^2y}{dx^2} = 6(x - \tfrac{11}{3})$$

it is obvious that $\frac{d^2y}{dx^2}$ is negative if x is a little less than $\frac{11}{3}$ and positive if x is a little greater than $\frac{11}{3}$. There is therefore a change in sign of $\frac{d^2y}{dx^2}$, and $x = \frac{11}{3}$ is a point of inflexion.

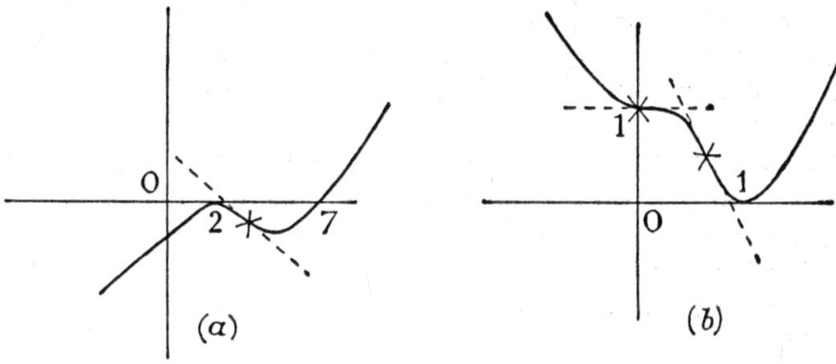

FIG. 58.

Example 7. Test $y = 3x^4 - 4x^3 + 1$ for stationary values and points of inflexion. Give a rough sketch of the curve.

$$y = 3x^4 - 4x^3 + 1 \qquad \text{(Fig. 58}(b))$$

$$\frac{dy}{dx} = 12x^3 - 12x^2 = 12x^2(x - 1).$$

$$\frac{d^2y}{dx^2} = 36x^2 - 24x = 12x(3x - 2).$$

$\therefore$ possible stationary values are $x = 0$ and $x = 1$.

We find that $x = 0$ makes $\frac{d^2y}{dx^2}$ zero, so that this value is a possible point of inflexion.

$x = 1$ makes $\frac{d^2y}{dx^2}$ positive, so that $x = 1$ is a minimum.

For possible points of inflexion

$$12x(3x - 2) = 0,$$

$$\therefore \quad x = 0 \text{ and } \tfrac{2}{3}.$$

If x is a small negative quantity

$$\frac{d^2y}{dx^2} = 12(-)(-) = +\text{ve}.$$

If x is a small positive quantity

$$\frac{d^2y}{dx^2} = 12(+)(-) = -\text{ve}.$$

$\therefore$ there is a change of sign, and $x = 0$ is a point of inflexion.

Similarly, $x = \frac{2}{3}$ is also a point of inflexion.

We therefore find:

(1, 0) is a minimum,
(0, 1) and $(\frac{2}{3}, \frac{11}{27})$ are points of inflexion.

EXERCISE 37

1. Find the points of inflexion on the following curves:
(a) $y = -x^3 + 6x^2 - 11x + 7$; (b) $y = 2x^3 - 3x^2 - 12x + 18$;
(c) $y = 3x^4 - 8x^3 + 6x^2 - 10$.

2. Prove that the point (3, 0) is a point of inflexion on

$$y = (x^2 - 5x + 6)/(x^2 - 3x + 3).$$

3. Find the turning points and points of inflexion of the following curves. In each case give a rough sketch.

(*a*) $y = x^2(x - 3)$; (*b*) $y = 2x^3 + 3x^2 - 12x + 6$;
(*c*) $y = x^4 - 8x^3 + 15x^2 + 4x - 20$.

4. Show that $y = 2x/(x^2 + 1)$ has three points of inflexion separated by one maximum and one minimum.

5. Find the points of inflexion for values of x between 0 and 2π, including the point 0 but excluding the point 2π, on:

(*a*) $y = \sin x$; (*b*) $y = \cos x$; (*c*) $y = \tan x$.

6. Show that the curve $y = e^x$ has no point of inflexion and find the point of inflexion on $y = xe^{-x}$.

7. Show that $y = x^4 - 6x^2 + 5x$ has points of inflexion at (1, 0) and (– 1, – 10).

8. Show that $y = 27x^3 - 54x^2 + 36x - 8$ has a point of inflexion on the x axis.

9. Show that $y = 4 \sin x - \sin 2x$ has points of inflexion at the points for which $x = n\pi$, $2n\pi \pm \pi/3$, where n is an integer.

10. Find $f(x)$, a cubic expression in x, such that $y = f(x)$ has a point of inflexion at (– 1, 16) and touches Ox at (1, 0).

11. Find $f(x)$, a quartic in x, such that $y = f(x)$ passes through O and has points of inflexion at (1, 7) and (– 1, – 17).

12. Find the equations of the tangents at the points of inflexion on $4y = x^4 + 4x^3 - 4x$.

13. Using the figure of 6·3, show by the Second Mean Value theorem that if $y = f(x)$ is the curve,

$$\begin{aligned} TQ &= \tfrac{1}{2}h^2 f''(a + \theta h) \\ &\simeq \tfrac{1}{2}h^2 f''(a) \end{aligned}$$

if $f''(x)$ is continuous at $x = a$ and h is small. Deduce that:

(*a*) A curve $y = f(x)$ is concave up at $x = a$, *i.e.*, lies above the tangent there in the neighbourhood of $[a, f(a)]$ if $f''(a)$ is positive; concave down if $f''(a)$ is negative.

(*b*) $f''(a) = 0$ and $f''(x)$ changes sign as we pass through $x = a$ if this is a point of inflexion so that the curve crosses its tangent at such a point.

14. By the process shown in Exercise 9, Nos. 7, 8, we can obtain the general Mean Value theorem

$$f(a + h) - f(a) = hf'(a) + \frac{h^2}{2!}f''(a) + \ldots + \frac{h^n}{n!}f^{(n)}(a + \theta h).$$

Deduce that if $f'(a)$ is zero and $f^{(n)}(x)$ is continuous at $x = a$ and is the first of the derivatives which does not vanish at $x = a$ then:

(*a*) If n is odd there is no turning point at $x = a$.

(*b*) If n is even there is a maximum there if $f^{(n)}(a) < 0$ and a minimum if $f^{(n)}(a) > 0$.

(*c*) If $n > 2$, $x = a$ is a point of inflexion if, and only if, n is odd.

15. Show that the stationary point $x = 0$ for:

(*a*) $\cos x - 1$ is a max. (*b*) $\cos x - 1 + x^2/2!$ is a min.;
(*c*) $\cos x - 1 + x^2/2! - x^4/4!$ is a max.;
(*d*) $\sin x - x + x^3/3!$ is a point of inflexion;
(*e*) $\sin x - x + x^3/3! - x^5/5!$ is a point of inflexion.

CHAPTER 18

INTEGRATION

18.1. The Form $\int x^n dx$

We know that

$$\int x^n dx = \frac{x^{n+1}}{n+1} + \text{const.} \qquad (n \neq -1).$$

A number of other integrals can be reduced to this form.

Example 1. To find $I = \int \frac{dx}{(3x+2)^4}$.

Put
$$z = 3x + 2,$$
$$\therefore \quad dz = 3dx,$$
$$\therefore \quad I = \int \frac{1}{z^4} \cdot \frac{dz}{3} = \frac{1}{3}\left(-\frac{1}{3} \cdot \frac{1}{z^3}\right) + \text{const.}$$
$$= -\frac{1}{9} \frac{1}{(3x+2)^3} + C.$$

(*a*) Note that having decided on a substitution we *must also substitute for dx in terms of the new variable.* When there are limits of integration these must also be changed over to their value in the new variable, *i.e.*, the new unit of measurement.

(*b*) The student should be able to do the above by inspection knowing that $\frac{1}{(3x+2)^4}$ will integrate to $\frac{1}{(3x+2)^3}$ multiplied by some constant to be found. This constant can be found by inspection or else as follows:

$$\frac{d}{dx}\left\{\frac{1}{(3x+2)^3}\right\} = -3 \cdot \frac{1}{(3x+2)^4} \cdot 3.$$

We must therefore put $-\frac{1}{9}$ in front of $\frac{1}{(3x+2)^3}$ to cancel the -9 obtained in the differentiation.

18.2. Integration by Inspection

Certain types of functions can be integrated by noticing that apart from numerical multipliers the integrand is evidently the differential coefficient of some part of it raised to a higher power.

Thus to find

$$I = \int \frac{7xdx}{\sqrt{8x^2 + 4}}$$

it is evident that if we differentiate $\sqrt{8x^2 + 4}$, we obtain

$$\frac{8x}{\sqrt{8x^2 + 4}}.$$

The integral is therefore

$$\tfrac{7}{8} \cdot \sqrt{8x^2 + 4},$$

7 as required by the integrand and 8 to cancel the 8 obtained in the differentiation.

A student who prefers another method should try

$$z = \sqrt{8x^2 + 4},$$

$$dz = \frac{8xdx}{\sqrt{8x^2 + 4}},$$

$$\frac{xdx}{\sqrt{8x^2 + 4}} = \tfrac{1}{8}dz.$$

$$\therefore \quad \mathrm{I} = \int \tfrac{7}{8}dz = \tfrac{7}{8}z + \mathrm{C}$$

$$= \tfrac{7}{8}\sqrt{8x^2 + 4} + \mathrm{C}.$$

Some integrals need a substitution method.

$$\mathrm{I} = \int x(3 - 2x)^4 dx.$$

[If the bracket contained $3 - 2x^2$ this integral could be done by inspection.]

Here we put $z = 3 - 2x$ and $x = \tfrac{1}{2}(3 - z)$,

$$dz = -2dx.$$

$$\therefore \quad \mathrm{I} = \int \tfrac{1}{2}(3 - z) \,.\, z^4 \,.\, \frac{dz}{-2}$$

$$= -\tfrac{1}{4}\int (3z^4 - z^5)dz$$

$$= -\tfrac{1}{4}\left(\tfrac{3}{5}z^5 - \frac{z^6}{6}\right) + \mathrm{C}$$

$$= -\tfrac{3}{20}(3 - 2x)^5 + \tfrac{1}{24}(3 - 2x)^6 + \mathrm{C}.$$

Example 2. To find $\mathrm{I} = \int \sin x \cos^3 x dx$.

It should be evident that

$$\frac{d}{dx}(\cos^4 x) = -4\cos^3 x \sin x,$$

$$\therefore \quad \mathrm{I} = -\frac{\cos^4 x}{4} + \mathrm{C}.$$

EXERCISE 38

Integrate the following. Each function should be written down with its integral sign and the differential dx before being integrated.

1. $1 + x + x^2$. 2. $(2 + x)(3 - x^2)$. 3. $(1 - x)^4$.

4. $2 - x^{-2} + x^{-3}$. 5. $\frac{(x^2 + x + 1)}{x^4}$. 6. $\frac{x^{\frac{3}{2}} - x^{\frac{5}{2}} + 1}{x^{\frac{1}{4}}}$.

7. $\left(x - \frac{1}{x}\right)^2$. 8. $\frac{(x + 1)^2}{x^4}$. 9. $16(3x + 2)^4$.

10. $\frac{1}{(2x - 1)^4}$. 11. $\sqrt{(1 - 4x)}$. 12. $\frac{1}{\sqrt{(5 - 3x)}}$.

13. $\frac{1}{(ax + b)^4}$. 14. $x(x^2 + 1)^3$. 15. $x\sqrt{(5 - 4x^2)}$.

16. $x^2\sqrt{(9 - 4x^3)}$. 17. $x(x - 4)^3$. 18. $\frac{x}{(2x + 1)^3}$.

19. $\frac{x}{\sqrt{5 - x}}$. 20. $x(a + bx)^{10}$. 21. $x\sqrt{(4x + 3)}$.

22. $\sec^2 4x$. 23. $\operatorname{cosec}^2 6x$. 24. $\sec^2 x - 1$.

25. $\tan^2 x$. 26. $\frac{\sin x}{\cos^2 x}$. 27. $\frac{\cos x}{\sin^2 x}$.

28. $\frac{\sin x}{\cos^6 x}$. 29. $\tan 3x \sec 3x$. 30. $\cos x \operatorname{cosec}^6 x$.

31. $(\sin x + \cos x)^2$. 32. $\tan^3 x \sec^2 x$. 33. $\cos x \sqrt{\sin x}$.

18.3. The Substitution of Circular Functions

A number of integrals contain expressions which simplify or lose their square roots when an obvious substitution is made of a circular function.

Example 3. Find $I = \int \sqrt{(a^2 - x^2)}dx$.

If we put $x = a \sin \theta$ the square root becomes

$$\sqrt{(a^2 - a^2 \sin^2 \theta)} = a \cos \theta.$$

Also
$$dx = a \cos \theta d\theta,$$

$$\therefore \quad I = \int a \cos \theta \,.\, a \cos \theta d\theta$$

$$= a^2 \int \cos^2 \theta d\theta = \frac{a^2}{2}\int (1 + \cos 2\theta)d\theta$$

$$= \frac{a^2}{2}\left(\theta + \frac{\sin 2\theta}{2}\right) + C$$

$$= \frac{a^2}{2}(\theta + \sin \theta \cos \theta) + C.$$

Since
$$x = a \sin \theta,$$

$$\theta = \sin^{-1}\left(\frac{x}{a}\right),$$

$$\cos \theta = \frac{1}{a}\sqrt{a^2 - x^2};$$

$$\therefore \quad I = \frac{a^2}{2}\left(\sin^{-1}\frac{x}{a} + \frac{x}{a} \cdot \frac{\sqrt{a^2 - x^2}}{a}\right) + C.$$

Example 4. Find $I = \int \frac{dx}{\sqrt{9 - 4x^2}}$.

This can be written as

$$I = \tfrac{1}{2}\int \frac{dx}{\sqrt{(\frac{3}{2})^2 - x^2}}.$$

But since

$$\frac{d}{dx}\left[\sin^{-1}\left(\frac{x}{a}\right)\right] = \frac{1}{\sqrt{a^2 - x^2}}, \qquad \text{(see 7.2)}$$

$$\therefore \quad \int \frac{dx}{\sqrt{a^2 - x^2}} = \sin^{-1}\left(\frac{x}{a}\right) + C.$$

(This is a " standard " form given in the table of integrals.)

$$\therefore \quad I = \tfrac{1}{2}\sin^{-1}\left(\frac{x}{\frac{3}{2}}\right) + C$$

$$= \tfrac{1}{2}\sin^{-1}\left(\frac{2x}{3}\right) + C.$$

The student should also use the substitution $x = \frac{3}{2}\sin\theta$.

EXERCISE 39

1. Find the integral by the substitution as given:

$$\int \frac{dx}{a^2 + x^2}; \quad x = a\tan\theta.$$

2. *Write down* the following integrals using the table of standard forms:

(a) $\int \frac{dx}{\sqrt{4 - x^2}}$; (b) $\int \frac{dx}{16 + x^2}$; (c) $\int \frac{dx}{16 + 9x^2}$; (d) $\int \frac{dx}{\sqrt{4 - 9x^2}}$;

(e) $\int \frac{dx}{3 + 7x^2}$; (f) $\int \frac{dx}{\sqrt{a^2 - b^2x^2}}$; (g) $\int \frac{dx}{\sqrt{2 - 3x^2}}$.

3. Find $\int \sqrt{\left(\frac{x}{1 - x}\right)}\,dx$ by $x = \sin^2\theta$.

4. Find $\int \frac{dx}{(1 + x^2)^{\frac{3}{2}}}$ by $x = \tan\theta$.

5. Find $\int \sqrt{\left(\frac{a + x}{a - x}\right)}\,dx$ by $x = a\cos 2\theta$.

6. Find $\int \frac{dx}{x\sqrt{x^2 - 1}}$ by $x = \sec\theta$.

18.4. Integrals giving Logarithms

(a) We have $\frac{d}{dx}(\log_e x) = \frac{1}{x}$, (see 5.7)

$$\therefore \quad \int \frac{dx}{x} = \log_e x + C.$$

Given $\log x$, it is understood that x is positive. In integration it may be necessary to emphasize this. Thus, if x is negative in the above integral, put $x = -y$ so that y is positive. We now have

$$I = \int \frac{dx}{x} = \int \frac{d(-y)}{-y} = \int \frac{dy}{y} = \log y$$
$$= \log(-x).$$

We then have

$$I = \log x \qquad x \text{ positive}$$
$$= \log(-x) \qquad x \text{ negative}$$

therefore $\qquad I = \log |x|$ always.

The modulus sign may be omitted in theoretical questions, but must be used in numerical problems. (See example after 18.6.)

In practice we often get the form

$$I = \int \frac{dx}{ax + b}.$$

Put $z = ax + b$, $dz = adx$,

$$\therefore \quad I = \int \frac{1}{z} \cdot \frac{dz}{a} = \frac{1}{a} \log z + C = \frac{1}{a} \log(ax + b) + C.$$

The student should know this "form" and integrate at sight, adjusting with the constant as required. Thus for

$$\int \frac{dx}{3 - 2x}$$

he should put down

$$\log(3 - 2x),$$

and then differentiating mentally he will get

$$\frac{1}{3 - 2x} \times -2.$$

He will then realize that the logarithm requires $-\frac{1}{2}$ in front to cancel the -2 obtained above. The required integral is therefore

$$-\tfrac{1}{2} \log(3 - 2x) + C.$$

(*b*) If $\qquad y = \log f(x),$

$$\frac{dy}{dx} = \frac{1}{f(x)} \times f'(x);$$

$$\therefore \quad \int \frac{f'(x)}{f(x)} dx = \log_e f(x) + C.$$

This result gives us the following important rule: if in the integrand the numerator is the differential coefficient of the denominator or can be made so with constants, then the integral will be of the form log (denominator).

Example 5. Find $\displaystyle\int \frac{(2 - 3x)dx}{3 + 4x - 3x^2}.$

This can be written
$$\tfrac{1}{2} \int \frac{4 - 6x}{3 + 4x - 3x^2} dx$$
$$= \tfrac{1}{2} \log(3 + 4x - 3x^2) + C.$$

The student should notice such a case as

$$\int \tan 2x dx = \int \frac{\sin 2x}{\cos 2x} dx$$
$$= -\tfrac{1}{2}\int \frac{-2\sin 2x}{\cos 2x} dx$$
$$= -\tfrac{1}{2}\log\cos 2x + C.$$

18.5. Integrals Involving e^x

If
$$y = e^{ax},$$
$$\frac{dy}{dx} = e^{ax} . a.$$
$$\therefore \quad \int e^{ax} dx = \frac{1}{a} e^{ax} + C.$$

Example 6.
$$\int e^{4x} dx = \tfrac{1}{4} e^{4x} + C.$$
$$\int \frac{e^x}{e^x + 1} dx = \log(e^x + 1) + C.$$
$$\int e^{\sin x} \cos x \, dx = e^{\sin x} + C.$$

EXERCISE 40

Integrate:

1. $\frac{1}{4x}$.
2. $\frac{1}{1 + x}$.
3. $\frac{1}{3 - 2x}$.
4. $\frac{x}{1 - x^2}$.
5. $\frac{x^2}{1 + 2x^3}$.
6. $\frac{6x + 4}{3x^2 + 4x + 7}$.
7. $4 \cot 2x$.
8. $3 \tan 5x$.
9. $\frac{\sec^2 x}{\tan x}$.
10. $\frac{\log x}{x}$.
11. $2e^{4x}$.
12. $7e^{-2x}$.
13. $\sqrt{e^x}$.
14. xe^{x^2}.
15. $e^{x \log 3}$.
16. $e^{3 \log x}$.

18.6. Partial Fractions

Certain types of functions are easily integrable when they have been put into partial fractions.

Example 7. Integrate $\frac{(x - 1)(x + 2)}{x(x + 1)}$.

This expression is
$$1 - \frac{2}{x(x + 1)}$$
$$= 1 - \frac{2}{x} + \frac{2}{x + 1} \quad \text{(see 4.2)}$$

$\therefore$ the integral is $\quad x - 2\log x + 2\log(x + 1) + C.$

Example 8. Integrate $\frac{1}{(x+1)^2(x^2+4)}$.

If
$$\frac{1}{(x+1)^2(x^2+4)} = \frac{A}{x+1} + \frac{B}{(x+1)^2} + \frac{Cx+D}{x^2+4}$$
$$= \frac{A}{x+1} + \frac{1}{5}\frac{1}{(x+1)^2} + \frac{Cx+D}{x^2+4},$$
then
$$1 = A(x+1)(x^2+4) + \frac{1}{5}(x^2+4) + (Cx+D)(x+1)^2.$$

Equate coefficients of:

x^3. $\quad 0 = A + C.$

x^2. $\quad 0 = A + \frac{1}{5} + 2C + D.$

x. $\quad 0 = 4A + C + 2D.$

$\therefore \quad A = \frac{2}{25}, \; D = -\frac{3}{25}, \; C = -\frac{2}{25}.$

$\therefore$ expression $= \frac{2}{25}\frac{1}{x+1} + \frac{1}{5}\frac{1}{(x+1)^2} - \frac{1}{25}\frac{2x+3}{x^2+4}.$

The integral is
$$\tfrac{2}{25}\int\frac{dx}{x+1} + \tfrac{1}{5}\int\frac{dx}{(x+1)^2} - \tfrac{1}{25}\int\frac{2x}{x^2+4} - \tfrac{3}{25}\int\frac{dx}{x^2+4}$$
$$= \tfrac{2}{25}\log(x+1) - \tfrac{1}{5}\frac{1}{(x+1)} - \tfrac{1}{25}\log(x^2+4) - \tfrac{3}{25}\cdot\tfrac{1}{2}\tan^{-1}\left(\frac{x}{2}\right) + C.$$

The student should note the following standard form:

since
$$\frac{1}{x^2-a^2} = \frac{1}{2a}\left(\frac{1}{x-a} - \frac{1}{x+a}\right),$$
$$\therefore \quad \int\frac{dx}{x^2-a^2} = \frac{1}{2a}(\log(x-a) - \log(x+a))$$
$$= \frac{1}{2a}\log\left(\frac{x-a}{x+a}\right) + C.$$

In this form the limits of integration will usually be such that x^2 is bigger than a^2 throughout the range of integration.

We also have
$$\frac{1}{a^2-x^2} = \frac{1}{2a}\left(\frac{1}{a-x} + \frac{1}{a+x}\right),$$
$$\therefore \quad \int\frac{dx}{a^2-x^2} = \frac{1}{2a}\log\left(\frac{a+x}{a-x}\right) + C.$$

In this form a^2 is usually bigger than x^2 throughout the range of integration. Thus in each case we will obtain the logarithm of a positive quantity. If not, in each case the modulus of the number must be taken as shown below.

As an example the curve $y = \frac{1}{(x^2-9)}$ is below the x axis for values of x between -3 and $+3$, and therefore the integral
$$\int_{-2}^{+1}\frac{dx}{x^2-9}$$
will be negative. By the formula its value is
$$\frac{1}{2\times 3}[\log|-\tfrac{1}{2}| - \log|-5|] = -\frac{1}{6}\log 10.$$

We could have taken the integral as

$$-\int_{-2}^{+1} \frac{dx}{9 - x^2} = -\frac{1}{6}\left[\log \frac{3+x}{3-x}\right]_{-2}^{+1} = -\frac{1}{6}\log 10$$

and so avoided the logarithms of negative numbers.

EXERCISE 41

Integrate the following:

1. $\dfrac{2x-1}{2x+3}$.
2. $\dfrac{x+1}{x^2-3x+2}$.
3. $\dfrac{1}{9-x^2}$.
4. $\dfrac{1}{x^2-4x+3}$.
5.* $\dfrac{x}{x^4-a^4}$.
6. $\dfrac{3x+1}{x(x^2-1)}$.
7. $\dfrac{1}{x(x+1)(x+2)}$.
8. $\dfrac{1+4x^2}{x(2x-1)^2}$.
9. $\dfrac{x^2}{(x-1)^2(x+1)}$.
10. $\dfrac{3x+2}{x(x^2+4)(x-1)}$.
11. $\dfrac{1}{x-3}$ with limits: (*a*) -2 to $+2$; (*b*) 4 to 8.
12. $\dfrac{1}{x^2-16}$ with limits: (*a*) -8 to -6; (*b*) -3 to $+3$; (*c*) 6 to 8.
13. $\dfrac{1}{16-x^2}$ with limits: (*a*) -8 to -6; (*b*) -3 to $+3$; (*c*) 6 to 8.

18.7. Trigonometrical Functions

A useful substitution is $t = \tan \dfrac{x}{2}$,

$$\therefore \quad \frac{dt}{dx} = \tfrac{1}{2}\sec^2\frac{x}{2} = \tfrac{1}{2}\left(1 + \tan^2\frac{x}{2}\right) = \tfrac{1}{2}(1+t^2),$$

$$\therefore \quad dx = \frac{2dt}{1+t^2}.$$

In using this substitution one also needs

$$\sin x = \frac{2\sin\frac{x}{2}\cos\frac{x}{2}}{\sin^2\frac{x}{2} + \cos^2\frac{x}{2}} \quad \left(\text{since } \sin^2\frac{x}{2} + \cos^2\frac{x}{2} = 1\right)$$

$$= \frac{2t}{t^2+1}$$

on dividing above and below by $\cos^2\left(\dfrac{x}{2}\right)$.

Similarly,

$$\cos x = \frac{\cos^2\frac{x}{2} - \sin^2\frac{x}{2}}{\cos^2\frac{x}{2} + \sin^2\frac{x}{2}} = \frac{1-t^2}{1+t^2}.$$

Thus to find $\int \frac{dx}{\sin x}$,

with the above substitution this becomes

$$\int \frac{t^2+1}{2t} \cdot \frac{2dt}{1+t^2} = \int \frac{dt}{t} = \log t = \log \left(\tan \frac{x}{2}\right) + \text{C}.$$

Also

$$\int \frac{dx}{\cos x} = \int \frac{1+t^2}{1-t^2} \cdot \frac{2dt}{1+t^2} = \int \frac{2}{1-t^2} dt = \int \left(\frac{1}{1-t} + \frac{1}{1+t}\right) dt$$

$$= \log \left(\frac{1+t}{1-t}\right) = \log \frac{1 + \tan \frac{x}{2}}{1 - \tan \frac{x}{2}} + \text{C}.$$

Since $1 = \tan \frac{\pi}{4}$, the above can be written

$$\log \left(\frac{\tan \left(\frac{\pi}{4}\right) + \tan \left(\frac{x}{2}\right)}{1 - \tan \left(\frac{\pi}{4}\right) \cdot \tan \left(\frac{x}{2}\right)} \right) + \text{C}$$

$$= \log \tan \left(\frac{\pi}{4} + \frac{x}{2}\right) + \text{C}.$$

The student should convert this to another form

$$\log (\sec x + \tan x) + \text{C}.$$

Example 9. To find $\int \frac{dx}{5 + 4 \cos x}$.

Put $t = \tan \frac{x}{2}$, $\therefore\ dx = \frac{2dt}{1+t^2}$.

$$5 + 4 \cos x = 5 + 4\frac{1-t^2}{1+t^2} = \frac{9+t^2}{1+t^2},$$

$$\therefore\ \text{I} = \int \frac{2dt}{1+t^2} \cdot \frac{1+t^2}{9+t^2} = 2\int \frac{dt}{9+t^2}$$

$$= 2 \cdot \tfrac{1}{3} \tan^{-1} \left(\frac{t}{3}\right)$$

$$= \tfrac{2}{3} \tan^{-1} \left(\tfrac{1}{3} \tan \frac{x}{2}\right) + \text{C}.$$

EXERCISE 42*

Integrate the following:

1. $\dfrac{1}{1 + \cos x}$.
2. $\dfrac{1}{1 + \sin x}$.
3. $\dfrac{1}{4 + 5 \cos x}$.
4. $\dfrac{1}{13 + 5 \sin x}$.
5. $\cos 2x \sec x$.
6. $\operatorname{cosec} x \sec x$.

18.8. The Form $\int \cos^m x \sin^n x dx$

(*a*) This important type of integral can be found easily when m or n is odd.

Example 10. To find $I = \int \sin^2 x \cos^5 x dx$.

Put $\sin x = s$ so that $\cos x dx = ds$,

$$\therefore \quad I = \int s^2 . \cos^4 x . ds$$
$$= \int s^2(1 - s^2)^2 ds.$$

Note that the effect of putting $\sin x = s$ (and not $\cos x = c$) is to reduce the *odd* power $\cos^5 x$ to an even power which can be changed easily into powers of $\sin x = s$.

$$I = \int (s^2 - 2s^4 + s^6)ds$$
$$= \frac{s^3}{3} - 2\frac{s^5}{5} + \frac{s^7}{7} + C$$
$$= \tfrac{1}{3}\sin^3 x - \tfrac{2}{5}\sin^5 x + \tfrac{1}{7}\sin^7 x + C.$$

(*b*) When m and n are both even and *small*, the integral is still easily found.

Example 11. To find $I = \int \sin^2 x \cos^4 x dx$.

$$\sin^2 x \cos^4 x = \left(\frac{1 - \cos 2x}{2}\right)\left(\frac{1 + \cos 2x}{2}\right)^2$$
$$= \tfrac{1}{8}(1 + \cos 2x - \cos^2 2x - \cos^3 2x).$$
$$\cos^2 2x = \tfrac{1}{2}(1 + \cos 4x)$$
$$\cos^3 2x = (1 - \sin^2 2x)\cos 2x.$$

$$\therefore \quad I = \tfrac{1}{8}\int (1 + \cos 2x)dx - \tfrac{1}{16}\int (1 + \cos 4x)dx - \tfrac{1}{8}\int (1 - \sin^2 2x)\cos 2x dx$$
$$= \tfrac{1}{8}\left(x + \frac{\sin 2x}{2}\right) - \tfrac{1}{16}\left(x + \frac{\sin 4x}{4}\right) - \tfrac{1}{8}\left(\frac{\sin 2x}{2} - \frac{\sin^3 2x}{6}\right) + C.$$

EXERCISE 43

Integrate:

1. $\sin^2 x \cos^3 x$.
2. $\sin^3 2x \cos 2x$.
3. $\sin^3 x$.
4. $\sin^2 2x$.
5. $\cos^3 3x$.
6. $7\sin^3\left(\frac{x}{2}\right)$.
7. $\tan^2\left(\frac{2x}{3}\right)$.
8. $\cos^5 x \sin x$.
9. $\sin^7 x \sec^8 x$.
10. $\cos^3 x \operatorname{cosec}^4 x$.
11. $\tan^3 2x \sec^3 2x$.
12. $\sin^2 2x \cos^3 2x$.
13. $\sin x \cos 2x$.

18.9. Integration by Parts

If u and v are both functions of x

$$u\frac{dv}{dx} + v\frac{du}{dx} = \frac{d}{dx}(uv).$$

Integrate this equation back again [noting that the sign of integration is $\int (\quad)dx$],

$$\therefore \quad \int u\frac{dv}{dx}dx + \int v\frac{du}{dx}dx = uv,$$

which can be written

$$\int \underset{(1)(2)}{u\frac{dv}{dx}}dx = \underset{(1)(2)}{uv} - \int \underset{(1)}{\frac{du}{dx}}\,\underset{(2)}{v}dx.$$

We note that $\frac{dv}{dx}$ on the L.H.S. becomes v on the R.H.S., and is therefore integrated, whilst u on the L.H.S. is differentiated in the integrand on the R.H.S. The formula may be stated in words, and should be known: Integral of 1st times 2nd equals 1st times integral of 2nd minus integral of d.c. of 1st times integral of 2nd.

Example 12.

$$\int \underset{(1)}{x}\,\underset{(2)}{\sin x}dx = x(-\cos x) - \int 1(-\cos x)dx$$
$$= -x\cos x + \int \cos x dx$$
$$= \underline{-x\cos x + \sin x + C.}$$

In integrating $\frac{dv}{dx}$ to v, we always omit the constant of integration, inserting one at the the very end. If we do insert a constant of integration we find

$$x(-\cos x + D) - \int 1(-\cos x + D)dx$$
$$= -x\cos x + Dx + \sin x - Dx + C$$
$$= -x\cos x + \sin x + C,$$

showing that D was unnecessary as it cancels.

If we take the integral as

$$\int \underset{(1)}{\sin x}\,.\,\underset{(2)}{x}dx = \sin x \cdot \frac{x^2}{2} - \int \cos x\frac{x^2}{2}dx,$$

we find that the second integral is more complicated than the original. In using integration by parts, the choice of the " first " and " second " is always fairly obvious. We choose as " first " the function that will become easier to deal with when differentiated or as " second " the function that can be integrated easily.

Example 13. $\int x^2e^xdx = x^2e^x - \int 2xe^xdx.$

Here we must integrate by parts again.

$$\int xe^xdx = xe^x - \int 1\,.\,e^xdx$$
$$= xe^x - e^x,$$
$$\therefore \quad \underline{\int x^2e^xdx = x^2e^x - 2xe^x + 2e^x + C.}$$

Example 14. To find $\int e^{ax}\cos bxdx$.

$$\int e^{ax}\cos bxdx = e^{ax}\frac{\sin bx}{b} - \int ae^{ax}\,.\,\frac{\sin bx}{b}dx.$$

We do not seem to be any nearer a solution, but if we integrate by parts again and call the required integral C

$$C = \frac{1}{b}e^{ax}\sin bx - \frac{a}{b}\left[e^{ax}\cdot\frac{-\cos bx}{b} - \int ae^{ax}\cdot\frac{-\cos bx}{b}dx\right]$$

$$= \frac{1}{b}e^{ax}\sin bx + \frac{a}{b^2}e^{ax}\cos bx - \frac{a^2}{b^2}C.$$

$$\therefore\quad C\left(1 + \frac{a^2}{b^2}\right) = \frac{e^{ax}}{b^2}(b\sin bx + a\cos bx),$$

$$C = \frac{e^{ax}}{a^2 + b^2}(b\sin bx + a\cos bx) + D.$$

The student should, in the same way, find

$$\int e^{ax}\sin bx dx = \frac{e^{ax}}{a^2 + b^2}(a\sin bx - b\cos bx) + D.$$

18.10. It will be noticed that each of the integrals found by this method is a product. Often a product has to be formed from the given integrand.

Example 15.

$$\int \log x dx = \int \log x \, . \, 1 dx$$

$$= \log x \, . \, x - \int \frac{1}{x}\cdot x dx$$

$$= x\log x - x + C.$$

Example 16.

$$\int \sin^n\theta d\theta = \int \sin^{n-1}\theta \, . \, \sin\theta d\theta$$

$$= \sin^{n-1}\theta \, . \, (-\cos\theta) - \int (n-1)\sin^{n-2}\theta\cos\theta \, . \, (-\cos\theta)d\theta.$$

$$= -\sin^{n-1}\theta\cos\theta + (n-1)\int \sin^{n-2}\theta(1 - \sin^2\theta)d\theta$$

$$= -\sin^{n-1}\theta\cos\theta + (n-1)\int \sin^{n-2}\theta d\theta - (n-1)\int \sin^n\theta d\theta.$$

If we denote the given integral by I_n so that

$$I_{n-2} \equiv \int \sin^{n-2}\theta d\theta$$

the above equation becomes

$$I_n = -\sin^{n-1}\theta\cos\theta + (n-1)I_{n-2} - (n-1)I_n.$$

$$\therefore\quad I_n = -\frac{\sin^{n-1}\theta\cos\theta}{n} + \frac{n-1}{n}I_{n-2}.$$

We have therefore connected the integral of $\sin^n\theta$ with one in which the index is two less. Such a formula is called a *reduction formula*, and in the next volume we will use these formulae to obtain some important results.

EXERCISE 44

Integrate the following:

1. $x^2\log x$.
2. $x\cos 2x$.
3. $\sin^{-1} x$.
4. $x\tan^{-1} x$.
5. $\tan^{-1} x$.
6. $x^2\sin 2x$.

7. xe^{2x}.　　8. $\dfrac{\sin 3x}{e^x}$.　　9. $x \sec^2 x$.

10. Obtain the formula

$$\int \cos^n \theta d\theta = \frac{\cos^{n-1}\theta \sin\theta}{n} + \frac{n-1}{n}\int \cos^{n-2}\theta d\theta.$$

11. Integrate $C \equiv \int e^{ax} \cos bxdx$ and $S \equiv \int e^{ax} \sin bxdx$ by parts once. Find C and S by solving the simultaneous equations thus obtained.

12. Assume that

$$\int e^{ax} \cos (bx)dx = e^{ax} [L \cos bx + M \sin bx]$$

Differentiate this equation, and hence find the unknown L and M.

13. Prove that the area bounded by the curve $y = x \sin (x/a)$ and the x axis between the ordinates at $x = 0$ and $x = \pi a$ is πa^2. Show also that the co-ordinates of the centroid of this area are

$$\left[a(\pi - 4\pi), \frac{a}{24}(2\pi^2 - 3)\right].$$

CHAPTER 19

DEFINITE INTEGRALS

19.1. Geometric Interpretation

Suppose that $y = f(x)$ is a finite single-valued and continuous curve in the interval (a, b). Divide this interval up into a large number n of sub intervals of lengths $\delta_1, \delta_2, \ldots \delta_s, \ldots \delta_n$ by the sequence of points $a, x_1, x_2, \ldots x_s, \ldots x_{n-1}, b$ so that

$$\begin{aligned}
\delta_1 &= x_1 - a \\
\delta_2 &= x_2 - x_1 \\
&\vdots \\
\delta_s &= x_s - x_{s-1} \\
&\vdots \\
\delta_n &= b - x_{n-1}.
\end{aligned}$$

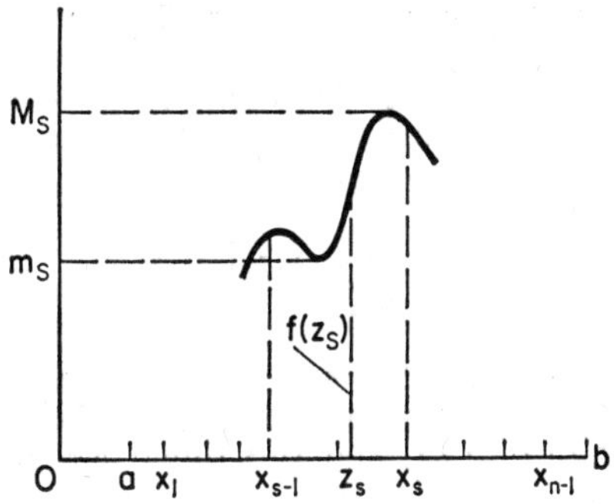

FIG. 59.

If z_s is any point in the interval δ_s and $f(z_s)$ the ordinate at this point, form the sum

$$\sum_1^n f(z_s)\, \delta_s,$$

where each of the n intervals provides a term. If the limit of this exists as $n \to \infty$ and the length of each interval tends to zero it is called the definite integral of $f(x)$ between the (lower) limit a and the (upper) limit b. This integral is written as

$$\int_a^b f(x)\,dx$$

The interpretation of this limit as an area enclosed by the curve, the ordinates at a and b and the x axis is evident, and it can be shown that it is evaluated as

$$\phi(b) - \phi(a),$$

where
$$f(x) = \phi'(x).$$

19.2. The Riemann Integral

To deal with more general functions than the simple one used above we will use an analytic method which need not be based on diagrams. Suppose that the function $f(x)$ is bounded in (a, b) so that it is also bounded in each of the sub-intervals δ_s. If in this sub-interval the bounds are m_s and M_s then

$$m \leqslant m_s \leqslant M_s \leqslant M$$

where m, M are respectively the lower and upper bounds for the *whole* interval. Form the two sums

$$s_n = \sum_1^n m_s\,\delta_s \qquad\qquad S_n = \sum_1^n M_s\,\delta_s.$$

If, as $n \to \infty$ and each length δ_s tends to zero, these two sums tend to the same limit, this common limit is called the integral of $f(x)$ between the limits a and b and *by definition* written as

$$\int_a^b f(x)\,dx,$$

which, so far, only means lim. s_n or lim. S_n. It is clear that for a continuous function there is little difference in the interval δ_s between m_s, M_s and the $f(z_s)$ of 19.1, and this difference vanishes as $\delta_s \to 0$. But now we can also cope with the case of $f(x)$ being discontinuous at any point in the interval (a, b) provided only that the " jump " in value is finite. If such a jump occurs in an interval δ_s, s_n will contain a single term $m_s\delta_s$ and S_n the term $M_s\delta_s$. As $\delta_s \to 0$, the effect of these terms on their respective sums is zero. Provided, then, that $f(x)$ has only a finite number of such points of discontinuity in (a, b), it can still be integrable in the Riemann sense.

It is sufficient for our purpose to state that this Riemann " limit sum " integral can be shown to exist provided $f(x)$ is bounded and has no more than a finite number of simple discontinuities in the interval of integration. A function continuous in an interval is bounded therein, has no discontinuities in the interval and is therefore integrable over it. If $f(x)$ is continuous except at one interior point $x = c$ where there is a simple jump, then $f(x)$ is still integrable over (a, b) and

$$\int_a^b f(x)dx = \int_a^c f(x)dx + \int_c^b f(x)dx.$$

Similarly if there is more than one such point.

Example 1. Evaluate $$\int_1^2 \frac{dx}{x^2}.$$

Any method of subdivision of the interval will do, provided each $\delta_s \to 0$ as $n \to \infty$. We will divide the interval into n parts in geometric progression, since in this case the summation is simplified.

(*a*) Suppose the points of division are

$$1, r, r^2 \ldots r^{n-1}, r^n \text{ where } r^n = 2.$$

(*b*) Since $y = 1/x^2$ is steadily decreasing as x increases 1 to 2, in each interval δ_s the upper bound is the left-hand ordinate and the lower bound is the right-hand ordinate. Hence

$$\Sigma M_s\delta_s = 1(r-1) + \frac{1}{r^2}(r^2 - r) + \frac{1}{r^4}(r^3 - r^2) + \ldots \frac{1}{r^{2n-2}}(r^n - r^{n-1})$$

$$= (r-1)\left[1 + \frac{1}{r} + \frac{1}{r^2} + \ldots + \frac{1}{r^{n-1}}\right]$$

$$= (r-1)\left(1 - \frac{1}{r^n}\right)\Big/\left(1 - \frac{1}{r}\right)$$

$$= r\left(1 - \frac{1}{r^n}\right) = r/2.$$

As $n \to \infty$, $r \to 1$, since

$$n \log r = \log 2 \text{ or } r = \exp[(\log 2)/n].$$

Hence $$\lim_{n\to\infty} M_s\delta_s = \tfrac{1}{2}.$$

Similarly,

$$\Sigma m_s\delta_s = \frac{1}{r^2}(r-1) + \frac{1}{r^4}(r^2 - r) + \ldots + \frac{1}{r^{2n}}(r^n - r^{n-1})$$

and the limit of this sum is also $\frac{1}{2}$. Hence the function is integrable and we have shown that

$$\int_1^2 \frac{dx}{x^2} = \frac{1}{2}.$$

19.3. Integration as the Inverse of Differentiation

We could build up the usual properties of definite integrals from the limit sums. Here we will be content with stating:

(1) We can prove that if $f(x)$ is continuous in (a, b) and $\mathrm{F}(x)$ is a function such that

$$\mathrm{F}'(x) = f(x) \qquad a \leqslant x \leqslant b$$

then

$$\int_a^x f(x)dx = \mathrm{F}(x) - \mathrm{F}(a) \quad \ldots\ldots \quad (1)$$

so that Riemann integrals are also found by reversing the process of differentiation and we have the usual formula for an indefinite integral

$$\int F'(x)dx = F(x) + C.$$

If in (1) $x \to b$ we have the fundamental formula

$$\int_a^b f(x)dx = F(b) - F(a) \quad . \quad . \quad . \quad . \quad . \quad . \qquad (2)$$

for a definite integral. Strictly it is

$$F(b - 0) - F(a + 0)$$

which is (2) if $F(x)$ is continuous at a and b.

(2) If, however, we are only given that $f(x)$ is *integrable* in (a, b) and write

$$\phi(x) = \int_a^x f(t)dt \qquad (a \leqslant x \leqslant b)$$

we can show that $\phi(x)$ is a continuous function such that

$$\phi'(x) = f(x)$$

for any value of x for which $f(x)$ is continuous.

(3) In most cases we can divide the range of integration up into sections in which $f(x)$ is continuous in each *open* interval and so integrable. If $f(x)$ is not continuous at one of these end points a special investigation may be needed unless the point is a simple discontinuity involving only a finite jump.

Example 2. Given

$$\int_{-1}^{+1} \frac{dx}{x^2}$$

we note that $f(x) \to \infty$ as $x \to 0$. Hence we should investigate

$$\int_{-1}^{0} \frac{dx}{x^2} \quad \text{and} \quad \int_{0}^{+1} \frac{dx}{x^2}$$

The first is

$$\lim_{b \to -0} \int_{-1}^{b} \frac{dx}{x^2} = -\lim_{b \to -0} \left(1 + \frac{1}{b}\right)$$

and has no finite value or the integral is non-existent.
The second is

$$\lim_{a \to +0} \int_{a}^{1} \frac{dx}{x^2} = \lim_{a \to +0} \left(\frac{1}{a} - 1\right)$$

which is also non-existent. Hence the entire integral has no meaning or value, and it would be incorrect to evaluate it as

$$\int_{-1}^{+1} \frac{dx}{x^2} = \left.-\frac{1}{x}\right)_{-1}^{+1} = -2.$$

19.4. Properties of the Integral

From the definition it can be shown that when $f(x)$ is integrable

(1) If
$$m \leqslant f(x) \leqslant M$$
then
$$m(b-a) \leqslant \int_a^b f(x)dx \leqslant M(b-a).$$

(1*a*) It follows that if $f(x) \geqslant 0$ then
$$\int_a^b f(x)dx \geqslant 0$$

(1*b*) Similarly if $f(x) \geqslant g(x)$ in (a, b)
$$\int_a^b f(x)dx \geqslant \int_a^b g(x)dx.$$

Example 3. In the interval (0, 1), where x is positive and less than 1, it can be seen that
$$x^3 > \frac{x^3}{(1+x^4)} > \frac{x^3}{2}.$$
Integration between the limits (0, 1) by the usual methods gives the inequality
$$1 > \log 2 > \tfrac{1}{2}.$$
If we use
$$x^3 > \frac{x^3}{(1+x^2)} > \frac{x^3}{2}$$
the closer limits are obtained
$$\underline{\tfrac{3}{4} > \log 2 > \tfrac{1}{2}.}$$

(1*c*) If $f(x)$ is continuous then for some value of z in (a, b)
$$\int_a^b f(x)dx = (b-a)f(z).$$

(2) If $f(x)$ and $g(x)$ are integrable in (a, b), so is their product $f(x) \,.\, g(x)$.
(3) If further $g(x) \geqslant 0$, then using (1) again
$$m\int_a^b g(x)dx \leqslant \int_a^b f(x)g(x)dx \leqslant M\int_a^b g(x)dx.$$
It follows that if $f(x)$ is continuous
$$\int_a^b f(x)g(x)dx = f(z)\int_a^b g(x)dx$$
where z is some point in the interval (a, b).

(4) Using an obvious shorthand, if λ and μ are two constants
$$\int_a^b (\lambda f + \mu g)^2 = \lambda^2\int_a^b f^2 + 2\lambda\mu\int_a^b fg + \mu^2\int_a^b g^2$$

since $(\lambda f + \mu g)^2 \geqslant 0$ it follows by (1a) that the integral and hence the right-hand side is also $\geqslant 0$ for all values of λ and μ. Hence by the usual quadratic equation formula we obtain **Schwarz's** inequality

$$\left(\int_a^b fg\right)^2 \leqslant \left(\int_a^b f^2\right)\left(\int_a^b g^2\right).$$

Example 4. Find an approximation to

$$I = \int_0^{\pi/2} \sqrt{(\sin x)}dx.$$

If we take $f(x) = \sqrt{(\sin x)}$, $g(x) = 1$ in the above inequality we find

$$I^2 = \left(\int_0^{\pi/2} \sqrt{(\sin x)}dx\right)^2 < \int_0^{\pi/2} \sin x dx \int_0^{\pi/2} dx$$

or
$$I < \sqrt{(\pi/2)} = 1{\cdot}2533.$$

The line joining the origin (0, 0) to the point ($\pi/2$, 1) on the curve $y = \sin x$ has the equation $y = 2x/\pi$, and the diagram provides a visual demonstration of the inequality

$$\frac{2x}{\pi} \leqslant \sin x \qquad \left(0 \leqslant x \leqslant \frac{\pi}{2}\right)$$

From this
$$\sqrt{\left(\frac{2}{\pi}\right)}\,.\,x^{\frac{1}{2}} \leqslant \sqrt{(\sin x)}.$$

Integration between 0 and $\frac{\pi}{2}$ gives

$$1{\cdot}0472 < I.$$

Hence we have

$$\underline{1{\cdot}0472 < I < 1{\cdot}2533.}$$

(5) If $f(x)$ is bounded and integrable in (a, b), then $|f(x)|$ is also bounded and integrable in (a, b) and

$$\left|\int_a^b f(x)dx\right| \leqslant \int_a^b |f(x)|\,dx.$$

If $f(x)$ is of one sign throughout (a, b) the equality sign holds.

Example 5. The curve $y = x(2 - x)$ has an area of 4/3 above the x axis. At $x = 2$ it crosses the x axis and from $x = 2$ onwards y is negative. We find

$$\left|\int_0^4 x(2-x)dx\right| = \left|\left(x^2 - \frac{x^3}{3}\right)_0^4\right| = \left|-\frac{16}{3}\right| = \underline{\frac{16}{3}}.$$

Since
$$|f(x)| = f(x) \text{ when } f(x) \text{ is positive}$$
$$= -f(x) \text{ when } f(x) \text{ is negative}$$

$$\int_0^4 |x(2-x)|\,dx = \int_0^2 x(2-x)dx + \int_2^4 [-x(2-x)]dx$$
$$= \frac{4}{3} + \frac{20}{3} = \underline{8.}$$

The result of 16/3 is due to an " internal " cancellation of positive and negative values. The final results 8 and 16/3 verify theorem (5) above.

19.5. Finally, as a resumé of the points that often occur in practice.

(1) Every continuous function $f(x)$ has an indefinite integral. If for the definite integral we insert a constant of integration C, then

$$\begin{aligned}\int_a^b f(x)dx &= [\mathrm{F}(x) + \mathrm{C}]_a^b \\ &= [\mathrm{F}(b) + \mathrm{C}] - [\mathrm{F}(a) + \mathrm{C}] \\ &= \mathrm{F}(b) - \mathrm{F}(a).\end{aligned}$$

Since C cancels it is usual to omit it from the very beginning when evaluating a definite integral.

(2)
$$\begin{aligned}\int_b^a f(x)dx &= \mathrm{F}(a) - \mathrm{F}(b) \\ &= -[\mathrm{F}(b) - \mathrm{F}(a)] \\ &= -\int_a^b f(x)dx,\end{aligned}$$

showing that a minus sign before a definite integral can be used to interchange the limits.

(3) Also for any continuous $f(x)$

$$\begin{aligned}\int_a^b f(x)dx + \int_a^c f(x)dx &= \mathrm{F}(b) - \mathrm{F}(a) + \mathrm{F}(c) - \mathrm{F}(b) \\ &= \mathrm{F}(c) - \mathrm{F}(a) \\ &= \int_a^c f(x)dx,\end{aligned}$$

or the range a to c may be subdivided into two (or more) sub-ranges such as a to b, b to c.

(4) Since $\mathrm{F}(x)$ is the integral of $f(x)$, $\mathrm{F}'(x) = f(x)$. If we use a variable upper limit x instead of b as above

$$\int_a^x f(x)dx = \mathrm{F}(x) - \mathrm{F}(a).$$

If we differentiate this relation

$$\begin{aligned}\frac{d}{dx}\int_a^x f(x)dx &= \frac{d}{dx}[\mathrm{F}(x) - \mathrm{F}(a)] \\ &= \mathrm{F}'(x) = f(x).\end{aligned}$$

In particular we will later require the relation

$$\frac{d}{dt}\int_0^t i\,dt = i.$$

i being the current at time t.

19.6. Integration with Infinite Limits

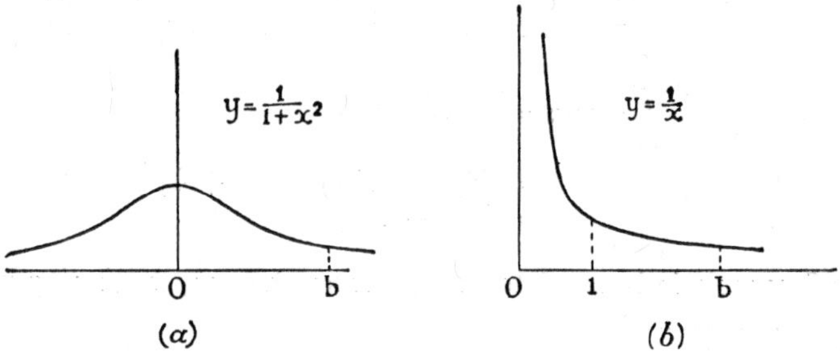

FIG. 60

For our purpose it is sufficient to consider the following examples.

We evaluate $\displaystyle\int_0^{\infty} \frac{dx}{1+x^2}$ or $\displaystyle\lim_{b\to\infty} \int_0^b \frac{dx}{1+x^2}$

as

$$[\tan^{-1}x]_0^{\infty} \qquad = \lim_{b\to\infty} \tan^{-1}(b)$$
$$= \tan^{-1}(\infty) - \tan^{-1}(0) \qquad = \frac{\pi}{2}.$$
$$= \frac{\pi}{2}.$$

(We may consider that we have found the area in the first quadrant under $y = \dfrac{1}{(1+x^2)}$ between $x = 0$ and b, and then found the limit of this area as b moves infinitely far to the right (Fig. 60(a)).

Similarly, in short,

$$\int_{-\infty}^{+\infty} \frac{dx}{a^2+x^2} = \left[\frac{1}{a}\tan^{-1}\left(\frac{x}{a}\right)\right]_{-\infty}^{+\infty} \qquad (a > 0).$$
$$= \frac{1}{a}[\tan^{-1}(\infty) - \tan^{-1}(-\infty)]$$
$$= \frac{1}{a}\left[\frac{\pi}{2} - \left(-\frac{\pi}{2}\right)\right] = \frac{\pi}{a}.$$

On the other hand, for the curve $y = \dfrac{1}{x}$ (Fig. 60(b))

$$\int_1^{\infty} \frac{dx}{x} = [\log x]_1^{\infty} \qquad \text{or} \qquad \lim_{b\to\infty} \int_1^b \frac{dx}{x}$$
$$= \log(\infty) - \log(1) \qquad = \lim_{b\to\infty} \log b$$
$$= \infty. \qquad \to \infty$$

Thus the area shown in the figure as b moves to the right becomes infinite when b becomes infinite.

EXERCISE 45

1. Find the area bounded by the axes, the curve $y(x^2 + b^2) = b^3$ and the ordinate $x = x_1$, where x is positive. Show that the area is always less than $\frac{1}{2}\pi b^2$, but tends to this value as $x_1 \to \infty$.

2. The area between the curve $y = \dfrac{c^2}{\sqrt{a^2 + x^2}}$, the x axis and the ordinates at $x = 0$ and $x = x_1$ revolves round the x axis. Show that the volume generated is always less than $\dfrac{\frac{1}{2}\pi^2 c^4}{a}$ and tends to this value as $x_1 \to \infty$.

3. Show that the area between the x axis, the curve $y = \dfrac{1}{x^2}$ and to the right of $x = 1$ is $\displaystyle\int_1^\infty \frac{dx}{x^2}$ and evaluate this integral.

4. Show that the total area between the x axis and the curve

$$y = \frac{c^3}{x^2 + c^2} \quad \text{is}$$

$$\int_{-\infty}^{+\infty} \frac{c^3}{x^2 + c^2} dx$$

and find this area.

5. Sketch the curve $xy^2 = 4(2 - x)$ and find the total area between the curve and the y axis.

6. Sketch the curve $y^2 = \dfrac{(x - 1)}{(4 - x)}$ and find the area between the curve and the line $x = 4$.

Find the value of the following infinite integrals:

7. $\displaystyle\int_0^\infty \frac{dx}{x^2 + 4}$.

8. $\displaystyle\int_{-\infty}^{+\infty} \frac{dx}{x^2 + 9}$.

9. $\displaystyle\int_2^\infty \frac{dx}{x^2 - 1}$.

10. $\displaystyle\int_{-\infty}^0 e^x dx$.

11. $\displaystyle\int_0^\infty \frac{xdx}{(x^2 + 4)(x^2 + 9)}$.

12. Show that $\displaystyle\int_0^\infty \cos xdx$ has no meaning.

13. In Fig. 61(*a*) a current I is passing along a very long wire, and it is given that the force at a point P distant r from it on a unit magnetic pole due to an element δx of the wire at Q is

$$\delta F = I \frac{\delta x}{PQ^2} \sin \theta.$$

Given that this force is perpendicular to the plane of the paper, show that the total force F is given by

$$F = 2\int_0^\infty I \frac{dx}{x^2 + r^2} \sin \theta = \frac{2I}{r}.$$

14. If $A = \int_0^{\infty} \frac{dx}{1+x^4}$, $B = \int_0^{\infty} \frac{xdx}{1+x^4}$, $C = \int_0^{\infty} \frac{x^2dx}{1+x^4}$

prove that:

(i) $B = \frac{1}{4}\pi$;

(ii) $A + C - \sqrt{2}B = \frac{\pi}{2\sqrt{2}}$;

(iii) $A = C$ by means of the substitution $x = \frac{1}{z}$;

(iv) $A = C = \frac{\pi}{2\sqrt{2}}$.

[For (ii) note that $1 + x^4 = (1 + x^2)^2 - (x\sqrt{2})^2$].

15. Show that (*a*) is non-existent but (*b*) is finite, although in each case $f(x) \to \infty$ as $x \to 0$.

(*a*) $$\int_0^b \frac{dx}{x} = \lim_{a \to +0} \int_a^b \frac{dx}{x}.$$

(*b*) $$\int_0^b \frac{dx}{x^{1/2}} = \lim_{a \to +0} \int_a^b \frac{dx}{x^{1/2}}.$$

16. Explain the following:

(*a*) $$\sec^2 x > 0 \text{ in } (0, \pi)$$

but $$\int_0^{\pi} \sec^2 x dx = \tan x \Big)_0^{\pi}$$

$$= \tan \pi - \tan 0 = 0.$$

(*b*) $$I = \int_{-1}^{+1} \frac{dx}{1+x^2} = \tan^{-1} x \Big)_{-1}^{+1} = \pi/2.$$

But the substitution $x = 1/y$ gives

$$I = -\int_{-1}^{+1} \frac{dy}{1+y^2} = -\pi/2.$$

17. Prove

$$\int_{-a}^{+a} f(x)dx = \int_0^a \{f(x) + f(-x)\}dx.$$

Hence show that

(*a*) $$\int_{-\pi/4}^{\pi/4} \frac{dx}{1+\sin x} = 2\int_0^{\pi/4} \sec^2 x dx = 2.$$

(*b*) $$\int_{-1}^{+1} \frac{dx}{1+e^{-x}} = 1.$$

18. Prove that $\int_0^a f(x)dx = \int_0^a f(a-x)dx.$

Hence show that

(a) $$\int_0^{\pi/2} \sin^2 x dx = \pi/4;$$

(b) $$\int_0^{\pi/2} \frac{a \sin x + b \cos x}{\sin x + \cos x} dx = \pi(a + b)/4.$$

19. If $f(x) = f(a - x)$, prove that

$$\int_0^a f(x)dx = 2\int_0^{a/2} f(x)dx$$

and that $$2\int_0^a xf(x)dx = a\int_0^a f(x)dx.$$

Hence show that

$$\int_0^{\pi} \frac{x \sin^3 xdx}{a + b \cos^2 x} = \frac{\pi}{b}\left[\frac{(a + b)}{\sqrt{ab}} \tan^{-1}\left(\sqrt{\frac{b}{a}}\right) - 1\right].$$

19.7. Change of Limits of Integration

We will end with worked examples involving change of the limits of integration.

Example 6. To find $I = \int_0^a \sqrt{a^2 - x^2}dx.$

[If we consider the curve $y = \sqrt{a^2 - x^2}$ or $y^2 + x^2 = a^2$ we see that the above is the area of a quadrant of the circle of radius a and the value of the integral is $\frac{1}{4}\pi a^2$.]

Put $x = a \sin \theta,$
∴ when $x = 0$, the lower limit, $0 = a \sin \theta$, ∴ $\theta = 0$;
$x = a$, the upper limit, $a = a \sin \theta$, ∴ $\theta = \pi/2$,
also $dx = a \cos \theta d\theta.$
We are now able to change every item of the integral into its value in the new unit of measurement.

$$I = \int_0^{\pi/2} \sqrt{a^2 - a^2 \sin^2 \theta}\, a \cos \theta d\theta$$
$$= a^2\int_0^{\pi/2} \cos^2 \theta d\theta = \frac{a^2}{2}\int_0^{\pi/2} (1 + \cos 2\theta)d\theta$$
$$= \frac{a^2}{2}\left[\theta + \frac{\sin 2\theta}{2}\right]_0^{\pi/2}$$
$$= \underline{\frac{\pi a^2}{4}}.$$

Example 7. To find $\int_{-\infty}^{+\infty} \frac{x^2}{(a^2 + x^2)^2}dx.$

Put $x = a \tan \theta,$
∴ when $x = -\infty, -\infty = a \tan \theta,$ $\tan \theta = -\infty,$ $\theta = -\pi/2;$
$x = +\infty, +\infty = a \tan \theta,$ $\tan \theta = +\infty,$ $\theta = +\pi/2,$
also $dx = a \sec^2 \theta d\theta.$

$$\therefore \quad \mathrm{I} = \int_{-\pi/2}^{+\pi/2} \frac{a^2 \tan^2 \theta}{(a^2 + a^2 \tan^2 \theta)^2} \cdot a \sec^2 \theta d\theta$$

$$= \frac{1}{a}\int_{-\pi/2}^{+\pi/2} \sin^2 \theta d\theta = \frac{1}{2a}\int_{-\pi/2}^{+\pi/2} (1 - \cos 2\theta) d\theta$$

$$= \underline{\underline{\frac{\pi}{2a}}}.$$

Example 8. To find $\mathrm{I} = \int_a^b \sqrt{\{(x-a)(b-x)\}}\,dx.$

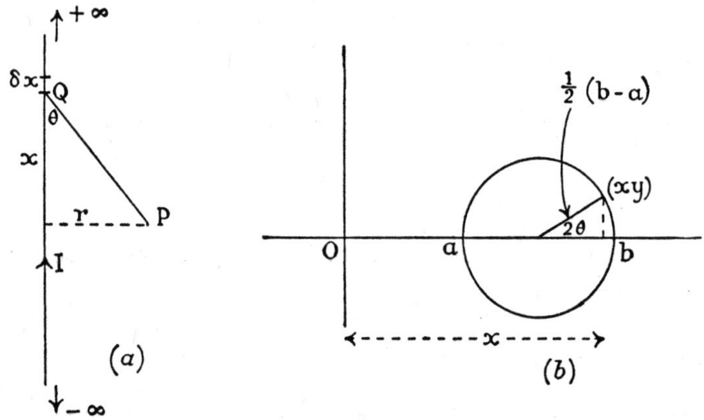

FIG. 61.

If we call the integrand y,

$$y = \sqrt{\{(x-a)(b-x)\}},$$

$$\therefore \quad x^2 + y^2 - x(a+b) + ab = 0$$

$$\left(x - \frac{a+b}{2}\right)^2 + y^2 = \left(\frac{b-a}{2}\right)^2.$$

This is the equation to a circle centre $\left(\frac{a+b}{2}, 0\right)$ and radius $\frac{1}{2}(b-a)$. The integral therefore represents the area of the upper half, and its value is

$$\tfrac{1}{2}\pi\left(\frac{b-a}{2}\right)^2 = \tfrac{1}{8}\pi(b-a)^2.$$

From Fig. 61(b) the following substitution for x is obvious. We put

$$x = \frac{a+b}{2} + \tfrac{1}{2}(b-a)\cos 2\theta$$

[2θ instead of the usual θ merely saves work.]

$$= \frac{a}{2}(1 - \cos 2\theta) + \frac{b}{2}(1 + \cos 2\theta)$$

$$= a \sin^2 \theta + b \cos^2 \theta.$$

$\therefore$ when $x = a$, the lower limit,

$$a = a \sin^2 \theta + b \cos^2 \theta,$$

$$a \cos^2 \theta = b \cos^2 \theta,$$

$a \neq b, \quad \therefore \cos^2 \theta = 0$ or $\theta = \pi/2$.

When $x = b$, the upper limit

$$b = a \sin^2\theta + b\cos^2\theta,$$
$$\therefore \quad b\sin^2\theta = a\sin^2\theta,$$
$$b \neq a, \quad \therefore \sin^2\theta = 0 \text{ or } \theta = 0,$$

also

$$dx = 2\sin\theta\cos\theta(a-b)d\theta$$
$$= -2\sin\theta\cos\theta(b-a)d\theta.$$

Finally,

$$x - a = a\sin^2\theta + b\cos^2\theta - a$$
$$= (b-a)\cos^2\theta,$$
$$b - x = b - a\sin^2\theta - b\cos^2\theta$$
$$= (b-a)\sin^2\theta.$$

$$\therefore \quad I = \int_{\pi/2}^{0} \sqrt{[(b-a)\cos^2\theta\,.\,(b-a)\sin^2\theta]}(-2\sin\theta\cos\theta)(b-a)d\theta$$
$$= 2(b-a)^2\int_0^{\pi/2}\sin^2\theta\cos^2\theta d\theta.$$

$$\sin^2\theta\cos^2\theta = \frac{\sin^2 2\theta}{4} = \frac{1-\cos 4\theta}{8},$$

$$\therefore \quad I = \frac{\pi}{8}(b-a)^2.$$

19.8. Two Important Limits

In integration the following limits occur:

(1) $\lim\limits_{x\to\infty} e^{-ax}\cos bx$, where $a > 0$.

Since a is +ve, $e^{-ax} \to 0$ as $x \to \infty$.

$|\cos bx|$ is never greater than 1 whatever bx is, $\therefore$ the limit is zero.

The same method and result apply to $e^{-ax}\sin bx$, $(a > 0)$.

(2) $\lim\limits_{x\to\infty} x^n e^{-x}$, where n is a positive integer.

This function may be written

$$\frac{x^n}{1 + x + \frac{x^2}{2!} + \ldots \frac{x^n}{n!} + \frac{x^{n+1}}{(n+1)!} + \ldots}$$

$$= \frac{1}{\frac{1}{x^n} + \frac{1}{x^{n-1}} + \frac{1}{2!x^{n-2}} + \ldots \frac{1}{n!} + \frac{x}{(n+1)!} + \frac{x^2}{(n+2)!} + \ldots},$$

$\therefore$ the limit as $x \to \infty$ is clearly zero.

Example 9. Find $\int_0^\infty e^{-2x}\cos 3x dx$.

The value is $\left[\frac{e^{-2x}}{2^2+3^2}(-2\cos 3x + 3\sin 3x)\right]_0^\infty$.

When $x \to \infty$ we have $e^{-2x}\cos 3x$ and $e^{-2x}\sin 3x \to 0$ by the first limit in 19.8.

$\therefore$ the value is $\frac{1}{13}\{0 - 1(-2+0)\} = \frac{2}{13}$.

Example 10. Find $I = \int_0^\infty x^2 e^{-x} dx$.

Integrating by parts: $I = \left[\frac{x^2e^{-x}}{-1}\right]_0^\infty - \int_0^\infty 2x(-e^{-x})dx$.

When $x \to \infty$, $x^2e^{-x} \to 0$ by the second limit in 19.8,

when $x = 0$, $x^2e^{-x} = 0$,

$$\therefore \quad I = 2\int_0^\infty xe^{-x}dx$$

$$= 2\left[\frac{xe^{-x}}{-1}\right]_0^\infty - \int_0^\infty 2(-e^{-x})dx$$

$$= 2[0 + \int_0^\infty e^{-x}dx].$$

Now $$\int_0^\infty e^{-x}dx = [-e^{-x}]_0^\infty = 0 - (-1) = 1,$$

$$\therefore \quad \underline{I = 2.}$$

19.9. An Important Formula

In the next volume we will prove the following formula:
If n is a positive integer

$$\int_0^{\pi/2} \sin^n \theta d\theta = \int_0^{\pi/2} \cos^n \theta d\theta$$

$$= \frac{(n-1)(n-3)\ \ldots\ 2}{n(n-2)\ \ \ldots\ 3} \quad (n \text{ odd})$$

or

$$\frac{(n-1)(n-3)\ \ldots\ 1}{n(n-2)\ \ \ldots\ 2} \times \frac{\pi}{2} \quad (n \text{ even}).$$

Thus $$\int_0^{\pi/2} \sin^4 \theta d\theta = \frac{3\,.\,1}{4\,.\,2} \times \frac{\pi}{2}$$

$$= \frac{3\pi}{16},$$

$$\int_0^{\pi/2} \cos^5 \theta d\theta = \frac{4\,.\,2}{5\,.\,3} \times 1 = \frac{8}{15}.$$

The student should use this formula to shorten the work required in examples 6, 7, 8 of this chapter.

EXERCISE 46

Find the values of the following integrals:

1. $\displaystyle\int_0^4 \frac{dx}{\sqrt{x}}$.
2. $\displaystyle\int_{-1}^{+1} (1 - x^2)^2 dx$.
3. $\displaystyle\int_{\frac{1}{2}}^1 \frac{dx}{\sqrt{(2x - 1)}}$.
4. $\displaystyle\int_{-1}^3 \frac{dx}{x + 4}$.
5. $\displaystyle\int_2^3 \frac{xdx}{x - 1}$.
6. $\displaystyle\int_{-\pi}^{+\pi} \sin\frac{x}{2}\, dx$.
7. $\displaystyle\int_{-\pi/2}^{+\pi/2} \cos^2 x dx$.
8. $\displaystyle\int_0^1 \frac{xdx}{\sqrt{1 - x^2}}$.
9. $\displaystyle\int_0^{\frac{1}{2}} \frac{dx}{\sqrt{1 - x^2}}$.
10. $\displaystyle\int_0^{\pi/2} \frac{\sin x dx}{1 + \cos^2 x}$.
11. $\displaystyle\int_2^3 \frac{dx}{x(x + 2)}$.
12. $\displaystyle\int_1^2 x^2 \log x dx$.

13. $\displaystyle\int_2^3 \frac{3x^2-1}{x(x^2-1)}dx.$ 14. $\displaystyle\int_0^{\pi/2} \frac{dx}{1+\cos x}.$ 15. $\displaystyle\int_0^1 \tan^{-1} x dx.$

16. $\displaystyle\int_1^e xe^x dx.$ 17. $\displaystyle\int_0^\pi \sin^2 x \cos^3 x dx.$ 18. $\displaystyle\int_0^\pi x^2 \sin x dx.$

19. $\displaystyle\int_0^\infty e^{-3x} \cos 4x dx.$ 20. $\displaystyle\int_0^\pi \frac{\sin x}{e^x} dx.$ 21. $\displaystyle\int_0^2 \frac{x dx}{(x+1)(x^2+9)}.$

22. $\displaystyle\int_0^\infty \frac{x^2 dx}{(x^2+4)(x^2+9)}.$ 23. $\displaystyle\int_0^\infty xe^{-x} dx.$ 24. $\displaystyle\int_0^{\pi/2} \frac{dx}{4+5\cos x}.$

25. $\displaystyle\int_0^{\pi/2} \frac{dx}{5+4\cos x}.$ 26. $\displaystyle\int_0^{\pi/2} \sin^6 x dx.$

27. If $\mathrm{I}_n = \displaystyle\int_0^\infty x^n e^{-x} dx$, prove that $\mathrm{I}_n = n\mathrm{I}_{n-1}$ (where $n > 1$). Hence find the value of I_n if n is a positive integer. [L.U.]

28. Write down the values of:

$$(a) \int_0^{\pi/2} \sin^2 \theta d\theta, \quad (b) \int_0^{\pi/2} \cos^3 \theta d\theta, \quad (c) \int_0^{\pi/2} \sin^7 \theta d\theta.$$

29. Show by a rough sketch that

$$\int_0^\pi \sin^4 \theta d\theta = 2\int_0^{\pi/2} \sin^4 \theta d\theta$$

and find the value of the first integral.

30. Using $\cos^2 \theta = 1 - \sin^2 \theta$, find

$$\int_0^{\pi/2} \sin^6 \theta \cos^4 \theta d\theta.$$

31. Find $$\int_0^{\pi/2} \sin^3 \theta \cos^5 \theta d\theta.$$

32. Show that $\displaystyle\int_a^b f(x)dx - \int_a^c f(x)dx = \int_c^b f(x)dx.$

33. Put $x = \mathrm{X} + a$ and prove that

$$\int_a^b f(x)dx = \int_0^{b-a} f(x+a)dx.$$

34. Show that the maximum and minimum values of

$$\int_0^x (9 - x^2)dx$$

occur when $x = +3$ and -3 respectively.

35. If $\mathrm{F}(x) = \displaystyle\int_x^a f(x)dx$ show that $\mathrm{F}'(x) = -f(x)$.

36. If $x\displaystyle\int_0^x f(x)dx = 2\int_0^x xf(x)dx$ prove that:

$$(1) \int_0^x f(x)dx = xf(x), \qquad (2)\ f'(x) = 0.$$

Deduce that $f(x)$ is a constant.

37. Give a rough sketch of an area represented by $\int_{-a}^{+a} f(x)dx$, when $f(x)$ is: (i) an even function, *i.e.*, consists of even powers of x only, (ii) an odd function.

Show that $$\int_{-a}^{+a} f(x)dx = 2\int_0^a f(x)dx \text{ in (i)}$$

and $$\int_{-a}^{+a} f(x)dx = 0 \qquad \text{in (ii)}.$$

38. Use the above example to evaluate as shortly as possible:

$$(a) \int_{-1}^{+1} 5(x^4 - x^2)dx, \quad (b) \int_{-1}^{+1} 6(x^5 - x^3)dx, \quad (c) \int_{-a}^{+a} \frac{xdx}{\sqrt{(9 + x^2)}}.$$

39. A text book on alternating currents contains the equations

$$L\frac{di}{dt} + Ri + \frac{Q}{C} = E \sin \omega t,$$

$$Q = \int_0^t idt,$$

$$\therefore \quad L\frac{d^2i}{dt^2} + R\frac{di}{dt} + \frac{i}{C} = \omega E \cos \omega t.$$

Obtain this last differential equation in i from the other two equations. [The electrical student should note that the limits of the integral 0 to t in the equation for Q are often regarded as obvious and omitted in many books.]

19.10. Mean Value of a Function

By the mean value of y with respect to x between $x = a$ and b we mean the value of

$$\frac{1}{b - a}\int_a^b ydx.$$

Thus if y is represented by a curve $y = f(x)$ the value found is the average height of the area enclosed by the curve, the x axis and the ordinates at $x = a$ and b.

Example 11. A large number N of shots are fired at a circular target of radius a ft., and it is found that they are scattered uniformly over the target area. Find their mean distance from the centre.

The number within a ring of radius x and width dx is $N(2\pi x dx/\pi a^2)$, and each of these is x from the centre,

$$\therefore \quad \bar{x} = \frac{1}{N}\int_0^a \left(\frac{N}{\pi a^2} \cdot 2\pi x dx\right)x$$

$$= \underline{\tfrac{2}{3}a}.$$

(This example is not based directly on the above formula.)

19.11. The Root Mean Square Value of a Function

This R.M.S. value over an interval is, as its title suggests, obtained as follows:

(1) square the function;
(2) find its mean value as above over the interval;
(3) take the square root of this mean value.

This value is required in electrical engineering, and is found for alternating electrical currents, etc.

Example 12. Find the R.M.S. value of

$$I_0 + I_1 \sin(\omega t + \phi_1) + I_2 \sin(2\omega t + \phi_2) + \ldots I_n \sin(n\omega t + \phi_n)$$

over the interval of time $2\pi/\omega$.

(1) When we square the function we obtain terms such as

$$I_0^2,\ I_s^2 \sin^2(s\omega t + \phi_s),\ 2I_rI_s \sin(r\omega t + \phi_r)\sin(s\omega t + \phi_s),\ 2I_0I_s \sin(s\omega t + \phi_s)$$

where r and s are any two *different* integers between 1 and n.

(2) The mean values of such terms are respectively:

(*a*) $$\frac{\omega}{2\pi}\int_0^{2\pi/\omega} I_0^2 dt = I_0^2,$$

(*b*) $$\frac{\omega}{2\pi}\int_0^{2\pi/\omega} I_s^2 \sin^2(s\omega t + \phi_s)dt$$

$$= \frac{\omega I_s^2}{4\pi}\int_0^{2\pi/\omega}[1 - \cos(2s\omega t + 2\phi_s)]dt$$

$$= \frac{\omega I_s^2}{4\pi}\left[t - \frac{\sin(2s\omega t + 2\phi_s)}{2s\omega}\right]_0^{2\pi/\omega}$$

$$= \frac{\omega I_s^2}{4\pi}\left[\left(\frac{2\pi}{\omega} - 0\right) - \frac{1}{2s\omega}\Big(\sin(4\pi s + 2\phi_s) - \sin(2\phi_s)\Big)\right]$$

$$= \frac{I_s^2}{2} \text{ for all values of } s \text{ from 1 to } n.$$

(*c*) $$\frac{\omega}{2\pi}\int_0^{2\pi/\omega} 2I_rI_s \sin(r\omega t + \phi_r)\sin(s\omega t + \phi_s)dt$$

$$= \frac{\omega I_rI_s}{2\pi}\int_0^{2\pi/\omega}[\cos(\overline{r - s}\,\omega t + \overline{\phi_r - \phi_s}) - \cos(\overline{r + s}\,\omega t + \phi + \phi_s)]dt$$

$= 0$, since each cosine term gives zero as in (*b*).

(*d*) $$\frac{\omega}{2\pi}\int_0^{2\pi/\omega} 2I_0I_s \sin(s\omega t + \phi_s)dt$$

$$= \frac{\omega I_0I_s}{\pi}\left[\frac{\cos(s\omega t + \phi_s)}{-s\omega}\right]_0^{2\pi/\omega}$$

$$= \frac{I_0I_s}{s\pi}\Big((\cos(\phi_s) - \cos(2\pi s + \phi_s)\Big)$$

$$= 0.$$

The final result is therefore

$$I_0^2 + \tfrac{1}{2}(I_1^2 + I_2^2 + \ldots I_n^2).$$

(3) The square root of this gives as the R.M.S. value

$$\underline{\sqrt{[I_0^2 + \tfrac{1}{2}(I_1^2 + I_2^2 + \ldots I_n^2)]}}.$$

EXERCISE 47

Find the mean value of:

1. $y = x^2$ in the interval $x = 1$ to 3.

2. $y = \sin 2x$ in the interval $x = 0$ to $\frac{\pi}{6}$.

3. The ordinate y in the first quadrant of the ellipse $\frac{x^2}{a^2} + \frac{y^2}{b^2} = 1$: (*a*) when y is given as a function of x; (*b*) when y is given as $y = b \sin \theta$, where θ is the eccentric angle.

4. Show that the mean area of all rectangles with a given perimeter $2a$ is $\frac{a^2}{6}$.

5. When a particle is projected with velocity V at an angle α to the horizontal its horizontal range is $V^2 \sin 2\alpha/g$. If all angles between 0 and $\pi/2$ are equally likely, find the mean value of the range.

6. The current in a circuit is $i = I_0 \sin \omega t$, and the voltage is obtained by means of the relation $v = L\, di/dt + Ri$. Find the mean value of vi over a period $2\pi/\omega$.

7. Find the R.M.S. value over a period $\frac{2\pi}{\omega}$ of

$$i = I_1 \sin (\omega t + \alpha) + I_2 \sin (2\omega t + \beta).$$

8. A current i is given by $i = a + bV + cV^2$, and when $V = V_0$, $i = i_0$. If $V = V_0 + V_s \sin \omega t$, show that

$$i = i_0 + \frac{cV_s^2}{2} + (bV_s + 2cV_0V_s) \sin \omega t - \frac{cV_s^2}{2} \cos 2\omega t,$$

and from this result prove that the mean value of i over the range $t = 0$ to $t = 2\pi/\omega$ exceeds i_0 by $\frac{1}{2}cV_s^2$.

9. If $e = 24 \cos pt + 4 \cos 3pt$ and $i = 4 \sin pt + \sin 3pt$, prove that

$$ei = 52 \sin 2pt + 20 \sin 4pt + 2 \sin 6pt.$$

Hence show that the mean value of ei over the range $t = 0$ to $t = \pi/2p$ is 33·5.

10. In a certain circuit the applied voltage is

$$v = 100 \sin \omega t + 16 \sin 3\omega t$$

and the corresponding current is

$$i = 5{\cdot}8 \sin \left(\omega t - \frac{\pi}{3}\right) + 1{\cdot}6 \sin \left(3\omega t - \frac{\pi}{6}\right).$$

Show that the mean value of the product iv taken over a period $2\pi/\omega$ is 156·1.

CHAPTER 20

AREAS AND VOLUMES

20.1. The Area under a Curve

Suppose the area included between the curve, the y axis, the x axis and an ordinate at the point E, where OE $= x$, is represented by A.

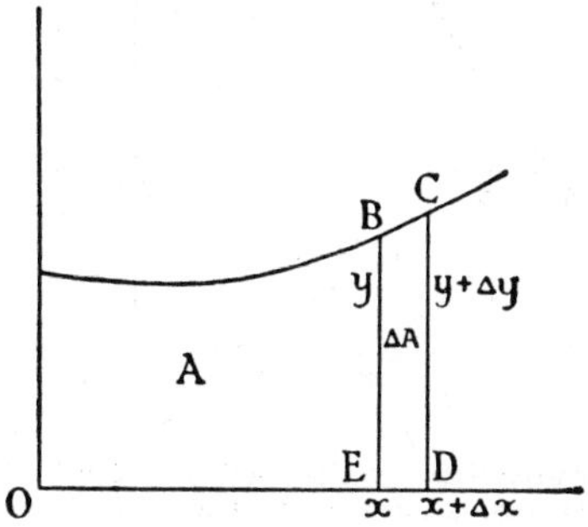

FIG. 62.

If we increase x by Δx to the point D $= x + \Delta x$ we obtain an increment of area ΔA, where ΔA tends to zero with Δx.

The area EBCD has a height varying from y to $y + \Delta y$, so we will assume its average height is $y + \alpha\Delta y$, where α is some fraction between -1 and $+1$.

$$\therefore \quad \Delta A = ED \times \text{av. height}$$
$$= \Delta x(y + \alpha\Delta y),$$
$$\therefore \quad \frac{\Delta A}{\Delta x} = y + \alpha\Delta y.$$

In the limit when $\Delta x \to 0$ this becomes, since $\Delta y \to 0$ with Δx,

$$\frac{dA}{dx} = y,$$
$$\therefore \quad A = \int y\,dx.$$

If the equation to the curve is $y = f(x)$ and F(x) is the indefinite integral of $f(x)$, this is

$$A = \int f(x)dx$$
$$= F(x) + C.$$

A is a function of x, and we will now denote it by $A(x)$,

$$\therefore \quad A(x) = F(x) + C.$$

When $x = a$, $\qquad A(a) = F(a) + C,$

$x = b$, $\qquad A(b) = F(b) + C,$

$$\therefore \quad A(b) - A(a) = F(b) - F(a),$$

which by definition $\qquad = \int_a^b f(x)dx,$

giving an expression for the area between the ordinates at $x = a$ and $x = b$.

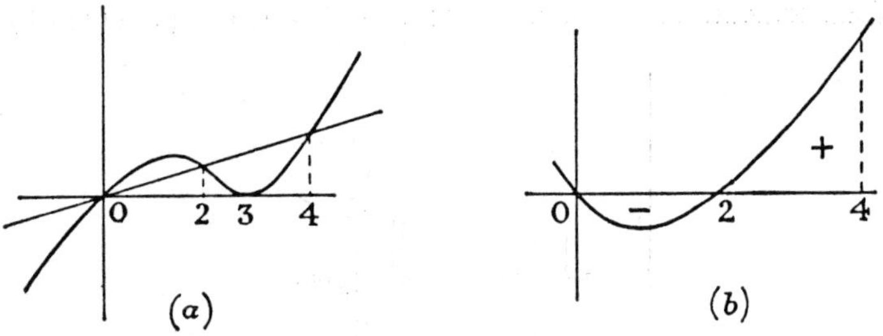

FIG. 63.

Example 1. Find the area between the curve $y = x(x-3)^2$ and the line $y = x$.

Fig. 63(a) shows that two separate areas are involved. Where the curves intersect

$$x = x(x-3)^2,$$
$$\therefore \quad x = 0 \text{ and } x^2 - 6x + 8 = 0,$$
$$\therefore \quad x = 0, 2, 4.$$

From $x = 0$ to 2 the area included is

$$\int_0^2 x(x-3)^2 dx - \int_0^2 x dx$$
$$= \int_0^2 (x^3 - 6x^2 + 9x)dx - [\tfrac{1}{2}x^2]_0^2$$
$$= \left[\frac{x^4}{4} - 6\frac{x^3}{3} + 9\frac{x^2}{2}\right]_0^2 - 2$$
$$= 6 - 2 = 4 \text{ sq. units.}$$

From $x = 2$ to 4 the line lies above the curve and the area is

$$\int_2^4 x dx - \int_2^4 x(x-3)^2 dx$$
$$= 4 \text{ sq. units.}$$

Total area = 8 sq. units.

20.2. The Sign of an Area

Integration is summation, and in finding an area by integration we are finding the limit of a sum of terms such as $y\Delta x$, this representing the area of a rectangle base Δx and height y. Δx is always a positive increment, so if y is negative, *i.e.*, the curve is below the x axis, we will be summing negative terms.

Consider the curve $y = x(x - 2)$ (Fig. 63(*b*)).

For the area between $x = 0$ and 2 we have

$$\int_0^2 x(x-2)dx = -\tfrac{4}{3},$$

a negative result, since the area is below the x axis. Integration between the limits 0 and 3 gives

$$\int_0^3 x(x-2)dx = 0,$$

since the area above the x axis happens to be equal to the area below. In integrating from 0 to 3 we are unknowingly adding negative values of $y\Delta x$ to positive values, and the final result is the difference of two areas. Finally, if we integrated from 0 to 4 we would obtain an answer of $\frac{16}{3}$, which would not be the area between the curve, the x axis and the ordinates at 0 and 4 but the *difference* of two areas, that between $x = 2$ and 4 less that between $x = 0$ and 2.

For the same reason

$$\int_0^{2\pi} \sin x dx = 0.$$

Whenever an area is involved the student should draw a rough sketch to help prevent mistakes due to this sign of an area.

Example 2. Find the area bounded by the curves $y^2 = x - 12$ and $2y^2 = x - 4$.

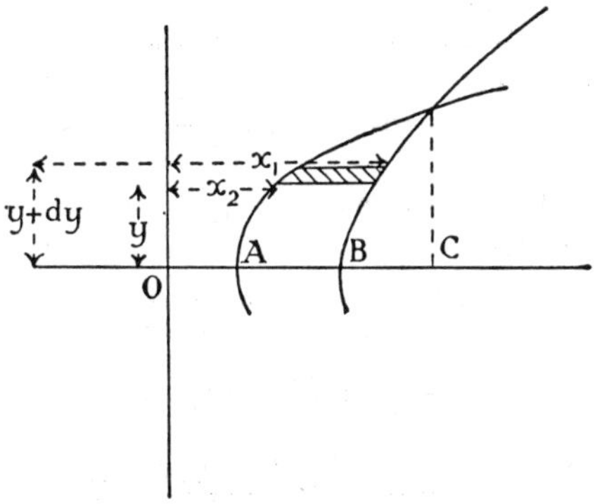

FIG. 64.

(1) If we integrate as usual with respect to x the area will have to be found in two separate parts, one part with AC as the range of integration and another with BC. We will integrate with respect to y, which requires only one integration.

(2) Since the curves are both symmetrical with respect to the x axis, we will find the area in the first quadrant and double it.

The curves intersect at $(20, \pm 2\sqrt{2})$,

$$\therefore \quad \text{area} = 2\int_0^{2\sqrt{2}} (x_1 - x_2)dy$$

$$= 2\int_0^{2\sqrt{2}} [(y^2 + 12) - (2y^2 + 4)]dy$$

$$= 2\int_0^{2\sqrt{2}} (8 - y^2)dy$$

$$= 2\left[8y - \frac{y^3}{3}\right]_0^{2\sqrt{2}}$$

$$= \frac{64\sqrt{2}}{3} \text{ sq. units.}$$

20.3. Areas from Parametric Equations

We can also find the area under a curve given by its parametric equations. (Some important problems of this type must wait until the student has become acquainted with " reduction formulae ".)

Example 3. Find the area of the ellipse given by $x = a \cos \theta$, $y = b \sin \theta$. The area in each quadrant is the same, so that

$$\text{total area} = 4\int_0^a ydx,$$

the limits being obtained from a knowledge of the curve.

We must now substitute for the *y, x and the limits of integration* in terms of the parameter.

Since $x = a \cos \theta$,

$\therefore$ when $x = 0$ the lower limit,

$$0 = a \cos \theta, \qquad \therefore \quad \theta = \pi/2.$$

When $x = a$ the upper limit,

$$a = a \cos \theta, \qquad \therefore \quad \theta = 0.$$

Also from $x = a \cos \theta$,

$$dx = -a \sin \theta d\theta.$$

The integral becomes

$$4\int_{\pi/2}^0 (b \sin \theta)(-a \sin \theta d\theta)$$

$$= -4ab\int_{\pi/2}^0 \sin^2 \theta d\theta$$

$$= -4ab\int_{\pi/2}^0 \frac{1 - \cos 2\theta}{2} \cdot d\theta$$

$$= -2ab\left[\theta - \frac{\sin 2\theta}{2}\right]_{\pi/2}^0$$

$$= \pi ab \text{ sq. units.}$$

$$\left[\text{Or,} \qquad -\int_{\pi/2}^0 \sin^2 \theta d\theta = \int_0^{\pi/2} \sin^2 \theta d\theta = \frac{1}{2} \cdot \frac{\pi}{2} \quad \text{(see 19.9).}\right]$$

EXERCISE 48

1. Draw a rough sketch of $y = x(x^2 - 1)$ and hence, without integration, state the value of

$$\int_{-1}^{+1} x(x^2 - 1)dx.$$

2. Find the areas cut off from the curve by the x axis for

$$y = (x + 2)(x - 1)(x - 4).$$

3. Prove by integration and also by a transfer of origin that

$$\int_2^3 (x + 1)(7 - x)dx = \int_3^4 x(8 - x)dx.$$

In each case give a sketch to show the area concerned.

4. Find the area bounded by $y = \dfrac{1}{(1 + x^2)}$, the x axis and the ordinates at $x = \pm 1$.

5. Find the area cut off from $y^2 = 4ax$ by the line $y = x$.

6. Find the area between the curves

$$y = x(11 - 2x) \quad \text{and} \quad y = 4(x - 1)(5 - x).$$

7. Find where the curve $y = \sin 2x - \sqrt{3} \sin x$ first cuts the x axis after the origin. Find the area bounded by this part of the curve and the x axis.

8. Find the area of the loop of the curve $y^2 = 16x^3(x - 5)^2$.

9. Find the area in the first quadrant bounded by the parabola $y^2 = 2 - x$ and the lines $y = x$ and $y = 2x$.

10. Find the area enclosed between $y = x(x - 4)$, $y + x = 0$ and $y + 3x = 0$.

11. Find the area bounded by the curve, the x axis and the ordinate at the point $x = at^2$, $y = 2at$ when t varies from 0 to 3.

By finding the area cut off from this parabola by the double ordinate at any point T, show that the area thus enclosed is two-thirds that of the circumscribing rectangle.

12. Find the area of each of the following curves as in the first part of Question 11 when the curve is given by:

(*a*) $x = a \sec \theta$, $y = b \tan \theta$ and θ varies from 0 to $\frac{\pi}{3}$.

(*b*) $x = ct$, $y = \frac{c}{t}$ and t varies from 1 to 4.

(*c*) $x = a\ (\theta - \sin \theta)$, $y = a(1 - \cos \theta)$ and θ varies from 0 to π

[In (*a*) note that $\int \sec^3 \theta d\theta = \frac{1}{2} \sec \theta \tan \theta + \frac{1}{2} \log \tan \left(\frac{\pi}{4} + \frac{\theta}{2}\right)$.]

13. Show that the curve $a^n y^m = b^m x^n$ divides the rectangle formed by the axes and $x = a$, $y = b$ into two parts whose areas are in the ratio $m : n$.

14. Find the area bounded by the curve $6xy = x^4 + 3$, the axis of x and the ordinates $x = 1$ and $x = 2$.

15. Find the area bounded by $y = \dfrac{(x-2)(x-3)}{(1-x^2)}$, the x axis and the lines $x = 2$, $x = 3$.

16. Find the area bounded by $y = \dfrac{x^4}{a^2(x+a)}$ and the lines $y = 0$, $x = a$.

17. Find where $y = 2\cos x \sin 3x$ first cuts the positive x axis after 0. Find the area thus enclosed by the curve and the x axis.

18. Give a rough sketch of the curve $y = \dfrac{x^2}{(3+x^2)}$ and show it has a point of inflexion at $x = \pm 1$. Find the area enclosed between the curve, its asymptote and the ordinates through the points of inflexion.

20.4. Volumes of Solids of Revolution

In exactly the same way as for areas in the previous section, we have that if ΔV is the increment in volume due to increasing the x co-ordinate by Δx, then

$$\Delta V = \pi(y + \alpha\Delta y)^2\Delta x,$$

$$\therefore \quad \frac{\Delta V}{\Delta x} = \pi(y + \alpha\Delta y)^2.$$

$\therefore$ in the limit when Δx and Δy tend to zero

$$\frac{dV}{dx} = \pi y^2,$$

$$\therefore \quad V = \int \pi y^2 dx,$$

where $y = f(x)$ is the curve whose revolution round the x axis generates the volume.

We also find in the same way that for the volume included between the ordinates at $x = a$ and b

$$V = \int_a^b \pi y^2 dx.$$

If the curve revolves round the y axis, then the volume included between the lines $y = c$ and $y = d$ is

$$V = \int_c^d \pi x^2 dy.$$

Example 4. Find the total volume formed when $y^2 = x^2(9 - x^2)$ rotates round the x axis. (The curve is similar to Fig. 55(c).)

The curve is symmetrical with regard to the y axis, therefore for the total volume,

$$\begin{aligned} V &= 2\int_0^3 \pi y^2 dx \\ &= 2\pi\int_0^3 (9x^2 - x^4)dx \\ &= 2\pi\Big[3x^3 - \frac{x^5}{5}\Big]_0^3 \\ &= \underline{64{\cdot}8\pi \text{ cu. units.}} \end{aligned}$$

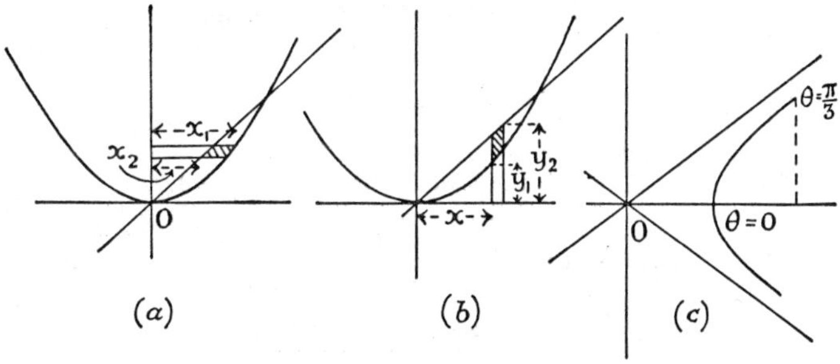

FIG. 65.

Example 5. The area bounded by the curves $x^2 = 4y$ and $y = 2x$ revolves round the y axis. Find the volume generated (Fig. 65(a)).

Where $x^2 = 4y$ meets $y = 2x$,

$$x^2 = 4(2x),$$

$$\therefore \quad x = 0 \text{ and } 8.$$

The corresponding y's are $\quad y = 0$ and 16.

For the volume we need $\quad \displaystyle\int_0^{16} \pi(x_1^2 - x_2^2)dy,$

where $x_1^2 = 4y$ and $x_2 = \dfrac{y}{2}$.

$$\begin{aligned} \therefore \quad V &= \pi\int_0^{16}\Big(4y - \frac{y^2}{4}\Big)dy \\ &= \pi\Big[2y^2 - \frac{y^3}{12}\Big]_0^{16} \\ &= \underline{\frac{512\pi}{3} \text{ cu. units.}} \end{aligned}$$

Example 6. In some cases it may be easier to solve the above problem by an integration with respect to x (Fig. 65(b)).

If y_2 denotes the height of the line above the x axis at a distance x from O and y_1 denotes the height of the curve, then on a base dx we have an area $(y_2 - y_1)dx$ which revolves round the y axis, describing the perimeter of a circle of radius x.

The element of volume generated is

$$\begin{aligned} &2\pi x(y_2 - y_1)dx \\ &= 2\pi x\Big[2x - \frac{x^2}{4}\Big]dx. \end{aligned}$$

$\therefore$ the total volume is
$$\int_0^8 2\pi x\left[2x - \frac{x^2}{4}\right]dx$$
$$= 2\pi\left[2\frac{x^3}{3} - \frac{x^4}{16}\right]_0^8$$
$$= \frac{512\pi}{3} \text{ cu. units.}$$

Example 7. Find the volume generated when the curve given by $x = a \sec \theta$, $y = b \tan \theta$, between $\theta = 0$ and $\theta = \pi/3$ revolves round the axis (Fig. 65(c)).

$$V = \int \pi y^2 dx$$
$$= \int_0^{\pi/3} \pi(b \tan \theta)^2(a \sec \theta \tan \theta d\theta)$$
$$= \pi ab^2 \int_0^{\pi/3} \frac{\sin^3 \theta}{\cos^4 \theta} d\theta.$$

Put $\cos \theta = c, \quad \therefore \quad -\sin \theta d\theta = dc.$

When $\theta = 0$ the lower limit, $c = \cos 0 = 1$.

$\theta = \pi/3$ the upper limit, $c = \cos(\pi/3) = 1/2$.

$$\therefore \quad V = \pi ab^2 \int_1^{1/2} \frac{\sin^2 \theta(-dc)}{c^4}$$
$$= -\pi ab^2 \int_1^{1/2} \frac{(1 - \cos^2 \theta)dc}{c^4}$$
$$= -\pi ab^2 \int_1^{1/2} \frac{1 - c^2}{c^4} dc$$
$$= -\pi ab^2\left[-\frac{1}{3c^3} + \frac{1}{c}\right]_1^{1/2}$$
$$= \tfrac{4}{3}\pi ab^2 \text{ cu. units.}$$

EXERCISE 49

1. The area cut off from $y^2 = 4ax$ by $x = h$ revolves round the x axis. Find the volume generated. Find the volume of the spindle generated if the rotation is about the y axis.

2. The part of the hyperbola $\dfrac{x^2}{a^2} - \dfrac{y^2}{4a^2} = 1$ which lies between the x axis and the line $y = 2a$ is rotated round the y axis. Prove that the volume generated is $\frac{8}{3}\pi a^3$.

3. The area bounded by the x axis, the curve $y = 3 + 2 \sin x$ and the lines $x = 0$, $x = \pi$ rotates round the x axis. Find the volume generated.

4. Find the volume generated when the loop of the curve $y^2 = x^2(x + 3)$ revolves round the x axis.

5. From the circle $x^2 + y^2 = 4$ the area of the ellipse $\dfrac{x^2}{4} + y^2 = 1$ is cut out. The remainder rotates round the x axis. Find the volume of the solid formed.

6. Find the volume generated when the area cut off from $y^2 = 4ax$ by the line $x = 2a$ rotates round this line.

7. The area bounded by the curve $y^2 = 4(x + 3)$ and the line $x = 1$ revolves round the line. Find the volume generated.

8. Find the volume generated when the loop of the curve

$$y^2 = \frac{x^2(1 + x)}{(1 - x)}$$

rotates round the x axis.

9. Find the volume generated when each of the following areas revolves round the x axis:

(*a*) The area bounded by $t = 1$ and $t = 4$, the x axis and the curve $x = ct$, $y = \frac{c}{t}$.

(*b*) The area bounded by $\theta = 1$ and $\theta = 2$, the x axis and the curve $x = 2c \log \theta$, $y = c\left(\theta + \frac{1}{\theta}\right)$.

10. Prove that the volume of the segment of a sphere whose height is h and the radius of whose base is c is $\frac{1}{6}\pi h(3c^2 + h^2)$. Hence or otherwise solve the following problem. Two equal spheres of radius a intersect, their centres being a apart. Show that the volume enclosed by the double sphere is $\frac{9}{4}\pi a^3$.

11. The area bounded by $y^2x = 4a^2(2a - x)$ and the ordinates $x = a$, $x = 2a$ revolves round Ox. Show that the volume generated is $4\pi a^3(2 \log 2 - 1)$.

12. The area bounded by the loop of $x^2 = y^2(2 - y)$ revolves round the y axis. Find the volume generated.

13. The curve $y = a + bx + cx^2$ is required to pass through the point (2, 0) and has a maximum value of 1 at $x = 1$. Show that the volume generated when that part of the curve for which y is positive rotates round the x axis is $\frac{16\pi}{15}$.

14. The area enclosed by $by^2 = c^2(x + b)$ and $ay^2 = c^2(a - x)$ revolves round the x axis to generate a solid of revolution. Show that the volume is $\frac{1}{2}\pi c^2(a + b)$.

15. A cylindrical hole is bored centrally through a sphere. If the hole is of length $2c$, show that the volume of the part left is $\frac{4}{3}\pi c^3$.

16. The area enclosed by the curve $y = \sin 4x + \sin 2x$ and the x axis from the origin to the next (positive) point where the curve crosses the x axis revolves round the x axis. Find the volume generated.

17. Repeat the above problem for the curve $y = 2 \cos 3x \cos 2x$.

CHAPTER 21

POLAR CO-ORDINATES

21.1. The Position of a Point in a Plane

The position of a point in a plane is often determined by giving its co-ordinates (x, y) relative to two fixed axes in the plane. It is just

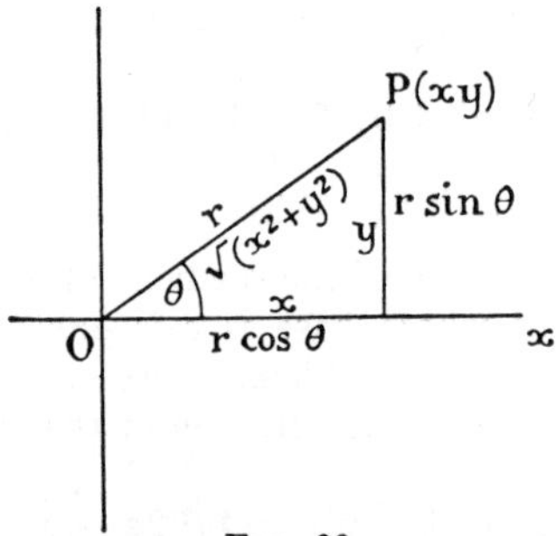

FIG. 66.

as often found convenient to fix the position of the point by " polar " co-ordinates. In this system a fixed line is chosen as the " initial " line, and we fix a point by saying that its co-ordinates are (r, θ), meaning that if O is the fixed " pole " on the line and P the point, then OP is of length r and the angle measured anticlockwise between Ox and the join OP (note this positive direction) is the angle θ.

Thus $\left(2, \frac{\pi}{4}\right)$ is a point in the first quadrant.

$\left(2, -\frac{3\pi}{4}\right)$ is the point in the third quadrant which is the reversal through the pole of the above point. We could also write this as $\left(-2, \frac{\pi}{4}\right)$, meaning that we rotate through $\frac{\pi}{4}$ from the initial line and then move -2 units from the pole, *i.e.*, not along the line making $\frac{\pi}{4}$ with the initial line but in the opposite direction.

21.2. To Interchange Cartesian and Polar Co-ordinates

From the above diagram we have the relations

$$x = r\cos\theta \qquad y = r\sin\theta$$

$$r^2 = x^2 + y^2 \qquad \tan\theta = \frac{y}{x}.$$

Example 1. Change the equation $x^2 + y^2 = 2ax$ into polar co-ordinates.
Using the above equations of transformation, we find

$$r^2 = 2ar\cos\theta.$$

$r = 0$ gives the one point 0, ignore this and obtain

$$\underline{r = 2a\cos\theta.}$$

Example 2. Change the equation $r^2 = a^2\cos 2\theta$ into Cartesian co-ordinates.
This is

$$r^2 = a^2(\cos^2\theta - \sin^2\theta),$$

$$= a^2\left(\left(\frac{x}{r}\right)^2 - \left(\frac{y}{r}\right)^2\right).$$

$$\therefore \quad r^4 = a^2(x^2 - y^2),$$

i.e.,

$$\underline{(x^2 + y^2)^2 = a^2(x^2 - y^2).}$$

The student will discover that in this case the polar equation is far easier to trace than the Cartesian equation.

EXERCISE 50

Change the following equations into polar co-ordinates:

1. $x^2 + y^2 = a^2$. 2. $ax + by + c = 0$. 3. $y = x\tan\alpha$.
4. $x^3 = y^2(2a - x)$. 5. $x^3 + y^3 = 3xy$.

Change the following equations into Cartesian co-ordinates:

6. $r = c$. 7. $r = a\cos\theta + b\sin\theta$. 8. $r = a\sec\theta$.
9. $\theta = \frac{\pi}{4}$. 10. $r^{\frac{1}{2}} = a^{\frac{1}{2}}\cos\frac{\theta}{2}$.

11. Show that $\frac{A}{r} = B\cos\theta + C\sin\theta$ is a straight line but that $\frac{A}{r} = B\cos\theta + C\sin\theta + D$ is NOT a line.

21.3. Curve Tracing

The method is best shown by examples. In some cases it may be better to turn the equation into the Cartesian form.

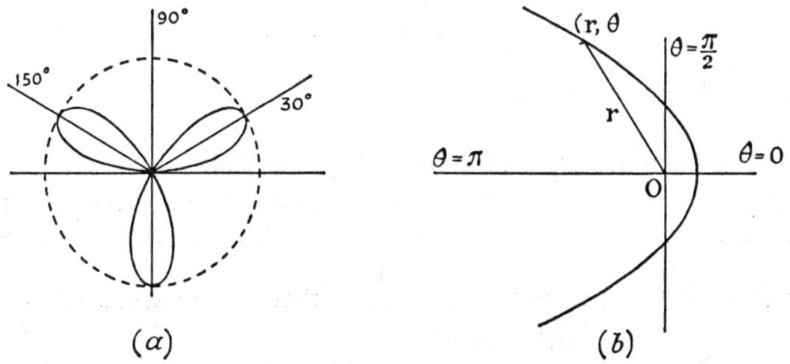

FIG. 67.

Example 3. Trace the curve $r = a \sin 3\theta$. (Fig. 67(*a*).)

(1) Since the maximum value of $\sin 3\theta$ is 1 and its minimum -1 the curve lies entirely in the circle $r = a$.

(2) When
$$\begin{aligned} \theta &= 30^\circ & r &= a \\ \theta &= 90^\circ & r &= -a \\ \theta &= 150^\circ & r &= a \\ \theta &= 210^\circ & r &= -a \\ \theta &= 270^\circ & r &= a \\ \theta &= 330^\circ & r &= -a. \end{aligned}$$

There is no need to go beyond $\theta = 360^\circ$.

(3) $r = 0$ when $3\theta = 0, \pi, 2\pi, 3\pi, \ldots$

$$i.e., \quad \theta = 0, \frac{\pi}{3}, \frac{2\pi}{3}, \pi, \ldots$$

(4) We could ignore the above general considerations and draw up a table giving r for say every value of θ increasing from 0 to 360 by 10° intervals.

(5) The curve is as shown in the figure.

Example 4. Trace the curve $r = \dfrac{2}{(1 + \cos\theta)}$ (Fig. 67(*b*)).

(1) When $\theta = 0, \quad r = 1$
$\theta = \pi, \quad r = \infty.$

(2) $\cos(-\theta) = \cos\theta$, $\therefore$ the curve is symmetrical with respect to the initial line, so that we need consider only values 0 to π.

(3) r is never imaginary for any value of θ, *i.e.*, there is a value in every direction round 0.

(4) When $\theta = \frac{\pi}{2}$, $r = 2$.

(5) We could draw up a table of values for r by finding $\dfrac{2}{1 + \cos\theta}$ for each value of 10° in the range 0 to 180°.

(6) The curve is as shown. The student should change the equation into Cartesians and show it is a parabola.

EXERCISE 51

Trace the following curves:

1. $r = 10$.
2. $\theta = \tan^{-1}(1)$.
3. $r = 16\cos\theta$.
4. $r\cos\theta = 6$.
5. $r\sin\theta = 4$.
6. $r = a(1 - \cos\theta)$.
7. $r^2 = a^2\cos 2\theta$.
8. $r = \dfrac{4}{(1 - \cos\theta)}$.
9. $r = \dfrac{8}{(1 - 2\cos\theta)}$.
10. Show that $r = 4(1 + 2\cos\theta)$ consists of two loops, one inside the other.
11. Trace $r = a(4 + b\cos\theta)$ for $b = 3, 4, 6$.

21.4. The Polar Equation of a Conic, Focus as Pole

Let S, the focus, be the pole and Sx the initial line. Suppose the conic has eccentricity e and semi latus rectum l so that $l = e\,.\,\text{SZ}$, where MZ is the directrix.

If P is any point (r, θ) on the curve so that $\text{SP} = r$ and $\angle \text{PS}x = \theta$,

$$\begin{aligned} \text{SP} &= e\text{PM} \\ &= e(\text{ZN}) = e(\text{ZS} + \text{SN}), \end{aligned}$$

i.e.,
$$r = e\left[\frac{l}{e} + r\cos\theta\right].$$
$$\therefore \quad \frac{l}{r} = 1 - e\cos\theta$$

is the connection between r and θ for any point on the curve, *i.e.*, it is the polar equation of the conic.

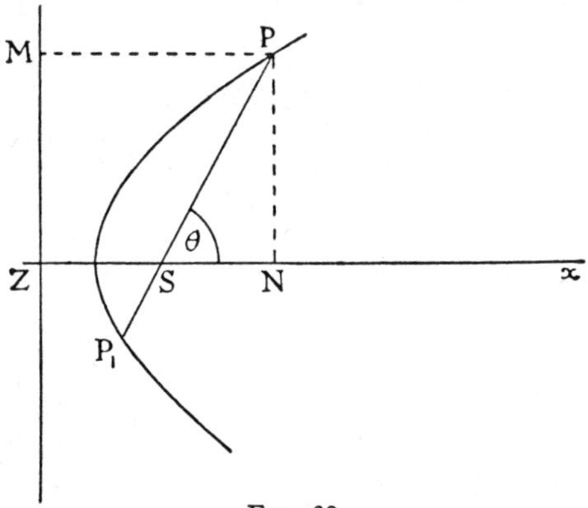

FIG. 68.

[If the initial line is measured in the direction SZ instead of Sx, then the equation becomes $\frac{l}{r} = 1 + e\cos\theta$, a form used in many books.]

Example 5. PSP′ is a focal chord of a conic. Prove that $\frac{1}{SP} + \frac{1}{SP'} =$ constant.

Let the equation to the conic, pole at a focus, be
$$\frac{l}{r} = 1 - e\cos\theta. \qquad \text{(Fig. 68.)}$$

If P is the point (r, θ)
$$\frac{l}{SP} = 1 - e\cos\theta.$$

P′ has $-(\pi - \theta)$ as its angular co-ordinate,
$$\therefore \quad \frac{l}{SP'} = 1 - e\cos(\pi - \theta)$$
$$= 1 + e\cos\theta.$$
$$\therefore \quad l\left[\frac{1}{SP} + \frac{1}{SP'}\right] = 2,$$
$$\frac{1}{SP} + \frac{1}{SP'} = \frac{2}{l} = \text{const.}$$

EXERCISE 52

1. Find the length of the line joining the points (r_1, θ_1), (r_2, θ_2).
2. Find the area of the triangle OPQ if P is (r_1, θ_1) and Q is (r_2, θ_2)
3. P is the point $\left(2, \frac{\pi}{4}\right)$. Q moves so that the area of the triangle OPQ is always 4 units. Find the polar equation to the locus of Q and by changing it into Cartesian form show it is a straight line.
4. Find the co-ordinates of the points where the ellipse

$$\frac{2}{r} = 1 - \tfrac{1}{2}\cos\theta$$

is cut by:

(i) the line $\theta = 30°$; (ii) the circle $r = 2$; (iii) the line $r\cos\theta = 2$.

5. Find the polar co-ordinates of the points of intersection of the parabola $\frac{2}{3r} = 1 - \cos\theta$ and the circle $r = 3\cos\theta$.
6. O is the focus of the conic $\frac{l}{r} = 1 - e\cos\theta$. Chords POP_1, QOQ_1 intersect at right angles at O. Prove that $\frac{1}{PP_1} + \frac{1}{QQ_1} =$ constant.
7. Show that: (i) is an ellipse, (ii) a hyperbola and (iii) a parabola. In the first two find the centre, and the lengths of the axes.

(i) $\frac{12}{r} = 5 - 4\cos\theta$; (ii) $\frac{40}{r} = 2 - 3\cos\theta$; (iii) $\frac{6}{r} = 1 - \cos\theta$.

21.5. Areas in Polar Co-ordinates

Let OC, OB be two fixed radii of a given curve which make angles α and β with the initial line Ox. Let P be the point (r, θ) so that

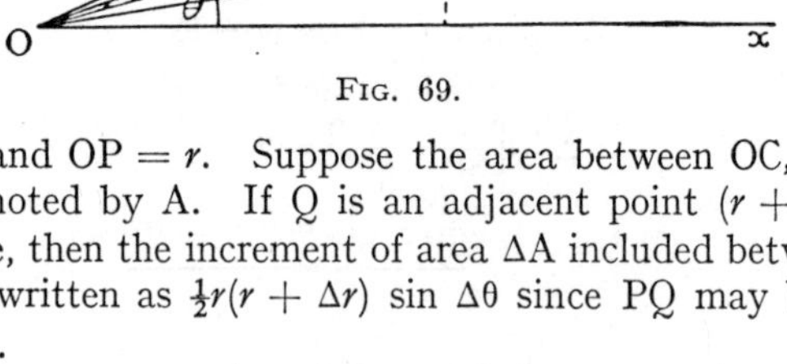

FIG. 69.

$\angle POx = \theta$ and $OP = r$. Suppose the area between OC, OP and the curve is denoted by A. If Q is an adjacent point $(r + \Delta r, \theta + \Delta\theta)$ on the curve, then the increment of area ΔA included between OP and OQ can be written as $\frac{1}{2}r(r + \Delta r)\sin\Delta\theta$ since PQ may be taken as a straight line.

$$\therefore \quad \Delta A = \tfrac{1}{2}r(r + \Delta r)\sin\Delta\theta,$$

$$\therefore \quad \frac{\Delta A}{\Delta\theta} = \tfrac{1}{2}r(r + \Delta r)\frac{\sin\Delta\theta}{\Delta\theta}.$$

But $\underset{\Delta\theta \to 0}{\mathcal{L}t.} \dfrac{\sin \Delta\theta}{\Delta\theta} = 1,$

$\therefore$ as Q approaches P we have, since $\Delta r \to 0$ with $\Delta\theta$,

$$\frac{dA}{d\theta} = \tfrac{1}{2}r^2,$$

$$\therefore \quad A = \int \tfrac{1}{2}r^2 d\theta,$$

and between the limits $\theta = \alpha$ and β,

$$A = \int_{\alpha}^{\beta} \tfrac{1}{2}r^2 d\theta.$$

Before this can be evaluated we must have r in terms of θ and make the usual substitution.

Example 6. Find the area of the curve $r = a \cos \theta$.

(1) Since $\cos(-\theta) = \cos \theta$ this curve is symmetrical about the initial line, and we need consider only the upper half.

(2) When $\theta = 0$, $r = a$ and r decreases steadily to zero as θ increases to $\frac{\pi}{2}$.

For $\theta = \frac{\pi}{2}$ to π, r is negative, *i.e.*, the curve is below the initial line.

A rough sketch shows that the area is given by

$$2\int_0^{\pi/2} \tfrac{1}{2}r^2 d\theta = \int_0^{\pi/2} a^2 \cos^2 \theta d\theta = a^2 \frac{1 \,.\, \pi}{2 \,.\, 2}$$

$$= \frac{\pi a^2}{4} \text{ sq. units.}$$

This curve is a circle of diameter a.

EXERCISE 53

1. Find the total area of the curve $r = a(1 + \cos \theta)$.
2. Find the area of one loop of $r^2 = a^2 \cos 2\theta$.
3. Find the area of one loop of $r = a \sin 4\theta$.
4. Find the area of the smaller segment of the circle $r = a \cos \theta$ cut off by the line $\theta = \frac{\pi}{4}$.
5. Find the area inside the circle $r = 6 \cos \theta$ and outside the circle $r = 3$.
6. Show that $r = a(\sqrt{2} \cos \theta - 1)$ consists of 2 loops and that the area of the smaller loop is $\frac{1}{2}a^2(\pi - 3)$ and of the larger loop $\frac{3}{2}a^2(\pi + 1)$.

21.6. Volumes of Solids of Revolution

We have seen that the element of area in polar co-ordinates is

$$dA = \tfrac{1}{2}r^2 d\theta.$$

This may be regarded as the triangle shown (Fig. 69) whose c.g. is two-thirds of the height of the triangle from the vertex so that its perpendicular distance from the initial line is $\frac{2}{3}r \sin \theta$.

Therefore by Pappus' Theorem (see 24.6) when this element dA revolves round the initial line, the element of volume generated is

$$\begin{aligned}&\text{area} \times \text{path travelled by c.g.}\\ &= \tfrac{1}{2}r^2 d\theta \times 2\pi \times \tfrac{2}{3}r \sin\theta\\ &= \pi\tfrac{2}{3}r^3 \sin\theta\, d\theta.\end{aligned}$$

$\therefore$ the total volume generated by the area enclosed between the radii making angles α and β with the initial line is $\int_\alpha^\beta \pi\frac{2}{3}r^3 \sin\theta d\theta$.

Example 7. Find the volume generated when the curve $r = a(1 + \cos\theta)$ revolves round its line of symmetry.

The upper half of this curve is given by the range $\theta = 0$ to $\theta = \pi$. The curve is symmetrical about the initial line.

$$\therefore \quad \text{Volume} = \frac{2\pi}{3}\int_0^\pi r^3 \sin\theta d\theta$$

$$= \frac{2\pi}{3}a^3\int_0^\pi (1 + \cos\theta)^3 \sin\theta d\theta.$$

It should be evident that since

$$\frac{d}{d\theta}(1 + \cos\theta)^4 = 4(1 + \cos\theta)^3 \times -\sin\theta,$$

$$\therefore \quad \int (1 + \cos\theta)^3 \sin\theta\, d\theta = \frac{(1 + \cos\theta)^4}{-4},$$

$$\therefore \quad \text{Volume} = \frac{2\pi a^3}{3}\left[\frac{(1 + \cos\theta)^4}{-4}\right]_0^\pi$$

$$= \frac{8}{3}\pi a^3 \text{ cu. units.}$$

EXERCISE 54

1. The curve $r = e^\theta$ between $\theta = 0$ and $\theta = \frac{\pi}{2}$ rotates round the initial line. Find the volume generated.

2. The curve $r = a$ between $\theta = 0$ and $\theta = \alpha$ revolves round the initial line. Find the volume generated and check your answer with the value $\alpha = \frac{\pi}{2}$.

3. The curve $r = a\theta^{\frac{1}{3}}$ between $\theta = 0$ and $\theta = \frac{\pi}{2}$ revolves round the initial line. Find the volume generated.

4. Find the volume when the curve $r = 2a\sin^2\left(\frac{\theta}{2}\right)$ between $\theta = 0$ and $\theta = \pi$ revolves round the initial line.

5. The area inside the cardioid $r = 2a(1 + \cos\theta)$, but outside the parabola $r(1 + \cos\theta) = 2a$ revolves round the initial line. Show that the volume generated is $18\pi a^3$.

CHAPTER 22

LENGTHS OF CURVES

22.1. The Length of a Plane Curve

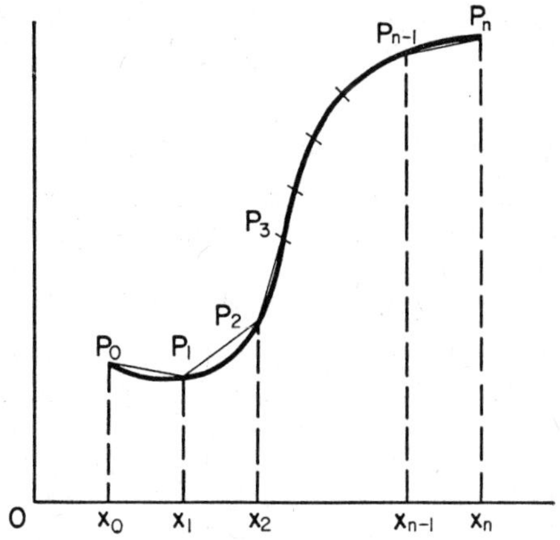

FIG. 70.

The length of a curve $y = f(x)$ between $x = a$ and $x = b$ may be defined as follows. Subdivide the curve by the points P_0, P_1, . . . P_n so that the points are $P_r = (x_r, f(x_r))$ for $r = 1$ to n, where $x_0 = a$, $x_n = b$. Then

$$l = P_0P_1 + P_1P_2 + \ldots + P_{n-1}P_n$$

is the perimeter of a polygon approximating to the length. If we choose another point, say P_1', between P_1 and P_2 it is clear that we have increased the sum l, since $P_1P_1' + P_1'P_2 > P_1P_2$ unless the curve is a line between P_1 and P_2. Hence as we increase the number of points of subdivision l may increase to a finite limit L or to $+\infty$. In the first case, of a finite limit L, the curve is said to be *rectifiable* and of length L. A formula is easily obtained. For

$$P_{r-1}P_r = \sqrt{[(x_r - x_{r-1})^2 + \{f(x_r) - f(x_{r-1})\}^2]}$$

If now $f(x)$ is differentiable in this range

$$f(x_r) - f(x_{r-1}) = (x_r - x_{r-1})f'(z_r)$$

by the first Mean Value theorem, where z_r is some number between x_r and x_{r-1}. Hence

$$P_{r-1}P_r = (x_r - x_{r-1})\sqrt{[1 + \{f'(z_r)\}^2]}.$$

This is

$$\Delta L/\Delta x = \sqrt{[1 + \{f'(z_r)\}^2]}.$$

Hence, if $f'(x)$ is continuous in the interval (a, b)

$$L = \int_a^b \sqrt{[1 + \{f'(x)\}^2]}\, dx.$$

An alternative method follows which, however, does not indicate when perhaps the length of the curve does not exist. Its assumption that lim. (arc AB/chord AB) $\to$ 1 can be verified whenever $f'(x)$ is continuous.

22.2. Given y in Terms of x

Let A (x, y) be a point on a given curve and B $(x + \Delta x, y + \Delta y)$ a near point also on the curve. If AB, the (straight line) chord, is of length Δs

$$(\Delta s)^2 = (\Delta x)^2 + (\Delta y)^2 \qquad \text{(Fig. 14)}$$

We now use our intuition and state that as B tends to A the ratio of the chord AB $= \Delta s$ to the differential element of arc AB $= ds$ tends to unity.

Since

$$(\text{arc AB})^2 = \left(\frac{\text{arc AB}}{\text{chord AB}}\right)^2 (\text{chord AB})^2$$

$$= \left(\frac{\text{arc AB}}{\text{chord AB}}\right)^2 ((\Delta x)^2 + (\Delta y)^2)$$

$\therefore$ in the limit

$$(ds)^2 = (dx)^2 + (dy)^2 \quad . \quad . \quad . \quad . \quad . \quad . \quad . \quad . \quad . \quad (1)$$

If we have y in terms of x so that $\dfrac{dy}{dx}$ can be obtained we divide this equation by $(dx)^2$ and obtain

$$\left(\frac{ds}{dx}\right)^2 = 1 + \left(\frac{dy}{dx}\right)^2$$

$$\frac{ds}{dx} = \pm\sqrt{1 + \left(\frac{dy}{dx}\right)^2}$$

$$s = \int\sqrt{1 + \left(\frac{dy}{dx}\right)^2}\, dx,$$

where we take the positive value of the result.

Example 1. Find the length of the curve $y^2 = x^3$ from the origin to the point $(8, 8^{\frac{3}{2}})$.

Keeping to the upper half of the curve on which the point lies

$$y = x^{\frac{3}{2}} \qquad \therefore \frac{dy}{dx} = \tfrac{3}{2}x^{\frac{1}{2}}, \qquad \text{and} \quad \left(\frac{ds}{dx}\right)^2 = 1 + \tfrac{9}{4}x.$$

$$\therefore \quad s = \int_0^8 \sqrt{1 + \frac{9x}{4}}\,dx$$

$$= \left[\tfrac{4}{9} \cdot \tfrac{2}{3}\left(1 + \frac{9x}{4}\right)^{\frac{3}{2}}\right]_0^8$$

$$= \tfrac{8}{27}\{19^{\frac{3}{2}} - 1\} = \underline{24{\cdot}3.}$$

22.3. Owing to the presence of the square root in the integrand few examples on lengths of arcs can be easily worked out. The student should always consider if the expression under the root is perhaps a perfect square as in the following example.

Example 2. Find the length of the loop of the curve $3ay^2 = x(x - a)^2$.
The curve is symmetrical about the x axis. We will keep to the upper half of the loop and double the integral to include the lower half.

$$y = \frac{1}{\sqrt{3a}}\,(x^{\frac{3}{2}} - ax^{\frac{1}{2}}),$$

$$\therefore \quad \frac{dy}{dx} = \frac{1}{\sqrt{3a}}\,(\tfrac{3}{2}x^{\frac{1}{2}} - \tfrac{1}{2}ax^{-\frac{1}{2}}),$$

$$\therefore \quad \left(\frac{ds}{dx}\right)^2 = 1 + \frac{1}{3a}\left(\tfrac{3}{2}x^{\frac{1}{2}} - \tfrac{1}{2}\frac{a}{x^{\frac{1}{2}}}\right)^2$$

$$= \frac{1}{3a}\left\{3a + \tfrac{9}{4}x - \tfrac{3}{2}a + \tfrac{1}{4}\frac{a^2}{x}\right\}$$

$$= \frac{1}{3a}\left\{\tfrac{9}{4}x + \tfrac{3}{2}a + \tfrac{1}{4}\frac{a^2}{x}\right\}$$

$$= \frac{1}{3a}\left\{\tfrac{3}{2}x^{\frac{1}{2}} + \frac{a}{2x^{\frac{1}{2}}}\right\}^2 \quad \text{(note this step)},$$

$$\therefore \quad \frac{ds}{dx} = \frac{1}{\sqrt{3a}}\left\{\tfrac{3}{2}x^{\frac{1}{2}} + \frac{a}{2x^{\frac{1}{2}}}\right\}.$$

$\therefore$ for whole loop

$$s = 2\int_0^a \frac{1}{\sqrt{3a}}\left\{\tfrac{3}{2}x^{\frac{1}{2}} + \frac{a}{2x^{\frac{1}{2}}}\right\}dx$$

$$= \frac{2}{\sqrt{3a}}\left[x^{\frac{3}{2}} + ax^{\frac{1}{2}}\right]_0^a \qquad = \underline{\frac{4a}{\sqrt{3}}}.$$

22.4. Given x in Terms of y

If we are given x in terms of y, then equation (1) must be divided through by $(dy)^2$ to give $\left(\frac{ds}{dy}\right)^2 = \left(\frac{dx}{dy}\right)^2 + 1$, from which s can be found.

Example 3. Find the length of the curve $6xy = 3 + y^4$ between the points for which $y = 1$ and 2.
It would be difficult to solve this equation for y. If we differentiate it as it stands, the equation for $\frac{dy}{dx}$ contains x and y and cannot easily be changed to an equation in one variable. However, we easily find

$$x = \frac{1}{2y} + \frac{y^3}{6}, \qquad \therefore \quad \frac{dx}{dy} = -\frac{1}{2y^2} + \frac{y^2}{2}.$$

$$\therefore \quad \left(\frac{ds}{dy}\right)^2 = 1 + \left(\frac{1}{4y^4} - \frac{1}{2} + \frac{y^4}{4}\right) = \left(\frac{1}{2y^2} + \frac{y^2}{2}\right)^2.$$

$$\therefore \quad s = \int_1^2 \left(\frac{1}{2y^2} + \frac{y^2}{2}\right) dy$$

$$= \left[-\frac{1}{2y} + \frac{y^3}{6}\right]_1^2 = \underline{\frac{17}{12}}.$$

22.5. Given x and y in Terms of Parameters

If we are given x and y in terms of parametric equations in θ we divide equation (1) by $(d\theta)^2$ to give $\left(\frac{ds}{d\theta}\right)^2 = \left(\frac{dx}{d\theta}\right)^2 + \left(\frac{dy}{d\theta}\right)^2$, from which s can be found.

Example 4. Find the length of one arch of the cycloid $x = a(\theta - \sin\theta)$, $y = a(1 - \cos\theta)$.

In this case

$$\left(\frac{ds}{d\theta}\right)^2 = a^2(1 - \cos\theta)^2 + (a\sin\theta)^2$$

$$= a^2\{1 - 2\cos\theta + \cos^2\theta + \sin^2\theta\}$$

$$= 2a^2(1 - \cos\theta)$$

$$= 4a^2\sin^2\frac{\theta}{2} \qquad \text{(note this step)}$$

$$\therefore \quad \frac{ds}{d\theta} = 2a\sin\frac{\theta}{2}.$$

For one arch θ varies from 0 to 2π,

$$\therefore \quad s = 2a\int_0^{2\pi} \sin\frac{\theta}{2}\,d\theta$$

$$= \left[-4a\cos\frac{\theta}{2}\right]_0^{2\pi}$$

$$= \underline{8a}.$$

22.6. Relations between dx, dy, ds

In Fig. 14, if AB makes angle α with the x axis

$$\frac{\Delta y}{\Delta x} = \tan\alpha, \quad \frac{\Delta y}{\Delta s} = \sin\alpha, \quad \frac{\Delta x}{\Delta s} = \cos\alpha.$$

As B tends to A this angle α tends to θ, where $\frac{dy}{dx} = \tan\theta$. We therefore have in the limit

$$\frac{dy}{dx} = \tan\theta, \quad \frac{dy}{ds} = \sin\theta, \quad \frac{dx}{ds} = \cos\theta.$$

These relations should be remembered by means of the right-angled triangle. They are important, in particular

$$\frac{dx}{ds} = \cos\theta = \frac{1}{\sec\theta} = \frac{1}{\pm\sqrt{1 + \tan^2\theta}}$$

$$= \pm\frac{1}{\sqrt{1 + \left(\frac{dy}{dx}\right)^2}}$$

will be required in finding a formula for the radius of curvature.

EXERCISE 55

Find the lengths of the arcs of the curves:

1. $9y^2 = (x + 2)^3$. The upper half between $x = 0$ and 2.
2. $ay^2 = 12x^3$. The total length cut off by $x = a$.
3. $y = \frac{1}{8} \log x - x^2$ between $x = 1$ and 2.
4. $y = \log (1 - x^2)$ from $x = 0$ to $\frac{1}{4}$.
5. $y = \log \cos x$ from $x = 0$ to $\frac{\pi}{3}$.
6. $6xy = x^4 + 3$ from $x = 2$ to 8.
7. $y = (x + 1)(x + 2) - \frac{1}{8} \log (2x + 3)$ from $x = 1$ to 2. [L.U.]
8. Draw a rough sketch of $6ay^2 = x(2a - x)^2$ and find the perimeter of its loop.
9. In the astroid $x = a \cos^3 \theta, y = a \sin^3 \theta$, show that $\frac{ds}{d\theta} = \frac{3}{2}a \sin 2\theta$.

Find the length of arc in the first quadrant and the total length.

10. Find the length of the curve between $\theta = \alpha$ and β for

$$x = a(\cos \theta + \theta \sin \theta),\ y = a(\sin \theta - \theta \cos \theta).$$

11. Show that for the hyperbola $xy = 12$ the length of curve between $x = 1$ and 4 is given by

$$s = \int_1^4 \sqrt{\left(1 + \frac{144}{x^4}\right)}\, dx.$$

Evaluate this approximately by Simpson's rule.

12. Show that the length of the arc of the curve $y = x^2$ between $x = 1$ and 2 is approximately 3·168.
13. For the curve $y^2 = 1 + x$ show that the upper half of the curve between $x = 0$ and 3 has an approximate length of 3·62.
14. A curve is given by the parametric equations

$$3x = 6 \cos \theta + 2 \cos 3\theta.$$
$$3y = 6 \sin \theta + 2 \sin 3\theta.$$

Show that between $\theta = 0$ and $\pi/3$ the length of the curve is $2\sqrt{3}$.

15. For the curve

$$x = \cos \theta \sin^2 \theta,\ y = \sin \theta\ (1 + \cos^2 \theta)$$

show that

$$\frac{ds}{d\theta} = \pm(2 \cos^2 \theta - \sin^2 \theta) = f(\theta).$$

If the curve $y = f(\theta)$ be drawn it will be zero at $\theta = \tan^{-1} (\sqrt{2})$ and change sign there. Any integration across this value will give then a difference of two values. Hence show that the length of arc between $\theta = 0$ and $\pi/2$ is $\tan^{-1} (\sqrt{2}) + \sqrt{2} - \pi/4$.

16. The parametric equations of an ellipse are

$$x = 4 \cos \theta, \; y = 2\sqrt{2} \sin \theta.$$

Show that the total perimeter is given by

$$s = 16\int_0^{\pi/2} \sqrt{(1 - \tfrac{1}{2} \cos^2 \theta)}d\theta.$$

Evaluate this by expanding the square .oot and using the formulae of 19.9 to evaluate the integrals to show that $s = 6{\cdot}89\pi$ approximately.

CHAPTER 23

CURVATURE

23.1. Curvature and Circle of Curvature

It is important to investigate the rate at which a curve is bending or curving away from its tangent at a given point. We do this by first defining the *curvature* at a point on the curve. If the tangent at a point P (Fig. 71(*a*)) on the curve makes an angle θ with the x axis,

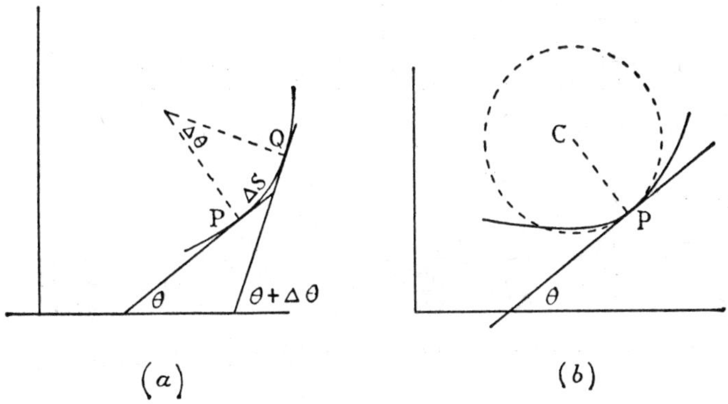

FIG. 71.

and the tangent at a near point Q a distance Δs along the curve from P makes angle $\theta + \Delta\theta$ with the x axis, then $\frac{\Delta\theta}{\Delta s}$ is the " average curvature " of the arc PQ. The curvature at P is defined as the limit of this ratio as Δs tends to zero, i.e.

$$\text{curvature at P} = \frac{d\theta}{ds}.$$

If PQ is the arc of a circle of radius ρ, then $\frac{d\theta}{ds}$ is $\frac{1}{\rho}$ a constant for any point on the circle. If ρ is very large the reciprocal is small to correspond with the fact that the amount of bending in a given (short) distance along a large circle is small. If ρ is small this amount of bending is comparatively large and so is $\frac{1}{\rho}$. We are therefore led to compare the curvature of a curve with that of a circle, the circle that corresponds as closely as possible with the curve near the point. This circle is called the circle of curvature at P, and is defined as that circle which has the same tangent at P as the curve, lies on the same side of the tangent as the curve and has a radius ρ given by $\frac{ds}{d\theta}$. The radius is called the radius of curvature and the centre of the circle the centre of curvature for the point P. We see that this circle has its centre on the normal at P, since it is to touch the tangent at P, and its centre at C, where CP $= \rho$. (Fig. 71(*b*)).

23.2. Radius of Curvature

The formula $\rho = \frac{ds}{d\theta}$ is used when we have an equation of the form $s = f(\theta)$. Since normally we have an equation in x and y we must find a formula in terms of these.

Since $\tan\theta = \frac{dy}{dx}$, $\theta = \tan^{-1}\left(\frac{dy}{dx}\right)$.

$$\therefore \quad \frac{d\theta}{ds} = \frac{d}{ds}\left[\tan^{-1}\left(\frac{dy}{dx}\right)\right] = \frac{d}{dx}\left[\tan^{-1}\left(\frac{dy}{dx}\right)\right]\cdot\frac{dx}{ds}$$

$$= \frac{1}{1+\left(\frac{dy}{dx}\right)^2}\cdot\frac{d^2y}{dx^2}\cdot\frac{dx}{ds}.$$

But (see 22.6)

$$\frac{dx}{ds} = \pm\frac{1}{\sqrt{1+\left(\frac{dy}{dx}\right)^2}}, \qquad \therefore \quad \frac{d\theta}{ds} = \pm\frac{\frac{d^2y}{dx^2}}{\left(1+\left(\frac{dy}{dx}\right)^2\right)^{\frac{3}{2}}}.$$

$\frac{d\theta}{ds} = \frac{1}{\rho}$, so that we have the formula $\left(\text{where } y_1 \equiv \frac{dy}{dx},\ y_2 \equiv \frac{d^2y}{dx^2}\right)$,

$$\rho = \pm\frac{(1+y_1{}^2)^{\frac{3}{2}}}{y_2}.$$

We choose the sign to obtain a positive answer.

Example 1. Find the radius of curvature at the point (2, 8) on the curve $y = x^3$.

$$\frac{dy}{dx} = 3x^2, \quad \frac{d^2y}{dx^2} = 6x,$$

$$\therefore \quad \rho = \pm\frac{(1+9x^4)^{\frac{3}{2}}}{6x} \text{ at the point } x$$

$$= \tfrac{1}{12}(1 + 9\times 2^4)^{\frac{3}{2}} \text{ at } x = 2$$

$$= \underline{145{\cdot}5.}$$

Example 2. Find the radius of curvature at the origin on the curve

$$x^3 + y^3 + 2x^2 - 4y + 3x = 0.$$

Differentiate the given equation :

$$3x^2 + 3y^2\frac{dy}{dx} + 4x - 4\frac{dy}{dx} + 3 = 0.$$

At (0, 0) this gives

$$\frac{dy}{dx} = \tfrac{3}{4}.$$

Again differentiate :

$$6x + 3y^2\frac{d^2y}{dx^2} + \frac{dy}{dx}\cdot 6y\frac{dy}{dx} + 4 - 4\frac{d^2y}{dx^2} = 0.$$

At (0, 0) with $\frac{dy}{dx} = \frac{3}{4}$ we find $\frac{d^2y}{dx^2} = 1.$

$$\therefore \quad \rho = \frac{(1 + \frac{9}{16})^{\frac{3}{2}}}{1} = \underline{\tfrac{125}{64}}.$$

EXERCISE 56A

Find the radius of curvature at the points:

1. (1, 4) on $y = 4x^2$.
2. (2, 4) on $y^2 = 2x^3$.
3. (1, 4) on $xy = 4$.
4. $\left(\frac{\pi}{6}, 2\right)$ on $y = 4 \sin x$.
5. (− 4, 0) on $xy = 16(x + 4)$.
6. (2, 2) on $x^3 + y^3 = 4xy$.
7. (x_1, y_1) on $y = c \log \sin \left(\frac{x}{c}\right)$.
8. (0, 1) on $y = \frac{1}{(x^2 + 1)}$.
9. (0, 1) on $y = e^x$.
10. (x_1, y_1) on $x^{\frac{2}{3}} + y^{\frac{2}{3}} = a^{\frac{2}{3}}$.

11. Prove that at any point on the curve $xy = c^2$, the radius of curvature is given by $\rho = \frac{r^3}{2c^2}$, where r is the distance of the point from the origin.

12. Prove that the curvature at any point on $y = a \text{ ch} \left(\frac{x}{a}\right)$ is $\frac{a}{y^2}$.

13. Find the radius of curvature at any point on $y = a + \frac{a^2}{x}$ and its minimum value.

14. When a body is moving on a curve, it experiences at any point an acceleration $\frac{v^2}{\rho}$ along the normal, where v is its velocity at the instant and ρ the radius of curvature at the point. Find this normal acceleration at the origin for the curve $y = x(x - 3)^2$ for a speed of 3 ft./sec.

15.* For the parabola $y = 1 + x - x^2$ show that the equation to the circle of curvature at (1, 1) is $x^2 + y^2 = 2$.

16. In problems on the deflection of a beam the gradient is usually so small that $y_1{}^2$ may be neglected. Show that the curvature is given by $\frac{1}{\rho} = \pm y_2$.

The deflection of the centre line of a beam under certain conditions is given by $y = \frac{w}{\text{EI}}\left(\frac{l}{2}x^2 - \frac{1}{6}x^3\right)$. Show that the curvature at $x = \frac{l}{2}$ is $\frac{wl}{2\text{EI}}$.

23.3. Newton's Method for ρ

When a curve touches the x or y axis at the origin, an alternative method exists for determining the radius of curvature there.

Suppose that the curve is given by

$$y = a_0 + a_1x + a_2x^2 + a_3x^3 + \ldots$$

and touches the x axis.

Since (0, 0) lies on it, $a_0 = 0$. Also

$$\left(\frac{dy}{dx}\right)_{x=0} = a_1, \quad \left(\frac{d^2y}{dx^2}\right)_{x=0} = 2a_2, \quad \ldots \quad (1)$$

and $a_1 = 0$ since the gradient at (0, 0) is zero. The equation is now

$$y = a_2x^2 + a_3x^3 + \ldots \quad (2)$$

and by the formula, using the values (1),

$$\rho = \frac{(1 + y_1{}^2)^{\frac{3}{2}}}{y_2} = \frac{1}{2a_2} \quad \ldots \quad (3)$$

where we will take the positive value of the result.

But from (2) $$\frac{y}{x^2} = a_2 + a_3x + \ldots$$

and taking the limit of each side as x (and therefore y) tends to zero

$$\lim_{x \to 0} \left(\frac{y}{x^2}\right) = \lim_{x \to 0} (a_2 + a_3x + \ldots) = a_2 \quad . \quad . \quad . \quad . \quad . \quad (4)$$

From (3) and (4) we obtain the formula

$$\lim_{x \to 0} \left(\frac{y}{x^2}\right) = \frac{1}{2\rho}$$

for the radius of curvature at the origin of a curve which touches the x axis there.

For the curve $$y = x^2 + x^3 \quad \text{[Fig. 56(}a\text{)]},$$

since $$\frac{y}{x^2} = 1 + x$$

$$\frac{1}{2\rho} = \lim_{x \to 0} \left(\frac{y}{x^2}\right) = \lim_{x \to 0} (1 + x) = 1 \text{ or } \underline{\rho = \tfrac{1}{2}.}$$

When the curve touches the y axis at the origin, a similar method gives

$$\frac{1}{2\rho} = \lim_{y \to 0} \left(\frac{x}{y^2}\right)$$

for ρ the radius of curvature there. Thus, for the curve $y^2 = 4ax$ [Fig. 45], $\frac{x}{y^2} = \frac{1}{4a}$ and $\frac{1}{2\rho} = \lim_{y \to 0} \left(\frac{x}{y^2}\right) = \lim_{y \to 0} \left(\frac{1}{4a}\right) = \frac{1}{4a}$ or $\underline{\rho = 2a.}$

Example 3. Find the radius of curvature at the point $(a, 0)$ on the ellipse $b^2x^2 + a^2y^2 = a^2b^2$.

Transfer to this point as origin by putting $x = \text{X} + a$ and we obtain an ellipse touching the y axis at the new origin, the point A in Fig. 49. The equation is now

$$b^2(\text{X} + a)^2 + a^2y^2 = a^2b^2$$

or $$b^2\text{X}^2 + 2ab^2\text{X} + a^2y^2 = 0$$

Here we need $\frac{\text{X}}{y^2}$ and from the equation form

$$b^2\text{X} \cdot \frac{\text{X}}{y^2} + 2ab^2\frac{\text{X}}{y^2} + a^2 = 0$$

Taking the limit as X, y tend to zero

$$b^2 \lim. \text{X} \cdot \lim. \left(\frac{\text{X}}{y^2}\right) + 2ab^2 \lim. \left(\frac{\text{X}}{y^2}\right) + \lim. a^2 = 0.$$

Since $\lim. \text{X} = 0$ whilst $\lim. \left(\frac{\text{X}}{y^2}\right) = \frac{1}{2\rho}$, the first term is zero. In total

$$2ab^2\left(\frac{1}{2\rho}\right) + a^2 = 0, \quad \underline{\rho = -\frac{b^2}{a}.}$$

EXERCISE 56B

1. For the circle centre $(a, 0)$ radius a, obtain the equation $x^2 - 2ax + y^2 = 0$ and hence, by the above method, the obvious answer $\rho = a$.
2. Show that at the point $(0, b)$ on $\frac{x^2}{a^2} + \frac{y^2}{b^2} = 1$, $\rho = \frac{a^2}{b}$.
3. Show that for $x^2 = 4by$, $\rho = 2b$ at the origin.
4. At a vertex of the hyperbola $x^2 - y^2 = a^2$, show that $\rho = a$.
5. Show that at the origin $\rho = 2$ for the curve
$$3x^2 + 4x^3 - 12y = 0$$
6. Show that at the point $(a, 0)$ on the curve
$$ay^2 = (x - a)(x - b)^2, \quad \rho = \frac{(a - b)^2}{2a}.$$

23.4. Centre of Curvature

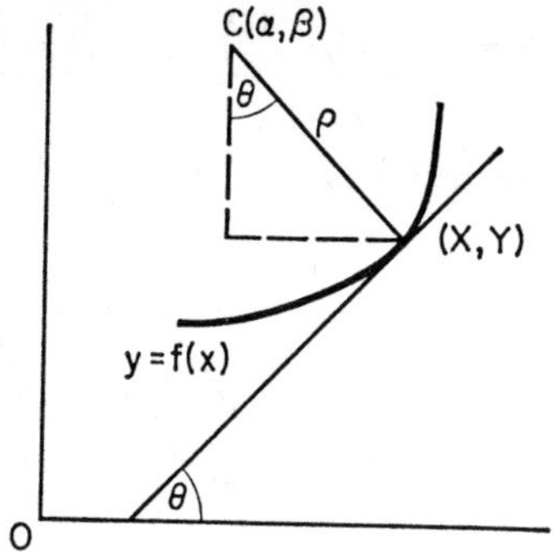

FIG. 72.

If the centre of curvature for the point (X, Y) on the curve $y = f(x)$ is (α, β), since this point is on the normal to the curve at (x, y) and a distance ρ from it,

$$\begin{aligned}\alpha &= X - \rho \sin \theta \\ &= X - \frac{(1 + y_1^2)^{\frac{3}{2}}}{y_2} \cdot \frac{y_1}{(1 + y_1^2)^{\frac{1}{2}}} \\ &= X - \frac{y_1}{y_2}(1 + y_1^2)\end{aligned}$$

where y_1, y_2 are the values of $f'(X)$ and $f''(X)$, *i.e.*, the first and second derivatives evaluated at the point (X, Y).
Similarly,

$$\begin{aligned}\beta &= Y + \rho \cos \theta \\ &= Y + \frac{(1 + y_1^2)^{\frac{3}{2}}}{y_2} \cdot \frac{1}{(1 + y_1^2)^{\frac{1}{2}}} \\ &= Y + \frac{(1 + y_1^2)}{y_2}.\end{aligned}$$

In these formulae the actual values of y_1 and y_2 with their signs must be used. For example, if y_1 is posit ve (as shown) but y_2 negative the curve at (X, Y) will be on the other side of the tangent and concave downwards. C will be on the other side of the tangent and have its co-ordinates α increased but β decreased. The formulae give this provided y_2 with its negative sign is used.

Example 4. Find the centre of curvature at (3, 4) on the curve $xy = 12$.

$$y = \frac{12}{x}$$

$$y_1 = -\frac{12}{x^2} = -\frac{4}{3} \text{ at } (3, 4)$$

$$y_2 = \frac{24}{x^3} = \frac{8}{9} \text{ at } (3, 4).$$

Hence
$$\alpha = 3 - \left(-\frac{4}{3}\right)\left(\frac{9}{8}\right)\left(1 + \frac{16}{9}\right) = \frac{43}{6}$$
$$\beta = 4 + \frac{9}{8}\left(1 + \frac{16}{9}\right) = \frac{57}{8}.$$

23.5. The Contact of Plane Curves

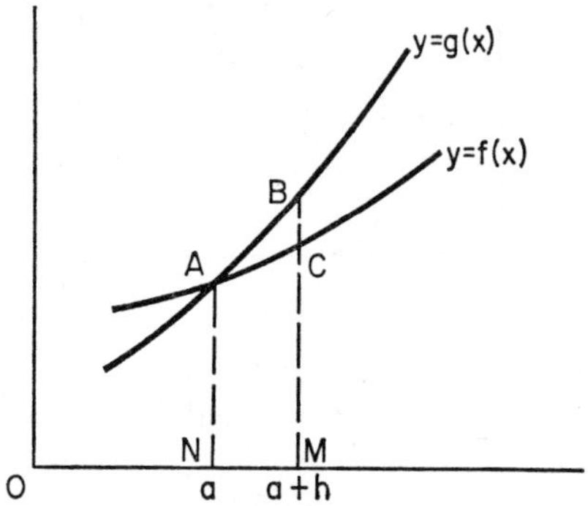

FIG. 73.

If the curves $y = f(x)$, $y = g(x)$ meet at the point A where $x = a$ then $f(a) = g(a)$. If in addition $f'(a) = g'(a)$, the curves touch at $x = a$ and have contact there of the *first order*. If also $f''(a) = g''(a)$ but $f^3(a) \neq g^3(a)$, then they are said to have contact at $x = a$ of the *second order* and so for higher orders of contact.

We can illustrate this as follows. By the Second Mean Value theorem if $x = a + h$ is the point M the ordinates there are given by

$$f(a + h) = f(a) + hf'(a) + \frac{h^2}{2!}f''(a + \theta_1 h)$$
$$g(a + h) = g(a) + hg'(a) + \frac{h^2}{2!}g''(a + \theta_2 h).$$

If now the curves have first-order contact only at A, so that $f(a) = g(a)$ and $f'(a) = g'(a)$ but no more, then the intercept BC between the curves at a distance $x = h$ from this point is given by

$$\mathrm{BC} = g(a + h) - f(a + h) = \frac{h^2}{2!}[g''(a + \theta_1 h) - f''(a + \theta_2 h)]$$

or as
$$h \to 0, \quad \lim_{h \to 0} \left(\frac{\mathrm{BC}}{h^2}\right) = \tfrac{1}{2}[g''(a) - f''(a)].$$

This shows that when curves *touch* at a point the difference of their ordinates at a near point is of the *second* order of smallness in h. Similarly, for higher orders of contact.

We will find the circle which has the highest possible order of contact with a given curve $y = f(x)$ at a point on it (x, y). If the equation is

$$(x - \alpha)^2 + (y - \beta)^2 = R^2 \quad . \quad . \quad . \quad . \quad . \quad (1)$$

differentiate:

$$2(x - \alpha) + 2(y - \beta)y_1 = 0 \quad . \quad . \quad . \quad . \quad . \quad (2)$$

Since y_1 must be the same as that of the given curve this rearranged as

$$\left(\frac{y - \beta}{x - \alpha}\right) = -\frac{1}{y_1}$$

shows that the join of the centre (α, β) of the circle to the point (x, y) is perpendicular to the tangent there, *i.e.*, (α, β) is on the normal at the point.

Differentiate again.

$$2 + 2(y - \beta)y_2 + 2y_1^2 = 0 \quad . \quad . \quad . \quad . \quad . \quad (3)$$

where again y_2 will be chosen to agree with that of the curve. We now have three equations which suffice to determine α, β, R the three unknowns in (1). Hencc generally a circle cannot have higher-order contact than two with a curve.

(3) gives

$$y - \beta = -\frac{1 + y_1^2}{y_2}$$

$$\beta = y + \frac{1 + y_1^2}{y_2}$$

using this, (2) gives

$$\alpha = x - \frac{y_1(1 + y_1^2)}{y_2}$$

and by (1)

$$R^2 = \frac{(1 + y_1^2)^3}{y_2^2}.$$

But these are the co-ordinates and radius of the circle of curvature. Hence this circle is also the circle of closest contact with a curve at a point on it.

Since the curves, the circle and $y = f(x)$ have only second-order contact at, say, $x = a$, the intercept BC of 23.5 can be shown to be

$$BC = \frac{h^3}{3!}[g^{(3)}(a + \theta_1 h) - f^{(3)}(a + \theta_2 h)]$$

by an extension of the Mean Value theorem to one more term. Assuming that $g^{(3)}(x)$ and $f^{(3)}(x)$ are continuous at $x = a$, their sign will not change as h changes from small positive to small negative. Hence the sign of BC is determined by that of h^3, which, being an odd function of h, changes sign as we move to below $x = a$ and have h negative. Hence a circle of curvature crosses the curve at the point of contact as shown in Fig. 71.

EXERCISE 56C

1. Find the values of a and b for which the parabola $y = ax(b - x)$ and the curve $y(x + 2) = x$ touch each other at the origin and have the same curvature there.

2. Show that the co-ordinates of the centre of curvature at the point (x, y) on a curve given by (a) $x = a(\log \cot (\theta/2) - \cos \theta), y = a \sin \theta$ are $x + a \cos \theta$ and a^2/y but for (b) $x = at^2$, $y = 2at$ they are $a(2 + 3t^2)$, $-2at^3$.

3. P is the point $t = \pi/3$ on the curve $x = \sin^3 t, y = 3 \cos^3 t$, and C is the centre of curvature at P. Show that CP has the equation $y\sqrt{3} = x$ and its length is $2\frac{1}{4}$.

4. Prove that the origin is a point of inflexion for $y = 3x^3 + 3x$. Show that the tangent at this point is $y = 3x$ and that the curve crosses the tangent at this point.

5. The curves $y^2 = 9x$ and $y = a + bx + x^2 + cx^3$ touch at (1, 3), and for the latter (1, 3) is a point of inflexion. Show that $a = \frac{11}{6}$, $b = \frac{1}{2}$, $c = -\frac{1}{3}$.

6. Show that the radius of curvature for the curve $x = a \cos^3 \theta$, $y = a \sin^3 \theta$ is given by $\rho = \frac{3}{2}a \sin 2\theta$. If C is the centre of curvature for the point P on the curve and if Q divides PC in the ratio 1 : 2, show that as P describes its curve Q describes the locus $x^2 + y^2 = a^2$.

7. Show that the curves

$$f(x) = x - \sin x, \; g(x) = x - \tfrac{1}{6}x^3 - \sin x$$

have contact of the second order only at the origin.

CHAPTER 24

CENTRES OF GRAVITY

24.1. Differentials

In Chapter 20 we wrote down an exact expression for the element of area of width Δx and found the limit of this as $\Delta x \to 0$. We obtained

$$\frac{dA}{dx} = y$$

and then integrated. We now wish to shorten the work involved and proceed as follows: we assume the width of the element is dx and its height y, *knowing by experience* that the small curvilinear area at the top of the rectangle does not affect the final result. The area of the element is then ydx, and since *integration sums* such elements, we integrate and obtain

$$A = \int ydx.$$

Similarly for volumes: when the height y rotates round the x axis the disc of width dx has a volume

$$\pi y^2 dx,$$

the volume due to the small area at the top of the rectangle being ignored. We then sum these elements of volume and write

$$V = \int \pi y^2 dx.$$

Finally, we will consider the formula for the element of area in polar co-ordinates (see Fig. 69). If we ignore the extra element of area due to OQ being different in length to OP, we can regard the element of area as a sector of a circle of radius r and angle $d\theta$ (the increase in θ). This element has area

$$\tfrac{1}{2}r^2 d\theta$$

and the total area is

$$\int \tfrac{1}{2}r^2 d\theta.$$

The expression ydx or $\pi y^2 dx$ or $\frac{1}{2}r^2 d\theta$ is called a *differential.*

In the following we will work with differentials. If ever the student is in doubt he should work with finite increments such as Δx and *find the limit concerned.*

24.2. Fundamental Formula

The fundamental formula obtained by moments is: The c.g. of a system of n particles of masses $m_1, m_2 \dots m_r \dots m_n$ is given by the formula

$$x = \frac{\Sigma m_r x_r}{\Sigma m_r}, \quad y = \frac{\Sigma m_r y_r}{\Sigma m_r},$$

where the mass m_r is supposed situated at the point (x_r, y_r). We will deal only with those cases where we have a continuous mass so that we have to integrate in order to sum the elements of mass and their contributions to the total " moment ".

Example 1. Find the centre of gravity of a rod the density of which varies as the square of the distance from one end.

Consider an element dx distant x from the end. We assume dx so small, that all of it is distant x from O and therefore its c.g. is also at this distance.

$$\text{Mass of element} = kx^2dx.$$

$$\therefore \quad \text{total mass, } i.e. \ \Sigma m = \int_0^l kx^2dx = \frac{kl^3}{3}.$$

The moment of this element about O is

$$(kx^2dx)x,$$

$\therefore$ total moment, *i.e.*

$$\Sigma mx = \int_0^l kx^3dx = \frac{kl^4}{4}.$$

$$\therefore \quad \bar{x} = \frac{\Sigma mx}{\Sigma m} = \frac{\frac{kl^4}{4}}{\frac{kl^3}{3}} = \underline{\tfrac{3}{4}l}.$$

24.3. Centre of Mass of a Lamina

Consider an element of area of height $y = \text{LM}$ and width dx. We will assume that its centre of mass is on LM, and therefore has co-ordinates $(x, y/2)$. (Fig. 74(a).)

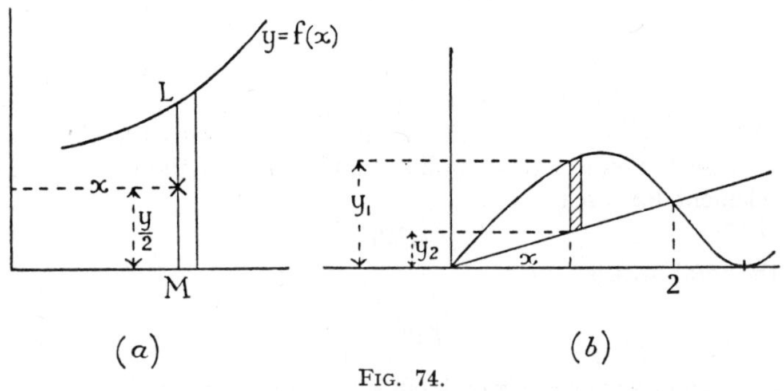

FIG. 74.

If ρ is the uniform density, the mass of the element is $\rho y dx$ and its moment about the y axis is

$$(\rho y dx)x,$$

$\therefore$ the total moment about the y axis is

$$\rho\int xydx.$$

Similarly, the total moment about the x axis is

$$\int(\rho ydx)\tfrac{1}{2}y = \rho\int\tfrac{1}{2}y^2dx.$$

The total mass is $\rho \times$ area involved

$$= \rho\int ydx.$$

Knowing the curve bounding the lamina $y = f(x)$, we can substitute for y and then evaluate these integrals between the limits as given.

We therefore have

$$x = \frac{\Sigma mx}{\Sigma m} = \frac{\rho\int xydx}{\rho\int ydx} = \frac{\int xydx}{\int ydx}$$

$$y = \frac{\Sigma my}{\Sigma m} = \frac{\rho\int \frac{1}{2}y^2dx}{\rho\int ydx} = \frac{\int \frac{1}{2}y^2dx}{\int ydx}.$$

Example 2. Find the centre of mass of the area nearest the origin in Example 1 of Chapter 20 (Fig. 74(*b*)).

From this example, area = 4 sq. units.

Consider an element of area as shown. We will consider this as a rectangle on base dx with the c.g. on the ordinate at x and half-way between the curves. Its co-ordinates are therefore x, $\frac{1}{2}(y_1 + y_2)$.

For moments about the y axis

$$\begin{aligned}\Sigma mx &= \int_0^2 \rho(y_1 - y_2)dx\,.\,x \\ &= \rho\int_0^2 x[x(x-3)^2 - x]dx \\ &= \rho\int_0^2 (x^4 - 6x^3 + 8x^2)dx = \rho\cdot\tfrac{56}{15},\end{aligned}$$

$$\therefore\quad \bar{x} = \frac{\frac{56}{15}}{4} = \underline{\tfrac{14}{15}}.$$

For moments about the x axis

$$\begin{aligned}\Sigma my &= \int_0^2 \rho(y_1 - y_2)dx\left(\frac{y_1 + y_2}{2}\right) \\ &= \frac{\rho}{2}\int_0^2 (y_1^2 - y_2^2)dx \\ &= \frac{\rho}{2}\int_0^2 [x^2(x-3)^4 - x^2]dx \\ &= \frac{\rho}{2}\int_0^2 (x^6 - 12x^5 + 54x^4 - 108x^3 + 80x^2)dx \\ &= \rho\tfrac{904}{105},\end{aligned}$$

$$\therefore\quad \bar{y} = \frac{\frac{904}{105}}{4} = \underline{\tfrac{226}{105}}.$$

24.4. Solids of Revolution

When the solid may be regarded as formed by the revolution of an area round the x axis, the c.g. is clearly on the x axis. We must therefore find only $\bar{x}$, the distance from O of the c.g.

The body may be considered as composed of discs each of thickness dx.

$$\therefore \quad x = \frac{\Sigma mx}{\Sigma m} = \frac{\rho\int \pi y^2 dx \, . \, x}{\rho\int \pi y^2 dx}.$$

For an application of this method see 24.5, where the c.g. of a hemispherical solid is found.

The same method applies for a surface of revolution, where if ds is the element that revolves round the x axis on a radius y

$$\bar{x} = \frac{\rho\int 2\pi y ds \, . \, x}{\rho\int 2\pi y ds}.$$

In this case ρ is the surface density.

For an application of this method see 24.5, where the c.g. of a zone of a sphere is found.

EXERCISE 57

1. Find the position of the c.g. of a rod of length a whose density varies as the nth power of the distance from one end.

2. Show that the centroid of the area of a quarter of a circle (radius a) is on the bisecting radius and distant $4a\sqrt{2}/3\pi$ from the centre.

3. Consider a semicircular area as composed of two quarter circles and use the result of Exercise 2 to show that the centroid of a semicircular area is on the bisecting radius and distant $4a/3\pi$ from the centre where a is the radius.

4. Find the c.g. of the area bounded by the parabolas $y^2 = 4ax$ and $x^2 = 4ay$.

5. Find the c.g. of the area bounded by the curve $y = \sin x$ between $x = 0$ and π and the x axis.

6. Find the centre of mass of the area of the loop of the curve $y^2 = x(1 - x)^2$.

7. The area of the parabola $y^2 = 4ax$ cut off by $x = a$ revolves round the x axis. Find the c.g. of the solid formed.

8. The area of the loop of $y^2 = x^3(1 - x)^2$ revolves round the x axis. Find the co-ordinates of the c.g. of this solid.

9. A segment of height h is cut off from a sphere of radius a ($>h$). Find the distance of the c.g. from the centre of the sphere.

Prove that the c.g. will be $a/4$ from the plane face of the segment, provided h/a satisfies the equation $x^2 - 5x + 3 = 0$. [L.U.]

10. Find the c.g. of the area bounded by $y^2 = 4ax$ and the line $y = mx$.

24.5. Some Standard Centres of Gravity

In this section we will find the position of the centre of gravity in a number of cases that frequently occur.

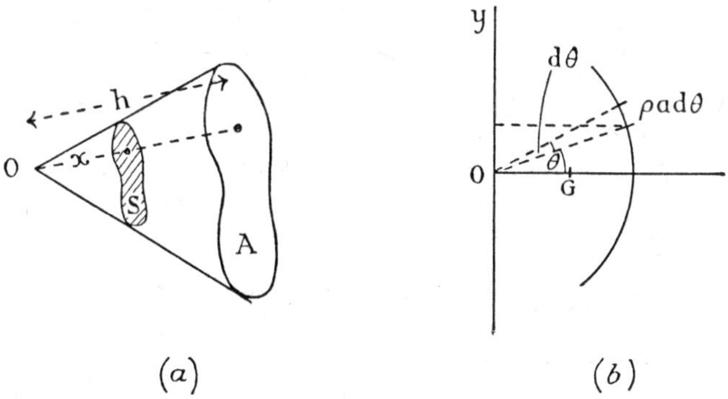

FIG. 75.

A Pyramid (Fig. 75(*a*))

By a pyramid we mean the body formed when a *plane* base of any shape is joined to a vertex.

Let A be the area of the plane base and h the perpendicular height. Suppose a section parallel to the base and x away from O to be of area S, and take as the element of volume Sdx, where dx is the thickness.

Since similar areas vary as the square of the distance from the vertex

$$\frac{S}{A} = \frac{x^2}{h^2}.$$

Since the element of volume is Sdx, the total volume is

$$\int_0^h S dx = \int_0^h A \frac{x^2}{h^2} dx = \tfrac{1}{3}Ah.$$

If ρ be the density, then by moments about the vertex O, the total moment of the pyramid is

$$\int_0^h \rho S dx \times x$$

$$= \rho \int_0^h A \frac{x^3}{h^2} dx = \rho A \frac{h^2}{4}.$$

$$\therefore \quad \bar{x} = \frac{\Sigma mx}{\Sigma m} = \frac{\rho A \frac{h^2}{4}}{\rho \frac{1}{3} A h}$$
$$= \tfrac{3}{4}h.$$

This lies on the line joining O to the c.g. of the base area. Note that a right circular cone is a special case of the above and has its c.g. on its axis, three-quarters of the way down from the vertex.

The Arc of a Circle (Fig. 75(*b*))

The c.g. clearly lies on the bisecting radius of the arc. We need to find its distance on this radius from O.

Consider an element of arc of length $ad\theta$ and mass $\rho a d\theta$.

If 2α is the angle of the arc, the total moment about Oy is

$$\int_{-\alpha}^{+\alpha} \rho a d\theta \times a \cos \theta = 2\rho a^2 \sin \alpha.$$

The mass of the wire is $\rho 2a\alpha$,

$$\therefore \quad OG = \bar{x} = \frac{2\rho a^2 \sin \alpha}{\rho 2a\alpha} = a\frac{\sin \alpha}{\alpha}.$$

In the case of a semicircle of wire $\alpha = \frac{\pi}{2}$,

$$\therefore \quad OG = \frac{a \sin \frac{\pi}{2}}{\frac{\pi}{2}} = \frac{2a}{\pi}.$$

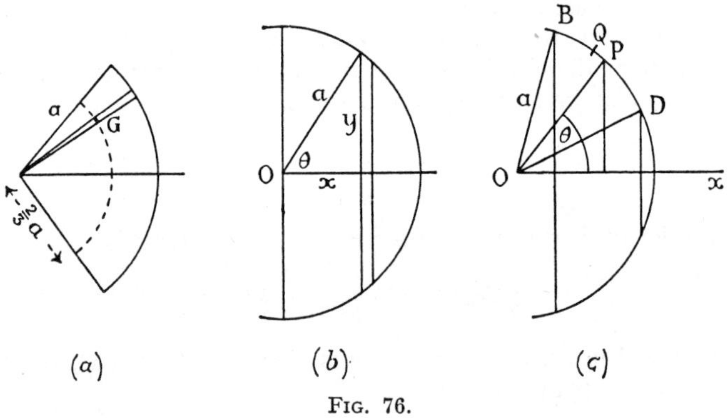

FIG. 76.

The Sector of a Circle (Fig. 76(*a*))

We may imagine the sector composed of equal elements of area, each a triangle as shown. The c.g. of each triangle is $\frac{2}{3}a$ from O.

Instead of the sector we may therefore consider an arc of centres of gravity and by the above the c.g. of this arc is given by

$$x = \tfrac{2}{3}a\frac{\sin\alpha}{\alpha}$$

where, as above, 2α is the angle of the sector and the c.g. lies on the bisecting radius.

In the case of a *semicircular area* $\alpha = \dfrac{\pi}{2}$ and

$$x = \frac{4a}{3\pi}.$$

As an illustration we will obtain this result directly by calculus (Fig. 76(*b*)):

$$\Sigma m = \rho \times \tfrac{1}{2}\pi a^2,$$

$$\Sigma mx = \int_0^a (\rho 2y\,dx)x$$

$$= 2\rho\int_0^a xy\,dx = 2\rho\int_0^a x\sqrt{(a^2 - x^2)}\,dx$$

$$= 2\rho\left[\frac{(a^2 - x^2)^{\frac{3}{2}}}{-3}\right]_0^a = \frac{2}{3}\rho a^3,$$

$$\therefore\quad \bar{x} = \frac{2\rho a^3/3}{\frac{1}{2}\rho\pi a^2} = \frac{4a}{3\pi}.$$

The Zone of a Sphere (Fig. 76(*c*))

A zone is the portion between two parallel planes. We are here concerned only with the thin " skin " formed by the rotation round Ox of an arc BD, where $\angle$BO$x = \alpha$ and $\angle$DO$x = \beta$.

Consider the contribution of the element due to the rotation of PQ round Ox, where $\angle$POQ $= d\theta$ and $\angle$PO$x = \theta$.

If the surface density is ρ

$$\text{mass of element} = \rho \times a\,d\theta \times 2\pi a \sin\theta,$$

$$\therefore\ \text{total mass} = 2a^2\rho\pi\int_\beta^\alpha \sin\theta\,d\theta$$

$$= 2\pi a^2\rho(\cos\beta - \cos\alpha).$$

For moments about Oy

$$\text{total moment} = \int_\beta^\alpha (\rho \times a\,d\theta \times 2\pi a\sin\theta) \times a\cos\theta$$

$$= 2\pi a^3\rho\int_\beta^\alpha \sin\theta\cos\theta\,d\theta$$

$$= \pi a^3\rho\left[\cos^2\theta\right]_\alpha^\beta$$

$$= \pi a^3\rho(\cos^2\beta - \cos^2\alpha).$$

$$\therefore \quad \bar{x} = \frac{\pi a^3\rho(\cos^2\beta - \cos^2\alpha)}{2\pi a^2\rho(\cos\beta - \cos\alpha)}.$$
$$= \frac{a}{2}(\cos\beta + \cos\alpha).$$

The c.g. is therefore half-way between the circular ends of the zone.

For a *hemispherical shell* $\beta = 0$ and $\alpha = \frac{\pi}{2}$,

$$\therefore \quad \bar{x} = \frac{a}{2}$$

and is half-way down the central radius.

A Solid Hemisphere

We will use Fig. 76(*b*), which now represents a central section of a hemisphere.

$$\Sigma m = \rho \times \tfrac{2}{3}\pi a^3,$$
$$\Sigma mx = \int_0^a (\rho\pi y^2 dx)x$$
$$[x^2 + y^2 = a^2] \qquad = \pi\rho\int_0^a (a^2 - x^2)x dx$$
$$= \pi\rho\tfrac{1}{4}a^4,$$
$$\therefore \quad \bar{x} = \tfrac{3}{8}a$$

and lies on the central radius.

EXERCISE 58

Whenever possible the following examples should be done without the use of calculus. Each body should be regarded as the sum or difference of bodies with known centres of gravity.

1. From a solid hemisphere of radius a, a right circular cone is scooped out, its base being the base of the hemisphere and its height a. Find the c.g. of the remaining solid.

2. A segment of a circle of radius a is bounded by a chord. Show that the distance of the c.g. from the centre is given by

$$\bar{x} = \frac{1}{12}\,\frac{(\text{chord})^3}{(\text{area of segment})}.$$

3. A hemispherical shell has its inner and outer radii a and b respectively. Show that the distance of its c.g. from the centre of the hemisphere is $\dfrac{3(a+b)(a^2+b^2)}{8(a^2+ab+b^2)}$.

4. A closed wire is bent to form a circular arc and the two bounding radii. It is found that the c.g. of the wire coincides with the centre of the circle of which the arc is a part. Show that the angle subtended at the centre by the arc is $2\tan^{-1}(-\tfrac{1}{2})$.

5. An arc of a circle of radius a subtends angle 2α at the centre. Prove that the area formed by this arc and the tangents at its ends has its centroid distant $\frac{(a \sin^3 \alpha)}{3 \cos^2 \alpha(\tan \alpha - \alpha)}$ from the centre.

6*. The figure shows a crank of uniform thickness with *semicircular* ends joined by straight lines and pierced by two circular holes. Find the distance of its c.g. from the centre of the smaller hole (Fig. 58).

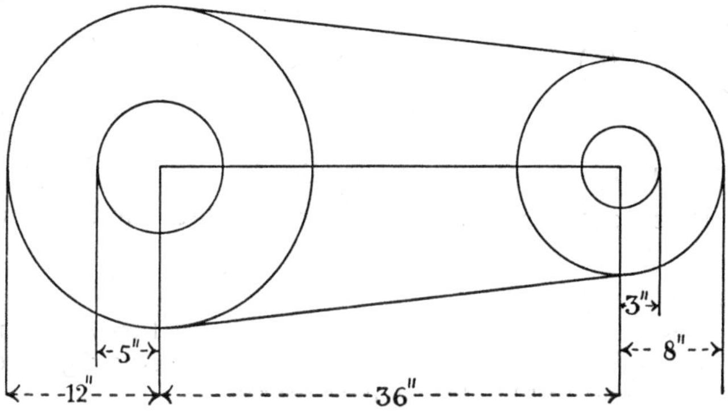

FIG. 77.

7. A thick conical shell without a base is bounded by two right circular cones each of semi-vertical angle α, the base radii being r and $r - t$. Show that the height of the c.g. above the base is $\frac{1}{6}(2r - 3t)\cot \alpha$ where the square of t/r is neglected.

8. A thin hemispherical shell with a base of the same material is filled with water and suspended from a point on the rim of the base. In this position the base makes angle α with the vertical. Show that the ratio of the weight of the water to that of the shell is $\frac{(\tan \alpha - \frac{1}{3})}{(\frac{3}{8} - \tan \alpha)}$.

9. The figure is composed of semicircular arcs of wire of radii a, $2a$. Find the distance of the c.g. from the common diameter (Fig. 78(a)).

10. A trapezium has 2 parallel sides a and b, distant h apart. Show that the distance of the c.g. from the side a is given by $\bar{x} = \frac{h}{3}\frac{(2b + a)}{(a + b)}$.

[The figure should be regarded as the sum of two triangles, on base a and base b, with weights proportional to the areas acting at the c.g. of each triangle.]

11. A casting uniform in material and thickness has the form given in the sketch. Find the distance of its mass centre from AB (Fig. 78(b)). [L.U.]

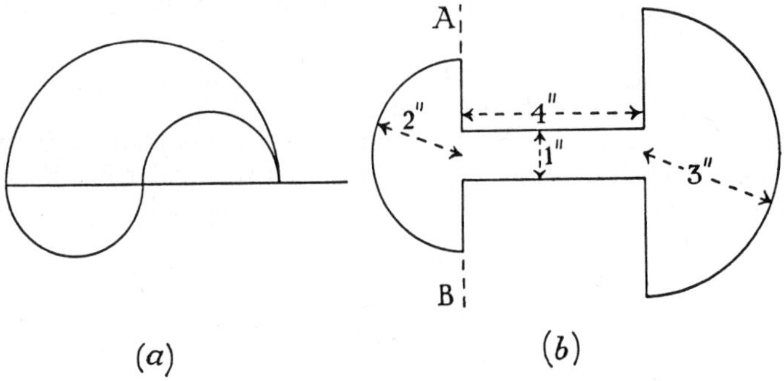

FIG. 78.

24.6. The Theorems of Pappus (or Guldinus)

For the sake of completeness we will repeat these two theorems.

Theorem 1

If a *curve* revolves round an axis which it does not cross, the area of the *surface* generated is equal to the length of the curve multiplied by the distance travelled by the c.g. of the *curve.*

Example 3. Find the area of the surface of an anchor ring generated by the revolution of a circle radius r round an axis distant R from its centre.

$$\begin{aligned} \text{Length of revolving curve} &= 2\pi r, \\ \text{Distance its c.g. travels} &= 2\pi R \\ \therefore \quad \text{area of surface generated} &= 2\pi r \times 2\pi R \\ &= \underline{4\pi^2 rR}. \end{aligned}$$

Note that there is no need for the curve to make a complete revolution. If its c.g. revolves through $60° = \frac{\pi}{3}$ about the axis, the surface generated in the above example is

$$2\pi r \times \frac{\pi}{3}R = \tfrac{2}{3}\pi^2 rR.$$

These theorems can also be used to find the position of a centre of gravity:

Example 4. Find the c.g. of a semicircular wire.

We know that it is on the bisecting radius. Let it be $\bar{x}$ distant from the bounding diameter.

Now if the arc rotates completely round the diameter, the surface of a sphere is generated.

$$4\pi a^2 = \pi a \times 2\pi\bar{x},$$

$$\therefore \quad \bar{x} = \underline{\frac{2a}{\pi}}.$$

Theorem 2

If an *area* revolves round an axis which it does not cross, the *volume* generated is equal to the area that revolves multiplied by the distance travelled by the c.g. of the *area.*

Example 5. An induction coil has the cross-section shown, and is generated by a trapezium rotating round the axis XX. Find the volume of the coil (Fig. 79).

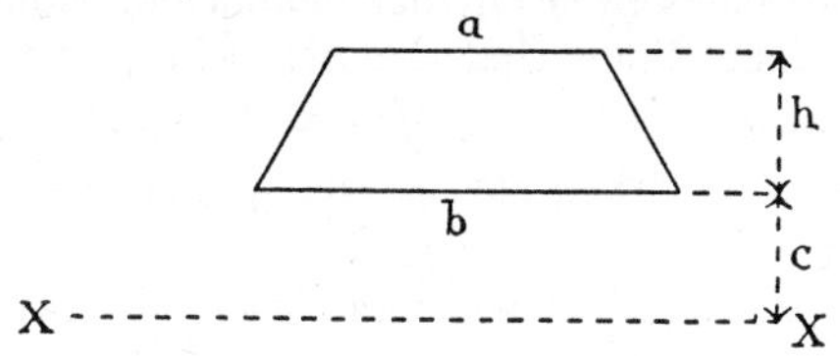

FIG. 79.

$$\text{Area of trapezium} = \frac{h}{2}(a + b).$$

$$\text{Height of c.g. of trapezium above base} = \frac{h}{3}\frac{(2a + b)}{(a + b)}.$$

$$\therefore \text{ height above axis of rotation} = \frac{h}{3}\frac{(2a + b)}{a + b} + c.$$

$$\therefore \text{ volume generated} = \frac{h}{2}(a + b) \,.\, 2\pi\left[\frac{h(2a + b)}{3(a + b)} + c\right]$$

$$= \frac{\pi h}{3}[h(2a + b) + 3c(a + b)].$$

EXERCISE 59

1. Find the position of the c.g. of a semicircular area.

2. Find the surface and volume generated when an equilateral triangle of side a rotates round its base.

3. A loudspeaker horn is formed by the revolution of a quadrant of a circle, radius R, about an axis parallel to the tangent at one corner and distant d from it. Show that the total area of its curved surface is $\pi^2 R(R + d) - 2\pi R^2$.

4. The cross-section of a bowl consists of two equal semi-circles with their bounding diameters perpendicular to the line (the base of the bowl) joining their lower ends. Show that the area of the inner surface of the bowl is $\frac{1}{4}\pi(d^2 - 2dh + 5h^2) + \frac{1}{2}\pi^2 h(d - h)$ where h is the height and d the diameter of the bowl.

5. Find the area between the curve $y = (x - 2)(x - 5)$ and the x axis. Find the volume when this area revolves round the x axis and use Pappus' theorem to deduce the distance of the c.g. of the area from the x axis.

6. Prove that the area enclosed between the curve and the axes in the first quadrant is $a^2/6$ for the curve $\sqrt{x} + \sqrt{y} = \sqrt{a}$. Find the position of the c.g. of this area, and the volume of revolution round the x axis and show that these results satisfy Pappus' theorem.

7. A circle, radius a, rotates round an axis in its own plane distant $b(>a)$ from the centre to form a closed ring. The surface of the ring is divided into two parts by a circular cylinder of radius $b - a\cos\theta$ co-axial with the ring. Show that the areas of the two parts are

$$4a\pi[b\theta - a\sin\theta] \text{ and } 4a\pi[b(\pi - \theta) + a\sin\theta]. \qquad \text{[L.U.]}$$

8. From a square ABCD of side a, the circular quadrant centre B radius $a/2$ and lying inside the square is removed. The remainder is revolved completely round AD to generate a solid of revolution. Show that its volume is $\pi a^3(13/12 - \pi/8)$.

9. The area A cut off from the parabola $y^2 = 4(x - 1)$ by the line $x = 2$ is rotated through four right angles about the y axis to form an anchor ring. By finding the centre of gravity of A and its area obtain $128\pi/15$ for the volume of the ring.

10. The ellipse $x^2/a^2 + y^2/b^2 = 1$ revolves round its tangent at the point on it $(a\cos\theta, b\sin\theta)$ and generates a volume. Show that the maximum volume possible is $2\pi^2a^2b$.

11. A uniform isosceles triangular lamina ABC, right angled at A is cut into 2 parts by a line DE parallel to BC so that AE/AC $= \lambda$, where $\lambda < 1$. Prove that the centre of mass of the quadrilateral BDEC is at a distance $\frac{1}{3}a(1 + \lambda + \lambda^2)/(1 + \lambda)$ from A, where a is the length of BC.

Show that if the quadrilateral is placed in a vertical plane with EC on the horizontal table it will not topple if

$$\lambda \leqslant \tfrac{1}{2}(\sqrt{3} - 1).$$

12. Find the centroid of the area enclosed by a curve drawn through the points

$$(1, 2), (1{\cdot}5, 2{\cdot}4), (2, 2{\cdot}7), (2{\cdot}5, 2{\cdot}8), (3, 3), (3{\cdot}5, 2{\cdot}6), (4, 2{\cdot}1)$$

the x axis and the ordinates at $x = 1$, $x = 4$.

13. Find the centroid of the area bounded by the curve drawn through the points given, the x axis and the extreme ordinates of the curve

$$(2, 1{\cdot}4), (3, 2), (4, 2{\cdot}3), (5, 1{\cdot}8), (6, 1{\cdot}2).$$

CHAPTER 25

INFINITE SERIES

25.1. Some Difficulties

(*a*) Suppose the student is asked to sum the infinite series

$$1 + \tfrac{1}{2} + \tfrac{1}{3} + \tfrac{1}{4} + \tfrac{1}{5} + \dots + \frac{1}{n} + \dots$$

a series which never terminates, each term being followed by yet more terms. The student may perhaps add the first twenty terms and find the sum to be about 3·6. Then, tiring of the process and noting that the terms are decreasing, he will hazard a guess that the sum is about 10 or even 20 or so.

However, suppose we group the terms as follows:

$$1 + \tfrac{1}{2} + (\tfrac{1}{3} + \tfrac{1}{4}) + (\tfrac{1}{5} + \dots + \tfrac{1}{8}) + (\tfrac{1}{9} + \dots + \tfrac{1}{16}) + (\tfrac{1}{17} + \dots + \tfrac{1}{32}) + \dots$$

Starting with the first bracket we note that

$$\tfrac{1}{3} + \tfrac{1}{4} > \tfrac{1}{4} + \tfrac{1}{4} = 2 \cdot \tfrac{1}{4} = \tfrac{1}{2}$$
$$\tfrac{1}{5} + \tfrac{1}{6} + \tfrac{1}{7} + \tfrac{1}{8} > \tfrac{1}{8} + \tfrac{1}{8} + \tfrac{1}{8} + \tfrac{1}{8} = 4 \cdot \tfrac{1}{8} = \tfrac{1}{2}$$
$$\tfrac{1}{9} + \dots + \tfrac{1}{16} > \tfrac{1}{16} + \dots + \tfrac{1}{16} = 8 \cdot \tfrac{1}{16} = \tfrac{1}{2}.$$

In this way we discover that the series is greater than

$$1 + \tfrac{1}{2} + \tfrac{1}{2} + \tfrac{1}{2} + \tfrac{1}{2} + \dots$$

In other words, so far from having a sum of 10 or 20 or even 20 million the sum is infinite, *i.e.*, however large a number N is given, by taking sufficient terms of the series the sum can be made to exceed N.

It can be shown that the sum of one million terms of this series lies between 13·8 and 14·8, whilst the sum of ten million terms lies between 16·1 and 17·1. Nevertheless, the sum of the series is infinite, so that by adding enough terms we can exceed in sum any given number.

(*b*) Consider an infinite series similar to the above:

$$1 - \tfrac{1}{2} + \tfrac{1}{3} - \tfrac{1}{4} + \tfrac{1}{5} - \tfrac{1}{6} \dots$$

If we denote the positive terms by S_1 and the negative by S_2

$$\begin{aligned} S_1 &= 1 + \tfrac{1}{3} + \tfrac{1}{5} + \tfrac{1}{7} + \dots \\ S_2 &= \tfrac{1}{2} + \tfrac{1}{4} + \tfrac{1}{6} + \dots \\ &= \tfrac{1}{2}(1 + \tfrac{1}{2} + \tfrac{1}{3} + \tfrac{1}{4} + \dots) \\ &= \tfrac{1}{2}\{(1 + \tfrac{1}{3} + \tfrac{1}{5} + \dots) + (\tfrac{1}{2} + \tfrac{1}{4} + \dots)\} \\ &= \tfrac{1}{2}\{S_1 + S_2\}. \end{aligned}$$

$$\therefore \quad 2S_2 = S_1 + S_2,$$
$$\therefore \quad S_2 = S_1,$$

or the sum of the negative terms equals the sum of the positive terms. But comparing term by term of S_1 with S_2 we note that

$$1 > \tfrac{1}{2}$$
$$\tfrac{1}{3} > \tfrac{1}{4}$$
$$\tfrac{1}{5} > \tfrac{1}{7}, \text{ etc.}$$

so that $S_1 > S_2$ and is not equal to it.

Difficulties such as these will lead the student to enquire whether in (*a*) we can show that an infinite series has or has not a definite sum and in (*b*) we can account for the contradictory results. We will now deal with the necessary theory, but only in an elementary way.

25.2. The Idea of a Limit

In connection with infinite series we are concerned only with finding the value of an expression in n as n tends to infinity, n being a positive integer.

We often use u_n to denote the nth term of a series which may be written

$$u_1 + u_2 + u_3 + \ldots u_n + \ldots = \sum_{n=1}^{\infty} u_n.$$

Consider a series for which

$$u_n = 2 + \frac{1}{n}.$$

Clearly as n becomes bigger and bigger u_n gets nearer and nearer to 2. Also by choosing n sufficiently large we can make u_n as near to 2 as we please. We therefore say that the limit of u_n as n tends to infinity is 2. In symbols

$$\lim_{n \to \infty} u_n = 2.$$

Example 1. Find the value of the following limits:

(*a*) $\displaystyle \lim_{n \to \infty} \frac{2n^2 + n - 4}{7n^2 + 6n - 20}$; (*b*) $\displaystyle \lim_{n \to \infty} \frac{n}{(2n - 1)(2n + 1)}$; (*c*) $\displaystyle \lim_{n \to \infty} \frac{n^4 + 3n^2 + 2}{n^2}$.

We will use the obvious limit

$$\lim_{n \to \infty} \frac{1}{n^s} = 0$$

for $s = 1, 2, 3 \ldots$

(*a*) Call the expression u_n and, dividing above and below by n^2, we have

$$u_n = \frac{2 + \frac{1}{n} - \frac{4}{n^2}}{7 + \frac{6}{n} - \frac{20}{n^2}},$$

$$\therefore \lim_{n \to \infty} u_n = \underline{\frac{2}{7}}.$$

(*b*)
$$u_n = \frac{\frac{1}{n}}{\left(2 - \frac{1}{n}\right)\left(2 + \frac{1}{n}\right)},$$

$$\therefore \lim_{n \to \infty} u_n = \frac{0}{4} = \underline{0}.$$

(c)
$$u_n = n^2 + 3 + \frac{2}{n^2}.$$

$$= n^2\left[1 + \frac{3}{n^2} + \frac{2}{n^4}\right]$$

$$\therefore \lim_{n \to \infty} u_n \to \infty \times 1$$

$$\to \underline{\infty}.$$

Apart from such simple examples, the product, powers and ratio of expressions that tend to infinity need to be treated with care.

EXERCISE 60

Find the limit of each of the following as $n \to \infty$:

1. $3 + \frac{4}{n^2}$. 2. $4 - \frac{10^4}{n}$. 3. $\frac{6n - 2}{3n + 20}$.

4. $2n^2 + 4n$. 5. $n + (-1)^n$. 6. $\frac{3^n}{1 + 3^n}$.

7. $(-\frac{1}{3})^n$. 8. $\frac{n - 1}{3n^2 + 1}$. 9. $\frac{1}{\sqrt{n}}$.

10. $\frac{\sqrt{n}}{2n + 1}$. 11. $\frac{(n + 2)(n + 3)}{n(n + 1)(n + 4)}$. 12. $\frac{n}{\sqrt{(n^2 - 3n)}}$.

If S_n denotes the sum of n terms, find S_n for each of the following series and the limits of this sum as $n \to \infty$.

13. $1 + 2 + 3 + 4 + \ldots n$.

14. $1 + \frac{1}{2} + \frac{1}{2^2} + \ldots \frac{1}{2^{n-1}} + \ldots$

15. $1 + \frac{1}{3} + \frac{1}{3^2} + \frac{1}{3^3} \ldots$

25.3. Definition of Convergent and Divergent Series

A series in which S_n, the sum of n terms of the series, tends to a definite value as n tends to infinity is called a *convergent* series.

For the series

$$1 + \frac{1}{2} + \frac{1}{2^2} + \ldots \frac{1}{2^{n-1}} + \ldots$$

$$S_n = \frac{1 - \frac{1}{2^n}}{1 - \frac{1}{2}} = 2 - \frac{1}{2^{n-1}},$$

$$\therefore \lim_{n \to \infty} S_n = 2$$

and the series is said to be convergent.

If S_n does not tend to a definite value as n tends to infinity, the series is said to be *divergent*.

For the series

$$1 + 2 + 2^2 + 2^3 + \ldots 2^{n-1} + \ldots$$

$$S_n = \frac{2^n - 1}{2 - 1} = 2^n - 1,$$

$$\therefore \lim_{n \to \infty} S_n = \infty$$

and the series is said to be divergent.

25.4. A Necessary Condition for Convergence

We will state without proof the following: a series cannot be convergent unless its terms ultimately tend to zero, *i.e.*, unless

$$\lim_{n \to \infty} u_n = 0.$$

Note that this theorem never proves the convergency of a series. It only states that if the above limit is *not* zero then the series must be divergent. It is still possible for the limit to be zero and for the series nevertheless to be divergent.

In the series

$$\frac{5}{11} + \frac{8}{21} + \frac{11}{31} + \ldots \frac{3n + 2}{10n + 1} + \ldots$$

$$u_n = \frac{\left(3 + \frac{2}{n}\right)}{\left(10 + \frac{1}{n}\right)},$$

$$\therefore \lim_{n \to \infty} u_n = \tfrac{3}{10}$$

and is not zero, *therefore* the series is divergent.

But in the harmonic series

$$1 + \frac{1}{2} + \frac{1}{3} + \ldots + \frac{1}{n} + \ldots$$

$$\lim_{n \to \infty} u_n = \lim_{n \to \infty} \frac{1}{n} = 0,$$

and yet the series has been proved divergent (25.1(*a*)).

25.5. The Comparison Test

We will state without proof the following theorem: a series of positive terms is convergent if its terms are less than the corresponding terms of a positive series which is known to be convergent. It is divergent if the terms are greater than the corresponding terms of a series of positive terms known to be divergent.

Example 2. (i) To test the series

$$1 + \frac{1}{2^2} + \frac{1}{3^3} + \frac{1}{4^4} + \ldots + \frac{1}{n^n} + \ldots$$

If we exclude the first two terms we can compare it with

$$\frac{1}{2^3} + \frac{1}{2^4} + \ldots + \frac{1}{2^n} + \ldots \qquad \ldots \ldots \qquad (a)$$

a known convergent series. The series

$$\frac{1}{3^3} + \frac{1}{4^4} + \ldots + \frac{1}{n^n} + \ldots$$

is therefore convergent, since it is less term by term than (a). The original series is therefore convergent, since it is a series proved convergent plus a finite sum.

(ii) To test the series

$$\sqrt{\tfrac{1}{2}} + \sqrt{\tfrac{2}{3}} + \sqrt{\tfrac{3}{4}} + \ldots \sqrt{\frac{n}{n+1}} + \ldots$$

$$\sqrt{\frac{n}{n+1}} = \sqrt{\frac{1}{1+\frac{1}{n}}} > \sqrt{\frac{1}{1+1}} \text{ for } n > 1,$$

$\therefore$ after the first term each term is greater than the corresponding term of the series

$$\sqrt{\tfrac{1}{2}} + \sqrt{\tfrac{1}{2}} + \sqrt{\tfrac{1}{2}} + \ldots \sqrt{\tfrac{1}{2}} + \ldots,$$

which is clearly divergent. Therefore the given series is also divergent.

We also note that

$$\lim_{n\to\infty} u_n = \lim_{n\to\infty} \sqrt{\frac{1}{1+\frac{1}{n}}} = 1.$$

Since this is not zero, the series is divergent (25.4).

To use this comparison test we need some standard series known to be convergent or divergent. A very useful series is provided by

$$\frac{1}{1^p} + \frac{1}{2^p} + \frac{1}{3^p} + \ldots + \frac{1}{n^p} + \ldots = \sum_{n=1}^{\infty} \frac{1}{n^p} \ldots \ldots \qquad (b)$$

It can be shown that if $p > 1$ the series converges but for $p \leqslant 1$ the series is divergent.

Thus $\sum \frac{1}{n^{1\cdot 01}}$ is convergent but $\sum \frac{1}{n^{0\cdot 99}}$ is divergent.

Example 3. Test the series $\sum \frac{1}{n^2 + a^2}$, where a is understood to be a constant.

Since $$n^2 + a^2 > n^2,$$

$$\therefore \quad \frac{1}{n^2 + a^2} < \frac{1}{n^2}.$$

But $\sum \frac{1}{n^2}$ is convergent since here $p = 2$, therefore the series being tested is convergent.

We will now give a proof, which also covers (b), the important series above.

25.6. The Integral Test

We are given that $f(1), f(2), \ldots f(n)$ represent a series of positive terms which decrease steadily in value as n takes the integral values $1, 2, 3, \ldots n, \ldots$. Suppose that these are set up as ordinates as shown $f(r)$ at the point $x = r$, an integer. $y = f(x)$ is the continuous curve joining the tops of these ordinates. It is continuous and so has an integral.

Since the ordinates are steadily decreasing

$$(\text{AE} =) f(1) > f(2) \, (= \text{BD})$$

$$\therefore \quad \text{rectangle AEFB} > \text{area AEDB} > \text{rectangle ACDB}$$

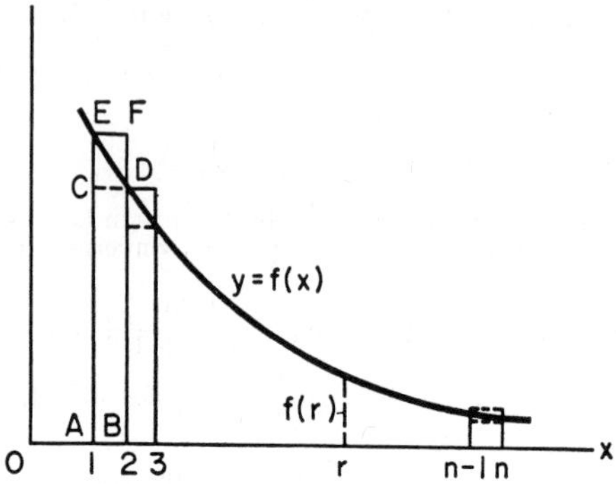

FIG. 80.

i.e., $$f(1) > \int_1^2 f(x)dx > f(2)$$

Similarly, $$f(2) > \int_2^3 f(x)dx > f(3)$$

finally, $$f(n-1) > \int_{n-1}^n f(x)dx > f(n).$$

If S_n denotes the sum of the first n terms of the series and I_n denotes the integral of $f(x)$ between the limits 1 and n, addition of the above inequalities gives

$$\sum_1^{n-1} f(s) > \int_1^n f(x)dx > \sum_2^n f(s)$$

or $$S_n - f(n) > I_n > S_n - f(1).$$

Since $f(n)$ is always positive, S_n and I_n are steadily increasing with n, and so either tend to a limit or to $+\infty$.

The right-hand inequality gives

$$I_n + f(1) > S_n$$

so that $$\lim_{n\to\infty}. I_n + f(1) \geqslant \lim_{n\to\infty}. S_n.$$

If, then, we can ascertain that the integral has a limit I, the series S_n is bounded above and so is convergent and

$$I + f(1) \geqslant S.$$

If we are given that S_n is convergent $\to$S, then from the left-hand inequality

$$S_n > I_n + f(n)$$

$\therefore$ $$\lim. S_n \geqslant \lim. I_n + \lim. f(n)$$

i.e. $$S \geqslant \lim. I_n$$

[lim. $f(n) = 0$ or the series could not be convergent.]

Hence the integral is bounded above and so is convergent, *i.e.*, finite in value.

We have thus proved that as $n \to \infty$

$$S_n = \sum_{s=1}^{n} f(s) \quad \text{and} \quad I_n = \int_1^n f(x)dx$$

converge or diverge together.

Example 4. Test the series $S_n = \Sigma n^{-p}$.

We find
$$I_n = \int_1^n \frac{dx}{x^p} = \log n \qquad (p = 1)$$
$$= \frac{n^{1-p} - 1}{1 - p} \qquad (p \neq 1).$$

Clearly if $p > 1$ $\quad I_n$ converges as $n \to \infty$

$p \leqslant 1$ $\quad I_n$ diverges as $n \to \infty$.

Hence $\quad \Sigma n^{-p}$ is divergent $p \leqslant 1$

convergent $p > 1$.

as stated above.

Example 5. Prove that

$$\tfrac{1}{2}(\pi + 1) > \frac{1}{2\sqrt{1}} + \frac{1}{3\sqrt{2}} + \frac{1}{4\sqrt{3}} + \ldots > \tfrac{1}{2}\pi.$$

Find
$$I = \int_1^\infty \frac{dx}{(x + 1)\sqrt{x}} \qquad (\text{put } x = \tan^2 \theta)$$
$$= \int_{\pi/4}^{\pi/2} 2d\theta = \frac{\pi}{2}.$$

Hence, since above

$$I + f(1) \geqslant S \geqslant I$$

here for a steadily decreasing series

$$\underline{\tfrac{1}{2}(\pi + 1) > S > \tfrac{1}{2}\pi.}$$

25.7. D'Alembert's Ratio Test for Positive Terms

If we could find S_n, the sum of n terms of a series, the question of its convergency could be settled. In most cases this is impossible or very difficult, and there is a very useful test which requires us only to know the nth term in terms of n. We will state this theorem without proof.

Let $u_1 + u_2 + \ldots u_n + \ldots$ denote a series of *positive* terms. Find the ratio $\frac{u_{n+1}}{u_n}$ and find the limit of this ratio as n tends to infinity. If this limit is less than 1 the series converges, if greater than 1 the series diverges, if equal to 1 the series may converge or diverge, and this test gives no information.

In symbols, if

$$\lim_{n \to \infty} \frac{u_{n+1}}{u_n} < 1. \quad \text{Cgt.}$$
$$> 1. \quad \text{Dgt.}$$
$$= 1. \quad \text{No information.}$$

Example 6. Test the series

(a) $\frac{1}{1}+\frac{3}{2}+\frac{5}{2^2}+\frac{7}{2^3}+\ldots$ (c) $\frac{1}{2}+\frac{2}{3}+\frac{3}{4}+\frac{4}{5}+\ldots$

(b) $\frac{1}{10}+\frac{2}{11}+\frac{2^2}{12}+\frac{2^3}{13}+\ldots$

(a) We note that $u_n = \dfrac{2n-1}{2^{n-1}}$.

$$\frac{u_{n+1}}{u_n} = \frac{2n+1}{2n}\cdot\frac{2n^{-1}}{2n-1} = \frac{1}{2}\cdot\frac{2n+1}{2n-1} = \frac{1}{2}\left(\frac{2+\frac{1}{n}}{2-\frac{1}{n}}\right)$$

$$\lim_{n\to\infty} \frac{u_{n+1}}{u_n} = \frac{1}{2},$$

∴ the series is convergent.

(b) $u_n = \dfrac{2^{n-1}}{10+(n-1)}$.

$$\frac{u_{n+1}}{u_n} = \frac{2^n}{10+n}\cdot\frac{9+n}{2^{n-1}} = 2\,\frac{(9+n)}{(10+n)} = 2\cdot\frac{\frac{9}{n}+1}{\frac{10}{n}+1},$$

$$\lim_{n\to\infty} \frac{u_{n+1}}{u_n} = 2,$$

∴ the series is divergent.

(c) $u_n = \dfrac{n}{n+1}$.

$$\frac{u_{n+1}}{u_n} = \frac{n+1}{n+2}\cdot\frac{n+1}{n} = \frac{\left(1+\frac{1}{n}\right)\left(1+\frac{1}{n}\right)}{\left(1+\frac{2}{n}\right)\cdot 1},$$

$$\lim_{n\to\infty} \frac{u_{n+1}}{u_n} = 1,$$

∴ the test does not give any information. We note, however, that since

$$u_n = \frac{1}{1+\frac{1}{n}},$$

$$\lim_{n\to\infty} u_n = 1,$$

and since this limit is *not* zero, the series is divergent (see 25.4).

Example 7. Prove that the series

$$x + \frac{x^2}{2} + \frac{x^3}{3} + \frac{x^4}{4} + \ldots$$

is convergent for $0 \leqslant x < 1$ and divergent for $x \geqslant 1$.

If $x = 0$ each term is 0, and the series is convergent. When $x \neq 0$ but is positive

$$u_n = \frac{x^n}{n},$$

$$\frac{u_{n+1}}{u_n} = \frac{x^{n+1}}{n+1}\cdot\frac{n}{x^n} = x\,\frac{n}{n+1} = x\,\frac{1}{1+\frac{1}{n}},$$

$$\lim_{n\to\infty} \frac{u_{n+1}}{u_n} = x.$$

since x is +ve, for $0 < x < 1$ series is cgt.
for $x > 1$ series is dgt.

For $x = 1$ the test gives no information, but since we obtain

$$1 + \tfrac{1}{2} + \tfrac{1}{3} + \tfrac{1}{4} + \ldots$$

we know the series is divergent.

We have therefore proved that for $0 \leqslant x < 1$ the series is convergent, but is divergent for $x \geqslant 1$.

EXERCISE 61

Find whether the following series converge or diverge:

1. $\dfrac{1}{2} + \dfrac{2}{2^2} + \dfrac{3}{2^3} + \dfrac{4}{2^4} + \ldots$

2. $\dfrac{2}{2 \,.\, 3} + \dfrac{2^2}{3 \,.\, 4} + \dfrac{2^3}{4 \,.\, 5} + \ldots + \dfrac{2^n}{(n+1)(n+2)} + \ldots$

3. $\dfrac{2}{1^2} + \dfrac{2^2}{2^2} + \dfrac{2^3}{3^2} + \ldots + \dfrac{2^n}{n^2} + \ldots$

4. $u_n = \dfrac{1}{(n+1)(n+2)}$. 5. $u_n = \dfrac{1 + 2n^2}{1 + n^2}$.

6. $u_n = \dfrac{(n\,!)^3}{(3n)\,!}$. $= \dfrac{1}{n\,!}$.

8. $u_n = \dfrac{n}{\sqrt{(2n^3 + 1)}}$. 9. $u_n = \sqrt{\left(\dfrac{n}{n^4 + 1}\right)}$.

10. $u_n = \dfrac{1}{n^2 - 100}$ $(n > 10)$.

In the following, x is a positive quantity. Find the range of values of x for which each series is convergent or divergent.

11. $1 + x + \dfrac{x^2}{2!} + \dfrac{x^3}{3!} + \dfrac{x^4}{4!} + \ldots$

12. $1 + 3x + 5x^2 + 7x^3 + 9x^4 + \ldots$

13. $x + \dfrac{3}{5}x^2 + \dfrac{8}{10}x^3 + \ldots + \dfrac{n^2 - 1}{n^2 + 1}x^n + \ldots$

14. $\dfrac{x}{1 \,.\, 2} + \dfrac{x^2}{2 \,.\, 3} + \dfrac{x^3}{3 \,.\, 4} + \ldots$

15. $\dfrac{2}{2} + \dfrac{4}{5}x + \dfrac{6}{10}x^2 + \ldots + \dfrac{2n}{n^2 + 1}x^n + \ldots$

16. $2x + \dfrac{3}{8}x^2 + \dfrac{4}{27}x^3 + \ldots + \dfrac{(n+1)}{n^3}x^n + \ldots$

17. Prove that

(a) $2\sqrt{n} - 2 < \dfrac{1}{\sqrt{1}} + \dfrac{1}{\sqrt{2}} + \ldots + \dfrac{1}{\sqrt{n}} < 2\sqrt{n} - 1$.

(b) $\dfrac{1}{4}\pi < \displaystyle\sum_{1}^{\infty} \dfrac{1}{n^2 + 1} \leqslant \dfrac{1}{2} + \dfrac{1}{4}\pi$.

18. By considering the area under the curve $y = 1/x$ prove that if $n > 1$

$$\log\left(\frac{n-1}{n}\right) > \frac{1}{n} > \log\left(\frac{n+1}{n}\right)$$

and that $\frac{1}{n} + \frac{1}{n+1} + \ldots + \frac{1}{n+r}$

lies between

$$\log\left(\frac{n+r}{n-1}\right) \quad \text{and} \quad \log\left(\frac{n+r+1}{n}\right)$$

Deduce that $\sum_{r=1}^{n} \frac{1}{n+r} \to \log 2$ as $n \to \infty$.

25.8. Alternating Series

There is another type of series for which the question of convergency is easily settled. Consider the series

$$u_1 - u_2 + u_3 - u_4 \ldots$$

where each u_r is positive and the signs alternate. Suppose that the terms are monotonic decreasing, *i.e.*, $u_n \geqslant u_{n+1}$ for $n = 1, 2, \ldots$ In this case for the sum of $2n$ terms, an even number,

$$S_{2n} = (u_1 - u_2) + (u_3 - u_4) + \ldots (u_{2n-1} - u_{2n})$$

every bracket is positive or zero, so that S_{2n} is a monotonic increasing series, *i.e.*,

$$S_{2n} \geqslant S_{2n-2} \quad \text{all } n = 1, 2, \ldots$$

Hence S_{2n} tends to a limit or to $+\infty$. But S_{2n} can be written

$$S_{2n} = u_1 - (u_2 - u_3) - (u_4 - u_5) \ldots - (u_{2n-2} - u_{2n-1}) - u_{2n}$$

so that S_{2n} is never greater than u_1. Hence S_{2n}, as $n \to \infty$, tends to a limit $\leqslant u_1$. (In most cases when $u_n > u_{n+1}$, *i.e.*, the terms are steadily decreasing, the two bracketed expressions show that S_n lies between u_1 and $u_1 - u_2$.)

Similarly, we can show that the sum of an odd number of terms S_{2n+1} is monotonic decreasing but is always greater (or equal to) $u_1 - u_2$. Hence S_{2n+1} decreases steadily to a limit $\geqslant (u_1 - u_2)$. These two series S_{2n} and S_{2n+1} could converge to different limits, and so the series not be " convergent ".

But clearly

$$S_{2n+1} = S_{2n} + u_{2n+1}$$

so that $\qquad \lim. S_{2n+1} = \lim. S_{2n} + \lim. u_{2n+1}$.

Hence if we know that

$$\lim. u_n = 0$$

the limit for n odd or even is the same and we have a convergent series for

$$\sum_{1}^{\infty} (-1)^{r-1} u_r$$

where: (1) the series is monotonic decreasing, *i.e.*, $u_n \geqslant u_{n+1}$; (2) $u_n \to 0$ as $n \to \infty$.

From the bracketing we note that the sum of such a series always lies between the sum of s and $s + 1$ terms for $s = 1, 2, \ldots$

Example 8. The following series are convergent

(*a*) $1 - \frac{1}{2} + \frac{1}{3} - \frac{1}{4} \ldots$

(*b*) $1 - \frac{1}{3} + \frac{1}{5} - \frac{1}{6} + \ldots$

(*c*) $\dfrac{1}{(x+1)} - \dfrac{1}{(x+2)} + \dfrac{1}{(x+3)} \ldots$

for all real values of x other than negative integers.

25.9. The Modulus Notation

The student will know that the symbol $|x|$ called modulus of x or mod. x stands for x if x is positive and $-x$ if x is negative, *i.e.*, it means the positive value of x. Thus $|3| = 3$ and $|-3| = 3$.

If we write $|x| < 1$, then if

x is +ve we have $x < 1$

x is −ve we have $-x < 1$ or $x > -1$,

$\therefore$ $|x| < 1$ is a convenient short way of writing

$$-1 < x < 1.$$

Similarly,
$$|x - 2| < 3$$
denotes
$$-1 < x < 5.$$

25.10. Series in General. Absolute Convergence

If $\Sigma u_n = u_1 + u_2 + u_3 + \ldots$

is a series of terms of which some are positive and some negative, then

$$\Sigma |u_n| = |u_1| + |u_2| + |u_3| + \ldots$$

is a series of positive terms.

Thus from the series

$$1 - \tfrac{1}{2} + \tfrac{1}{3} - \tfrac{1}{4} \ldots \qquad \ldots \ldots \quad (1)$$

we could form the series of positive terms

$$1 + \tfrac{1}{2} + \tfrac{1}{3} + \tfrac{1}{4} \ldots \qquad \ldots \ldots \quad (2)$$

(1) is convergent and is $\log_e 2$ (see 26.10), whilst (2) is divergent so that Σu_n can be convergent, whilst $\Sigma |u_n|$ is divergent. However, it can be proved that if $\Sigma |u_n|$ is convergent, then Σu_n is also convergent and is said to be *absolutely* convergent. The force of the word absolutely is that Σu_n is not only convergent as it stands but even has a definite finite sum when all the negative terms are made positive.

If Σu_n is convergent but $\Sigma|u_n|$ is divergent then Σu_n is said to be *conditionally* convergent. The series (1) above is an example of this.

Example 9. Test the series

$$\frac{1}{1} - \frac{3}{2} + \frac{5}{2^2} - \frac{7}{2^3} + \ldots$$

If we consider the series with all terms positive

$$\frac{1}{1} + \frac{3}{2} + \frac{5}{2^2} + \frac{7}{2^3} + \ldots$$

we can now apply D'Alembert's test as in Example 4(*a*) and show that this series is convergent. Therefore the original series is absolutely convergent and therefore convergent.

25.11. The Ratio Test for General Series

Given any series Σu_n, we can form from it a series of positive terms $\Sigma\,|u_n|$ and apply the ratio test to this latter series. In this way we will find conditions under which the original series Σu_n is absolutely convergent and therefore necessarily convergent.

Since
$$\frac{|u_{n+1}|}{|u_n|} = \left|\frac{u_{n+1}}{u_n}\right|,$$
the test for the series $\Sigma\,|\,u_n\,|$ may be written

$$\lim_{n\to\infty} \left|\frac{u_{n+1}}{u_n}\right| < 1. \quad \text{Absolute convergence}$$
$$> 1. \quad \text{Divergence}$$
$$= 1. \quad \text{No information.}$$

It should be noticed that if

$$\lim_{n\to\infty} \left|\frac{u_{n+1}}{u_n}\right| > 1$$

the series Σu_n is not merely not absolutely convergent but is in fact divergent, since in this case u_n does not tend to zero.

Before applying this test we will deal with power series, the type of series of most concern to an engineering student.

25.12. Power Series

A series such as

$$a_0 + a_1x + a_2x^2 + \ldots + a_nx^n + \ldots$$

where the coefficients $a_0, a_1, \ldots a_n, \ldots$ are independent of x is called a power series in x.

To apply the above test we consider

$$\lim_{n\to\infty} \left|\frac{a_nx^n}{a_{n-1}x^{n-1}}\right| = \lim_{n\to\infty} \left|\frac{a_n}{a_{n-1}}\right| |\,x\,|.$$

If we find

$$\lim_{n\to\infty} \left|\frac{a_n}{a_{n-1}}\right| = \frac{1}{\text{R}},$$

where R is, of course, a positive quantity, the above limit becomes $\frac{|x|}{\text{R}}$. The test then gives for $|x| < \text{R}$, absolute convergence of Σa_nx^n and therefore convergence. For $|x| > \text{R}$, divergence of $\Sigma\,|a_nx^n|$

and therefore of $\Sigma a_n x^n$. This shows that a power series is always convergent—also absolutely convergent—for all values of x within a certain range, $-$ R to $+$ R, and diverges for all values of x outside that range. At the ends of this range $\frac{|x|}{R} = 1$, and further investigation is needed.

Example 10. Test the series

$$(a)\ 1 + x + \frac{x^2}{2!} + \frac{x^3}{3!} + \ldots + \frac{x^n}{n!} + \ldots$$

$$(b)\ x - \frac{x^2}{2} + \frac{x^3}{3} - \frac{x^4}{4} \ldots + (-1)^{n-1}\frac{x^n}{n} + \ldots$$

$$(c)\ x - \frac{x^3}{3!} + \frac{x^5}{5!} - \frac{x^7}{7!} \ldots + (-1)^{n-1}\frac{x^{2n-1}}{(2n-1)!} + \ldots$$

$$(d)\ 1 - \frac{x^2}{2!} + \frac{x^4}{4!} \ldots + (-1)^{n-1}\frac{x^{2n-2}}{(2n-1)!} + \ldots$$

(a) $u_n = \frac{x^{n-1}}{(n-1)!}$,

$$\frac{u_{n+1}}{u_n} = \frac{x^n}{n!} \cdot \frac{(n-1)!}{x^{n-1}} = \frac{x}{n},$$

$$\lim_{n \to \infty} \left|\frac{u_{n+1}}{u_n}\right| = \lim_{n \to \infty} \left|\frac{x}{n}\right| = 0 \text{ for all values of } x.$$

$\therefore$ the series is absolutely convergent for all values of x.

(b) $u_n = (-1)^{n-1}\frac{x^n}{n}$,

$$\frac{u_{n+1}}{u_n} = (-1)^n \frac{x^{n+1}}{n+1} \cdot (-1)^{1-n}\frac{n}{x^n} = -x\frac{n}{n+1} = -x\frac{1}{1+\frac{1}{n}},$$

$$\lim_{n \to \infty} \left|\frac{u_{n+1}}{u_n}\right| = |x|.$$

$\therefore$ the series is absolutely convergent if $|x| < 1$, divergent if $|x| > 1$. If $x = +1$ the series is

$$1 - \tfrac{1}{2} + \tfrac{1}{3} - \tfrac{1}{4} \ldots$$

which we know to be convergent.

If $x = -1$ the series is

$$-1 - \tfrac{1}{2} - \tfrac{1}{3} - \tfrac{1}{4} \ldots$$

which we know to be divergent.

We have therefore proved that this series is:

(1) convergent for $-1 < x \leqslant 1$;
(2) absolutely convergent for $-1 < x < 1$;
(3) divergent for $|x| > |$ and $x = -1$.

(c) $u_n = (-1)^{n-1}\frac{x^{2n-1}}{(2n-1)!}$,

$$\left|\frac{u_{n+1}}{u_n}\right| = \left|\frac{x^{2n+1}}{(2n+1)!} \cdot \frac{(2n-1)!}{x^{2n-1}}\right| = \left|\frac{x^2}{(2n+1)2n}\right|,$$

$$\lim_{n \to \infty} \left|\frac{u_{n+1}}{u_n}\right| = 0 \text{ for all } x.$$

$\therefore$ the series is absolutely convergent for all x.

(d) is proved similarly and gives the same result.

In the next chapter these expansions will be obtained for: (a) e^x, (b) $\log(1 + x)$, (c) $\sin x$, (d) $\cos x$.

EXERCISE 62

1. For the Binomial series $(1 + x)^m$ show that

$$\left|\frac{u_{n+1}}{u_n}\right| = \left|\frac{m - n + 1}{n}\right| |x|$$

and deduce that the series converges if $|x| < 1$ and diverges if $|x| > 1$. [m is not a positive integer.]

Test the following power series:

2. $\dfrac{x^2}{1} - \dfrac{x^4}{2} + \dfrac{x^6}{3} - \dfrac{x^8}{4} \ldots$

3. $\dfrac{2x}{1\,.\,3} - \dfrac{4x^2}{2\,.\,9} + \dfrac{8x^3}{3\,.\,27} \ldots + (-1)^{n-1}\dfrac{2^n x^n}{n\,.\,3^n} + \ldots$

4. $\dfrac{x}{2\,.\,5} + \dfrac{x^2}{3\,.\,5^2} + \dfrac{x^3}{4\,.\,5^3} + \ldots$

5. $1 - 2x + 3x^2 - 4x^3 + \ldots$

6. $\dfrac{x^2}{2^2 + 1} + \dfrac{x^3}{3^2 + 1} + \dfrac{x^4}{4^2 + 1} + \ldots$

7. $\dfrac{x}{1\,.\,2} + \dfrac{x^2}{2\,.\,3} + \dfrac{x^3}{3\,.\,4} + \ldots$

8. $1 - \dfrac{x^2}{2^2} + \dfrac{x^4}{2^2\,.\,4^2} - \dfrac{x^6}{2^2\,.\,4^2\,.\,6^2} + \ldots$

9. $\dfrac{x^2}{2\,.\,4} - \dfrac{x^4}{2^2\,.\,4\,.\,6} + \dfrac{x^6}{2^2\,.\,4^2\,.\,6\,.\,8} - \dfrac{x^8}{2^2\,.\,4^2\,.\,6^2\,.\,8\,.\,10} + \ldots$

10. $u_n = \dfrac{n + 3}{(n + 1)(n + 2)}x^n.$

11. $u_n = \dfrac{(n + 1)}{n^2}x^n.$

12. $\dfrac{x}{1} + \dfrac{1}{2}\dfrac{x^3}{3} + \dfrac{1\,.\,3}{2\,.\,4}\dfrac{x^5}{5} + \dfrac{1\,.\,3\,.\,5}{2\,.\,4\,.\,6}\dfrac{x^7}{7} + \ldots$

[When the limit in D'Alembert's test is 1, the next test is

$$\lim_{n\to\infty}\left\{n\left(\left|\frac{u_n}{u_{n+1}}\right| - 1\right)\right\} \begin{matrix} > 1. & \text{Convergent.} \\ < 1. & \text{Divergent.}\end{matrix}$$

Check that in Example 12 this limit for $x = 1$ is $\frac{3}{2}$ and hence the series is convergent for $x = 1$.]

13. $\dfrac{4}{5}x + \dfrac{4\,.\,7}{5\,.\,8}x^2 + \dfrac{4\,.\,7\,.\,10}{5\,.\,8\,.\,11}x^3 + \ldots$

14. Show that if n is a positive integer

$$1 + \frac{5}{6} + \frac{5^2}{6^2} + \ldots + \frac{5^n}{6^n} < 6.$$

Deduce that the infinite series

$$1 + \frac{5}{1!} + \frac{5^2}{2!} + \ldots + \frac{5^n}{n!} + \ldots$$

is convergent and its sum does not exceed

$$1 + \frac{5}{1!} + \frac{5^2}{2!} + \frac{5^3}{3!} + \frac{5^4}{4!} + \frac{625}{4}.$$

15. Show that the infinite series

$$\frac{1}{1\,.\,2}+\frac{1}{3\,.\,4}+\frac{1}{5\,.\,6}+\ldots$$

is convergent. If the sum is S, show also by using partial fractions and rebracketing that S is also

$$1-\frac{1}{2\,.\,3}-\frac{1}{4\,.\,5}-\frac{1}{6\,.\,7}-\ldots$$

and hence that

$$\frac{37}{60}<S<\frac{47}{60}.$$

CHAPTER 26

EXPANSIONS IN SERIES

26.1. We have used the expansions

$$e^x = 1 + x + \frac{x^2}{2!} + \ldots + \frac{x^n}{n!} + \ldots$$

and $$(1 + x)^n = 1 + nx + \frac{n(n-1)}{2!}x^2 + \ldots$$

in which the function of x on the left-hand side is " expanded " in a series of terms which are in ascending powers of x.

We will now investigate a method by which a given general function $f(x)$ may be expanded in this way. We will obtain a " formula " or theorem which may be applied to a large number of functions.

26.2. In the following work successive differentiations of $f(x)$ are denoted by $f'(x), f''(x) \ldots f^n(x)$, the last meaning that $f(x)$ has been differentiated with respect to x n times. Also $f^n(0)$ means that *after* the nth differentiation x has been put equal to 0.

26.3. Maclaurin's Theorem

(1) Suppose

$$f(x) = a + bx \qquad \ldots \ldots \quad (1)$$

and we wish to investigate whether the constants a and b can be represented in terms of the special values of $f(x)$ at say $x = 0$.

If we put $x = 0$ in (1) we obtain

$$f(0) = a.$$

Now differentiate (1):

$$f'(x) = b.$$

To correspond to the above we will again put $x = 0$ in this and obtain

$$f'(0) = b.$$

$$\therefore \; a + bx = f(0) + xf'(0).$$

(2) Suppose $\qquad f(x) = a + bx + cx^2 \qquad \ldots \quad (2)$

Again $\qquad f(0) = a.$

Differentiate (2) $\qquad f'(x) = b + 2cx \qquad \ldots \quad (3)$

$$\therefore \; f'(0) = b.$$

Differentiate (3) $\qquad f''(x) = 2c,$

$$\therefore \; f''(0) = 2c, \text{ or } c = \tfrac{1}{2}f''(0).$$

$$\therefore \; a + bx + cx^2 = f(0) + xf'(0) + \frac{x^2}{2}f''(0),$$

where $f''(0)$ means that we have differentiated the given function $a + bx + cx^2$ twice and then placed $x = 0$.

(3) The student should assume $f(x) = a + bx + cx^2 + dx^3$ and show that in this case

$$f(x) = f(0) + xf'(0) + \frac{x^2}{1\,.\,2}f''(0) + \frac{x^3}{1\,.\,2\,.\,3}f'''(0).$$

(4) We may now prove the general theorem. Assuming that $f(x)$ is a function that can be expanded in ascending powers of x, let

$$f(x) = a_0 + \frac{a_1}{1!}x + \frac{a_2}{2!}x^2 + \frac{a_3}{3!}x^3 + \ldots \frac{a_n}{n!}x^n + \ldots \quad (4)$$

We wish to find the unknown coefficients $a_0, a_1 \ldots a_n \ldots$ in terms of the value of $f(x)$ and its differential coefficients at $x = 0$.

Put $x = 0$ in (4):

$$f(0) = a_0.$$

Now differentiate (4) and note that

$$\frac{n}{n!} = \frac{1}{(n-1)!}.$$

We have

$$f'(x) = a_1 + \frac{a_2}{1!}x + \frac{a_3}{2!}x^2 + \ldots \frac{a_n}{(n-1)!}x^{n-1} + \ldots \quad (5)$$

Put $x = 0$ in this:

$$f'(0) = a_1.$$

Differentiate (5)

$$f''(x) = a_2 + \frac{a_3}{1!}x + \ldots \frac{a_n}{(n-2)!}x^{n-2} + \ldots \quad (6)$$

Put $x = 0$ in this:

$$f''(0) = a_2.$$

Differentiate (6)

$$f'''(x) = a_3 + \ldots \frac{a_n}{(n-3)!}x^{n-3} + \ldots \quad (7)$$

Put $x = 0$ in this:

$$f'''(0) = a_3.$$

Proceeding in this way, we will find that

$$f^n(0) = a_n$$

for $n = 1, 2, 3 \ldots$

We have now obtained Maclaurin's Theorem which states that if $f(x)$ can be expanded in ascending powers of x, then

$$f(x) = f(0) + \frac{x}{1!}f'(0) + \frac{x^2}{2!}f''(0) + \frac{x^3}{3!}f'''(0) + \ldots \frac{x^n}{n!}f^n(0) + \ldots$$

26.4. To Expand $f(x) = e^x$

Here $f(x) = e^x$, $\therefore$ $f(0) = e^0 = 1$;
$f'(x) = e^x$, $f'(0) = 1$;
$f''(x) = e^x$, $f''(0) = 1$ and so on.

$$\therefore \quad e^x = 1 + \frac{x}{1!}\cdot 1 + \frac{x^2}{2!}\cdot 1 + \frac{x^3}{3!}\cdot 1 + \ldots \frac{x^n}{n!}\cdot 1 + \ldots$$
$$= 1 + x + \frac{x^2}{2!} + \frac{x^3}{3!} + \ldots$$

as obtained previously by another method. This expansion is true for all values of x.

26.5. To Expand $f(x) = \sin x$

$$\begin{aligned} f(x) &= \sin x, & \therefore \quad f(0) &= \sin 0 = 0; \\ f'(x) &= \cos x, & f'(0) &= \cos 0 = 1; \\ f''(x) &= -\sin x, & f''(0) &= -\sin 0 = 0; \\ f'''(x) &= -\cos x, & f'''(0) &= -\cos 0 = -1; \\ f''''(x) &= \sin x, & f''''(0) &= \sin 0 = 0. \end{aligned}$$

Evidently $f^n(0)$ is zero whenever n is an even integer and $+1$ or -1 alternately when n is an odd integer.

$$\therefore \quad \sin x = 0 + \frac{x}{1!}\,.\,1 + \frac{x^2}{2!}\,.\,0 + \frac{x^3}{3!}(-1) + \frac{x^4}{4!}(0) + \frac{x^5}{5!}(1) + \ldots$$
$$= x - \frac{x^3}{3!} + \frac{x^5}{5!} - \frac{x^7}{7!} + \ldots$$

26.6. To Expand $f(x) = \cos x$

We can proceed as above. Another way is to differentiate the above relation, which gives

$$\cos x = 1 - \frac{x^2}{2!} + \frac{x^4}{4!} - \frac{x^6}{6!} + \ldots$$

26.7. Note that the sine and cosine expansions are valid for all values of x. In these expansions x is understood to be in radians. This is implied when we differentiate $\sin x$ as $\cos x$ and not $\frac{\pi}{180}\cos x$.

26.8. As an illustration of the use of these series we will put $x = 0{\cdot}1$ in the sine series. This will give us the sine of $0{\cdot}1$ radians or $\sin(5{\cdot}73°)$.

$$\sin(0{\cdot}1) = (0{\cdot}1) - \frac{(0{\cdot}1)^3}{3\,!} + \frac{(0{\cdot}1)^5}{5\,!} - \frac{(0{\cdot}1)^7}{7\,!} + \ldots$$

$$\begin{aligned} 0{\cdot}1 &= 0{\cdot}100\ 000\ 00, \\ (0{\cdot}1)^5/5\,! &= \underline{0{\cdot}000\ 000\ 08}, \\ & \ 0{\cdot}100\ 000\ 08 \\ (0{\cdot}1)^3/3\,! &= \underline{0{\cdot}000\ 166\ 67}. \\ & \ 0{\cdot}099\ 833\ 41 \end{aligned}$$

$\therefore \quad \sin(0{\cdot}1) = \sin(5{\cdot}73°) = 0{\cdot}099\ 833$ correct to six decimal places.

26.9. To Expand $f(x) = \log_e (1 + x)$

We will now obtain an expansion which is used in the calculation of logarithm tables.

Let
$$f(x) = \log(1+x), \qquad \therefore \quad f(0) = \log 1 = 0;$$
$$f'(x) = \frac{1}{1+x}, \qquad f'(0) = 1;$$
$$f''(x) = \frac{(-1)}{(1+x)^2}, \qquad f''(0) = -1;$$
$$f'''(x) = \frac{(-1)(-2)}{(1+x)^3}, \qquad f'''(0) = 2\,!;$$
$$f''''(x) = \frac{(-1)(-2)(-3)}{(1+x)^4}, \qquad f''''(0) = -3\,!.$$

$$\therefore \quad \log_e (1+x) = 0 + \frac{x}{1!} + \frac{x^2}{2!}(-1) + \frac{x^3}{3!}2\,! + \frac{x^4}{4!}(-3!) + \ldots$$
$$= x - \frac{x^2}{2} + \frac{x^3}{3} - \frac{x^4}{4} + \frac{x^5}{5} - \ldots$$

This expansion is only true for $-1 < x \leqslant +1$, *i.e.*, x must lie between -1 and $+1$, but we may also put $x = +1$.

26.10. If we put $x = 1$ in the series for $\log(1 + x)$ we obtain

$$\log 2 = 1 - \tfrac{1}{2} + \tfrac{1}{3} - \tfrac{1}{4} + \tfrac{1}{5} \ldots$$

It would be necessary to evaluate one million terms of this series in order to have the value of log 2 correct to four decimal places. We will now obtain a more useful series.

$$\log(1+x) = x - \frac{x^2}{2} + \frac{x^3}{3} - \frac{x^4}{4} \ldots$$

Change the sign of x in this

$$\therefore \quad \log(1-x) = -x - \frac{x^2}{2} - \frac{x^3}{3} - \frac{x^4}{4} \ldots$$

(true for $-1 \leqslant x < +1$).

Subtract and note that

$$\log(1+x) - \log(1-x) = \log\left(\frac{1+x}{1-x}\right)$$

$$\therefore \quad \log\left(\frac{1+x}{1-x}\right) = 2\left\{x + \frac{x^3}{3} + \frac{x^5}{5} + \ldots \frac{x^{2n-1}}{2n-1} + \ldots\right\}$$

an expansion which is true for $-1 < x < +1$.

Put $x = \frac{1}{3}$ in this:

$$\log\left(\frac{1+\frac{1}{3}}{1-\frac{1}{3}}\right) = \log 2,$$

$$\therefore \quad \log 2 = 2\left\{\tfrac{1}{3} + \frac{(\frac{1}{3})^3}{3} + \frac{(\frac{1}{3})^5}{5} + \frac{(\frac{1}{3})^7}{7} + \ldots\right\}$$

$$= 2\{u_1 + u_2 + u_3 + u_4 + \ldots\}.$$

$\frac{1}{3} = 0{\cdot}333\ 333$	$u_1 = 0{\cdot}333\ 333$
$\frac{1}{3^3} = 0{\cdot}037\ 037$	$u_2 = 0{\cdot}012\ 345$
$\frac{1}{3^5} = 0{\cdot}004\ 115$	$u_3 = 0{\cdot}000\ 823$
$\frac{1}{3^7} = 0{\cdot}000\ 457$	$u_4 = 0{\cdot}000\ 065$
$\frac{1}{3^9} = 0{\cdot}000\ 051$	$u_5 = 0{\cdot}000\ 006$
	$0{\cdot}346\ 572$

$$\therefore \quad \log 2 = 2 \times 0{\cdot}346\ 572$$
$$= 0{\cdot}693\ 144$$
$$= 0{\cdot}6931 \text{ correct to four decimal places.}$$

26.11. The student may remark that we use an artificial function $\log(1 + x)$ instead of $\log x$. Unfortunately $\log x$ cannot be expanded by Maclaurin's Theorem, since if $f(x) = \log x$, $f(0)$ is infinite and so is $f'(0), f''(0) \ldots f^n(0)$.

EXERCISE 63

Use Maclaurin's Theorem to expand the functions in Nos. 1–4 in ascending powers of x.

1. e^{ax}. 2. $\cos ax$. 3. $\sin bx$. 4. $(1 + x)^n$.

5. Show that when x is so small that powers above x^5 may be neglected, $\tan x \simeq x + \frac{1}{3}x^3 + \frac{2}{15}x^5$.

6. Verify that $\log(1 + \cos x) = \log 2 - \frac{1}{4}x^2 - \frac{1}{96}x^4$ approximately for x small.

7. If x is small show that approximately:

(a) $\sin^{-1} x = x + \frac{1}{6}x^3$.

(b) $\log(1 + \sin x) = x - \frac{1}{2}x^2 + \frac{1}{6}x^3$.

(c) $\sec x = 1 + \frac{1}{2}x^2 + \frac{5}{24}x^4$.

8. Show that

$$e^x \log(1 + x) = x + \frac{x^2}{2!} + \frac{2x^3}{3!} + \frac{9x^5}{5!} + \ldots$$

9. In the series of Section 10 of this chapter put $x = \frac{1}{4}$ and show that $\log(0{\cdot}75) = -0{\cdot}2877$.

10. Obtain the series for $\log(1+x)$. Deduce that

$$\log\left(\frac{n+1}{n-1}\right) = \frac{2n}{n^2+1} + \frac{1}{3}\left(\frac{2n}{n^2+1}\right)^3 + \frac{1}{5}\left(\frac{2n}{n^2+1}\right)^5 + \ldots$$

Hence find $\log(\frac{4}{3})$ correct to five decimal places.

11. Obtain the series for $\log\left\{\frac{1+x}{1-x}\right\}$. Put $\frac{1+x}{1-x} = \frac{n+1}{n}$ and obtain $\log(n+1) =$

$$\log n + 2\left\{\frac{1}{(2n+1)} + \frac{1}{3}\frac{1}{(2n+1)^3} + \frac{1}{5}\frac{1}{(2n+1)^5} + \ldots\right\}$$

In this series put $n = 1$ and find $\log 2$. Then put $n = 2$, and using the value of $\log 2$ find $\log 3$. In this way build up the logarithms of the numbers 2 to 5.

12. An endless belt passes over two pulleys of diameters D, d with their centres l apart. Show that, ignoring the sag, the length of belt L required is given by

$$L = 2l\cos\alpha + \frac{(D+d)\pi}{2} + (D-d)\alpha.$$

where $\sin\alpha = \frac{1}{2l}(D-d).$

If α is such that α^3 and higher powers may be ignored show that an approximate formula is

$$L = 2l + \frac{(D-d)^2}{4l} + 1{\cdot}57(D+d).$$

13. ABC is an arc of a circle of centre O and radius r, B being the mid point of the arc. If $\angle AOB = \theta$, show that $AB(=b) = 2r\sin(\frac{1}{2}\theta)$ and $AC(=a) = 2r\sin\theta$. Deduce from these the usual approximation that arc $AC = \frac{1}{3}(8b-a)$ by showing that $8b - a = 6r\theta$ if θ^5 and higher powers may be neglected.

14. If in the above question S denotes the area of the segment ABC and h is the height of B above AC, show that:

(i) $S = r^2(\theta - \frac{1}{2}\sin 2\theta) = \frac{2}{3}r^2\theta^3$ approx.
(ii) $h(6a + 8b) = 10r^2\theta^3$ approx.

Hence deduce the usual rule

$$S = \frac{h}{15}(6a + 8b).$$

26.12. Other Methods

In certain cases there are simple methods for obtaining an expansion in series without using Maclaurin's Theorem. These apply if the given function has a differential coefficient which can be expanded by the Binomial Theorem.

Example 1. Expand $y = \tan^{-1}(x)$ in ascending powers of x.

We have $$\frac{dy}{dx} = \frac{1}{1+x^2} = 1 - x^2 + x^4 - x^6 + x^8 \ldots$$
if $|x^2| < 1$, *i.e.*, $|x| < 1$.
Now integrate back again:
$$y = x - \frac{x^3}{3} + \frac{x^5}{5} - \frac{x^7}{7} + \frac{x^9}{9} \ldots \quad + \text{Const.}$$
When $x = 0$, $y = \tan^{-1}(0) = 0$, so that the constant of integration is zero.
$$\therefore \quad \tan^{-1}(x) = x - \frac{x^3}{3} + \frac{x^5}{5} \ldots + (-1)^{n-1}\frac{x^{2n-1}}{2n-1} + \ldots$$
It can be shown that this series is true for $-1 \leqslant x \leqslant +1$.

The student should use this method to show
$$\log(1+x) = x - \frac{x^2}{2} + \frac{x^3}{3} \ldots \qquad (-1 < x \leqslant +1)$$
$$\sin^{-1}(x) = x + \frac{1}{2}\frac{x^3}{3} + \frac{1.3}{2.4}\frac{x^5}{5} + \ldots . \qquad (-1 \leqslant x \leqslant +1).$$

EXERCISE 64

Obtain the following expansions by any convenient method. Expansions already obtained should be used if necessary.

1. $x\tan^{-1}x - \frac{1}{2}\log(1+x^2) = \frac{x^2}{1.2} - \frac{x^4}{3.4} + \frac{x^6}{5.6} \ldots$
2. $e^x \cos x = 1 + x - \frac{2}{3!}x^3 - \frac{2^2}{4!}x^4 \ldots$
3. $\log(1+x+x^2) = x + \frac{x^2}{2} - \frac{2}{3}x^3 + \frac{x^4}{4} \ldots$
4. $e^x \sec x = 1 + x + x^2 + \frac{2}{3}x^3 + \frac{1}{2}x^4 + \ldots$
5. $x \cot x = 1 - \frac{1}{3}x^2 - \frac{1}{45}x^4 \ldots$
6. $\log(x + \sqrt{1+x^2}) = x - \frac{1}{2}\frac{x^3}{3} + \frac{1.3}{2.4}\frac{x^5}{5} - \frac{1.3.5}{2.4.6}\frac{x^7}{7} \ldots$
7. $x\sin x + \cos x = 1 + \frac{x^2}{2} - \frac{x^4}{2!4} + \frac{x^6}{4!6} \ldots$
8. $e^x \log(1+x) = x + \frac{1}{2}x^2 + \frac{1}{3}x^3 + \frac{3}{40}x^5 + \ldots$

By expanding the function and integrating term by term show:

9. $\int_0^x \frac{\sin x}{x}\,dx = x - \frac{x^3}{3!3} + \frac{x^5}{5!5} \ldots$
10. $\int_0^1 \frac{\log(1+x)}{x}\,dx = \frac{1}{1^2} - \frac{1}{2^2} + \frac{1}{3^2} \ldots$
11. $\int_0^1 \frac{\log(1-x)}{x}\,dx = -\left(\frac{1}{1^2} + \frac{1}{2^2} + \frac{1}{3^2} + \ldots\right).$
12. $\int_0^{1/2} \frac{\cos x}{1+x}\,dx = 0{\cdot}3914.$
13. $\int_0^{1/3} e^x \log(1+x)\,dx = 0{\cdot}0628.$

26.13. Evaluation of Limits

The work done W in compressing a gas from volume v_1 to volume v_2 is given by

$$W = \int_{v_1}^{v_2} p\,dv,$$

where p is the pressure at volume v.

If the gas is compressed according to the law $pv^n = C$, we find

$$W = C\int_{v_1}^{v_2} \frac{dv}{v^n} = \frac{C}{1-n}(v_2^{1-n} - v_1^{1-n}) \quad . \quad . \quad . \quad (1)$$

When the law is $pv = C$ we obtain

$$W = C\int_{v_1}^{v_2} \frac{dv}{v} = C \log_e \left(\frac{v_2}{v_1}\right). \quad . \quad . \quad . \quad . \quad . \quad . \quad . \quad (2)$$

We naturally expect to obtain this result from (1) when n is put equal to 1, yet we then find

$$W = C \cdot \frac{v_2^0 - v_1^0}{1-1} = C \cdot \frac{1-1}{1-1} = C\frac{0}{0}.$$

An expression such as $\frac{0}{0}$ is called an " indeterminate form ", since the value may be anything whatsoever according to the functions concerned. We evaluate such an expression by finding its limit (in this case as n tends to 1). We write

$$W = C \lim_{n \to 1} \frac{v_2^{1-n} - v_1^{1-n}}{1-n}.$$

Put $\qquad 1 - n = h$ where $h \to 0$ as $n \to 1$,

$$\therefore \quad \frac{v_2^{1-n} - v_1^{1-n}}{1-n} = \frac{v_2^h - v_1^h}{h}$$

$$= \frac{1}{h}(e^{h \log v_2} - e^{h \log v_1})$$

$$= \frac{1}{h}\left(\left[1 + h \log v_2 + \frac{h^2}{2!}(\log v_2)^2 + \ldots\right] - \left[1 + h \log v_1 + \frac{h^2}{2!}(\log v_1)^2 + \ldots\right]\right)$$

$$= \log\left(\frac{v_2}{v_1}\right) + \frac{h}{2!}((\log v_2)^2 - (\log v_1)^2) + \text{further positive powers of } h.$$

We may now put $h = 0$, for we have cancelled above and below by an h that made numerator and denominator zero when h was put equal to 0.

We find, as in (2),

$$W = C \log\left(\frac{v_2}{v_1}\right).$$

Such indeterminate forms occur and are evaluated by the above process of finding a limit.

Example 2. Find $\lim_{x \to 0} \dfrac{\sin x - x}{\sin x - x \cos x}$

$$\sin x - x = -\frac{x^3}{3!} + \frac{x^5}{5!} - \dots$$

$$\sin x - x \cos x = \left(x - \frac{x^3}{3!} + \frac{x^5}{5!} \dots\right) - x\left(1 - \frac{x^2}{2!} + \frac{x^4}{4!} \dots\right)$$

$$= \frac{x^3}{3} - \frac{x^5}{30} \dots$$

$\therefore$ if y denotes the expression,

$$y = \frac{-\dfrac{x^3}{3!} + \dfrac{x^5}{5!} \dots}{\dfrac{x^3}{3} - \dfrac{x^5}{30} \dots} = \frac{-\dfrac{1}{6} + \dfrac{x^2}{5!} + \text{other +ve powers of } x}{\dfrac{1}{3} - \dfrac{x^2}{30} + \text{other +ve powers of } x}.$$

$$\therefore \quad \lim_{x \to 0} y = \frac{-\dfrac{1}{6}}{\dfrac{1}{3}} = -\underline{\frac{1}{2}}.$$

EXERCISE 65

Evaluate the following limits:

1. $\lim_{\theta \to 0} \dfrac{1 - \cos \theta}{\theta \sin \theta}$.

2. $\lim_{x \to 0} \dfrac{x - \sin x}{x^3}$.

3. $\lim_{x \to 4} \dfrac{\log \left(\frac{4}{x}\right)}{x - 4}$.

4. $\lim_{x \to 0} \dfrac{\log (1 + x) - x}{\sin^2 x}$.

By division of the series for $\sin x$ by that for $\cos x$ show

$$\tan x = x + \tfrac{1}{3}x^3 + \tfrac{2}{15}x^5 + \dots$$

Hence evaluate:

5. $\lim_{x \to 0} \dfrac{x - \sin x}{\tan^3 x}$.

6. $\lim_{x \to 0} \dfrac{\tan px - p \tan x}{\sin px - p \sin x}$.

7. $\lim_{x \to 0} \dfrac{\tan 2x - 2x}{x^3}$.

8. Find $\lim_{x \to 0} \dfrac{2^x - 1}{x}$.

9. Show $\lim_{x \to 3} \dfrac{e^x - e^3}{x - 3} = e^3$.

10. Prove that the curve $x = a(\theta + \sin \theta)$, $y = a(1 - \cos \theta)$ touches the x axis at the origin and show that $\rho = 4a$ there by evaluating $\lim_{x \to 0} \left(\dfrac{x^2}{2y}\right)$.

Note: it will be shown in volume 2 that so long as the substitution $x = a$ in the ratio gives 0/0,

$$\lim_{x \to a} \frac{f(x)}{g(x)} = \lim_{x \to a} \frac{f'(x)}{g'(x)} = \lim_{x \to a} \frac{f''(x)}{g''(x)} = \dots$$

until a definite result is obtained, *e.g.*

$$\lim_{x \to 0} \frac{x - \sin x}{x^3} = \lim_{x \to 0} \frac{1 - \cos x}{3x^2} = \lim_{x \to 0} \frac{\sin x}{6x}$$

and $$\lim_{x \to 0} \frac{\sin x}{6x} = \lim_{x \to 0} \frac{\cos x}{6} = \frac{1}{6}.$$

Each of the limits in Exercise 65 should be evaluated in this way.

CHAPTER 27

PARTIAL DIFFERENTIATION

27.1. The Meaning

If V is the volume of a right circular cylinder of radius r and height h

$$V = \pi r^2 h.$$

Now suppose that the height h remains constant whilst the radius r changes. Since h is constant it may be considered as another constant like π and on differentiating with respect to r, we have

$$\left(\frac{dV}{dr}\right)_{h \text{ const.}} = (\pi h) \,.\, 2r,$$

giving the rate of change of V with respect to r when h remains constant.

Similarly, if r is constant whilst h varies

$$\left(\frac{dV}{dh}\right)_{r \text{ const.}} = (\pi r^2) \,.\, 1.$$

This notation, which shows precisely what has been done, is rather clumsy, and a special notation is introduced. We write

$$\frac{\partial V}{\partial r} = \pi h \,.\, 2r$$

and

$$\frac{\partial V}{\partial h} = \pi r^2 \,.\, 1.$$

The "curly" d is used to show that the expression to be differentiated contains more than one variable, and that we regard as constant all but the one used in the denominator of the left-hand side. We differentiate in the usual way with respect to this stated variable, regarding all the others as constant. No mention is made on the left-hand side of the variables which are regarded as constant.

Example 1. If $V = x^2y^3z^4 + 6x + 7y + 9z$, find $\frac{\partial V}{\partial x}, \frac{\partial V}{\partial y}, \frac{\partial V}{\partial z}$.

We find

$$\frac{\partial V}{\partial x} = y^3z^4 \,.\, 2x + 6;$$

$$\frac{\partial V}{\partial y} = x^2z^4 \,.\, 3y^2 + 7;$$

$$\frac{\partial V}{\partial z} = x^2y^3 \,.\, 4z^3 + 9.$$

Example 2. If $V = f(ax + by)$,

show

$$b\frac{\partial V}{\partial x} = a\frac{\partial V}{\partial y}.$$

In a problem such as this it is given by means of $f(ax + by)$ that $ax + by$ occurs as a unit in the function. It may help to call it z.

$$\therefore \quad V = f(z), \text{ where } z = ax + by.$$

From which $$\frac{dV}{dz} = f'(z) \text{ and } \frac{\partial z}{\partial x} = a, \frac{\partial z}{\partial y} = b.$$

In ordinary differentiation

$$\frac{dV}{dx} = \frac{dV}{dz} \cdot \frac{dz}{dx}.$$

Similarly here, $$\frac{\partial V}{\partial x} = \frac{dV}{dz} \cdot \frac{\partial z}{\partial x},$$

the curly d being used to show, where necessary, that y has been treated as a constant.

$$\therefore \quad \frac{\partial V}{\partial x} = f'(z) \,.\, a.$$

Similarly, $$\frac{\partial V}{\partial y} = \frac{dV}{dz} \cdot \frac{\partial z}{\partial y}$$
$$= f'(z) \,.\, b,$$

$$\therefore \quad b\frac{\partial V}{\partial x} = a\frac{\partial V}{\partial y} = abf'(z).$$

After a little practice the substitution stage can be dispensed with and we can differentiate by the usual stage-by-stage method. Thus if

$$V = f(ax + by),$$
$$\frac{\partial V}{\partial x} = f'(ax + by) \times a,$$

where we differentiate $f(\quad)$ first as $f'(\quad)$ and then "go inside" and differentiate the function inside with respect to the variable concerned.

Similarly, if $$V = f(xy) \qquad [xy \text{ is the unit}],$$
$$\frac{\partial V}{\partial x} = f'(xy) \,.\, y,$$

whilst $$\frac{\partial V}{\partial y} = f'(xy) \,.\, x.$$

EXERCISE 66

In each of the following examples find $\dfrac{\partial V}{\partial x}, \dfrac{\partial V}{\partial y}$:

1. $V = 3x^2 + 2xy + 4y^2.$
2. $V = \dfrac{x}{y}.$
3. $V = \tan^{-1}\left(\dfrac{y}{x}\right).$
4. $V = \sin^{-1}\left(\dfrac{x}{y}\right).$
5. $V = \dfrac{1}{\sqrt{(x^2 + y^2)}}.$
6. $V = \dfrac{(2x - y)}{(x + y)}.$

Show that if:

7. $V = f(x + y)$, then $\dfrac{\partial V}{\partial x} = \dfrac{\partial V}{\partial y}.$
8. $z = f(x - y)$, then $\dfrac{\partial z}{\partial x} + \dfrac{\partial z}{\partial y} = 0.$
9. $z = f\left(\dfrac{x}{y}\right)$, then $x\dfrac{\partial z}{\partial x} + y\dfrac{\partial z}{\partial y} = 0.$
10. $z = f(x^2 + y^2)$, then $x\dfrac{\partial z}{\partial y} - y\dfrac{\partial z}{\partial x} = 0.$

11. $z = xf(x + y)$, then $\dfrac{\partial z}{\partial x} - \dfrac{\partial z}{\partial y} = \dfrac{z}{x}$.

12. $z = x^2f(x - y)$, then $\dfrac{\partial z}{\partial x} + \dfrac{\partial z}{\partial y} = \dfrac{2z}{x}$.

13. $V = x^2 + y^2 + z^2$, then $x\dfrac{\partial V}{\partial x} + y\dfrac{\partial V}{\partial y} + z\dfrac{\partial V}{\partial z} = 2V$.

14. $V = \tan^{-1}\left(\dfrac{x}{y + z}\right)$, then $x\dfrac{\partial V}{\partial x} + y\dfrac{\partial V}{\partial y} + z\dfrac{\partial V}{\partial z} = 0$.

27.2. Successive Derivatives

If

$$z = \sin(3x + 2y),$$
$$\frac{\partial z}{\partial x} = 3\cos(3x + 2y).$$

This is still a function of x and y, and can be differentiated with respect to x or y. We find

$$\frac{\partial}{\partial x}\left(\frac{\partial z}{\partial x}\right) \text{ or } \frac{\partial^2 z}{\partial x^2} = -9\sin(3x + 2y),$$
$$\frac{\partial}{\partial y}\left(\frac{\partial z}{\partial x}\right) \text{ or } \frac{\partial^2 z}{\partial y \partial x} = -6\sin(3x + 2y).$$

Also

$$\frac{\partial z}{\partial y} = 2\cos(3x + 2y),$$
$$\therefore \quad \frac{\partial}{\partial x}\left(\frac{\partial z}{\partial y}\right) \text{ or } \frac{\partial^2 z}{\partial x \partial y} = -6\sin(3x + 2y),$$
$$\frac{\partial}{\partial y}\left(\frac{\partial z}{\partial y}\right) \text{ or } \frac{\partial^2 z}{\partial y^2} = -4\sin(3x + 2y).$$

This notation for successive derivatives is easy to extend when necessary.

The student will notice that

$$\frac{\partial^2 z}{\partial y \partial x} = \frac{\partial^2 z}{\partial x \partial y}.$$

This will be true for all the functions that occur in this book, and means that we may differentiate a function z of x and y first with respect to x and then y, or vice versa, when finding $\dfrac{\partial^2 z}{\partial x \partial y}$.

Example 3. If $V^2 = x^2 + y^2 + z^2$, show that

$$\frac{\partial^2 V}{\partial x^2} + \frac{\partial^2 V}{\partial y^2} + \frac{\partial^2 V}{\partial z^2} = \frac{2}{V}.$$

$$V = (x^2 + y^2 + z^2)^{\frac{1}{2}},$$
$$\therefore \quad \frac{\partial V}{\partial x} = \frac{x}{(x^2 + y^2 + z^2)^{\frac{1}{2}}},$$
$$\frac{\partial^2 V}{\partial x^2} = \frac{(x^2 + y^2 + z^2)^{\frac{1}{2}} \cdot 1 - x \cdot \dfrac{x}{(x^2 + y^2 + z^2)^{\frac{1}{2}}}}{(x^2 + y^2 + z^2)}$$
$$= \frac{y^2 + z^2}{(x^2 + y^2 + z^2)^{\frac{3}{2}}}.$$

Similarly for the others.

$$\therefore \quad \frac{\partial^2 V}{\partial x^2} + \frac{\partial^2 V}{\partial y^2} + \frac{\partial^2 V}{\partial z^2} = \frac{(y^2 + z^2) + (z^2 + x^2) + (x^2 + y^2)}{(x^2 + y^2 + z^2)^{\frac{3}{2}}}$$

$$= \frac{2}{(x^2 + y^2 + z^2)^{\frac{1}{2}}} = \frac{2}{V}.$$

Example 4. Show that

$$V = \left(Ar^n + \frac{B}{r^n}\right) \cos (n\theta - a)$$

satisfies the equation

$$\frac{\partial^2 V}{\partial r^2} + \frac{1}{r}\frac{\partial V}{\partial r} + \frac{1}{r^2}\frac{\partial^2 V}{\partial \theta^2} = 0.$$

We find
$$\frac{\partial V}{\partial r} = \left(nAr^{n-1} - \frac{nB}{r^{n+1}}\right) \cos (n\theta - a),$$

$$\frac{\partial^2 V}{\partial r^2} = \left[n(n-1)Ar^{n-2} + \frac{n(n+1)B}{r^{n+2}}\right] \cos (n\theta - a),$$

$$\frac{\partial V}{\partial \theta} = \left(Ar^n + \frac{B}{r^n}\right)[- n \sin (n\theta - a)],$$

$$\frac{\partial^2 V}{\partial \theta^2} = \left(Ar^n + \frac{B}{r^n}\right)[- n^2 \cos (n\theta - a)].$$

$$\therefore \quad \frac{\partial^2 V}{\partial r^2} + \frac{1}{r}\frac{\partial V}{\partial r} + \frac{1}{r^2}\frac{\partial^2 V}{\partial \theta^2} = \Big[n(n-1)Ar^{n-2} + \frac{n(n+1)B}{r^{n+2}} + nAr^{n-2} - \frac{nB}{r^{n+2}}$$
$$+ \left(Ar^{n-2} + \frac{B}{r^{n+2}}\right)(- n^2)\Big] \cos (n\theta - a)$$
$$= 0,$$

since the coefficients of A and B vanish separately.

EXERCISE 67

Find $\frac{\partial^2 f}{\partial x^2}, \frac{\partial^2 f}{\partial x \partial y}, \frac{\partial^2 f}{\partial y \partial x}, \frac{\partial^2 f}{\partial y^2}$ for the function $f(x, y)$ in numbers 1–6.

1. x^2y^3.
2. $ax^3 + hx^2y + by^3$.
3. $\log xy$.
4. e^{2x+3y}.
5. $x \cos y - y \cos x$.
6. $\operatorname{sh} 2x \operatorname{ch} 3y$.

7. If $V = \log (x^2 + y^2)$ prove that $\frac{\partial^2 V}{\partial x^2} + \frac{\partial^2 V}{\partial y^2} = 0$.

8. If $z = f(x + ct) + g(x - ct)$ prove that $\frac{\partial^2 z}{\partial t^2} = c^2\frac{\partial^2 z}{\partial x^2}$.

9. If $z = \frac{y}{x} \log x$ verify that $\frac{\partial^2 z}{\partial x \partial y} = \frac{\partial^2 z}{\partial y \partial x}$.

10. If $z = \log \sqrt{x^2 + y^2} + \frac{1}{2} \tan^{-1}\frac{y}{x}$ show that $\frac{\partial^2 z}{\partial x^2} + \frac{\partial^2 z}{\partial y^2} = 0$.

11. Show that $v = \frac{A}{t^{\frac{1}{2}}}e^{-\frac{x^2}{4a^2t}}$, where A and a are constant, satisfies the equation
$$\frac{\partial v}{\partial t} = a^2\frac{\partial^2 v}{\partial x^2}.$$

12. Show that if $U = Ae^{-gx} \sin (nt - gx)$ satisfies the equation

$$\frac{\partial U}{\partial t} = \mu \frac{\partial^2 U}{\partial x^2},$$

then $g^2 = \frac{n}{2\mu}$. A, g, n are positive constants.

13. Find c if $\phi = Ae^{-\frac{1}{2}kt} \sin pt \cos qx$ satisfies the equation

$$\frac{\partial^2 \phi}{\partial x^2} = \frac{1}{c^2}\left[\frac{\partial^2 \phi}{\partial t^2} + k\frac{\partial \phi}{\partial t}\right].$$

[The student may be interested to learn that numbers 10–13 above are a very few of the expressions that occur in the application of mathematics to practical engineering problems.]

27.3. The Total Differential

So far we have considered only the case when the variables vary one at a time, all the others concerned remaining constant. We will now consider the case when they all vary independently of each other.

Consider the example of a right circular cylinder volume V which is being heated so that its height h and radius r are increasing with time. If ΔV is the increase in volume in time Δt, when r has changed to $r + \Delta r$ and h to $h + \Delta h$, then

$$\begin{aligned} \Delta V &= \pi(r + \Delta r)^2(h + \Delta h) - \pi r^2 h \\ &= \pi\{2rh\Delta r + r^2\Delta h + h(\Delta r)^2 + 2r\Delta r\Delta h + (\Delta r)^2\Delta h\}. \end{aligned}$$

$$\therefore \quad \frac{\Delta V}{\Delta t} = \pi\left\{2rh\frac{\Delta r}{\Delta t} + r^2\frac{\Delta h}{\Delta t} + h\frac{\Delta r}{\Delta t}\cdot \Delta r + 2r\frac{\Delta r}{\Delta t}\cdot \Delta h + (\Delta r)^2\frac{\Delta h}{\Delta t}\right\}.$$

Now as $\Delta t \to 0$ so do ΔV, Δr, Δh.

Therefore we have

$$\frac{dV}{dt} = \pi \,.\, 2rh\frac{dr}{dt} + \pi r^2\frac{dh}{dt},$$

since each other term contains a zero multiplier.

But $$\frac{\partial V}{\partial r} = 2\pi rh \text{ and } \frac{\partial V}{\partial h} = \pi r^2.$$

Therefore the above can be written

$$\frac{dV}{dt} = \frac{\partial V}{\partial r}\frac{dr}{dt} + \frac{\partial V}{\partial h}\frac{dh}{dt}.$$

In order not to confine ourselves to t we write this as

$$dV = \frac{\partial V}{\partial r}dr + \frac{\partial V}{\partial h}dh.$$

In this form we may state this as: the *Total Differential* is the *sum* of the *separate partial differentials.*

We have given a simple demonstration to show the meaning of the theorem which is true however many variables there may be. Thus if

$$z = f(x, y, u, v \ldots),$$

$$dz = \frac{\partial z}{\partial x}dx + \frac{\partial z}{\partial y}dy + \frac{\partial z}{\partial u}du + \ldots$$

If $x, y \ldots$ are all varying with time t, then the rate of change of z with time is given by

$$\frac{dz}{dt} = \frac{\partial z}{\partial x}\frac{dx}{dt} + \frac{\partial z}{\partial y}\frac{dy}{dt} + \ldots$$

$$= \Sigma \frac{\partial z}{\partial x}\frac{dx}{dt} \text{ or } \Sigma \frac{\partial f}{\partial x}\frac{dx}{dt}.$$

In these general expressions we use z or f on the right-hand side indifferently since $z = f(x, y, \ldots)$.

Example 5. A box with sides of length x, y, z inches is expanding along the x and y sides at a rate of 2 and 3 inches per second but contracting along the z side at a rate of 4 inches per second. Find the rate of change of volume when $x = y = 10$ inches, $z = 20$ inches.

$$V = xyz,$$

$$\therefore \quad \frac{\partial V}{\partial x} = yz, \quad \frac{\partial V}{\partial y} = xz, \quad \frac{\partial V}{\partial z} = xy.$$

Now
$$\frac{dV}{dt} = \frac{\partial V}{\partial x}\frac{dx}{dt} + \frac{\partial V}{\partial y}\frac{dy}{dt} + \frac{\partial V}{\partial z}\frac{dz}{dt}$$

$$= yz\frac{dx}{dt} + xz\frac{dy}{dt} + xy\frac{dz}{dt}$$

$$= 10 \,.\, 20 \,.\, (2) + 10 \,.\, 20 \,.\, (3) + 10 \,.\, 10(-4)$$

$$= \underline{600 \text{ cu. in. per sec.}}$$

Example 6. Find du when:

(a) $u = x^2y + \dfrac{y}{x}$;

(b) $u = e^r(\cos\phi + j\sin\phi)$.

(a) The variables are x and y,

$$\therefore \quad du = \frac{\partial u}{\partial x}dx + \frac{\partial u}{\partial y}dy$$

$$= \underline{\left(2xy - \frac{y}{x^2}\right)dx + \left(x^2 + \frac{1}{x}\right)dy.}$$

(b) The variables are r and ϕ,

$$\therefore \quad du = \frac{\partial u}{\partial r}dr + \frac{\partial u}{\partial \phi}d\phi$$

$$= \underline{e^r(\cos\phi + j\sin\phi)dr + e^r(-\sin\phi + j\cos\phi)d\phi.}$$

EXERCISE 68

Find du when:

1. $u = x^2y + 3xz^2$.

2. $u = x^2 + y^2 - z^2$.

3. $u = \tan^{-1}\left(\dfrac{yz}{x^2}\right)$.

4. If $p = \dfrac{RT}{V - b} - \dfrac{a}{V^2}$, find dp if V and T are the independent variables, a, b, R being constant.

5. The radius of a right circular cone is increasing at 2 in. per sec., whilst the height is increasing at 5 in. per sec. Find the rate of increase of the volume when $r = 4$ in. and $h = 12$ in.

27.4. Small Errors

The theorem of total differential gives for $u = f(x, y \ldots)$

$$du = \frac{\partial u}{\partial x}dx + \frac{\partial u}{\partial y}dy + \ldots$$

If instead of differentials we have small finite changes $\Delta x, \Delta y \ldots$, then the finite change in u, Δu, is given approximately by

$$\Delta u = \frac{\partial u}{\partial x}\Delta x + \frac{\partial u}{\partial y}\Delta y + \ldots \quad \ldots \quad (1)$$

This formula is used in finding an approximate value for the change (or error) caused by small changes (or errors) in the variables.

Example 7. The area of a triangle is found by $S = \frac{1}{2}bc \sin A$, and it is known that b, c, A are measured correctly to within 1%. If the angle A is measured as 45°, prove that the percentage error in S is not more than about 2·8%.

$S = \frac{1}{2}bc \sin A$ contains 3 variables, b, c and A,

∴ by (1) above,

$$\Delta S = \frac{\partial S}{\partial b}\Delta b + \frac{\partial S}{\partial c}\Delta c + \frac{\partial S}{\partial A}\Delta A$$
$$= \tfrac{1}{2}c \sin A \,.\, \Delta b + \tfrac{1}{2} b \sin A \,.\, \Delta c + \tfrac{1}{2}bc \cos A \,.\, \Delta A.$$

We are given

$$\Delta b = \pm 0{\cdot}01b,\ \Delta c = \pm 0{\cdot}01c,\ \Delta A = \pm 0{\cdot}01A;$$
$$\therefore\ \Delta S = \tfrac{1}{2}bc \sin A[\pm 0{\cdot}01 \pm 0{\cdot}01 \pm 0{\cdot}01A \cot A],$$
$$\therefore\ \frac{\Delta S}{S} = \pm 0{\cdot}01[2 + A \cot A].$$

Note that A is in radians,

$$\therefore\ \frac{\Delta S}{S} = \pm 0{\cdot}01\left[2 + \frac{\pi}{4}\right] = \pm 0{\cdot}01 \times 2{\cdot}8,$$

showing that the percentage error is about 2·8.

When the function to be differentiated is a product of several variables it is often useful to take logs before differentiating.

$$\log S = \log \tfrac{1}{2} + \log b + \log c + \log \sin A,$$
$$\therefore\ \frac{dS}{S} = \frac{db}{b} + \frac{dc}{c} + \cot A \,.\, dA,$$

from which we deduce the approximate relation

$$\frac{\Delta S}{S} = \frac{\Delta b}{b} + \frac{\Delta c}{c} + \cot A \,.\, \Delta A$$
$$= \pm 0{\cdot}01 \pm 0{\cdot}01 \pm 0{\cdot}01\, A \cot A$$
$$= \pm 0{\cdot}01[2 + A \cot A] \text{ as above.}$$

EXERCISE 69

1. The sides of a rectangle are measured as 3 ft. × 2 ft. If there is a possible error of 0·01 ft. in each side, find the greatest possible error in the stated area.

2. If the radius of a right circular cone increases at the rate of 1 in. per minute and the height by 3 in. per minute, find the rate at which the volume is increasing when $r = 6$ in. and $h = 3$ ft.

3. The H.P. required for a ship varies as the cube of the speed and the square of the length. Prove that a 3 per cent. increase in speed

and a 2 per cent. increase in length requires a 13 per cent. increase in H.P.

4. The deflection at the centre of a rod under certain conditions is proportional to Wl^3/d^4. What is the percentage increase in the deflection if the load W increases by 2 per cent., the length l by 3 per cent. and the diameter d decreases by 2 per cent.?

5. The coefficient of rigidity n of a wire under certain conditions varies as $Tl/\phi a^4$. If an error of 1 per cent. too much is made in measuring l, 2 per cent. too little in measuring a, what is the error per cent. in n?

6. Under certain conditions the discharge over a weir is $3(c - \frac{1}{5}l)l^{\frac{3}{2}}$ cu. ft. per sec. Find the approximate increase in discharge if c increases by 3 in. and l by 1 in. when $c = 10$ ft. and $l = 9$ ft.

7. The height of a mast is calculated from the observed elevation θ at a measured distance a from its base. Find the error in the height due to small errors $\Delta\theta$, Δa in the observations.

If the observed values of θ and a are 30° and 100 ft. and the true values 30·2° and 99·8 ft., find the error in the calculated height.

8. The quantity G gals./min. of water supplied through a pipe D in. in diameter and L yd. long to a point H ft. below the reservoir level is given by

$$G = \sqrt{[(3D)^5 H/L]}.$$

Show that if D decreases by 1 per cent. and H by 2 per cent., then G will decrease by $3\frac{1}{2}$ per cent.

9. A formula for turbulent gas flow is

$$v = 5{\cdot}3h^{\frac{5}{4}}D^{\frac{1}{4}}/C_p^{\frac{5}{4}}T^{\frac{5}{8}}.$$

If the measurements of D and T are subject to errors of $\pm 1{\cdot}5$ per cent. and ± 1 per cent. respectively, show that the maximum error in the value of v will be 1·2 per cent. approximately.

10. The side a of a triangle is calculated by

$$a^2 = b^2 + c^2 - 2bc \cos A.$$

If b, c, A are respectively 3 ft., 5 ft., $\pi/3$ and the errors in these are respectively +0·1 ft., +0·2 ft., +3°, show that the error in a is 0·328 ft.

11. Find the area between the curve $y = e^{0{\cdot}1x} \sin x$ the x axis and the ordinates at $x = 0$ and π. If the coefficient 0·1 is increased to $0{\cdot}1 + \theta$, where θ is small, find the change in the area.

12. The heat generated H in a resistance weld is given by the formula

$$H = Ki^2Rt,$$

where K is a constant, i is the current between the electrodes, R is the initial resistance between the electrodes and t is the time for which the current flows. For constant weld quality H must not vary by more than 5 per cent. If the machine controls i to within 1 per cent. and t to within 0·5 per cent., show that the maximum possible percentage variation in R is 2·5 per cent.

13. Holes A, B, C are to be bored in a jig plate such that AB = 5 in., AC = 6 in., and angle BAC = 45°. If lengths can be measured to the nearest 0·01 in. and angles to the nearest 0·5°, show that the maximum error in BC is about $\frac{1}{40}$ in.

CHAPTER 28

COMPLEX NUMBERS

28.1. Introduction

Since $$(+3) \times (+3) = +9$$
and $$(-3) \times (-3) = +9$$
the square root of -9 cannot be either $+3$ or -3 and must be a new kind of number. We must therefore invent an algebra to deal with this new number. This algebra is of great importance to the engineer, although originally it was a piece of " pure " mathematics. We begin by inventing a symbol j to denote $\sqrt{-1}$ so that $j \equiv \sqrt{-1}$. For example,

$$\sqrt{-7} = \sqrt{-1 \times 7} = \sqrt{-1} \times \sqrt{7} = j\sqrt{7}.$$

In this way these new numbers can be reduced to our usual ordinary numbers, called *real* numbers, multiplied by the symbol j.

We will also define

$$j^2 = \sqrt{-1} \times \sqrt{-1} = -1$$
$$j^3 = j^2 \times j = -j$$
$$j^4 = (j^2)^2 = (-1)^2 = +1.$$

In this way any power of j higher than the first can be reduced, and the first power is the only power of j we need consider. (Throughout this chapter the engineering convention of using j to represent $\sqrt{(-1)}$ is followed. This avoids confusion with the current unit i.)

28.2. A Complex Number

If a and b are real numbers then $a + jb$ (*i.e.*, $a + \sqrt{-1}b$) is called a complex number. a is called the " real " part, and b the " imaginary " or j part. A number such as jb, which is $0 + jb$, is called pure imaginary.

If a and b are not real numbers we cannot say what $a + jb$ is, and one of our tasks is to separate into a real and j part any given mixture of real and j parts. Until this is done nothing much can be stated about the given expression containing them.

We agree to deal with these numbers as follows:

$$(3 + j4) + (2 - j5) = (3 + 2) + j(4 - 5) = 5 - j1,$$
$$(3 + j4) - (2 - j5) = (3 - 2) + j(4 + 5) = 1 + j9,$$
$$\begin{aligned}(3 + j4)(2 - j5) &= 3(2 - j5) + j4(2 - j5)\\ &= 6 - j15 + j8 - j^2 20\\ &= 6 - j7 - (-1)(20)\\ &= 26 - j7.\end{aligned}$$

This means that we regard a complex number as the sum of two separate components and must always group together the corresponding components—real and imaginary. In multiplying numbers we act as with real numbers, but put -1 for j^2 and then again group together corresponding parts.

EXERCISE 70

1. Multiply out and simplify:
   (a) $3(1 + j2)$; (b) $5j(1 - j)$; (c) $(2 + 3j)(2 - 5j)$;
   (d) $(3 + 4j)(3 - 4j)$; (e) $(a + jb)^2$;
   (f) $(\cos\theta + j\sin\theta)(\cos\phi + j\sin\phi)$;
   (g) $(x - \cos\theta - j\sin\theta)(x - \cos\theta + j\sin\theta)$.
2. Solve the equations:
   (a) $x^2 + 36 = 0$; (b) $x^2 - 16x + 100 = 0$;
   (c) $x^4 - 3x^2 - 4 = 0$; (d) $x^3 + x - 2 = 0$.
3. Simplify:
   (a) $3 + j2 + 5 - j^2 10 + j^3 15 - 4$;
   (b) $(2 + j3)^3 - (2 - 3j)^3$.
4. Factorize:
   (a) $x^2 + y^2$; (b) $x^4 - y^4$.

28.3. Conjugate Numbers

When two complex numbers differ only in the sign of the j part they are called conjugate, *e.g.*, $a + jb$ and $a - jb$ are conjugate.

Note that the product

$$(a + jb)(a - jb) = a^2 + b^2$$

is a real number.

28.4. Rationalization

It is often necessary to separate a ratio of complex numbers into real and j parts. We do this by using the conjugate of the denominator as shown, in a process called rationalization.

$$\frac{a + jb}{c + jd} = \frac{a + jb}{c + jd} \times \frac{c - jd}{c - jd} \quad \left(\text{since } \frac{(c - jd)}{(c - jd)} = 1\right)$$

$$= \frac{(ac + bd)}{c^2 + d^2} + \frac{j(bc - ad)}{c^2 + d^2}$$

showing the two components.

28.5. A Fundamental Theorem

If a, b, c, d are real and

$$a + jb = c + jd,$$

then we will show that $a = c$ and $b = d$.

Since $a + jb = c + jd$,

$$\therefore \quad a - c = j(d - b),$$

$$\therefore \quad (a - c)^2 = -1(d - b)^2 \qquad \text{. . . . . . (1)}$$

Now $(a - c)^2$ and $(d - b)^2$ being the squares of expressions involving real numbers only are either positive or zero. If positive then the equation (1) shows that a positive is equal to a negative. The only possible conclusion is that each side is zero.

$$\therefore \quad a = c \text{ and } d = b.$$

i.e., when two complex numbers are equal we can equate their respective real and imaginary parts.

Example 1. If
$$\frac{(2 - j)(3 + 2j)}{3 - 4j} = r(\cos\theta + j\sin\theta)$$
find r.

$$\begin{aligned} \text{L.H.S.} &= \frac{8 + j}{3 - 4j} \\ &= \frac{8 + j}{3 - 4j} \times \frac{3 + 4j}{3 + 4j} \\ &= \frac{20 + 35j}{3^2 + 4^2} = \frac{4}{5} + j\frac{7}{5}, \end{aligned}$$

$$\therefore \quad \frac{4}{5} + j\frac{7}{5} = r\cos\theta + jr\sin\theta.$$

By our fundamental theorem

$$r\cos\theta = \frac{4}{5},$$

$$r\sin\theta = \frac{7}{5};$$

$$\therefore \quad r^2(\cos^2\theta + \sin^2\theta) = \frac{16 + 49}{25} = \frac{65}{25},$$

$$\underline{r = \sqrt{2{\cdot}6}}$$

EXERCISE 71

1. Rationalize:

(a) $\dfrac{1 + 2j}{1 + j}$; (b) $\dfrac{2 - 3j}{1 + 2j}$; (c) $\dfrac{1 + j}{(1 - j)^2}$; (d) $\dfrac{1}{1 - \cos\theta + j\sin\theta}$.

2. Find z if $z(3 + 4j) = 2 + 3j$.
3. If $(2 + j3)(3 - j4) = x + jy$, find x and y.
4. Find x and y if
$$x + jy = \frac{3}{2 + \cos\theta + j\sin\theta}.$$
5. Find R_1 and L, given that
$$\frac{R_1 + j\omega L}{R_3} = \frac{R_2}{R_4 - j\dfrac{1}{\omega C}},$$
where all symbols denote real quantities but $j \equiv \sqrt{-1}$.
6. When a voltage $\overline{V} = 40 + j20$ acts on a certain circuit, the current $\overline{I}$ is $-4 + j5$. Given that $R + jX = \overline{V}/\overline{I}$, find R and X.

7. In a certain electric circuit

$$z = z_1 + \frac{z_2 z_3}{z_2 + z_3},$$

where $z_1 = 2 + 3j$, $z_2 = 3 - 4j$, $z_3 = -5 + 12j$. If $\overline{E} = \overline{I}z$, find $\overline{E}$ when $\overline{I} = 5 + 6j$.

8. If $\alpha + j\beta = \sqrt{\{(R + j\omega L)(G + j\omega C)\}}$,

show that $\alpha^2 - \beta^2 = RG - \omega^2 LC$

and $2\alpha\beta = \omega(RC + LG)$.

Hence prove that

$$2\alpha^2 = RG - \omega^2 LC + \sqrt{\{(R^2 + \omega^2 L^2)(G^2 + \omega^2 C^2)\}}.$$

28.6. The Argand Diagram (Fig. 81(*a*)).

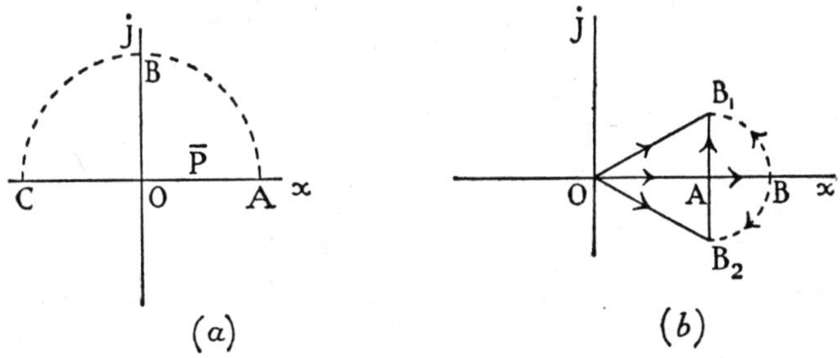

FIG. 81.

Let q be an operator which when applied to a vector rotates it through $+90°$ without change of magnitude.

If then (Fig. 61(*a*))

$$\overline{OA} = \overline{P},$$

$$\overline{OB} = q\overline{P}$$

and $\overline{OC} = q\overline{OB} = q \cdot q\overline{P} = q^2\overline{P}$,

$\therefore$ $\overline{OC} = q^2 \cdot \overline{OA}$.

But $\overline{OC} = -\overline{OA}$,

$\therefore$ $q^2 = -1$ and $q = \sqrt{-1}$.

$\therefore$ $j \equiv \sqrt{-1}$ can be interpreted as an operator which rotates a vector through $+90°$.

$\therefore$ j^2 rotates twice through $+90°$, *i.e.*, through $+180°$.

Similarly, j^3 rotates through $+270°$,

but $j^3 = j^2 \times j = -j$,

$\therefore$ $-j$ can be taken as rotating through $-90°$, which gives the same final position as a rotation through $+270°$. We can therefore regard $a + jb$ as the *sum of two perpendicular vectors*, which must, of course, *be added vectorially.* Thus in Fig. 81(*b*) if OA = 2 units and AB = 1 unit

$$\overline{OA} + \overline{AB} = 2 + 1 = 3 = \overline{OB}.$$

But $$2 + j1 = \overline{OA} + \overline{AB_1} = \overline{OB_1}$$

and $$2 - j1 = \overline{OA} + \overline{AB_2} = \overline{OB_2}.$$

In this method of representation on an *Argand Diagram,* Ox is the x or real axis and Oj the j or imaginary axis. Note that $AB_1 = 1$ not $j1$ and $AB_2 = -1$ not $-j1$. The j indicates that the number with it is measured parallel to the j axis, but the j *does not occur* in the actual magnitude.

Thus $$OB_1^2 = OA^2 + AB_1^2$$
$$= 2^2 + 1^2 = 5$$

and *NOT* $$OB_1^2 = 2^2 + (j1)^2 = 4 - 1 = 3.$$

It is often useful to regard the complex number $a + jb$ as the point (a, b) on the Argand diagram. Thus $2 + j3$ would be the point (2, 3), whilst $2 - j3$ is $2 + j(-3)$ and is the point $(2, -3)$.

Example 2. If $\overline{OA} = 3 + 4j$ and $\overline{OB} = j\overline{OA}$, show that $AB^2 = OA^2 + OB^2$ (Fig. 82(*b*)).

$$j\overline{OA} = j(3 + 4j) = -4 + 3j,$$
$$\therefore \quad A = (3, 4), \quad B = (-4, 3),$$
$$\therefore \quad AB^2 = (3 + 4)^2 + (4 - 3)^2 = 50,$$

also $$OA^2 + OB^2 = 5^2 + 5^2 = 50.$$

Thus verifying that $\angle AOB = 90°$, or to multiply $\overline{OA}$ by j is to rotate it through $+ 90°$, whatever its inclination to the x axis.

28.7. The Polar Form

We often need to express the complex number $a + jb$ in the form

$$r(\cos\theta + j\sin\theta).$$

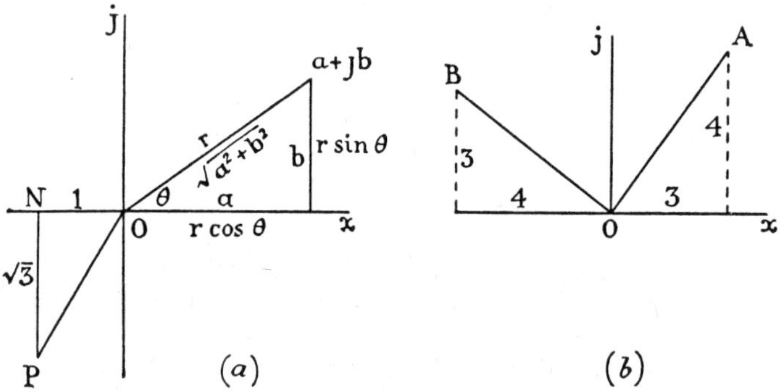

FIG. 82.

If $$a + jb = r\cos\theta + jr\sin\theta \text{ (Fig. 82(}a\text{))},$$

then $$r\cos\theta = a,$$
$$r\sin\theta = b,$$

$$\therefore \quad r^2 = a^2 + b^2$$

and $$r = +\sqrt{a^2 + b^2}$$

also $$\tan\theta = \frac{b}{a},$$

so that r and θ can be obtained.

In any given case it is best to put the point (a, b) on an Argand diagram, r is then the distance of the point from O, and the angle θ is carefully chosen so that a line initially along Ox must revolve through θ so as finally to pass through (a, b). It can clearly revolve positively or negatively to do this. It is usual to choose the smaller of the two angles. We therefore choose θ so that

$$-\pi < \theta \leqslant +\pi$$

which means that we will always choose an angle between $-\pi$ and $+\pi$, but if ever the point is on the negative x axis we will give the angle as $+\pi$ and not $-\pi$ (although of course either will do).

Example 3. Put into polar form $-1 - j\sqrt{3}$.
This is the point P (Fig. 82(a)).

$$\text{OP} = 2 = r.$$

$\angle$NOP $= 60°$, but we require the angle through which a line lying along Ox must rotate to coincide with OP. We could give $+240°$ for the positive rotation or $-120°$ for the negative rotation. Since the rule is to choose an angle between $-180°$ and $+180°$ we choose $-120°$.

$$\therefore \quad -1 - j\sqrt{3} = 2\{\cos(-120) + j\sin(-120)\}$$
$$= \underline{2\{\cos 120 - j\sin 120\}}.$$

This can be written as $2\angle(-120°)$ or $2\angle(-2\pi/3)$.

EXERCISE 72

Put into polar form the numbers:

1. 2. 2. $3j$. 3. -2. 4. $-2j$.
5. $3 + 4j$. 6. $3 + j\sqrt{3}$. 7. $-4 - 3j$. 8. $-3 + j\sqrt{3}$.
9. $2 + j2$. 10. $\sqrt{3} - j$. 11. $-\sqrt{3} - j$.

Express in the form $r\angle\theta$:

12. $(2 - 3j)(4 + 3j)$. 13. $2/(2 + 3j)$.
14. $(3 - 4j)/(4 + 5j)$.
15. Express the roots of $x^2 + 4x + 13 = 0$ in polar form.
16. Show that $\sqrt{[(5 + 3j)/(2 - 5j)]} = 0{\cdot}67 + 0{\cdot}79j$.
17. An expression in telephony is $n = \sqrt{[(r + lqj)(s + kqj)]}$. Evaluate n when $q = 5000$, $r = 18$, $l = 0{\cdot}0039$, $k = 0{\cdot}008 \times 10^{-6}$, $s = 10^{-6}$, and show it is $0{\cdot}0122 + 0{\cdot}0302j$.

28.8. Modulus and Argument

If P is the point $a + jb$ on the Argand diagram, the magnitude of OP is called the *modulus* of $a + jb$ and written $|a + jb|$.

Thus $$|a + jb| = +\sqrt{a^2 + b^2}.$$

The angle xOP is called the *argument* of $a + jb$ and written $\arg(a + jb)$.

Thus
$$\arg(a + jb) = \tan^{-1}\left(\frac{b}{a}\right)$$
where we carefully choose the correct value for θ, the angle made by OP with the positive x axis.

We can generalize the idea of modulus as follows. If z_1 denotes the vector (or point) $x_1 + jy_1$ and $z_2 \equiv x_2 + jy_2$, then
$$\begin{aligned}|z_1 - z_2| &= |(x_1 + jy_1) - (x_2 + jy_2)|\\ &= |(x_1 - x_2) + j(y_1 - y_2|\\ &= \sqrt{(x_1 - x_2)^2 + (y_1 - y_2)^2} \text{ by the definition.}\end{aligned}$$
Therefore $|z_1 - z_2|$ is the actual length of the join of the point z_2 to z_1.

Similarly, $|z_1 + z_2| = |z_1 - (-z_2)|$ is the actual length of the join $-z_2$ to z_1.

From this it follows that $|z_1| = |z_1 - 0|$ is the length of the join of O to the point z_1.

In the following z will be used to denote the general point $x + jy$.

Example 4. What is the locus of the point z if
$$|z + 3j|^2 - |z - 3j|^2 = 12.$$
We have
$$|x + j(y + 3)|^2 - |x + j(y - 3)|^2 = 12,$$
$$\therefore \quad \{x^2 + (y + 3)^2\} - \{x^2 + (y - 3)^2\} = 12,$$
$$\therefore \quad y = 1,$$
or the point (x, y) describes the line $y = 1$.

EXERCISE 73

1. What is the locus:
   (*a*) $|z| = 2$;
   (*b*) $|z - z_1| = 3$, where z_1 is a fixed point;
   (*c*) $\arg z =$ constant.
2. Prove that if $2|z - 1| = |z - 2|$, then $3(x^2 + y^2) = 4x$.
3. If $|2z - 1| = |z - 2|$, prove that $x^2 + y^2 = 1$.
4. What is the locus, if k is real and positive, given by
$$|z + jk|^2 + |z - jk|^2 = 10k^2.$$
5. If the ratio $(z - j)/(z - 1)$ is purely imaginary, show that the point z lies on a circle, centre at the point $\frac{1}{2}(1 + j)$ and radius $1/\sqrt{2}$. [L.U.]
6. If the argument of $(z - 1)/(z + 1)$ is $\pi/4$, show that z lies on a circle, radius $\sqrt{2}$ and centre $(0, 1)$.
7. Find: (*a*) $|(2 + 3j)^2 (3 - 4j)^2|$;
   (*b*) $|(2 + 3j)^2/(3 + 4j)^2|$.
8. Show that the modulus of $r(\cos\theta + j\sin\theta)$ is r.

28.9. The Exponential Form for a Complex Number

(*a*) We have the expansion

$$e^x = 1 + x + \frac{x^2}{2!} + \frac{x^3}{3!} + \frac{x^4}{4!} + \dots \frac{x^n}{n!} + \dots$$

If we substitute $j\theta$ for x, this becomes

$$e^{j\theta} = 1 + j\theta + \frac{(j\theta)^2}{2!} + \frac{(j\theta)^3}{3!} + \frac{(j\theta)^4}{4!} + \frac{(j\theta)^5}{5!} + \dots$$

$$= 1 + j\theta - \frac{\theta^2}{2!} - \frac{j\theta^3}{3!} + \frac{\theta^4}{4!} + \frac{j\theta^5}{5!} + \dots$$

$$= \left(1 - \frac{\theta^2}{2!} + \frac{\theta^4}{4!} \dots\right) + j\left(\theta - \frac{\theta^3}{3!} + \frac{\theta^5}{5!} \dots\right).$$

$$\therefore \quad e^{j\theta} = \cos\theta + j\sin\theta \qquad \text{(see 26.6)}$$

Similarly,

$$e^{-j\theta} = \cos\theta - j\sin\theta.$$

We now have several ways of representing a complex number:

(1) $a + jb$; (2) $r(\cos\theta + j\sin\theta)$;
(3) $r\angle\theta$; (4) $re^{j\theta}$;

since we have just established the equivalence of (2) and (4). (3) is a useful shorthand, (1) is useful in addition, whilst (2) or (4) are useful in multiplication or division and more advanced work to be dealt with later on.

(*b*) We have

$$\begin{aligned} e^{jx} . e^{jy} &= (\cos x + j\sin x)(\cos y + j\sin y) \\ &= \cos x\cos y - \sin x\sin y + j(\sin x\cos y + \cos x\sin y) \\ &= \cos(x + y) + j\sin(x + y) \\ &= e^{j(x+y)}, \end{aligned}$$

which proves that the Law of Indices,

$$e^m \times e^n = e^{m+n},$$

remains true when m and n are pure imaginaries.

We shall assume these laws always true, *e.g.*,

$$(e^m)^n = e^{mn},$$

for all m and n real or complex.

Since $\qquad (e^{j\theta})^2 = e^{j.2\theta}$

$$\therefore \quad (\cos\theta + j\sin\theta)^2 = \cos 2\theta + j\sin 2\theta$$

or $\quad \cos^2\theta - \sin^2\theta + j2\sin\theta\cos\theta = \cos 2\theta + j\sin 2\theta.$

Equating real and imaginary parts,

$$\cos 2\theta = \cos^2\theta - \sin^2\theta.$$

and $\qquad \sin 2\theta = 2\sin\theta\cos\theta.$

Many useful relations can be obtained in this way.

Example 5. Find $\int e^{ax} \cos bx dx.$

Let $C \equiv \int e^{ax} \cos bxdx$

and $S \equiv \int e^{ax} \sin bxdx.$

$$\therefore \quad C + jS \equiv \int e^{ax} (\cos bx + j \sin bx)dx$$
$$= \int e^{ax} . e^{jbx}dx$$
$$= \int e^{(a+jb)x}dx$$
$$= \frac{e^{(a+jb)x}}{a + jb} + \text{const.}$$

Having now finished the integration, we must express the R.H.S. in the usual form A + jB so that we may find C and S.

$$\text{R.H.S.} = \frac{e^{ax} . e^{jbx}}{a + jb} + \text{const.}$$
$$= e^{ax} \frac{(\cos bx + j \sin bx)}{a + jb} \times \frac{a - jb}{a - jb} + \text{const.}$$
$$= \frac{e^{ax}}{a^2 + b^2}\{(a \cos bx + b \sin bx) + j(a \sin bx - b \cos bx)\} + \text{const.}$$

$\therefore$ equating real and imaginary parts,

$$C = \frac{e^{ax}}{a^2 + b^2}(a \cos bx + b \sin bx) + \text{const.}$$
$$S = \frac{e^{ax}}{a^2 + b^2}(a \sin bx - b \cos bx) + \text{const.}$$

EXERCISE 74

1. Using $e^{jx} . e^{jy} = e^{j(x+y)}$,
prove
$$\cos x \cos y - \sin x \sin y = \cos (x + y),$$
$$\sin x \cos y + \cos x \sin y = \sin (x + y).$$
2. Using $(e^{j\theta})^3 = e^{j.3\theta}$,
find expressions for sin 3θ, cos 3θ and hence tan 3θ in terms of tan θ.
3. Find $\int e^{-3x} \sin 4xdx$ and $\int e^{-4x} \cos 3xdx$ without substituting in the formulae of Example 5.
4. Express $1 + j\sqrt{3}$ in the form $re^{j\theta}$, finding r and θ. Hence find, without expanding, $(1 + j\sqrt{3})^{20}$.
5. If $z = 0{\cdot}3 + 0{\cdot}3j$, show that $e^z = 1{\cdot}290 + 0{\cdot}399j$.

28.10. Multiplication and Division

Suppose two given numbers z_1 and z_2 are expressed in polar form as

$$z_1 = r_1 (\cos \theta_1 + j \sin \theta_1) = r_1 e^{j\theta_1},$$
$$z_2 = r_2 (\cos \theta_2 + j \sin \theta_2) = r_2 e^{j\theta_2},$$
$$\therefore \quad z_1 z_2 = r_1 r_2 e^{j(\theta_1 + \theta_2)}.$$

(*a*) Since r_1r_2 is the modulus of the R.H.S. and $\theta_1 + \theta_2$ its argument, we have

$$|z_1z_2| = r_1r_2$$
$$= |z_1|\,|z_2|$$

or in words: the modulus of a product is the product of the separate moduli. The proof clearly holds for three or more numbers, and so the statement is true for any number, *i.e.*,

$$|z_1z_2 \ldots z_n| = |z_1|\,|z_2| \ldots |z_n|.$$

If $z_1 = z_2 = \ldots = z_n$ then

$$|z_1{}^n| = |z_1|^n$$

(*b*) Also
$$\arg(z_1z_2) = \theta_1 + \theta_2$$
$$= \arg z_1 + \arg z_2,$$

or in words: the argument of a product is the sum of the separate arguments. This statement is also true for three or more numbers.

If we divide the numbers,

$$\frac{z_1}{z_2} = \frac{r_1e^{j\theta_1}}{r_2e^{j\theta_2}} = \frac{r_1}{r_2}e^{j(\theta_1-\theta_2)},$$

$$\therefore \quad \left|\frac{z_1}{z_2}\right| = \frac{r_1}{r_2} = \frac{|z_1|}{|z_2|}$$

and
$$\arg\left(\frac{z_1}{z_2}\right) = \theta_1 - \theta_2$$
$$= \arg z_1 - \arg z_2.$$

In words: the modulus of a quotient is the quotient of the separate moduli and the argument of a quotient is the difference of the arguments (in the order shown).

Example 6. Find the modulus and argument of

$$z = \frac{(2+3j)^2(3+4j)^4}{(3-4j)^3(2-3j)^3}.$$

$$|z| = \frac{|2+3j|^2\,|3+4j|^4}{|3-4j|^3\,|2-3j|^3} = \frac{(\sqrt{13})^2(5)^4}{(5)^3(\sqrt{13})^3} = \frac{5}{\sqrt{13}}.$$

For the argument we have

$$\text{argument }(z) = 2\arg(2+3j) + 4\arg(3+4j) - 3\arg(3-4j) - 3\arg(2-3j)$$
$$= 2(56°\ 18') + 4(53°\ 8') - 3(-53°\ 8') - 3(-56°\ 18')$$
$$= 653°\ 26'.$$

Since we usually express the argument as an angle in the range $-180°$ to $+180°$, this angle becomes $-66°\ 34'$,

$$\therefore z = \frac{5}{\sqrt{13}}\angle(-66°\ 34').$$

28.11. Demoivre's Theorem

Since
$$(e^{j\theta})^n = e^{j(n\theta)} \quad \text{for all } n,$$

$$\therefore \quad (\cos\theta + j\sin\theta)^n = \cos n\theta + j\sin n\theta.$$

Hence, for all values of n, $\cos n\theta + j\sin n\theta$ is one of the values of $(\cos\theta + j\sin\theta)^n$. This is known as Demoivre's Theorem. Later the student will see the importance of the words " one of the values of ".

(*a*) This theorem, as already shown, can be used to obtain the expansions of $\cos n\theta$ or $\sin n\theta$ in terms of the powers of $\cos\theta$ and $\sin\theta$. Thus since

$$\begin{aligned}\cos 3\theta + j\sin 3\theta &= (\cos\theta + j\sin\theta)^3\\ &= \cos^3\theta + 3\cos^2\theta\, j\sin\theta + 3\cos\theta\,(j\sin\theta)^2 + (j\sin\theta)^3\\ &= (\cos^3\theta - 3\cos\theta\sin^2\theta) + j(3\cos^2\theta\sin\theta - \sin^3\theta),\end{aligned}$$

$$\therefore\quad \cos 3\theta = \cos^3\theta - 3\cos\theta\sin^2\theta,$$
$$\sin 3\theta = 3\cos^2\theta\sin\theta - \sin^3\theta;$$

$$\therefore\quad \tan 3\theta = \frac{\sin 3\theta}{\cos 3\theta} = \frac{3\cos^2\theta\sin\theta - \sin^3\theta}{\cos^3\theta - 3\cos\theta\sin^2\theta} = \frac{3\tan\theta - \tan^3\theta}{1 - 3\tan^2\theta}$$

on dividing above and below by $\cos^3\theta$.

(*b*) The theorem can be used to simplify complex fractions in polar form.

$$\frac{(\cos 3\theta + j\sin 3\theta)^5(\cos\theta - j\sin\theta)^3}{(\cos 5\theta - j\sin 5\theta)^3} = \frac{(\cos\theta + j\sin\theta)^{15}(\cos\theta + j\sin\theta)^{-3}}{(\cos\theta + j\sin\theta)^{-15}},$$

since, for example,

$$\begin{aligned}\cos 5\theta - j\sin 5\theta &= \cos(-5\theta) + j\sin(-5\theta)\\ &= (\cos\theta + j\sin\theta)^{-5}.\\ \therefore\quad \text{expression} &= (\cos\theta + j\sin\theta)^{15-3+15}\\ &= (\cos\theta + j\sin\theta)^{27}\\ &= \cos 27\theta + j\sin 27\theta.\end{aligned}$$

(*c*) The theorem can be used to find simply such expansions as $(1 + j)^{15}$.

$$1 + j = \sqrt{2}\left(\cos\frac{\pi}{4} + j\sin\frac{\pi}{4}\right)$$

$$\begin{aligned}\therefore\quad (1 + j)^{15} &= 2^{15/2}\left(\cos\frac{\pi}{4} + j\sin\frac{\pi}{4}\right)^{15}\\ &= 2^{15/2}\left(\cos\frac{15\pi}{4} + j\sin\frac{15\pi}{4}\right)\\ &= 2^{15/2}\left(\cos\frac{\pi}{4} - j\sin\frac{\pi}{4}\right)\\ &= 2^7(1 - j).\end{aligned}$$

(*d*) The theorem is used for finding the roots of a given expression, and we will now consider this in the next section.

28.12. The q qth Roots of a Number

Consider $$e^{\frac{j\theta}{3}} = \cos\frac{\theta}{3} + j\sin\frac{\theta}{3},$$
$$e^{j\left(\frac{\theta+2\pi}{3}\right)} = \cos\frac{\theta+2\pi}{3} + j\sin\frac{\theta+2\pi}{3},$$
$$e^{j\left(\frac{\theta+4\pi}{3}\right)} = \cos\frac{\theta+4\pi}{3} + j\sin\frac{\theta+4\pi}{3}.$$

These three complex numbers are all different, as can be seen by assuming say $\theta = 0$ and putting the three numbers on an Argand diagram. If, however, we cube them we obtain

$$\left(\cos\frac{\theta}{3} + j\sin\frac{\theta}{3}\right)^3 = \cos\theta + j\sin\theta,$$
$$\left(\cos\frac{\theta+2\pi}{3} + j\sin\frac{\theta+2\pi}{3}\right)^3 = \cos(\theta+2\pi) + j\sin(\theta+2\pi)$$
$$= \cos\theta + j\sin\theta,$$
$$\left(\cos\frac{\theta+4\pi}{3} + j\sin\frac{\theta+4\pi}{3}\right)^3 = \cos(\theta+4\pi) + j\sin(\theta+4\pi)$$
$$= \cos\theta + j\sin\theta.$$

Since three different numbers when cubed give the same result, $\cos\theta + j\sin\theta$, each must be a cube root of the number. We note the law of formation, and might be tempted to try

$$\cos\frac{\theta+6\pi}{3} + j\sin\frac{\theta+6\pi}{3}$$

as another cube root. This number when cubed does give

$$\cos\theta + j\sin\theta,$$

but it is

$$\cos\left(\frac{\theta}{3} + 2\pi\right) + j\sin\left(\frac{\theta}{3} + 2\pi\right)$$
$$= \cos\frac{\theta}{3} + j\sin\frac{\theta}{3}$$

and is therefore the first cube root repeated. We have not therefore found a fourth cube root of $\cos\theta + j\sin\theta$. We will now deal with the general case and show that there are only three separate cube roots of a number, or only q qth roots.

Exercise: Show that the fourth powers of each of the following give the same result:

$$\cos\alpha + j\sin\alpha,$$
$$\cos\left(\alpha + \frac{\pi}{2}\right) + j\sin\left(\alpha + \frac{\pi}{2}\right),$$
$$\cos\left(\alpha + \frac{2\pi}{2}\right) + j\sin\left(\alpha + \frac{2\pi}{2}\right),$$
$$\cos\left(\alpha + \frac{3\pi}{2}\right) + j\sin\left(\alpha + \frac{3\pi}{2}\right).$$

Show also that the fourth power of $\cos\left(\alpha + \frac{5\pi}{2}\right) + j\sin\left(\alpha + \frac{5\pi}{2}\right)$ gives the same result, but that this number is included in the previous four numbers.

28.13. To Find the q qth Roots of $a + jb$

(1) Put the number into polar form as $r(\cos\theta + j\sin\theta)$.

(2) Express this in the general form

$$r[\cos(\theta + 2n\pi) + j\sin(\theta + 2n\pi)],$$

where n is any integer, positive or negative.

(3) We now have

$$a + jb = r[\cos(\theta + 2n\pi) + j\sin(\theta + 2n\pi)],$$

$$\therefore\quad (a + jb)^{\frac{1}{q}} = r^{\frac{1}{q}}[\cos(\theta + 2n\pi) + j\sin(\theta + 2n\pi)]^{\frac{1}{q}}$$

$$= r^{\frac{1}{q}}\left[\cos\frac{\theta + 2n\pi}{q} + j\sin\frac{\theta + 2n\pi}{q}\right] \quad . \quad . \quad . \quad \text{(A)}$$

by Demoivre's Theorem.

The number n is still at our disposal. If we put n equal to 0, 1, 2 . . . $(q - 1)$ in turn in (A) we will obtain q different values, and each of these is a qth root of $a + jb$. If, for example, we put $n = q$, we obtain

$$r^{\frac{1}{q}}\left[\cos\frac{\theta + 2q\pi}{q} + j\sin\frac{\theta + 2q\pi}{q}\right]$$

$$= r^{\frac{1}{q}}\left[\cos\frac{\theta}{q} + j\sin\frac{\theta}{q}\right],$$

which is the value obtained when $n = 0$. In this way it can be shown that only q different values can be obtained.

Example 7. Find the cube roots of 1 and show them on an Argand diagram.

(1) $1 = 1[\cos 0 + j\sin 0]$;

(2) $\therefore$ $1 = 1\,[\cos 2n\pi + j\sin 2n\pi]$, where n is any integer;

(3) $\therefore$ $1^{\frac{1}{3}} = 1^{\frac{1}{3}}\,[\cos 2n\pi + j\sin 2n\pi]^{\frac{1}{3}}$

$$= 1^{\frac{1}{3}}\left[\cos\frac{2n\pi}{3} + j\sin\frac{2n\pi}{3}\right].$$

It will be noticed that on the R.H.S. we take the arithmetical value of the root of the modulus which here is 1.

When $n = 0$ we have $1[\cos 0 + j\sin 0] = 1$,

$n = 1$,, $1\left[\cos\frac{2\pi}{3} + j\sin\frac{2\pi}{3}\right] = -\frac{1}{2} + j\frac{\sqrt{3}}{2}$,

$n = 2$,, $1\left[\cos\frac{4\pi}{3} + j\sin\frac{4\pi}{3}\right] = -\frac{1}{2} - j\frac{\sqrt{3}}{2}$.

(*a*) It will be noticed that in each case we have the same modulus, so that each root lies on a circle on the Argand Diagram radius $r^{\frac{1}{q}}$, which here is 1. Also the arguments always increase in arithmetical progression, so that the join of the roots on the circle forms a regular polygon inscribed in the circle.

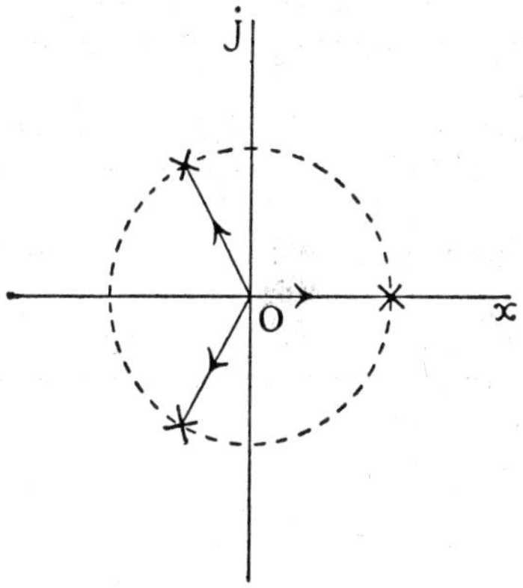

FIG. 83.

(*b*) In this example we have solved $x^3 = 1$,

$$\therefore \quad x^3 - 1 = 0,$$

$$(x - 1)(x^2 + x + 1) = 0,$$

$$\therefore \quad x = 1 \text{ and } \frac{-1 \pm \sqrt{-3}}{2}$$

$$= 1 \text{ and } \frac{-1 \pm j\sqrt{3}}{2}.$$

as found by Demoivre's Theorem.

Example 8. Find the fourth roots of $3 - 4j$.

$$3 - 4j = 5[\cos 53° \, 8' - j \sin 53° \, 8']$$
$$= 5[\cos (n \, . \, 360 + 53° \, 8') - j \sin (n \, . \, 360 + 53° \, 8')],$$
$$\therefore \quad (3 - 4j)^{\frac{1}{4}} = 5^{\frac{1}{4}}[\cos (n \, . \, 360 + 53° \, 8') - j \sin (n \, . \, 360 + 53° \, 8')]^{\frac{1}{4}}$$
$$= 5^{\frac{1}{4}}[\cos (n \, . \, 90 + 13° \, 17') - j \sin (n \, . \, 90 + 13° \, 17')].$$

We now put $n = 0, 1, 2, 3$ in order to obtain the 4 roots which are:

$$5^{\frac{1}{4}} [\cos 13° \, 17' - j \sin 13° \, 17'],$$
$$5^{\frac{1}{4}} [\cos 103° \, 17' - j \sin 103° \, 17'],$$
$$5^{\frac{1}{4}} [\cos 193° \, 17' - j \sin 193° \, 17'],$$
$$5^{\frac{1}{4}} [\cos 283° \, 17' - j \sin 283° \, 17'].$$

These roots all lie on a circle centre O and radius $5^{\frac{1}{4}} = 1{\cdot}495$. In the form $a + jb$ they are:

$$1{\cdot}495 \, [0{\cdot}973 - 0{\cdot}230j] = 1{\cdot}46 - 0{\cdot}34j,$$
$$1{\cdot}495 \, [-0{\cdot}230 - 0{\cdot}973j] = -0{\cdot}34 - 1{\cdot}46j,$$
$$1{\cdot}495 \, [-0{\cdot}973 + 0{\cdot}230j] = -1{\cdot}46 + 0{\cdot}34j,$$
$$1{\cdot}495 \, [0{\cdot}230 + 0{\cdot}973j] = 0{\cdot}34 + 1{\cdot}46j.$$

EXERCISE 75

1. Find expressions for $\cos 4\theta$ and $\sin 4\theta$ by Demoivre's Theorem, and hence find $\tan 4\theta$ in terms of $\tan\theta$ and powers of $\tan\theta$.

2. Show that:

$$\cos 5\theta = \cos^5\theta - 10\cos^3\theta\sin^2\theta + 5\cos\theta\sin^4\theta;$$
$$\sin 5\theta = 5\cos^4\theta\sin\theta - 10\cos^2\theta\sin^3\theta + \sin^5\theta.$$

3. Find simply $(3 + 4j)^5$.

4. Find the square roots of: $\cos 6\theta + j\sin 6\theta$; $\cos\theta - j\sin\theta$; j; $1 + j$.

5. Find the cube roots of: $\cos 9\theta + j\sin 9\theta$; $-j$.

6. Find the four fourth roots of $1 + 2j$ in the form $a + jb$.

7. Solve the equations:

(a) $x^6 + 1 = 0$;
(b) $x^9 - x^5 + x^4 - 1 = 0$ $(= (x^5 + 1)(x^4 - 1))$;
(c) $x^7 + x^4 + x^3 + 1 = 0$.

8. A formula giving the voltage at the end of a long telephone wire is

$$10^{-3}\left(\frac{3 + 30j}{6 + 18j}\right)^{\frac{1}{2}}.$$

Show that this can be written as $0{\cdot}00126\angle 6{\cdot}35°$.

9. The current I through a telephone line of length l is given by

$$I = \frac{2V_0}{\left(R + \frac{r}{n}\right)e^{ln}}$$

where $r = 88$, $l = 40$, and $n = \sqrt{(rkqj)}$, where $k = 0{\cdot}05 \times 10^{-6}$, $q = 5000$, $j = \sqrt{-1}$, $V_0 = 10\sin 5000t$, and $R = 100 + 0{\cdot}04qj$.

Show that:

(1) $n = 0{\cdot}1483\sqrt{j} = 0{\cdot}1483\angle 45°$;

(2) $\frac{r}{n} = 593\angle(-45°)$;

(3) $R + \frac{r}{n} = 563\ \angle(-22{\cdot}9°)$;

(4) $ln = 4{\cdot}196(1 + j)$;

(5) $e^{ln} = 66{\cdot}42\angle 240{\cdot}43°$;

(6) $I = 0{\cdot}0005348\sin(5000t - 217{\cdot}5°)$, if we may put $10e^{j5000t}$ for V_0, evaluate the complex expression for I and then pick out its j component in order to find I.

CHAPTER 29

HYPERBOLIC FUNCTIONS

29.1. Origin and Definition

The student will have appreciated the use of two functions such as $\sin\theta$ and $\cos\theta$, the *sum* of whose squares is one. Two functions the *difference* of whose squares is one would be just as useful, and these functions have been invented.

We define $\sinh x$ (written $\operatorname{sh} x$) as

$$\operatorname{sh} x = \frac{e^x - e^{-x}}{2}$$

and $\cosh x$ (written $\operatorname{ch} x$) as

$$\operatorname{ch} x = \frac{e^x + e^{-x}}{2}.$$

From these we have

$$\operatorname{ch} x + \operatorname{sh} x = e^x$$
$$\operatorname{ch} x - \operatorname{sh} x = e^{-x},$$
$$\therefore\ \operatorname{ch}^2 x - \operatorname{sh}^2 x = e^x \times e^{-x} = 1 \quad . \quad . \quad . \quad . \quad (1)$$

These functions are pronounced shine (x) and cosh (x). They and others to be obtained are called hyperbolic functions, since it can be shown that they bear much the same relation to a rectangular hyperbola that the sine and cosine (called circular functions) bear to the circle.

To correspond to the other circular functions we extend the number of hyperbolic functions as follows:

Since $$\tan\theta = \frac{\sin\theta}{\cos\theta}$$

we define $\tanh x$ (written $\operatorname{th} x$ and pronounced than x) as

$$\operatorname{th} x = \frac{\operatorname{sh} x}{\operatorname{ch} x} = \frac{e^x - e^{-x}}{e^x + e^{-x}}.$$

Similarly, $\coth x = \dfrac{1}{\operatorname{th} x}$, $\operatorname{cosech} x = \dfrac{1}{\operatorname{sh} x}$ and $\operatorname{sech} x = \dfrac{1}{\operatorname{ch} x}$.

We have by (1) $\qquad \operatorname{ch}^2 x - \operatorname{sh}^2 x = 1.$

Divide by $\operatorname{ch}^2 x$ and obtain

$$1 - \operatorname{th}^2 x = \operatorname{sech}^2 x$$

(cf. $1 + \tan^2\theta = \sec^2\theta$).

If we divide by $\operatorname{sh}^2 x$ we obtain

$$\coth^2 x - 1 = \operatorname{cosech}^2 x$$

(cf. $\cot^2\theta + 1 = \operatorname{cosec}^2\theta$).

K

29.2. Graphs and Properties

From the definitions we can easily obtain the rough sketches shown of the graphs of cosh x and sinh x, each built up from the separate graphs of e^x and e^{-x} or $-e^{-x}$. In each case P, the point on the curve $y = \text{ch}\, x$ or $\text{sh}\, x$ is the mid point of the intercept AB made by the curves on an ordinate erected at any point N on the x axis.

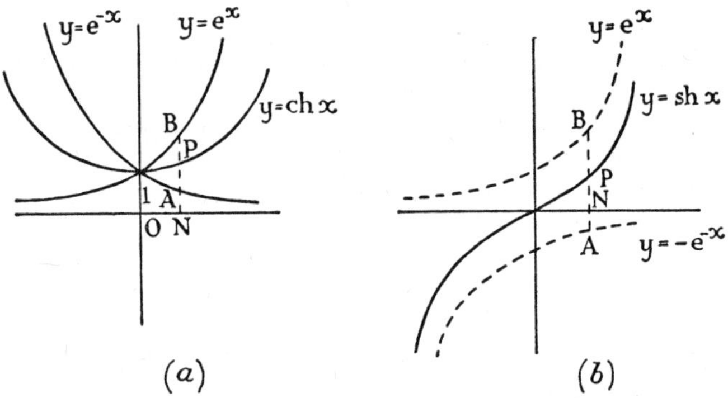

FIG. 84.

ch x. (Fig. 84 (a).)

From the definition:

(1) $\text{ch}\,(0) = \frac{1}{2}(e^0 + e^{-0}) = 1$.

(2) For x +ve ch x is +ve.

(3) $\text{ch}\,(-x) = \frac{1}{2}(e^{-x} + e^x) = \text{ch}\, x$, so that $y = \text{ch}\, x$ is symmetrical about the y axis. Therefore $y = \text{ch}\, x$ lies entirely in the 1st and 2nd quadrants.

(4) As $x \to \infty$, $\text{ch}\, x \to \frac{1}{2}e^x$, since $e^{-x} \to 0$.

(5) $\text{ch}\, x = \frac{1}{2}(e^x + e^{-x}) = 1 + \frac{x^2}{2!} + \frac{x^4}{4!} + \ldots \frac{x^{2n}}{(2n)!} + \ldots$

sh x. (Fig. 84 (b).)

From the definition:

(1) $\text{sh}\,(0) = \frac{1}{2}(1 - 1) = 0$.

(2) For x +ve sh x is +ve.

(3) $\text{sh}\,(-x) = \frac{1}{2}(e^{-x} - e^x) = -\text{sh}\, x$, so that $y = \text{sh}\, x$ is symmetrical with respect to the origin and lies entirely in the 1st and 3rd quadrants.

(4) As $x \to \infty$, $\text{sh}\, x \to \frac{1}{2}e^x$ since $e^{-x} \to 0$, $\therefore$ sh x and ch x tend to the same value as $x \to \infty$.

(5) $\text{sh}\, x = \frac{1}{2}(e^x - e^{-x}) = x + \frac{x^3}{3!} + \frac{x^5}{5!} + \ldots \frac{x^{2n-1}}{(2n-1)!} + \ldots$

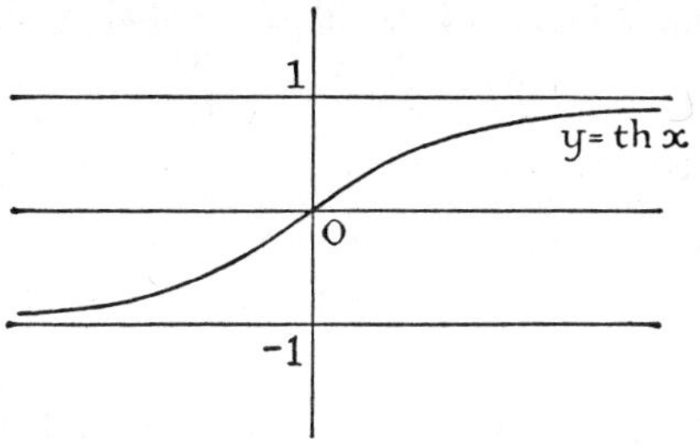

FIG. 85.

th x. (Fig. 85.)

(1) $\text{th}(0) = \frac{\text{sh}(0)}{\text{ch}(0)} = \frac{0}{1} = 0.$

(2) From the definition th x is +ve when x is +ve, and is always less than 1 for x +ve, but since

$$\text{th}\, x = \frac{e^x - e^{-x}}{e^x + e^{-x}} = \frac{1 - e^{-2x}}{1 + e^{-2x}},$$

$\therefore$ th $x \to +1$ as $x \to +\infty$ since then $e^{-2x} \to 0$.

$\therefore$ $y = \text{th}x$ for x +ve starts at 0 and increases to 1 for x infinite.

(3) $\text{th}(-x) = \frac{\text{sh}(-x)}{\text{ch}(-x)} = \frac{-\text{sh}\, x}{\text{ch}\, x} = -\text{th}\, x.$

$\therefore$ $y = \text{th}x$ is symmetrical with regard to the origin and so lies in the 1st and 3rd quadrants.

From these considerations we obtain the graph shown.

The slope of each curve for $x = 0$ will be apparent when we have differentiated these functions.

EXERCISE 76

1. If sh $x = \frac{3}{4}$, what is ch x?
2. If ch $x = 3$, what is sh x?
3. If th $x = \frac{1}{3}$, what is sech x?
4. If sh $x = 2$, what is th x?
5. If th $x = \frac{1}{2}$, what is ch x?
6. If th $x = \frac{1}{3}$, find e^{2x} and hence show $x = \frac{1}{2}\log 2$.
7. If $3e^x + 4e^{-x} = A\,\text{ch}\, x + B\,\text{sh}\, x$, find A and B.
8. Eliminate θ from the two equations $x = a\,\text{ch}\,\theta$, $y = b\,\text{sh}\,\theta$.
9. Give rough sketches of the curves $y = \text{sech}\, x$, $y = \text{cosech}\, x$ and $y = \text{coth}\, x$.
10. If $2\,\text{ch}\, x + 4\,\text{sh}\, x = Ae^x + Be^{-x}$, find A and B.
11. Show that:

$$\tfrac{1}{2}(\text{sh}\, x + \sin x) = x + \frac{x^5}{5!} + \frac{x^9}{9!} + \ldots \frac{x^{4n-3}}{(4n-3)!} + \ldots$$

$$\tfrac{1}{2}(\text{ch}\, x + \cos x) = 1 + \frac{x^4}{4!} + \frac{x^8}{8!} + \ldots \frac{x^{4n-4}}{(4n-4)!} + \ldots$$

12. The speed, V knots, of waves over a shallow bottom is given by

$$V^2 = 1{\cdot}8\,L\,\text{th}\left(\frac{6{\cdot}3d}{L}\right),$$

where d is the depth of the water in feet and L the wave length. Find V if $d = 30'$ and $L = 300'$.

13. Simplify sh (log x) and ch (log x).

14. If 4 cosech² $x - 8\coth x + 7 = 0$, find the value of coth x and hence that of x.

15. If $x = \log_e \tan\left(\frac{\pi}{4} + \frac{1}{2}\theta\right)$, find e^x, e^{-x} and hence show that $\sinh x = \tan\theta$.

16. If $z = 0{\cdot}3(1 + j)$, find e^z and e^{-z} in the form $a + jb$. Hence show that $\text{ch}(0{\cdot}3 + 0{\cdot}3j) = 0{\cdot}999 + 0{\cdot}090j$ and $\text{sh}(0{\cdot}3 + 0{\cdot}3j) = 0{\cdot}291 + 0{\cdot}309j$.

29.3. Further Relations

(a) We will obtain some relations between hyperbolic functions to correspond to those between circular functions.

Thus sh A ch B + ch A sh B

$$= \frac{e^A - e^{-A}}{2}\cdot\frac{e^B + e^{-B}}{2} + \frac{e^A + e^{-A}}{2}\cdot\frac{e^B - e^{-B}}{2}$$

$$= \tfrac{1}{4}\{(e^{A+B} + e^{A-B} - e^{-A+B} - e^{-A-B}) + (e^{A+B} - e^{A-B} + e^{-A+B} - e^{-A-B})\}$$

$$= \frac{e^{A+B} - e^{-(A+B)}}{2}$$

$$= \text{sh}\,(A + B)$$

Similarly, we can prove

$$\text{sh A ch B} - \text{ch A sh B} = \text{sh}\,(A - B),$$
$$\text{ch A ch B} \pm \text{sh A sh B} = \text{ch}\,(A \pm B).$$

[Note the signs in this last formula which are opposite to those found in the corresponding formula

$$\cos x \cos y \mp \sin x \sin y = \cos(x \pm y).]$$

$$\text{th}\,(A \pm B) = \frac{\text{sh}\,(A \pm B)}{\text{ch}\,(A \pm B)}$$
$$= \frac{\text{sh A ch B} \pm \text{ch A sh B}}{\text{ch A ch B} \pm \text{sh A sh B}}$$
$$= \frac{\text{th A} \pm \text{th B}}{1 \pm \text{th A th B}}$$

[Note that $\tan(x \pm y) = \dfrac{\tan x \pm \tan y}{1 \mp \tan x \tan y}$.]

(b) If we put A = B in the above we deduce:

(1) $\text{sh}\,2A = 2\,\text{sh A ch A}$;

(2) $\text{ch}\,2A = \text{ch}^2 A + \text{sh}^2 A$
$= 1 + 2\,\text{sh}^2 A$

or
$$= 2\,\text{ch}^2 A - 1;$$
$$\therefore \quad \text{sh}^2 A = \tfrac{1}{2}(\text{ch}\,2A - 1),$$
$$\text{ch}^2 A = \tfrac{1}{2}(\text{ch}\,2A + 1).$$

The student should re-write these with $\frac{A}{2}$ for A, thus giving the half-angle formulae.

Example 1. Prove from the definition that $4\text{sh}^3 x = \text{sh}\,3x - 3\text{sh}\,x$.

$$\text{sh}^3 x = \left(\frac{e^x - e^{-x}}{2}\right)^3$$
$$= \tfrac{1}{8}\{e^{3x} - 3e^{2x}e^{-x} + 3e^x e^{-2x} - e^{-3x}\}$$
$$= \tfrac{1}{8}\{e^{3x} - 3e^x + 3e^{-x} - e^{-3x}\}$$
$$= \tfrac{1}{8}\{(e^{3x} - e^{-3x}) - 3(e^x - e^{-x})\}$$
$$= \underline{\tfrac{1}{4}\{\text{sh}\,3x - 3\text{sh}\,x\}}.$$

Example 2. Simplify $\dfrac{1 + \text{sh}\,A + \text{ch}\,A}{1 - \text{sh}\,A - \text{ch}\,A}$.

$$1 + \text{sh}\,A + \text{ch}\,A = 1 + 2\text{sh}\,\frac{A}{2}\,\text{ch}\,\frac{A}{2} + 2\,\text{ch}^2\frac{A}{2} - 1$$
$$= 2\,\text{ch}\,\frac{A}{2}\left(\text{sh}\,\frac{A}{2} + \text{ch}\,\frac{A}{2}\right);$$
$$1 - \text{sh}\,A - \text{ch}\,A = 1 - 2\,\text{sh}\,\frac{A}{2}\,\text{ch}\,\frac{A}{2} - \left(1 + 2\,\text{sh}^2\frac{A}{2}\right)$$
$$= -2\,\text{sh}\,\frac{A}{2}\left(\text{sh}\,\frac{A}{2} + \text{ch}\,\frac{A}{2}\right);$$
$$\therefore \text{ the given expression} = \frac{2\,\text{ch}\,\frac{A}{2}\left(\text{sh}\,\frac{A}{2} + \text{ch}\,\frac{A}{2}\right)}{-2\,\text{sh}\,\frac{A}{2}\left(\text{sh}\,\frac{A}{2} + \text{ch}\,\frac{A}{2}\right)}$$
$$= \underline{-\coth\frac{A}{2}}.$$

EXERCISE 77

Prove the following from the definitions, converting one side to the other:

1. $1 + \text{ch}\,x = 2\text{ch}^2\left(\dfrac{x}{2}\right)$.
2. $1 - \text{ch}\,x = -2\,\text{sh}^2\left(\dfrac{x}{2}\right)$.
3. $\text{th}\,2x = \dfrac{2\,\text{th}\,x}{(1 + \text{th}^2 x)}$.
4. $\text{sh}\,\theta - \text{sh}\,\phi = 2\,\text{ch}\,\dfrac{\theta + \phi}{2}\,\text{sh}\,\dfrac{\theta - \phi}{2}$.
5. $\text{ch}\,\theta - \text{ch}\,\phi = 2\,\text{sh}\,\dfrac{\theta + \phi}{2}\,\text{sh}\,\dfrac{\theta - \phi}{2}$.
6. $\dfrac{1 + \text{th}\,x}{1 - \text{th}\,x} = \text{ch}\,2x + \text{sh}\,2x$.
7. $\coth\dfrac{\theta}{2} - \coth\theta = \text{cosech}\,\theta$.
8. Factorize $x^2 - 2xy\,\text{ch}\,\alpha + y^2$.
9. Solve the equation $x^2 - 2x\,\text{ch}\,\alpha + 1 = 0$.

10. Using the formula for $\tan^{-1} A - \tan^{-1} B$, prove that

$$\tan^{-1}(e^x) - \tan^{-1}\left(\text{th}\frac{x}{2}\right) = \frac{\pi}{4}.$$

11. Prove:

(*a*) $4 \text{ ch}^3 x = \text{ch } 3x + 3 \text{ ch } x$;

(*b*) $8 \text{ sh}^4 x = \text{ch } 4x - 4 \text{ ch } 2x + 3$;

(*c*) $8 \text{ ch}^4 x = \text{ch } 4x + 4 \text{ ch } 2x + 3$.

12. Show that any point on the rectangular hyperbola $x^2 - y^2 = a^2$ may be represented by the parametric equations $x = a \text{ ch } \theta, y = a \text{ sh } \theta$. If this be the point θ, show that the chord joining the points θ, ϕ is

$$x \text{ ch } \frac{\theta + \phi}{2} - y \text{ sh } \frac{\theta + \phi}{2} = a \text{ ch } \frac{\theta - \phi}{2}.$$

13. Prove that $\sin^2 \theta \text{ ch}^2 \phi + \cos^2 \theta \text{ sh}^2 \phi = \frac{1}{2}(\text{ch } 2\phi - \cos 2\theta)$.

29.4. Differentiation of Hyperbolic Functions

We have $$\frac{d}{dx}(\text{sh } x) = \frac{d}{dx}\left(\frac{e^x - e^{-x}}{2}\right) = \frac{e^x + e^{-x}}{2},$$

$$\therefore \quad \frac{d}{dx}(\text{sh } x) = \text{ch } x.$$

Similarly, $$\frac{d}{dx}(\text{ch } x) = \text{sh } x.$$

Note that the differential coefficient of sh (ax) can be found as usual by the " stage-by-stage " method, thus :

$$\frac{d}{d(ax)} \text{ sh } (ax) = \text{ch } (ax).$$

Now " go inside " the sinh function

$$\frac{d}{dx}(ax) = a,$$

$$\therefore \quad \frac{d}{dx}[\text{sh } (ax)] = a \text{ ch } ax.$$

Similarly, $$\frac{d}{dx}[\text{ch } (ax)] = a \text{ sh } ax.$$

From these two results all the other differential coefficients can be deduced.

$$\begin{aligned}\frac{d}{dx}(\text{th } x) &= \frac{d}{dx}\left(\frac{\text{sh } x}{\text{ch } x}\right) \\ &= \frac{\text{ch } x \,.\, \text{ch } x - \text{sh } x \,.\, \text{sh } x}{\text{ch}^2 x} \\ &= \frac{\text{ch}^2 x - \text{sh}^2 x}{\text{ch}^2 x} = \frac{1}{\text{ch}^2 x} = \text{sech}^2 x;\end{aligned}$$

$$\begin{aligned}\frac{d}{dx}(\text{sech } x) &= \frac{d}{dx}[(\text{ch } x)^{-1}] \\ &= -1 \, (\text{ch } x)^{-2} \times \text{sh } x = -\frac{\text{sh } x}{\text{ch}^2 x};\end{aligned}$$

$$\frac{d}{dx}(\text{cosech } x) = \frac{d}{dx}[(\text{sh } x)^{-1}]$$

$$= -1\,(\text{sh } x)^{-2} \times \text{ch } x = -\frac{\text{ch } x}{\text{sh}^2 x}.$$

Example 3. Differentiate $\tan^{-1}\left(\text{th } \frac{x}{2}\right)$.

(1) d.c. of $\tan^{-1}\left(\text{th } \frac{x}{2}\right) = \dfrac{1}{1 + \text{th}^2 \frac{x}{2}}$.

(2) d.c. of $\text{th}\left(\frac{x}{2}\right) \quad = \text{sech}^2 \frac{x}{2}$.

(3) d.c. of $\frac{x}{2} \quad = \frac{1}{2}$.

result $\quad = \dfrac{1}{1 + \text{th}^2 \frac{x}{2}} \times \text{sech}^2 \frac{x}{2} \times \frac{1}{2}$

$$= \frac{\text{ch}^2 \frac{x}{2}}{\text{ch}^2 \frac{x}{2} + \text{sh}^2 \frac{x}{2}} \times \frac{1}{\text{ch}^2 \frac{x}{2}} \times \frac{1}{2} = \underline{\frac{1}{2 \text{ ch } x}}.$$

EXERCISE 78

1. Differentiate the following:

(a) $\text{sh } \frac{x}{3}$; (b) $3 \text{ ch } 5x$; (c) $2 \text{ th } 3x$; (d) $\text{ch}^3 2x$;

(e) $\text{sh}^2 3x$; (f) $\text{sh } 2x \text{ ch } 2x$; (g) $\text{cosech } 4x$; (h) $\text{sech } \frac{x}{2}$;

(i) $\text{th}^2 \frac{x}{4}$; (j) $\log (\text{ch } 3x)$; (k) $\log\left(\text{th } \frac{x}{2}\right)$; (l) $x - \text{coth } x$;

(m) $\sin 2x \text{ ch } 3x$; (n) $x^{\text{sh} x}$; (o) $e^{ax} \text{ ch } bx$; (p) $\dfrac{\tan x}{\text{th } x}$;

(q) $\dfrac{x}{\text{ch } x}$; (r) $\dfrac{\text{sh } 2x}{x^2}$; (s) $(\cosh x)^x$.

2. Find the minimum value of $5 \text{ ch } x + 3 \text{ sh } x$ and give a rough sketch to illustrate.

3. Prove that $e^{-x} \text{ sh } \frac{x}{2}$ has a maximum at $x = \log 3$.

4. If $y = a \text{ ch } nx + b \text{ sh } nx$, show that $\dfrac{d^2y}{dx^2} = n^2y$.

5. If $x = \tan^{-1} (\text{sh } pt + \text{ch } pt)$, show that

$$\frac{dx}{dt} = \frac{1}{2} p \text{ sech } pt.$$

6. Solve the equation $\text{ch} (\log x) = \text{sh}\left(\log \frac{x}{2}\right) + \frac{7}{4}$.

7. Using the series for each function in powers of x, find the limit of each of the following as $x \to 0$.

(a) $\dfrac{\text{sh}\, x}{x}$; (b) $\dfrac{x}{\text{th}\, x}$;

(c) $\dfrac{1}{x^2} - \coth^2 x$; (d) $\dfrac{\text{sh}\, x - \sin x}{x^3}$.

8. Show that $\text{sh}\, x - \text{th}\, x = \frac{1}{2}x^3$ approximately if x is small.

9. Show that if θ is small,

$$\frac{\text{cosec}\,\theta + \text{cosech}\,\theta}{\theta^3} - \frac{2}{\theta^4} = \frac{7}{180}.$$

10. Find the equation of the tangent at any point of the curve

$$x = a\,\text{ch}\,2\theta, \quad y = b\,\text{sh}\,\theta.$$

Show that the two tangents which pass through the origin have equations $b\sqrt{2}\,x \pm 4\,ay = 0$.

11. Solve the equation $1{\cdot}02z = \text{sh}\, z$ correct to three decimals.

12. Solve the equation $\dfrac{z}{2} + 1 = \text{ch}\, z$ correct to three decimals.

[The student will discover later that the equations in nos. 11 and 12 occur in catenary problems, such as to find the clearance of overhead lines above the road.]

29.5. Integration of Hyperbolic Functions

Since $$\frac{d}{dx}(\text{sh}\, ax) = a\,\text{ch}\, ax,$$

$$\int \text{ch}\, ax\, dx = \frac{1}{a}\,\text{sh}\, ax + \text{const.}$$

Similarly, $$\int \text{sh}\, ax\, dx = \frac{1}{a}\,\text{ch}\, ax + \text{const.}$$

and $$\int \text{sech}^2\, ax\, dx = \frac{1}{a}\,\text{th}\, ax + \text{const.}$$

But
$$\begin{aligned}\int \text{th}\, ax\, dx &= \int \frac{\text{sh}\, ax}{\text{ch}\, ax}\,dx\\ &= \frac{1}{a}\int \frac{a\,\text{sh}\, ax}{\text{ch}\, ax}\,dx\\ &= \frac{1}{a}\int \frac{d(\text{ch}\, ax)}{\text{ch}\, ax}\\ &= \frac{1}{a}\log(\text{ch}\, ax) + \text{const.}\end{aligned}$$

$$\begin{aligned}\int \text{sh}^2\, x dx &= \int \frac{\text{ch}\, 2x - 1}{2}\,dx\\ &= \frac{1}{4}\,\text{sh}\, 2x - \frac{x}{2} + \text{const.}\end{aligned}$$

Example 4. The curve $y = a \operatorname{ch}\frac{x}{a}$ revolves round the x axis. Find the volume generated between the ordinates at $x = 0$ and $x = a$.

$$\text{Vol.} = \int_0^a \pi y^2 dx = \pi \int_0^a a^2 \operatorname{ch}^2 \frac{x}{a} dx$$

$$= \frac{\pi a^2}{2} \int_0^a \left(\operatorname{ch}\frac{2x}{a} + 1\right) dx$$

$$= \frac{\pi a^2}{2} \left[\frac{a}{2} \operatorname{sh}\frac{2x}{a} + x\right]_0^a$$

$$= \frac{\pi a^2}{2} \left[a \frac{\operatorname{sh} 2}{2} + a\right]$$

$$= \frac{\pi a^3}{4} \left[\frac{e^2 - e^{-2}}{2} + 2\right].$$

EXERCISE 79

1. Integrate:

(*a*) $4 \operatorname{ch} 3x$; (*b*) $5 \operatorname{sh} \frac{3x}{2}$; (*c*) $\operatorname{th} \frac{x}{2}$;

(*d*) $\operatorname{sh}^2 3x$; (*e*) $2 \operatorname{sech}^2 5x$; (*f*) $4 \operatorname{ch}^2 7x$.

2. Integrate by parts:

(*a*) $x \operatorname{sh} 2x$; (*b*) $x^2 \operatorname{ch} x$; (*c*) $x \operatorname{sech}^2 x$.

3. Find:

(*a*) $\int_{-1}^{+1} \operatorname{ch} 2x dx$; (*b*) $\int_0^2 \operatorname{sh}^2 \frac{x}{2} dx$.

4. Show that the curves $y = 4e^x$ and $y = 9 \operatorname{sh} x$ intersect where $x = \log 3$ and find the area bounded by these curves and the y axis.

5. Find the area bounded by the curve $y = \operatorname{ch} x$ and the line $y = 2$ and also the volume generated by rotating this area about the x axis.

6. Find $$\int_0^{\log 3} \frac{\operatorname{ch} x}{1 + 3 \operatorname{sh} x} dx.$$

7. Find the area bounded by $y = \operatorname{th} x$, the line $x = \frac{4}{5}$ and the x axis.

8. If (a, b) is a point on the curve $y = c \operatorname{ch} \frac{x}{c}$, show that the volume generated by rotating about the x axis the area bounded by this curve, the axes and the line $x = a$ is

$$\frac{\pi c}{2} [b\sqrt{b^2 - c^2} + ca].$$

29.6. The Inverse Hyperbolic Functions (Fig. 86)

(*a*) When $x = \text{ON}$ is given, we can through N, a point on the x axis of the curve $y = \operatorname{sh} x$ (Fig. 64(*b*)), erect NP to meet the curve in P and thus find $\text{NP} = \operatorname{sh} x$. In this case x is the given or " independent " variable and we find $\text{NP} = y$ the " dependent " variable.

We wish to consider the case where it is NP that is given and ON is to be found. In this case we may measure off OM = NP on the y axis and draw MP parallel to the x axis to meet the curve in P. With inverse functions, since OM is the independent variable we will measure it along the x axis and call it x and we will call MP y, so that the curve is now $x = \text{sh}\, y$ or $y = \text{sh}^{-1} x$ as shown (Fig. 86(*a*)). x is now a number whose hyperbolic sine is y. We note that for any given value of x positive or negative, there is a unique value of y, *i.e.*, MP will meet the curve once only.

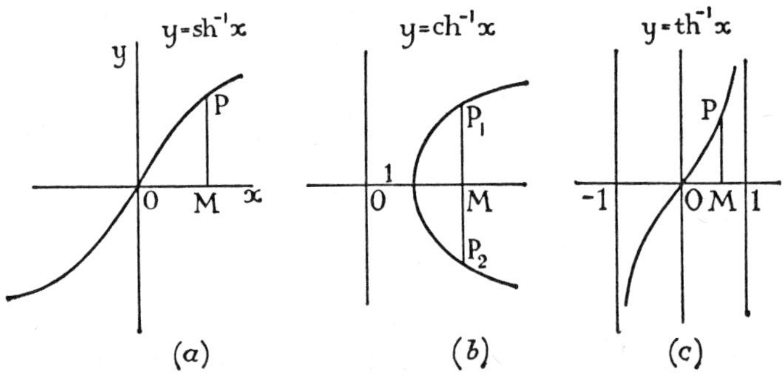

FIG. 86.

(*b*) Similarly, for $y = \text{ch}^{-1}(x)$ (Fig. 86(*b*)), x being given, $\text{ch}^{-1}(x)$ is a number whose hyperbolic cosine is y. The graph is as shown, and we note that for $\text{ch}^{-1}(x)$ to exist x must be positive and greater than 1. In this case there are two values, MP_1 and MP_2, which are equal and opposite. We always keep to *the positive value.*

(*c*) Similarly, for $y = \text{th}^{-1}(x)$ where the graph is as shown (Fig. 86(*c*)). For this to exist $x = \text{OM}$ must lie between $+1$ and -1, and then there is only one value.

29.7. Logarithmic Equivalents

If
$$y = \text{sh}^{-1}\left(\tfrac{3}{4}\right),$$
then
$$\text{sh}\, y = \tfrac{3}{4};$$
$$\therefore \quad \text{ch}\, y = +\sqrt{1 + \left(\tfrac{3}{4}\right)^2} = \tfrac{5}{4};$$
we take the plus sign for the square root, since $\text{ch}\, y$ is positive,
$$\text{sh}\, y + \text{ch}\, y = 2,$$
i.e.,
$$e^y = 2,$$
$$\therefore \quad y = \log_e 2 = \text{sh}^{-1}\left(\tfrac{3}{4}\right).$$

We will now do this in general terms to obtain a general formula.

(*a*) $\text{sh}^{-1}\left(\frac{x}{a}\right)$.

Let
$$y = \text{sh}^{-1}\left(\frac{x}{a}\right),$$
$$\text{sh}\, y = \frac{x}{a},$$
$$\therefore \quad \text{ch}\, y = +\sqrt{1 + \frac{x^2}{a^2}},$$
$$\text{sh}\, y + \text{ch}\, y = \frac{x}{a} + \sqrt{1 + \frac{x^2}{a^2}},$$
i.e.,
$$e^y = \frac{x + \sqrt{a^2 + x^2}}{a},$$
$$\therefore \quad y = \log\left(\frac{x + \sqrt{a^2 + x^2}}{a}\right) = \text{sh}^{-1}\left(\frac{x}{a}\right),$$
giving a logarithmic equivalent for $\text{sh}^{-1}\left(\frac{x}{a}\right)$.

Example 5. $\text{sh}^{-1}\left(\frac{4}{3}\right) = \log_e\left(\frac{4 + \sqrt{3^2 + 4^2}}{3}\right) = \underline{\log_e 3}.$

(*b*) $\text{ch}^{-1}\left(\frac{x}{a}\right)$.

Let
$$y = \text{ch}^{-1}\left(\frac{x}{a}\right)$$
where we have taken the positive value so that y is positive.
$$\text{ch}\, y = \frac{x}{a},$$
$$\therefore \quad \text{sh}\, y = +\sqrt{\frac{x^2}{a^2} - 1},$$
$$\text{ch}\, y + \text{sh}\, y = \frac{x}{a} + \sqrt{\frac{x^2}{a^2} - 1},$$
i.e.,
$$e^y = \frac{x + \sqrt{x^2 - a^2}}{a},$$
$$\therefore \quad y = \log\left(\frac{x + \sqrt{x^2 - a^2}}{a}\right) = \text{ch}^{-1}\left(\frac{x}{a}\right).$$

Example 6.
$$\text{ch}^{-1}\left(\frac{13}{5}\right) = \log\left(\frac{13 + \sqrt{13^2 - 5^2}}{5}\right)$$
$$= \log\left(\frac{13 + 12}{5}\right) = \underline{\log_e 5}.$$

(*c*) $\text{th}^{-1}\left(\frac{x}{a}\right)$.

Let
$$y = \text{th}^{-1}\left(\frac{x}{a}\right),$$
$$\text{th}\, y = \frac{x}{a},$$

i.e.,
$$\frac{e^{2y}-1}{e^{2y}+1}=\frac{x}{a},$$
$$e^{2y}=\frac{a+x}{a-x},$$
$$\therefore \quad y=\frac{1}{2}\log\left(\frac{a+x}{a-x}\right).$$

Example 7. $\text{th}^{-1}\left(\frac{1}{3}\right)=\frac{1}{2}\log\frac{3+1}{3-1}=\underline{\frac{1}{2}\log 2.}$

EXERCISE 80

1. Show that:
(*a*) $\text{sh}^{-1}(\frac{3}{4})=\log 2$;
(*b*) $\text{ch}^{-1}(\frac{5}{4})=\log 2$;
(*c*) $\text{th}^{-1}(\frac{2}{7})=\frac{1}{2}\log(\frac{9}{5})$;
(*d*) $\text{sh}^{-1}(0{\cdot}6)=0{\cdot}569$;
(*e*) $\text{ch}^{-1}(3)=1{\cdot}763$;
(*f*) $\text{th}^{-1}(0{\cdot}7)=0{\cdot}867$.
2. Show that $x=\frac{1}{2}\log 3$ is a root of the equation
$$4\,\text{th}^2 x+3=8\,\text{th}\,x.$$

29.8. Differentiation of Inverse Hyperbolic Functions

(*a*) Since
$$\text{sh}^{-1}\left(\frac{x}{a}\right)=\log\frac{x+\sqrt{x^2+a^2}}{a},$$
$$\frac{d}{dx}\left\{\text{sh}^{-1}\left(\frac{x}{a}\right)\right\}=\frac{d}{dx}\{\log(x+\sqrt{x^2+a^2})-\log a\}$$
$$=\frac{1}{x+\sqrt{x^2+a^2}}\times\left(1+\frac{x}{\sqrt{x^2+a^2}}\right)$$
$$=\frac{1}{\sqrt{x^2+a^2}},$$
$$\therefore \quad \int\frac{dx}{\sqrt{x^2+a^2}}=\text{sh}^{-1}\left(\frac{x}{a}\right)+\text{const.}$$
$$\text{or }\log\frac{x+\sqrt{x^2+a^2}}{a}+\text{const.}$$

Note that some tables of integrals omit the a in the denominator of the logarithm, since it may be regarded as part of the constant of integration.

(*b*) Similarly,
$$\frac{d}{dx}\left\{\text{ch}^{-1}\left(\frac{x}{a}\right)\right\}=\frac{d}{dx}\{\log(x+\sqrt{x^2-a^2})-\log a\}$$
$$=\frac{1}{x+\sqrt{x^2-a^2}}\times\left(1+\frac{x}{\sqrt{x^2-a^2}}\right)$$
$$=\frac{1}{\sqrt{x^2-a^2}},$$

$$\therefore \int \frac{dx}{\sqrt{x^2 - a^2}} = \text{ch}^{-1}\left(\frac{x}{a}\right) + \text{const.}$$

$$\text{or } \log \frac{x + \sqrt{x^2 - a^2}}{a} + \text{const.}$$

(*c*) $$\frac{d}{dx}\left\{\text{th}^{-1}\left(\frac{x}{a}\right)\right\} = \frac{d}{dx}\left\{\frac{1}{2}\log\frac{a+x}{a-x}\right\}$$

$$= \frac{1}{2}\frac{d}{dx}\{\log(a+x) - \log(a-x)\}$$

$$= \frac{1}{2}\left\{\frac{1}{a+x} - \frac{-1}{a-x}\right\}$$

$$= \frac{a}{a^2 - x^2},$$

$$\therefore \int \frac{a}{a^2 - x^2}dx = \text{th}^{-1}\left(\frac{x}{a}\right) + \text{const.}$$

$$\text{or } \frac{1}{2}\log\frac{a+x}{a-x} + \text{const.}$$

or, as a standard form, dividing by a,

$$\int \frac{dx}{a^2 - x^2} = \frac{1}{2a}\log\frac{a+x}{a-x} + \text{const.} \quad . \quad . \quad . \quad \text{(A)}$$

Result (A) is the more important in section (*c*) and is usually obtained by putting $\dfrac{1}{(a^2 - x^2)}$ into partial fractions and integrating each part.

Example 8. (*a*) $$\frac{d}{dx}\text{sh}^{-1}\left(\frac{3x}{4}\right) = \frac{1}{\sqrt{\left(\frac{3x}{4}\right)^2 + 1^2}} \times \frac{3}{4}$$

$$= \underline{\frac{3}{\sqrt{9x^2 + 16}}}$$

Note that we regard $\frac{3x}{4}$ as z and differentiate $\text{sh}^{-1}\left(\frac{z}{1}\right)$. We then differentiate the next stage $\frac{3x}{4}$ to obtain the factor $\frac{3}{4}$.

(*b*) $$\frac{d}{dx}\text{th}^{-1}\left(\frac{2x}{3}\right) = \frac{1}{1 - \left(\frac{2x}{3}\right)^2} \times \frac{2}{3}$$

$$= \underline{\frac{6}{9 - 4x^2}}.$$

EXERCISE 81

Differentiate Nos. 1–9.

1. $\text{sh}^{-1}\left(\frac{2}{3}x\right)$. 2. $\text{ch}^{-1}\left(\frac{3x}{4}\right)$. 3. $\text{th}^{-1}\left(\frac{3x}{2}\right)$.

4. $\text{ch}^{-1}(3 + 2x)$. 5. $\text{th}^{-1}\tan\left(\frac{x}{2}\right)$. 6. $\text{sh}^{-1}\sqrt{(x^2 - 1)}$.

7. $\text{sh}^{-1}(\tan x)$. 8. $\text{ch}^{-1}(\sec x)$. 9. $\text{th}^{-1}(\sin x)$.

10. If
$$y = \text{sh}^{-1}\left(\frac{a \text{ sh } x - b}{a + b \text{ sh } x}\right),$$
show that
$$\frac{dy}{dx} = \frac{\sqrt{a^2 + b^2}}{a + b \text{ sh } x}.$$

29.9. Integration by Substitution

The previous results are so important that we will obtain them by another method.

To find
$$\int \frac{dx}{\sqrt{a^2 + x^2}}.$$

If we can find a substitution for x that will combine $a^2 + x^2$ into a function with an easy square root we may hope to find the integral just as the substitution $x = a \sin \theta$ gives an easy method of finding
$$\int \frac{dx}{\sqrt{a^2 - x^2}}.$$

In this case we try
$$x = a \text{ sh } \theta,$$
$$\therefore \quad dx = a \text{ ch } \theta \, d\theta$$
and
$$a^2 + x^2 = a^2 + a^2 \text{ sh}^2 \theta = a^2 \text{ ch}^2 \theta.$$
$\therefore$ the integral becomes
$$\int \frac{a \text{ ch } \theta \, d\theta}{\sqrt{a^2 \text{ ch}^2 \theta}} = \int d\theta = \theta + \text{const.}$$

But since $x = a \text{ sh } \theta, \quad \theta = \text{sh}^{-1}\left(\frac{x}{a}\right),$
$$\therefore \quad \text{integral} = \text{sh}^{-1}\left(\frac{x}{a}\right) + \text{const.}$$

The student should find
$$\int \frac{dx}{\sqrt{x^2 - a^2}}$$
by the substitution $x = a \text{ ch } \theta.$

He may also find
$$\int \frac{dx}{a^2 - x^2}$$
by the substitution $x = a \text{ th } \theta$, but should note specially the partial fraction method.

Example 9.
$$\int \frac{dx}{\sqrt{4x^2 - 9}} = \frac{1}{2}\int \frac{dx}{\sqrt{x^2 - (\frac{3}{2})^2}}$$
$$= \frac{1}{2} \text{ ch}^{-1}\left(\frac{x}{\frac{3}{2}}\right) + \text{const.}$$

[It is always best to make the coefficient of x^2 unity as above and then use the standard form.]

If, however, we are given limits of integration so that a numerical answer is required we use the log form. Thus

$$\int_2^3 \frac{dx}{\sqrt{4x^2 - 9}} = \tfrac{1}{2}\int_2^3 \frac{dx}{\sqrt{x^2 - (\frac{3}{2})^2}}$$

$$= \tfrac{1}{2}\left[\log \frac{x + \sqrt{x^2 - \frac{9}{4}}}{\frac{3}{2}}\right]_2^3$$

$$= \tfrac{1}{2}\log\left(\frac{3 + \sqrt{9 - \frac{9}{4}}}{2 + \sqrt{4 - \frac{9}{4}}}\right)$$

$$= \tfrac{1}{2}\log_e\left(\frac{6 + 3\sqrt{3}}{4 + \sqrt{7}}\right)$$

$$= \tfrac{1}{2}[\log 11{\cdot}196 - \log 6{\cdot}646]$$

$$= \underline{0{\cdot}261.}$$

Example 10. Find $I = \int \sqrt{a^2 + x^2}dx.$

Put $x = a \text{ sh } z$ then $dx = a \text{ ch } z dz$

and $a^2 + x^2 = a^2 + a^2 \text{ sh}^2 z = a^2 \text{ ch}^2 z,$

$$\therefore \quad I = \int a \text{ ch } z \,.\, a \text{ ch } z dz$$

$$= \tfrac{1}{2}a^2\int (\text{ch } 2z + 1)dz$$

$$= \tfrac{1}{2}a^2[\tfrac{1}{2} \text{ sh } 2z + z] + C$$

$$= \tfrac{1}{2}a^2[\text{sh } z \text{ ch } z + z] + C.$$

But $\text{sh } z = \frac{x}{a}$, $\quad\therefore\quad \text{ch } z = \frac{1}{a}\sqrt{a^2 + x^2}$ and $z = \text{sh}^{-1}\left(\frac{x}{a}\right)$,

$$\therefore \quad \underline{I = \tfrac{1}{2}a^2\left[\frac{x}{a} \cdot \frac{\sqrt{a^2 + x^2}}{a} + \text{sh}^{-1}\frac{x}{a}\right] + C.}$$

There is an alternative method, as follows. Integrating by parts

$$\int 1 \,.\, \sqrt{a^2 + x^2}dx = \sqrt{a^2 + x^2} \,.\, x - \int \frac{x}{\sqrt{a^2 + x^2}} \cdot x dx,$$

now

$$\frac{x^2}{\sqrt{a^2 + x^2}} = \frac{(a^2 + x^2) - a^2}{\sqrt{a^2 + x^2}} = \sqrt{a^2 + x^2} - \frac{a^2}{\sqrt{a^2 + x^2}},$$

$$\therefore \quad \int \frac{x^2}{\sqrt{a^2 + x^2}}dx = \int \sqrt{a^2 + x^2}dx - a^2 \text{ sh}^{-1}\left(\frac{x}{a}\right).$$

$\therefore$ if I denotes the required integral

$$I = x\sqrt{a^2 + x^2} - \left[I - a^2 \text{ sh}^{-1}\left(\frac{x}{a}\right)\right],$$

$$\therefore \quad 2I = x\sqrt{a^2 + x^2} + a^2 \text{ sh}^{-1}\left(\frac{x}{a}\right),$$

$$\therefore \quad \underline{I = \frac{x}{2}\sqrt{a^2 + x^2} + \frac{a^2}{2} \text{ sh}^{-1}\left(\frac{x}{a}\right) + C,}$$

where the constant C is added at the last stage.

EXERCISE 82

Integrate nos. 1–9.

1. $\dfrac{1}{\sqrt{x^2 + 4}}$. 2. $\dfrac{1}{\sqrt{x^2 - 9}}$. 3. $\dfrac{1}{\sqrt{4x^2 - 25}}$.

4. $\dfrac{1}{\sqrt{9x^2+1}}$. 5. $\dfrac{1}{\sqrt{a^2x^2+b^2}}$. 6. $\dfrac{1}{\sqrt{a^2-b^2x^2}}$.

7. $\dfrac{1}{\sqrt{16-9x^2}}$. 8. $\dfrac{2x}{\sqrt{x^4+1}}$. 9. $\dfrac{2x}{\sqrt{x^4-a^2}}$.

Find:

10. $\displaystyle\int_4^5 \frac{dx}{\sqrt{x^2-9}}$. 11. $\displaystyle\int_3^4 \frac{dx}{\sqrt{25-x^2}}$. 12. $\displaystyle\int_0^4 \frac{dx}{\sqrt{x^2+9}}$.

By substitution or integration by parts integrate:

13. $\sqrt{9x^2+16}$. 14. $\sqrt{x^2-9}$.

15. Find $\displaystyle\int_0^4 \sqrt{x^2+9}\,dx$.

16. Find the area between the curve $y = \sqrt{x^2-16}$, the x axis and the ordinate at $x = 5$.

17. Find the length of the arc of $y^2 = 4ax$ from the origin to one of the points for which $x = 3a$.

18. The arc of the catenary $y = c \operatorname{ch}\left(\dfrac{x}{c}\right)$ from the point $(0, c)$ to the point (x, y) revolves about Ox. Show that the area of the surface generated is

$$\pi c\left\{x + y \operatorname{sh}\left(\frac{x}{c}\right)\right\}.$$

19. Show that the area of the region bounded by two arcs of the parabolas is $ab/3$ for the curves

$$y^2 = ax,\ x^2 = by \qquad (a, b > 0)$$

Show that when $b = a$ the perimeter of the region is

$$a\{\tfrac{1}{2}\log(2+\sqrt{5}) + \sqrt{5}\}.$$

20. The area lying between the curve $y = ch(x/2a)$, the ordinates $x = \pm a^2$ and the x axis is rotated about this axis. Prove that the volume of the solid of revolution so formed is

$$\pi a(a + \operatorname{sh} a).$$

Show that the volume given by $a = 1$, $a = 1 + \delta$ differ by $\pi(2 + e)\delta$ when δ is small.

CHAPTER 30

MOMENTS OF INERTIA

30.1. Definition

If every element of mass of a body be multiplied by the square of its distance from a given axis and the result summed for the whole body, the sum is called the *Moment of Inertia* of the body *about the given axis.*

For separate particles of mass $m_1, m_2 \ldots m_n$, distant $r_1, r_2 \ldots r_n$ from the axis, we would obtain

$$\sum_{i=1}^{n} m_i r_i^2.$$

For a continuous body with an element of mass dm distant y from the x axis, we would need to integrate to sum and obtain

$$\int y^2 dm.$$

In the special case of a piece of wire of density ρ, if an element of length ds is distant y from the x axis, then the m. of i. of the wire about the x axis is

$$\int (\rho ds)y^2.$$

In each of the above cases the result has as dimensions mass $\times$ (length)^2. If we divide the result, the m. of i. of the body, by its total mass we are left with a number which is of dimensions (length)^2. We denote this by K^2, and K is called the radius of gyration of the body about the given axis. The m. of i. of a body is denoted in symbols by MK^2, and K is such that if the mass of the body was concentrated at a distance K from the axis the resulting m. of i. would be the same.

In certain problems, *e.g.*, on bending beams, we are concerned with an element of area dA and not of mass dm. If this element dA is distant y from an axis, then

$$\int y^2 dA$$

is called the *second moment* of the area about the axis, and is denoted by AK^2, where A is the total area and K, as above, the radius of gyration.

30.2. Some Standard Formulae

Certain standard results have already been obtained and will be found in the list of formulae. These (and others to be obtained later) can be remembered by a single rule.

Routh's Rule.

With respect to an axis of symmetry

$$MK^2 = M \times \frac{\text{sum of squares of perpendicular semi-axes}}{3,\ 4 \text{ or } 5}$$

where the denominator is

3 if the body is rectangular
4 ,, circular
5 ,, spherical

Examples

(1) For a rod of length $2a$ with respect to a perpendicular axis through its centre the perpendicular semi-axes are of length a and 0,

$$\therefore \quad MK^2 = M\frac{a^2 + 0^2}{3} = M\frac{a^2}{3}.$$

(2) For a perpendicular axis at one end of the above rod

$$MK^2 = M\frac{(2a)^2 + 0^2}{3} = M\frac{4a^2}{3}.$$

(3) For a disc of radius a and a central axis perpendicular to its plane, the perpendicular semi-axes are each of length a,

$$\therefore \quad MK^2 = M\frac{a^2 + a^2}{4} = M\frac{a^2}{2}.$$

The student should obtain the results for an axis in the plane of the disc and for a sphere.

30.3.

Example 1. Find the m. of i. of a right circular cone about its axis.
If ρ is the density and M the mass,

$$\rho\tfrac{1}{3}\pi a^2 h = M.$$

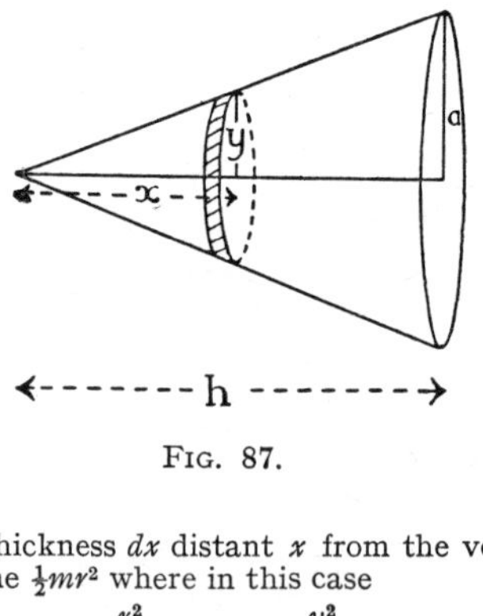

FIG. 87.

A disc of radius y and thickness dx distant x from the vertex has as its m. of i. about the axis of the cone $\frac{1}{2}mr^2$ where in this case

$$m\frac{r^2}{2} = (\rho\pi y^2 dx)\frac{y^2}{2}.$$

$\therefore$ for the whole cone

$$MK^2 = \int_0^h (\rho\pi y^2 dx)\frac{y^2}{2}.$$

But $$\frac{y}{x} = \frac{a}{h}, \quad \therefore \ y = \frac{ax}{h},$$

$$\therefore \ MK^2 = \frac{\rho\pi}{2}\int_0^h \frac{a^4x^4}{h^4}dx$$

$$= \frac{\rho\pi}{2}\frac{a^4}{h^4}\cdot\frac{h^5}{5} = \frac{\rho\pi a^4}{10}h$$

$$= M\frac{3}{10}a^2.$$

Example 2. To find the moment of inertia about the x axis of a piece of wire in the shape of one arch of a cycloid.

If ρ is the linear density of the wire,

$$MK^2 = \int (\rho ds)y^2.$$

We will express all variables in terms of the parameter θ, so that

$x = a(\theta - \sin\theta)$, $y = a(1 - \cos\theta)$, where θ varies from 0 to 2π.

Since $$ds = 2a\sin\frac{\theta}{2}d\theta \qquad \text{(see 22.4)},$$

$$\therefore \ MK^2 = \int_0^{2\pi} \rho \,.\, 2a\sin\frac{\theta}{2}d\theta \,.\, a^2(1-\cos\theta)^2$$

$$= \rho 2a^3\int_0^{2\pi}\sin\frac{\theta}{2}\left(2\sin^2\frac{\theta}{2}\right)^2 d\theta = 8\rho a^3\int_0^{2\pi}\sin^5\frac{\theta}{2}d\theta.$$

Put $\frac{\theta}{2} = \phi$, $d\theta = 2d\phi$ and the new limits are 0 and π,

$$\therefore \ MK^2 = 16\rho a^3\int_0^{\pi}\sin^5\phi d\phi = 16\rho a^3 \,.\, 2\int_0^{\pi/2}\sin^5\phi d\phi$$

$$= 32\rho a^3\frac{4\,.\,2}{5\,.\,3} \qquad \text{(see 19.9)}$$

$$= \frac{256}{15}\rho a^3.$$

But $8a\rho = M$, since the length of one arch is $8a$,

$$\therefore \ MK^2 = M\frac{32}{15}a^2.$$

EXERCISE 83

1. Find the m. of i. of an isosceles triangle of height h about a line through the vertex parallel to the base.
2. Repeat the above for any triangle of height h.
3. Repeat example 2, but take the base of the triangle as the axis.
4. Find the m. of i. of a truncated cone about its axis in terms of the mass M of the truncated cone and the radii r_1 and r_2 of the ends.
5. Find the m. of i. about the x axis of the segment of the parabola $y^2 = 4ax$ cut off by $x = b$.
6. If the above segment rotates round the x axis, find the m. of i.

of the paraboloid of revolution about this axis in terms of the mass M and the radius r of the base.

7. Find the m. of i. of the rod CD of mass M about the axis AB (Fig. 88). [L.U.]

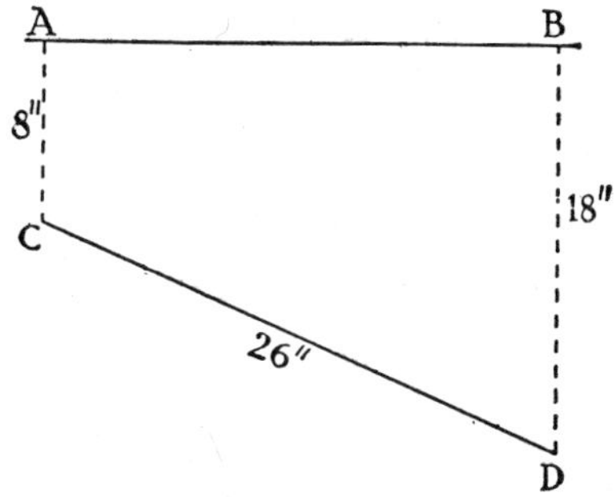

FIG. 88.

8. Working from first principles, prove that the moment of inertia of a triangle, base b in., height h in., about an axis through the vertex and parallel to the base is $\frac{1}{4}bh^3$ in.^{4}.

In a quadrilateral ABCD, AD = 1 in., BC = 3 in., AB = 4 in., and AD and BC are both perpendicular to AB. CD and BA are produced to meet at O, and OY is drawn parallel to AD. Using the above result or otherwise, find the moment of inertia of the quadrilateral ABCD about OY. [U.L.C.I.]

9. A wheel and axle are made of the same material of density ρ. The axle is of radius r ft. and length a ft., whilst the wheel has an overall radius of R ft. and is of thickness b ft. Find the radius of gyration of this composite body about its axis.

30.4. The Parallel Axis Theorem

The following theorem has been proved: If Mk^2 is the m. of i. about an axis through the c.g., then the m. of i. about a parallel axis distant d from it is $M(k^2 + d^2)$.

Note 1. This theorem shows that of all axes in a given direction the axis through the c.g. of the body gives a minimum m. of i. for the body.

Note 2. We can only " step out " from an axis through the c.g. to a parallel axis or back from a given axis to a parallel axis through the c.g. We *cannot* transfer directly from one axis to a parallel one unless one of them passes through the c.g.

Note 3. If in a given expression $3Mk^2$, 3M is the mass, then the m. of i. about a parallel axis d away is $3M(k^2 + d^2)$, but if M is the mass, then the m. of i. is $M(3k^2 + d^2)$. In using the above theorem it is necessary to make sure of the " M ".

Note 4. It is usual to use k for a radius of gyration about an axis through the c.g. and K when the axis does not pass through the c.g. Thus the above theorem could be stated

$$MK^2 = M(k^2 + d^2).$$

Example 3. Given that the m of. i. of a rod (mass M, length $2a$) is $M\frac{4}{3}a^2$ about one end, find its m. of i. about a parallel axis distant $\frac{a}{3}$ from this end.

$$\text{m. of i. (axis through c.g.)} = M\left(\frac{4}{3}a^2 - a^2\right) = M\frac{a^2}{3},$$

$$\therefore \quad \text{m. of i. (axis } \tfrac{2}{3}a \text{ from c.g.)} = M\left(\frac{a^2}{3} + \left(\frac{2a}{3}\right)^2\right) = M\frac{7}{9}a^2.$$

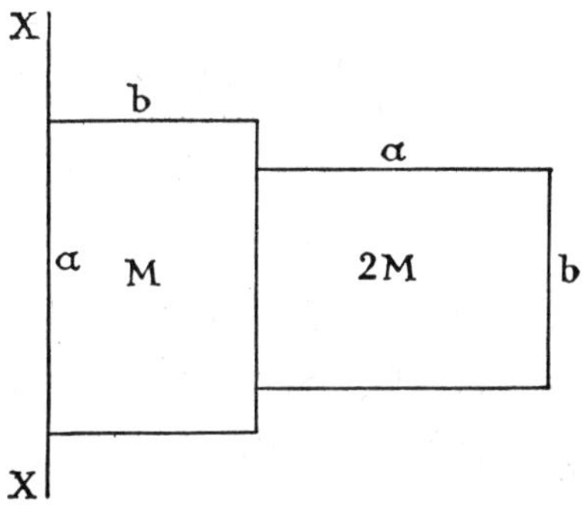

FIG. 89.

Example 4. A sign board consists of 2 separate parts as shown. Find its radius of gyration about the axis XX (Fig. 89) [L.U.]

$$\text{m. of i. of mass M} = M\frac{b^2}{3}$$

$$\text{m of i. of mass 2M} = 2M\left[\frac{a^2}{12} + \left(b + \frac{a}{2}\right)^2\right].$$

∴ if K denotes the required radius of gyration

$$3MK^2 = M\left[\frac{b^2}{3} + \frac{a^2}{6} + 2\left(b + \frac{a}{2}\right)^2\right],$$

$$K^2 = \frac{2a^2 + 6ab + 7b^2}{9}.$$

Example 5. Find the m. of i. and the radius of gyration of an angle section as shown about an axis through the c.g. parallel to a side. (Fig. 90.)

We will regard this as consisting of ABCD, which is $6 \times \frac{1}{2}$ in., and EFLC, which is $5\frac{1}{2} \times \frac{1}{2}$ in., and find the m. of i. about the axis through G parallel to the side DL.

Taking moments about the side DL to find $\bar{z}$ the distance of G from DL

$$(6 \times \tfrac{1}{2}) \times 3 + (5\tfrac{1}{2} \times \tfrac{1}{2}) \times \tfrac{1}{4} = (6 \times \tfrac{1}{2} + 5\tfrac{1}{2} \times \tfrac{1}{2})\bar{z},$$

$$\therefore \quad \bar{z} = 1{\cdot}685 \text{ in.}$$

$$\therefore \text{ distance of } G_1 \text{ from ZZ} = 3 - 1{\cdot}685 = 1{\cdot}315 \text{ in.}$$

$$\therefore \text{ distance of } G_2 \text{ from ZZ} = 1{\cdot}685 - 0{\cdot}25 = 1{\cdot}435 \text{ in.}$$

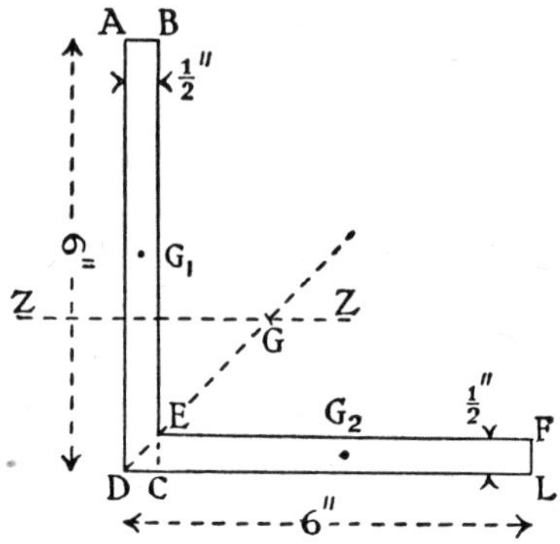

FIG. 90.

For ABCD

$$I_{ZZ} = Ak^2 + A(1{\cdot}315)^2$$
$$= \frac{6^3 \times \frac{1}{2}}{12} + 6 \times \tfrac{1}{2} \times (1{\cdot}315)^2$$
$$= 14{\cdot}188 \text{ in.}^4.$$

For CEFL

$$I_{ZZ} = \frac{(\frac{1}{2})^3 \times 5\frac{1}{2}}{12} + 5\tfrac{1}{2} \times \tfrac{1}{2} \times (1{\cdot}435)^2$$
$$= 5{\cdot}720 \text{ in.}^4.$$

$$\text{Total } I_{ZZ} = 14{\cdot}188 + 5{\cdot}720 = 19{\cdot}908 \text{ in.}^4,$$
$$\text{total area } A = 5{\cdot}75 \text{ in.}^2,$$
$$\therefore \quad 5{\cdot}75\, k^2 = 19{\cdot}908,$$
$$k = 1{\cdot}86 \text{ in.}$$

30.5. The Theorem of Perpendicular Axes

A Lamina

It has already been proved that if we know the m. of i. of a plane area about each of two perpendicular axes in the plane then the m. of i. of the area about the axis perpendicular to the area and *through the*

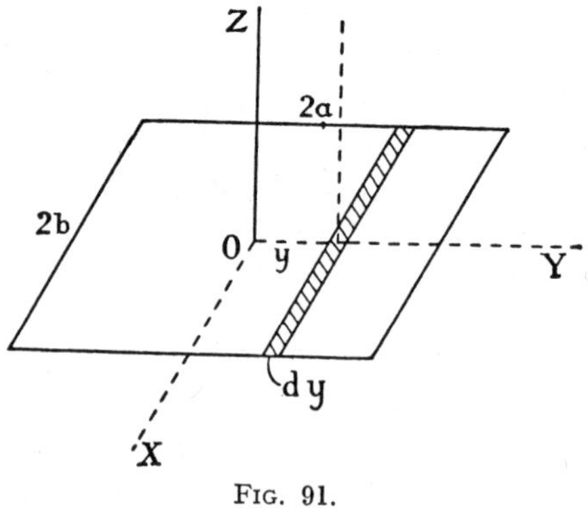

FIG. 91.

point of intersection of the other two axes is given by the sum. In obvious symbols

$$I_z = I_x + I_y,$$

where I_z denotes the m. of i. about the axis perpendicular to the plane.

From this we can at once deduce the m. of i. of the rectangular area shown about OZ, where O is at the c.g.

$$\begin{aligned} I_z &= I_x + I_y \\ &= M\frac{a^2}{3} + M\frac{b^2}{3} \\ &= M\frac{a^2 + b^2}{3}. \end{aligned}$$

This result can be recalled by the aid of Routh's Rule. The student should also obtain the result by using the Parallel Axis theorem on the m. of i. of a rod thickness dy and y distant from OZ.

EXERCISE 84

1. Find the m. of i. of a rod (mass M, length a) about an axis perpendicular to the rod and distant d from its centre.

2. Find the m. of i. of a disc mass M, radius a: (1) about a tangent line parallel to a diameter; (2) about a line parallel to the axis and touching the disc.

3. Find the m. of i. of a rectangular area mass M and sides a, b about an edge, length a or b.

4. Find the m. of i. of a triangular area about an axis through the c.g. parallel to the base. (The triangle has mass M and height h.)

5. Find the m. of i. of a solid hemisphere, mass M, radius a, about: (1) a diameter of the base; (2) a parallel axis through the c.g.

6. Find the m. of i. of a right circular cone mass M, height h, radius of base r, about: (1) a diameter of the base; (2) a parallel axis through the c.g.

7. Find the second moment for the area shown, about an axis through the c.g. parallel to HK.

AB = CL = 6 in., FH = 4 in., HK = 10 in.
AE = DC = 2 in., (Fig. 92(a)). [L.U.]

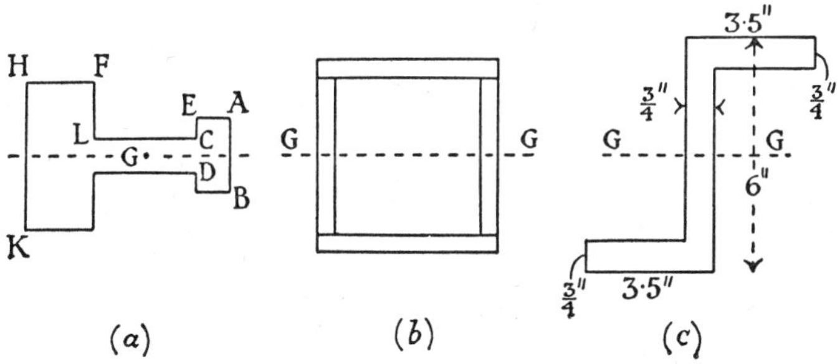

FIG. 92.

8. Find the second moment of a plane normal section of a box girder consisting of four 2×12-in. planks with respect to the axis GG. (Fig. 92(*b*)).

9. Find the second moment of the z bar section shown with respect to the axes GG (Fig. 92 (*c*)).

10. A right circular cylinder is of height h and radius r. Show that its m. of i. about a diameter of the base is

$$M\left[\frac{r^2}{4} + \frac{h^2}{3}\right].$$

11. A connecting rod is of length 4 ft., its mass is 200 lb., its c.g. is 2·8 ft. from the little end and its radius of gyration about an axis through the c.g. perpendicular to its plane is $\sqrt{2}$ ft. Find an equivalent system of two masses m_1, m_2 of which m_1 is at the little end if (*a*) the total mass, (*b*) its c.g., (*c*) its m. of i. about the axis through the c.g., are all to be unchanged. How far is m_2 from the c.g.?

12. A thin square plate ABCD of side a has a section OAB removed where O is the centre of the square. Show that the radius of gyration of the remainder about an axis through O parallel to AB is $\frac{1}{12}a\sqrt{10}$.

13. An equilateral triangle ABC is made of three identical thin rods, each of length l. Show that the radius of gyration of the body about an axis through A perpendicular to the plane ABC is $l/2$.

14. Show that the moment of inertia about the x axis of a uniform lamina of mass M bounded by the curve $y^2 = 4x$, the x axis and the ordinate at $x = 1$ is $4M/5$.

15. The area bounded by the curve $y^2 = 4a(b - x)$ and the y axis is rotated round the x axis. Given that a, b are both positive, show that the volume of the solid generated is $2\pi ab^2$ and its radius of gyration is $\sqrt{(4ab/3)}$ about the x axis and $\sqrt{\{(4ab + b^2)/6\}}$ about the y axis.

CHAPTER 31

CENTRES OF PRESSURE

31.1. The Perfect Fluid

In problems on hydrostatics we assume that water is a perfect fluid. The word perfect is used in a mathematical sense to denote the following properties:

(*a*) At any point in the fluid the stress is normal to any and every small plane area at the point, whatever its direction.

(*b*) There is no viscosity in the fluid or resistance to any force tending to separate the particles of the fluid. From this it follows that the liquid will never support a tension, and any stress is due to pressure.

(*c*) The pressure at any point of the fluid is the same in all directions about the point.

(*d*) Any pressure applied at any point in the fluid is transmitted to every other point.

(*e*) The fluid is incompressible.

31.2. Pressure at a Point (Fig. 93(*a*))

Consider the equilibrium of a vertical cylinder of water, height x and base of area ΔA, at a depth x below the surface of the water.

Since there is no viscosity, there are no supporting forces round the curved surface, and the only supporting force is the total pressure which acts perpendicular to the horizontal base ΔA. If p is the pressure per unit area on this base, then for the equilibrium of the cylinder composed of water weight w per unit volume

$$p\Delta A = wx\Delta A,$$
$$\therefore \quad p = wx.$$

If it is intended to take the pressure of the atmosphere, P lb./sq. ft., into account, then since it acts vertically downwards on the area ΔA in the surface, we have in this case

$$p\Delta A = wx\Delta A + P\Delta A,$$
$$\therefore \quad p = wx + P.$$

We will, unless it is specifically mentioned, neglect this pressure P. We then have that the pressure at any point in the fluid is $w \times$ (vertical depth below the surface). Usually w is given in lb./cu. ft., and x in ft., so that p is in lb./sq. ft.

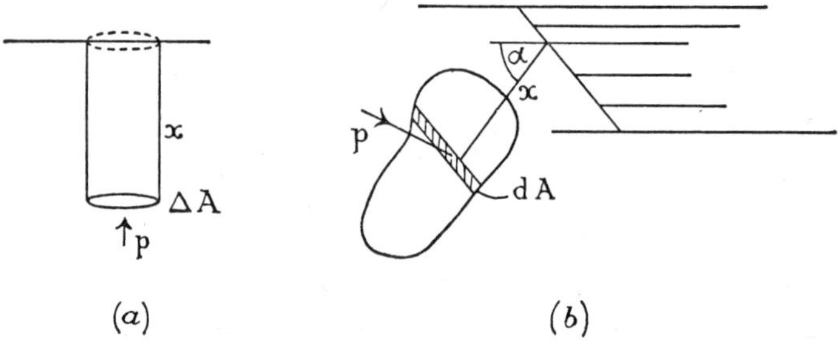

FIG. 93.

31.3. Total Pressure on a Plane Area (Fig. 93(*b*))

Suppose a plane area is immersed in water with its plane making an angle α with the surface. At a depth x, measured down the plane, the pressure on a strip of the plane of area $d\text{A}$ is $wx \sin\alpha d\text{A}$ if the area $d\text{A}$ is bounded by two horizontal lines near together so that the pressure may be considered as uniform over the whole width.

The total pressure is

$$\int wx \sin\alpha d\text{A} = w \sin \alpha \int x d\text{A}.$$

But if we were finding the depth $\bar{x}$ of the c.g. of the area we would have

$$\bar{x} = \frac{\int x d\text{A}}{\int d\text{A}} = \frac{\int x d\text{A}}{\text{A}},$$

$$\therefore \quad \int x d\text{A} = \text{A}\bar{x},$$

$$\therefore \text{ total pressure} = w \sin \alpha \,.\, \text{A}\bar{x} = w\text{A}\bar{z},$$

where $\bar{z}$ is the *vertical* depth of the c.g. of the area.

(1) We note that when $\bar{z}$ is measured as the vertical depth, the inclination of the plane does not matter.

(2) If the atmospheric pressure P is taken into account, then since this is added on to every element of pressure the formula becomes

$$(w\bar{z} + \text{P})\text{A}.$$

Example 1. A semicircular area, radius a, is immersed vertically in water with its diameter in the surface. Find the total pressure on it.

By the formula

$$\text{pressure} = w\text{A}\bar{z}$$

$$= w \cdot \tfrac{1}{2}\pi a^2 \cdot \frac{4a}{3\pi} = \underline{\tfrac{2}{3}wa^3.}$$

The student should obtain this result by integration of the pressure over a horizontal strip of width dx at depth x.

EXERCISE 85

Find the total pressure on:

1. A rectangular vertical area $a \times b$ with the side a in the surface of the water.
2. The above area if the side a is horizontal, but at depth c.
3. The above area if the side a is horizontal and at depth c, but the plane of the area is inclined at angle θ to the horizontal.
4. A circular plate in the side of a ship. The plate is inclined at 10° to the vertical, it is 6 in. in radius and its centre is 10 ft. below the water level. In this case assume that the air pressure is equivalent to an extra 30 ft. of water above the surface level and that $w = 64$ lb./cu. ft. for sea-water.
5. Water is supplied to a tap from a reservoir 250 ft. above its level. If the area of the tap's plate is 1·5 sq. in., find the total thrust on it. ($w = 62{\cdot}5$ lb./cu. ft.)
6. A rectangular vertical dock gate has a width of 50 ft. and on one side there is salt water (sp. gr. 1·03) to a depth of 25 ft. On the other side there is fresh water. If the thrusts on the two sides are equal, find the depth of the fresh water.

31.4. Centre of Pressure

We will consider plane areas only. Since the pressure on any element of area is perpendicular to it, the total pressure will be the sum of a number of such parallel forces or pressures. The point of action of this resultant force is called the *centre of pressure* of the area considered.

Since the pressure on an element of area increases with its depth below the surface, in finding the centre of pressure (C.P.) of an area we are, as it were, finding the c.g. of a body whose density increases with the depth below the surface. Such a body will clearly have its c.g. below that of the same body with a uniform density. This shows that the C.P. of a plane area is always below the c.g.—except for a horizontal area when they coincide.

The student must be careful not to confuse the C.P. with the c.g. The total pressure on an area is $wA\bar{z}$, where $\bar{z}$ is the vertical depth of the c.g. of the area, but the point of application of this total pressure is at the C.P., which is below the c.g.

31.5. The C.P. of a Rectangle (Fig. 94(*a*))

Consider a vertical rectangle of width a with its upper side horizontal and at depth d_1 and the lower side at depth d_2 below the surface.

The pressure on an element of area adz at depth z is

$$wadz \,.\, z.$$

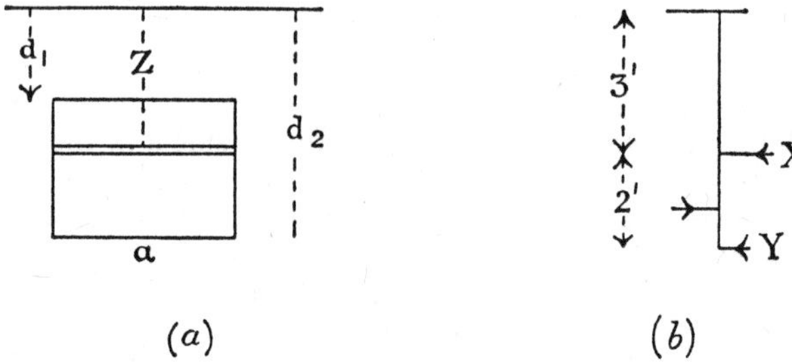

FIG. 94.

The moment of this pressure about the surface line is

$$(wadz\,.\,z)z.$$

Therefore the total moment is

$$wa\int_{d_1}^{d_2} z^2dz = \frac{wa}{3}(d_2^3 - d_1^3).$$

The total pressure is $\qquad w\text{A}\bar{z} = w\,.\,a(d_2 - d_1)\cdot\frac{d_2 + d_1}{2}$

$$= \frac{wa}{2}(d_2^2 - d_1^2),$$

∴ if the depth of the C.P. is denoted by $\bar{\bar{z}}$

$$\bar{\bar{z}} = \frac{\frac{wa}{3}(d_2^3 - d_1^3)}{\frac{wa}{2}(d_2^2 - d_1^2)} = \frac{2}{3}\frac{(d_2 - d_1)(d_2^2 + d_2d_1 + d_1^2)}{(d_2 - d_1)(d_2 + d_1)}$$

$$= \frac{2}{3}\cdot\frac{d_2^2 + d_2d_1 + d_1^2}{d_2 + d_1}.$$

If one side is in the surface, $d_1 = 0$ and $\bar{\bar{z}} = \frac{2}{3}d_2$.

Example 2. A door 1 ft. wide and 2 ft. deep is in the vertical side of a tank filled with water so that the centre of the door is 4 ft. below the surface of the water. If the door is bolted at the top and bottom only, find the pressures X and Y on these bolts (Fig. **94**(*b*)).

Total pressure on door $= w\text{A}z$
$= w \times 2 \times 4$
$= 8w.$

This pressure acts at a depth

$$\bar{\bar{z}} = \frac{2}{3}\frac{d_2^2 + d_2d_1 + d_1^2}{d_2 + d_1},$$

where $d_1 = 3$, $d_2 = 5$.

$$\therefore \qquad \bar{\bar{z}} = \frac{2}{3}\frac{5^2 + 5\,.\,3 + 3^2}{5 + 3} = \frac{49}{12}\text{ ft.}$$

Since the door is in equilibrium,

(1) Equating horizontal forces on the door

$$\text{X} + \text{Y} = 8w.$$

(2) Moments about the line of the lower bolts

$$X \,.\, 2 = 8w\left(5 - \frac{49}{12}\right),$$

$$\therefore \quad X = 4w \cdot \frac{11}{12} = \frac{11w}{3} = \underline{229{\cdot}2 \text{ lb. wt.}}$$

$$Y = 8w - X = \frac{13w}{3} = \underline{270{\cdot}8 \text{ lb. wt.}}$$

EXERCISE 86

1. Show that the depth of the C.P. of a vertical triangle with one side in the surface is $\frac{1}{2}h$, if h is the perpendicular height.

2. For a triangle with the base horizontal and vertex in the surface, show that the C.P. is at a depth of $\frac{3}{4}h$, where h is the perpendicular height.

3. A vertical trapezium is immersed in water with the side of length L in the surface and the parallel side of length l at depth d. Prove that $\bar{\bar{z}} = \dfrac{d(L + 3l)}{2(L + 2l)}$.

4. The depth of water on either side of a rectangular sea wall is d_1 and d_2. Prove that the resultant pressure acts at a height above the base of the wall of $\dfrac{1}{3}\dfrac{(d_1^2 + d_1d_2 + d_2^2)}{d_1 + d_2}$.

5. The segment of $y^2 = 4ax$ cut off by the ordinate $x = d$ is placed with the origin in the surface and Ox vertically downwards. Find the depth of the C.P.

31.6. A General Formula (Fig. 93(b))

A lamina is immersed with its plane making an angle α with the horizontal and its c.g. at a depth h, measured down the plane. Suppose the lamina divided by horizontal lines into narrow strips over which the pressure may be assumed uniform.

If the area of such a strip is dA at a depth x (measured down the inclined plane), then the total pressure on the strip is

$$wx \sin \alpha \, dA$$

and acts perpendicular to the area.

Therefore the total moment of these elements of pressure about the line in which the lamina meets the surface is

$$\int (wx \sin \alpha \, dA)\, x = w \sin \alpha \int x^2 dA.$$

But $\int x^2 dA$ is the moment of inertia of the total area A about this line, therefore the total moment is $\quad w \sin \alpha \, AK^2,$
where AK^2 is the second moment (or m. of i.), A being the area and K

the radius of gyration about the line in which the plane of the area cuts the surface.

The total pressure is $wAh \sin \alpha$.

Therefore the depth of the C.P. is

$$\bar{\bar{z}} = \frac{w \sin \alpha \, AK^2}{w \sin \alpha \, Ah} = \frac{K^2}{h} \quad . \quad . \quad . \quad . \quad . \quad . \quad (1)$$

If k is the radius of gyration of the area about a horizontal coplanar line through the c.g.

$$K^2 = k^2 + h^2,$$

and the formula now becomes

$$\bar{\bar{z}} = \frac{h^2 + k^2}{h} = h + \frac{k^2}{h} \quad . \quad . \quad . \quad . \quad . \quad . \quad (2)$$

where $\bar{\bar{z}}$ like h is measured down the plane.

The C.P. is therefore always below the c.g. of the area, but the distance between them decreases as the depth of the c.g. increases.

Example 3. A rectangle is immersed vertically with its horizontal sides at depths d_1 and d_2 respectively. Find the depth of the C.P.

Since the vertical length of the rectangle is $d_2 - d_1$ its k^2 about a horizontal axis through the c.g. is

$$\frac{(d_2 - d_1)^2}{12},$$

$$\therefore \quad \bar{\bar{z}} = \frac{d_2 + d_1}{2} + \frac{(d_2 - d_1)^2}{12} \Big/ \left(\frac{d_2 + d_1}{2}\right)$$

$$= \frac{d_2 + d_1}{2} + \frac{1}{6}\frac{(d_2 - d_1)^2}{d_2 + d_1}$$

$$= \frac{2}{3}\frac{(d_2^2 + d_2 d_1 + d_1^2)}{d_2 + d_1}$$

as found previously.

Example 4. A circle radius a is immersed vertically with its centre at a depth h. Find the position of its C.P.

For a horizontal axis through the c.g. in the plane of the circle

$$k^2 = \frac{a^2}{4},$$

$$\therefore \quad \bar{\bar{z}} = h + \frac{a^2/4}{h}$$

$$= h + \frac{a^2}{4h}.$$

In all cases dealt with the areas have been symmetrical about a vertical line through the c.g. so that the C.P. was clearly on this line and we were only concerned with its depth. Other cases require a consideration of "products of inertia". These cases both in moments of inertia and centres of pressure will be dealt with in the next volume.

EXERCISE 87

1. A rectangular area of sides a and b is immersed with the side b horizontal but the plane of the area making angle θ with the horizontal. Show that the vertical depth of the C.P. is

$$\frac{a^2}{12h}\sin\theta$$

below the c.g., if the c.g. is at (an inclined) depth h.

2. A circular hole in the side of a tank is closed by a door pinned at the highest and lowest points only. The radius of the hole is 1 ft. and the centre is 5 ft. below the surface of the water. Find the forces exerted on the upper and lower pins.

3. A lockgate 12 ft. wide has fresh water (weighing 62·5 lb. per cu. ft.) on one side to a depth of 10 ft. and sea-water (weighing 64 lb. per cu. ft.) to a depth of 6 ft. on the other. Find the resultant pressure on the gate and the point where it acts. [L.U.]

4. A lamina in the form of a quadrant of a circle is immersed with one bounding radius in the surface. Prove that the C.P. is at a distance $\frac{3\pi a}{16}$ from this radius. [L.U.]

5. Show that the relation

$$Z = \frac{I}{A\bar{x}}$$

gives the depth Z of the centre of pressure of a lamina of area A immersed in a liquid with its plane vertical, $\bar{x}$ being the depth of the centroid of the lamina and I the moment of inertia of the lamina about the line in which its plane meets the surface of the liquid.

Use this relation to determine the depth of the centre of pressure in the case of each of the following laminae immersed vertically in a liquid:

(i) A right-angled isosceles triangle PQR with the hypotenuse PQ, length 6 ft., in the surface.

(ii) A circle, diameter 8 ft., with its centre at depth 5 ft. below the surface. [U.L.C.I.]

CHAPTER 32

LINEAR VELOCITY AND ACCELERATION

32.1. Definitions

Linear velocity is defined as the rate of change of distance with regard to time.

If x ft. denote the distance travelled in time t sec., then by the definition

$$\text{velocity } (v) = \frac{dx}{dt} \text{ ft./sec.}$$

Linear acceleration is defined as the rate of change of linear velocity with regard to time.

Therefore if v ft./sec. is the velocity at time t sec.

$$\text{acceleration} = \frac{dv}{dt} \text{ ft./sec.}^2.$$

Or since $\quad v = \dfrac{dx}{dt}, \qquad \dfrac{dv}{dt} = \dfrac{d}{dt}\left(\dfrac{dx}{dt}\right) = \dfrac{d^2x}{dt^2}.$

In some problems on acceleration the time t is not involved, and it is useful to have an expression without t. We obtain this as

$$\text{acceleration} = \frac{dv}{dt} = \frac{1}{dt} \cdot \frac{dv}{1} = \frac{dx}{dt} \cdot \frac{dv}{dx} = v\frac{dv}{dx}.$$

We therefore have three expressions for acceleration and must choose the one required in any given problem. They are

$$\frac{dv}{dt}, \; \frac{d^2x}{dt^2}, \; v\frac{dv}{dx}.$$

By linear we mean here motion along a line or curve as opposed to motion round a point measured in terms of the angle turned through. In the case of motion along a curve, s is sometimes used instead of x, where s is the distance travelled along the curve from some fixed point on it.

32.2. The Direction of the Expressions for Velocity and Acceleration

It must be noticed that the above expressions for velocity and acceleration give the velocity and acceleration in the direction of x *increasing*. If a body is moving in the opposite direction or is subject to a retardation, the appropriate negative sign must be inserted.

Example 1. A body is moving in a straight line so that its velocity at time t is given by $v = 2t + 3t^2$. Find its distance from the origin after 2 seconds if it started 3 feet away and is moving: (i) towards the origin; (ii) away from the origin.

Choose an origin O on a line, and a point A on it where OA = + 3 ft. Then OA is the positive direction, the direction of x increasing.

(i) Since the body is moving towards O, its velocity in the positive direction is $-(2t + 3t^2)$, and it is this velocity which is given by $\frac{dx}{dt}$.

$$\therefore \quad \frac{dx}{dt} = -(2t + 3t^2).$$

Integrate:

$$x = -t^2 - t^3 + C,$$

but $x = 3$ when $t = 0$,

$$\therefore \quad 3 = 0 + 0 + C \text{ or } C = 3,$$

$$x = 3 - t^2 - t^3;$$

when $t = 2$,

$$x = 3 - 2^2 - 2^3$$
$$= \underline{-9 \text{ ft.}},$$

so that the body has crossed over the origin and is 9 ft. away on the other side.

(ii) When the body is moving in the direction $\overline{OA}$

$$\frac{dx}{dt} = 2t + 3t^2,$$

$$\therefore \quad x = t^2 + t^3 + C.$$

$x = 3$, when $t = 0$.

$$3 = 0 + 0 + C, \qquad \therefore \quad C = 3,$$

$$\therefore \quad x = 3 + t^2 + t^3.$$

when $t = 2$,

$$x = 3 + 2^2 + 2^3.$$
$$= \underline{15 \text{ ft.}}$$

Example 2. A body is projected vertically upwards under gravity and is subject also to a retardation av^2 ft./sec.², where a is a constant and v the velocity at the instant. Put down the equations of motion when the body is moving: (1) upwards: (2) downwards.

Choose the origin on the ground and the positive direction as upwards (Fig. 95(a)).

(1) g, the acceleration due to gravity acts downwards, and is therefore negative. Since the body is moving upwards, the retardation also acts downwards, in the negative direction of x, and so is also negative. The equation of motion is therefore

$$v\frac{dv}{dx} = -g - av^2.$$

(2) With the same origin and positive direction g is still negative, but the retardation now acts upwards to oppose the motion. The equation is now

$$v\frac{dv}{dx} = -g + av^2.$$

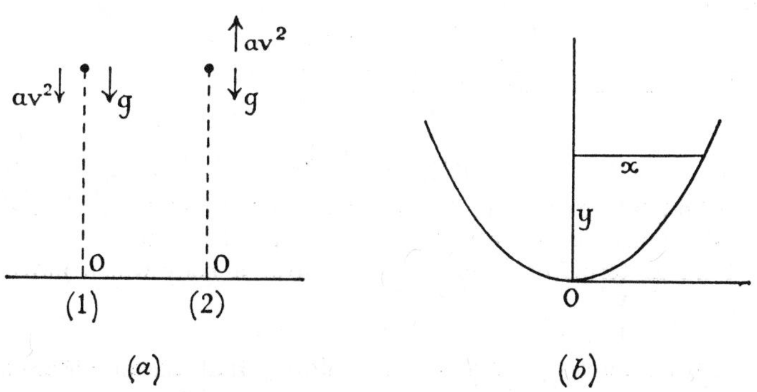

FIG. 95.

Example 3. The curve $y = x^2$ rotates round the y axis, generating a parabolic cup. Water enters at 2 cu. ft. per sec. Find the rate at which the surface is (1) rising, (2) expanding, when the height of the water is 4 ft. If the influx is stopped and water begins to trickle out through a hole in the base at a rate $k\sqrt{y}$, where y is the height of water, find the rate at which the water surface is falling when its height is 1 ft. (Fig. 95(*b*)).

When the height of the water is y, the volume V is given by

$$V = \int_0^y \pi x^2 dy = \int_0^y \pi y dy = \pi\frac{y^2}{2},$$

$$\therefore \quad \frac{dV}{dt} = \frac{\pi}{2}\cdot 2y\frac{dy}{dt} \quad \quad (a)$$

(1) Now $\frac{dV}{dt} = +2$, and when $y = 4$ the above equation gives

$$\frac{dy}{dt} = \frac{1}{2\pi}\text{ ft./sec.},$$

giving the rate at which the height is rising.

(2) Since $y = x^2$,

$$V = \frac{\pi}{2}x^4,$$

$$\therefore \quad \frac{dV}{dt} = 2\pi x^3\frac{dx}{dt}.$$

When $y = 4$, $x = 2$,

$$2 = 2\pi 2^3\frac{dx}{dt},$$

$$\therefore \quad \frac{dx}{dt} = \frac{1}{8\pi}\text{ ft./sec.},$$

giving the rate at which the radius of the surface is expanding.

(3) When the water is flowing out

$$\frac{dV}{dt} = -k\sqrt{y}$$

(note the minus sign, since $\frac{dV}{dt}$ is the rate of *increase* of V with t),

$\therefore$ equation (a) gives

$$-k\sqrt{y} = \pi y\frac{dy}{dt},$$

or

$$\frac{dy}{dt} = -\frac{k}{\pi\sqrt{y}}.$$

When $y = 1$,

$$\frac{dy}{dt} = -\frac{k}{\pi}\text{ ft./sec.},$$

the sign showing that the surface is falling.

EXERCISE 88

1. A body moves so that $v^2 = ax$, where a is a constant. Find by a single differentiation, an expression for the acceleration.

2. Find in terms of x the acceleration of a body which moves so that $v = 2 + \frac{x}{4}$.

3. A body moves so that $x = t^{\frac{1}{2}}$. Prove that the acceleration is negative and varies as v^3.

4. If the relation between x and t is of the form $t = Ax^2 + Bx$, where A, B are constants, find v in terms of x and prove that the retardation is $2Av^3$.

5. A body moves so that $x = t^3 - 6t^2 + 9t + 4$. Find the maximum and minimum values, if any, of x, the velocity v and the acceleration.

6. A body moves so that the retardation is proportional to v^3. If the initial velocity is u, show that

$$x = \frac{1}{k}\left(\frac{1}{v} - \frac{1}{u}\right),$$

$$t = \frac{1}{2k}\left(\frac{1}{v^2} - \frac{1}{u^2}\right),$$

where k is a positive constant.

7. The distance s moved in a straight line by a particle in time t is given by $s = at^2 + bt + c$, where a, b and c are constants. If v is the velocity after time t, show that $4a(s - c) = v^2 - b^2$. [L.U.]

8. A bucket in the form of an inverted right circular cone 15 ft. deep and 4 ft. base radius is receiving water at the rate of 1 cu. ft./min. Find the rate at which the water level is rising when the water is 5 ft. deep. Find also the depth when the rate of rise of the water level is $\frac{1}{\pi}$ ft./min.

9. Water is flowing into a hemispherical bowl of radius a ft. at 3 cu. ft./min. Show that when the height of the water is h ft. $V = \frac{1}{3}\pi h^2(3a - h)$ and that when $h = \frac{1}{2}a$ the rate at which the surface of the water is rising is $\frac{4}{\pi a^2}$ ft./min.

10. A rectangular tank has a base 3 ft. by 3 ft. and is 6 ft. high. When the depth of the water is h ft. the outflow per sec. through a hole in the base of 6 sq. in. area is given by $v^2 = 2gh$, but the jet of water is found to cover 60 per cent. only of the area of the hole. (*a*) Find the rate of fall of the level of water in the tank when the height is h ft. (*b*) If the tank is full to begin with, how long does it take to empty itself? (*c*) How long does it take to empty the top half? [Take $g = 32$ ft./sec.^{2}].

11. Water is flowing out of a reservoir through a right-angled notch forming the sides of a triangle with vertex downwards and its sides equally inclined to the vertical. Given that the rate of outflow at depth h ft. below the surface is $k\sqrt{h}$ ft./min., where k is a constant, find the total outflow per minute if the water through the notch is of constant depth H ft.

Example 4. A cyclist rides at a speed v m.p.h., given by

$$v = \frac{10x + 3}{x + 2},$$

where x miles is the distance travelled from the start. Find his acceleration after 10 miles and the time taken to travel this distance.

With x in miles and t in hours we have

$$\frac{dx}{dt} = \frac{10x + 3}{x + 2},$$

$$\therefore \quad dt = \frac{x + 2}{10x + 3}dx.$$

Integrate:

$$t = \int \frac{x + 2}{10x + 3}dx$$

$$= \frac{1}{10}\int \left(1 + \frac{1\frac{7}{10}}{x + \frac{3}{10}}\right) dx$$

$$= \frac{1}{10}\left[x + \frac{17}{10}\log\left(x + \frac{3}{10}\right)\right] + \text{C}.$$

When $t = 0$, $x = 0$,

$$\therefore \quad 0 = \frac{1}{10}\left[0 + \frac{17}{10}\log\frac{3}{10}\right] + \text{C}.$$

Subtract:
$$t = \frac{1}{10}\left[x + \frac{17}{10}\log\left(\frac{10x + 3}{3}\right)\right].$$

When $x = 10$,

$$t = \frac{1}{10}\left[10 + \frac{17}{10}\log\frac{103}{3}\right] \text{ hr.}$$

$$= \frac{1}{10}\left[10 + \frac{17}{10} \times 3{\cdot}5362\right] \text{ hr.}$$

$$= \underline{1{\cdot}60 \text{ hr.}}$$

From
$$\frac{dx}{dt} = \frac{10x + 3}{x + 2},$$

we have
$$\frac{d^2x}{dt^2} = \frac{d}{dt}\left(\frac{10x + 3}{x + 2}\right)$$

$$= \frac{d}{dx}\left(\frac{10x + 3}{x + 2}\right) \times \frac{dx}{dt}$$

$$= \frac{17}{(x + 2)^2} \times \frac{10x + 3}{(x + 2)}$$

$$= \frac{17(10x + 3)}{(x + 2)^3},$$

so that when $x = 10$,

$$\text{acceleration} = \frac{17 \times 103}{12^3} = \underline{1{\cdot}01 \text{ m./hr.}^2}$$

EXERCISE 89

1. A man walks so that after t hours his speed is $\dfrac{24}{(6 + t)}$ m.p.h. How far has he walked before his speed is reduced to 2 m.p.h., and how long does he take to walk 10 miles?

2. A body starts with a velocity u ft./sec. and moves subject to a retardation kx ft./sec.^{2}, where x is the distance travelled from the start. Show that before it stops the body will have travelled a distance $\dfrac{u}{\sqrt{k}}$ ft.

3. A car is moving on a horizontal road, and at the instant the speed is V ft./sec. the engine is cut off. If the retardation is now $0{\cdot}0004\ v^2$

ft./sec.^{2} at velocity v, find the distance travelled before the speed is reduced to $\frac{V}{2}$ ft./sec.

4. A particle moves in a straight line subject only to a retardation kv^2. If u is its initial velocity, show that the distance travelled in time t is

$$\frac{1}{k}\log(1 + kut).$$

5. A body is projected vertically upwards, and the air resistance produces a retardation proportional to the speed v at the instant. Show that

$$\frac{dv}{dt} = -g - kv$$

if the origin is taken on the ground and the positive direction vertically upwards.

Hence obtain

$$t = \frac{1}{k}\log\left(\frac{g + ku}{g + kv}\right)$$

connecting v and t, if u is the velocity of projection. Solve this equation for $v = \frac{dx}{dt}$, and hence show that the height x after time t is

$$x = \frac{1}{k}\left(u + \frac{g}{k}\right)(1 - e^{-kt}) - \frac{gt}{k}.$$

6. A particle of mass m moves in a straight line under no forces except a resistance mkv^3, where v is the velocity and k is a constant. If the initial velocity is u and x is the distance covered in time t, prove that

$$kx = \frac{1}{v} - \frac{1}{u}, \quad t = \frac{x}{u} + \frac{1}{2}kx^2.$$

The initial velocity of a bullet fired horizontally from a point O is 2500 ft./sec., and after moving 400 ft. its velocity is reduced to 2450 ft./sec. Neglecting gravity and assuming the air resistance to be proportional to the whole of the velocity, find the time for a bullet to cover a distance of 3000 ft. from O. [L.U.]

7. A particle moving in a horizontal straight line is subject to a retardation $av(v^2 + u^2)$, where v is the velocity at any time and u the initial velocity. Show that the particle moves a distance $\pi/(12au)$ before its velocity is reduced to $u/\sqrt{3}$ and find the time taken. [L.U.]

8. The differential equation $d^2x/dt^2 + K/x^2 = 0$, where K is a constant, represents the motion of a missile projected vertically from the earth's surface, the pull of gravity at a distance x from its centre being inversely proportional to x^2. If the radius of the earth is R and the magnitude of the acceleration due to gravity at the earth's surface is g, prove that the speed v at a distance $x(>R)$ from the centre of the earth is given by

$$V^2 = v^2 + 2gR\left(\frac{x - R}{x}\right),$$

where V is the velocity of projection.

Taking R = 3960 miles and $g = 32$ ft./sec.^{2}, calculate in miles per hour the minimum speed of projection in order that the missile shall *just* pass beyond the gravitational effect of the earth. [L.U.]

32.3. The Limiting Velocity

When a raindrop falls vertically the air resistance, acting vertically upwards, can be assumed to vary as the square of the speed. If then, the origin is taken at the initial position and the positive direction as vertically downwards, the equation of motion is

$$v\frac{dv}{dx} = g - kv^2.$$

We see from this that the acceleration is a little less than g in the early stages of the motion, when v is small, and decreases steadily as v increases. Finally, we get to the stage when

$$g - kv^2 = 0$$

or

$$v = \sqrt{\frac{g}{k}}.$$

From this point onwards the acceleration is zero, and the fall continues with a uniform speed called the *limiting velocity*. It is obtained by equating the expression for the acceleration to zero.

Example 5. A particle falls from a height under gravity, the resistance of the air varying as the square of the speed v. After a time the body acquires a velocity V and continues to fall with this velocity. Show that

$$\frac{dv}{dt} = g\left(1 - \frac{v^2}{V^2}\right)$$

gives the acceleration and that

$$t = \frac{V}{2g}\log\left(\frac{V + v}{V - v}\right)$$

is the time taken from the start to reach velocity v.

With the origin at the initial position and the positive direction downwards, the equation of motion is

$$\frac{dv}{dt} = g - kv^2.$$

When $\frac{dv}{dt} = 0$, $v = V$,

$$\therefore \quad 0 = g - kV^2,$$

and

$$k = \frac{g}{V^2}.$$

The equation of motion can now be written

$$\frac{dv}{dt} = g - \frac{g}{V^2}v^2$$

$$= g\left(1 - \frac{v^2}{V^2}\right).$$

Since we require the time t, we write this

$$\frac{V^2}{V^2 - v^2}dv = gdt.$$

Integrate:

$$\int \frac{V^2}{V^2 - v^2}dv = gt + C.$$

The integral on the left-hand side is a " standard form ". We could quote this or proceed

$$gt + C = \tfrac{1}{2}V\int\left(\frac{1}{V-v}+\frac{1}{V+v}\right)dv$$
$$= \tfrac{1}{2}V\{-\log(V-v)+\log(V+v)\}$$
$$= \frac{V}{2}\log\frac{V+v}{V-v}.$$

We measure the time t from the instant when the velocity is zero, *i.e.*, the commencement of the motion, so that $t = 0$, $v = 0$, satisfies this equation, an equation which holds throughout the motion.

$$\therefore \quad C = \frac{V}{2}\log 1 = 0,$$

and
$$t = \frac{V}{2g}\log\left(\frac{V+v}{V-v}\right).$$

32.4. Horse-power and Effective Force

Suppose an engine of horse-power H to be exerting a thrust, or pull, or force, F lb. wt. at any instant. If the body affected moves a distance δx in time δt, then $F\delta x$ is the work done in time δt.

$$\therefore \quad F\frac{\delta x}{\delta t} = \text{rate of doing work},$$
$$= 550H.$$

We thus obtain the important formula

$$Fv = 550H$$

connecting horse-power and force exerted.

32.5. Units

In the following examples we shall adopt the usual engineering units as fundamental: force (F) in pounds weight (lb. wt.), distance (x) in feet (ft.), and time (t) in seconds (sec.). We shall use the acceleration due to gravity (g) in feet per second per second (ft./sec.^{2}). From these we obtain the definition of *mass* (M), as the word appears in Newton's second law of motion, to be

$$M = \frac{W}{g}$$

where W lb. is the weight of the body whose acceleration due to a force F lb. wt. is being found. Newton's law now becomes

$$F = \frac{W}{g}\ddot{x}, \; i.e., \; F(\text{lb.}) = \frac{W(\text{lb.})}{g(\text{ft./sec.}^2)}\ddot{x}(\text{ft./sec.}^2).$$

In this system of units the slight change in the value of W that would occur at different points of the earth's surface due to the variation in the value of g is ignored. $\frac{W}{g}$ is of course constant.

In order to cope with problems set on the *absolute* system of units the student must also know Newton's law, in the form

$$P = M\ddot{x},$$

where the pound of *mass* is the fundamental unit and the *derived* unit of *force* is the *poundal* which is the pound of mass multiplied by g. In this system all forces must be expressed in poundals. Note that in a problem such as Ex. 90 no. 1, reference is made to a mass M. This means that the *absolute* system is being used and we therefore conclude that the force P (units not stated) is in poundals. If the mass M occurred amongst the forces it would have to appear as Mg, *i.e.*, in poundals. In question 4 again there is reference to a mass M tons, but we are told that the force is P tons wt. This force therefore appears in the equation of motion as 2240Pg (*i.e.*, in poundals).

Example 6. The resistance to the motion of a motor car varies as the square of the speed, and the horse-power exerted by the engine is constant and equal to 22. If the weight of the car is 1 ton and its maximum speed against its resistance is 45 m.p.h., prove that the car will travel about 58 yd. in increasing its speed from 15 to 30 m.p.h.

$$\left[\log_e\left(\frac{26}{19}\right) = 0{\cdot}315\right].$$ [L.U.]

When the speed is v ft./sec., let the resistance be kv^2 lb. wt. and the force exerted by the engine F lb. wt.

By Newton's Law of motion

$$F - kv^2 = \frac{W}{g} v \frac{dv}{dx}.$$

where

$$Fv = 550H = 12{,}100.$$

Substitute for F in the equation:

$$\frac{12{,}100}{v} - kv^2 = \frac{2240}{32} v \frac{dv}{dx}.$$

The limiting velocity is 66 ft./sec., so that at this velocity the acceleration is zero.

$$\therefore \quad \frac{12{,}100}{66} - k(66)^2 = 0,$$

or

$$k = \frac{12{,}100}{(66)^3}.$$

The equation now becomes

$$\frac{12{,}100}{v} - \frac{12{,}100}{(66)^3} v^2 = 70v\frac{dv}{dx}$$

or

$$\frac{12{,}100}{v}\left[1 - \left(\frac{v}{66}\right)^3\right] = 70v\frac{dv}{dx},$$

which can be written

$$\frac{1210}{7} dx = \frac{v^2 dv}{1 - \left(\frac{v}{66}\right)^3}.$$

On the right-hand side the numerator can be made the differential of the denominator by means of constants only so that the integral will be of the form log (denominator).

Integrate:

$$\frac{1210}{7} x + C = -\frac{66^3}{3} \log\left(1 - \left(\frac{v}{66}\right)^3\right).$$

If we now measure x from the instant when the speed is 15 m.p.h. or 22 ft./sec., then $x = 0$ when $v = 22$.

$$\therefore \quad 0 + C = -\frac{66^3}{3} \log\left(1 - \frac{1}{27}\right).$$

Subtract:

$$\frac{1210}{7} x = \frac{66^3}{3} \log\left(\frac{26}{27}\Big/\left[1 - \left(\frac{v}{66}\right)^3\right]\right);$$

When $v = 30$ m.p.h. $= 44$ ft./sec.,

$$x = \frac{7}{1210} \times \frac{66^3}{3} \log \left(\frac{26}{27} \Big/ \frac{19}{27}\right)$$
$$= \frac{7}{1210} \times \frac{66^3}{3} \times 0{\cdot}315 \text{ ft.}$$
$$= \underline{58{\cdot}21 \text{ yd.}}$$

EXERCISE 90

1. The pull in the rope used to tow a vessel of mass M at a uniform speed V is P. Prove that if the resistance varies as the square of the speed at any instant and the rope is cast off when the vessel is moving at speed V, the distance then travelled in time t is $\frac{MV^2}{P} \log\left(1 + \frac{Pt}{MV}\right)$.

2. A particle of mass m is projected vertically upwards under gravity with speed u in a medium in which the resistance is mkv^2 when the speed of the particle is v. Prove that the greatest height attained by the particle is $\frac{1}{2k} \log\left(1 + \frac{ku^2}{g}\right)$.

Prove also that the speed v with which the particle returns to its point of projection is $u\left\{\frac{g}{g + ku^2}\right\}^{\frac{1}{2}}$. [L.U.]

3. A railway engine weighing 32 tons exerts a constant horse-power of 448, and the motion of the engine is opposed by a constant force equal to $\frac{5}{4}$ tons weight. Prove that the equation of motion of the engine is $v^2\frac{dv}{dx} = \frac{5}{4}(88 - v)$, where v is the speed in ft./sec., x is the distance travelled in feet and g has the value 32 ft./sec.².

Find the maximum speed of the engine in miles per hour, and prove that the engine attains a speed of 30 m.p.h., starting from rest in approximately 423 ft. [Take $\log_e 2 = 0{\cdot}6932$.] [L.U.]

4. The driving force on a ship of mass M tons is a constant force P tons wt. The resistance to the motion is proportional to the square of the speed, and the limiting velocity is V ft./sec. If when the ship is going at full speed the engines are reversed, show that the ship is brought to rest in a time $\frac{\pi MV}{4Pg}$ sec. after going a distance $\frac{MV^2 \log 2}{2Pg}$ ft.

5. A train is going at 30 m.p.h. when steam is shut off. If the resistance at velocity v ft./sec. is $8 + \frac{v^2}{726}$ lb. per ton wt. of train, show that the train stops in about 349 sec. after going 2439 yd.

[$\log_e (\frac{4}{3}) = 0{\cdot}288$.] [L.U.]

6. A particle is projected vertically upwards in a resisting medium whose resistance is kv^2 per unit mass, where k is a constant and v is

the velocity of the particle. U is the velocity of projection, V is the velocity of the particle when it returns to the point of projection and T is the time taken by the particle to reach its highest point. Prove that

$$U = \sqrt{\left(\frac{g}{k}\right)} \tan\{T\sqrt{(gk)}\},$$

$$V = \sqrt{\left(\frac{g}{k}\right)} \sin\{T\sqrt{(gk)}\}.$$

7. The resistance to the motion of a train is 160 lb. wt. per ton mass at all speeds. It is moving on the level with uniform speed V and comes to an incline of 1 in 70. The engine continues to work at the same rate as before; prove that if v is the velocity and x the distance travelled up the incline in time t, then

$$v^2 = V^2 - \frac{g}{35}(6x - 5Vt).$$

8. A particle of mass m is shot up vertically under gravity with velocity u, the air resistance being proportional to the square of the velocity. The particle returns to the point of projection with velocity v. Prove that its terminal velocity is $uv(u^2 - v^2)^{-1/2}$. [L.U.]

9. A train of mass m lb. moves on straight horizontal rails against a resistance kv lb. wt., where v ft./sec. is the velocity and k is a constant. The engine works at a constant rate of 400 k ft. lb./sec. Show that the time taken to increase the speed of the train from 4 to 10 ft./sec. is $(m/2kg) \log (\frac{32}{25})$ sec. [L.U.]

10. The air resistance on a car moving at a speed v may be assumed to be kv^2, where k is a constant. The power transmitted from its engine may take any value up to a given maximum. Write down the equation for motion up a slope of constant gradient α, assuming air resistance, engine drive and gravity to be the only operative forces.

If the maximum possible speed of the car on a level road ($\alpha = 0$) is 60 m.p.h. and if the greatest speed at which the car can coast, without using the engine, down a slope α is 45 m.p.h., show that the greatest speed at which it can ascend the same slope is $15x$ m.p.h., where $x^3 + 9x - 64 = 0$. Find x to two figures. [L.U.]

11. A train whose weight (including the engine) is 270 tons is pulled on the level by an engine which develops $20v(1 - v/100)$ H.P. when the speed is v m.p.h. The frictional resistance is proportional to the square of the speed, and the maximum speed is 50 m.p.h. If a speed of v m.p.h. is attained starting from rest in t hours, prove that

$$\frac{dv}{dt} = \frac{15}{77}(50 - v)(100 + v)$$

and show that the time taken to attain a speed of 20 m.p.h. is about 1·4 min. [$g = 32$ ft./sec.^{2}] [L.U.]

12. A car of mass 12 cwt. stands at rest on a hill inclined at an angle θ to the horizontal where $\sin\theta = \frac{1}{20}$. When the brakes are released it descends under a resistance which at any instant is proportional to the speed. If this resistance is 21 lb. wt. when the speed is 15 m.p.h., show that the speed cannot exceed 48 m.p.h. and that in f.p.s. units the equation of motion may be written

$$220v\frac{dv}{dx} = (352 - 5v).$$

Hence find the distance travelled by the car from rest before its speed is 16 m.p.h. [L.U.]

CHAPTER 33

EQUATIONS OF ROTATION. THE TORQUE EQUATION

33.1. Definitions

If a point P is moving in a fixed plane, the angular velocity of P about a fixed point O in the plane is the rate of increase of angle POx, the angle that the join OP makes with a line Ox fixed in the plane. If this angle is θ radians at time t, then (Fig. 96)

$$\text{angular velocity of P} = \frac{d\theta}{dt} \text{ radians per second.}$$

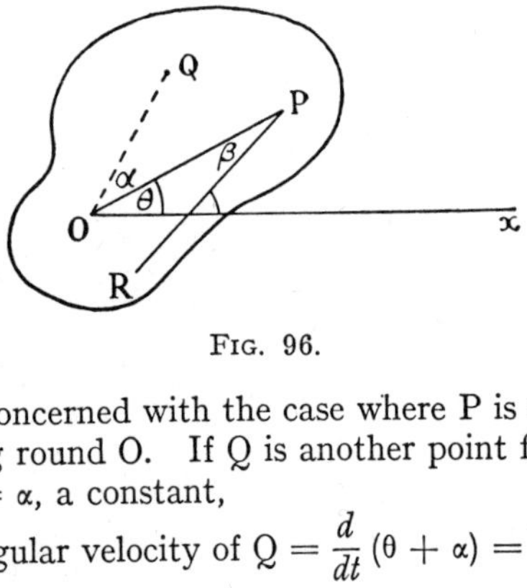

FIG. 96.

We will often be concerned with the case where P is a fixed point in a rigid body rotating round O. If Q is another point fixed in the body, then angle QOP = α, a constant,

$$\therefore \text{ angular velocity of Q} = \frac{d}{dt}(\theta + \alpha) = \frac{d\theta}{dt}.$$

We note then that every point of the body has the same angular velocity about O. If PR is a line fixed in the body so that β is constant, the rate of rotation of PR is

$$\frac{d}{dt}(\theta + \beta) = \frac{d\theta}{dt},$$

showing that every line in the body has the same rate of rotation or angular velocity. We may therefore refer to the angular velocity of a point, or of a body containing the point, round some fixed point.

Angular velocity is often denoted by ω or Ω (omega),

$$\therefore \quad \omega \equiv \frac{d\theta}{dt}.$$

Angular acceleration is the rate of change of angular velocity with regard to time,

$$\therefore \quad \text{angular acceleration} = \frac{d\omega}{dt} = \frac{d^2\theta}{dt^2} \text{ rad./sec.}^2$$

As an expression not involving time,

$$\frac{d\omega}{dt} = \frac{1}{dt} \cdot \frac{d\omega}{1} = \frac{d\theta}{dt} \cdot \frac{d\omega}{d\theta} = \omega \frac{d\omega}{d\theta}.$$

We now have three expressions for angular acceleration

$$\frac{d\omega}{dt}, \quad \frac{d^2\theta}{dt^2}, \quad \omega \frac{d\omega}{d\theta}.$$

As in linear motion, care must be taken with the signs, since each means the value in the direction of θ increasing.

33.2. The Equations of Rotation

As an example, we will obtain the equations of rotation for a body rotating with *constant* angular acceleration α.

(*a*) Given $\frac{d^2\theta}{dt^2} = \alpha$, $\therefore \frac{d\theta}{dt} = \alpha t + \text{A}$ (by integration). If the body started with angular velocity Ω, then $\frac{d\theta}{dt} = \Omega$, when $t = 0$. Substitute in the equation:

$$\Omega = 0 + \text{A},$$

$$\therefore \quad \frac{d\theta}{dt} = \Omega + \alpha t$$

or

$$\omega = \Omega + \alpha t \qquad [\text{cf. } v = u + at]$$

giving the relation between the initial angular velocity Ω, and the final ω after time t for a body rotating with a constant angular acceleration α.

(*b*) Return to

$$\frac{d\theta}{dt} = \Omega + \alpha t,$$

$$\therefore \quad \theta = \Omega t + \alpha\frac{t^2}{2} + \text{B},$$

but if the angle θ is measured from the instant $t = 0$ and is zero, then we have $\theta = 0$ when $t = 0$,

$$0 = 0 + 0 + \text{B},$$

$$\therefore \quad \theta = \Omega t + \tfrac{1}{2}\alpha t^2 \qquad [\text{cf. } s = ut + \tfrac{1}{2}at^2]$$

giving the angle θ radians turned through by the body in time t.

(*c*) If we use the expression $\omega\frac{d\omega}{d\theta}$ for acceleration, we are given

$$\omega\frac{d\omega}{d\theta} = \alpha.$$

Noting that $\frac{d}{d\theta}(\omega^2) = 2\omega\frac{d\omega}{d\theta}$, we have on integration

$$\frac{\omega^2}{2} = \alpha\theta + \text{C}.$$

If $\omega = \Omega$ when $\theta = 0$,

$$\frac{\Omega^2}{2} = 0 + \text{C},$$

$$\therefore \quad \omega^2 = \Omega^2 + 2\alpha\theta \qquad [\text{cf. } v^2 = u^2 + 2as]$$

giving the final angular velocity ω in terms of the initial angular velocity Ω and the angle θ turned through.

Example 1. A flywheel is started rotating with angular velocity Ω rad./sec., and is subject to a retardation $a + b\omega^2$ rad./sec.^{2}, where a, b are positive constants and ω is the angular velocity. Find the number of revolutions made and the time taken to come to rest.

Number of Revolutions Made

This does not involve time, therefore, noting that we are concerned with a retardation, the equation is

$$\omega\frac{d\omega}{d\theta} = -(a + b\omega^2),$$

and from this we must find θ in terms of Ω. We will write the equation

$$\frac{\omega}{a + b\omega^2}d\omega = -d\theta.$$

Each side now integrates easily to give

$$\frac{1}{2b}\log_e(a + b\omega^2) = -\theta + C.$$

But $\omega = \Omega$ when $\theta = 0$, since we will measure θ from the position when the rotation began.

$$\therefore \quad \frac{1}{2b}\log(a + b\Omega^2) = 0 + C,$$

and

$$\frac{1}{2b}\log\left(\frac{a + b\Omega^2}{a + b\omega^2}\right) = \theta.$$

When the flywheel stops $\omega = 0$ and

$$\theta = \frac{1}{2b}\log\left(1 + \frac{b}{a}\Omega^2\right),$$

$$\therefore \quad \text{no. of revs.} = \frac{\theta}{2\pi} = \frac{1}{4\pi b}\log\left(1 + \frac{b}{a}\Omega^2\right).$$

Time Taken to Come to Rest

We now use

$$\frac{d\omega}{dt} = -(a + b\omega^2),$$

$$\frac{d\omega}{a + b\omega^2} = -dt,$$

$$\frac{1}{b}\int\frac{d\omega}{\frac{a}{b} + \omega^2} = -t + C.$$

or

$$\frac{1}{b}\sqrt{\frac{b}{a}}\tan^{-1}\left(\omega\sqrt{\frac{b}{a}}\right) = -t + C.$$

But $\omega = \Omega$ when $t = 0$,

$$\therefore \quad \frac{1}{b}\sqrt{\frac{b}{a}}\tan^{-1}\left(\Omega\sqrt{\frac{b}{a}}\right) = 0 + C.$$

Finally

$$t = \frac{1}{\sqrt{ab}}\left\{\tan^{-1}\left(\Omega\sqrt{\frac{b}{a}}\right) - \tan^{-1}\left(\omega\sqrt{\frac{b}{a}}\right)\right\},$$

giving the time t taken for the angular velocity to reduce from Ω to ω. When the body ceases to rotate $\omega = 0$,

$$\therefore \quad t = \frac{1}{\sqrt{ab}}\tan^{-1}\left(\Omega\sqrt{\frac{b}{a}}\right) \text{ sec.}$$

33.3. The Torque Equation

We will state without proof the following theorem: If a body is rotating round a fixed axis under the action of a torque C lb. ft. the angular acceleration is given by

$$C = \frac{WK^2}{g}\frac{d^2\theta}{dt^2}.$$

C lb. ft. is the moment of the external forces about the fixed axis, K ft. is the radius of gyration of the body about the fixed axis, g ft./sec.^{2} is the acceleration due to gravity, $\frac{d^2\theta}{dt^2}$ rad./sec.^{2} is the angular acceleration produced.

It is usual to denote $\frac{d\theta}{dt}$ by $\dot{\theta}$ and $\frac{d^2\theta}{dt^2}$ by $\ddot{\theta}$. The above equation then becomes

$$C = \frac{WK^2}{g}\ddot{\theta}.$$

Example 2. A door 8 ft. by 4 ft. stands open perpendicular to the wall. If it is closed by a constant torque of 20 lb. ft., find its angular velocity when it shuts. The door weighs 120 lb.

Here $W = 120$ lb., $K^2 = \frac{4^2}{3}$ ft.^{2}, $C = 20$ lb. ft., $g = 32$ ft./sec.^{2},

$$\therefore \quad 20 = \frac{120}{32}\cdot\frac{16}{3}\cdot\ddot{\theta},$$

or $\ddot{\theta} = 1$ rad./sec.^{2}.

Using $\omega^2 = \Omega^2 + 2\alpha\theta$,

$$\omega^2 = 0 + 2.1.\frac{\pi}{2},$$

$$\therefore \quad \underline{\omega = \sqrt{\pi}\text{ rad./sec.}}$$

Example 3. The diagram (Fig. 97) represents a wheel and axle of radii 2 ft. and 3 in. respectively, total weight 3 cwt. and radius of gyration 18 in., free to turn about a horizontal axis. Loads as shown hang from light cords wound round rim and axle. Neglect friction and find the angular acceleration. The observed angular acceleration was 1·74 rad./sec.^{2}. Calculate the frictional torque. [L.U.]

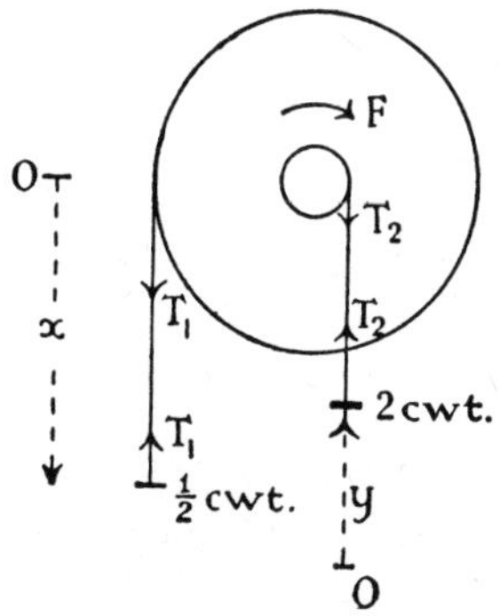

FIG. 97.

Suppose at time t the wheel and axle has rotated through an angle θ radians, the 56 lb. wt. has descended x ft. and the 224 lb. wt. has ascended y ft. The amount of string unwound from the wheel is 2θ ft., whilst the amount wound up round the axle is $\frac{1}{4}\theta$ ft.,

$$\therefore \quad x = 2\theta \quad \text{and} \quad y = \tfrac{1}{4}\theta.$$

Differentiate these equations with respect to time,

$$\dot{x} = 2\dot{\theta} \quad \text{and} \quad \dot{y} = \tfrac{1}{4}\dot{\theta}.$$

Again:

$$\ddot{x} = 2\ddot{\theta} \quad \text{and} \quad \ddot{y} = \tfrac{1}{4}\ddot{\theta} \quad \ldots\ldots\ldots \quad (1)$$

Let T_1 lb. wt. be the tension in the string attached to the 56 lb. wt., T_2 lb. wt. that in the other string and F lb. ft. the frictional torque opposing the rotation caused by the descent of the 56 lb. wt.

The equation of linear motion for the 56 lb. wt. is

$$56 - T_1 = \frac{56}{g}\ddot{x}.$$

For the upward motion of the 226 lb. wt.

$$T_2 - 224 = \frac{224}{g}\ddot{y}.$$

For the rotation of the wheel and axle, assuming the frictional torque F to be acting,

$$T_1 . 2 - T_2 \cdot \frac{1}{4} - F = \frac{3 \times 112}{g}\left(\frac{3}{2}\right)^2\ddot{\theta}.$$

Substitute from (1) for $\ddot{x}$ and $\ddot{y}$ and obtain

$$56 - T_1 = \frac{112}{g}\ddot{\theta},$$

$$T_2 - 224 = \frac{56}{g}\ddot{\theta},$$

$$2T_1 - \frac{1}{4}T_2 - F = \frac{756}{g}\ddot{\theta}.$$

Multiply the first equation all through by 2, the second equation by $\frac{1}{4}$ and add to the third. We find

$$112 - 56 - F = \frac{\ddot{\theta}}{g}(224 + 14 + 756),$$

$$\therefore \quad \ddot{\theta} = \frac{56 - F}{994}g.$$

If now F = 0, we find

$$\ddot{\theta} = \frac{56}{994} \times 32{\cdot}2 = \underline{1{\cdot}81 \text{ rad./sec.}^2}$$

If $\ddot{\theta} = 1{\cdot}74$, then

$$1{\cdot}74 = \frac{56 - F}{994} \times 32{\cdot}2,$$

or

$$\underline{F = 2{\cdot}29 \text{ lb. ft.}}$$

[We have here taken $g = 32{\cdot}2$ ft./sec.², the usual " accurate " value.]

33.4. Work Done by a Couple

If a couple or torque C lb. ft. rotates through an angle $d\theta$, the work it does is $Cd\theta$ and the total work done in a rotation through an angle θ_1 is

$$\int_0^{\theta_1} Cd\theta.$$

If C is constant, this becomes

$$C\int_0^{\theta_1} d\theta = C\theta_1.$$

For a complete revolution this gives $2\pi C$ ft. lb.

Example 4. A door 3 ft. broad and weighing 50 lb. is subject to a constant frictional couple of 3 lb. ft. at the hinges. If it stands open perpendicular to the wall, find the initial angular velocity with which it must be swung in order just to close.

The work done against the frictional couple is $3 \cdot \frac{\pi}{2}$ ft. lb. If ω is the initial angular velocity of the door, this work comes from the K.E. of the door.

$$\therefore \quad \frac{1}{2} \cdot \frac{50}{g} \cdot \frac{3^2}{3} \omega^2 = 3 \cdot \frac{\pi}{2} \qquad \text{(see 33.5)},$$

$$\therefore \quad \omega = \frac{4}{5}\sqrt{\pi} = \underline{1{\cdot}4 \text{ rad./sec.}}$$

33.5. Kinetic Energy of a Rotating Body

If a body W lb. is rotating round a fixed axis about which its radius of gyration is K ft., then the K.E. of the body is

$$\frac{1}{2}\frac{WK^2}{g}\dot{\theta}^2 \text{ ft. lb.}$$

at any instant when its angular velocity is $\dot{\theta}$.

If during the motion $\dot{\theta}$ is increased from $\dot{\theta}_1$ to $\dot{\theta}_2$, this change in K.E. must equal the work done by the external forces, *i.e.*,

$$\frac{1}{2}\frac{WK^2}{g}(\dot{\theta}_2{}^2 - \dot{\theta}_1{}^2) = \text{increase in K.E.}$$

$$= \text{work done on the system by the external forces.}$$

Example 5. Find the acceleration of the system in Example 3 when friction is neglected.

The 56 lb. wt. descends x ft. and does $56x$ ft. lb. of work and its K.E. is $\frac{1}{2} \cdot \frac{56\dot{x}^2}{g}$.

The 224 lb. wt. has ascended y ft., and $224y$ ft. lb. of work has been done on it. Its K.E. is $\frac{1}{2} \cdot \frac{224\dot{y}^2}{g}$. (Note that K.E. is always positive and independent of whether the weight is moving up or down.)

The wheel and axle has a K.E.

$$\frac{1}{2} \cdot \frac{3 \times 112}{g}\left(\frac{3}{2}\right)^2\dot{\theta}^2.$$

Since gain in K.E. = work done,

$$\frac{1}{2}\frac{56}{g}\dot{x}^2 + \frac{1}{2}\frac{224}{g}\dot{y}^2 + \frac{1}{2}\frac{336}{g} \cdot \frac{9}{4}\dot{\theta}^2 = 56x - 224y.$$

In terms of θ and $\dot{\theta}$, this is

$$56(4\dot{\theta}^2) + 224(\tfrac{1}{16}\dot{\theta}^2) + 756\dot{\theta}^2 = 2g(56 \times 2\theta - 224 \times \tfrac{1}{4}\theta),$$

or

$$994\dot{\theta}^2 = 112g\theta.$$

If we differentiate this equation with respect to time

$$994(2\dot{\theta}\,\ddot{\theta}) = 112g\dot{\theta}$$

cancel by $\dot{\theta}$ and

$$\ddot{\theta} = \frac{56}{994}g$$

as in the previous example.

This method of writing down the energy equation and then differentiating is most useful. It avoids the internal forces such as the tensions in the strings.

33.6. The Compound Pendulum

A body of any shape swinging about a fixed axis is known as a compound pendulum. When the body is a point mass connected to the axis by a light string we call it a simple pendulum.

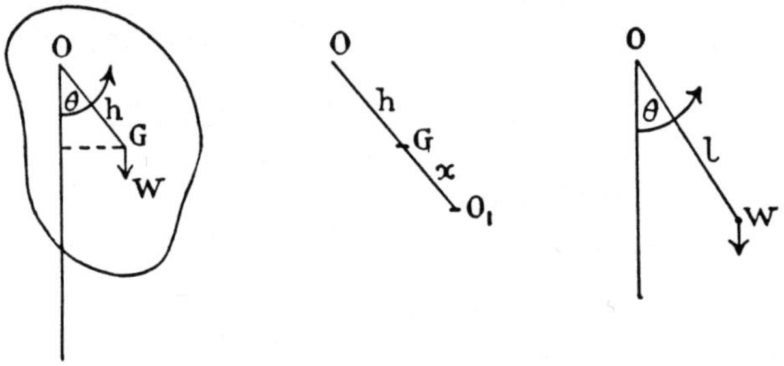

FIG. 98.

Let the body be of weight W lb. swinging about a fixed horizontal axis O distant h ft. from its centre of gravity G. k is the radius of gyration of the body about a parallel axis through the c.g. and K the radius of gyration about the axis of swing, so that

$$K^2 = k^2 + h^2 \qquad . \quad . \quad . \quad . \quad . \quad (1)$$

At any instant when OG makes an angle θ with the vertical, the torque equation gives

$$\frac{WK^2}{g}\ddot{\theta} = -\,Wh\sin\theta.$$

If θ is small, *i.e.*, the body is making small oscillations, $\sin\theta = \theta$ approximately and the equation becomes

$$\frac{K^2}{g}\ddot{\theta} = -\,h\theta,$$

$$\therefore \quad \ddot{\theta} = -\frac{gh}{K^2}\theta.$$

This shows that (for small oscillations) the motion is simple harmonic (see 34.10) and the periodic time is given by

$$T = 2\pi\sqrt{\frac{K^2}{gh}} \text{ sec.} \qquad . \quad . \quad . \quad . \quad . \quad . \quad . \quad (2)$$

In the case of a simple pendulum of length l, $K^2 = l^2$ and $h = l$. The periodic time is

$$T = 2\pi\sqrt{\frac{l}{g}} \text{ sec.}$$

Therefore a simple pendulum (l) and a compound pendulum will have the same time of swing if

$$\frac{K^2}{h} = l.$$

Thus, if $\frac{K^2}{h}$ be evaluated for a body swinging about an axis and a simple pendulum is set up beside it of length $l = \frac{K^2}{h}$, the two pendulums will have the same time of swing. This length $\frac{K^2}{h}$ is called the equivalent simple pendulum (E.S.P.) for the body relative to the given axis.

33.7. We wish to find if there are any other points on OG which, taken as axis of swing, will give the same time of oscillation as when the axis at O is used. Produce OG to O_1, where $GO_1 = x$. Then for an axis at O_1, K^2 is $k^2 + x^2$ and h is x, therefore if T is the same,

$$2\pi\sqrt{\frac{k^2 + h^2}{hg}} = 2\pi\sqrt{\frac{k^2 + x^2}{xg}},$$

$$\therefore \quad \frac{k^2 + h^2}{h} = \frac{k^2 + x^2}{x},$$

$$x^2h - x(k^2 + h^2) + hk^2 = 0,$$
$$(xh - k^2)(x - h) = 0,$$

$$\therefore \quad x = \frac{k^2}{h} \text{ and } h.$$

$x = h$ gives the original axis O, and we have found a new axis that will give the same periodic time of swing. Notice that O_1 may be in any direction from G provided $GO_1 = \frac{k^2}{h}$.

When O_1 is on OG produced

$$OO_1 = h + \frac{k^2}{h} = \frac{K^2}{h} = l$$

the length of the E.S.P. For a given O, O_1 can be found by experiment. T can be found accurately by timing a large number of swings. Therefore in the equation

$$T = 2\pi\sqrt{\frac{l}{g}}$$

g will be the only unknown. This method for determining g is the basis of Kater's method which was used as a preliminary to a national survey.

Example 6. A rod of weight W and length l ft. has attached to an end a disc of weight w and radius r ft. The rod swings about a horizontal axis at the other end. Find the E.S.P. (1) when the plane of the disc is vertical, its centre being l ft. from the axis; (2) when the plane of the disc is horizontal, its centre being attached to the end of the rod.

(1) For the compound body:

To find K^2, $\qquad (W + w)K^2 = W\frac{l^2}{3} + w\left(\frac{r^2}{2} + l^2\right).$

To find h, $$(W + w)h = W\frac{l}{2} + wl.$$

$$\therefore \quad \frac{K^2}{h} = \frac{2Wl^2 + 3w(r^2 + 2l^2)}{3l(W + 2w)}.$$

(2) $$(W + w)K^2 = W\frac{l^2}{3} + w\left(\frac{r^2}{4} + l^2\right).$$

$$(W + w)h = W\frac{l}{2} + wl.$$

$$\therefore \quad \frac{K^2}{h} = \frac{4Wl^2 + 3w(r^2 + 4l^2)}{6l(W + 2w)}.$$

Example 7. A rigid body performs small oscillations under gravity about a horizontal axis. If K is the radius of gyration about and h the distance of the centre of gravity from the axis, show that the length of the equivalent simple pendulum is $\frac{K^2}{h}$.

A connecting-rod is swung about the axes of the big- and little-end bearings successively, and the lengths of the equivalent simple pendulums are found to be 9·5 in. and 15·5 in. respectively. Given that the distance between the axes is 20 in., find the position of the centre of gravity and the radius of gyration about a parallel axis through it. [L.U.]

(i) See 33.6.

(ii) Let k be the radius of gyration about the c.g. and h in. its distance from the big-end, so that $(20 - h)$ in. is its distance from the small-end.

Using E.S.P. $= \frac{K^2}{h} = \frac{k^2 + h^2}{h}$ and working in inches,

$$9{\cdot}5 = \frac{(k^2 + h^2)}{h}$$

and $$15{\cdot}5 = \frac{[k^2 + (20 - h)^2]}{(20 - h)},$$

$$\therefore \quad 9{\cdot}5h - h^2 = 15{\cdot}5(20 - h) - (20 - h)^2,$$

since each equals k^2. This gives $h = 6$ in.

Using the first equation $$9{\cdot}5 = \frac{(k^2 + 36)}{6},$$

or $$\underline{k = \sqrt{21} \text{ in.}}$$

EXERCISE 91

1. A body is rotating so that: (1) $\theta = 3t + 1$; (2) $\theta = 2t^2 + 7t + 5$; (3) $\omega = 5 + 14\theta$. Find in (1) and (2) the angular velocity and acceleration at time t and when $t = 3$, and in (3) the angular acceleration when $\theta = 2$.

2. A wheel is rotating with uniform angular acceleration. If its angular velocity increases from 10 rad./sec. to 50 rad./sec. in 10 sec., find the number of radians turned through in that time.

3. A flywheel is rotating with an angular retardation proportional to its angular velocity. If its angular velocity diminishes by 5 per cent. in 1 min., find by how much it will decrease in the next minute.

4. A wheel of weight 160 lb. and radius of gyration 18 in., is rotating at 10 revs./sec. Find the frictional couple that will stop it in 1 min.

5. A flywheel of uniform thickness has an inner radius of 6 in., an outer radius of 2 ft. and weighs 120 lb. It is mounted on a horizontal axis and is rotated by a weight of 80 lb. hanging by a string from its outer rim. Find the velocity of this weight when it has fallen 4 ft.

6. A flywheel whose m. of i. is 200 lb. ft.^{2} is revolving at 5 revs./sec. and its velocity is reduced in 10 secs. to 2 revs./sec. by a resistance which produces a torque $k\omega$ lb. ft., where ω is the instantaneous angular velocity of the wheel. Find the initial value of this torque if k is a constant.

7. The frictional torque acting on a flywheel equals $k(\omega^2 + c^2)$ lb. ft., where k and c are constants and ω is the angular velocity at the instant. Show that if the flywheel be set rotating with angular velocity $c \tan \lambda$, the angular velocity after time t is $c \tan (\lambda - At)$, where $A = kcg/I$ and I is the m. of i. of the wheel. [L.U.]

8. A square trapdoor of side 3 ft. and weight 40 lb. is hinged at one side so as to be horizontal when closed and to open upwards. In the hinge is a spring which tends to close the door, exerting a couple proportional to the angle through which the door has turned from its position when shut. The door is opened through 180°, and can just be held in position by its own weight, together with a weight of 20 lb. placed on the edge farthest from the hinge. If this extra weight is suddenly removed, find the angular velocity of the door when it shuts. [L.U.]

9. The radius of a flywheel weighing 1 ton is 4 ft. It is set rotating about its axis and when revolving at 10 rev./sec. a brake is applied to the rim and stops the wheel in 9 sec. If the frictional force of the brake is $\frac{1}{10}$ of a ton, find the radius of gyration of the wheel about its axis.

10. A flywheel in the form of a uniform circular disc of radius 2 ft. and weight 100 lb. is rotating at 50 r.p.m. when a brake, whose normal pressure is 20 lb. wt., is applied to the rim. If the coefficient of friction between the rim and the brake is 0·1, find the number of revolutions and the time taken by the wheel to stop.

11. A flywheel weighing 10,000 lb. is suspended by an axis at its rim so that it can swing in a vertical plane. This axis is parallel to and 3 ft. from the wheel's axis. If the time of a complete swing is 2·5 sec., find the radius of gyration about its central axis.

12. A flywheel whose m. of i. about its horizontal axis is I, is set in motion about this axis by means of a cord wrapped round the axle (of radius r) which carries a load P at its free end. If there is a frictional torque $k\omega^2$, where ω is the angular speed of the wheel at any instant and k is a constant, find the angular velocity acquired by the wheel when P has descended a vertical distance x. [L.U.]

13. A flywheel mounted on a horizontal axle of diameter 2 in. is set in motion by weights attached to a cord wrapped round the axle and allowed to fall vertically. The times taken to fall 5 ft. from rest

for weights of 10 and 20 lb. are respectively 9·5 and 5·5 sec. Show that the moment of inertia of the flywheel is (approximately) 1440 lb. in.^{2} and determine the frictional torque (assumed constant) in the bearings. [$g = 32{\cdot}2$ ft./sec.^{2}] [L.U.]

14. A thin uniform rod of length $4a$ and mass m has a uniform disc of mass m and radius a attached to one end, its centre and plane being in line with the rod. Find the radius of gyration about an axis perpendicular to the plane of the disc through the mass centre.

If the body oscillates as a pendulum about an axis through the end of the rod perpendicular to the plane of the disc, find the period. (The disc's centre is at the end of the rod.) [L.U.]

15. A compound pendulum is made by suspending from an end a straight rod of mass m and length l. At a distance x from the point of suspension a mass nm is fixed to the rod. As x varies from 0 to l, show that there is a value of x which renders the time of oscillation a minimum. Show that for a minimum time of oscillation $x = \frac{1}{3}l$ nearly when n is small and $l/\sqrt{(3n)}$ nearly when n is large. By giving n suitable values, determine the time of oscillation of a uniform rod oscillating about one end and the time of oscillation of a simple pendulum of length x. [L.U.]

16. A uniform piece of wire of length $18a$ and mass m is bent to form a right angle ABC, in which AB $= 12a$, BC $= 6a$. It is smoothly hinged at A and oscillates in its own plane, which is vertical.

Prove: (i) that the moment of inertia about the axis of rotation is $84ma^2$, and (ii) that the length of the equivalent simple pendulum is $84a/\sqrt{65}$. [L.U.]

17. A and B are two points at a distance l apart in a thin, straight non-uniform rod. When the rod is pivoted at A it swings in the same period as a simple pendulum of length a, and when pivoted at B the corresponding length is b. Prove that if the centre of gravity G is between A and B and if k is the radius of gyration about an axis through G at right angles to AB, then

$$k^2 = l(a - l)(b - l)(a + b - l)/(a + b - 2l)^2. \qquad \text{[L.U.]}$$

CHAPTER 34

DIFFERENTIAL EQUATIONS

34.1. An equation involving differential coefficients is called a differential equation. The equations

$$\frac{dx}{dt} = 3, \qquad L\frac{di}{dt} + Ri = 0$$

are equations of the first order. The equations

$$EI\frac{d^2y}{dx^2} = W(l - x), \qquad L\frac{d^2Q}{dt^2} + R\frac{dQ}{dt} + \frac{Q}{C} = E_0 \cos \omega t$$

are equations of the second order, the *order* of the equation referring to the *highest* differential coefficient involved. The student has already solved a large number of first-order differential equations. Each time he has found an area A as

$$\int f(x)dx = F(x) + C$$

he has really solved the equation

$$\frac{dA}{dx} = f(x)$$

and found as the general solution

$$A = \int f(x)dx = F(x) + C.$$

Our object is to solve various simple types of differential equations such as often occur in engineering problems. By solving, we mean to obtain an equation between the two variables (that occur in the differential coefficients) which does not involve any differential coefficients and satisfies the given differential equation when substituted in it. Thus from the differential equation in x and y

$$\frac{d^2y}{dx^2} + 3\frac{dy}{dx} + 2y = 0,$$

later, we will obtain as the general solution the relation between x and y

$$y = Ae^{-x} + Be^{-2x},$$

where A and B are two unknown constants which can be found when sufficient data is given.

34.2. The Type $\frac{dy}{dx} = f(x)$

Example 1. Solve $x^2\frac{dy}{dx} = 1 + x$.

This can be written $$\frac{dy}{dx} = \frac{1}{x^2} + \frac{1}{x},$$

$$\therefore \quad y = \int \left(\frac{1}{x^2} + \frac{1}{x}\right) dx$$

$$= -\frac{1}{x} + \log x + C.$$

In simple cases the integral sign should not be put in but the integration performed at once.

We could have stated this problem as: find the curve whose gradient at the point (x, y) is $\frac{1}{x^2} + \frac{1}{x}$. The solution shows that there are an infinite number of such curves, one to every possible value of C. We could now particularize and ask for the curve satisfying the given condition and also passing through the point (1, 2).

We have

$$y = -\frac{1}{x} + \log x + C.$$

If this is satisfied by (1, 2)

$$2 = -1 + \log 1 + C,$$

$$\therefore \quad C = 3.$$

The required curve is

$$y = -\frac{1}{x} + \log x + 3.$$

34.3. The Type $\frac{dy}{dx} = f(y)$

We write this as $$\frac{dy}{f(y)} = dx,$$

$$\therefore \quad \int \frac{dy}{f(y)} = x + C.$$

Example 2. Solve $\frac{dy}{dx} + ay + b = 0$.

This is $$\frac{dy}{ay + b} = -dx,$$

$$\therefore \quad \frac{1}{a} \log (ay + b) = -x + C.$$

Example 3. Solve $\frac{dT}{d\theta} - \mu T = 0$, given that $T = T_0$ when $\theta = 0$.

We have $$\frac{dT}{T} = \mu d\theta,$$

$$\therefore \quad \log T = \mu\theta + C.$$

But $T = T_0$ when $\theta = 0$, $\quad \therefore \log T_0 = C.$

Subtract: $$\log_e \left(\frac{T}{T_0}\right) = \mu\theta,$$

$$T = T_0 e^{\mu\theta}.$$

EXERCISE 92

Solve the following equations:

1. $x^3\dfrac{dy}{dx} = 2x + 3.$

2. $\dfrac{dy}{dx} = \dfrac{1}{(ax + b)}.$

3. $\tan x\dfrac{dy}{dx} = 3.$

4. Find a given that $x^3\dfrac{dp}{dx} = a - x$ and that $p = 0$ when $x = 2$ and when $x = 6$. [L.U.]

5. Find the curve whose gradient at the point (x, y) is $2x$ and which passes through the point (1, 2).

6. Solve $\dfrac{dy}{dx} = \dfrac{3y^2 + 2y}{3y + 1}.$

7. Solve $\dfrac{dy}{dx} = \dfrac{3y^2 + 2}{3y + 1}.$

8. Solve $L\dfrac{di}{dt} + Ri = 0$, given $i = i_0$ when $t = 0$.

9. Solve $R\dfrac{dq}{dt} + \dfrac{q}{C} = 0$, given $q = EC$ when $t = 0$.

10. The adiabatic expansion of a gas is governed by the equation

$$C_p\frac{dv}{v} + C_v\frac{dp}{p} = 0,$$

where C_p and C_v are constants. Prove that $pv^n =$ constant, where $n = \dfrac{C_p}{C_v}.$

11. The velocity of a chemical reaction is governed by $\dfrac{dx}{dt} = k(a - x)$, where k, a are constants and x, the amount of substance transformed at time t, is initially zero. Show that $x = a(1 - e^{-kt})$.

12. Find the equation of the curves given by $2y\,dy = x^2dx$. Find also the special curve of the family that passes through the point (1, 2).

13. Find the solution of $\dfrac{dy}{dx} = x - \dfrac{8}{x^2}$ if the minimum value of y is 7.

14. The gradient curve of a function is $x(4 + 3x^2)$, and the curve makes an intercept of 2 on the y axis. Find the equation of the curve.

The following equations require two integrations. The student should, when possible, find each constant of integration as it appears.

15. Solve $\dfrac{d^2s}{dt^2} = \dfrac{2}{t^2} - \dfrac{10}{t^3} + 3.$

16. Solve $\dfrac{d^2s}{dt^2} = t^2(t + 7)$, given that $\dfrac{ds}{dt} = 2$ when $t = 1$ and $s = 0$ when $t = 0$.

17. Solve $\dfrac{d^2\theta}{dt^2} = 2 - \frac{1}{2}t$, given that $\dfrac{d\theta}{dt} = \frac{1}{2}$, when $t = 2$ and $\theta = 2$ when $t = 0$.

18. Find the equation of the curve which is such that $\dfrac{d^2y}{dx^2} = \dfrac{1}{x^4}$ and passes through the points (1, 4), (2, 5).

19. The form of a horizontal cantilever of length l, fixed horizontally at one end which is chosen as the origin and with a load W at the other, is given by $\mathrm{EI}\dfrac{d^2y}{dx^2} = \mathrm{W}(l - x)$. Find y, noting that $y = 0$, when $x = 0$ (since the origin is on the beam) and $\dfrac{dy}{dx} = 0$ when $x = 0$ (since the beam is horizontal at the fixed end).

20. In the above problem if the load is w per unit length and there is no load at the free end, the equation of bending is

$$\mathrm{EI}\frac{d^2y}{dx^2} = \frac{1}{2}w(l - x)^2.$$

Find y, noting that the " end " conditions are as above.

34.4. The Type " Variables Separable "

The two previous types are special cases of a type that can be written, with the " variables separated " as

$$\mathrm{F}(x)dx = f(y)dy,$$

which integrates as

$$\int \mathrm{F}(x)dx = \int f(y)dy + \mathrm{C}.$$

Example 4. Solve $\dfrac{dy}{dx} = e^{2x+3y}$.

As this stands it looks difficult, but we write it

$$e^{-3y}dy = e^{2x}dx,$$

and now, having " separated the variables ", we integrate as

$$-\tfrac{1}{3}e^{-3y} = \tfrac{1}{2}e^{2x} + \mathrm{C}.$$

Example 5. A constant e.m.f. E is introduced into an (L, R) circuit. Find the current at time t.

If i is the current at the instant t in a given direction caused by E, there is an e.m.f. $\mathrm{L}\dfrac{di}{dt}$ in the reverse direction due to the inductance L. From the point of view of obtaining the differential equation of the circuit this " back e.m.f. " is the sole effect of an inductance. The total e.m.f. in the circuit is then $\mathrm{E} - \mathrm{L}\dfrac{di}{dt}$. By Ohm's Law the current is given by

$$\mathrm{E} - \mathrm{L}\frac{di}{dt} = \mathrm{R}i.$$

We write this as

$$\frac{di}{\mathrm{E} - \mathrm{R}i} = \frac{1}{\mathrm{L}}dt.$$

Integrate:

$$-\frac{1}{\mathrm{R}}\log(\mathrm{E} - \mathrm{R}i) = \frac{1}{\mathrm{L}}t + \text{const.}$$

At the instant the e.m.f. is introduced the current is nil, *i.e.*, $i = 0$ when $t = 0$. Substitute in the above equation:

$$-\frac{1}{\mathrm{R}}\log \mathrm{E} = 0 + \text{const.}$$

Subtract:

$$-\frac{1}{R}\log_e\left(\frac{E - Ri}{E}\right) = \frac{1}{L}t,$$

or

$$i = \frac{E}{R}\left(1 - e^{-Rt/L}\right).$$

EXERCISE 93.

Solve the equations:

1. $\frac{dy}{dx} = \frac{\sin 2x}{4y}$.

2. $\frac{dy}{dx} = \tan x \cot y$.

3. $x(1 + y^2)^{\frac{1}{2}} + y(1 + x^2)^{\frac{1}{2}}\frac{dy}{dx} = 0$.

4. $xy\frac{dy}{dx} = 1 + y^2$.

5. $\frac{dq}{dt} + \frac{1}{RC}q = \frac{E}{R}$, given that $q = 0$ when $t = 0$. (E, R, C constant.)

6. $x\frac{dy}{dx} - y = xy$.

7. $\frac{dy}{dx} = \sqrt{\frac{1 - y^2}{1 - x^2}}$.

8. The equation $r\frac{dp}{dr} + p(1 - a) + b = 0$ gives the pressure p at distance r from the axis in the material of a thick cylinder subject to internal pressure. Given that $p = p_1$ when $r = r_1$ (the internal radius) and $p = 0$ when $r = r_0$ (the outside radius), show that $r_0 = r_1\left\{p_1\left(\frac{1 - a}{b}\right) + 1\right\}^{\frac{1}{1-a}}$.

9. The velocity v ft./sec. of water through a circular pipe is given by $v = k(a^2 - x^2)$ at x ft. from the centre, where a ft. is its radius and k is a constant for the pipe. Find the quantity Q cu. ft. discharged by the pipe per second.

10. A cylindrical tank has its axis vertical. Its cross-section is A sq. ft. and its height H ft. It is filled with water which flows out through a hole in the base of area a sq. ft. If it is given that when the height of the water is h ft., the rate of outflow is given by

$$A\frac{dh}{dt} = -8ka\sqrt{h},$$

where k is a constant, show that the time taken to empty the tank is $\frac{A\sqrt{H}}{4ka}$ sec.

11. If $y = Ae^{px} + Be^{qx}$, show that

$$\frac{d^2y}{dx^2} - (p + q)\frac{dy}{dx} + pqy = 0.$$

12. If $y = e^{-px}(L\cos qx + M\sin qx)$, show that

$$\frac{d^2y}{dx^2} + 2p\frac{dy}{dx} + (p^2 + q^2)y = 0.$$

34.5. The General Solution

We have seen that the solution of a first-order differential equation involves one unknown constant, introduced when we integrate once. Similarly, a second-order equation will contain two unknown constants, one introduced at each integration, from $\frac{d^2y}{dx^2}$ to $\frac{dy}{dx}$ and then $\frac{dy}{dx}$ to y. This is a general rule which must be appreciated. A *general* solution will always contain a number of unknown constants equal to the *order* of the equation. Any solution with less constants is called a *particular* integral or solution. Thus we will soon show that the solution of

$$\frac{d^2y}{dx^2} - (p + q)\frac{dy}{dx} + pqy = 0$$

is $$y = Ae^{px} + Be^{qx}. \quad \text{(see also Ex. 93, no. 11.)}$$

Since this contains two unknown constants, A and B, and the differential equation is of the second order, this solution is the general solution. The student should show that $y = Ae^{px}$ or $y = Be^{qx}$ alone will satisfy the equation. Each of these is a particular solution, since it contains only one unknown constant.

Also consider the second-order differential equation

$$\frac{(1 + y_1^2)^{\frac{3}{2}}}{y_2} = 3$$

This states that the radius of curvature at any point of the curve we require is equal to 3. Clearly the solution we will obtain must be a circle, and any circle, whatever its centre, will do, provided its radius is 3. We will in fact obtain as the solution

$$(x - a)^2 + (y - b)^2 = 3^2,$$

an equation with *two* unknown constants, a and b, as required, since we have solved a *second*-order equation. The result, when obtained, can be interpreted as showing that any centre will do.

34.6. The Type $a\frac{d^2y}{dx^2} + b\frac{dy}{dx} + cy = 0$

(a) Suppose a disc of moment of inertia I lb. ft.^{2} is suspended from a wire which gives a restoring torque of $k\theta$ lb. ft. when the disc is

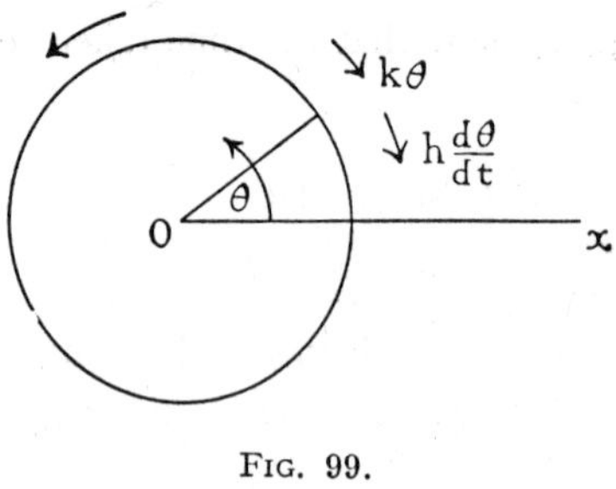

FIG. 99.

turned through θ. Also let the disc be immersed in a resisting medium which opposes its rotation by a torque $h\frac{d\theta}{dt}$ lb. ft. when its angular velocity of rotation is $\frac{d\theta}{dt}$.

For the rotation of the disc, by the torque equation

$$\frac{I}{g}\frac{d^2\theta}{dt^2} = -h\frac{d\theta}{dt} - k\theta,$$

or

$$\frac{I}{g}\frac{d^2\theta}{dt^2} + h\frac{d\theta}{dt} + k\theta = 0.$$

an equation of the type we wish to solve.

(*b*) Suppose a condenser charged to a given potential v is then discharged through an R, L circuit. If i is the current at time t, then the e.m.f. due to v is in the same direction but $L\frac{di}{dt}$ acts in opposition.

$$\therefore \quad v - L\frac{di}{dt} = Ri \qquad \ldots\ldots\ (1)$$

But since the condenser is discharging, if q is the charge on it at this instant t,

$$i = -\frac{dq}{dt},$$

since $\frac{dq}{dt}$ is the rate of increase of charge with time.

Since $q = Cv$, therefore $i = -\frac{d}{dt}(Cv) = -C\frac{dv}{dt}$.

Differentiate (1)

$$\frac{dv}{dt} - L\frac{d^2i}{dt^2} = R\frac{di}{dt}.$$

Substitute for $\frac{dv}{dt}$ and obtain

$$\frac{d^2i}{dt^2} + \frac{R}{L}\frac{di}{dt} + \frac{1}{CL}i = 0,$$

again an equation of the same type. Note that the coefficients R, L, C and I, h, k *are all constant.*

We note then that in solving this type we shall be dealing with equations that occur in mechanical and electrical problems.

34.7. Real Roots

To solve $\frac{d^2y}{dx^2} + \frac{dy}{dx} - 20y = 0.$

It is usual to use D for $\frac{d}{dx}$ and D^2 for $\frac{d^2}{dx^2}$. The equation can be written

$$(D^2 + D - 20)y = 0 \qquad \ldots\ (i)$$

We will try $y = Ae^{mx}$ as a solution.
Since $Dy = Ame^{mx}$ and $D^2y = Am^2e^{mx}$, we find by substitution

$$Am^2e^{mx} + Ame^{mx} - 20Ae^{mx} = 0$$

$$Ae^{mx}(m^2 + m - 20) = 0.$$

e^{mx} is not zero for finite values of the index. A is not zero, for this would give $y = 0$ always.

$$\therefore \quad m^2 + m - 20 = 0, \quad \ldots \ldots \quad \text{(ii)}$$

a quadratic equation with *real* roots

and $m = -5$ and 4.

Therefore $y = Ae^{-5x}$ and $y = Ae^{4x}$ are solutions whatever A is. But this is a second-order equation, and we need two unknown constants, therefore we take $y = Ae^{-5x} + Be^{4x}$
as the general solution, A and B being two unknown constants which can be found when sufficient data is given.

[Note that (ii) can be obtained from (i) by substituting m for D.]

Example 6. A particle moves so that its distance x from a fixed origin at time t is given by

$$\frac{d^2x}{dt^2} + 3\frac{dx}{dt} + 2x = 0.$$

Solve this equation, given that at time $t = 0$, $x = 0$ and also $\frac{dx}{dt} = 5$.

We have $(D^2 + 3D + 2)x = 0$, where $D \equiv \frac{d}{dt}$.

Let $x = Ae^{mt}$, $\therefore \; m^2 + 3m + 2 = 0$,

$m = -2$ and -1,

$\therefore \; x = Ae^{-2t} + Be^{-t}$.

$x = 0, t = 0$, $\therefore \; 0 = A + B$.

Also $\frac{dx}{dt} = -2Ae^{-2t} - Be^{-t}$.

$\frac{dx}{dt} = 5, t = 0$, $\therefore \; 5 = -2A - B$.

Solve for A and B: $A = -5, B = 5$.

$\therefore \; \underline{x = 5(e^{-t} - e^{-2t})}$,

giving the displacement of the particle at any time t.

EXERCISE 94

Solve the equations:

1. $(D^2 - 9)y = 0$.
2. $(D^2 - D - 20)y = 0$.
3. $(D^2 + 5D + 6)y = 0$.
4. $(D^2 - 2D - 3)x = 0$, where $D \equiv \frac{d}{dt}$.
5. $\frac{d^2x}{dt^2} = 25x$, given that when $t = 0$, $x = 1$ and $\frac{dx}{dt} = 2$.

6. $\frac{d^2r}{d\theta^2} + 4\frac{dr}{d\theta} + 3r = 0$, given that $r = 2$ and $\frac{dr}{d\theta} = 3$ when $\theta = 0$.

7. Show by differentiation that $y = Ae^{-3x} + Be^{-4x}$ satisfies the equation $(D^2 + 7D + 12)y = 0$.

34.8. Complex Roots

An important case in engineering occurs when the equation in m obtained above has complex roots.

Consider $$(D^2 + 4D + 9)y = 0.$$

Let $y = Ae^{mx}$,

$$\therefore \quad m^2 + 4m + 9 = 0,$$

$$m = -2 \pm \sqrt{-5} = -2 \pm j\sqrt{5} \quad . \quad . \quad \text{(i)}$$

As usual
$$y = Ae^{(-2+j\sqrt{5})x} + Be^{(-2-j\sqrt{5})x}$$
$$= e^{-2x}\{Ae^{j\sqrt{5}x} + Be^{-j\sqrt{5}x}\}.$$

We have shown (see 28.9) that

$$e^{jx} = \cos x + j \sin x, \quad e^{-jx} = \cos x - j \sin x,$$

$$\therefore \quad y = e^{-2x}\{A(\cos \sqrt{5}x + j \sin \sqrt{5}x) + B(\cos \sqrt{5}x - j \sin \sqrt{5}x)\}$$
$$= e^{-2x}\{(A + B) \cos \sqrt{5}x + j(A - B) \sin \sqrt{5}x\}.$$

y, being a real displacement or a real current, etc., cannot be equal to a complex expression. In practice, it is always found that A and B are complex conjugate numbers.

E.g.,
$$A = 3 + j4,$$
$$B = 3 - j4,$$
$$\therefore \quad A + B = 6, \text{ a real number,}$$
$$j(A - B) = j \times 8j = -8, \text{ a real number.}$$

We may therefore write the expression for y as

$$y = e^{-2x}\{L \cos \sqrt{5}x + M \sin \sqrt{5}x\} \quad . \quad . \quad . \quad . \quad . \quad \text{(ii)}$$

where L and M are two real unknown constants. When the student is familiar with this method he should pass directly from (i) to (ii).

Example 7. Solve $(D^2 + 4D + 13)y = 0$ $\quad \left[D \equiv \frac{d}{dt}\right]$.

Let $y = Ae^{mt}$, $\quad \therefore \quad m^2 + 4m + 13 = 0,$

$$m = \frac{-4 \pm \sqrt{(-36)}}{2} = -2 \pm j3,$$

$$\therefore \quad \underline{y = e^{-2t}\{L \cos 3t + M \sin 3t\}} \quad . \quad . \quad . \quad (1)$$

Suppose further, that $y = 0$ when $t = 0$, *i.e.*, we measure time from the instant when the body in motion is at a certain point which we choose as O. Also, let $\frac{dy}{dt} = 2$ when $t = 0$, *i.e.*, at this instant the body's velocity is 2 units in the direction of y increasing. We then have

(*a*) $y = 0$, $t = 0$, therefore from (1)

$$0 = 1\{L + 0\}, \text{ or } L = 0,$$
$$\therefore \quad y = Me^{-2t} \sin 3t.$$

(*b*) Differentiate: $\frac{dy}{dt} = M\{e^{-2t} . 3 \cos 3t + \sin 3t . -2e^{-2t}\}$.

$\dfrac{dy}{dt} = 2,\ t = 0$, therefore $2 = \mathrm{M}\{3 + 0\}$, or $\mathrm{M} = \frac{2}{3}$.

$$\therefore\quad y = \tfrac{2}{3}e^{-2t}\sin 3t.$$

34.9. Equal Roots

If the equation is of the form

$$(\mathrm{D} + a)^2 y = 0,\ \text{or}\ \frac{d^2y}{dx^2} + 2a\frac{dy}{dx} + a^2 y = 0,$$

the usual trial solution $y = \mathrm{A}e^{mx}$ gives

$$(m + a)^2 = 0, \qquad \therefore\quad m = -a,\ -a.$$

The usual method, if followed, gives

$$y = \mathrm{A}e^{-ax} + \mathrm{B}e^{-ax} = \mathrm{L}e^{-ax},$$

where $\mathrm{L} = \mathrm{A} + \mathrm{B}$ and is a single unknown constant. We require two unknown constants, and $\mathrm{L}e^{-ax}$ is a particular solution only. We must proceed as follows. Write the equation

$$\frac{d^2y}{dx^2} + a\frac{dy}{dx} = -a\left(\frac{dy}{dx} + ay\right).$$

$$\therefore\quad \frac{\dfrac{d^2y}{dx^2} + a\dfrac{dy}{dx}}{\dfrac{dy}{dx} + ay} = -a.$$

This can be written $\dfrac{d}{dx}\left\{\log\left(\dfrac{dy}{dx} + ay\right)\right\} = -a.$

Integrate: $\log\left(\dfrac{dy}{dx} + ay\right) = -ax + \mathrm{C}$

i.e., $\dfrac{dy}{dx} + ay = e^{-ax+\mathrm{C}} = \mathrm{B}e^{-ax}.$

This can be written $e^{ax}\dfrac{dy}{dx} + yae^{ax} = \mathrm{B}$

or $\dfrac{d}{dx}(ye^{ax}) = \mathrm{B},$

$$\therefore\quad ye^{ax} = \mathrm{A} + \mathrm{B}x$$

or $y = (\mathrm{A} + \mathrm{B}x)e^{-ax}$

a solution with two arbitrary constants as required and which the student should check, by substitution, satisfies the given differential equation. [This is a " trick " method for dealing with the difficulty. In the next volume we will meet with a more general and easier method.]

Example 8. Solve $(\mathrm{D}^2 + 6\mathrm{D} + 9)x = 0.\quad \left(\mathrm{D} \equiv \dfrac{d}{dt}\right).$

Let $x = \mathrm{A}e^{mt}$, $\therefore\quad m^2 + 6m + 9 = 0$

and $m = -3,\ -3$, two equal roots.

$$\therefore\quad x = (\mathrm{A} + \mathrm{B}t)e^{-3t}.$$

34.10. Simple Harmonic Motion

A body is said to be moving with S.H.M. when it moves in a straight line under the action of a force directed to a fixed point on the line, the magnitude of the force being proportional to the distance of the body from the fixed point.

If the distance is x at time t, let the force be kx lb. wt. If W is the weight of the body, the equation of motion is

$$\frac{W}{g}\frac{d^2x}{dt^2} = -kx,$$

the minus sign being due to the fact that the force is acting towards the origin, so that $-kx$ is the force in the direction of x increasing, which is the direction of $\frac{d^2x}{dt^2}$.

We can write this $\frac{d^2x}{dt^2} + n^2x = 0$, where $n^2 = \frac{kg}{W}$,

i.e., $$(D^2 + n^2)x = 0, \qquad \left[D \equiv \frac{d}{dt}\right].$$

Let $x = Ae^{mt}$, then $m^2 + n^2 = 0$,

$$m = \pm jn = 0 \pm jn.$$

As usual
$$\begin{aligned} x &= e^{ot}\{A\cos nt + B\sin nt\} \\ &= A\cos nt + B\sin nt \\ &= \sqrt{A^2+B^2}\cos(nt-\alpha). \qquad \left[\tan\alpha = \frac{B}{A}\right]. \end{aligned}$$

The motion is therefore purely periodic with period $\frac{2\pi}{n}$, which is independent of A and B, depending only on W, g and k. A and B depend on the circumstances of the motion, the initial displacement and velocity, etc. We thus find that the periodic time of an oscillation between $-\sqrt{A^2+B^2}$ and $+\sqrt{A^2+B^2}$ and back again is independent of the "initial" or "boundary" conditions.

It should be noted that in S.H.M. there is no resistance to the motion proportional to the speed, *i.e.*, no term in $\frac{dx}{dt}$ or Dx occurs in the differential equation. Hence the real part of the roots for m is zero and there is no "damping factor" such as occurs in Example 7, where it is e^{-2t}.

Example 9. A body moves with S.H.M. so that $\ddot{s} = -16s$. If $s = 3$ and $\dot{s} = 16$ when $t = 0$, find the motion.

Since $\ddot{s} = -16s$, $\quad s = A\cos 4t + B\sin 4t$,

$s = 3,\ t = 0,\quad \therefore\ 3 = A,$

also $\quad \dot{s} = -4A\sin 4t + 4B\cos 4t$

$\dot{s} = 16,\ t = 0,\quad 16 = 4B,\quad B = 4.$

We now have $\quad \underline{s = 3\cos 4t + 4\sin 4t.}$

We can also obtain a useful equation relating velocity to distance from the origin and not involving time. The equation can be written

$$v\frac{dv}{dx} = -n^2x.$$

Integrate: $$\frac{v^2}{2} = -\frac{1}{2}n^2x^2 + C.$$

Suppose $v = 0$ when $x = a$,

$$0 = -\tfrac{1}{2}n^2a^2 + C,$$

$$\therefore\quad v^2 = n^2(a^2 - x^2).$$

When $v = 0$ $x = \pm a$, showing that the motion is between $+a$ and $-a$.

Example 10. A body moves with S.H.M., and its velocity at three points 1 ft. apart is $2\sqrt{15}$, $4\sqrt{3}$, $2\sqrt{7}$ ft./sec. Find the position of these points relative to the centre, the amplitude of the motion and the periodic time.

If the distances are x, $x + 1$, $x + 2$ ft. from the centre, then using $v^2 = n^2(a^2 - x^2)$,

$$60 = n^2\{a^2 - x^2\},$$
$$48 = n^2\{a^2 - (x + 1)^2\},$$
$$28 = n^2\{a^2 - (x + 2)^2\}.$$

$\therefore$ $x = 1$, showing that the points are 1, 2, 3 ft. from 0.

$n^2 = 4$, $\quad\therefore\quad T = \frac{2\pi}{2} = \pi$ sec.

$a^2 = 16$, $\quad a = 4$, giving the amplitude.

34.11. Summary

We will now summarize the different types of motion which a body can perform when it moves subject to the second-order equation we have been considering.

If we take the equation as

$$\frac{d^2x}{dt^2} + a\frac{dx}{dt} + bx = 0,$$

then in practice a and b will be positive.

(1) Roots real or $a^2 > 4b$. The solution is of the form

$$x = Ae^{-m_1t} + Be^{-m_2t},$$

where m_1 and m_2 are positive. The motion is not oscillatory, and the final position of rest is approached slowly (Fig. 100(b)).

(2) Roots imaginary or $a^2 < 4b$. The solution is of the form

$$x = e^{-m_1t}[A\cos m_2t + B\sin m_2t],$$

where m_1 is positive. The motion is oscillatory, consisting of damped oscillations of decreasing amplitude about the final position (Fig. 100(a)).

If $a = 0$, then $m_1 = 0$, and we have S.H.M., *i.e.*, oscillatory motion with constant amplitude.

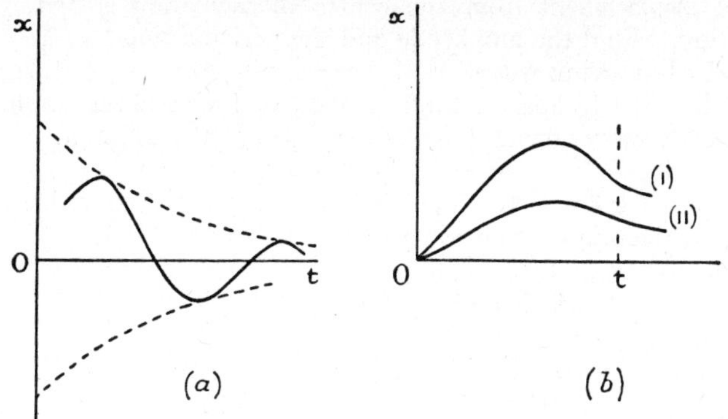

ROOTS IMAGINARY

(i) ROOTS REAL AND DIFFERENT

(ii) ROOTS REAL AND EQUAL

FIG. 100.

(3) Roots equal or $a^2 = 4b$. The solution is of the form

$$x = (A + Bt)e^{-m_1 t},$$

where m_1 is positive. The motion is non-oscillatory. We regard a as having been made just large enough to equal $2\sqrt{b}$ and so render the motion non-oscillatory. The motion is said to be "critically damped" (Fig. 100(b)).

It will be seen that at any time t the displacement from the equilibrium position when the roots are equal is less than when the roots are unequal, other conditions of course being equal.

EXERCISE 95

Solve the equations:

1. $(D^2 + D + 1)y = 0.$

2. $(D^2 + 4)y = 0.$

3. $\dfrac{d^2x}{dt^2} - 2\dfrac{dx}{dt} + 5x = 0.$

4. $(D^2 + 4D + 4)y = 0.$

5. $\dfrac{d^2x}{dt^2} - 2a\dfrac{dx}{dt} + (a^2 + b^2)x = 0$, where a and b are real constants.

6. $L\dfrac{d^2Q}{dt^2} + \dfrac{1}{C}Q = 0.$

7. $(D^2 + 4D + 29)y = 0$, given that $\dfrac{dy}{dx} = 15$ and $y = 0$ when $x = 0$.

8. $\dfrac{d^2x}{dt^2} + 4\dfrac{dx}{dt} + 5x = 0$, given that $x = 0$ and $\dfrac{dx}{dt} = 2$ when $t = 0$.

9. $\ddot{x} = -16x$, given that $x = 2$ and $\dot{x} = 10$ when $t = 0$.

10. A body moving with S.H.M. has velocities of $5\sqrt{96}$, $5\sqrt{51}$ ft./sec

when its displacement from the centre of oscillation is 2 ft., 7 ft. respectively. Find the amplitude and the periodic time.

11. A body moving with S.H.M. has velocities of 8, 7, 4 ft./sec., at 3 points distant 1 ft. apart. Find the periodic time and the amplitude.

12. A body moves on a straight line subject to the equation

$$5\ddot{x} + 2\dot{x} + 40x = 0.$$

Show that it oscillates, the amplitude of the oscillations reducing to about $\frac{1}{20}$ of the original value in 15 secs.

13. Solve the equation

$$\frac{d^2i}{dt^2} + \frac{R}{L}\frac{di}{dt} + \frac{i}{LC} = 0,$$

given that $R^2C = 4L$. Solve also if in addition to $R^2C = 4L$, $i = 2$ when $t = 0$ and $\frac{di}{dt} = \frac{R}{L}$ when $t = 0$.

34.12. Bending Beams

For our purpose a beam can be represented by a line, the central axis, which passes through the centroid of every section of the beam perpendicular to its length. During bending this line is unchanged in length.

If ρ is the radius of curvature at any point (x, y) on the curved line and M the bending moment of the external forces acting on the beam about this point, then it can be shown that

$$\frac{EI}{\rho} = M \quad . \quad . \quad . \quad . \quad . \quad . \quad . \quad . \quad (1)$$

In this formula E is Young's Modulus for the material of the beam, I is the second moment of a section of the beam perpendicular to the length about a line in the section through the centroid and perpendicular to the plane in which the beam is bending.

We consider only cases in which the deflection and therefore the gradient is quite small. Since (see 23.2)

$$\rho = \pm \frac{(1 + y_1^2)^{\frac{3}{2}}}{y_2},$$

we assume that the gradient is sufficiently small for y_1^2 to be neglected. This gives

$$\rho = \pm \frac{1}{y_2},$$

and the formula (1) now becomes

$$EIy_2 = \pm M.$$

From this, by integration, y is obtained in terms of x when M is known in terms of x.

34.13. Concave and Convex

In the following it will be necessary to remember that when a curve has its convex side upwards in the direction of the positive y axis, then

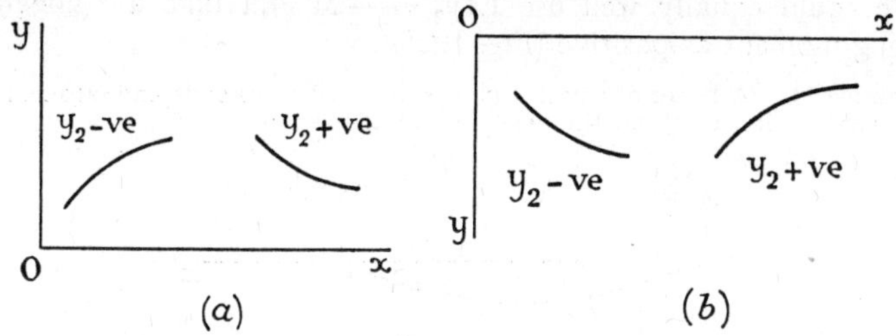

FIG. 101.

$\frac{d^2y}{dx^2}$ (*i.e.*, y_2) is negative over this part of the curve. Similarly, y_2 is positive when the concave side faces the direction in which the positive y axis is drawn. The student may find it useful to remember the rules for maxima and minima. Thus in Fig. 101(*b*) the curve over which y_2 is negative can be considered as part of a curve having a maximum a little to the right, and for a maximum y_2 is negative. The curve over which y_2 is positive can be considered as part of a curve having a minimum to the right, and for a minimum y_2 is positive.

34.14. The Sign of M

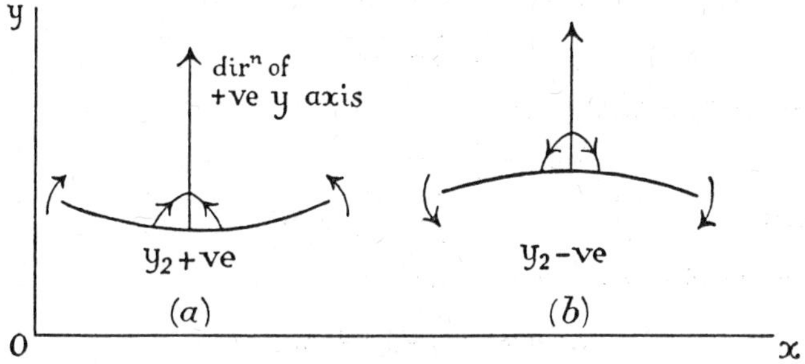

FIG. 102.

In Fig. 102(*a*), $\frac{d^2y}{dx^2}$ is positive as the result of a " sagging " bending moment acting on the beam. In the equation

$$EIy_2 = \pm M$$

the left-hand side will be positive for this case, and therefore we must make the right-hand side positive too, to equal it. We can therefore decide that a sagging bending moment is positive and from now onwards use

$$EIy_2 = + M \quad . \quad . \quad . \quad . \quad . \quad . \quad . \quad (1)$$

where the bending moment at a point is taken as positive when it tends to turn the beam to the left of the point in a clockwise direction or to the right of the point in an anti-clockwise direction.

[We could equally well use $EIy_2 = -M$ and take a "hogging" bending moment as positive (Fig. 102(*b*).]

Example 11. A beam of length l ft. is supported at its ends and sags under its own weight w lb./ft. Find the deflection at the centre.

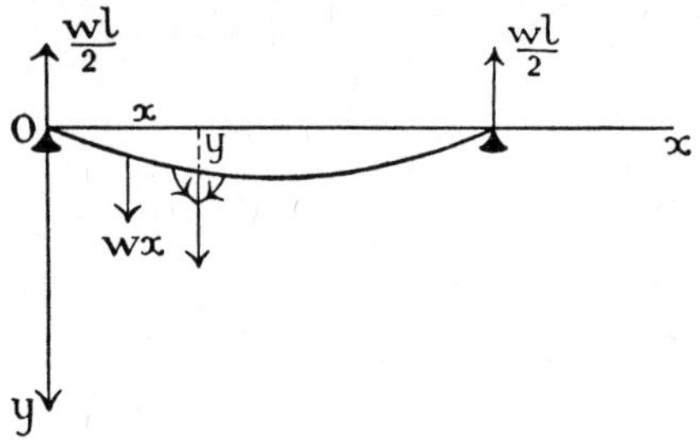

FIG. 103.

Choose axes as shown with Oy downwards. The reaction at each support is $\frac{wl}{2}$.

Consider any point (x, y) on the beam. It may help to draw a line through this point in the direction of Oy and put in the positive direction of the bending moment as shown, arrows directed inwards towards the line.

We consider the external forces to the left or right of the point as is more convenient. In this case we choose those to the left.

The bending moment (B.M.) in the positive direction is

$$wx\frac{x}{2} - \frac{wl}{2}x.$$

The equation (1) in **34.14** becomes

$$EIy_2 = \frac{w}{2}(x^2 - lx).$$

Integrate: $$EIy_1 = \frac{w}{2}\left(\frac{x^3}{3} - l\frac{x^2}{2}\right) + A.$$

At the centre, where $x = \frac{l}{2}$, y_1 is clearly 0,

$$\therefore \quad 0 = \frac{w}{2}\left(\frac{l^3}{24} - \frac{l^3}{8}\right) + A.$$

Subtract: $$EIy_1 = \frac{w}{2}\left(\frac{x^3}{3} - \frac{lx^2}{2} + \frac{l^3}{12}\right).$$

Integrate: $$EIy = \frac{w}{2}\left(\frac{x^4}{12} - \frac{lx^3}{6} + \frac{l^3x}{12}\right) + B.$$

At the origin $y = 0$ when $x = 0$, therefore $B = 0$.

We find for the sag y at any point distant x from O

$$y = \frac{w}{24EI}(x^4 - 2lx^3 + l^3x),$$

$\therefore$ when $x = \frac{1}{2}l$ $$\delta = \frac{5wl^4}{384EI}.$$

Example 12. In the above problem the beam is 14 ft. long and weighs 1 ton. Its cross-section is I-shaped, the upper flange being 6 in. × 2 in., the web 2 in. × 6 in. and the lower flange 10 in. × 4 in. If $E = 25 \times 10^6$ lb. wt./sq. in., find the central deflection.

As above $$\delta = \frac{5wl^4}{384\text{EI}} = \frac{5\text{W}l^3}{384\text{EI}},$$
where $\text{W} = wl$, the weight of the beam.

The second moment about the base of length 10 in. = 2293·3 in.^{4}. The area is 64 sq. in., and the distance of the centroid from the base = $\frac{296}{64}$ in.,

$$\therefore \text{ the second moment} \quad \text{I} = 2293{\cdot}3 - 64 \times \left(\frac{296}{64}\right)^2$$
$$= 924{\cdot}3 \text{ in.}^4,$$
$$\therefore \quad \delta = \frac{5 \times 2240 \times (14 \times 12)^3}{384 \times 25 \times 10^6 \times 924{\cdot}3} = \underline{0{\cdot}006 \text{ in.}}$$

Example 13. A light beam (l) is fixed horizontally at one end and carries a load W at the other. Find the equation of the curve assumed by the beam.

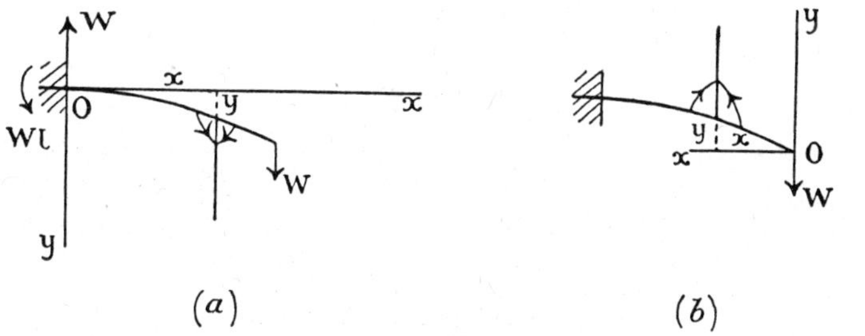

FIG. 104.

Since the weight of the beam is negligible the forces acting on it are: (1) the weight W at the free end; (2) a vertical reaction W at the fixed end to balance this, and (3) a couple Wl as shown to balance the couple on the beam caused by the weight W. It is this couple that keeps the end horizontal.

If we choose axes as shown [Fig. 104(a)] at the fixed end, the equation for the B.M. is, choosing the forces to the left of the point

$$\text{EI}y_2 = \text{W}l - \text{W}x.$$

Integrate: $$\text{EI}y_1 = \text{W}\left(lx - \frac{x^2}{2}\right) + \text{A}.$$

But $y_1 = 0$ when $x = 0$ (at the fixed end),
$$0 = 0 + \text{A}, \qquad \therefore \quad \text{A} = 0.$$

Integrate: $$\text{EI}y = \text{W}\left(\frac{lx^2}{2} - \frac{x^3}{6}\right) + \text{B}.$$

Since $y = 0$ when $x = 0$, $\text{B} = 0$,
$$\therefore \quad y = \underline{\frac{\text{W}x^2}{\text{EI}}\left(\frac{l}{2} - \frac{x}{6}\right)}.$$

Alternative Method.

If we choose axes at the free end [Fig. 104(b)] the equation using the forces on the right of a point (x, y) is

$$\text{EI}y_2 = -\text{W}x,$$
$$\therefore \quad \text{EI}y_1 = -\text{W}\frac{x^2}{2} + \text{A},$$

but $y_1 = 0$ when $x = l$,

$$\therefore \quad 0 = -\text{W}\frac{l^2}{2} + \text{A}.$$

Subtract: $$EIy_1 = \frac{W}{2}(l^2 - x^2),$$

$$\therefore \quad EIy = \frac{W}{2}\left(l^2x - \frac{x^3}{3}\right),$$

since $y = 0$ when $x = 0$.

To find the deflection at the free end, we put $x = l$ in this equation and find the height of the fixed end above it.

Example 14. A beam of length l and total load w lb./ft. is clamped horizontally at each end. Find the deflection at any point.

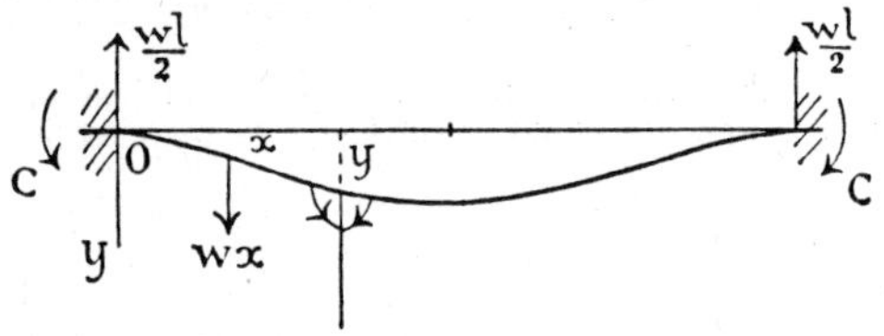

FIG. 105.

There is a vertical reaction at each end $\frac{1}{2}lw$. Also there is a couple at each end keeping the end horizontal. We cannot find this couple by resolving and taking moments, and will call it C.

With axes as shown and using the forces to the left of the point (x, y)

$$EIy_2 = C + \tfrac{1}{2}wx^2 - \tfrac{1}{2}lwx.$$

C is a constant, therefore integration gives

$$EIy_1 = Cx + \tfrac{1}{6}wx^3 - \tfrac{1}{4}lwx^2 + A.$$

$y_1 = 0$ when $x = 0$, $\therefore$ A = 0. Also $y_1 = 0$ when $x = l$,

$$\therefore \quad 0 = Cl + \tfrac{1}{6}wl^3 - \tfrac{1}{4}wl^3,$$

or $$C = \tfrac{1}{12}wl^2.$$

A further integration, noting that $y = 0$ when $x = 0$, gives

$$EIy = \frac{wx^2}{24}(l - x)^2.$$

34.15. The Equation $EI\dfrac{d^4y}{dx^4} = w$

Problems such as that solved above, where forces or couples are acting which cannot be found by the ordinary methods of statics, usually require further equations which will now be found.

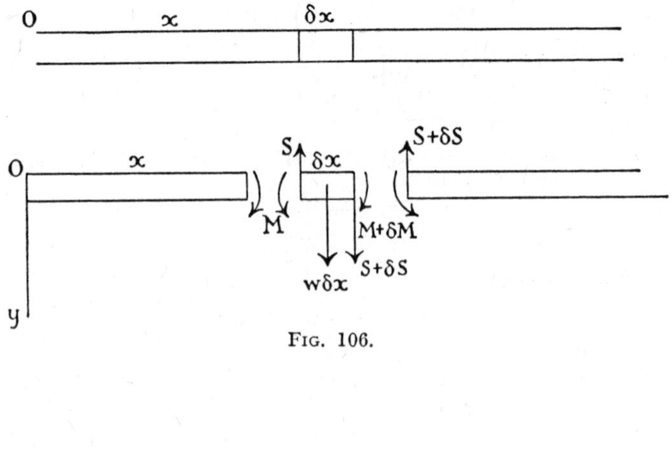

FIG. 106.

In the above figure a section δx of the beam, of weight $w\delta x$, is shown isolated. If we assume the shearing force S to act upwards on the left of the section, then a distance δx further on this force is $S + \delta S$ also acting upwards on the left of the section. Therefore $S + \delta S$ will be acting downwards on the length δx at its right-hand end. Similarly, for the bending moment M.

The length δx is in equilibrium under the forces, therefore:

(1) Equating the vertical forces acting on the length δx,

$$w\delta x + S + \delta S = S,$$

$$\therefore \quad \frac{\delta S}{\delta x} = -w.$$

In the limit as $\delta x \to 0$

$$\frac{dS}{dx} = -w \quad . \quad . \quad . \quad . \quad . \quad . \quad . \quad . \quad . \quad (1)$$

(2) Taking moments about a point on the line of action of S,

$$M = w\delta x \cdot \frac{\delta x}{2} + (S + \delta S)\delta x + M + \delta M.$$

$$\therefore \quad 0 = w\frac{\delta x}{2} + S + \delta S + \frac{\delta M}{\delta x}.$$

In the limit

$$\frac{dM}{dx} = -S \quad . \quad . \quad . \quad . \quad . \quad . \quad . \quad . \quad . \quad (2)$$

Differentiate this and use (1)

$$\frac{d^2M}{dx^2} = -\frac{dS}{dx} = w \quad . \quad . \quad . \quad . \quad . \quad . \quad . \quad (3)$$

But $$M = EIy_2$$

$$\therefore \quad \frac{d^2}{dx^2}\left(EI\frac{d^2y}{dx^2}\right) = w \quad . \quad . \quad . \quad . \quad . \quad (4)$$

If I is constant, *i.e.*, the beam is of uniform cross-section throughout its length, and is of uniform material so that E is constant, (4) may be written

$$EI\frac{d^4y}{dx^4} = w \quad . \quad . \quad . \quad . \quad . \quad . \quad . \quad . \quad . \quad (5)$$

When EI is constant (2) may be written

$$S = -\frac{dM}{dx} = -\frac{d}{dx}\left(EI\frac{d^2y}{dx^2}\right) = -EI\frac{d^3y}{dx^3} \quad . \quad . \quad . \quad (6)$$

We now have the equations

$$M = EIy_2 \quad . \quad . \quad . \quad . \quad . \quad . \quad . \quad . \quad . \quad (7)$$

$$S = -EIy_3 \quad . \quad . \quad . \quad . \quad . \quad . \quad . \quad . \quad (8)$$

$$w = EIy_4 \quad . \quad . \quad . \quad . \quad . \quad . \quad . \quad . \quad . \quad (9)$$

(*a*) Since at a free end of a beam

$$M = 0, \qquad \therefore \quad y_2 = 0 \text{ by (7).}$$

$$S = 0, \qquad \therefore \quad y_3 = 0 \text{ by (8).}$$

(*b*) At a freely supported end M = 0, $\therefore\ y_2 = 0$ and y is known.

(*c*) At a clamped end the value of M generally cannot be found from the external forces, but y is known and $\dfrac{dy}{dx}$ is generally zero.

Equation (9) and the above considerations are sufficient for most problems. This equation, however, requires four integrations, and therefore when possible we use Equation (7).

Example 15. A beam of length $2l$ and total load w lb./ft. is supported at each end and also at the mid-point, the supports being at the same level. Find the pressures on the supports.

We cannot find the pressures by equating forces, etc., and therefore use Equation (9). The beam will consist of two symmetrical parts, and we will consider the left-hand part only. With the origin at the left end and the y axis downward, we begin with

$$\mathrm{E}\mathrm{I}y_4 = w,$$

$$\therefore\ \mathrm{E}\mathrm{I}y_3 = wx + \mathrm{A},$$

$$\therefore\ \mathrm{M} = \mathrm{E}\mathrm{I}y_2 = \frac{wx^2}{2} + \mathrm{A}x + \mathrm{B}.$$

But at the free end ($x = 0$) $\mathrm{M} = 0$, $\therefore\ \mathrm{B} = 0$.

Integrate: $$\mathrm{E}\mathrm{I}y_1 = \frac{wx^3}{6} + \frac{\mathrm{A}x^2}{2} + \mathrm{C}.$$

At $x = l$, $y_1 = 0$ by symmetry,

$$\therefore\ 0 = \frac{wl^3}{6} + \frac{\mathrm{A}l^2}{2} + \mathrm{C}.$$

We now have $$\mathrm{E}\mathrm{I}y_1 = \frac{w}{6}(x^3 - l^3) + \frac{\mathrm{A}}{2}(x^2 - l^2),$$

$$\therefore\ \mathrm{E}\mathrm{I}y = \frac{w}{6}\left(\frac{x^4}{4} - l^3x\right) + \frac{\mathrm{A}}{2}\left(\frac{x^3}{3} - l^2x\right),$$

for since $y = 0$ when $x = 0$, the constant is zero.

Also $y = 0$ when $x = l$,

$$\therefore\ 0 = -\tfrac{3}{24}wl^4 - \mathrm{A}\,.\,\tfrac{1}{3}l^3,$$

or $$\mathrm{A} = -\tfrac{3}{8}wl.$$

But from Equation (8)

$$\mathrm{S} = -\mathrm{E}\mathrm{I}y_3 = -(wx + \mathrm{A})$$

$$= \tfrac{3}{8}wl - wx,$$

$\therefore$ at $x = 0$ $$\mathrm{S} = \tfrac{3}{8}wl = \tfrac{3}{16}\ \text{(total load)}.$$

The pressure on the support at the other end of the beam is the same, leaving $\tfrac{10}{16}$(total load) for the centre support.

34.16. Discontinuous Loading

In all the above problems the loading is uniform over the beam, or else the concentrated loads are at an end of the beam. In the last problem we were able to avoid the difficulty of a change in the shearing force at the centre by considering one of the symmetrical halves of the beam. Whenever this occurs due to a concentrated load not at an end or a change in the distributed loading, the above equations cannot be applied over the whole beam, but only to each section over which the loading is uniform and there is no concentrated load.

Example 16. A light beam freely supported at the ends carries a concentrated load W distant a, b from the ends. Find the deflection at the load.

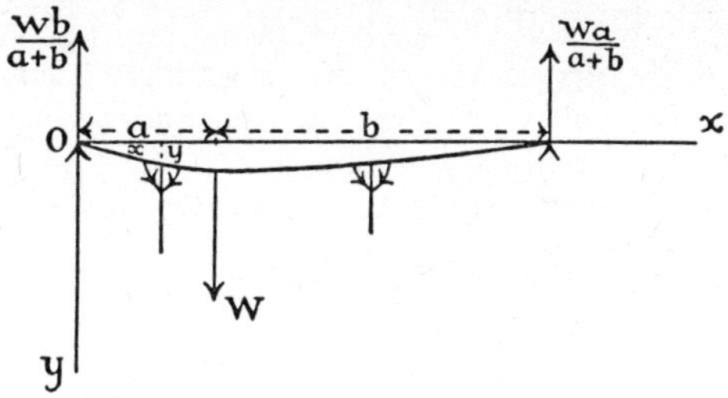

FIG. 107.

With axes as shown, we note that M varies according to whether the point considered is to the left or right of the load W.

for $x < a$ $\qquad EIy_2 = -\dfrac{Wb}{a+b}x = -Rx,$

$x > a$ $\qquad EIy_2 = -\dfrac{Wb}{a+b}x + W(x-a)$

$$= -Rx + W(x-a).$$

Dealing with these in parallel

$x < a$	$x > a$
$EIy_2 = -Rx$	$EIy_2 = -Rx + W(x-a)$
$EIy_1 = -R\dfrac{x^2}{2} + A_1$	$EIy_1 = -R\dfrac{x^2}{2} + \dfrac{W}{2}(x-a)^2 + A_2$

The gradient at the load W is continuous, so that these two expressions must agree when $x = a$,

$$\therefore \quad A_1 = A_2.$$

Integrate again

$EIy = -R\dfrac{x^3}{6} + A_1x + B_1$	$EIy = -R\dfrac{x^3}{6} + \dfrac{W}{6}(x-a)^3 + A_1x + B_2$

The deflection y is the same for both equations when $x = a$, therefore $B_1 = B_2$.

Using the left-hand equation, $y = 0$ when $x = 0$, $\therefore B_1 = 0$. Using the right-hand equation, $y = 0$ when $x = a + b$,

$$\therefore \quad 0 = -\frac{R}{6}(a+b)^3 + \frac{W}{6}b^3 + A_1(a+b).$$

Since $\qquad R = \dfrac{Wb}{(a+b)},$

we find $\qquad A_1 = \dfrac{Wab(a+2b)}{6(a+b)}.$

From the left-hand equation

$$EIy = -\frac{Wb}{a+b}\frac{x^3}{6} + \frac{Wab(a+2b)}{6(a+b)}x.$$

When $x = a$,

$$\delta = \frac{1}{EI}\frac{Wa^2b^2}{3(a+b)}$$

The student will note that the right-hand equation for M is the same as that on the left-hand plus an extra term involving $(x - a)$. We integrated this each time as $\frac{1}{2}(x-a)^2 + A_2$, etc., instead of $\frac{1}{2}x^2 - ax + C$, etc. By this means it remains an expression which vanishes when $x = a$ and thus we found that $A_2 = A_1$ and $B_2 = B_1$. This trick often simplifies the work.

34.17. Theory of Struts (Euler's Formula)

So far all external forces acting on a beam have been perpendicular to its length. We will now deal with axial forces, as these give a different type of differential equation.

We will find the least load, *i.e.*, compressive force, which, applied axially, will cause the beam to bend.

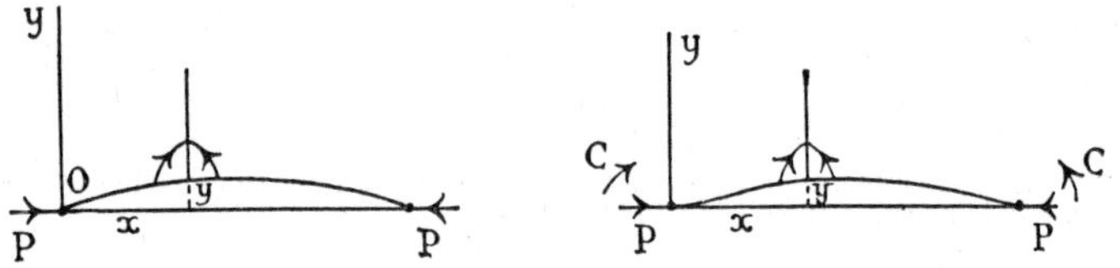

FIG. 108.

(*a*) When the beam (l) is free at each end to take up a position inclined to the x axis, let P be the axial force at each end which has caused the beam (or strut) to bend.

With axes as shown, the equation of bending is *

$$EIy_2 = -Py,$$

$$\therefore \quad \frac{d^2y}{dx^2} + \frac{P}{EI}y = 0.$$

Put $n^2 = \dfrac{P}{EI}$, and solving this equation

$$y = A \sin nx + B \cos nx.$$

But $y = 0$ when $x = 0$, $\quad \therefore B = 0$,

$$\therefore \quad y = A \sin nx.$$

But $y = 0$ also when $x = l$,

$$\therefore \quad 0 = A \sin nl.$$

$A \neq 0$ or $y = 0$ for all x, which means that no bending has occurred,

$$\therefore \quad \sin nl = 0,$$

$$nl = 0, \pi, 2\pi, 3\pi, \ldots$$

nl cannot be zero, therefore the *smallest* value of n is given by

$$nl = \pi,$$

$$\therefore \quad \sqrt{\frac{P}{EI}} \cdot l = \pi,$$

$$\therefore \quad P = \frac{\pi^2 EI}{l^2},$$

* We must now take the sign of y into account. Here y is positive. Had the beam been taken as bending under the line PP, then with the y axis as shown, the deflection y is negative and the B.M. equation $EIy_2 = P(-y)$, giving the same final solution.

giving the least force that will cause buckling when the ends are free to turn.

(*b*) When the ends are fixed to lie along the original axis of the beam, let C be the couple at each end causing this.

The B.M. equation now is

$$EIy_2 = C - Py,$$

$$\therefore \quad \frac{d^2y}{dx^2} + \frac{P}{EI}y = \frac{C}{EI}$$

or

$$\frac{d^2y}{dx^2} + n^2y = n^2a,$$

where $n^2 = \frac{P}{EI}$ and $a = \frac{C}{P}$.

In the next section we will deal with second-order differential equations having a term on the right-hand side. Here we will put $y - a = z$, and since $\frac{d^2y}{dx^2} = \frac{d^2z}{dx^2}$ the equation becomes

$$\frac{d^2z}{dx^2} + n^2z = 0.$$

$$\therefore \quad z = A \sin nx + B \cos nx \quad \text{(see 34.10)},$$

i.e.,

$$y - a = A \sin nx + B \cos nx.$$

Now $\frac{dy}{dx} = 0$ when $x = 0$. Here

$$\frac{dy}{dx} = nA \cos nx - nB \sin nx,$$

$$\therefore \quad 0 = nA \text{ or } A = 0,$$

we now have $\quad y - a = B \cos nx.$

Also $y = 0$ when $x = 0$, $\quad \therefore \quad -a = B,$

and now $$y = a(1 - \cos nx).$$

Finally, $y = 0$ when $x = l$,

$$\therefore \quad 0 = a(1 - \cos nl).$$

$a \neq 0$, $\quad \therefore \quad \cos nl = 1,$

and $$nl = 0, 2\pi, 4\pi, \ldots$$

$nl \neq 0$, therefore the smallest value of n is given by

$$nl = 2\pi,$$

i.e.,

$$\sqrt{\frac{P}{EI}} \cdot l = 2\pi,$$

or

$$P = \frac{4\pi^2EI}{l^2},$$

giving the least axial force required to cause buckling when the ends are clamped.

EXERCISE 96

1. A light beam of length l is fixed horizontally at one end and carries a load W at the other. Show that the slope of the beam at the load is $\frac{Wl^2}{2EI}$ and the deflection there is $\frac{Wl^3}{3EI}$.

2. A beam of length l ft. is fixed horizontally at one end and carries a uniform load w lb./ft. Show that the deflection and the slope at the free end are respectively $\frac{wl^4}{8EI}$ ft. and $\frac{wl^3}{6EI}$.

3. A light beam of length l is freely supported at its ends and carries a load W at the centre. Show that the deflection there is $\frac{Wl^3}{48EI}$.

4. If the above beam is clamped horizontally at each end, show that the couple acting at each end is $\frac{1}{8}Wl$. Find also the points of inflexion on the beam and the maximum deflection of the beam.

5. A beam of length l ft. is clamped horizontally at one end and supported at the same level at the other. If its load is uniformly distributed at w lb./ft., find the pressure on the support and the position of the points of inflexion.

6. A uniform beam w lb./ft. and of length $6a$ rests symmetrically upon two supports distant $2a$ apart. Find the height of the highest point of the beam above the line of the supports.

7. A beam of length l is uniformly loaded, and rests on supports at its ends. A third support is introduced at the middle point so that the pressure on each support is the same. Find how much the middle support is lower than the end ones.

8. A beam of length l and total weight W is built in at one end and supported on a column at the other so as to be, originally, horizontal. Prove that after the equilibrium position has been reached the load on the column is $\frac{3W}{8(1 + 3EI/l^3F)}$, where F is the force required to produce unit depression in the column.

9. A beam of length l ft. supported at each end carries a point load W lb. at the centre and a distributed load w lb./ft. Find the central deflection.

10. A beam of length l ft. carries a load w lb./ft. One end is fixed horizontally and the other freely supported so that it is d ft. below the fixed end. Find the reaction at the supported end.

11. A beam 20 ft. long is clamped horizontally at one end and carries a load of 2 tons per ft. If it is supported by a column 5 ft. from the other end at the same height as the clamped end, find the load on the column.

34.18. The General Equation

So far we have dealt with equations of the form

$$(aD^2 + bD + c)y = 0$$

where a, b and c are constants. It will be noted that when all the terms containing the symbol y, the dependent variable, are put on one side of the equation, the other side is zero.

Suppose now that in Fig. 99 (page 332) there is another item, an anticlockwise torque of A sin wt lb. ft. acting on the disc. The torque equation is now

$$\frac{I}{g}\frac{d^2\theta}{dt^2} = A \sin wt - h\frac{d\theta}{dt} - k\theta$$

or

$$\left(\frac{I}{g}D^2 + hD + k\right)\theta = A \sin wt$$

an equation similar to those solved above but with a non-zero term in t, the independent variable, on the right-hand side.

As another example. For an (L, R, C) series circuit acted on by an electromotive force $e = E_0 \sin wt$ we could obtain the equation

$$L\frac{d^2i}{dt^2} + R\frac{di}{dt} + \frac{1}{C}i = \frac{de}{dt}$$

or

$$\left(LD^2 + RD + \frac{1}{C}\right)i = wE_0 \cos wt$$

the solution of which gives the current i in terms of the time t. Again there is a non-zero term in the independent variable t, on the right-hand side.

We will now deal with the solution of such equations.

34.19. The General Solution

As usual, we will work in terms of y and x to solve

$$(aD^2 + bD + c)y = F(x) \quad . \quad . \quad . \quad . \quad . \quad (1)$$

where $F(x)$ is any non-zero expression in the independent variable x. In a simple case it could be a constant.

If this equation has a solution $y = u$, substitution gives

$$(aD^2 + bD + c)u = F(x)$$

where so far u is some unknown function of x. The difference of these two equations gives

$$(aD^2 + bD + c)[y - u] = 0$$

or for convenience with $y - u = v$

$$(aD^2 + bD + c)v = 0 \quad . \quad . \quad . \quad . \quad . \quad (2)$$

We now have the type of equation with zero on the right-hand side which we can solve completely to find v. Since the order of this equation (2) is the same as that of (1) the solution will contain two unknown constants as required for the general solution of (1). If then we could find a function u, in any way whatsoever, u not containing any unknown constants, the sum $u + v = y$ will be the general solution required for (1).

The method of solution is then as follows:

(*a*) Solve as usual (2) above *i.e.*, using for convenience the original variable y, given (1) solve

$$(aD^2 + bD + c)y = 0 \quad . \quad . \quad . \quad . \quad . \quad . \quad (3)$$

This solution is now called the **Complementary Function** (or C.F.).

(*b*) Obtain any solution (as shown below) of the complete original equation (1).

This solution will not contain any unknown constants and is called the **Particular Integral** (or P.I.).

(*c*) The general solution is given by the sum of the two separate expressions *i.e.* by

$$y = \text{(the complementary function)} + \text{(the particular integral)}.$$
$$= \text{C.F.} + \text{P.I.}$$

34.20. The Particular Integral

It is clear that our concern is with finding the P.I. in any given case since the solution of (3) above has been dealt with.

(*a*) The right-hand side $F(x)$ = a constant.

To solve

$$(D^2 + 3D + 2)y = 10 \quad . \quad . \quad . \quad . \quad . \quad (3)$$

Since R.H.S. = a constant, try $y = C$, a constant, as a P.I. Substitution gives

$$(D^2 + 3D + 2)C \equiv 10$$

or since $\quad D^2(C) = 0, \quad D(C) = 0,$

$$2C = 10, \ C = 5$$

Since the C.F. obtained in the usual way is

$$Ae^{-2x} + Be^{-x},$$

the general solution is

$$y = \text{C.F.} + \text{P.I.}$$
$$= Ae^{-2x} + Be^{-x} + 5$$

as can be checked by substitution in (3).

(*b*) $F(x)$ = a polynomial.

To solve $\quad (D^2 + 3D + 2)y = 2x + 7.$

Assume as P.I. $y = ax + b$. Substitution gives

$$(D^2 + 3D + 2)(ax + b) \equiv 2x + 7$$
$$2ax + (3a + 2b) \equiv 2x + 7$$

Equating the coefficients of like powers of x

$$2a = 2, \qquad 3a + 2b = 7$$

or $\quad a = 1, \quad b = 2, \quad \text{P.I.} = x + 2$

General solution: $y = Ae^{-2x} + Be^{-x} + x + 2$

(c) $F(x)$ = an exponential function.

To solve $(D^2 + 4)y = 3e^{-4x}$.

The simplest function which when differentiated will produce e^{-4x} is itself so assume as P.I. $y = Ae^{-4x}$.

Substitution gives

$$(D^2 + 4)(Ae^{-4x}) \equiv 3e^{-4x}$$

i.e., $\quad (16A + 4A)e^{-4x} \equiv 3e^{-4x}, \; A = \frac{3}{20}.$

General solution: $y = L\cos 2x + M\sin 2x + \frac{3}{20}e^{-4x}$

(d) $F(x)$ = a sine or cosine.

To solve $(D^2 + 4D + 5)y = 5\sin 3x$.

Clearly a P.I. of $A\sin 3x$ will not do, since this gives on substitution

$$-4A\sin 3x + 12A\cos 3x \equiv 5\sin 3x$$

which requires $A = -\frac{5}{4}$ and also $A = 0$, since there is no cosine term on the right-hand side.

If we try as P.I. $y = A\sin 3x + B\cos 3x$,

$$(D^2 + 4D + 5)(A\sin 3x + B\cos 3x) \equiv 5\sin 3x,$$

or $\quad (44A - 12B)\sin 3x + (12A + 44B)\cos 3x \equiv 5\sin 3x$

which can be satisfied by

$$44A - 12B = 5$$
$$12A + 44B = 0.$$

Solve: $A = \frac{11}{104}$, $B = -\frac{3}{104}$.

The P.I. is $\dfrac{11\sin 3x - 3\cos 3x}{104}$.

The general solution is

$$y = e^{-2x}(L\cos x + M\sin x) + \frac{1}{104}(11\sin 3x - 3\cos 3x)$$

34.21. After the particular integral has been found there still remain the arbitrary constants of the complementary function. Given sufficient " boundary conditions ", we can determine these constants (as in 34.8, Example 7) and so obtain a solution satisfying a specific problem.

Example 17. Solve the equation

$$(D^2 + 3D + 2)y = 10$$

given that $y = 0$ and $Dy = 4$ when $t = 0$.

As above the complete solution is

$$y = Ae^{-2t} + Be^{-t} + 5 \quad . \quad . \quad . \quad . \quad . \quad . \quad . \quad (1)$$

and so far the boundary conditions have not been used.

Since the complete solution holds for the specific case $y = 0$, $t = 0$ substitution in (1) gives

$$0 = A + B + 5$$

Further, from (1)

$$Dy = -2Ae^{-2t} - Be^{-t}$$

Since $Dy = 4$, $t = 0$ holds for this derivative of the complete solution

$$4 = -2A - B$$

Finally $A = 1$, $B = -6$. $y = e^{-2t} - 6e^{-t} + 5$.

EXERCISE 97

1. Show by substitution for y that

$$y = Ae^{-2x} + Be^{3x} - 2$$

satisfies the equation

$$(D^2 - D - 6)y = 12$$

2. Show that

$$y = (A + Bx)e^{-x} + x^2 - 4x + 6$$

satisfies the equation

$$(D^2 + 2D + 1)y = x^2.$$

Find A and B given that $y = 0$ and $Dy = 1$ when $x = 0$.

Find the P.I. for the following equations:

3. $(D^2 + 4D + 7)y = 6$.
4. $(D^2 + 2D + 3)y = 2x + 3$.
5. $(D^2 - 5D - 14)y = 4e^{3x}$.
6. $(D^2 + 9)y = 4 \cos 2x$.

Find the general solution of the equations:

7. $(D^2 + 3D + 2)y = e^{-4x}$.
8. $(D^2 + 5D + 6)x = 2 \sin 3t$.
9. $(D^2 + 4D + 29)x = 3 \sin 4t$.
10. $(D^2 - 8D + 25)y = 7 \cos 5t + 50$.
11. $(D^2 + 4D - 5)x = t^2 + 3t + 5$.
12. $(D^2 - 6D + 10)y = 20 - e^{2x}$.

Solve the differential equations:

13. $(D^2 + 3D + 2)y = e^{2x}$ where $y = 0$, $Dy = 1$ when $x = 0$.
14. $(D^2 + 1)y = 2 \cos^2 x$ where $y = 0$, $Dy = 1$ when $x = 0$. (Express $\cos^2 x$ in terms of $\cos 2x$.)
15. $(D^2 - 3D - 4)y = \sin 2x$ where $y = 2$, $Dy = 4$ when $x = 0$.
16. $(3D^2 - 2D - 1)x = 2t - 1$, given that $x = 7$, $Dx = 2$ when $t = 0$.
17. $(D^2 + 6D + 25)y = 104e^{3x}$ given that $y = 2$ when $x = 0$ and $y = 0$ when $x = \frac{1}{8}\pi$.

18. A body which weighs 32 lb. is moving in a straight line, and it is subject to the following forces along the line when it is x ft. from a fixed point O in the line: (*a*) $5x$ lb. wt. towards O; (*b*) a resistance $4\dot{x}$ lb. wt.; (*c*) a force $2 \cos t$ lb. wt. in the positive direction.

(i) Obtain its equation of motion as

$$(D^2 + 4D + 5)x = 2 \cos t$$

(ii) Obtain also the general solution if $x = 1$ and $\dot{x} = 0$ at $t = 0$.

(iii) Give the steady state solution in the form

$$x = A \sin (wt + \phi),$$

finding A, w and ϕ.

19. A point A moves along OX starting at O with a speed of 2 ft./sec. in the direction OX. Its distance x from O at time t is given by

$$(D^2 + 3D + 2)x = 3t + 2$$

Solve the equation completely and hence find its speed and acceleration at $t = 2$ seconds.

20. A uniform horizontal strut of length l and weight w per unit length is freely supported at its ends and is also subject to a horizontal axial thrust P at each end. With the origin at one end, the x axis measured along the axis of the strut and the y axis measured downwards show that the deflection is given by

$$EI \frac{d^2y}{dx^2} + Py = -\tfrac{1}{2}wx(l - x).$$

or

$$(D^2 + n^2)y = -\frac{w}{2EI} x(l - x) \qquad \left[n^2 = \frac{P}{EI}\right]$$

Solve this completely using the data $y = 0$ when $x = 0$, $Dy = 0$ when $x = \tfrac{1}{2}l$. Hence find the deflection at the centre of the beam.

34.22. Some Special Cases

It is seen that in every case the form assumed for the P.I. is suggested by the right-hand side of the equation. There are, however, difficulties even in simple cases.

(*a*) If we solve

$$(D^2 + 3D)y = 10$$

or

$$D(D + 3)y = 10$$

the C.F. will be found to contain a constant. If we assume a P.I. of $y = C$, a constant, we get an absurd result. This happens because the P.I. assumed occurs already in the C.F. In such a case a working rule is to multiply the assumed P.I. by x. Here we therefore try $y = Cx$, and by substitution

$$D(D + 3)[Cx] \equiv 10$$

$$3C \equiv 10, \ C = \tfrac{10}{3}.$$

General solution: $y = A + Be^{-3x} + \frac{10}{3}x$.

(*b*) In solving $(D^2 + 4D + 3)y = 7e^{-x}$

the C.F. is $Ae^{-x} + Be^{-3x}$.

Since the term e^{-x} of the right-hand side occurs in this C.F. we cannot find the P.I. by assuming $y = Ce^{-x}$. However, $y = Cxe^{-x}$ when substituted will give $C = \frac{7}{2}$.

General solution: $y = Ae^{-x} + Be^{-3x} + \frac{7}{2}xe^{-x}$.

Note: If the differential equation is

$$(D + 1)^2y = 7e^{-x}$$

so that the C.F. is $(A + Bx)e^{-x}$, then since both e^{-x} and xe^{-x} occur in this we must assume $y = Cx^2e^{-x}$ for the P.I. Substitution gives

$$(D + 1)^2[Cx^2e^{-x}] \equiv 7e^{-x}$$

$$2C \equiv 7, \quad C = \tfrac{7}{2}$$

General solution: $y = (A + Bx)e^{-x} + \frac{7}{2}x^2e^{-x}$.

(*c*) In solving $(D^2 + 4)y = \cos 2x$

the C.F. is $A \cos 2x + B \sin 2x$, so we must assume for the P.I.

$$y = x(L \cos 2x + M \sin 2x)$$

substitution gives

$$(D^2 + 4)[x(L \cos 2x + M \sin 2x)] \equiv \cos 2x$$

which reduces to

$$-4L \sin 2x + 4M \cos 2x \equiv \cos 2x$$

$L = 0$, $M = \frac{1}{4}$, P.I. is $\frac{1}{4}x \sin 2x$

General solution: $y = A \cos 2x + B \sin 2x + \frac{1}{4}x \sin 2x$.

The above should be sufficient for most cases. More general methods are given in Volume Two.

EXERCISE 98

Solve completely the equations 1–5.

1. $(D^2 + 4D)y = 6$.
2. $(D^2 - D - 2)y = 3e^{2x}$.
3. $(D^2 + 9)x = 4 \cos 3t$.
4. $(D^2 + 1)y = 3 \sin x$ where $y = 2$, $Dy = 3$ when $x = \dfrac{\pi}{2}$.
5. $(D^2 + 4D + 4)x = e^{-2t}$ where $x = 0$, $Dx = 1$ when $t = 0$.
6. Solve $(D^2 + n^2)x = A \cos wt$

given that $x = a$, $Dx = b$ when $t = 0$.

Write your solution in the form

$$x = a \cos nt + \frac{b}{n} \sin nt + A\left(\frac{\cos wt - \cos nt}{n^2 - w^2}\right)$$

and by evaluating the indeterminate form provided by the last term solve the equation as above when $n \longrightarrow w$, *i.e.*, solve

$$(D^2 + w^2)x = A \cos wt$$

with the above boundary conditions.

7. An inductance L is in series with a condenser C, and this circuit contains an e.m.f. $E_0 \cos nt$ but is of negligible resistance. If i is the current at time t, Q the charge on the condenser plate caused by i and V the p.d. between the plates obtain the equations

$$E_0 \cos nt - L\frac{di}{dt} - V = 0$$

$$i = \frac{dQ}{dt} = C\frac{dV}{dt}.$$

Eliminate i to obtain

$$\frac{d^2V}{dt^2} + \frac{1}{LC}V = \frac{E_0}{LC}\cos nt$$

If $\frac{1}{LC} = n^2$ solve the resulting equation

$$(D^2 + n^2)V = n^2E_0 \cos nt$$

and interpret the result to show that the voltage V becomes very large as t increases.

8. The equation of motion of a particle moving in a straight line under damping is

$$(D^2 + 4D + 5)x = 2a \sin t.$$

Show that x in terms of t, if $x = a$ and $Dx = 0$ when $t = 0$, is given by

$$x = \tfrac{1}{4}ae^{-2t}(9 \sin t + 5 \cos t) + \tfrac{1}{4}a(\sin t - \cos t)$$

and show that as $t \longrightarrow \infty$ the particle tends to describe simple harmonic oscillations with amplitude $\frac{1}{4}a\sqrt{2}$.

9. A particle moves along the x axis, its displacement x at time t being given by

$$(D^2 + 3D + 2)x = 0.$$

show that whatever the initial conditions the particle's final condition is of rest at the origin.

10. A particle's motion is given by

$$(D^2 + 2D + 2)x = \cos t.$$

Show that when t is large the motion is approximately S.H.M. with period 2π.

CHAPTER 35

STATISTICS *

35.1. Introduction

By statistics we will mean the mathematical methods of dealing with large amounts of numerical data. Thus if we measure three 1-inch screws cut by a machine and find their lengths to be 0·95, 1·00, 1·03 in., we shall not need statistics to assess these figures. If, however, we have several thousand such figures, we would need a method or technique to help " size up " the mass of numerical data.

(1) The average or mean length of the screws clearly gives a standard by which to judge the machine's performance.

(2) Since 0·50 and 1·50 in., also 0·99 and 1·01 in., each have a mean value of 1 in., we need an estimate of the distribution of lengths around the mean value. If every screw has a length far removed (above or below) from the mean value of 1, then the machine is not functioning properly. If every length is within the tolerance of say $\pm$ 0·05 we would be well satisfied. A function of the values known as the " standard deviation " has been invented to provide a measure of the dispersion of the values around the mean.

We have referred only to a machine cutting screws. The technique of statistics is used in many branches of engineering and chemistry, *e.g.*, time-and-motion studies, coal and coke burning, textiles, electric lamps, building materials, brewing and the manufacture of chemicals.

35.2. The Arithmetic Mean

If we have N values $x_1, x_2 \dots x_N$ the A.M. or mean is defined as the sum of the values divided by their total number. In symbols

$$\bar{x} = \frac{1}{N}\sum_{r=1}^{N} x_r \quad \dots \dots \dots \quad (1)$$

Amongst these values there may be f_1 with the same value x_1, f_2 of x_2 and generally f_r of x_r, where $\Sigma f_r = N$. In this case

$$\bar{x} = \frac{1}{N}\sum_{r=1}^{N} f_r x_r \quad \dots \dots \dots \quad (2)$$

where some of the f's may be 1.

Suppose we subtract the value x_0 from each value before finding (2).

We have

$$\frac{1}{N}\Sigma f_r(x_r - x_0) = \frac{1}{N}\Sigma f_r x_r - \frac{1}{N}x_0 \Sigma f_r$$

$$= \frac{1}{N}\Sigma f_r x_r - x_0$$

$$= \bar{x} - x_0 \quad . \quad . \quad . \quad . \quad . \quad . \quad . \quad . \quad (3)$$

We will use this method to simplify the multiplication required by (2). We subtract a convenient value x_0 from each value x_r, and after performing the calculations required, $\bar{x}$ is obtained by adding back x_0, according to (3).

Example 1. As a check on a machine filling tins with 1 lb. wt. orange juice, 100 tins were chosen at random from various orders awaiting despatch, and the contents carefully weighed. The following results were found. Find the mean weight.

Weight (lb. wt.), x_r.	Frequency, f_r.	$f_r x_r$.	$x_r - 1$.	$f_r(x_r - 1)$.
0·94	1	0·94	− 0·06	− 0·06
0·95	0	0	− 0·05	0
0·96	3	2·88	− 0·04	− 0·12
0·97	4	3·88	− 0·03	− 0·12
0·98	12	11·76	− 0·02	− 0·24
0·99	19	18·81	− 0·01	− 0·19
1·00	24	24·00	0	− 0·73
1·01	17	17·17	+ 0·01	+ 0·17
1·02	12	12·24	+ 0·02	+ 0·24
1·03	8	8·24	+ 0·03	+ 0·24
	100	99·92		+ 0·65

(*a*) The second column shows the number of tins that have the weight given in the first column.

(*b*) To simplify the arithmetic 1 has been subtracted from each value of x_r and the result shown in column 4.

(*c*) In column 5 the zero value due to 24×0 has been replaced by the sum of the negative values in the column, whilst the sum of the positive values only is shown at the foot of the column.

By formula (2), $\bar{x} = \dfrac{99{\cdot}92}{100} = \underline{0{\cdot}9992.}$

By formula (3) we find

$$\bar{x} = \frac{-0{\cdot}73 + 0{\cdot}65}{100} + 1$$

$$= -0{\cdot}0008 + 1 = \underline{0{\cdot}9992}$$

(we add back $x_0 = 1$ to find $\bar{x}$).

In giving the weight of a tin of juice as 0·94, we really mean $0{\cdot}94 \pm 0{\cdot}005$ lb. wt. The items in the first column of Example 1 could therefore have been given as

$$0{\cdot}935 - 0{\cdot}945, \quad 0{\cdot}945 - 0{\cdot}955, \quad 0{\cdot}955 - 0{\cdot}965, \text{ etc.}$$

Statistical data is often given in this form. Thus the figure 19 in the second column would be opposite 0·985 − 0·995, and would be taken to mean that 19 tins were of weight from 0·985 lb. wt. inclusive, up to but *not including* 0·995 lb. wt. A tin of weight 0·995 lb. wt. is put in the next higher group (or counted as ½ tin in each group). Data not given in this form is often so grouped for convenience of calculation. In the calculation we assume that the value of the group is the value of its mid point.

Example 2. The breaking strength of 150 joins, spot welded under certain conditions, was found and the data grouped as shown. Find the mean value of the breaking strength of a join.

Breaking strength.	Frequency, f_r.	Mid point of interval, x_r.	$x_r - 62\frac{1}{2}$. (Z_r).	$X_r = \frac{1}{5}Z_r$.	f_rX_r.
40–45	2	$42\frac{1}{2}$	-20	-4	-8
45–50	6	$47\frac{1}{2}$	-15	-3	-18
50–55	10	$52\frac{1}{2}$	-10	-2	-20
55–60	28	$57\frac{1}{2}$	-5	-1	-28
60–65	50	$62\frac{1}{2}$	0	0	-74
65–70	31	$67\frac{1}{2}$	$+5$	$+1$	$+31$
70–75	15	$72\frac{1}{2}$	$+10$	$+2$	$+30$
75–80	8	$77\frac{1}{2}$	$+15$	$+3$	$+24$
	150				$+85$

(*a*) We assume that the two joins whose breaking strength is in the range 40–45 each have a breaking strength of the mid value of the range $42\frac{1}{2}$. We therefore replace column (1) by column (3).

(*b*) To simplify the arithmetic we subtract $62\frac{1}{2}$ from each value in column (3) to give column (4).

(*c*) Further to simplify the work we choose a new unit X_r, which is $\frac{1}{5}$ of the values in column (4).

$$\Sigma f_rX_r = -74 + 85 = +11,$$

$$\therefore \quad \bar{x} = 5 \times \tfrac{11}{150} + 62\tfrac{1}{2} = \underline{62{\cdot}9.}$$

35.3. The Standard Deviation

As already stated, the two pairs of measurements 0·50 and 1·50, 0·99 and 1·01 each have a mean value of 1. In the first pair each value is far removed from the required value of 1, whilst in the second pair each value is suitably near to this required mean. We therefore need a measure of the extent of the scattering of the values about the mean. The sum of the deviations from the mean will not do, for this is zero.

$$\sum_1^N(x_r - \bar{x}) = \sum_1^N x_r - \sum_1^N \bar{x} = N\bar{x} - N\bar{x} = 0.$$

To avoid this, we square the values before adding and divide by their number N to find the average value of the sum of the squares. To reduce this result back to the same units as the original values, we then take the square root of this average value. This result is called the standard deviation and denoted by σ (sigma).* In words, the standard deviation is the square root of the average of the squares of the deviations of the values from their mean. In symbols

$$\sigma = \sqrt{\left\{\frac{1}{N}\{(x_1 - \bar{x})^2 + (x_2 - \bar{x})^2 + \ldots (x_N - \bar{x})^2\}\right\}}$$

$$= \sqrt{\left\{\frac{\Sigma(x_r - \bar{x})^2}{N}\right\}} \quad . \quad . \quad . \quad . \quad . \quad . \quad . \quad . \quad . \quad . \quad . \quad (4)$$

* σ^2, *i.e.* (4) or (5) without the square root sign is called the *variance*.

If a number of these values are the same so that we have f_1 values of x_1, f_2 values of x_2, etc., then

$$\sigma = \sqrt{\left\{\frac{1}{N}\Sigma f_r(x_r - \bar{x})^2\right\}} \quad . \quad . \quad . \quad . \quad . \quad . \quad (5)$$

As an illustration we will find σ in two simple examples.

I			II		
Number, x_r.	Deviation, $x_r - 50$.	(Deviation)^2.	Number, x_r.	Deviation, $x_r - 50$.	(Deviation)^2.
49·9 50 50·1	− 0·1 0 0·1	+ 0·01 0 0·01	5 50 95	− 45 0 + 45	2025 0 2025
150	0	0·02	150	0	4050
$\bar{x} = \frac{150}{3} = 50$ $\sigma = \sqrt{\frac{0\cdot02}{3}} = 0\cdot082$			$\bar{x} = \frac{150}{3} = 50$ $\sigma = \sqrt{\frac{4050}{3}} = 36\cdot7$		

These results show that two sets of values can have the same mean, but their different distribution around this mean will result in very different values for their respective standard deviations.

35.4. Short Method for Calculation of Standard Deviation

If the mean of a set of values is not an integer, the work required to subtract it from the values and square the result can be heavy. We can reduce this by working with an arbitrary origin or fictitious mean and then adjust the result according to a formula now to be obtained.

We have N values $x_1, x_2, x_3 \ldots x_N$, whose mean is $\bar{x}$.

Let A be a chosen convenient fictitious mean; $d = \bar{x} - A$, the deviation of the mean from A; S the fictitious standard deviation using A as the mean.

By the definition of standard deviation

$$S^2 = \frac{1}{N}\Sigma f_r(x_r - A)^2,$$

$$\therefore \quad NS^2 = \Sigma f_r[(x_r - \bar{x}) + (\bar{x} - A)]^2 = \Sigma f_r[(x_r - \bar{x}) + d]^2,$$

where we have introduced $\bar{x}$ on the R.H.S. in an obvious way.

$$\therefore \quad NS^2 = \Sigma f_r(x_r - \bar{x})^2 + 2\Sigma f_r(x_r - \bar{x})d + \Sigma f_r d^2$$
$$= \Sigma f_r(x_r - \bar{x})^2 + 2d\Sigma f_r(x_r - \bar{x}) + d^2\Sigma f_r,$$

but $\Sigma f_r(x_r - \bar{x}) = 0$, being the sum of the deviations from the mean.

Also $\qquad \Sigma f_r = N, \quad \Sigma f_r(x_r - \bar{x})^2 = N\sigma^2,$

$$\therefore \quad NS^2 = N\sigma^2 + Nd^2,$$
$$\sigma^2 = S^2 - d^2$$
$$= S^2 - (\bar{x} - A)^2.$$

We may therefore find S, the fictitious standard deviation from any convenient number A and reduce it to σ the required true standard deviation from the mean by this formula.

It may help to note that S, σ, d are the three sides of a right-angled triangle with S as the hypotenuse.

There is another useful form. Put $X_r = x_r - A$, where A, as above, is any convenient number chosen usually so as to reduce the size of the numbers x_r, and hence the arithmetic; it can, of course, be zero. Add up the series of equations

$$X_r = x_r - A \qquad (r = 1, 2, \ldots)$$

to obtain
$$\Sigma f_r X_r = \Sigma f_r x_r - NA.$$

Divide by N:
$$\bar{X} = \bar{x} - A$$

hence
$$(\bar{x} - A)^2 = \bar{X}^2 = [\Sigma(f_r X_r)/N]^2$$

and
$$S^2 = \frac{1}{N}\Sigma f_r(x_r - A)^2 = \frac{1}{N}\Sigma f_r X_r^2.$$

Instead of
$$\sigma^2 = S^2 - (\bar{x} - A)^2$$

we now have

$$\sigma^2 = \frac{1}{N}\Sigma f_r X_r^2 - \left[\frac{\Sigma f_r X_r}{N}\right]^2$$

$$= \frac{1}{N}\left\{\Sigma f_r X_r^2 - \frac{(\Sigma f_r X_r)^2}{N}\right\}$$

where each value X_r occurs f_r times. This formula is particularly useful for grouped data where there could be p groups, so that $r = 1, 2, \ldots p$ and $\sum_1^p f_r = N$ the total frequency. Example 3 following uses this formula in the alternative solution.

Example 3. 143 samples of metal were tested for hardness with results shown in the table. Find the standard deviation of the results.

Degrees of hardness. (1)	Mid. point. x_r. (2)	Frequency, f_r. (3)	$x_r - 94$. (4)	New unit $X_r = \frac{1}{2}(x_r - 94)$ (5)	$f_r X_r$. (6)	$f_r X_r^2$. (7)
89–91	90	17·5	− 4	− 2	− 35	70
91–93	92	21·5	− 2	− 1	− 21·5	21·5
					− 56·5	
93–95	94	32	0	0		0
95–97	96	38	2	1	+ 38	38
97–99	98	17	4	2	+ 34	68
99–101	100	17	6	3	+ 51	153
		143			+ 123	350·5
					+ 66·5	

(*a*) The value 17·5 for the number of samples whose degree of hardness was in the range 89–91 means that an odd number of samples were found whose degree was exactly 91. For accuracy these were regarded as half in group 89–91 and half in group 91–93.

(*b*) The figures in column (4) are not large, but to show the general method we have chosen a new unit.

(*c*) Owing to the choice of a new unit, column (6) is half of its proper value and column (7) one quarter. Therefore

$$S^2 = \frac{4\Sigma f_r X^2_r}{N} = \frac{4 \times 350{\cdot}5}{143} = 9{\cdot}804$$

$$\bar{x} = \frac{2\Sigma f_r X_r}{N} + 94 = 0{\cdot}932 + 94 = 94{\cdot}932.$$

$$\sigma^2 = S^2 - d^2$$

$$= 9{\cdot}804 - (94{\cdot}932 - 94)^2 = 8{\cdot}935$$

$$\sigma = \underline{2{\cdot}99 \text{ units of hardness.}}$$

OR

$$\sigma^2 = \frac{1}{143}\left\{350{\cdot}5 - \frac{(66{\cdot}5)^2}{143}\right\}$$

$$= 2{\cdot}236 \text{ new units}$$

$$= 4 \times 2{\cdot}236 \text{ original units}$$

$$\sigma = \underline{2{\cdot}99} \text{ units of hardness}$$

35.5. Histograms and Frequency Curves. The Normal Curve

It is found very useful to draw graphs of the "frequency tables" given in the above examples. Thus for Example 1 we will draw the usual graph of the frequency f_r against the weight x_r of the tins. Instead of erecting an ordinate of height 1 over the value 0·94 we prefer to draw a rectangle of height 1 and base 0·935—0·945, a range which has 0·94 as its mid point and covers half the distance to the next given value 0·95. In this way a "histogram" is obtained (Fig. 109)

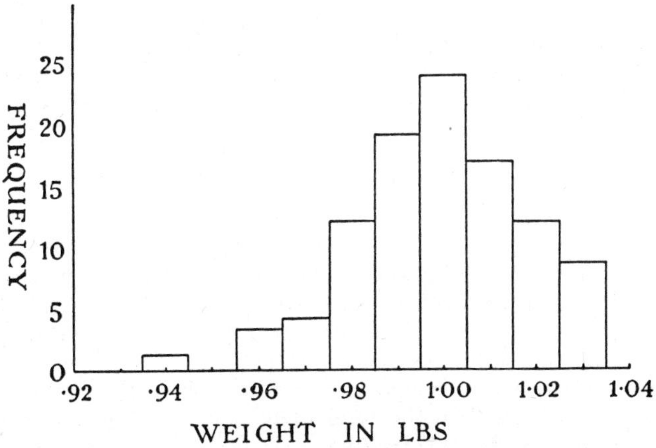

FIG. 109.

Histogram of the number of tins of a given weight. (Example 1.)

in which the area of each rectangle is proportional to the number of items it represents since the bases are all equal.

From our experience in drawing such figures when the total frequency is very large instead of being such a small figure as 100, we believe that the irregularities are due to the paucity of data, and a very large amount of data would give a figure with a smoother outline as shown in Fig. 110. Thus in the above example we cannot weigh the

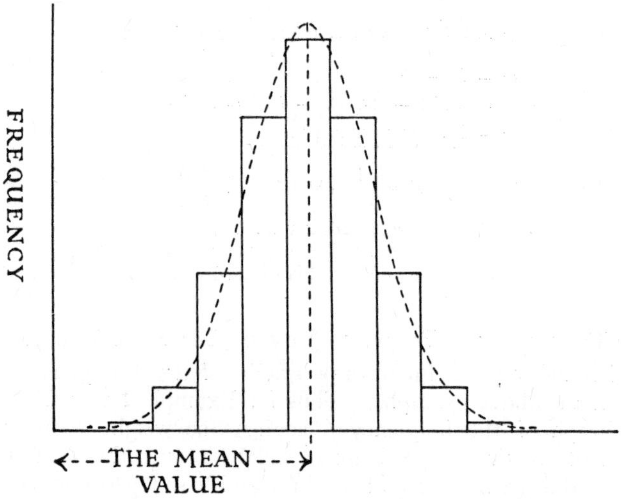

FIG. 110.

The histogram shows the shape expected for Fig. 109 if several thousand tins had been tested.

tins to the nearest 0·001 lb. for with the grouping 0·9395–0·9405 lb., 0·9405–0·9415 lb., etc., we would find that many of the groups had no tins of that weight and the resulting histogram would be very irregular. With a large number of tins we find that the smaller the unit of measurement on the base the more regular the outline of the histogram becomes. Finally we would have a series of rectangles varying so that their outline would represent, in many (but not all) cases of interest to the scientist, a smooth continuous curve known as the " normal curve of distribution ". The various stages in the change of outline of curve towards this normal curve are shown in Fig. 111.

In Fig. 110 by drawing a smooth curve approximately through the mid points of the upper boundaries of the rectangles, we have a curve the area beneath which is equal to the total area of the rectangles and therefore proportional to the total frequency. As the base per rectangle becomes smaller this task becomes easier, and finally we have a normal curve " fitted " to the data, a normal curve whose area is proportional to the total frequency involved. Since the area between the

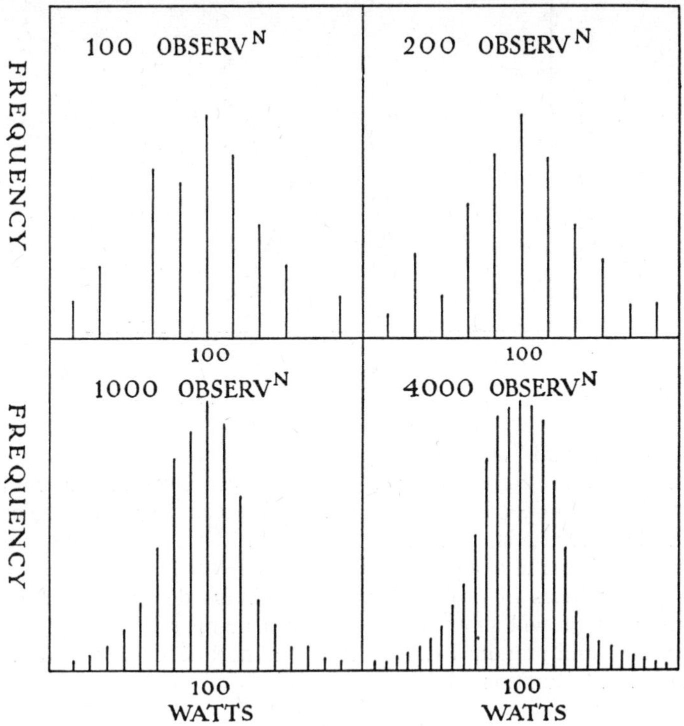

FIG. 111.

Frequency distributions for various numbers of 100 watt lamps tested for power consumption in watts.

ordinates erected at x_1 and x_2 is the sum of a large number of rectangles between x_1 and x_2, with their upper boundaries on the curve, and each such rectangle represents a frequency, we see that the area between x_1 and x_2 represents a frequency which is the number of items in the given data which have a value between x_1 and x_2. If the normal curve is $y = \phi(x)$, then the total area under the curve may be written as

$$\int_{-\infty}^{+\infty} \phi(x)dx.$$

even if $\phi(x)$ in practice is zero outside a certain range.

The area between x_1 and x_2 will be

$$\int_{x_1}^{x_2} \phi(x)dx.$$

The ratio of these two areas will be the proportion of the total frequency between x_1 and x_2.

The data obtained in engineering and other investigations is often

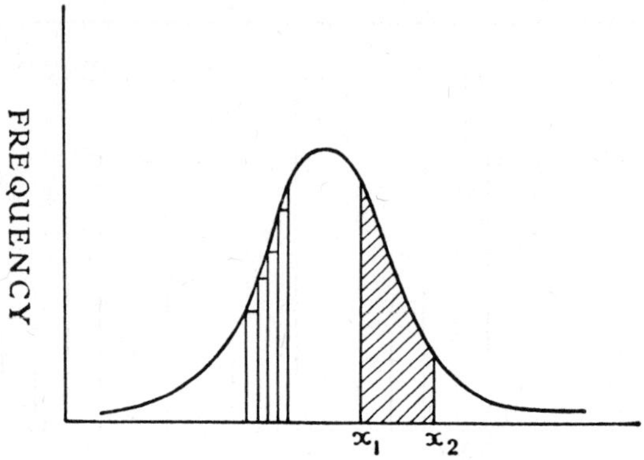

FIG. 112.
The Normal Curve of Distribution.

in this " normal " form. Even when it is not accurately so, the error in taking it to be " normal " is not great. Once this assumption is made, the properties of the normal curve can be used and enable valuable conclusions to be drawn from such data, even when present only in " small samples ". To proceed further requires some elementary ideas in probability. This will be dealt with later. In Chapter 38 we will show that for a given number N of values whose mean is $\bar{x}$ and standard deviation σ, the normal curve fitted to the data has the equation

$$y = \frac{N}{\sigma\sqrt{(2\pi)}} e^{-\frac{1}{2\sigma^2}(x-\bar{x})^2}$$

EXERCISE 99

1. Find the mean value for the following two series of figures:

(a)

x_r.	f_r.
61·5–62·5	1
62·5–	2
63·5–	3
64·5–	4
65·5–	8
66·5–	12
67·5–	13
68·5–	18
69·5–	14
70·5–	10
71·5–	5
72·5–	4
73·5–	3
74·5–	2
75·5–76·5	1
Total	100

(b)

x_r.	f..
80	3
82	10
84	6·5
86	10·5
88	16·5
90	17·5
92	21·5
94	32
96	38
98	17
100	17
102	8·5
104	6·5
106	6
108	1·5
110	2
Total	214

2. Find the standard deviation for each of the following sets of figures:

(*a*) 74, 75, 78, 72, 77, 78, 79, 78, 81, 76, 72, 72, 77, 74, 70, 78, 79, 80, 81, 74, 80, 75, 71, 73.

(*b*) 89, 88, 80, 84, 86, 85, 86, 82, 82, 79, 86, 80, 82, 76, 86, 89, 87, 83, 80, 88, 86, 81, 84, 87.

3. A batch of 200 metal bars was made to a supposed length of 34 in. On measurement the number n of bars of length l was found to be:

l . .	30	31	32	33	34	35	36	37	38	39
n . .	4	8	23	35	62	44	18	4	1	1

Draw a frequency diagram and calculate: (i) the mean length; (ii) the standard deviation from the mean. [L.U.]

4. Define the *mean* and *standard deviation* of a set of observations. In the following table f is the frequency of an observation x.

x . .	2·7	2·9	3·1	3·3	3·5	3·7
f . .	2	7	15	21	12	3

Calculate the mean and standard deviation of x. [L.U.]

5. The table below gives the annual sunshine in hours, rounded to the nearest 10 hours, at a certain meteorological station. Find the mean annual sunshine in this 10-year period and the standard deviation.

Year	1940	1941	1942	1943	1944	1945	1946	1947	1948	1949
Sunshine, hrs. . . .	1470	1200	1330	1470	1190	1470	1300	1430	1360	1580

[L.U.]

6. Two separate distributions have numbers, mean and standard deviations as shown.

$$n_1 = 20,\ \bar{x}_1 = 5,\ \sigma_1 = 3$$
$$n_2 = 30,\ \bar{x}_2 = 7,\ \sigma_2 = 4.$$

Show that when these are combined in one distribution of 50 values the mean is 6·2 and the standard deviation 3·76.

7. The mean of 50 readings of a variable was 7·43 and their standard deviation 0·28. The following 10 additional readings became available:

6·80, 7·81, 7·58, 7·70, 8·05, 6·98, 7·78, 7·85, 7·21, 7·40.

If these are included with the original 50 readings show that the mean and standard deviation of the 60 readings are 7·44 and 0·30 respectively.

8. The standard deviations of two samples, each of n observations are s_1 and s_2, their respective means being m_1 and m_2. Show that the standard deviation s of the combined sample of $2n$ observations is

$$s^2 = \tfrac{1}{2}(s_1{}^2 + s_2{}^2) + \tfrac{1}{4}(m_1 - m_2)^2.$$

9. Two samples have (n_1, m_1, s_1), (n_2, m_2, s_2) observations, mean value and standard deviation respectively. Show that the standard deviation s of the combined samples is given by

$$s^2 = \frac{n_1 s_1{}^2 + n_2 s_2{}^2}{n_1 + n_2} + \frac{n_1 n_2 (m_1 - m_2)^2}{(n_1 + n_2)^2}.$$

10. Four boys sit for an examination. The average of their marks is M and the standard deviation σ. The marks are converted to a new scale by the formula

$$y = 50 - 20(\mathrm{M} - x)/\sigma$$

where y, x are respectively the new and old marks. (*a*) Find the mean and standard deviation of the new marks.

(*b*) If the original marks were 47, 57, 65, 71 find the new marks, each to the nearest integer. [L.U.]

11. Given that

$$f(x) = x(4 - x) \qquad 0 \leqslant x \leqslant 4$$

is a frequency distribution so that $f(x)dx$ is the number of values between x and $x + dx$. Use the formula of 24.3 on centres of gravity to find the mean value $\bar{x}$ of the distribution. Find also the square of the radius of gyration of the area about the y axis and hence, by using

$$\sigma^2 = \mathrm{S}^2 - \bar{x}^2,$$

the variance of the distribution.

12. For the distribution

$$y = 100 \exp(-10x) \qquad 0 \leqslant x \leqslant \infty$$

find the mean and variance.

13. The second moment about the line $x = A$ of the distribution $y = f(x)$ is given by

$$y = \int_{-\infty}^{+\infty} (x - A)^2 f(x)dx \qquad \left[\text{where} \int_{-\infty}^{+\infty} f(x)dx = 1\right]$$

Show that y is a minimum when $A = \bar{x}$, the mean value of the distribution. Hence the variance is the minimum value possible of the second moment. [Assume that the processes of differentiation and integration may be interchanged and solve for $dy/dx = 0$.]

CHAPTER 36

PROBABILITY

36.1. Introduction

If a penny is tossed repeatedly and the outcome, heads or tails, noted a sequence, perhaps the following, is obtained.

H T T H H H T H T . . .

This is an example of the repeatable similar events with which probability theory is concerned. In the above sequence the occurrence of an H or T is random, *i.e.*, unpredictable, but the **proportion** of the whole number of tosses in which they occur is usually predictable within known limits.

In three separate experiments, in each of which a coin was tossed 1000 times the proportion of heads obtained each time was 0·476, 0·529 and 0·497 respectively, confirming our belief that for the usual coin the **theoretical** proportion is one half.

Our aim is to develop a method for obtaining and using such results. In the above example probability theory will provide the theoretical value of 1/2 for the proportion of heads. Statistical theory will provide a formula for the range within which the experimental value should lie if the coin is unbiased. If N is the number of tosses per experiment and p the theoretical proportion of heads, a formula is

$$p \pm 1{\cdot}96\sqrt{[p(1-p)/N]}.$$

Here $p = \frac{1}{2}$, $N = 1000$. Substitution gives for the range a value

$$0{\cdot}500 \pm 0{\cdot}062.$$

Since the results obtained above lie within this range, we have no reason to suspect the balance of the coin used. If this data referred to industrial mass production, the results could be used as a check on the quality of the components produced. It is the aim of Theoretical Statistics to use Probability Theory to find such appropriate tests but requiring only a small number of " experiments ".

36.2. The Definition

If we throw the usual six-faced die in the hope of obtaining a 4 there are six faces which are " equally likely " to show up, of these only one will show the value 4. We would therefore take the ratio (one face showing the required outcome of 4)/(six faces that could show up), *i.e.*, 1/6 as the probability of obtaining a 4 in a single throw. In effect, the proportion of times we could **expect** a 4 to show in a large number of throws is 1/6.

This leads to the definition:

The probability of the occurrence of a given event A is equal to the ratio of the number of cases which are favourable to A to the total number of possible cases, provided that all these cases are equally likely.

If P(A) denotes the probability of the event A happening, n the number of cases favourable to A and N the total number of possible cases in the experiment

$$P(A) = \frac{n}{N} = \frac{\text{Number of favourable cases}}{\text{Total number of possible cases}}.$$

Example 1. If two dice are thrown on to a table and the faces uppermost noted there are 36 equally likely combinations of the faces, since each face on one can occur with any one of the six faces on the other. If we require a total of 4, there are only 3 ways in which this can occur by the two faces showing respectively (1, 3) or (2, 2) or (3, 1). By the definition P (obtaining a 4) = 3/36 = 1/12.

36.3. Another Definition

If 10 rubber tyres are tested and 3 found to be defective the proportion of tyres defective is 3/10, a value which could be taken as applying to the rest of the batch. Suppose the tyres as tested give the sequence

G, D, G, G, D, G, G, G, G, D,

where G denotes a good and D a defective tyre. If the proportion of tyres defective is calculated after each test we have the sequence of proportions

$$\tfrac{0}{1}, \tfrac{1}{2}, \tfrac{1}{3}, \tfrac{1}{4}, \tfrac{2}{5}, \tfrac{2}{6}, \tfrac{2}{7}, \tfrac{2}{8}, \tfrac{2}{9}, \tfrac{3}{10}.$$

The final figure must be taken as the limit of the sequence and called the proportion of the event, for we, presumably, have no more data.

This variation in the value of the proportion shows the necessity for testing as large a random batch as possible if the result obtained is to be of any use as a guide to the quality of the main batch. This leads to another definition of probability:

A batch of size N is tested and *n* of this batch are found to have the feature A. The probability of the feature A in the batch is given by

$$P(A) = \lim. (n/N).$$

The limit means that N is taken as large as possible, and the final value of the ratio is used as the proportion or probability required. The two definitions can easily be shown to imply the same result in most cases. We will regard them as equivalent and obtain the value of the probability by whichever method can be applied to the data of a problem. In both cases the same probability laws apply.

Example 2. A carton contains 100 batteries, of which 10 are defective. If 5 are chosen at random from the 100 and sold to a customer, find the chance that he receives: (*a*) no defective; (*b*) one defective; (*c*) at most one defective.

There are ${}_{100}C_5$ ways of choosing 5 out of 100, and this is the total number of possible outcomes to the experiment.

(*a*) The number of ways in which a sample of no defectives can be chosen is ${}_{90}C_5$, since we must choose 5 good from the 90 good batteries. Hence

$$P \text{ (no defective)} = {}_{90}C_5/{}_{100}C_5 = \frac{90!}{5!\ 85!} \times \frac{5!\ 95!}{100!} = \frac{90!\ 95!}{85!\ 100!} = \underline{0{\cdot}5837.}$$

[log (90!)		138·1719
(95!)		148·0141
		286·1860
(85!)	128·4498	
(100!)	157·9700	286·4198
		$\bar{1}$·7662]

(see footnote *)

If trays of batteries, 100 per tray, were tested by an inspector who extracted at random 5 per tray for testing, in some 584 trays per 1000 examined he would find no defectives in the sample of 5 tested, although each tray contained 10 defective.

(*b*) The number of ways of choosing 1 defective from the 10 is ${}_{10}C_1$. The independent number of ways of choosing 4 good from the 90 good batteries is ${}_{90}C_4$. Hence

$${}_{10}C_1 \times {}_{90}C_4$$

is the total number of favourable outcomes and

$$P \text{ (1 def. and 4 good)} = \frac{{}_{10}C_1 \times {}_{90}C_4}{{}_{100}C_5}$$

$$= 10 \times \frac{90!}{4!\ 86!} \times \frac{5!\ 95!}{100!} = \underline{0{\cdot}3394.}$$

This result could be tested by an experiment in which we use a large basin containing 90 white beads and 10 red, all of the same weight and size. These represent respectively the good and defective components above. After stirring well 5 beads are drawn at random and it is noted when only 1 red bead occurs in the draw. The 5 are returned to the basin and after stirring the draw is repeated. As this proceeds it will be found that the ratio (number of draws in which only 1 red bead occurs)/(total number of draws) varies within a range which appears to be narrowing down on the above ratio of 0·3394.

(*c*) Since the number of ways in which at most 1 defective can occur is the sum of the number of ways in which 1 or none can occur, it is

$${}_{10}C_1 \times {}_{90}C_4 + {}_{90}C_5.$$

Hence the probability of this event is the above sum divided by the total number of ways in which the 5 can be drawn or

$$\begin{aligned} P \text{ (1 or none def.)} &= ({}_{10}C_1 \times {}_{90}C_4 + {}_{90}C_5)/{}_{100}C_5 \\ &= P \text{ (1 def.)} + P \text{ (none def.)} \\ &= 0{\cdot}3394 + 0{\cdot}5837 = \underline{0{\cdot}9231.} \end{aligned}$$

It will be noticed that these two events are mutually exclusive, *i.e.*, only one can occur in a given draw of 5. It will be proved later that, as shown above, in such a case the separate probabilities are added to give the probability of either one or the other event happening.

* Log factorial tables are given at the end of the book.

36.4. If we test N components and find n of them with a special feature, clearly

$$0 \leqslant n \leqslant N$$

Division by N changes this to

$$0 \leqslant n/N \leqslant 1 \quad \text{or} \quad 0 \leqslant p \leqslant 1$$

where p denotes the chance of a random choice of one from the batch of N giving a component with this special feature.

This shows that a probability is always a positive number between 0 and 1. If $n = 0$, the event cannot happen, then $p = 0$ and is the chance of an impossible event. If $n = N$ so that the event of choosing a specially marked component is certain to happen, then $p = 1$, the chance of a certain event.

Since $N - n$ do not show this special feature, the chance of not picking a special one from the batch of N is

$$(N - n)/N = N/N - n/N = 1 - p.$$

This chance of failing in the event is usually denoted by q if p is the chance of a success. Hence

$$q = 1 - p \text{ or } p + q = 1$$

an important relation between the chances of an event happening and not happening. Since one of these mutually exclusive events is certain to happen, the sum of the chances is the chance of a certain event or 1, another illustration of the theorem referred to above in Example 2.

EXERCISE 100

1. A six-sided die is thrown once. What is the chance of it showing: (*a*) 2; (*b*) an even number; (*c*) the numbers 3 or 5; (*d*) a number greater than 4?

2. When two coins are tossed what are the chances that: (*a*) both show heads; (*b*) one head and one tail is shown?

3. A 3-digit number is formed by randomly choosing three of the digits 1, 2, 3, 4, 5 without repetition. What is the chance that the number is: (*a*) even; (*b*) odd; (*c*) a multiple of 5?

4. A coin is tossed 3 times. Find the chance that the outcomes are (*a*) H, H, T in this order; (*b*) H appears twice only; (*c*) T appears at least once.

5. A die is thrown 3 times and we require the chance that the total sum shown is 9. By listing the possible favourable outcomes show that the given table applies. Hence complete the question.

Outcome of first throw.	Number of ways of getting a total of 9.
1	5
2	6
3	5
4	4
5	3
6	2

Show that the coefficient of x^9 in

$$(x + x^2 + \ldots + x^6)^3 = x^3(1 - x^6)^3/(1 - x)^3$$

gives the same total of number of ways.

6. Two dice are thrown on to a table. Find the number of ways in which a total of (*a*) 7, (*b*) 8 can be obtained. Find the chance that a total of (*c*) 7, (*d*) 8, (*e*) either 7 or 8 points is obtained.

7. There are 5 nuts and 5 bolts, of which 1 nut and 2 bolts are defective. (*a*) How many different combinations, nut plus bolt, can be made? (*b*) How many of these pairs are defective due to at least one member being defective? (*c*) If a completed pair is chosen at random, what is the chance that it is defective?

8. There are 6 tickets to be sold in the order of application. A queue of 6 men and 4 women will apply. Find the chance that the tickets are sold to: (*a*) the 6 men; (*b*) 4 men and 2 women; (*c*) at least 2 women.

9. A man fires at a circular target of radius 10 in. and 80 per cent. of his shots are hits. If a successful shot is equally likely to hit any part of the target, find the chance that: (*a*) any shot scores an "inner" if the outer radius of this inner area is 4 in.; (*b*) a successful shot lands on an annulus of inner and outer radii 4 in. and 8 in. respectively; (*c*) any shot lands in this area.

10. A sample of 3 is to be selected from a batch of 20 articles. (*a*) How many different samples are possible? (*b*) If the batch contains 1 defective, how many samples will contain it? (*c*) What is the chance that a random sample will contain the defective?

11. A random sample of 4 is chosen from a batch of 12 articles, of which 3 are defective. Find the chance that the sample will contain 2 or more defective.

12. A biased coin is tossed a large number of times and gives a head 3 times out of 5. Find the chance that in 4 throws, 2 heads and 2 tails are obtained.

13. A sample of 10 springs contains 3 defective. If 2 are chosen from the sample for a test find the chance that: (*a*) both are defective; (*b*) none is defective.

14. A bag holds 3 white and 4 red balls, all identical except for colour. If 3 are drawn at random, find the chance that one is white and two are red. Find this chance if the balls are drawn one at a time, the colour noted, the ball replaced and the bag well shaken before the next draw.

15. A group consists of 10 men and 4 girls. If a committee is formed by choosing 3 of the group, find the chance that it contains 2 men and 1 girl.

16. A batch of 20 articles contains 3 defective. A random sample of 5 is chosen. What are the chances that the sample contains 0, 1, 2 or 3 defective? Find the sum of these four chances of mutually exclusive events and explain the result.

17. A group of 30 articles contains 10 defectives. What is the chance that a sample of 4 will contain: (*a*) no defective; (*b*) 1 defective? Find in the easiest way available: (*c*) the chance that the sample contains more than 1 defective.

18. A consignment of switches is packed in boxes of 100 each. A box is inspected by testing 20 chosen at random from it and the box rejected if any one of the 20 is found to be faulty. What is the chance of rejecting a box containing 2 defective?

19. An insecticide is used on flies. It is found that 80 per cent. are killed on the first application, but that those which survive develop a resistance so that the *proportion* of survivors killed in any subsequent application is only one-half of the proportion of the immediately preceding application. Find the probability that: (*a*) a fly will survive 5 applications of insecticide; (*b*) having survived the first it will survive 4 more applications.

[Consider the successive survivals of an original group of 100 flies.]

36.5. Compound Characteristics

Suppose that two machines A and B are being compared for output and efficiency. The output is shown in the following table. The number per machine $(n_1 + n_3)$ from A and $(n_2 + n_4)$ from B are further subdivided according to the number produced of defective (D) or good (G). Thus, of the total of $N = n_1 + n_2 + n_3 + n_4$ machine A produced $n_1 + n_3$, of which n_1 were defective and n_3 good. Similar figures for B are as given.

		STATE		
		D	G	Total
MACHINE	A	n_1	n_3	$n_1 + n_3$
	B	n_2	n_4	$n_2 + n_4$
	Total	$n_1 + n_2$	$n_3 + n_4$	N $[= n_1 + n_2 + n_3 + n_4]$.

It will be noticed that an article can only occur in one of the four categories, *i.e.*, the " events " are mutually exclusive and no component is counted more than once.

From this table we can put down the various probabilities, *e.g.*, that an article chosen from the total batch of N will have come from one of the four main groups.

The chance that an article drawn from the N is made by machine A is

$$\mathrm{P(A)} = (n_1 + n_3)/\mathrm{N} \quad . \; . \; . \; . \; . \; . \; . \quad (1)$$

Similarly,

$$\mathrm{P(D)} = (n_1 + n_2)/\mathrm{N} \quad . \; . \; . \; . \; . \; . \; . \quad (2)$$

and so for the others.

If A∪D means that the article was made by A or was defective D or both defective and also made by A, since $n_1 + n_2 + n_3$ have this characteristic

$$\mathrm{P(A \cup D)} = (n_1 + n_2 + n_3)/\mathrm{N} \quad . \; . \; . \; . \quad (3)$$

If AD means that the article was both in the A and D groups

$$\mathrm{P(AD)} = \frac{n_1}{\mathrm{N}} \quad . \; . \; . \; . \; . \; . \; . \; . \quad (4)$$

Now (3) can be rearranged as

$$\mathrm{P(A \cup D)} = \frac{(n_1 + n_3) + (n_1 + n_2) - n_1}{\mathrm{N}}$$

$$= \mathrm{P(A)} + \mathrm{P(D)} - \mathrm{P(AD)} \quad . \; . \; . \; . \quad (5)$$

giving the *Addition Rule*:

The chance that at least one of two events occurs is equal to the sum of the separate probabilities of each event less the probability of both events occurring simultaneously.

Example 3. A batch of 10 pencils contain 4 red (R), 5 black (B) and 1 yellow (Y). These pencils are also hard (H) or soft (S) as shown by the following scheme:

R R R R B B B B B Y
S H H H H H S H H S

e.g., the first column showing that the first pencil is both red and soft.

Since

$$\mathrm{P(R)} = \frac{4}{10}, \; \mathrm{P(H)} = \frac{7}{10}, \; \mathrm{P(RH)} = \frac{3}{10}$$

the probability of choosing at random a pencil that is either red or hard or both is

$$\mathrm{P(R \cup H)} = \frac{4}{10} + \frac{7}{10} - \frac{3}{10} = \frac{8}{10}.$$

If we group the pencils as above, by counting,

	R	not R	
H	(3)	(4)	7
not H	(1)	2	3
	4	6	(10)

the same result is obtained immediately from the figures in brackets.

36.6. Mutually Exclusive Events

If the events A and D are mutually exclusive so that they cannot both occur, *i.e.*, $n_1 = 0$, then P(AD) = 0 and (5) now becomes

$$P(A \cup D) = P(A) + P(D) \quad . \quad . \quad . \quad . \quad . \quad (6)$$

This can be generalized for a number of *mutually exclusive* events to give

$$P(A \cup B \cup C \ . \ . \ .) = P(A) + P(B) + P(C) + \ . \ . \ . \ . \quad (7)$$

which is called the *theorem of total probability*:

The chance of the occurrence of at least one of a number of mutually exclusive events is the sum of the separate chances of occurrence of each event.

We have already used this theorem in the examples on the original definition. Thus, if 2 dice are tossed and we want the chance of getting a 4 we can consider that there are 3 ways of getting this, by the pairs (1, 3), (2, 2), (3, 1). The probability is then 3/36. But these are three mutually exclusive events, since the pair of dice can show only one sum per toss. Hence

$$\begin{aligned} P(4) &= P(1, 3) + P(2, 2) + P(3, 1) \\ &= \frac{1}{36} + \frac{1}{36} + \frac{1}{36} = \frac{3}{36}. \end{aligned}$$

Suppose A* denotes the opposite event to A, *i.e.*, the event which occurs when A does not. A and A* are then mutually exclusive events, and since $A \cup A^*$ is a certain event where $P(AA^*) = 0$,

$$1 = P(A \cup A^*) = P(A) + P(A^*)$$

or the sum of the chances of an event and its opposite is always unity. This has already been shown with the more usual notation

$$p + q = 1.$$

Similarly, if a series of mutually exclusive events cover every possible outcome to an experiment the sum of their respective probabilities is the chance of a certain event, *i.e.*, 1.

Example 4. Find the chance of getting at least one 6 in four throws of a die.
There are $5 \times 5 \times 5 \times 5 = 5^4$ ways of not getting a 6 in four throws. There are 6^4 possible combinations of the faces. Hence the chance of not getting a 6 is $(5/6)^4$. Since the opposite of " no 6 " is " at least one 6 "

$$P \text{ (at least one 6)} = 1 - (5/6)^4 = \underline{0{\cdot}518.}$$

Example 5. A batch of 100 total contains 10 defective. An inspector tests 20 from the batch. If he finds more than 1 defective he will reject the entire batch. Find the proportion of batches rejected.

If $P(n)$ denotes the chance of finding n defective we require to evaluate

$$P(2) + P(3) + \ldots + P(10).$$

But

$$P(0) + P(1) + P(2) + \ldots + P(10)$$

is the chance of a certain event, and this sum is therefore 1. Hence an easier way is to find

$$\begin{aligned} & 1 - [P(0) + P(1)] \\ &= 1 - \left[\frac{{}_{90}C_{20}}{{}_{100}C_{20}} + \frac{{}_{10}C_1 \times {}_{90}C_{19}}{{}_{100}C_{20}}\right] \\ &= 1 - (0{\cdot}0951 + 0{\cdot}2679) \\ &= \underline{0{\cdot}637.} \end{aligned}$$

Some 64 per cent. of the batches tested will be rejected by this inspection scheme.

36.7. The Multiplication Law

We will now make a further use of the basic 2×2 table of section 5.

By P(D/A) we will mean the chance of choosing a D article given that it is an A article, *i.e.*, that it is chosen from the sub-group of A articles. This is called the conditional (or relative) probability relative to A whilst P(D) is called an absolute probability.

From the table

$$P(D/A) = n_1/(n_1 + n_3)$$

hence

$$\begin{aligned} P(AD) = n_1/N &= \frac{(n_1 + n_3)}{N} \cdot \frac{n_1}{(n_1 + n_3)} \\ &= P(A) \,.\, P(D/A) \quad \ldots \quad (8) \end{aligned}$$

Alternatively,

$$\begin{aligned} n_1/N &= \frac{(n_1 + n_2)}{N} \cdot \frac{n_1}{(n_1 + n_2)} \\ &= P(D) \,.\, P(A/D) \quad \ldots \quad (9) \end{aligned}$$

From either relation we find that the chance of both of two events occurring is equal to the product of the absolute chance of one event and the conditional chance of the other relative to the first.

Example 6. Two articles are drawn from a batch of 20 known to contain 5 defective. Find the chance that both are defective.

Without the use of the above law, using only the fundamental definition

$$\begin{aligned} p &= \text{(no. of ways in which 2 defective can be drawn from 5 defective)/} \\ &\qquad \text{(no. of ways in which 2 can be drawn from 20 total)} \\ &= {}_5C_2/{}_{20}C_2 \\ &= \frac{5!}{2!\;3!} \times \frac{2!\;18!}{20!} = \frac{1}{19}. \end{aligned}$$

Using the above law requires the following. The chance of drawing the first defective is an absolute chance of 5/20. A "second" can only be drawn provided that there has been a "first". We are now in this conditional state of a total of 19, of which 4 are defective. Hence by (8) above

$$p = \frac{5}{20} \cdot \frac{4}{19} = \frac{1}{19}.$$

It is clear that this can be extended to three or more dependent events. The probability of three such events all occurring is (the absolute probability of the first happening) multiplied by (the probability of the second given that the first has happened) multiplied by (the probability of the third given that the first two have happened). In the usual notation

$$P(ABC) = P(A) \,.\, P(B/A) \,.\, P(C/AB) \quad . \quad . \quad . \quad (10)$$

If the events are all *independent, i.e.*,

$$P(B/A) = P(B),\ P(C/AB) = P(C)$$

so that the chance of B or C is independent of whether the other events singly or in pairs have happened or not

$$P(ABC) = P(A)\, P(B)\, P(C) \quad . \quad . \quad . \quad . \quad (11)$$

and this is true for any number of such independent events.

Example 7. Find the chance of drawing 3 spade cards from the usual pack of 52 cards if: (*a*) each card is replaced and the pack shuffled before the next draw; (*b*) there is no replacement.

(*a*) Each act of drawing is independent of the others. For any one act the chance is $\frac{13}{25} = \frac{1}{4}$. Hence by (11) above

$$p = \frac{1}{4} \cdot \frac{1}{4} \cdot \frac{1}{4} = \frac{1}{64}.$$

(*b*) For the first card the chance is 13/25. For the second card when the first has been drawn the chance is 12/51. For the third card the chance is 11/50. Hence for the compound event, by (10) above,

$$p = \frac{13}{52} \cdot \frac{12}{51} \cdot \frac{11}{50} = \frac{11}{850}.$$

Example 8. The chance of A hitting a target is 0·8, whilst with B it is 0·7. If both fire together, a total of 100 shots each, find the proportion of times the target is hit at least once per round of 2 shots.

Since their results are independent the chance of both hitting the target is by (11) above

$$P(AB) = 0{\cdot}8 \times 0{\cdot}7 = 0{\cdot}56.$$

This is easily checked. Per 100 shots A hits 80 times. Since B misses 3 times out of 10, of A's 80 hits B misses $8 \times 3 = 24$ times in his simultaneous firing. Hence both hit $80 - 24 = 56$ times per 100 shot pairs.

Now
$$\begin{aligned} P(A \cup B) &= P(A) + P(B) - P(AB) \\ &= 0{\cdot}8 + 0{\cdot}7 - 0{\cdot}56 \\ &= \underline{0{\cdot}94.} \end{aligned}$$

This result is again easily checked. When A fires his 100 shots, 80 hits will be recorded. Of the 20 misses since B hits 7 times in 10, B will score 14 hits during these 20 misses by A. Hence the target is hit by A or B or both

$$80 + 14 = 94 \text{ times per 100 shot/pairs.}$$

Example 9. A bookcase contains three shelves, the first having 30 books, of which 5 are on mathematics, the second has 20 books, of which 6 are on mathematics, whilst for the third shelf the numbers are respectively 10 and 3. Owing to the different heights, the chance of a child choosing the shelves are respectively 3/12, 4/12, 5/12. If the child removes a book, find the chance that it was: (*a*) a mathematics book from the third shelf; (*b*) a mathematics book.

(*a*) p = (Chance third shelf is chosen) × (chance the book removed is on mathematics)

$$= \frac{5}{12} \times \frac{3}{10} = \frac{1}{8}.$$

(*b*) Chance first shelf is chosen and such a book removed $= \frac{3}{12} \times \frac{5}{30} = \frac{1}{24}$.

For the second shelf this chance is $\frac{4}{12} \times \frac{6}{20} = \frac{1}{10}$.

For the third shelf it is as above $\frac{1}{8}$.

These are 3 mutually exclusive events, since the child chooses only one shelf and a book on it. Hence

$$p = \frac{1}{24} + \frac{1}{10} + \frac{1}{8} = \frac{4}{15}.$$

Example 10. A and B throw a die, the winner being the first to throw a 6. If A throws first, what are their respective chances of winning?

A wins either on the first throw or the second or a subsequent throw. There is only a second throw for him if both he and B failed in their first throws. He will have a third throw only if both have failed previously. Similarly for further throws. Hence

$$P(\text{A wins}) = \tfrac{1}{6} + \tfrac{5}{6} \cdot \tfrac{5}{6} \cdot \tfrac{1}{6} + (\tfrac{5}{6})^2 (\tfrac{5}{6})^2 \cdot \tfrac{1}{6} + \ldots$$

This is a geometrical progression summed to infinity. The sum is given by

$$S = \frac{a}{1-r} = \frac{\frac{1}{6}}{1 - \frac{25}{36}} = \frac{6}{11} \quad \ldots \ldots \quad (1)$$

where a is the first term and r the common ratio of this G.P.

Since A or B wins the game

$$P(\text{B wins}) = 1 - \frac{6}{11} = \frac{5}{11} \quad \ldots \ldots \quad (2)$$

as can be checked by summing the G.P. representing B's chance.

EXERCISE 101

1. The chance that A solves a problem is p_1, whilst for B in an independent attempt the chance is p_2. What is the chance that: (*a*) A solves it but B does not; (*b*) A does not solve it but B does; (*c*) A and B both solve it when working independently?

Hence, find the chance that the problem is solved. Show that your solution is the same as the expression

$$1 - (1 - p_1)(1 - p_2)$$

and explain the reason for the correctness of this form of solution.

2. An assembly consists of 2 parts made independently. p_1 is the chance that the first part is defective and p_2 for the second part.

What is the chance that in the assembly: (*a*) both parts are defective; (*b*) first is defective, but the second good; (*c*) first good, but the second defective; (*d*) both parts are good? Find the sum of these four probabilities and explain the result.

3. Four per cent. of the valves made by a firm are defective. Find the chance of getting at least one defective valve in a random sample of four.

4. A bag contains 7 black and 4 white balls. They are drawn one by one from the bag, without replacement. Find the chance that the drawings are first a black and then a white, and so on alternately until only black remain.

5. There are two separate sets, each of 10 discs, the discs being numbered consecutively 0 to 9. A disc is chosen from each set. Find the chance that: (*a*) both numbers are odd; (*b*) one is odd and the other even; (*c*) the sum of the numbers is not greater than 5.

6. If 3 dice are thrown together, what is the chance of obtaining: (*a*) 3 fives; (*b*) 1, and only 1, five; (*c*) at least 1 five?

7. There are 2 independent furnaces in a works. The probability that one breaks down on a given day is p. Find the probabilities that in a week of 7 days: (*a*) neither breaks down; (*b*) only one breaks down; (*c*) both break down.

8. Two bags contain respectively (1B, 2W) and (2B, 1W) where B denotes a

black and W a white ball. One ball is chosen at random from the first bag and put in the second, which is then well shaken. What is the chance that a ball drawn from the second bag is: (*a*) white; (*b*) black?

9. Three bags contain respectively (1W, 2B), (3W, 1B) and (2W, 3B) balls. One ball is drawn from each. Find the probability that the three chosen consist of 2W and 1B ball.

10. Two bags contain respectively (3W, 7R, 15B) and (10W, 6R, 9B) balls, and one ball is drawn from each. Find the chance that they are both of the same colour.

11. A bag contains 6 six-faced dice. Four are marked as usual (1, 2, 3, 4, 5, 6), one is marked (1, 1, 2, 3, 3, 4) and the sixth is marked (3, 3, 3, 4, 5, 6). A die is drawn at random and thrown on to the table. What is the chance it will show 3?

12. A die is thrown n times. Show that the chance of obtaining at least one 6 is

$$1 - (5/6)^n.$$

Find the least number of throws if this chance is to be greater than 1/2.

13. If the chance of the face of a die coming up when it is thrown on to a table is proportional to the number shown on the face, find the chance of getting: (*a*) the number 3; (*b*) an even number.

14. A continuous production of components is known to be 5 per cent. defective, *i.e.*, the chance of drawing a defective from the stream is constant and equal to 0·05. Denoting this value by p show that if 3 are drawn out the chance of obtaining: (*a*) 3 defective is p^3; (*b*) 2 defective and 1 non-defective is $3p^2q$; (*c*) 1 defective and 2 non-defective is $3pq^2$; (*d*) 3 non-defective is q^3; (*e*) show that $(p + q)^3$ gives the same sequence of terms. Evaluate each of these chances for $p = 0{\cdot}05$ and check that their sum is 1.

15. If p is the constant chance of drawing a defective from a large batch of goods, put down a formula for the chance of finding r defective and $n - r$ non-defective in a random sample of n drawn from this batch.

If a random sample of 25 is taken from a stream of goods 20 per cent. defective, what is the chance that it will contain exactly 5 defective?

16. What is

$$\underset{p \to 0}{\text{£t.}}\ (1 - p)^{\frac{1}{p}}?$$

The chance of being hit by flying glass was in a certain instance 0·005. If on this occasion there were 5 pieces flying at random, show that the chance of at least one hit is approximately

$$1 - \exp\left(-\tfrac{1}{40}\right).$$

17. A batch consists of 80 components, of which 15 are defective. A test sample of 20 is chosen at random from the batch. If this is found to contain 2 or more defective the whole batch is rejected. Find the proportion of batches rejected under this sampling scheme.

18. A carton of 50 plugs is tested by a sample of 10. If no defectives are found the carton is passed. Find the chance that a carton, containing 2 defective amongst the 50, is rejected.

19. During a flight the chance an engine fails is p, independent of the number of engines in the aeroplane. To complete a flight at least one-half of the engines must not fail. Put down the probabilities that a flight will be completed by an aeroplane with: (*a*) two engines; (*b*) four engines. Find the range of values of p for which (*c*) a four-engine, (*d*) a two-engine plane is to be preferred.

20. A and B take turns to throw 2 dice, the first to throw a total of 9 being the winner. If A begins the game, show that the respective chances are as 9 : 8.

21. Three men in succession toss a coin, the winner being the first to throw a head. Show that their chances are respectively 4/7, 2/7, 1/7.

36.8. The Expectation

Suppose that in a certain game your chance of a win of £3 is $\frac{1}{10}$, of a win of £2 is $\frac{7}{10}$, and of a loss of £5 is $\frac{2}{10}$. What is a fair price to pay for a ticket to participate in this game?

If £P is this fair price per game, since in 10 games you expect to win £3 once, £2 seven times and lose £5 twice, but buy 10 tickets,

$$10\text{P} = (3)\,.\,(1) + (2)\,.\,(7) + (-5)\,.\,(2)$$
$$\text{P} = (3)(\tfrac{1}{10}) + (2)(\tfrac{7}{10}) + (-5)(\tfrac{2}{10})$$
$$= £(0{\cdot}70).$$

This is the sum of a number of products consisting of each possible outcome multiplied by the probability of its occurrence. It will be noticed that the sum of the probabilities is unity, showing that every possible outcome has been included, and one of these mutually exclusive events is certain to occur.

On this understanding we define the expectation of an event as

$$\Sigma f(x)p_x$$

where $f(x)$ is one of the outcomes, p_x is its probability. The summation is over every possible outcome, so that $\Sigma p_x = 1$.

Example 11. A firm estimates that over the coming year it will produce 10,000 articles. The amount of gain or loss per article with the corresponding probability is as shown. Find the expected gain: (*a*) per article; (*b*) on the whole batch.

Gain per article	$£f(x)$	5	3	1	0	-10
Probability	p_x	0·2	0·4	0·1	0·16	0·14

(*a*) Expected gain per article (over all articles)

$$= \Sigma f(x)p_x$$
$$= 5(0{\cdot}2) + 3(0{\cdot}4) + 1(0{\cdot}1) + 0(0{\cdot}16) + (-10)(0{\cdot}14)$$
$$= \underline{£0{\cdot}9.}$$

(*b*) Per 10,000 articles this is

$$10{,}000 \times (0{\cdot}9) = \underline{£9000.}$$

Suppose that we are dealing with continuous variation and the probability* is $f(x)dx$ of an "outcome" $g(x)$. In this case the expectation $E[g(x)]$ is given by

$$E[g(x)] = \int_{-\infty}^{+\infty} g(x)f(x)dx \qquad \left[\int_{-\infty}^{+\infty} f(x)dx = 1\right]$$

If $g(x)$ is taken as x we have the mean value, if as x^2 we have the second moment (about the value $x = 0$).

Example 12. A man shoots at a target which is in the shape of

$$y = 4 - x^2 \qquad 0 \leqslant x \leqslant 2$$

All shots land but their distribution over the target is uniform. For every shot that lands at a point whose x value is X, he receives $£1/(1 + X^2)$. Find his expectation.

$$\text{Area under curve} = 2\int_0^2 (4 - x^2)\,dx = 32/3.$$

Hence $$f(x) = 3(4 - x^2)/32 \qquad 0 \leqslant x \leqslant 2$$

* *i.e.* a reward $g(x)$ is given whenever a result between x and $x + dx$ in value is obtained.

satisfies the condition above (and its use will save the need for a denominator in the following integral).

The proportion of shots which land in the area between x and $x + dx$ is $f(x)dx$. Hence the expectation is

$$2\int_0^2 \frac{3}{32}(4 - x^2)dx \cdot \frac{1}{1 + x^2}$$

$$= \frac{3}{16}\int_0^2 \frac{5 - (1 + x^2)}{1 + x^2}\,dx = \frac{3}{16}[5 \tan^{-1} x - x]_0^2$$

$$= \frac{3}{16}[5 \tan^{-1} 2 - 2]$$

$$= \underline{\underline{£0{\cdot}663.}}$$

EXERCISE 102

1. The usual die of 6 faces showing the numbers 1 to 6 is tossed on to a table. Find the expected value of the number shown if: (*a*) all numbers are equally likely to appear; (*b*) the chance of a number is inversely proportional to the number.

2. A firm makes articles at a cost of P pence each to be sold at 2P pence each. 84 per cent. are within the tolerances and immediately saleable. 10 per cent. are too big and have to be reworked at a further cost of 0·1P pence each before sale. 6 per cent. are too small and only fit for scrap, sold at 0·05P pence each. Find the profit per article made.

3. A contract between 2 firms stipulates that £1000 will be paid for a machine but £750 only if it has to be returned. To test a machine just before delivery will cost the makers £10, and the cost of repair of a returned machine is £50. If it is known that 2 per cent. of machines are faulty at delivery, should the makers test before delivery or not? At what percentage defective of machines should they change their practice?

4. Two dice are tossed. If a total of 7 appears the player receives £1 and nothing in other cases. Find the value of his expectation.

5. The chance that there will be n persons in a hired car on a given journey is given by

n	1	2	3	4	5	6
Chance	0·05	0·20	0·20	0·45	0·08	0·02

(*a*) What is the expected number of people per journey?

(*b*) What minimum cost per person should be charged per journey if the cost to the car owner is £20 per journey and in addition £5 per person if less than 4 persons are carried but £3 per person if the number carried is 4 or more?

6. A die is tossed repeatedly until a 6 appears, when the game is ended. If a 6 appears at the nth throw the player receives £n. Find his expectation.

CHAPTER 37

THE BINOMIAL PROBABILITY DISTRIBUTION

37.1. Outcomes of Constant Probability

There are many experiments which consist of the repetition of an event such as the tossing of a coin or die. In this event the chance of each outcome is constant and independent of previous outcomes. Another example is provided by continuous industrial production of components with a proportion p defective. The chance that any component picked out at random is defective is p, and p^n is the chance that in a sample of n all are defective. Again if a large batch, such as 10,000, is 2 per cent. defective the chance that a random choice is defective is 0·02. The chance that a second is defective given that the first was defective (and not replaced) is $199/9999 = 0{\cdot}01990$. The chance that a third drawn at random from the remaining batch of 9998 is defective given that the first two are defective and not replaced is $198/9998 = 0{\cdot}01980$. Provided we do not proceed too far, these numbers can be regarded as constant at the value of 0·02 and the chance that a small group of n are all defective taken as $(0{\cdot}02)^n$.

We will consider the distribution of probabilities provided by such an experiment, in which we have a sequence of n repeated similar but independent events, the chance of a given outcome in each event being a constant, denoted by p.

37.2. The Binomial Probability Expansion

If in a given case $n = 3$ and p is the constant chance of finding a defective, whilst $q = 1 - p$ is the constant chance of finding a non-defective, then in a choice of 3 articles the chance that we find:

(*a*) all defective is $p \cdot p \cdot p = p^3$

(*b*) two defective and one non-defective is either ppq or pqp or qpp. Either of these mutually exclusive events will satisfy the requirement that in the sample of 3 there are two defective and one non-defective. Hence the probability of this event is the sum of these $= 3p^2q$

(*c*) one defective and two non-defective $= 3pq^2$

(*d*) all non-defective $= q^3$.

We have stated every possible outcome to the experiment and note that these terms come from

$$(p + q)^3.$$

The method is quite general and for an experiment of n repetitions of an event (such as choosing a component from a batch) of constant probability the expansion of

$$(p + q)^n$$

gives the probabilities of each possible outcome. Thus

$$\begin{aligned} p^n &= \text{chance of } n \text{ successes.} \\ {}_nC_1 p^{n-1}q &= \text{chance of } (n-1) \text{ successes, 1 failure.} \\ &\vdots \\ {}_nC_r p^r q^{n-r} &= \text{chance of } r \text{ successes, } (n-r) \text{ failures.} \\ &\vdots \\ q^n &= \text{chance of 0 successes, } n \text{ failures.} \end{aligned}$$

These $(n + 1)$ terms give every possible outcome to the experiment. They are mutually exclusive, and therefore their sum is, since one of them must occur,

$$(p + q)^n = 1$$

as expected.

Example 1. (*a*) The chance of 8 throws of a good die giving exactly 3 sixes is

$${}_8C_3(\tfrac{1}{6})^3(\tfrac{5}{6})^5 = \underline{0{\cdot}10489}$$

since the chance of a six is $p = \frac{1}{6}$.

(*b*) The chance of 10 tosses of a penny giving 6 tails is

$${}_{10}C_6(\tfrac{1}{2})^6(\tfrac{1}{2})^4 = \underline{0{\cdot}20508.}$$

(*c*) The chance of at least 8 heads in 12 tosses of a coin is

$${}_{12}C_8(\tfrac{1}{2})^8(\tfrac{1}{2})^4 + {}_{12}C_9(\tfrac{1}{2})^9(\tfrac{1}{2})^3 + {}_{12}C_{10}(\tfrac{1}{2})^{10}(\tfrac{1}{2})^2 + {}_{12}C_{11}(\tfrac{1}{2})^{11}(\tfrac{1}{2}) + (\tfrac{1}{2})^{12} = \underline{0{\cdot}19385.}$$

Note.

(*a*) Since ${}_nC_r = {}_nC_{n-r}$, the student will use, in evaluation, the form giving the least calculation. Thus, above

$${}_{12}C_{11} = {}_{12}C_1 = 12.$$

(*b*) The approximate evaluation of binomial terms and sums such as above can be performed by the use of the areas of the Normal curve (see 38.7).

Example 2. An inspection scheme is: take 170 and test. If 3 or more are defective, reject the whole batch from which the 170 were chosen. If the batch is 2 per cent. defective and large, find the proportion of batches accepted under this scheme. The chance p of choosing a defective is taken as constant at 0·02.

We could expand

$$(0{\cdot}02d + 0{\cdot}98g)^{170}$$

but this begins with the chance of 170 defectives being found, so reverse and use

$$(0{\cdot}98g + 0{\cdot}02d)^{170}.$$

The g stands for good, d for defective and the coefficient of, say, $g^{160}d^{10}$ would be the chance of finding 160 good and 10 defective in the sample,

chance of no defective	$(0{\cdot}98)^{170}$	$= 0{\cdot}032$
chance of 1 defective	$170(0{\cdot}98)^{169}(0{\cdot}02)$	$= 0{\cdot}112$
chance of 2 defective	$\frac{170 \cdot 169}{1 \cdot 2}(0{\cdot}98)^{168}(0{\cdot}02)^2$	$= \underline{0{\cdot}193}$
chance of 0, 1 or 2 defective		$0{\cdot}337.$

Some 34 per cent. of the batches will be accepted and 66 per cent. rejected under this scheme.

37.3. If this series of n events is repeated N times the expected number of occurrences of the event of r successes is

$$N[{}_nC_r p^r q^{n-r}]$$

and the expected number of each possible result is given by the terms of

$$N(p + q)^n.$$

Example 3. Components for testing are packed in trays of 50. If the process average defective is 2 per cent., find the number of trays which will be found to contain 0, 1 or 2 defective in a batch of 1000 trays.

We require the first 3 terms in

$$1000(0{\cdot}98g + 0{\cdot}02d)^{50}$$

Number of trays with

(*a*) no defective	$1000(0{\cdot}98)^{50}$	$= 364$
(*b*) one defective	$1000\ {}_{50}C_1(0{\cdot}98)^{49}(0{\cdot}02)$	$= 372$
(*c*) two defective	$1000\ {}_{50}C_2(0{\cdot}98)^{48}(0{\cdot}02)^2$	$= 186.$
		922

If trays containing less than 3 defective result in the original batch being passed, then some 92 per cent. of batches containing 2 per cent. defective will be passed.

37.4. Mean and Variance

Suppose that we have N batches of the same component, each batch having the same proportion p defective. A sample of n components is chosen at random from each batch. We will find the mean (or average or expected) number of defectives per sample and its variance.

The mean number per batch is given by

$$\bar{X} = \frac{1}{N}\sum_{r=0}^{n} N[{}_nC_r p^r q^{n-r}] \times r$$

$$= \sum_{1}^{n} {}_nC_r p^r q^{n-r} \times r.$$

To evaluate this consider the expansion

$$(q + px)^n = \sum_{r=0}^{n} {}_nC_r p^r q^{n-r} x^r.$$

If we differentiate with respect to x:

$$n(q + px)^{n-1} \,.\, p = \sum_{r=1}^{n} {}_nC_r p^r q^{n-r} \,.\, rx^{r-1} \quad . \quad . \quad . \quad (1)$$

The substitution $x = 1$ in the right-hand side reproduces exactly the expression for $\bar{X}$. Hence,

$$\bar{X} = n(q + px)^{n-1} \,.\, p]_{x=1} = np \quad . \quad . \quad . \quad (2)$$

We will find the fictitious variance S^2 about the origin and from it deduce σ^2 the variance about the mean by using the formula

$$\sigma^2 = S^2 - (\bar{X})^2.$$

The variance about the origin is

$$S^2 = \frac{1}{N} \sum_{0}^{n} N[{}_nC_r p^r q^{n-r}] \times r^2 = \sum_{1}^{n} {}_nC_r p^r q^{n-r} \times r^2.$$

To obtain this expression multiply (1) throughout by x.

$$np(q + px)^{n-1} x = \sum_{r=1}^{n} {}_nC_r p^r q^{n-r} \,.\, rx^r.$$

Differentiate this with respect to x

$$np[(q + px)^{n-1} + x(n - 1)(q + px)^{n-2} \,.\, p] = \sum_{r=1}^{n} {}_nC_r p^r q^{n-r} \,.\, r^2 x^{r-1}.$$

The substitution of $x = 1$ gives a right-hand side of S^2. Hence

$$np[1 + p(n - 1)] = S^2.$$

By the formula

$$\sigma^2 = np[q + pn] - (np)^2 = npq. \quad . \quad . \quad . \quad (3)$$

Example 4. A sample of constant size is taken from each of 100 batches, and the number of defectives found is shown. Given that the chance of finding a defective is constant, find this chance and the sample size.

Using these values calculate the expected binomial distribution of values.

No. of defectives per sample (x)	0	1	2	3	4	Total
No. of samples (f)	4	31	35	25	5	100

(*a*) $\text{Mean} = np = \Sigma fx/\Sigma f = \frac{196}{100} = 1{\cdot}96.$

(*b*) $$\text{Variance} = npq = \frac{1}{100}\left[\Sigma fx^2 - \frac{(\Sigma fx)^2}{100}\right]$$

$$= \frac{1}{100}\left[476 - \frac{(196)^2}{100}\right] = 0{\cdot}9184.$$

$$q = npq/np = 0{\cdot}9184/1{\cdot}96 = 0{\cdot}4686$$

$$p = 1 - q \qquad = \underline{0{\cdot}5314}$$

$$n = 1{\cdot}96/0{\cdot}5314 = 3{\cdot}69 \rightarrow \underline{4}.$$

(*c*) The expected terms are obtained from

$$100(0{\cdot}4686g + 0{\cdot}5314d)^4$$
$$= 4{\cdot}8,\ 22{\cdot}3,\ 37{\cdot}2,\ 28{\cdot}2,\ 7{\cdot}5 = \underline{100.}$$

The correspondence with the given data (f) is evident. This latter is a sample set of data, *i.e.*, if the experiment was repeated with another 100 batches of the same production, a somewhat different set of f values would be obtained, and so for each repeat of the experiment. Hence exact correspondence is not to be expected, but the values obtained by the mathematical process are the graduated or averaged values.

37.5. The Most Likely Number

The chance of r successes in n trials is

$$_nC_r p^r q^{n-r} \quad . \quad . \quad . \quad . \quad . \quad . \quad . \quad (1)$$

If we find the value of r for which this expression is a maximum we will have the greatest value of the successive probabilities for $r =$ 0, 1, 2, . . . n successes. This number of successes is the one most likely to occur, since its probability is the greatest of the series.

The term (1) will be the greatest if it is greater than the term before and the term after. Hence we must find r, a positive integer, such that

$$_nC_{r-1}p^{r-1}q^{n-r+1} \leqslant {_nC_r}p^r q^{n-r} \geqslant {_nC_{r+1}}p^{r+1}q^{n-r-1}.$$

From the first pair

$$\frac{n!}{(r-1)!(n-r+1)!}\,p^{r-1}q^{n-r+1} \leqslant \frac{n!}{r!(n-r)!}\,p^r q^{n-r}.$$

After cancellation

$$\frac{1}{(n-r+1)}\,q \leqslant \frac{1}{r}\,p$$

or
$$r(1-p) \leqslant p(n-r+1)$$

giving
$$r \leqslant np + p.$$

Similarly, from the second pair,

$$r \geqslant np - (1-p).$$

Together, r is subject to the inequalities

$$np + p \geqslant r \geqslant np - (1-p)$$

and can be found.

Example 5. The proportion of defectives produced by a machine is constant at 2·14 per cent. If these components are packed in cartons of 1000, what is the most likely number of defectives to be found in a carton?
If r is the number required

$$1000(0{\cdot}0214) + 0{\cdot}0214 \geqslant r \geqslant 1000(0{\cdot}0214) - 0{\cdot}9786$$
$$21{\cdot}4214 \geqslant r \geqslant 20{\cdot}4214$$

hence
$$\underline{r = 21.}$$

If the outer values are both integers, with, of course, a difference between them of 1, then either value for r will give the same maximum probability.

EXERCISE 103

1. A machine produces articles 1 per cent. defective. What is the chance that a sample of 4 will contain: (*a*) no defective; (*b*) exactly one defective; (*c*) at most one defective?

2. 400 coins are tossed on to a table. What is the expected value and variance of the number of coins which show a head?

3. A six-sided die is tossed 1620 times. What is the mean and the standard deviation of the number of 6's shown?

4. If on the average rain falls on twelve days in every thirty, find the chance that:

(*a*) the first three days of a given week are fine and the remainder wet;
(*b*) rain will fall on exactly three days of a given week. [L.U.]

5. How many aces are most likely to be found in a random choice of 13 cards from the normal pack of 52 containing 4 aces?

6. A process produces articles 2·52 per cent. defective. How many defective will most likely be found in a carton of 60 articles?

7. A large box of components is known to be 10 per cent. defective. A random sample of 10 is chosen. What is the chance that the sample contains: (*a*) no defective; (*b*) one defective; (*c*) two defectives; (*d*) more than two defectives? (*e*) What is the most likely number of defectives to be found in a box?

8. In sampling from a large number of parts made by a machine the mean number of defectives in a sample of 20 is 2. Out of a 1000 such samples, how many would be expected to contain at least 3 defectives?

9. As an acceptance procedure an inspector will choose a sample of 75 from a batch of 500 and pass the batch if at most 2 defective are found. If a batch is 20 per cent. defective, show that the chance it passes is about $3{\cdot}2 \times 10^{-6}$.

10. In a binomial distribution it is known that the mean is 60 and the variance 40. Find the values of n, p, q.

11. The production of a component is checked by testing samples of 4. The table gives the distribution of defectives found in 200 samples. Find the proportion defective, and assuming the distribution is binomial, find the theoretical values.

No. of defectives	0	1	2	3	4	Total
No. of samples	62	85	40	11	2	200

12. In the above question neither the first nor last frequencies are zero. If the distribution is binomial $62 = 200q^4$, $2 = 200p^4$. From the ratio evaluate p as an approximation to its true value.

13. A foreman states that he can tell at sight when a process is finished, and so dispense with an expensive test. You decide to test him in 10 cases and grant his claim if he is correct in at least 8 cases. Put down the formula for calculating this chance if p is his chance of being correct. Show that if he has some skill ($p = 0{\cdot}85$ say), then his chance of establishing his claim is 0·820, whilst if he has no skill at all, so that $p = 0{\cdot}5$, the chance of success is only 0·055.

14. A machine normally makes goods which are 5 per cent. defective. The product is inspected every hour by a sample of 10, and if no defectives are found the machine is allowed to run on for another hour. What is the chance that this method of inspection will lead to the machine being let run on when in fact it is producing goods 10 per cent. defective?

How large a sample should be inspected to ensure that if $p = 0{\cdot}10$ the chance that the machine will not be stopped is less than or equal to 0·01?

15. A process produces a mixture of two kinds, types P and Q respectively. This mixture is satisfactory if one-third is P and the rest Q. As an inspection test the following is used: choose 6 at random and test. (*a*) If 2 are type P pass the batch. If 3 are type P choose another 6 and test. If now 1 or 2 are of P pass the batch. (*b*) If only 1 of the first test is of P choose another 6 after the test and accept only if 2 or 3 are of type P.

If the mixture is exactly as required one-third P, two-thirds Q, find the chance p of acceptance. Is this testing scheme satisfactory?

[If $P(r)$ denotes the probability of finding r of type P in a sample of 6, show that

$$p = P(2) + P(3)[P(1) + P(2)] + P(1)[P(2) + P(3)]$$

and evaluate this.]

16. A sampling inspection is as follows. Select 8 from the (large) batch and test. If all are good pass the batch, but if more than one is defective reject the batch. If one (and only one) is defective 12 more are chosen and the batch passed if, and only if, the 12 are all good. If a batch which is 5 per cent. defective is subjected to this test, find the chance: (*a*) it is accepted; (*b*) the test on the first 8 is decisive and the batch accepted.

17. A process produces large batches of components, of which a high proportion are defective, but the output is still satisfactory if no more than one-quarter are defective. An inspection test is as follows: Choose 12 at random and test. (*a*) If no more than 3 are defective pass the batch. (*b*) If 4 are defective choose another 8 and pass the batch only if no more than 1 defective is found in this second test. In all other cases the batch is rejected. Find the chance of acceptance of a batch exactly one-quarter defective.

18. Show that the probability of exactly r successes in n trials is the coefficient of t^r in the expression of $(1 - p + pt)^n$, where p is the probability of success in any one trial.

On an expedition a machine is taken which fails to start on the average once in c attempts owing to the breakage of a certain part. If s spare parts of this kind are carried, show that the probability that the last spare part will fail at the nth attempt is equal to the coefficient of t^s in the expansion

$$\frac{1}{c}\left(1 + \frac{t-1}{c}\right)^{n-1}. \qquad \text{[L.U.]}$$

19. A competition consists of filling in a form of N spaces, and each space has to be filled up in one of n ways. There is a unique correct solution. If the spaces are filled up in a random manner, prove that the chance of there being r mistakes is the coefficient of x^r in the expansion of

$$n^{-N}\{1 + x(n-1)\}^N. \qquad \text{[L.U.]}$$

CHAPTER 38

THE NORMAL CURVE

38.1. Probability Density Functions

In Chapter 35.5 is drawn a histogram for the distribution of weights of tins. In this example there were 19 tins of weights varying from 0·985 to 0·995 lb. If a tin is chosen at random from the total of 100 the chance that a tin of weight within this range is picked is (no. of such tins)/(total no. of tins) or 19/100. Since the rectangles of the histogram have areas representing the number of tins in each range, a ratio of the corresponding areas will also give this probability. If now we change the scale, *e.g.*, measure proportions instead of actual numbers along the y axis, each area represents the proportion within a certain range, and the total area is now unity. Hence each area represents a probability and the area beneath the curve and between the values x_1 and x_2 is the probability of a tin picked at random from the batch having a weight between x_1 and x_2.

If $y = f(x)$ is this curve, $y\Delta x$ is the probability of obtaining a value in the range x to $x + \Delta x$. As $\Delta x \to 0$ so does $y\Delta x$ and the probability of a value exactly x is zero. This result emphasizes the difference, discrete data where we cannot measure to more than, say, 6 decimals and data requiring continuous variation. Clearly no experiment can provide us with a value for, say, $\pi = 3{\cdot}14159 \ldots$ in all its infinity of decimals.

Such a curve showing the distribution of the proportions or probabilities within the range $-\infty$ to $+\infty$ is called the probability distribution or probability density function (p.d.f.). If this curve is

$$y = f(x) \qquad (f(x) \geqslant 0, \text{ all } x)$$

we have

$$\int_{-\infty}^{+\infty} f(x)dx = 1$$

and

$$\int_{x_1}^{x_2} f(x)dx$$

is the probability that a result will fall within the range x_1 to x_2. We may regard the end values included or not, as is most convenient.

Example 1. Given

$$\begin{aligned} f(x) &= 6x(1 - x) \qquad & 0 < x < 1 \\ &= 0 & \text{otherwise} \end{aligned}$$

is a p.d.f. for a random variable x, check that the area enclosed is unity. Find $P(\frac{1}{3} < x < \frac{2}{3})$, also the mean and variance of this distribution.

$$\int_{-\infty}^{+\infty} y dx = \int_0^1 6x(1 - x)dx = 1$$

$$P(\tfrac{1}{3} < x < \tfrac{2}{3}) = \int_{1/3}^{2/3} 6x(1 - x)dx = \underline{\frac{13}{27}}.$$

The mean value is

$$\bar{x} = \int_0^1 6x(1 - x)dx \,.\, x = \underline{\frac{1}{2}}.$$

For the variance

$$\sigma^2 = \int_0^1 6x(1 - x)dx \,.\, x^2 - (\bar{x})^2 = \frac{6}{20} - \frac{1}{4} = \underline{\frac{1}{20}}.$$

38.2. The Normal Distribution

There is one probability distribution function of supreme importance

$$y = \frac{1}{\sigma\sqrt{(2\pi)}} \exp\left(-\frac{(x - \bar{x})^2}{2\sigma^2}\right) \quad . \quad . \quad . \quad . \quad (1)$$

where $\bar{x}$ is the mean value and σ the standard deviation (as will be proved). This can be obtained in several ways.

(*a*) If we assume that any measurement made is subject to a large number of errors of equal importance, some acting positively and others negatively, the chance of a total error between x and $x + dx$ in the value of a single measurement is given by ydx.

(*b*) Similarly if we assume that when a number of measurements are made of a given unknown magnitude, their mean is its most probable value.

(*c*) We have had the probability of r successes in a binomial distribution

$$_nC_r p^r q^{n-r} \quad . \quad . \quad . \quad . \quad . \quad . \quad . \quad . \quad . \quad (2)$$

This can be converted directly to the Normal curve form on a deviation from the mean np with a variance npq.

(*d*) A curve may be drawn with ordinates proportional to the above probability (2) for $r = 0, 1, \ldots n$. When n is large this binomial curve is indistinguishable from the Normal curve with mean np and variance npq of the binomial distribution. This can be proved by the " Central Limit Theorem " and will be assumed here. It follows that any area under the binomial curve or sum of ordinates is given by the area under the corresponding part of the Normal curve.

38.3. Properties

We will assume the basic result (proved in Volume 2).

$$\int_{-\infty}^{+\infty} \exp(-z^2)dz = \sqrt{\pi}.$$

The Normal curve is symmetrical about the value $x = \bar{x}$, so that $\bar{x}$ is the mean value. Referred to this mean value as origin, is the easier form

$$y = \frac{1}{\sigma\sqrt{(2\pi)}} \exp\left(-\frac{x^2}{2\sigma^2}\right).$$

(*a*) The total area under the curve is unity.

Put $x/\sigma\sqrt{2} = z$ in the expression for the area to obtain

$$\int_{-\infty}^{+\infty} y dx = \int_{-\infty}^{+\infty} \frac{1}{\sigma\sqrt{(2\pi)}} \exp(-z^2) \,.\, (\sigma\sqrt{2}dz)$$

$$= \frac{1}{\sqrt{\pi}} \int_{-\infty}^{+\infty} \exp(-z^2) dz$$

$$= \frac{1}{\sqrt{\pi}} \cdot \sqrt{\pi} = \underline{1}.$$

(*b*) The variance is given by

$$\int_{-\infty}^{+\infty} y dx \,.\, x^2 = \frac{2\sigma^2}{\sqrt{\pi}} \int_{-\infty}^{+\infty} z^2 \exp(-z^2) dz.$$

This can be integrated by parts

$$\int_{-\infty}^{+\infty} z\{z \exp(-z^2)\} dz = \left[z \frac{\exp(-z^2)}{-2}\right]_{-\infty}^{+\infty} - \int_{-\infty}^{+\infty} \frac{\exp(-z^2)}{-2} dz.$$

Since $$\lim_{z \to \pm\infty} \{z \exp(-z^2)\} = 0$$

the integral reduces to

$$\tfrac{1}{2} \int_{-\infty}^{+\infty} \exp(-z^2) dx = \tfrac{1}{2}\sqrt{\pi}.$$

The variance is therefore

$$\frac{2\sigma^2}{\sqrt{\pi}} \cdot \tfrac{1}{2}\sqrt{\pi} = \underline{\sigma^2}.$$

These two values $\bar{x}$ and σ determine a Normal curve and must be evaluated from any data to which a Normal curve is to be fitted.

(*c*) The maximum value of the ordinate is at $x = 0$, the curve being a " cocked hat " symmetrical about the y axis ($x = 0$), with the x axis as an asymptote at each end ($x = \pm\infty$). The points of inflexion are given by

$$\frac{d^2y}{dx^2} = \frac{1}{\sigma\sqrt{(2\pi)}} \frac{d^2}{dx^2}\left[\exp\left(-\frac{x^2}{2\sigma^2}\right)\right] = 0.$$

This gives $$x = \pm\sigma$$

At $$x = \sigma, \quad y = \frac{1}{\sigma\sqrt{(2\pi)}} \exp(-\tfrac{1}{2}).$$

The tangent at this point of inflexion is easily shown to meet the x axis at the point $x = 2\sigma$. We are now able to place freehand a Normal curve over a histogram using the above data. [If, however, the histogram represents N values and not unity and the intervals in the histogram are of length h and not unity, the appropriate curve is

$$y = \frac{Nh}{\sigma\sqrt{(2\pi)}} \exp\left(-\frac{x^2}{2\sigma^2}\right)$$

where h, σ, x are measured in the same units.]

Example 2. Fit a Normal curve to the histogram of values given below.

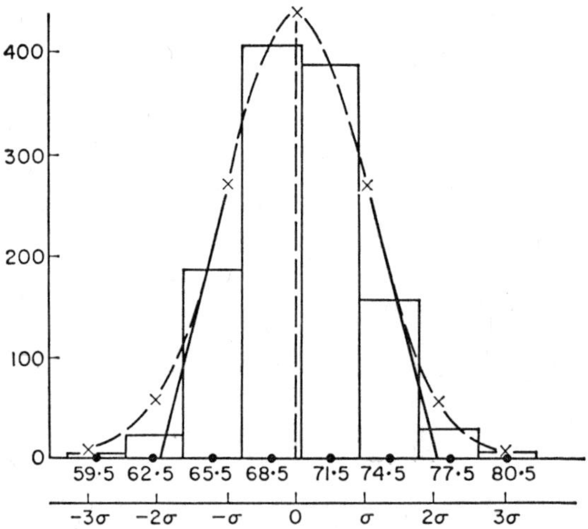

FIG. 113.

A Normal curve fitted to the data of example 2. The actual values on which the histogram is based and also the standardized values by which the curve is constructed are both given.

Central Value x (in.).	Frequency f.	$(x - 68{\cdot}5)$ X.	$z = \frac{X}{3}$.	fz.	fz^2.
59·5	4	−9	−3	−12	36
62·5	24	−6	−2	−48	96
65·5	188	−3	−1	−188	188
68·5	404	0	0		
71·5	387	3	1	387	387
74·5	158	6	2	316	632
77·5	30	9	3	90	270
80·5	5	12	4	20	80
	1200			−248	1689
				+813	
				+565	

$$\bar{z} = \tfrac{565}{1200} = 0{\cdot}4708 \text{ units of } z$$
$$\bar{x} = 68{\cdot}5 + 3(\tfrac{565}{1200}) = \underline{69{\cdot}9125} \text{ in.}$$
$$\sigma^2 = \frac{1}{1200}\left\{1689 - \frac{(565)^2}{1200}\right\} \text{ units of } z$$
$$= 9 \times 1{\cdot}186 \text{ units of } x$$
$$\sigma = 3 \times 1{\cdot}089 = \underline{3{\cdot}267} \text{ in.}$$

Referred to the mean as origin, the equation to the curve is

$$y = \frac{1200 \times 3}{3{\cdot}267\sqrt{(2\pi)}} \exp\left(-\frac{X^2}{2(3{\cdot}267)^2}\right).$$

At X = 0 the ordinate at the mean value is

$$y_0 = \frac{1200 \times 3}{3{\cdot}267\sqrt{(2\pi)}} = 439{\cdot}67.$$

At X = 3·267 (= σ)

$$y = y_0 \exp(-\tfrac{1}{2}) = 0{\cdot}60653y_0 = 266{\cdot}67.$$

At X = 2σ

$$y = y_0 \exp(-2) = 0{\cdot}13534y_0 = 59{\cdot}50.$$

At X = 3σ

$$y = y_0 \exp(-4{\cdot}5) = 0{\cdot}01111y_0 = 4{\cdot}88.$$

The actual mean is marked on the histogram and the above values put in relative to the mean. The join of the point of inflexion to the point (2σ, 0) provides a tangent to the curve at the point of inflexion, and the positive half of the curve can be drawn. The other half is exactly similar on the other side of the mean line.

The figure shows that a Normal curve with the mean and standard deviation obtained from the actual data provides a good fit to this data represented as a histogram. In practice, we are concerned with obtaining the area under various parts of the curve. The probabilities obtained from the histogram are regarded as sample values. Those obtained from the Normal curve are the *graduated* values and less subject to sampling errors. We will now consider areas under the Normal curve and then obtain the graduated values for the above data.

38.4. Areas under the Normal Curve

To use tables of this area, standardized values must be obtained for the x variate.

In
$$\int \frac{1}{\sigma\sqrt{2\pi}} \exp\left(-\frac{(x-\bar{x})^2}{2\sigma^2}\right) dx$$

put $(x - \bar{x})/\sigma = z$. We now have

$$\Phi(z) = \frac{1}{\sqrt{(2\pi)}}\int_{-\infty}^{z} \exp\left(-\frac{z^2}{2}\right) dz$$

for the area to the left of a *standardized variate* z, as shown by the shaded area (Fig. 114). This integral cannot be evaluated in finite terms, and tables of its values for a given z must be consulted. Usually only positive values of z are tabulated, since the curve is symmetrical about the y axis. A few values are given below. Other tables give different portions of the area for a given z, *e.g.*, the shaded area less 0·5 (= area 0 to z only) or 1 − shaded area (= area above the value z).

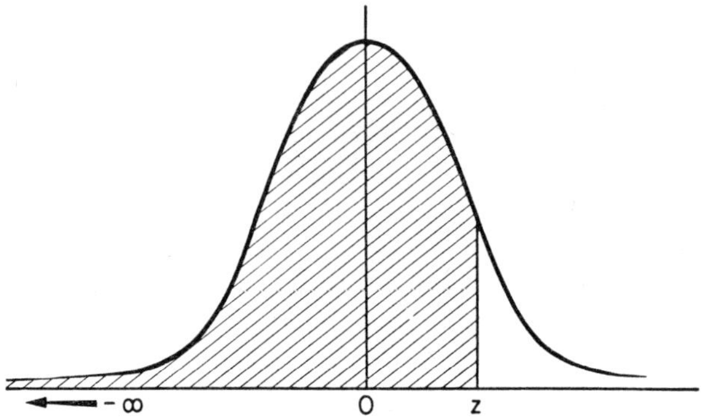

Shaded area $= \Phi(z) = \frac{1}{\sqrt{(2\pi)}} \int_{-\infty}^{z} \exp\left(-\frac{z^2}{2}\right) dz.$

FIG. 114

z.	$\Phi(z)$.	z.	$\Phi(z)$.	z.	$\Phi(z)$.	z.	$\Phi(z)$.
0	0·500	1·0	0·841	2·0	0·977	3·0	0·99865
0·2	0·579	1·2	0·885	2·2	0·986	3·2	0·99931
0·4	0·655	1·4	0·919	2·4	0·992	3·4	0·99966
0·6	0·726	1·6	0·945	2·6	0·995	3·6	0·99984
0·8	0·788	1·8	0·964	2·8	0·997	3·8	0·99993

Values often required are (see also the table at the end of the book):

area between

$\pm\sigma$ is 0·683 $\quad\pm 0{\cdot}67\sigma$ is 0·500

$\pm 1{\cdot}96\sigma$ is 0·950 $\quad\pm 2\sigma$ is 0·956

$\pm 3{\cdot}09\sigma$ is 0·998 $\quad\pm 3\sigma$ is 0·997

We note, for example, that above the ordinate $3{\cdot}09\sigma$ distant from the mean there is only 0·001 unit of the total area of unity and a similar area below $-3{\cdot}09\sigma$. Thus, if the total area is taken to represent 1000 measurements of a component whose parameters are $\bar{x}$, σ, then one of these components will have a value greater than $\bar{x} + 3{\cdot}09\sigma$ and one other a value less than $\bar{x} - 3{\cdot}09\sigma$. Some 25 will have values greater than $\bar{x} + 1{\cdot}96\sigma$ and 25 values below $\bar{x} - 1{\cdot}96\sigma$. By the use of tables the proportion of output with values between any two given measurements can be found.

Example 3. A Normal curve has a mean of 3·0 with a standard deviation of 2·0. Find the area: (*a*) above the value $x = 3{\cdot}4$; (*b*) below $x = 1{\cdot}6$; (*c*) between $x = 1{\cdot}0$ and 3·8.

(*a*) The standardized value for use with the table is

$$z = (3{\cdot}4 - 3{\cdot}0)/2 = 0{\cdot}2.$$

From the table $\Phi(0{\cdot}2) = 0{\cdot}5793.$

Area above this is $1 - 0{\cdot}5793 = \underline{0{\cdot}4207.}$

(*b*) $z = |\,1{\cdot}6 - 3\,|\,/2 = 0{\cdot}7.$

The area above 0·7 is $1 - \Phi(0{\cdot}7) = 1 - 0{\cdot}7580.$

By symmetry, area below $x = 1{\cdot}6$ is $\underline{0{\cdot}2420.}$

(*c*) $(3{\cdot}8 - 3)/2 = 0{\cdot}4.$

Area between 3 and 3·8 $= \Phi(0{\cdot}4) - 0{\cdot}5$
$= 0{\cdot}6554 - 0{\cdot}5$
$= 0{\cdot}1554$

Area between 1 and 3 $= \Phi(1) - 0{\cdot}5$
$= 0{\cdot}8413 - 0{\cdot}5$
$= 0{\cdot}3413$

Total area between $x = 1{\cdot}0$ and 3·8 is $0{\cdot}1554 + 0{\cdot}3413 = \underline{0{\cdot}4967}.$

Example 4. Tests on a certain type of valve show that the lifetimes are Normally distributed about a mean value of 2000 hours with a standard deviation of 100 hours. To what value must the standard deviation be reduced if it is required that 95 per cent. of the output have a life of more than 1900 hours?

We require $z = |\,1900 - 2000\,|/\sigma = 100/\sigma$ to give $\Phi(z) = 0{\cdot}95$. Enter the tables inversely to find $z = 1{\cdot}645$. Hence

$$100/\sigma = 1{\cdot}645, \quad \underline{\sigma = 61 \text{ hours.}}$$

38.5. To Fit a Normal Curve

We are now in a position to find the graduated values between any two limits when given an experimental result.

Example 5. Find the graduated values between the class limits in Example 2.

Since the central value of the first class is 59·5 with a class interval of 3, the lower limit to this class is 59·5 − 1·5 = 58.

Lower class limit (X).	$z = \dfrac{X - 69{\cdot}9125}{3{\cdot}267}$.	Area to right of (z).	Diff. (d).	1200d.	Actual frequency.
58	−3·65	0·99987			
			0·00304	3·65	4
61	−2·73	0·99683			
			0·03198	38·38	24
64	−1·81	0·96485			
			0·15158	181·90	188
67	−0·89	0·81327			
			0·32524	390·29	404
70	0·03	0·48803			
			0·31697	380·36	387
73	0·95	0·17106			
			0·13962	167·54	158
76	1·86	0·03144			
			0·02872	34·46	30
79	2·78	0·00272			
			0·00261	3·13	5
82	3·70	0·00011			
				1199·71	1200

Column (1). The lower limit of each class interval. Since we wish to obtain the number in the last interval 77–82, we must end with the lower limit of the first interval omitted, *i.e.*, 82.

Column (2). The standardized value z has been found. The reciprocal of 3·267 will be used to simplify the arithmetic.

Column (3). The area to the right of z in the Normal curve is found from the tables.

Column (4). The areas in column (3) are differenced to give the area between any two consecutive class limits.

Column (5). The area in (4) is multiplied by 1200, the total number, to turn the proportions between the limits into the actual (graduated) numbers.

Note.

(1) The sum of the graduated values is not quite 1200, because the areas below 58 and above 82 have been omitted. These values when taken to the nearest integer could have the last figure of 3 adjusted up to 4 to give a corrected sum of 1200.

(2) The close correspondence between the actual and graduated values will be noted. (There is a Chi squared test to check if the differences are large enough to cast doubt upon the assumption that a Normal curve is a good enough representation of the given data.)

38.6. Sheppard's Correction

In calculating the mean and variance of the above distribution of values we assumed that the values in a class interval were uniformly scattered over the interval, and so could be assumed to have the value of the mid-point of the interval. But the shape of the histogram shows that in an interval there are more values nearer to the mean value of the whole distribution and the spread over an interval is not uniform. It can be shown that the resultant error in the *mean value* found is zero but that the variance found is too large. If h is the length of an interval the corrected variance is given by

$$\sigma^2 \text{ (corrected)} = \sigma^2 \text{ (uncorrected)} - \frac{h^2}{12}.$$

In the above example, where $h = 3$,

$$\begin{aligned} \sigma^2 \text{ (corrected)} &= (3{\cdot}267)^2 - \tfrac{9}{12} \\ &= 9{\cdot}923 \\ \sigma &= \underline{3{\cdot}15.} \end{aligned}$$

This corrected value could be used instead of 3·267 in all applications. However, this correction assumes that the histogram of values shows signs, like the Normal curve, of hugging the x axis at each end, *i.e.*, running into it asymptotically.

EXERCISE 104

1. If
$$c/(1 + x^2) \qquad (-\infty < x < +\infty)$$
is a p.d.f., find the value of c. Find also $P(-1 < x < +1)$.

2. A p.d.f. is given by
$$\begin{aligned} f(x) &= ce^{-cx} & (x \geqslant 0) \\ &= 0 & (x < 0) \end{aligned}$$
where c is positive. Find the mean and variance of this distribution.

3. A variable x is distributed at random between the values 0 and 4, so that the equation of the frequency curve is
$$y = \text{A}x^3(4 - x)^2 \qquad (0 < x < 4)$$
where A is a constant. Determine A so that the above is a probability distribution function. Find also its mean and standard deviation.

4. A variate can assume values only between 0 and 1. The equation of its frequency curve is
$$y = \text{A}e^{-2x} \qquad (0 < x < 1)$$
where A is a constant such that the area under the curve is unity. Determine A to three decimal places. Find also the mean and variance of the distribution.

5. A variate x can assume only values between 0 and 5. The frequency curve is

$$y = \text{A} \sin\left(\frac{\pi x}{5}\right) \qquad (0 \leqslant x \leqslant 5)$$

where A is a constant such that the area under the curve is unity. Find A. Show also that the variance of the distribution is

$$50\left(\frac{1}{8} - \frac{1}{\pi^2}\right).$$

6. A p.d.f. is given by

$$y = a + bx + cx^2. \qquad (0 \leqslant x \leqslant 6)$$

The mean is 2·5 and the variance 2·15. Find the values of a, b and c.

7. For the Normal curve

$$y = \frac{1}{\sigma\sqrt{(2\pi)}} \exp\left(-\frac{x^2}{2\sigma^2}\right).$$

(*a*) the mean deviation is given by

$$\eta = \int_{-\infty}^{+\infty} y \mid x \mid dx$$

evaluate this to obtain

$$\eta = \sigma\sqrt{(2/\pi)} = 0{\cdot}797\sigma.$$

(*b*) The probable error ρ is given by the definition that the area between $\pm\rho$ is 0·5. Obtain

$$\rho = 0{\cdot}6745\sigma = 0{\cdot}8454\eta.$$

(*c*) The rth moment is defined as

$$\mu_r = \int_{-\infty}^{+\infty} y \,.\, x^r dx.$$

Show that $\mu_3 = 0$, $\mu_4 = 3\sigma^4$.

[It follows that for a Normal curve the 4th moment about the mean divided by the 4th power of the standard deviation is 3. The value of this ratio for any other distribution (*i.e.*, its approximation to the value 3) is a measure of the normality of it.]

8.
$$f(t) = \frac{1}{1000} e^{-t/1000} \qquad (t \geqslant 0)$$

is a frequency function for the life of a vacuum tube. For how many hours should a maker guarantee the tube if he wishes to be 90 per cent. certain of fulfilling the guarantee ?

9. A random variable has a frequency function

$$f(x) = a + bx^2 \qquad (0 \leqslant x \leqslant 1)$$

Find a and b if the mean is 2/3.

10. Assume that the length of a telephone conversation x min. has a frequency function

$$f(x) = a \exp(-ax) \qquad (x \geqslant 0)$$

Show that the chance of a conversation lasting more than $t_1 + t_2$ minutes given that it has already lasted at least t_1 minutes is equal to the absolute probability that it will last more than t_2 minutes.

11. Using Normal probability tables find:

(*a*) $\text{P}(x > 1{\cdot}23)$ (*b*) $\text{P}(x < -1{\cdot}2)$ (*c*) $\text{P}(-2{\cdot}1 < x < 1{\cdot}95)$.

12. The following values of a quantity x were obtained by experiment:

x	18	19	20	21	22	23	24	25	26
f	1	5	8	12	10	7	4	1	2

Find the equation of the Normal curve fitting this data.

13. 100 specimens when tested gave breaking strengths as shown where the mid-point of each interval is given and values are in 1000-lb. units. Show that

the mean is 71·1 and the standard deviation 2·02. Fit a Normal curve to this and obtain the graduated frequencies.

Mid-pt.	65·5	66·5	67·5	68·5	69·5	70·5
Freq.	1	0	4	10	14	22
Mid-pt.	71·5	72·5	73·5	74·5	75·5	76·5
Freq.	18	14	8	5	3	1

14. The weights in pounds of 100 men are as shown.

Mid-pt.	125	135	145	155	165	175	185	195	205
Freq.	1	1	14	22	25	19	13	3	2

Calculate the mean and standard deviation. Find the graduated Normal values for the above intervals.

15. The following is the distribution of 346 values believed Normally distributed. Show that the mean is 67·84 and the standard deviation (corrected) is 2·17. Obtain the graduated values for the class limits given.

Class interval.	Freq.	Class interval.	Freq.
58–60	1	66–68	131
60–62	2	68–70	102
62–64	9	70–72	40
64–66	48	72–74	13

16. Sacks of coal filled by a machine that is set to deliver 112 lb. each time are found to contain 8 per cent. of sacks that are 114 lb. or more in weight. Find the standard deviation of the machine. The regulations are that only 5 per cent. of the sacks are to be under the prescribed weight. To what new delivery weight must the machine be set?

17. A certain make of lamp has an average consumption of 120 watts with a standard deviation of 10 watts. Find the proportion which will have a consumption: (*a*) more than 127 watts; (*b*) more than 110 watts; (*c*) between 115 and 130 watts.

18. A large consignment of components are tested, and it is found that 45 per cent. are above the upper gauge limit of 5·7 mm. and 25 per cent. below the lower gauge limit of 2·4 mm. Find the mean and standard deviation of this batch and hence the percentage that will be rejected if new gauge limits of 2·5–5·4 mm. are introduced.

19. A random sample of fifteen 2-lb. packets as delivered by an automatic machine are found to have weights in oz. of:

32·11	31·97	32·18	32·03	32·25
32·07	32·05	32·14	32·19	31·98
32·07	31·99	32·16	32·03	32·18

Find the mean and standard deviation of this set of values.

If the distribution is Normal, estimate the percentage of underweight packets which the machine is delivering.

The regulations are that not more than 5 per cent. of packets may be underweight. To what value must the mean be changed if the machine is to comply with this regulation?

20. A process produces components whose lengths are normally distributed about a mean of 1·00 in. with a S.D. of 0·02 in. The specification is $1{\cdot}00 \pm 0{\cdot}04$ in. giving the maximum and minimum lengths. Components of the correct length are sold at a profit of 5*d*. Those too long can be reworked at a cost of 3*d*. and then sold with the rest. Those too short are a total loss of 1*d*. per component. Show that the expected profit is 4·79*d*. per part.

21. The tolerances on a product are $\pm 0{\cdot}003$ in. about a mean of 0·503 in., but the machine used has a S.D. of 0·0015 in. Undersize components are scrapped and oversize can be reworked. Find the objective setting of the machine mean for the most economical product and the resultant average cost per part given that

Cost of material	3·7*d*. per part
Cost of preliminary operation	6·3*d*. ,, ,,
Cost of final operation	4·1*d*. ,, ,,
Scrap value	0·3*d*. ,, ,,

22. A manufacturer sells an article at a fixed price of £1. He guarantees to refund the purchase money to any customer who receives an article of weight less than 8 oz. The articles are made by a process which has a standard deviation of 1 oz., and the cost £c per article is related to the mean weight w oz. by the equation

$$c = 0{\cdot}05w + 0{\cdot}30.$$

Find the mean weight which should be used to maximize the expected profit per article.
[If P is the profit per article, explain and solve the equation $dP/dw = 0$, where

$$P = 1 - (0{\cdot}05w + 0{\cdot}30) - \frac{1}{\sqrt{2\pi}}\int_{(w-8)}^{\infty} \exp\left(-\frac{x^2}{2}\right) dx\Big].$$

23. A firm makes components by a process with a standard deviation of 3. These parts cost 4*d.* each. If the dimension is between 95 and 105 the part is acceptable. If less than 95 it is scrapped, but if greater than 105 it can be reworked at a cost of 2*d.* per part. Find the process average to be used for a maximum profit per article.

38.7. Evaluation of Binomial Terms

We have shown how terms such as

$$_nC_r p^r q^{n-r} \quad . \quad . \quad . \quad . \quad . \quad . \quad . \quad . \quad . \quad (1)$$

can be evaluated exactly. Tables of these values and their sums also exist. We have also stated a form of the *Central Limit Theorem* that if r is the number of successes in n trials, where p is the constant probability of success per trial

$$\frac{(r - np)}{\sqrt{(npq)}}$$

is approximately normally distributed with mean zero and standard deviation 1, the approximation improving as n increases. We will now

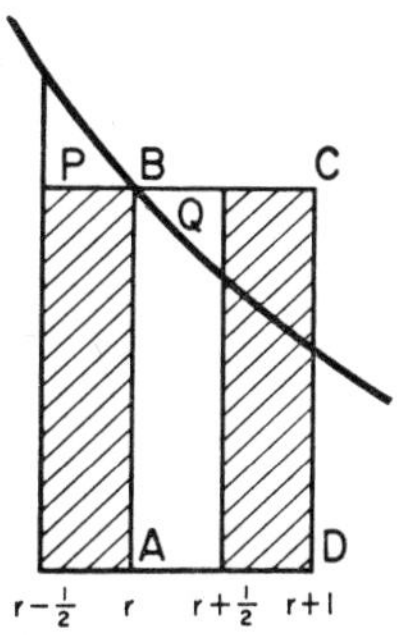

FIG. 115.

The area ABCD, a rectangle on unit base r to $(r + 1)$, where AB is an ordinate of the Normal curve is well represented by the area under the Normal curve on base $(r - \frac{1}{2})$ to $(r + \frac{1}{2})$.

apply this but note first that a minor adjustment improves considerably the degree of the approximation.

The figure shows a rectangle of a histogram of base r to $r + 1$, *i.e.*, width 1 and height given by (1) above. This has been placed within a Normal curve, so that the area under the curve from r onwards is shown. It is seen that the area ABCD is greater than the area under the curve on the same base AD. If, however, we move one-half a unit nearer to the mean and find the area under the curve from $(r - \frac{1}{2})$ to $(r + \frac{1}{2})$ we appear to have a very good approximation, with the area P included under the curve compensating for the area Q of the rectangle that is omitted.

This suggests that we use an ordinate $\frac{1}{2}$ nearer to the mean than that given, *i.e.*, we use, for example, the standardized value

$$\frac{(r - np - \frac{1}{2})}{\sqrt{(npq)}}$$

when concerned with the right-hand tail of the curve, *i.e.*, $r > np + \frac{1}{2}$.

Example 5. Evaluate:

(*a*) ${}_{25}C_5(0{\cdot}10)^5(0{\cdot}90)^{20}$ (*b*) ${}_{100}C_5(0{\cdot}10)^5(0{\cdot}90)^{95}$ (*c*) $\sum_{r=30}^{100} {}_{100}C_r(0{\cdot}25)^r(0{\cdot}75)^{100-r}$.

(*a*) Using log factorial tables the exact value is

$$\underline{0{\cdot}0646.}$$

Here $np = 25 \times 0{\cdot}1 = 2{\cdot}5 \qquad \sqrt{(npq)} = 1{\cdot}5.$

We require the area between x_1 and x_2 where

$$x_1 = \frac{(5 - \frac{1}{2} - 2{\cdot}5)}{1{\cdot}5} = 1{\cdot}33 \qquad x_2 = \frac{(6 - \frac{1}{2} - 2{\cdot}5)}{1{\cdot}5} = 2{\cdot}00$$

$$\Phi(1{\cdot}33) = 0{\cdot}9082 \qquad \Phi(2{\cdot}00) = 0{\cdot}9773$$

Area between $= \underline{0{\cdot}0691.}$

(*b*) The exact value is $\underline{0{\cdot}0339.}$

Here $np = 100 \times 0{\cdot}10 = 10, \qquad \sqrt{(npq)} = 3.$

Since $r = 5$ is below the mean of 10, we need the area between the standardized values of $4\frac{1}{2}$ and $5\frac{1}{2}$.

$$x_1 = \frac{(10 - 4\frac{1}{2})}{3} = 1{\cdot}833 \qquad x_2 = \frac{(10 - 5\frac{1}{2})}{3} = 1{\cdot}500$$

$$\Phi(1{\cdot}833) = 0{\cdot}0334 \qquad \Phi(1{\cdot}5) = 0{\cdot}0668$$

Area between $= \underline{0{\cdot}0334.}$

(*c*) A continuous stream of goods 25 per cent. type A, 75 per cent. type B passes an inspector. He picks out at random 100 for testing. The expression to be evaluated is the chance that he obtains 30 or more of type A.

(i) Binomial tables give the exact value as $\underline{0{\cdot}1495.}$

(ii) Here $np = 100 \times 0{\cdot}25 = 25, \qquad \sqrt{(npq)} = \sqrt{(18{\cdot}75)} = 4{\cdot}33.$

Since the area beyond the upper value is negligible, we need only calculate that beyond

$$x = \frac{(30 - 25 - \frac{1}{2})}{4{\cdot}33} = 1{\cdot}04.$$

$$\text{Area} = 1 - \Phi(1{\cdot}04) = 1 - 0{\cdot}8508 = \underline{0{\cdot}1492.}$$

EXERCISE 105

1. Two dice are tossed 100 times. What is the chance of obtaining a total of 12: (*a*) exactly 3 times; (*b*) at least 3 times?
2. If the chance of success in a trial is 1/5, what is the chance of exactly 215 successes in 1000 trials?
3. The chance of success in a certain experiment is 0·6. What is the chance of 35 or more successes in 50 such experiments?
4. It is known that 1 per cent. of articles delivered are defective. What is the chance that in a carton of 400 such articles there are 5 or more defectives?
5. If the chance of success in a single trial is $\frac{1}{4}$, find the chance that in 2000 trials the number of successes is between 460 and 540.
6. 100 coins are tossed as a batch 10,000 times. Show that exactly 65 heads will be obtained about 9 times and that 65 or more heads will occur about 18·7 times (*i.e.*, about 187 times in 100,000 tosses).
7. Show that the exact value of ${}_{25}C_8(0{\cdot}23)^8(0{\cdot}77)^{17}$ is 0·09960, whilst the Normal curve approximation gives the value 0·10710.
8. A process at a given stage has delivered articles which are 10 per cent. defective. How many articles must be produced if we want a final number of at least 200 and are prepared to take: (*a*) about a 5 per cent. risk; (*b*) no risk of having less? [If n are produced, show that

$$\frac{(200 - 0{\cdot}9n)}{\sqrt{n(0{\cdot}9)(0{\cdot}1)}} = -1{\cdot}645 \qquad (a)$$
$$= -4 \qquad (b).]$$

38.8. The Addition of Variances

Suppose that we have a batch of resistances each $x = 10$ ohms (mean value) with a standard deviation of 0·2 ohms and another batch for which $y = 100$ ohms (mean) and $\sigma = 3$ ohms. To make a circuit of total resistance $z = 270$ ohms we would combine 7 of the 10 ohms and 2 of the 100 ohms in series. This is

$$z = 7x + 2y \quad . \; . \; . \; . \; . \; . \; . \; . \quad (1)$$

Owing to the variation in each value x and y the question arises of the total resistance of such a circuit and its standard deviation—if we kept on forming such combinations of 7 of the x's and 2 of the y's.

To be general let

$$z_r = ax_r + by_r \qquad (r = 1, 2, \ldots n) \; (2)$$

where a and b are constants. If we put down the n such equations and add

$$\sum_1^n z_r = a\sum_1^n x_r + b\sum_1^n y_r.$$

Division by n gives the relation

$$\bar{z} = a\bar{x} + b\bar{y} \quad . \; . \; . \; . \; . \; . \; . \; . \quad (3)$$

[This shows that in (1) above, since the mean values are 10 and 100 respectively, the *mean* value of the combination is 270, the required value.]

From (2) and (3) we have the n equations

$$z_r - \bar{z} = a(x_r - \bar{x}) + b(y_r - \bar{y}) \quad (r = 1, 2, \ldots n)$$

Square each and add the n results:

$$\sum(z_r - \bar{z})^2 = a^2\sum(x_r - \bar{x})^2 + b^2\sum(y_r - \bar{y})^2 + 2ab\sum(x_r - \bar{x})(y_r - \bar{y}).$$

Since x_r and y_r are independent variables, *i.e.*, their variations about their respective means have no connection with each other, the third term on the right-hand side is zero. [It will be seen later that this summation term is the numerator in the formula for the coefficient of correlation between the x's and the y's, and so is necessarily zero when there is no connection between their variations.]

We now have

$$\sum(z_r - \bar{z})^2 = a^2\sum(x_r - \bar{x})^2 + b^2\sum(y_r - \bar{y})^2.$$

If V is used to denote the variance of, division by n gives the relation

$$\mathrm{V}(z) = a^2\mathrm{V}(x) + b^2\mathrm{V}(y) \quad \ldots \ldots \quad (4)$$

(*a*) The special case

$$z = x \pm y$$

should be noted. Here $a = 1$, $b = \pm 1$. It follows that

$$\bar{z} = \bar{x} \pm \bar{y},$$

but in either case

$$\mathrm{V}(z) = \mathrm{V}(x) + \mathrm{V}(y),$$

so that the variance of the sum or difference of two independent variables is the *sum* of their separate variances.

(*b*) The above method is clearly applicable to any number of independent variables, *i.e.*, if

$$z = a_1x_1 + a_2x_2 + \ldots + a_sx_s = \sum_1^s a_rx_r \quad \ldots \quad (5)$$

where the a's are constant

$$\mathrm{V}(z) = \sum a_r^2\mathrm{V}(x_r) \quad \ldots \ldots \ldots \quad (6)$$

(*c*) The above formula (6) is a special case of a formula for the variance of a general function of n *mutually independent variables.* Thus if

$$z = f(x_1, x_2 \ldots x_n)$$
$$\mathrm{V}(z) = \sum_{r=1}^{n}\left(\frac{\partial z}{\partial x_r}\right)^2\mathrm{V}(x_r).$$

It is seen that for the linear function (5) this formula immediately produces the result (6). In other cases, owing to the neglect of higher-order differentials, it provides a good working result if the standard deviation of any variable is not, say, more than 20 per cent. of its mean value.

Example 6. Cylindrical rods are made to a mean diameter of 2·01 cm., with a standard deviation of 0·03 cm. The sockets into which they fit are mean diameter 2·11 cm., S.D. of 0·04 cm. If assembled at random, what proportion of rods will not fit?

If $x =$ the diameter of a socket

$y =$ the diameter of a rod

let $z = x - y$

so that $\bar{z} = \bar{x} - \bar{y} = \underline{0{\cdot}1}$

and
$$\begin{aligned} V(z) &= V(x) + V(y) \\ &= (0{\cdot}04)^2 + (0{\cdot}03)^2 \\ \sigma_z &= \underline{0{\cdot}05.} \end{aligned}$$

The difference $z = x - y$ forms a normal distribution, mean 0·1 cm. and standard deviation 0·05 cm. A fit occurs provided $x > y$. We therefore need that proportion of the area below $z = 0$ as the proportion of cases in which $y > x$ and so a fit does not occur.

The standardized normal deviate is

$$X = \frac{(0{\cdot}1 - 0)}{0{\cdot}05} = 2.$$

Since $\Phi(X) = 0{\cdot}9772$

the proportion required $= 1 - 0{\cdot}9772 = \underline{0{\cdot}0228.}$
Some $2\frac{1}{4}$ per cent. of rods will not fit.

Example 7. Department A checks N articles and passes on a proportion p_1 as good to department B, which after a test passes on a proportion p_2 to department C. This department in a final check passes on a proportion p_3 to the packing section. Find N so that at least 100 should be received for packing if $p_1 = 0{\cdot}93$, $p_2 = 0{\cdot}90$, $p_3 = 0{\cdot}80$.

Let $z = p_1p_2p_3$

$$\therefore \quad V(z) = \left(\frac{\partial z}{\partial p_1}\right)^2 V(p_1) + \left(\frac{\partial z}{\partial p_2}\right)^2 V(p_2) + \left(\frac{\partial z}{\partial p_3}\right)^2 V(p_3)$$

Since the variance of a proportion p based on a sample size n is pq/n,

$$\begin{aligned} V(z) &= (p_2p_3)^2\frac{p_1q_1}{N} + (p_1p_3)^2\frac{p_2q_2}{p_1N} + (p_1p_2)^2\frac{p_3q_3}{p_1p_2N} \\ &= \frac{(p_1p_2p_3)^2}{N}\left[\frac{q_1}{p_1} + \frac{q_2}{p_1p_2} + \frac{q_3}{p_1p_2p_3}\right] \\ &= \frac{(0{\cdot}6696)^2}{N}\left[\frac{0{\cdot}07}{0{\cdot}93} + \frac{0{\cdot}10}{0{\cdot}837} + \frac{0{\cdot}20}{0{\cdot}6696}\right] = \frac{0{\cdot}221236}{N}. \end{aligned}$$

Assuming the proportion to be Normally distributed and using the $-3{\cdot}09\sigma$ limit as a minimum, the number received will be greater than

$$N[p_1p_2p_3 - 3{\cdot}09\sqrt{V(z)}] = N\left[0{\cdot}6696 - \frac{1{\cdot}4534}{\sqrt{N}}\right].$$

Since this is to be 100, we must solve the quadratic equation in $\sqrt{N}$

$$0{\cdot}6696(\sqrt{N})^2 - 1{\cdot}4534\sqrt{N} - 100 = 0$$
$$\sqrt{N} = 13{\cdot}354$$
$$N = \underline{178.}$$

About 178 articles are required. The risk of error is about 1 in 1000.

EXERCISE 106

1. In a relay race the times of the 4 runners for their distances are respectively:

Mean	22·3	23·2	54·7	123·6 (sec.)
S.D.	0·5	0·2	1·2	2·1 (sec.)

If these times are independently distributed, find the mean and S.D. for their total time in the race. Find the chance that on a certain day they will return a total time of less than 3 min. 40 sec.

2. A process makes resistances mean value 50, S.D. 2 ohms. If the distribution of values is Normal, find what tolerances should be imposed if it is desired that not more than one in a thousand should fail to be accepted.

The resistances are paired at random to give a total of 100 ohms. What tolerances should be imposed in this case if not more than one in a thousand should fail?

3. A batch of nuts (mean diameter 3·21 cm., S.D. 0·05 cm.) is to be matched with an equal batch of bolts (mean diameter 3·08 cm., S.D. 0·07 cm.). Find what proportion will not be matched. If a batch is 100, what is the chance that all fit?

4. Three gears are made for assembly on the same shaft, being held on one side by an enlargement of the shaft and on the other by a bearing housing so that they are held together. If their dimensions are:

Gear-wheel	A	mean	width	0·5000 in.	S.D.	0·0010 in.
,,	B	,,	,,	0·3000 in.	,,	0·0009 in.
,,	C	,,	,,	0·7000 in.	,,	0·0015 in.

show that the overall width is

$$\overline{X} = 1{\cdot}5000 \text{ in. with a S.D. of } 0{\cdot}0020 \text{ in.}$$

If the tolerances are $\overline{X} \pm 3\sigma$, show that only some 3 in 1000 assemblies are excluded by this.

5. A wagon load consists of 200 cartons, each containing 50 boxes, where each box has 1 dozen reels of cotton. The weights are given as:

Wooden reel	mean	weight	2 oz.	S.D.	0·3 oz.
Hank of cotton	,,	,,	1·5 oz.	,,	0·1 oz.
Box	,,	,,	5 oz.	,,	0·4 oz.
Carton	,,	,,	12 oz.	,,	1·0 oz.

Find the mean weight of a wagon load and its standard deviation. Hence find the 95 per cent. confidence limits for the weight of a load.

6. A resistance of 30,000 ohms is made by combining in series: 4 of 5000 ohms (mean) S.D. 20 with 5 of 2000 ohms (mean) S.D. 13. Find the least possible resistance (the -4σ limit) that can occur in such a circuit.

7. A machine applies to screws a torque average 4 lb. ft. with a standard deviation of 1·2 lb. ft. The screw-heads have an average strength of 6 lb. ft. with a standard deviation of 1·3 lb. ft. Find the proportion of screw-heads which break.

8. A resistance of 24,000 ohms is obtained by a series join of 2 of 10,000 each, S.D. = 200 and 4 of 1000 each, S.D. = 50. Show that there is an even chance that the constructed resistance is within 300 ohms of the required value.

9. A machine filling tins with juice is governed by the total weight, tin plus juice, but has a standard deviation of 0·30 oz. The tins have a mean weight of 7·2 oz. with a standard deviation of 0·40 oz. What mean total weight must the machine be set to deliver if it is required that only 5 per cent. of the contents of the tins should be under the advertised weight of 20 oz ?

10. If $z = xy$, where x, y are two independent variables, show that

$$\frac{V(z)}{(\bar{z})^2} = \frac{V(x)}{(\bar{x})^2} + \frac{V(y)}{(\bar{y})^2}.$$

11. The percentage of usable material in a sample of coal is found by burning a weight x gm. noting the weight y gm. of ash and finding

$$z = \frac{x - y}{x} = 1 - \frac{y}{x}$$

expressed as a percentage.
Show that

$$\frac{V(z)}{(\bar{z})^2} = \left(\frac{\bar{y}}{\bar{x} - \bar{y}}\right)^2 \left[\frac{V(x)}{(\bar{x})^2} + \frac{V(y)}{(\bar{y})^2}\right].$$

The average weight of coal used is 5 gm. per test and leaves an average weight of ash of 1 gm. Each weighing has a standard deviation of 0·01 gm. Find the 95 per cent. confidence limits for the percentage of usable material in this type of coal.

MISCELLANEOUS EXERCISES

Section A

Use the table of natural logarithims for Nos. 1–4.

1. The law governing the decay of radioactivity is

$$I = I_0 e^{-kt}$$

where I_0 is the initial intensity and I the intensity after time t. If it is known that $I = \frac{1}{2}I_0$ when $t = 2000$ years, find when I becomes $\frac{1}{10}I_0$.

2. Evaluate $e^{0 \cdot 892}$ and $e^{-0 \cdot 892}$; hence find sinh (0·892) and cosh (0·892). Solve the equation

$$\frac{e^{2x} - 1}{e^{2x} + 1} = 0 \cdot 537. \qquad \text{[U.L.C.I.]}$$

3. Find i from the formula

$$i = \frac{E}{R}(1 - e^{-Rt/L}),$$

given that $E = 500$, $R = 50$, $L = 5 \cdot 5$ and $t = 1$.

4 (*a*). Find q from the formula

$$q = \frac{T_2}{L_2}\left\{\frac{q_1 L_1}{T_1} + \log_e \frac{T_1}{T_2}\right\},$$

when $T_1 = 632$, $T_2 = 849$, $q_1 = 1 \cdot 362$, $L_1 = 946$ and $L_2 = 957$.

(*b*) Evaluate T_1 given by

$$T_1 = T_0 e^{\mu\theta},$$

when $T_0 = 132$, $\mu = 0 \cdot 2$ and $\theta = 2\pi$.

5. An acute angle x (degrees) is such that

$$x \cos 2x - 28 \cdot 65 \sin 2x + 45 = 0.$$

Show that the value of x lies between 50 and 60 degrees, and by a graphical method or otherwise, find this value correct to one decimal place.

6. Show graphically that if allowance be made for errors of observation, a law of the form $V = aU^n$ connects the following corresponding values of two quantities U and V, and determine the most probable values of the constants a and n:

U . .	2·60	3·02	3·42	4·15	4·92
V . .	16·6	19·5	23·6	30·9	37·5

7. (*a*) Find $\frac{dy}{dx}$ when $y = x\frac{(1 + x)}{(1 - x)}$.

(*b*) If $s = t^n e^{nt}$ where n is a constant, show that $t\frac{ds}{dt} = ns(1 + t)$.

(*c*) At time t the displacement x of a body moving in a straight path is given by $x = A\sin(\omega t + \alpha) + B\cos(\omega t + \alpha)$, where A, B, ω, α, are constants. Show that the ratio of the acceleration $\frac{d^2x}{dt^2}$ to the displacement x is constant.

8. (*a*) Given that $r = 5 + 4\cos\theta$ and that $\frac{d\theta}{dt}$ has a constant value ω, find $\frac{dr}{dt}$ when $\theta = \frac{\pi}{6}$.

(*b*) A quantity W is proportional to the expression

$$v(10 - v)^2 - 0{\cdot}32v^3.$$

Find the value of v for which W is greatest.

9. Differentiate with respect to x:

(i) x^4e^{-2x}, (ii) $\frac{(2x^2 - 5)}{(x^2 + 1)}$, (iii) $\sinh^2 x$.

Find $\frac{d^2s}{dt^2}$ when $s = \sqrt{2t} - 3$.

A10. (*a*) If $i = 10\sin 100t$ and $e = 5i + 0{\cdot}035\frac{di}{dt}$, express e in the form $E_m\sin(100t + \alpha)$, where E_m is a positive constant and α an acute angle in radian measure.

(*b*) Find the minimum value of the expression $\frac{1}{x}(x^3 + 54)$.

11. Differentiate with respect to x:

(i) $x^2\log_e x$; (ii) $\frac{\sqrt{x}}{(1 - x)}$; (iii) $\sqrt[4]{(2x^4 + 1)^3}$; (iv) $\cos^4 x$.

12. (*a*) Evaluate:

$$\int_{-1}^{3}\frac{1}{\sqrt{6x + 7}}dx \quad \text{and} \quad \int_{-1}^{3}\frac{1}{6x + 7}dx.$$

(*b*) Show that $(1 - \cos\theta)^2 = \frac{3}{2} - 2\cos\theta + \frac{1}{2}\cos 2\theta$; hence find $\int_0^{\pi}(1 - \cos\theta)^2 d\theta$.

(*c*) The gradient $\frac{dy}{dx}$ at any point (x, y) on a curve is given by

$$\frac{dy}{dx} = \sinh\frac{x}{100}.$$

If $y = 100$ when $x = 0$, find the equation of the curve.

13. Evaluate:

(i) $\int_8^{27}\left(\frac{4}{\sqrt[3]{u^2}} - 1\right)du$; (ii) $\int_0^1 (x + 1)^{-2}dx$;

(iii) $\int x\sin x\,dx$; (iv) $\int_0^{0{\cdot}002}\sin^2 500\pi t\,dt$.

14. Show that if $y = \frac{20}{\sqrt{x^3}}$ the integrals $\int_0^9 x^2y\,dx$ and $\int_1^{10} xy^2dx$ have equal values.

Evaluate:

(i) $\int_0^{\pi/9} \cos\left(3t + \frac{\pi}{6}\right)dt$; (ii) $\int_1^2 \frac{u}{3u^2 - 2}du$; (iii) $\int (1 + x)e^x dx$.

15. Using the same axes of reference, sketch the grapns of $\sin \theta$ and $\sin^2 \theta$ between $\theta = 0$ and $\theta = 2\pi$. Find by integration the mean height of each curve over the range $\theta = 0$ to $\theta = \pi$. Deduce the root-mean-square value of $\sin \theta$, *i.e.*, the square root of the mean value of $\sin^2 \theta$.

16. (*a*) Find the mean value of xe^{-x} over the range $x = 0$ to $x = 0{\cdot}5$.

(*b*) If $v\frac{dv}{dx} = -\frac{k}{x^2}$ where k is a constant and $v = 0$ when $x = a$, show that $v^2 = 2k\left(\frac{1}{x} - \frac{1}{a}\right)$. Deduce the value of v when $x = b$ and a is infinitely great.

17. A ring made of metal weighing 0·26 lb. per cu. in. is generated by one complete revolution about the x axis of the area bounded by the two curves $y = \sqrt{x} + 3$ and $y = \sqrt{x} + 4$ and the ordinates at $x = 0$ and $x = 1$, the unit of length along the x and y axes being 1 in. Find the weight of the ring. (Assume $\sqrt{x}$ to be positive.)

18. State and prove the theorem of Pappus (or Guldinus) concerning the volume of a solid of revolution.

The section of a metal collar is in the form of a trapezium ABCD in which the side AB, length 3 in., is perpendicular to the parallel sides AD and BC, lengths 2 in. and 1 in. respectively. Determine the distance of the centroid of the section from AB.

The collar may be regarded as generated by the rotation of the section ABCD through one revolution about an axis PQ parallel to AB and 3 in. beyond the corner C in the direction BC. Find the volume of metal in the collar.

19. An I section of a girder consists of three rectangles, namely, the upper flange 6 in. by 1 in., the lower flange 9 in. by 2 in., and the web 6 in. by 1 in., which connects the flanges. The longer sides of the flanges are horizontal, and those of the web vertical. Determine: (*a*) the height of the centroid G of the section above the bottom edge AB of the lower flange; (*b*) the moment of inertia of the section about the axis through G parallel to AB.

A20. Solve the following differential equations:

(i) $\frac{d^2s}{dt^2} = -4 \sin 2t$, given that when $t = 0$, $\frac{ds}{dt} = 2$ and $s = 0$;

(ii) $(1 + \theta)\frac{dy}{d\theta} = y^2$, given that y is infinite when $\theta = 0$;

(iii) $v\dfrac{dv}{dx} = -\mu x$, where μ is a constant, given that $v = 0$ when $x = a$.

21. Solve the following differential equations:

(i) $\omega\dfrac{d\omega}{d\theta} = 2$, given that $\omega = 4$ when $\theta = 0$;

(ii) $\dfrac{dy}{dx} = 3y$, given that $y = 1$ when $x = 0$.

The bending moment $EI\dfrac{d^2y}{dx^2}$ of a certain beam at distance x from the centre is given by $EI\dfrac{d^2y}{dx^2} = \dfrac{w}{2}\left(\dfrac{1}{4}l^2 - x^2\right)$, and when $x = 0$, $\dfrac{dy}{dx} = 0$, and $y = 0$. Express y in terms of x.

22. Solve the differential equation $\dfrac{d^2y}{dx^2} = -\dfrac{P}{EI}y$, where P, E, I are constants.

Using the conditions $y = 0$ when $x = 0$ and also when $x = l$, show that $P = \dfrac{k^2\pi^2 EI}{l^2}$, where k is an integer.

23. In the plane figure ABCD shown in the diagram, the straight parallel sides AB and DC are 2 in. apart and the breadth PQ of the figure measured parallel to AB and at any distance x in. from AB is given by $PQ = 2 - x + \frac{1}{4}x^2$ in. Determine:

(i) the area of ABCD;

(ii) the distance above AB of the centroid of the figure;

(iii) the volume of the ring generated by the rotation of the figure about an axis OO parallel to AB and $\frac{3}{4}$ in. below it.

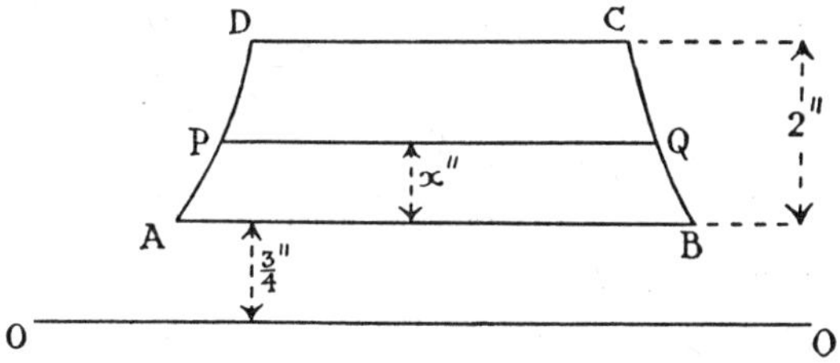

FIG. 116.

24. The area included by the curve $y = f(x)$, the axis of x, and the ordinates at $x = a$ and $x = b$ is rotated round the x axis through one revolution. Prove that the moment of inertia of the uniform solid thus generated about the axis of revolution is $\frac{1}{2}\pi m\int_a^b \{f(x)\}^4 dx$, where m is the mass of the solid per unit volume. Deduce that the moment of inertia I of a uniform solid right circular cone, mass M, radius of base r, about the axis of the cone is given by $I = M\frac{3}{10}r^2$.

SECTION B

B1. (*a*) Differentiate $\dfrac{(1 - \cos 2x)}{(1 + \cos 2x)}$.

(*b*) Find $\dfrac{dy}{dx}$ if $1 + xy^2 + 2x^2y = 0$.

(*c*) Show that $y = e^x\{A \cos \sqrt{5}x + B \sin \sqrt{5}x\}$ satisfies the equation

$$\frac{d^2y}{dx^2} - 2\frac{dy}{dx} + 6y = 0.$$

2. (*a*) Differentiate:

(i) $x^3\sqrt{a^2 - x^2}$; (ii) $\cosh^{-1}(3 + 2x)$; (iii) using logarithmic differentiation, find the value of $\dfrac{dy}{dx}$ when $x = 6$ for $y = \dfrac{(x-4)^2}{\sqrt[3]{(4x+3)}}$.

(*b*) If $x = a \sec \theta$, $y = b \tan \theta$, prove that

$$\frac{dy}{dx} = \frac{b}{a \sin \theta}, \qquad \frac{d^2y}{dx^2} = -\frac{b}{a^2 \tan^3 \theta}.$$

3. (*a*) Differentiate:

$$\text{(i) } e^{-3x} \cos 2x; \qquad \text{(ii) } 2x^3 \log_e \left(\frac{3x - 2}{7 - 4x}\right).$$

(*b*) Verify that $i = \dfrac{E_m}{R^2 + \omega^2L^2}\{R \sin \omega t - \omega L \cos \omega t\}$ satisfies the equation $L\dfrac{di}{dt} + Ri = E_m \sin \omega t$.

4. (*a*) Differentiate:

$$\text{(i) } \frac{\cos 2x}{1 + x^2}; \quad \text{(ii) } \log\sqrt{\left(\frac{2 + 3x}{3 + 2x}\right)}; \quad \text{(iii) } \sinh^{-1}(a + bx).$$

(*b*) Given that $y = A \cos 2x + B \sin 2x$ is a solution of the equation $\dfrac{d^2y}{dx^2} + 12\dfrac{dy}{dx} + 45y = \sin 2x$, determine the values of A and B.

5. By writing $\dfrac{x}{(1 + x)}$ as $1 - \dfrac{1}{(1 + x)}$, prove that

$$\sqrt{\frac{x}{1+x}} = 1 - \frac{1}{2(1+x)} - \frac{1}{8(1+x)^2} - \frac{1}{16(1+x)^3} - \frac{5}{128(1+x)^4} \cdots$$

and hence evaluate, correct to two decimal places, the integral

$$\int_1^2 \sqrt{\frac{x}{1+x}}\, dx.$$

6. The potential V at a point P due to AB, a bar magnet of length l and pole strength m, is given by $V = m\left(\dfrac{1}{AP} - \dfrac{1}{BP}\right)$,

where
$$AP^2 = r^2 + \frac{l^2}{4} - rl \cos \theta,$$
$$BP^2 = r^2 + \frac{l^2}{4} + rl \cos \theta,$$

where θ is the angle the line of length r joining P to the midpoint of AB makes with AB. Show that if l is small $V = \dfrac{ml \cos \theta}{r^2}$.

7. A current I of frequency $\frac{p}{2\pi}$ has the value given by

$$I = I_0 e^{-hx} \sin(pt - gx),$$

where x miles is the distance from the sending end and h, g are given by the expression

$$\sqrt{\frac{kpr}{2}}\sqrt{\left[\sqrt{\left(1+\frac{p^2l^2}{r^2}\right)} \pm \frac{pl}{r}\right]},$$

the minus sign giving h and the plus sign giving g. When $\frac{pl}{r}$ is very large, what are the approximate values of h and g.

If $k = 0{\cdot}05 \times 10^{-6}$, $r = 88$, $p = 5000$, and $l = 0{\cdot}3$, find the distance x at which the amplitude of I is halved.

8. Find:

(i) $\int x \cos 2x\, dx$; (ii) $\int \frac{dx}{\sqrt{49 - 4x^2}}$;

(iii) $\int \frac{dx}{x^2 + 4x + 13}$; (iv) $\int \frac{(x-2)dx}{(x+1)(x-4)}$.

9. (*a*) Find:

(i) $\int \frac{dx}{\sqrt{4x^2 - 25}}$; (ii) $\int_5^6 \frac{dx}{x^2 - 7x + 12}$.

(*b*) Under certain conditions the horizontal thrust H on an arch is given by

$$H = \frac{WR^4\int_0^{\pi/6}\left(\frac{1}{4} - \sin^2\theta\right)\left(\cos\theta - \frac{\sqrt{3}}{2}\right)d\theta}{2R^3\int_0^{\pi/6}\left(\cos\theta - \frac{\sqrt{3}}{2}\right)d\theta}.$$

Find H if W = 0·1 ton/ft., R = 40 ft.

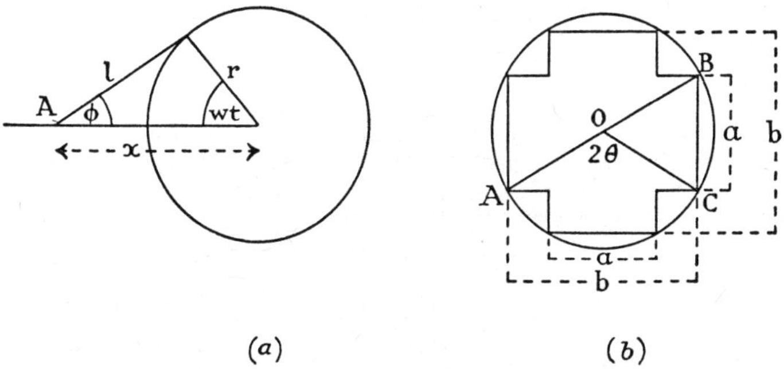

FIG. 117.

B10. In Fig. 117(a) show that

$$x = r\cos\omega t + l\cos\phi$$
$$= r\cos\omega t + l\sqrt{\left(1 - \frac{r^2}{l^2}\sin^2\omega t\right)}$$
$$= r\cos\omega t + l\left(1 - \frac{r^2}{4l^2}\right) + \frac{r^2}{4l}\cos 2\omega t \text{ (approx.)}.$$

Hence find an expression for the acceleration of the crosshead A.

11. When steam is flowing from a vessel at pressure p_1 into the atmosphere and p is the pressure at the orifice, the weight of steam per second passing through is proportional to $x^{2n} - x^{1+n}$, where $x = \frac{p}{p_1}$ and $n = 0{\cdot}8850$. For what value of x is the flow a maximum?

12. The discharge Q gallons per hour through a circular pipe of radius R is given by

$$Q = kR^{\frac{3}{2}}\sqrt{\frac{(\theta - \sin\theta)^3}{\theta}},$$

where θ is the angle subtended at the centre of the circular section of the pipe by the wetted perimeter. Show that when the discharge is a maximum $\sin\theta = \theta(3\cos\theta - 2)$. Verify that $\theta = 308°$ is an approximate solution of this equation.

13. The Fig. 117(b) within the circle represents the cross-section of a limb of a core-type power transformer, which is required to have a maximum cross-sectional area. The diameter AB = D being given, express the required area in terms of angle AOC = 2θ and D. Hence show that when the area is a maximum $b = 1{\cdot}62a$.

14. Find the area of the segment cut off from $y^2 = 4ax$ by the line $y = x$. Find also the volume of the solid of revolution formed when this area rotates round the x axis.

15. Show that the area bounded by the curves $pv^n = C$, the lines $v = v_1$, $v = v_2$, and $p = 0$ is $\frac{(p_1v_1 - p_2v_2)}{(n-1)}$. (Assume $v_2 > v_1$.)

16. Find the equation of the parabola passing through the points B, A, C as shown in Fig. 118. If this represents a section of a hill, and a mast is erected at P and just visible at C, find its height. Find the area of the cross-section BAC.

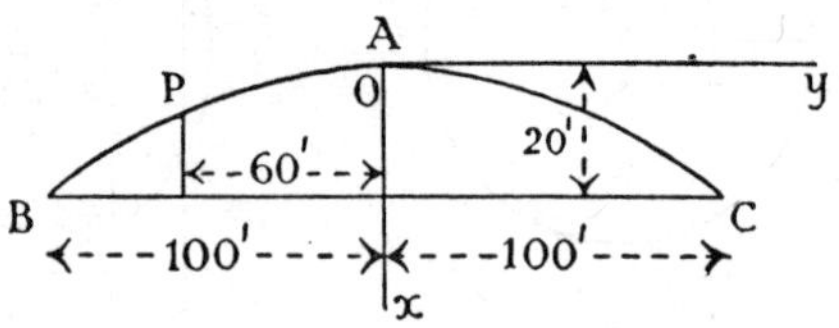

FIG. 118.

17. Give a rough sketch of the curve $y = x\sin x$ between $x = 0$ and $x = 2\pi$. Find the areas enclosed between the curve and the x axis within this range.

18. Find the values of x at which the turning points and point of inflexion occur on $y = \frac{2x^3}{3} - 7x^2 + 20x + 5$. Hence find the area enclosed by the curve, the axis of x and the ordinates passing through the points where y is a maximum and the point of inflexion.

19. Sketch the graphs of $y = 5x - x^2$ and $y = 15 - 3x$. The area enclosed by the graphs and the axis of x is rotated about the x axis, forming a solid of revolution. Find the volume of the solid generated. If only the curve $y = 5x - x^2$ from $x = 0$ to $x = 5$ is rotated about the x axis, find the position of the centre of gravity of the solid generated.

B20. Find the height above the x axis of the centroid of the area enclosed by the curves $y = 3 + 2x - x^2$, $y = 2x - x^2$, and the x axis.

21. The area enclosed by the curves $y = 4e^{\frac{1}{2}x}$ and $x^2 + y^2 = 16$ and the ordinates at $x = 0$ and $x = 4$ is rotated about the x axis. Find the volume of the solid generated.

22. For a beam length l ft., loaded w lb. per ft., fixed at both ends, the deflection y ft. at distance x ft. from one end is given by

$$y = \frac{wx^2}{24\mathrm{EI}}(l - x)^2,$$

where E, I are constants.

(*a*) Find the area between the curve of deflection and the original horizontal line of the beam.

(*b*) If the bending moment M at any point is given by $\mathrm{M} = \mathrm{EI}\frac{d^2y}{dx^2}$, find in terms of l (i) where M is a minimum; (ii) where M is zero.

23. A distance piece is shaped from the zone of a sphere as shown by the shaded part of Fig. 119(*a*). The radius of the sphere is 12 in., the faces of the zone are 3 in. and 6 in. from the centre of the sphere. The hole through the shaded area is central and has a radius of 2 in.

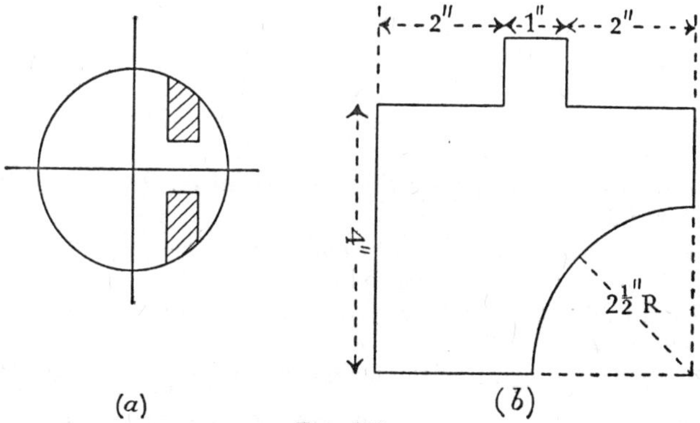

FIG. 119.

Find the volume of the distance piece and the distance of its centre of gravity from the larger face.

24. The two curves $pv =$ constant, $pv^{1\cdot4} =$ constant intersect at the point (1, 10). Find the area of the figure bounded by the two curves and the two ordinates at $v = 3$ and $v = 5$. Find also the volume swept out by the complete revolution of this area round the v axis. [v is measured along the x axis.]

25. The Fig. 119(b) shows a plate of uniform thickness. Find the co-ordinates of the centre of gravity of the plate referred to the bottom left hand corner as origin and the sides through it as axes. [The upper projection is a square of side 1 in.]

26. (a) Prove from first principles that the radius of gyration of a circular lamina about a central axis perpendicular to its plane is $\frac{r}{\sqrt{2}}$, where r is the radius.

(b) A metal casting has the form of a frustum of a cone. Its height is 6 in., the radius of the base 5 in., and the radius of the other plane surface is 2 in. Through this is drilled centrally a hole of radius 1 in., its axis coinciding with the axis of the frustum. Find the moment of inertia of the casting about its axis if the metal weighs 0·3 lb./cu. in.

27. Fig. 120 shows a vertical gate retaining water to a height h. The gate is hinged at A and is supported by a stop B. Find the maximum possible value of h and the maximum force per foot width on the stop B. (The density of water is 62·5 lb./cu. ft.).

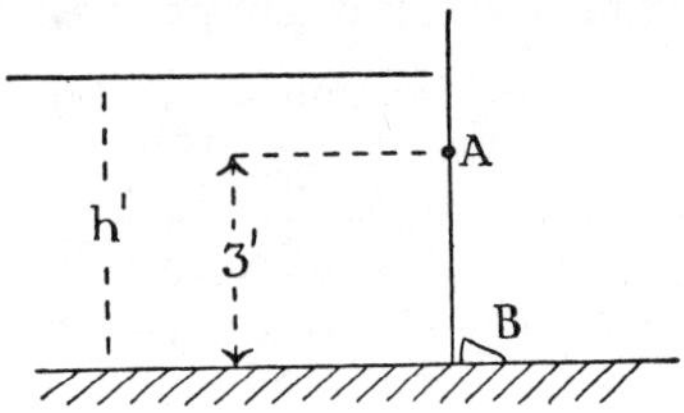

FIG. 120.

28. A dam 30 ft. high has a triangular cross-section. If the water side of the dam is vertical and the base is 20 ft. thick, determine the density of the material constituting the dam, given that the water surface is level with the top and that the resultant of the water pressure and weight of the dam passes through a point on the base 14 ft. from the water side.

29. (a) If $v = V_0(1 + \sin \omega t)$ and $i = I_0(1 + \sin \omega t)$, find the mean value of vi over half a period.

(b) Find the root mean square (R.M.S.) value of i over half a period if $i = 60 \cos (100\pi t + 2)$.

B30. Find by integration the form factor (R.M.S. value/mean value) of the wave $e = E_1 \sin \omega t + E_3 \sin 3\omega t$ over the range $t = 0$ to $t = \frac{\pi}{\omega}$.

31. (*a*) If $x + jy = Re^{j\omega t}$, find $x^2 + y^2$.

(*b*) Express $2 - 3j$ in the form $r(\cos\theta + j\sin\theta)$.

(*c*) Express $\dfrac{4(\cos 30 + j\sin 30)}{(16 - 4j)}$ in the form $a + jb$.

(*d*) Express $\cos 4\theta$ in terms of functions of θ only.

32. (*a*) Express $\dfrac{(2 + 3j)(1 - 4j)}{(-4 + j)(-1 - j)}$ in the form $re^{j\theta}$.

(*b*) Express $(2 - j)^4$ in the form $r(\cos\theta + j\sin\theta)$.

33. (*a*) Solve the equation $\dfrac{d^2y}{dx^2} + 5\dfrac{dy}{dx} + 6y = 0$.

(*b*) Find y if $\dfrac{d^4y}{dx^4} = \dfrac{w}{\text{EI}}$ and $y = 0$ at $x = 0$ and $x = l$, $\dfrac{dy}{dx} = 0$ at $x = 0$ and $\dfrac{d^2y}{dx^2} = 0$ at $x = l$.

34. The equation $\text{L}\dfrac{di}{dt} + \text{R}i = 0$ gives the current i at time t sec. in a circuit where L is the inductance and R the resistance. Find i in terms of t given that $i = i_0$ when $t = 0$.

If R = 5 ohms and L = 2 henrys, find after what time the current will have fallen to $\frac{1}{4}$ of its original value.

35. Solve the equations:

(*a*) $\dfrac{d^2y}{dx^2} + 3\dfrac{dy}{dx} + 2y = 0$, given that $y = 3$ and $\dfrac{dy}{dx} = 0$ when $x = 0$.

(*b*) $\dfrac{d^2x}{dt^2} + 4x = 0$, given that $x = 4$, $\dfrac{dx}{dt} = 8$ when $t = 0$.

36. (*a*) The distance x from the axis of a thick cylindrical tube is related to the internal pressure p by the equation $\dfrac{dp}{dx} = \dfrac{a - 2p}{x}$, where a is a constant. Show that, with C a constant $p = \dfrac{1}{2}a + \dfrac{\text{C}}{x^2}$.

(*b*) A body moving in a straight line with simple harmonic motion is governed by the equation $\dfrac{d^2x}{dt^2} + \omega^2 x = 0$, where x is the distance from the origin at time t and ω is a constant. Show that if the body starts from its equilibrium position with velocity v, its displacement t seconds later is $x = \dfrac{v}{\omega}\sin\omega t$.

SECTION C

C1. Obtain from first principles the differential coefficient of $2\cos 3x$ with respect to x. Find the x derivative of x^2e^{-3x}, $\dfrac{(x^2 - 1)}{(x^2 + 1)}$ and $\log_e\left(\tan\dfrac{x}{2}\right)$.

2. If y is a function of x, and x is a function of t, show that

$$\frac{dy}{dt} = \frac{dy}{dx}\frac{dx}{dt}.$$

If s, v, t represent distance, speed, and time respectively for a body in motion, show that $\frac{d^2s}{dt^2} = \frac{d}{ds}\left(\frac{1}{2}v^2\right)$. If $v = \omega\sqrt{(a^2 - s^2)}$, where a and ω are constants, find $\frac{d^2s}{dt^2}$ in terms of s.

3. Establish the formula for the derivative of a product. Find the derivatives of: x^2e^{-2x}, $\log_e \frac{(x+1)}{(x-1)}$, $\sqrt{\cos 2x}$. If $y = xv$, where v is a function of x, express $\frac{d^2y}{dx^2}$ in terms of x and the derivatives of v.

4. Show, from first principles, that if v is any differentiable function of x, then $\frac{d}{dx}\left(\frac{1}{v}\right) = -\frac{1}{v^2}\frac{dv}{dx}$. Give the x derivatives of $\sec x$, $\log_e \left\{\frac{(1-x)}{(1+x)}\right\}$ and $\sec^{-1} x$.

If $z = \sin\theta$ and ω is a function of θ (and therefore also of z), express $\frac{d\omega}{d\theta}$ and $\frac{d^2\omega}{d\theta^2}$ in terms of z and the z derivatives of ω.

5. An open rectangular tank is to have a volume of 50 cu. ft. and is to be 4 ft. wide. Find the length and depth if the least area of metal is to be used in its construction.

6. A sector of angle θ is cut from a circle of radius a, and the remainder is bent to form a right circular cone. Find the value of θ which makes the volume of the cone a maximum and show that the maximum volume is $\frac{2\pi\sqrt{3}a^3}{27}$.

7. Find the semi-vertical angle of the right circular conical shell of minimum surface area which with its rim resting on a table can cover a sphere of radius r and show that the area is $(3 + 2\sqrt{2})\pi r^2$.

8. A cylindrical hole is drilled through a hemispherical casting of radius R, the axis of the hole and of the hemisphere coinciding. Find the length of the cylindrical wall of the hole when its volume is a maximum and find the volume of metal remaining in this case.

9. (i) Find the maxima and minima of $2\sin^2 x - 3(1 + \cos x)^2$ in the range $0 \leqslant x < 360°$.

(ii) The total perimeter of a sector of a circle is given. Find the angle of the sector when its area is greatest, giving your answer in degrees.

C10. The equation $x^3 - 3x^2 + 3{\cdot}9 = 0$ has two roots in the neighbourhood of 2. Find the larger of these correct to two decimals.

11. Show graphically or otherwise that the equation

$$\cos x - x\sin x = 0,$$

where x is in radians, has an infinite number of real roots, and find the smallest positive root correct to three places of decimals.

12. Show that the equation $x = e^{-x}$ has one and only one real root and find it correct to three decimals.

13. Find:

(a) $\int \frac{x^2 + x + 1}{x + 2} dx$; (b) $\int \frac{x + 2}{x^2 + x + 1} dx$; (c) $\int \frac{x + 2}{\sqrt{(x^2 + x + 1)}} dx$.

Find correct to three decimals: $\int_0^{\pi/2} x^2 \sin x \, dx$.

14. Find:

(i) $\int \cos^5\theta \, d\theta$; (ii) $\int x\sqrt{(1 + x)} dx$;

(iii) $\int x^2 e^{-\frac{1}{2}x} \, dx$; (iv) $\int \frac{du}{\sinh u}$.

15. Find correct to three significant figures:

(i) $\int_0^{\pi/4} \tan\theta \, d\theta$; (ii) $\int_0^1 \frac{x^4 dx}{1 + x^2}$; (iii) $\int_0^{\pi/2} \sin^3 \theta(\sin^3 \theta + \cos^3 \theta)d\theta$.

16. Show that:

$$\frac{d}{dx}\left\{\cot^{-1}\left(\frac{\cot \alpha \cos x}{1 + \operatorname{cosec} \alpha \sin x}\right)\right\} = \frac{\cos \alpha}{1 + \sin \alpha \sin x}.$$

Deduce a value of $\int \frac{dx}{A + B \sin x}$ $(B < A)$.

17. Find the area included between the parabola $y^2 = x$ and the straight line $x - 5y + 6 = 0$. Find the co-ordinates of the centroid of this area.

18. Show that the parabola and the hyperbola $8y = 8 + 5x - 2x^2$, $2y = x + \frac{1}{x}$ intersect in three points, and find the abscissæ of these points. Sketch the curves for $x = -4$ to $+4$ and find the area in the first quadrant common to both curves.

19. Prove that $\frac{d}{dx}\left\{\tan^{-1}\left(\frac{x}{a}\right)\right\} = \frac{a}{a^2 + x^2}$.

Hence or otherwise, find the expansion of $\tan^{-1}\left(\frac{x}{a}\right)$ in: (i) ascending powers of x; (ii) ascending powers of $\frac{1}{x}$. For what range of values of x are these expansions valid?

C20. If $y = \tan^{-1}(1 + x)$ find $\frac{dy}{dx}$.

By expanding the result in ascending powers of x and integrating (or otherwise) obtain the series for y to sufficient terms to calculate $\tan^{-1}(1{\cdot}1)$ correct to four decimals and carry out the calculation

$$\left(\frac{\pi}{4} = 0{\cdot}785398 \ldots\right).$$

21. Obtain in any manner the series for $\sin\theta$ in ascending powers of θ.

If $y = \dfrac{A}{m^2}\left\{\dfrac{\sin mx}{\sin ml} - \dfrac{x}{l}\right\}$, find the limit to which y tends as $m \to 0$.

22. Prove that $\dfrac{d}{dx}\log_e(1+x) = \dfrac{1}{1+x}$, and hence, assuming that $x^2 < 1$, expand $\log_e(1+x)$ in ascending powers of x.

Obtain a series in ascending powers of x for $\log_e\dfrac{(1+x)}{(1-x)}$ and use the expansion to calculate $\log_e\left(\dfrac{11}{9}\right)$ correct to three places of decimals.

23. Define $\cosh x$ and $\sinh x$, show that each is the derivative of the other, and write down their expansions in series of ascending powers of x.

Find the limit as $\alpha \to 0$ of the expression $\dfrac{\alpha b(\cosh\alpha b - \cosh\alpha x)}{\alpha b\cosh\alpha b - \sinh\alpha b}$.

24. Obtain in any manner the series for $\sec\theta$ as far as the term in θ^4.

If a beam of length l is subject to a uniformly distributed load of intensity w and to an end thrust P, the central deflection is given by $\dfrac{wEI}{P^2}(\sec\frac{1}{2}ml - 1) - \dfrac{wl^2}{8P}$, where $m^2 = \dfrac{P}{EI}$. Show that as $P \to 0$ this tends to the limit $\dfrac{5wl^4}{384EI}$.

25. Obtain by Maclaurin's Theorem or otherwise the series for $\log_e(1+x)$ in ascending powers of x and deduce the series for $\log_e\dfrac{(1+x)}{(1-x)}$.

By putting $x = \frac{1}{3}$ in this latter series calculate $\log_e 2$ correct to four places of decimals.

26. Show that $\tan\left(\dfrac{\pi}{4} + x\right) = 1 + 2x + 2x^2 + \dfrac{8}{3}x^3 + \dfrac{10}{3}x^4 + \ldots$

Evaluate tan 46° 30′ correct to four decimals.

27. Prove the formula

$$\frac{1}{\rho} = \frac{d^2y}{dx^2}\Big/\left[1 + \left(\frac{dy}{dx}\right)^2\right]^{\frac{3}{2}}$$

for the radius of curvature ρ of a plane curve.

Find the radius of curvature and the co-ordinates of the centre of curvature at the point $(\frac{1}{2}, \frac{5}{8})$ on the curve $y = x^3 + 2x^2 - 2x + 1$.

28. Find the value of $\int e^{-at}\cos bt\,dt$.

A particle of mass m moves so that its velocity at time t is $Ve^{-kt}\sin pt$. Write down its kinetic energy at time t and find its average kinetic energy in the interval from $t = 0$ to $t = \dfrac{\pi}{p}$.

29. Sketch the curve whose equation is $y^2 = 25(x+1)(x-2)^2$ for

values of x between -1 and 4, showing both positive and negative values of y.

Prove that the area of the loop is $24\sqrt{3}$.

C30. The curve whose equation is $y = ax^3 + bx^2 + cx + d$ passes through the points (1, 3), (0, 1) and has a tangent parallel to the x axis at the point (2, 1). Prove that the maximum and minimum points on the curve are at the points where $x = \frac{2}{3}$ and $x = 2$ respectively. Draw a sketch of the curve.

31. Prove the theorem of Pappus relating to the surface obtained by rotating a curve about an axis in its own plane.

A circle of radius a is rotated about an axis in its own plane distant $b(>a)$ from its centre so as to form a closed ring. The surface of the ring is divided into two parts by a circular cylinder of radius $b - a\cos\theta$ coaxial with the ring. Show that the area of the two parts is $4a\pi[b\theta - a\sin\theta]$ and $4a\pi[b(\pi - \theta) + a\sin\theta]$.

32. Find the position of the centre of gravity of a piece of uniform wire in the form of an arc of a circle. Using this result or otherwise, find the position of the centroid of a semicircular area.

A semicircle ABC, of radius a, revolves about a line parallel to and at a distance b from the bounding diameter AC so that the point B of the circumference of the area is at a distance $a + b$ from the axis of rotation. Find: (i) the area of the surface and (ii) the volume of the solid formed.

33. A shell has the form of a cylinder of length 12 in. and diameter 6 in. with a pointed nose of axial length 9 in. The meridian length (see Fig. 121) of the nose is an arc of a circle tangential to the generator of the cylinder at the junction. Find the total volume of the shell.

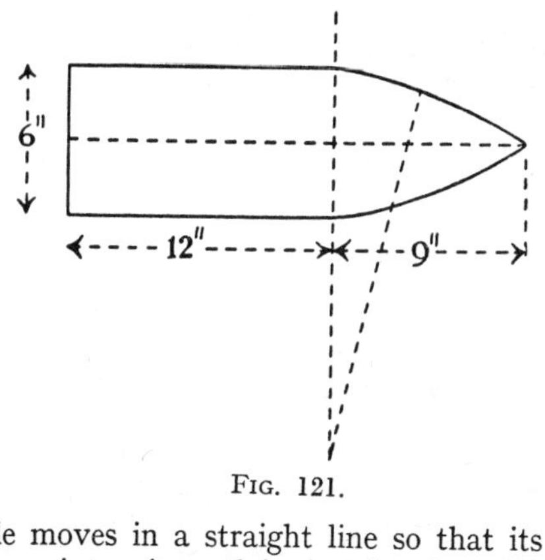

FIG. 121.

34. A particle moves in a straight line so that its velocity v at a distance x from a point on its path is given by $v^2 + \alpha^2x^2 + 2\beta x + \gamma = 0$. Show that the particle's motion is simple harmonic. Find the centre, period and amplitude of the motion.

35. Show that when a locomotive is travelling at a constant speed, the vertical motion of the coupling-rod is simple harmonic.

If the driving-wheels are 6 ft. in diameter and the coupling-rod cranks are 15 in. long, find the greatest vertical velocity and acceleration of the coupling-rod when the locomotive is travelling at 45 m.p.h.

36. A train of weight W tons moves on the level under the action of a pull P tons wt. against a resistance R tons wt., and the speed at any instant is v ft./sec. Show that the distance travelled while the speed varies from from v_0 to v_1 is $\frac{W}{g}\int_{v_0}^{v_1}\frac{vdv}{P-R}$.

If $W = 300$ and $R = 0{\cdot}9 + 0{\cdot}007v^2$, show that the distance travelled in slowing down from 45 to 30 m.p.h. with power cut off is about 520 ft.

37. A beam of length l and negligible weight which is fixed horizontally at one end and freely supported at the same level at the other end, carries a load W at its middle point. Show that there is a point of inflexion at a distance $\frac{8l}{11}$ from the free end and that the maximum deflection is $\frac{\sqrt{5}Wl^3}{240EI}$, where E is Young's modulus and I is the second moment of area of the cross section about the neutral axis.

38. Define the standard deviation σ of a set of observations x_1, x_2, . . . x_n of frequencies f_1, f_2, f_3 . . . f_n.

If $\bar{x}$ is the mean of the observations, A any arbitrary number and s is the root-mean-square deviation from A, prove that

$$\sigma^2 = s^2 - (\bar{x} - A)^2.$$

Calculate the mean and standard deviation of the following observations:

x (variate)	0	1	2	3	4	5	6	7	8	9	10
f (frequency)	10	40	72	85	78	55	32	18	7	2	1

ANSWERS

Exercise 1.

1. $-0{\cdot}4055$ or $-0{\cdot}6932$.
2. $0{\cdot}4055$ or $0{\cdot}2231$.
3. $-0{\cdot}6932$.
4. $\frac{1}{9}$ or $\frac{25}{4}$.
5. $\frac{1}{2}(1 \pm i\sqrt{11})$.
6. $\dfrac{1}{2LC}\{\pm C\sqrt{Z^2 - R^2} \pm \sqrt{(C^2Z^2 - C^2R^2 + 4LC)}\}$.

Exercise 2.

1. $3{\cdot}59$.
2. $1{\cdot}51$.
3. $2{\cdot}41$, $-0{\cdot}41$.
4. $0{\cdot}23$.

Exercise 3.

1. $10{\cdot}003{,}332{,}222{,}84$.
2. $1{\cdot}709{,}978$.
3. $1{\cdot}245{,}730{,}9$.
4. (i) $|x| < \frac{3}{2}$; $\dfrac{1}{9} - \dfrac{4x}{27} + \dfrac{4x^2}{27}$. (ii) $|x| > \frac{3}{2}$; $\dfrac{1}{4x^2} - \dfrac{3}{4x^3} + \dfrac{27}{16x^4}$.

8. $1 + \dfrac{3x}{2} + \dfrac{3x^2}{8} - \dfrac{1}{16}x^3$.
9. $|x| < \frac{2}{3}$: $\dfrac{1}{16}\left(1 - 6x + \dfrac{45}{2}x^2\right)$.

10. $\frac{1}{3} - \frac{71}{360}x$.
13. (i) $+12\%$; (ii) $+8\%$.
14. 15% too small.
15. $+1\%$.
17. $\frac{1}{2}[n^2(a + b + c) + n(3a + b - c) + 2a]$ $\quad a = 0, b = 1, c = 1$.

Exercise 4.

1. $\dfrac{1}{x + 2} + \dfrac{1}{x + 3}$.
2. $\dfrac{3}{x - 2} + \dfrac{1}{x - 5}$.
3. $\dfrac{7(x + 1)}{3(x^2 + 2x - 2)} - \dfrac{4}{3(x + 1)}$.
4. $\dfrac{3x - 1}{x^2 - x - 1} - \dfrac{2}{x - 1}$.
5. $-\dfrac{1}{x - 3} + \dfrac{1}{(x - 3)^2}$.
6. $\dfrac{25}{8(x - 3)^2} + \dfrac{55}{64(x - 3)} + \dfrac{9}{64(x + 5)}$.
7. $\dfrac{7}{9(x - 1)} - \dfrac{2}{3(x - 1)^2} - \dfrac{7x + 1}{9(x^2 + 2)}$.
8. 130; $|x| < \frac{1}{2}$.
9. $\frac{115}{972}$.

11. $\dfrac{1}{13}\log(x - 3) - \dfrac{1}{26}\log(x^2 + 4) - \dfrac{3}{26}\tan^{-1}\left(\dfrac{x}{2}\right) + C$.
12. $-\dfrac{3}{7}\dfrac{5!}{(x - 2)^6} - \dfrac{4}{7}\dfrac{5!}{(x + 5)^6}$
13. $-\dfrac{1}{2 + x} - \dfrac{1}{1 - x} + \dfrac{2}{(1 - x)^2}$; $7\frac{1}{16}x^3$; $8\frac{31}{32}x^4$.
14. $\dfrac{2}{(1 - x)^2} - \dfrac{1}{1 - x} + \dfrac{1}{2 + x}$.
15. $\dfrac{1}{n - 1} - \dfrac{1}{n}$.
16. $V_n = \dfrac{1}{3n} - \dfrac{1}{2(n + 1)} + \dfrac{1}{6(n + 3)}$

$$S_n = \frac{7}{36} - \frac{1}{3(n + 1)} + \frac{1}{6(n + 2)} + \frac{1}{6(n + 3)}.$$

Exercise 5.

4. $-\frac{23}{27}$.
5. $\frac{11}{16}$.
7. $\frac{2}{3}$; $\frac{5}{24}$.
8. $\dfrac{2}{3}$; $\dfrac{5\sqrt{2}}{12}$.
9. $\dfrac{43\sqrt{2}}{120}$.
11. $\frac{1}{2}E_mI_m(\cos a \pm 1)$.

Exercise 6.

1. $\sqrt{29}\cos(x - 21^\circ\,48')$.
2. $2\sin(x - 30)$.
3. $2\cos(x - 150)$.
4. $3\sqrt{5}\sin(2\pi ft - 0{\cdot}4636)$.
5. $A_0 = 100$, $A_1 = 4{\cdot}58$, $A_2 = -1{\cdot}5$, $\tan a_1 = \frac{13}{8}$, $\tan a_2 = -\frac{3}{4}$.
6. $Z^2 = R^2 + \left(\omega L - \dfrac{1}{\omega C}\right)^2$, $\tan a = \dfrac{\left(\omega L - \dfrac{1}{\omega C}\right)}{R}$.
7. $A = E^2 + I^2(R^2 + X^2)$, $B = 2EI\sqrt{(R^2 + X^2)}$, $a = \tan^{-1}(R/X)$.

Exercise 7.

6. The two expressions denote the same thing in (*a*), (*b*) or (*c*).

Exercise 8D.

1. (*a*) -3; (*b*) ± 3; (*c*) 1; (*d*) $x = n\pi + (-1)^n\frac{\pi}{2}$.

Exercise 8E.

1. (*a*) $\frac{1}{2}$; (*b*) $\frac{4}{3}$; (*c*) $\frac{2a+b}{3}$.

Exercise 9.

1. (*a*) $\frac{1}{2}$; (*b*) $\frac{\{\sqrt{(a^2+ah+\frac{1}{3}h^2)}-a\}}{h}$;

(*c*) $\theta = \log\frac{\{(\exp h - 1)/h\}}{h}$. $0 < \log\{(\exp h - 1)/h\} < h$.

5. (*a*) $-\sin x$; (*b*) $-\frac{1}{x^2}$.
13. 2·984.
14. 1·675.

Exercise 10.

1. $6x^2 + 6x - 2$.
2. $-\frac{1}{4}x^{-\frac{3}{2}} + 16x^{-5}$.
3. $-14x(1+x^2)^{-2}$.
4. $\frac{(x+2)}{2(x^2+x+1)^{\frac{3}{2}}}$.
5. $-\frac{3}{2}x(a^2-x^2)^{-\frac{1}{4}}$.
6. $4(3x_1^2 + x_1 + 1)^3(6x_1+1)$.
7. $x_1(a^2 - x_1^2)^{-\frac{3}{2}}$.
8. $-\frac{(ax_1+hy_1)}{(hx_1+by_1)}$.
9. $-\frac{(x_1^2-2x_1+3)}{(x_1-1)^2}$.
12. $2y = x + 3$.

Exercise 11.

1. $6\cos 2x$.
2. $-pa\sin(ax+b)$.
3. $-\cos(-x)$.
4. $-\frac{1}{2}\sec^2\left(\frac{\pi}{4}-\frac{x}{2}\right)$.
5. 0.
6. $2x\cos 2x + \sin 2x$.
7. $8\sec^2(2x)$.
8. $-a\operatorname{cosec}^2(ax+b)$.
9. $-\frac{1}{x^3}(2x\sin 2x + 2\cos 2x)$.
10. $2\cos x\cos 2x - \sin x\sin 2x$.
11. $\frac{2\sec^2(x)}{(1-\tan x)^2}$.
12. $\frac{\sec x}{(1+\sec x)}$.
13. $2\sin 2x$.
16. $12\sin(1-4x)$.
17. $6\sin 3x\cos 3x$.
18. $\frac{1}{6}\cos\frac{x}{3}\left(\sin\frac{x}{3}\right)^{-\frac{1}{2}}$.
19. $-\sin 2x(\cos 2x)^{-\frac{1}{2}}$.
20. $6\sec^2(3x)\tan 3x$.
21. 0.
22. $6\tan^2(2x)\sec^2(2x)$.
23. $3\sec^4(x)$.
24. $3\sec x\tan^3(x)$.
25. $-\frac{2}{x^3}\cos x(x\sin x + \cos x)$.
26. $-\frac{1}{(1+\sin x)}$.
27. $-\cot^2(x)$.
28. $2x\cos x(\cos x - x\sin x)$.
29. $2y - 1 = \sqrt{3}\left(x - \frac{\pi}{6}\right)$.
30. $\pi y + x - \pi = 0$.
31. $y = 4x - \pi + 1$.
34. $20e^{4x}$.
35. $-14e^{-2x}$.
36. $e^{2x}(2x+1)$.
37. $2xe^{x^2}$.
38. $2e^{2x}(\sin 4x + 2\cos 4x)$.
39. $2xe^{-4x}(1-2x)$.
42. 3 or 2.
43. $\frac{2}{x}$.
44. $\frac{(2x+2)}{(x^2+2x+3)}$.
45. $-4\tan 4x$.
46. $2x$.
47. $x + 2x\log x$.
48. $\frac{(1-\log 2x)}{x^2}$.
49. $\frac{1}{\sqrt{x^2+a^2}}$.
50. $\frac{1}{\sqrt{x^2-a^2}}$.
51. $\frac{4(\log x)^3}{x}$.
52. $\frac{1}{x\log x}$.

Exercise 12.

4. (*a*) $x = +1$ (min.), $x = -1$ (max.); (*b*) $x = 3{\cdot}41$ (min.), $x = 0{\cdot}59$ (max.); (*c*) $x = 0$ (max.), $x = \frac{4}{3}$ (min.).
5. $4 : \pi$.
6. (i) $2ab$; (ii) $a + b + 2\sqrt{ab}$.
7. 18 ft. from 27 C.P.
8. T (min.) = 3 for $\theta = 161° \ 34'$. T (max.) = 13 for $\theta = 71° \ 34'$.
9. $b - \dfrac{av}{\sqrt{u^2 - v^2}}$.
11. $r = \frac{4}{3}$ in., $h = 3\frac{2}{3}$ in.
13. $+3\sqrt{3}$ (max.), $-3\sqrt{3}$ (min.).
14. 2 tons.
16. Diam. of circles $\dfrac{220}{\pi}$ yd., length of rect. 110 yd.
19. (i) $2\tan^{-1}(\sqrt{2})$; (ii) $2\tan^{-1}\left(\dfrac{1}{\sqrt{2}}\right)$.
24. $R = \frac{3}{8}wl$, $u = \dfrac{w^2l^5}{640EI}$.
25. 28/27 gall.

Exercise 13.

1. $5(x^2 + 3x - 4)^4(2x + 3)$.
2. $6x^2(4 - x^3)^{-3}$.
3. $-x(1 - x^2)^{-\frac{1}{2}}$.
4. $-20 \sin 4x$.
5. $-14x \sec^2(1 - x^2)$.
6. $4x \cos(x^2 - 1)$.
7. $6 \sec^2(2x) \cot 2x$.
8. $e^{5x}(2x + 5x^2)$.
9. $12 \operatorname{ch} 4x$.
10. $-4x \operatorname{sh}(1 - x^2)$.
11. $e^{\sin 3x} . 3 \cos 3x$.
12. $e^{x^2} . 14x$.
13. $(9 - 2x^2)(9 - x^2)^{-\frac{1}{2}}$.
14. $9(9 - x^2)^{-\frac{3}{2}}$.
15. $-\dfrac{2}{x^2\sqrt{x^2 + 2}}$.
16. $-6 \sin(2 - 3x) \cos(2 - 3x)$.
17. $-\dfrac{n}{2}\cos^{n-1}\left(\dfrac{x}{2}\right)\sin\left(\dfrac{x}{2}\right)$.
18. $\dfrac{\sec^2\sqrt{x}}{2\sqrt{x}}$.
19. $-8 \operatorname{cosec}^2(2x) \cot 2x$.
20. $2x(1 + x^2)^{-\frac{1}{2}}(1 - x^2)^{-\frac{3}{2}}$.
21. $\dfrac{2(\operatorname{ch} 4x \operatorname{ch} 2x - 2 \operatorname{sh} 4x \operatorname{sh} 2x)}{\operatorname{ch}^2(4x)}$.
22. $\dfrac{1}{\sqrt{x^2 - 1}}$.
23. $\dfrac{1}{\sqrt{x^2 + a^2}}$.
24. $30 \operatorname{cosec}^2(2 - 3x) \cot(2 - 3x)$.
25. $70 \sec^2(5x) \tan 5x$.
26. $-24 \cot 4x \operatorname{cosec}^2(4x)$.

Exercise 14A.

1. $8x^3 + 3x^2 + 10x + 4$.
2. $-\dfrac{2(x^2 + 6x - 5)^2(x^3 + 15x^2 - 26x - 18)}{(x^2 + 2)^5}$.
3. $5e^{2x} \sin 3x \cos 4x\{2 + 3 \cot 3x - 4 \tan 4x\}$.
4. $e^{ax}\{a \cos bx - b \sin bx\}$.
5. $10^x \log_e 10$.
6. abe^{bx}.
7. $2xe^{x^2}$.
8. $a^{ax+b}a \log_e a$.
9. $(\cos x)^x\{\log \cos x - x \tan x\}$.
10. $x^x(1 + \log x) + x^{3/x} \cdot \dfrac{3}{x^2}(1 - \log x)$.
11. $x^3a^x \log a + a^x 3x^2 + x^{\sin^{-1}x}\left(\dfrac{1}{x}\sin^{-1}x + \dfrac{\log x}{\sqrt{1 - x^2}}\right)$.
13. $-9(2 - 3x)^2$.
14. $-10(3 - 4x)^{\frac{3}{2}}$.
15. $2\left(x - \dfrac{1}{x^3}\right)$.
16. $\dfrac{1}{2}\left(x - \dfrac{1}{x}\right)^{-\frac{1}{2}}\left(1 + \dfrac{1}{x^2}\right)$.
17. $6x(1 + 2x)^2(1 + 3x)^{-3}$.
18. $-(1 - x)^{-\frac{1}{2}}(1 + x)^{-\frac{3}{2}}$.
19. $2a^2x(a^2 + x^2)^{-\frac{1}{2}}(a^2 - x^2)^{-\frac{3}{2}}$.
20. $a^2(a^2 + x^2)^{-\frac{3}{2}}$.
21. $(1 + x)^3(1 - x)^2(1 - 7x)$.
22. $-2a^2x(a^2 - x^2)^{-\frac{1}{2}}(a^2 + x^2)^{-\frac{3}{2}}$.
23. $2nx\dfrac{(a + x)^{n-1}}{(a - x)^{n+1}}$.
24. $-\dfrac{2a}{\sqrt{a^2 - x^2}(\sqrt{a + x} - \sqrt{a - x})^2}$.
25. $n^2x^{n-1}(1 + x^n)^{n-1} - n^2x^{n-1}(1 - x^n)^{n-1}$.
28. 0·347.
29. 1·51.
30. 4·49.
31. (*a*) 5·36; (*b*) 2·32.
32. 0·74.
33. 54·6°.
34. 2·506.
35. 1·276.
36. 1·184.
37. 2·310.
38. (*a*) 2·11; (*b*) 2·22.
39. 0·9010.
40. 1·257.
41. 1·9 and − 0·33; 1·896.
42. 0·567.
43. 0·416.
44. 7·8.
45. $x = 1{\cdot}201$; 6·304.
46. 1·55.

Exercise 14B.

1. $x \cos x + \sin x - \sin x \cos x$.
2. (*a*) $(\cos x - 1)^2/(\cos x + 2)^2$. (*b*) $(\cos x - 1)(2 \cos x + 1)/\cos^2 x$.

Exercise 15.

1. $\dfrac{1}{\sqrt{9a^2 - x^2}}$. 2. $\dfrac{2a}{a^2 + 4x^2}$. 3. $\dfrac{2}{\sqrt{(15 + 4x - 4x^2)}}$.
4. $-\dfrac{3}{(2 - 6x + 9x^2)}$. 5. $-\dfrac{6}{\sqrt{(6 - 9x^2)}}$. 6. $\dfrac{1}{2\sqrt{x(1 - x)}}$.
7. $-\dfrac{m}{\sqrt{(1 - m^2x^2)}}$. 8. 1. 9. 2.
10. $1 + 2x \tan^{-1} x$. 11. $\dfrac{2}{(1 + x^2)}$. 12. $1 - \dfrac{x \sin^{-1} x}{\sqrt{(1 - x^2)}}$.
13. $\dfrac{-\sin x}{1 + (1 + \cos x)^2}$. 14. $\dfrac{\cos x}{2\sqrt{\sin x(1 - \sin x)}}$.

Exercise 16.

1. (i) 5; (ii) 5; (iii) $2b$; (iv) $5\sqrt{5}$. 2. $2\sqrt{2}$.
6. $(\frac{7}{5}, \frac{9}{5})$, $(\frac{4}{5}, \frac{13}{5})$, $(\frac{1}{5}, \frac{17}{5})$, $(-\frac{2}{5}, \frac{21}{5})$. 7. $(-\frac{1}{5}, 0)$; $(7, -12)$.
8. (i) $y = 2x - 4$; (ii) $y = \frac{4}{3}x + \frac{1}{2}$; (iii) $y = -\frac{1}{4}x - 2$; (iv) $y = x - 3$; (v) $y = x \tan 170 + 4 = -0{\cdot}176x + 4$.
9. $m =$ (i) $\frac{3}{2}$; (ii) $-\frac{3}{4}$; (iii) 2.
   y intercept = (i) -2; (ii) $-\frac{7}{4}$; (iii) $-\frac{1}{2}$.
   x intercept = (i) $\frac{4}{3}$; (ii) $-\frac{7}{3}$; (iii) $\frac{1}{4}$.
10. (i) $4y - 3x + 10 = 0$; (ii) $7y + 2x + 1 = 0$; (iii) $y = x\sqrt{3} + \sqrt{3} + 2$; (iv) $y + x + 1 = 0$; (v) $y = x$; (vi) $y = x \tan \alpha$.
11. (i) $y = 2$; (ii) $x + 2 = 0$.
12. (i) $y + x = 0$; (ii) $y + x = a + b$; (iii) $y = 2x$; (iv) $y - 3 = 0$; (v) $2t^2y + x - 3ct = 0$; (vi) $2y + 4x - 5 = 0$.
13. (i) $x + y = 1$; (ii) $y - x = 1$; (iii) $\dfrac{x}{2} - \dfrac{y}{3} = 1$; (iv) $4x + 3y + 12 = 0$.
15. (i) 1; (ii) $\dfrac{7}{\sqrt{17}}$; (iii) $\pm\dfrac{(a - b)}{\sqrt{2}}$; (iv) 0, point is on line.
16. (i) 32° 54′; (ii) 78° 41′; (iii) 59° 2′; (iv) 90°.
17. (i) $3y + 2x + 13 = 0$; (ii) $3y + 4x = 0$; (iii) $y = 2x - 5$.
19. $-\frac{7}{4}$; 2; $\frac{3}{2}$. 20. 1·3. 21. 1·5.
22. (4, 2); $y = 6x - 22$, $3y = x + 2$, $5y + 4x = 26$.
23. 20; $4y = 3x + 2$.

Exercise 17A.

1. (i) $y = x$; (ii) $x + y = 4$; (iii) $x^2 + y^2 = 16$; (iv) $3x = 4y$.
2. $4x - 2y + 10 = 0$. 4. $2(x^2 + y^2) = k^2 - 2a^2$.
6. $2y - 6x - 13 = 0$; 3 : 1. 8. $2x - 2y + 1 = 0$.

Exercise 17B.

1. $(0, 2b)$; $\left(\dfrac{2a}{3}, \dfrac{2b}{3}\right)$. 4. OC at $\left(\dfrac{ab^2}{a^2 + ab + b^2}, \dfrac{ab(a + b)}{a^2 + ab + b^2}\right)$.
OD at $\left(\dfrac{ab(a + b)}{a^2 + ab + b^2}, \dfrac{a^2b}{a^2 + ab + b^2}\right)$
11. (*a*) $64x + 112y - 61 = 0$, $14x - 8y + 9 = 0$;
   (*b*) $x + 2y + 1 = 0$, $2x - y - 3 = 0$.
12. (*a*) $11x - 20 = 0$; (*b*) $11x - 11y + 19 = 0$; (*c*) $17x - 9y + 1 = 0$.
13. $7y - 14x + 40 = 0$, $2y - 2x + 3 = 0$, $10x + 4y - 53 = 0$, orthocentre $(\frac{59}{14}, \frac{19}{7})$.

Exercise 18B.

1. 11. 2. $\frac{11}{7}$.
3. 100 lb. of the cheap, 50 lb. of the dearer mixture. Return is £17 10*s*.
4. $x = \frac{26}{17}$, $y = \frac{29}{17}$; about 312 oz. of D only unused.
5. 200 of A and 600 of B.
6. First depot sends 70 tons to first market and 30 tons to second. Second depot sends none to first and 60 tons to second market.
7. 200 of A, 150 of B and 150 of C.
8. 873 of A, 109 of B. M_1 and M_3 are fully used, but M_2 is idle for about 33·6 hours.

9.

	C_1	C_2	C_3
D_1	5	15	10
D_2	15	0	0

Minimum cost 150 units.

10. 41*s*.

Exercise 19.

1. $(x - 2)^2 + (y + 1)^2 = 9$.
2. 5.
3. (i) (3, 4), 5; (ii) (1, 3), 2; (iii) (1, 3), 2; (iv) $(\frac{4}{3}, -\frac{5}{3})$, $\frac{1}{6}\sqrt{254}$.

Exercise 20.

1. $(\frac{11}{5}, \frac{27}{5})$, $(-3, -5)$; $(-68, 34)$.
3. (*a*) $x^2 + y^2 - 2x - 5y - 24 = 0$; (*b*) $x^2 + y^2 - 7x - 5y + 16 = 0$.
5. $\frac{1}{5}(9 \pm 2\sqrt{14})$.
6. $x^2 + y^2 = \dfrac{a^2}{4}$.
7. If A, B are $(\pm 2, 0)$ locus is $x^2 + y^2 = 4$.
8. (i) $3x + 4y = 25$; (ii) $x - 7y = 50$; (iii) $x - 2y + 12 = 0$; (iv) $3x + 11y - 63 = 0$.
9. (i) $\sqrt{71}$; (ii) $\sqrt{85}$; (iii) $\sqrt{82}$.
10. (i) without; (ii) without; (iii) within.

Exercise 21.

1. $x^2 + y^2 = 4$.
2. $y = x$.
5. $(\frac{25}{3}, \frac{25}{2})$.
7. $(\frac{7}{2}, \frac{11}{2})$; 126° 52′.
8. (*a*) $(\frac{19}{2}, -\frac{9}{2})$, (3, 2), $(-\frac{11}{5}, -\frac{3}{5})$; $x^2 + y^2 - 6x + 9y - 13 = 0$.
   (*b*) A $= -1$, B $= 3$.
9. (*a*) $L_1L_2 + AL_2L_3 + BL_3L_1 = 0$; (*b*) $x^2 + y^2 - 2x - 4 = 0$.
10. $x - 2y + 8 = 0$, $x - 2y - 2 = 0$.

Exercise 23.

1. $\dfrac{(3t^2 - 2t)}{(2t + 1)}$.
2. $2t - 1$.
3. $\dfrac{(\cos t + \sin t)}{(\cos t - \sin t)}$.
4. $\dfrac{b}{a} \sin \theta$.
5. $\dfrac{1}{2}\left(t - \dfrac{1}{t}\right)$.
6. $ty - x = at^2$; $y + tx = 2at + at^3$.
7. $\dfrac{x}{a}\cos\theta + \dfrac{y}{b}\sin\theta = 1$; $ax \sec\theta - by \operatorname{cosec}\theta = a^2 - b^2$.
8. $y - \dfrac{3at^2}{1 + t^3} = \dfrac{t(2 - t^3)}{(1 - 2t^3)}\left\{x - \dfrac{3at}{1 + t^3}\right\}$;
   $y - \dfrac{3at^2}{1 + t^3} = -\dfrac{(1 - 2t^3)}{t(2 - t^3)}\left\{x - \dfrac{3at}{1 + t^3}\right\}$.
9. $y - \cos 2\theta = -2 \sin\theta(x - 2\sin\theta)$;
   $y - \cos 2\theta = \frac{1}{2}\operatorname{cosec}\theta(x - 2\sin\theta)$.
11. $y - x\sqrt{3} = a(2 - \frac{1}{3}\sqrt{3}\pi)$; $y + \dfrac{1}{\sqrt{3}}x = \dfrac{\pi a}{3\sqrt{3}}$.
13. 45°.

Exercise 24.

1. $y^2 = 4ax$.
2. $xy = c^2$.
3. $\dfrac{x^2}{a^2} + \dfrac{y^2}{b^2} = 1$.
4. $y = 1 - \frac{1}{2}x^2$.
5. $2y = (x - 1)(x - 3)$.
6. $\dfrac{y^2}{b^2} - \dfrac{x^2}{a^2} = 1$.
7. $x^3 + y^3 = 3axy$.
8. $x^{\frac{2}{3}} + y^{\frac{2}{3}} = a^{\frac{2}{3}}$.
9. $x^{\frac{2}{3}} + y^{\frac{2}{3}} = 4^{\frac{2}{3}}$.
10. $xy^2 = 4a^3$.
11. $(x - a)^2 + (y - b)^2 = r^2$.
12. $\dfrac{x^2}{a^2} - \dfrac{y^2}{b^2} = 1$.

Exercise 25.

1. $\tan \dfrac{1}{2b}(a + 2b)\theta$.
2. $x = 2\sqrt{2}b$.
3. $x + \sqrt{3}y = 2b$.
4. $2(a + b)\sin\dfrac{a\theta}{2b}$; $\dfrac{8(a + b)b}{a}$.
5. 3 : 1.

6. $y = nt^{n-1}x - (n-1)at^n$; $nt^{n-1}(y - at^n) + x - at = 0$.
7. (*a*) 90°. (*b*) 3° 20′; 36° 2′. (*c*) 71° 34′. (*d*) 71° 1′.

Exercise 26.

1. $2y = x + 6$; $y + 2x = 18$.
2. $y = x + \frac{3}{4}$, $y + x = \frac{9}{4}$; $y + x + \frac{3}{4} = 0$, $y = x - \frac{9}{4}$.
3. $y = x + \frac{1}{2}$, $(\frac{1}{2}, 1)$.
4. $4y = x + 36$, $4y = 9x + 4$.
5. $\frac{125}{6}$ sq. units.

Exercise 27.

7. $4x + 2y + a = 0$.

Exercise 28.

2. 8·8 ft.
3. 207·1 ft.
4. 266 ft. from lower and 14·7 ft. below it.

Exercise 29.

2. $\frac{x^2}{16} + \frac{y^2}{12} = 1$.
3. (*a*) $(\pm\sqrt{3}, 0)$; (*b*) $(\pm\sqrt{\frac{3}{20}}, 0)$.
4. $\frac{x^2}{\frac{32}{3}} + \frac{y^2}{\frac{32}{5}} = 1$.

Exercise 30.

6. $a^2 = 5$, $b^2 = 11$.
14. (4, 2·4), (3, 3·2); 1·28.
15. (3, 1·6), (4, 1·2); 11° 22′.
17. (*a*) $\frac{4}{3}\pi ab^2$; (*b*) $\frac{4}{3}\pi a^2 b$.
18. $\frac{198}{7\pi}$.
20. (i) 3·68 tons/in.²; (ii) 3·46 tons/in.².
21. $c = \pm 4$, $\theta = \frac{1}{6}\pi, \frac{7}{6}\pi$.

Exercise 31.

1. $(2, -1)$, $(1, 0)$, $(0, -7)$.
2. (i) $2x + 4y + 3 = 0$; (ii) $x + 4y = 0$.
3. $5y^2 - 5x^2 - 2 = 0$.
5. $x^2 + y^2 = 4$. A circle has the same equation referred to any perpendicular axes through its centre.
6. $3x^2 + 2y^2 = 6$.

Exercise 32.

3. (*a*) $(\pm\sqrt{13}, 0)$; $\frac{1}{2}\sqrt{13}$. (*b*) $(\pm 4, 0)$; $\frac{4}{3}$. (*c*) $(\pm\frac{2}{3}\sqrt{10}, 0)$; $\frac{1}{3}\sqrt{10}$. (*d*) $(\pm\frac{5}{2}, 0)$; $\frac{5}{4}$.
4. $3x - \sqrt{3}y = 3$; $y\sqrt{3} + x - 13 = 0$.
5. $\frac{x}{a}\sec\theta - \frac{y}{b}\tan\theta = 1$.
6. $(-3, -1)$.
7. $x + y \pm 1 = 0$.
10. $x \pm y \pm 2 = 0$.
11. $y^2 = -\frac{1}{2}ax$.
12. $x = ct\frac{(t^4 - 1)}{(t^4 + 1)}$, $y = -c\frac{(t^4 - 1)}{t(t^4 + 1)}$. $yx(x^2 + y^2)^2 + c^2(x^2 - y^2)^2 = 0$.
13. $3x^2 - y^2 = 3(550)^2$; 60°.
14. 24π; 96π.
15. $\left(\frac{a}{2}, \frac{2c^2}{a}\right)$; $\tan^{-1}\sqrt{2}$.
17. 2.
18. $y = 3x - 4$, $3y + x = 28$.

Exercise 36.

1. $y = 0$, $y = 1$, $x = 0$, $x = 1$.
2. $y = 0$, $x = a$, $x = -a$.
3. $y = 0$, $x = 0$.
5. Max. $(1, -1)$; min. $(5, 7)$.

Exercise 37.

1. (*a*) $(2, 1)$; (*b*) $(\frac{1}{2}, \frac{23}{2})$; (*c*) $(\frac{1}{3}, -\frac{259}{27})$, $(1, -9)$.
3. (*a*) T.P. $x = 0$ and 2. Inflexⁿ $x = 1$;
   (*b*) T.P. $x = -2$ and 1. Inflexⁿ $x = -\frac{1}{2}$;
   (*c*) T.P. $x = 2, \frac{1}{2}(4 \pm 3\sqrt{2})$. Inflexⁿ $x = \frac{1}{2}(4 \pm \sqrt{6})$.
4. T.P. $x = -1$ (min.). $x = +1$ (max.). Inflexⁿ $x = 0, \pm\sqrt{3}$.
5. (*a*) $0, \pi$; (*b*) $\frac{\pi}{2}, \frac{3\pi}{2}$; (*c*) $0, \pi$.
6. $x = 2$.
8. $x = \frac{2}{3}$.
10. $x^3 + 3x^2 - 9x + 5$.
11. $x^4 - 6x^2 + 12x$.
12. $y + x = 0$, $y - 3x = 4$.

Exercise 38.

The constant of integration is omitted.

1. $x + \frac{1}{2}x^2 + \frac{1}{3}x^3$.
2. $6x + \frac{3}{2}x^2 - \frac{2}{3}x^3 - \frac{1}{4}x^4$.
3. $-\frac{1}{5}(1 - x)^5$.
4. $2x + x^{-1} - \frac{1}{2}x^{-2}$.
5. $-x^{-1} - \frac{1}{2}x^{-2} - \frac{1}{3}x^{-3}$.
6. $\frac{4}{9}x^{\frac{9}{4}} - \frac{4}{13}x^{\frac{13}{4}} + \frac{4}{3}x^{\frac{3}{4}}$.
7. $\frac{1}{3}x^3 - 2x - \frac{1}{x}$.
8. $-x^{-1} - x^{-2} - \frac{1}{3}x^{-3}$.
9. $\frac{16}{15}(3x + 2)^5$.
10. $-\frac{1}{6}(2x - 1)^{-3}$.
11. $-\frac{1}{6}(1 - 4x)^{\frac{3}{2}}$.
12. $-\frac{2}{3}(5 - 3x)^{\frac{1}{2}}$.
13. $-\frac{1}{3a}(ax + b)^{-3}$.
14. $\frac{1}{8}(x^2 + 1)^4$.
15. $-\frac{1}{12}(5 - 4x^2)^{\frac{3}{2}}$.
16. $-\frac{1}{18}(9 - 4x^3)^{\frac{3}{2}}$.
17. $\frac{1}{5}x^5 - 3x^4 + 16x^3 - 32x^2$ or $\frac{1}{5}(x - 4)^5 + (x - 4)^4$.
18. $-\frac{1}{4} \cdot \frac{1}{(2x + 1)} + \frac{1}{8} \cdot \frac{1}{(2x + 1)^2}$.
19. $\frac{2}{3}(5 - x)^{\frac{3}{2}} - 10(5 - x)^{\frac{1}{2}}$.
20. $\frac{1}{12b^2}(a + bx)^{12} - \frac{a}{11b^2}(a + bx)^{11}$.
21. $\frac{1}{40}(4x + 3)^{\frac{5}{2}} - \frac{1}{8}(4x + 3)^{\frac{3}{2}}$.
22. $\frac{1}{4}\tan 4x$.
23. $-\frac{1}{6}\cot 6x$.
24. $\tan x - x$.
25. $\tan x - x$.
26. $\frac{1}{\cos x}$.
27. $-\frac{1}{\sin x}$.
28. $\frac{1}{5\cos^5 x}$.
29. $\frac{1}{3}\sec 3x$.
30. $-\frac{1}{5}\operatorname{cosec}^5 x$.
31. $x - \frac{1}{2}\cos 2x$.
32. $\frac{1}{4}\tan^4 x$.
33. $\frac{2}{3}\sin^{\frac{3}{2}} x$.

Exercise 39.

The constant of integration is omitted.

1. $\frac{1}{a}\tan^{-1}\frac{x}{a}$.
2. (*a*) $\sin^{-1}\left(\frac{1}{2}x\right)$; (*b*) $\frac{1}{4}\tan^{-1}\left(\frac{x}{4}\right)$; (*c*) $\frac{1}{12}\tan^{-1}\left(\frac{3x}{4}\right)$; (*d*) $\frac{1}{3}\sin^{-1}\left(\frac{3x}{2}\right)$; (*e*) $\frac{1}{\sqrt{21}}\tan^{-1}\left(x\sqrt{\frac{7}{3}}\right)$; (*f*) $\frac{1}{b}\sin^{-1}\left(\frac{bx}{a}\right)$; (*g*) $\frac{1}{\sqrt{3}}\sin^{-1}\left(x\sqrt{\frac{3}{2}}\right)$.
3. $\sin^{-1}\sqrt{x} - \sqrt{x(1 - x)}$.
4. $\frac{x}{(1 + x^2)^{\frac{1}{2}}}$.
5. $-a\left[\cos^{-1}\left(\frac{x}{a}\right) + \frac{1}{a}\sqrt{a^2 - x^2}\right]$.
6. $\sec^{-1} x$.

Exercise 40.

The constant of integration is omitted.

1. $\frac{1}{4}\log x$.
2. $\log(1 + x)$.
3. $-\frac{1}{2}\log(3 - 2x)$.
4. $-\frac{1}{2}\log(1 - x^2)$.
5. $\frac{1}{6}\log(1 + 2x^3)$.
6. $\log(3x^2 + 4x + 7)$.
7. $2\log\sin 2x$.
8. $-\frac{3}{5}\log\cos 5x$.
9. $\log\tan x$.
10. $\frac{1}{2}[\log x]^2$.
11. $\frac{1}{2}e^{4x}$.
12. $-\frac{7}{2}e^{-2x}$.
13. $2e^{x/2}$.
14. $\frac{1}{2}e^{x^2}$.
15. $\frac{1}{\log 3}e^{x\log 3}$.
16. $\frac{1}{4}x^4$.

Exercise 41.

The constant of integration is omitted.

1. $x - 2\log(2x + 3)$.
2. $3\log(x - 2) - 2\log(x - 1)$.
3. $\frac{1}{6}\log\left(\frac{3 + x}{3 - x}\right)$.
4. $\frac{1}{2}\log\left(\frac{x - 3}{x - 1}\right)$.
5. $\frac{1}{4a^2}\log\left(\frac{x^2 - a^2}{x^2 + a^2}\right)$.
6. $-\log x + 2\log(x - 1) - \log(x + 1)$.
7. $\frac{1}{2}\log x(x + 2)(x + 1)^{-2}$.
8. $\log x - 2(2x - 1)^{-1}$.
9. $\frac{1}{4}\log(x + 1)(x - 1)^3 - \frac{1}{2}(x - 1)^{-1}$.
10. $-\frac{1}{2}\log x + \log(x - 1) - \frac{1}{4}\log(x^2 + 4) - \frac{1}{2}\tan^{-1}\left(\frac{x}{2}\right)$.
11. (*a*) $-\log 5$; (*b*) $\log 5$.
12. (*a*) $\frac{1}{8}\log\frac{5}{3}$; (*b*) $-\frac{1}{8}\log 49$; (*c*) $\frac{1}{8}\log\frac{5}{3}$.
13. (*a*) $-\frac{1}{8}\log\frac{5}{3}$; (*b*) $\frac{1}{8}\log 49$; (*c*) $-\frac{1}{8}\log\frac{5}{3}$.

Exercise 42.

The constant of integration is omitted.

1. $\tan\frac{x}{2}$.
2. $-\frac{2}{(1+\tan(x/2))}$.
3. $\frac{1}{3}\log\frac{3+\tan(x/2)}{3-\tan(x/2)}$.
4. $\frac{1}{6}\tan^{-1}\left\{\frac{1}{12}\left(13\tan\frac{x}{2}+5\right)\right\}$.
5. $2\sin x - \log\tan\left(\frac{x}{2}+\frac{\pi}{4}\right)$.
6. $\log\tan x$.

Exercise 43.

The constant of integration is omitted.

1. $\frac{1}{3}\sin^3 x - \frac{1}{5}\sin^5 x$.
2. $\frac{1}{8}\sin^4 2x$.
3. $-\cos x + \frac{1}{3}\cos^3 x$.
4. $\frac{1}{2}x - \frac{1}{8}\sin 4x$.
5. $\frac{1}{3}\sin 3x - \frac{1}{9}\sin^3 3x$.
6. $-14\cos\frac{x}{2} + \frac{14}{3}\cos^3\frac{x}{2}$.
7. $\frac{3}{2}\tan\frac{2x}{3} - x$.
8. $-\frac{1}{6}\cos^6 x$.
9. $\frac{1}{7}(\cos x)^{-7} - \frac{3}{5}(\cos x)^{-5} + (\cos x)^{-3} - (\cos x)^{-1}$.
10. $-\frac{1}{3}(\sin x)^{-3} + (\sin x)^{-1}$.
11. $\frac{1}{10}(\cos 2x)^{-5} - \frac{1}{6}(\cos 2x)^{-3}$.
12. $\frac{1}{6}\sin^3 2x - \frac{1}{10}\sin^5 2x$.
13. $-\frac{2}{3}\cos^3 x + \cos x$.

Exercise 44.

The constant of integration is omitted.

1. $\frac{1}{3}x^3\log x - \frac{1}{9}x^3$.
2. $\frac{1}{2}x\sin 2x + \frac{1}{4}\cos 2x$.
3. $x\sin^{-1}x + \sqrt{1-x^2}$.
4. $\frac{1}{2}x^2\tan^{-1}x - \frac{1}{2}x + \frac{1}{2}\tan^{-1}x$.
5. $x\tan^{-1}x - \frac{1}{2}\log(1+x^2)$.
6. $-\frac{1}{2}x^2\cos 2x + \frac{1}{2}x\sin 2x + \frac{1}{4}\cos 2x$.
7. $\frac{1}{2}xe^{2x} - \frac{1}{4}e^{2x}$.
8. $-\frac{1}{10}e^{-x}(\sin 3x + 3\cos 3x)$.
9. $x\tan x + \log\cos x$.
11. See example 14 of 18.9.
12. $L = a/(a^2+b^2)$, $M = b/(a^2+b^2)$.

Exercise 45.

3. 1.
4. πc^2.
5. 4π.
6. 3π.
7. $\frac{1}{4}\pi$.
8. $\frac{1}{3}\pi$.
9. $\frac{1}{2}\log 3$.
10. 1.
11. $\frac{1}{10}\log\frac{9}{4}$.

Exercise 46.

1. 4.
2. $\frac{16}{15}$.
3. 1.
4. $\log(\frac{7}{3})$.
5. $1+\log 2$.
6. 0.
7. $\frac{\pi}{2}$.
8. 1.
9. $\frac{1}{6}\pi$.
10. $\frac{1}{4}\pi$.
11. $\frac{1}{2}\log(\frac{6}{5})$.
12. $\frac{8}{3}\log 2 - \frac{7}{9}$.
13. $2\log 2$.
14. 1.
15. $\frac{1}{4}\pi - \frac{1}{2}\log 2$.
16. $e^e(e-1)$.
17. 0.
18. $\pi^2 - 4$.
19. $\frac{3}{25}$.
20. $\frac{1}{2}(1+e^{-\pi})$.
21. $\frac{1}{20}\log\frac{13}{81} + \frac{3}{10}\tan^{-1}(\frac{2}{3})$.
22. $\frac{1}{10}\pi$.
23. 1.
24. $\frac{1}{3}\log 2$.
25. $\frac{2}{3}\tan^{-1}(\frac{1}{3})$.
26. $\frac{5\pi}{32}$.
27. $n!$.
28. (*a*) $\frac{1}{4}\pi$; (*b*) $\frac{2}{3}$; (*c*) $\frac{16}{35}$.
29. $\frac{3}{8}\pi$.
30. $\frac{3\pi}{512}$.
31. $\frac{1}{24}$.
38. (*a*) $-\frac{4}{3}$; (*b*) 0; (*c*) 0.

Exercise 47.

1. $4\frac{1}{3}$.
2. $\frac{3}{2\pi}$.
3. (*a*) $\frac{1}{4}\pi b$; (*b*) $\frac{2b}{\pi}$.
5. $\frac{2V^2}{\pi g}$.
6. $\frac{1}{2}RI_0^2$.
7. $\sqrt{\frac{1}{2}(I_1^2+I_2^2)}$.

Exercise 48.

1. 0.
2. $20\frac{1}{4}$; $20\frac{1}{4}$.
4. $\frac{\pi}{2}$.
5. $\frac{8}{3}a^2$.
6. $1\frac{1}{8}$.
7. $x = \frac{\pi}{6}$; $1\frac{3}{4} - \sqrt{3}$.
8. $\frac{800}{7}\sqrt{5}$.
9. 0·297
10. $4\frac{1}{3}$.
11. $36a^2$.
12. (*a*) $ab[\sqrt{3} - \frac{1}{2}\log(2+\sqrt{3})]$; (*b*) $c^2\log 4$; (*c*) $\frac{3}{2}\pi a^2$.

14. $\frac{5}{8} + \frac{1}{2}\log 2$.

15. $11\log 2 - 6\log 3 - 1$.

16. $a^2(\log 2 - \frac{7}{12})$.

17. $\frac{\pi}{3}$; $\frac{9}{8}$.

18. $\frac{\pi}{\sqrt{3}}$.

Exercise 49.

1. $2\pi ah^2$; $\frac{4}{5}\pi a^{\frac{1}{2}}h^{\frac{5}{2}}$.
3. $\pi(11\pi + 24)$.
4. $\frac{27}{4}\pi$.
5. 8π.
6. $\frac{128}{15}\sqrt{2}\pi a^3$.
7. $\frac{1024}{15}\pi$.
8. $\pi[2\log 2 - \frac{4}{3}]$.
9. (*a*) $\frac{3}{4}\pi c^3$; (*b*) $2\pi c^3[\frac{15}{8} + 2\log 2]$.
12. $\frac{4}{3}\pi$.
16. $\frac{\pi}{96}(32\pi + 27\sqrt{3})$.
17. $\frac{\pi}{120}(20\pi + 27\sqrt{3})$.

Exercise 50.

1. $r = a$.
2. $ar\cos\theta + br\sin\theta + c = 0$.
3. $\theta = \alpha$.
4. $r\cos\theta = 2a\sin^2\theta$.
5. $r(\cos\theta + \sin\theta)(1 - \cos\theta\sin\theta) = 3\cos\theta\sin\theta$.
6. $x^2 + y^2 = c^2$.
7. $x^2 + y^2 = ax + by$.
8. $x = a$.
9. $y = x$.
10. $[2(x^2 + y^2) - ax]^2 = a^2(x^2 + y^2)$.

Exercise 52.

1. $\sqrt{[r_1{}^2 + r_2{}^2 - 2r_1r_2\cos(\theta_1 - \theta_2)]}$.
2. $\frac{1}{2}r_1r_2\sin(\theta_1 - \theta_2)$.
3. $r\sin\left(\theta - \frac{\pi}{4}\right) = \pm 4$.
4. (i) $\frac{8}{13}(4 + \sqrt{3})$, 30°; (ii) 2, ± 90°; (iii) 3, ± 48° 11′.
5. (1, ± 70° 32′); (2, ± 48° 11′).
7. (i) $(\frac{16}{3}, 0)$; (ii) $(-24, 0)$. (i) $a = 6\frac{2}{3}$, $b = 4$; (ii) $a = 16$, $b = 8\sqrt{5}$.

Exercise 53.

1. $\frac{3\pi a^2}{2}$.
2. $\frac{1}{2}a^2$.
3. $\frac{1}{16}\pi a^2$.
4. $\frac{1}{16}a^2(\pi - 2)$.
5. $\frac{3}{2}(2\pi + 3\sqrt{3})$.

Exercise 54.

1. $\frac{\pi}{15}(3e^{3\pi/2} + 1)$.
2. $\frac{2}{3}\pi a^3(1 - \cos\alpha)$.
3. $\frac{2}{3}\pi a^3$.
4. $\frac{8}{3}\pi a^3$.

Exercise 55.

1. 2·64.
2. 7·3*a*.
3. $\frac{1}{8}\log 2 + 3$.
4. $\log(\frac{5}{3}) - \frac{1}{4}$.
5. $\log(2 + \sqrt{3})$.
6. $84\frac{3}{16}$.
7. $6 + \frac{1}{8}\log\frac{7}{5}$.
8. $\frac{8}{\sqrt{3}}a$.
9. $\frac{3}{2}a$; $6a$.
10. $\frac{a}{2}(\beta^2 - \alpha^2)$.
11. 9·76.

Exercise 56A.

1. 65·5.
2. $\frac{4}{3}(10)^{\frac{3}{2}}$.
3. 8·74.
4. 23·5.
5. $\frac{1}{2}(17)^{\frac{3}{2}}$.
6. $\frac{1}{4}\sqrt{2}$.
7. $c\operatorname{cosec}\left(\frac{x_1}{c}\right)$.
8. $\frac{1}{2}$.
9. $2\sqrt{2}$.
10. $3(ax_1y_1)^{\frac{1}{3}}$.
13. $\frac{1}{2a^2}\left(x^2 + \frac{a^4}{x^2}\right)^{\frac{3}{2}}$; $a\sqrt{2}$.
14. 0·15 ft./sec.².

Exercise 56C.

1. $a = \pm\frac{1}{4}$, $b = \pm 2$.

Exercise 57.

1. $\frac{n+1}{n+2}a$.
4. $\left(\frac{9a}{5}, \frac{9a}{5}\right)$.
5. $\left(\frac{\pi}{2}, \frac{\pi}{8}\right)$.
6. $(\frac{3}{7}, 0)$.

7. $(\frac{2}{3}a, 0)$. 8. $(\frac{4}{7}, 0)$. 9. $\frac{3(4a^2 - 4ah + h^2)}{4(3a - h)}$. 10. $\left(\frac{8a}{5m^2}, \frac{2a}{m}\right)$.

Exercise 58.

1. $\frac{1}{2}a$. 6. 21·2 in. 9. $\frac{2a}{\pi}$. 11. 3·2 in.

Exercise 59.

1. $\frac{4a}{3\pi}$. 2. $\sqrt{3}\pi a^2$; $\frac{1}{4}\pi a^3$. 5. 0·9. [A = 4·5, V = 8·1π].
6. V = $\frac{1}{15}\pi a^3$, $\bar{y} = \frac{1}{5}a$. 12. $\bar{x}$ = 2·52, $\bar{y}$ = 1·31. 13. (3·95, 0·96).

Exercise 60.

1. 3. 2. 4. 3. 2. 4. ∞. 5. ∞. 6. 1.
7. 0. 8. 0. 9. 0. 10. 0. 11. 0. 12. 1.
13. $\frac{1}{2}n(n+1)$; ∞. 14. $2 - \frac{1}{2^{n-1}}$; 2. 15. $\frac{3}{2}\left(1 - \frac{1}{3^n}\right)$; $\frac{3}{2}$.

Exercise 61. (Note that x is positive and $x < 1$ means $0 \leqslant x < 1$).

1. C. 2. D. 3. D. 4. C. 5. D. 6. C.
7. C. 8. D. 9. C. 10. C. 11. C, all positive x.
12. C, $x < 1$; D, $x \geqslant 1$. 13. C, $x < 1$; D, $x \geqslant 1$. 14. C, $x \leqslant 1$; D, $x > 1$.
15. C, $x < 1$; D, $x \geqslant 1$. 16. C, $x \leqslant 1$; D, $x > 1$.

Exercise 62. (A.C. $\equiv$ absolutely convergent.)

2. A.C., $|x| < 1$; D, $|x| > 1$; C, $x = \pm 1$.
3. A.C., $|x| < \frac{3}{2}$; D, $|x| > \frac{3}{2}$; C, $x = \frac{3}{2}$; D, $x = -\frac{3}{2}$.
4. A.C., $|x| < 5$; D, $|x| > 5$; D, $x = +5$; C, $x = -5$.
5. A.C., $|x| < 1$; D, $|x| > 1$; D, $x = \pm 1$.
6. A.C., $|x| < 1$; D, $|x| > 1$; C, $x = \pm 1$.
7. A.C., $|x| < 1$; D, $|x| > 1$; C, $x = \pm 1$.
8. A.C., all values of x.
9. A.C., all values of x.
10. A.C., $|x| < 1$; D, $|x| > 1$; C, $x = -1$; D, $x = +1$.
11. A.C., $|x| < 1$; D, $|x| > 1$; C, $x = -1$; D, $x = +1$.
12. A.C., $|x| < 1$; D, $|x| > 1$; C, $x = \pm 1$.
13. $|x| < 1$, C. $|x| \geqslant 1$, D.

Exercise 63.

1. $1 + ax + \frac{a^2x^2}{2!} + \frac{a^3x^3}{3!} + \ldots$ 2. $1 - \frac{a^2x^2}{2!} + \frac{a^4x^4}{4!} \ldots$
3. $bx - \frac{b^3x^3}{3!} + \frac{b^5x^5}{5!} \ldots$ 4. $1 + nx + \frac{n(n-1)}{1.2}x^2 + \ldots$
10. 0·28767

Exercise 65.

1. $\frac{1}{2}$. 2. $\frac{1}{6}$. 3. $-\frac{1}{4}$. 4. $-\frac{1}{2}$.
5. $\frac{1}{6}$. 6. -2. 7. $\frac{8}{3}$. 8. log 2.

Exercise 66.

1. $6x + 2y$; $2x + 8y$. 2. $\frac{1}{y}$; $-\frac{x}{y^2}$.
3. $-\frac{y}{x^2 + y^2}$; $\frac{x}{x^2 + y^2}$. 4. $\frac{1}{\sqrt{y^2 - x^2}}$; $-\frac{x}{y\sqrt{y^2 - x^2}}$.
5. $-x(x^2 + y^2)^{-\frac{3}{2}}$; $-y(x^2 + y^2)^{-\frac{3}{2}}$. 6. $\frac{3y}{(x+y)^2}$; $-\frac{3x}{(x+y)^2}$.

Exercise 67.

1. $2y^3$; $6xy^2$; $6xy^2$; $6x^2y$. 2. $6ax + 2hy$; $2hx$; $2hx$; $6by$.
3. $-\frac{1}{x^2}$; 0; 0; $-\frac{1}{y^2}$.

4. $4e^{2x+3y}$; $6e^{2x+3y}$; $6e^{2x+3y}$; $9e^{2x+3y}$.
5. $y\cos x$; $-\sin y + \sin x$; $-\sin y + \sin x$; $-x\cos y$.
6. $4\,\mathrm{sh}\,2x\,\mathrm{ch}\,3y$; $6\,\mathrm{ch}\,2x\,\mathrm{sh}\,3y$; $6\,\mathrm{ch}\,2x\,\mathrm{sh}\,3y$; $9\,\mathrm{sh}\,2x\,\mathrm{ch}\,3y$.
13. $4c^2q^2 = k^2 + 4p^2$.

Exercise 68.

1. $(2xy + 3z^2)dx + x^2dy + 6xzdz$.
2. $2xdx + 2ydy - 2zdz$.
3. $\dfrac{1}{x^4 + y^2z^2}(-2xyzdx + x^2zdy + x^2ydz)$.
4. $\dfrac{\mathrm{R}}{\mathrm{V} - b}d\mathrm{T} + \left(\dfrac{2a}{\mathrm{V}^3} - \dfrac{\mathrm{RT}}{(\mathrm{V} - b)^2}\right)d\mathrm{V}$.
5. $90\frac{2}{3}\pi$ cu. in. per sec.

Exercise 69.

1. 0·05 sq. ft.
2. 180π cu. in. per min.
4. + 19%.
5. + 9%.
6. $28\frac{1}{8}$ cu. ft. per sec.
7. $\Delta h = (a\sec^2\theta)\Delta\theta + (\tan\theta)\Delta a$; 0·35 ft.
11. 2·34; increase by $3{\cdot}79\theta$.

Exercise 70.

1. (*a*) $3 + j6$; (*b*) $5 + 5j$; (*c*) $19 - 4j$; (*d*) 25; (*e*) $a^2 - b^2 + j2ab$; (*f*) $\cos(\theta + \phi) + j\sin(\theta + \phi)$; (*g*) $x^2 - 2x\cos\theta + 1$.
2. (*a*) $\pm 6j$; (*b*) $8 \pm 6j$; (*c*) ± 2, $\pm j$; (*d*) 1, $-\frac{1}{2} \pm 1{\cdot}322j$.
3. (*a*) $14 - 13j$; (*b*) $18j$.
4. (*a*) $(x + jy)(x - jy)$; (*b*) $(x - y)(x + y)(x + jy)(x - jy)$.

Exercise 71.

1. (*a*) $\frac{3}{2} + \frac{1}{2}j$; (*b*) $-\frac{1}{5}(4 + 7j)$; (*c*) $\frac{1}{2}(-1 + j)$; (*d*) $\dfrac{1}{2}\left(1 - j\cot\dfrac{\theta}{2}\right)$.
2. $\frac{1}{25}(18 + j)$.
3. $x = 18$, $y = 1$.
4. $x = \dfrac{3(2 + \cos\theta)}{(5 + 4\cos\theta)}$; $y = -\dfrac{3\sin\theta}{(5 + 4\cos\theta)}$.
5. $\mathrm{R}_1 = \dfrac{\mathrm{R}_2\mathrm{R}_3\mathrm{R}_4}{\left(\mathrm{R}_4^2 + \dfrac{1}{\omega^2\mathrm{C}^2}\right)}$; $\mathrm{L} = \dfrac{\mathrm{R}_2\mathrm{R}_3\mathrm{C}}{1 + \mathrm{R}_4^2\omega^2\mathrm{C}^2}$.
6. $\mathrm{R} = -\frac{60}{41}$, $\mathrm{X} = -\frac{280}{41}$.
7. $\frac{1}{34}(1811 + 1124j)$.

Exercise 72.

1. $2(\cos 0 + j\sin 0)$.
2. $3\left(\cos\dfrac{\pi}{2} + j\sin\dfrac{\pi}{2}\right)$.
3. $2(\cos\pi + j\sin\pi)$.
4. $2\left(\cos\dfrac{\pi}{2} - j\sin\dfrac{\pi}{2}\right)$.
5. $5(\cos 53°\,8' + j\sin 53°\,8')$.
6. $2\sqrt{3}(\cos 30 + j\sin 30)$.
7. $5(\cos 143°\,8' - j\sin 143°\,8')$.
8. $2\sqrt{3}(\cos 150 + j\sin 150)$.
9. $2\sqrt{2}(\cos 45 + j\sin 45)$.
10. $2(\cos 30 - j\sin 30)$.
11. $2(\cos 150 - j\sin 150)$.
12. $18{\cdot}028\,(\cos 19°\,26' - j\sin 19°\,26')$.
13. $\dfrac{\sqrt{52}}{13}(\cos 56°\,19' - j\sin 56°\,19')$.
14. $0{\cdot}781\,(\cos 104°\,28' - j\sin 104°\,28')$.
15. $\sqrt{13}\,(\cos 123°\,41' \pm j\sin 123°\,41')$.

Exercise 73.

1. (*a*) circle centre O radius 2; (*b*) circle centre z_1 radius 3; (*c*) line through O.
4. Circle centre O radius $2k$.
7. (*a*) 325; (*b*) $\frac{13}{25}$.

Exercise 74.

2. $\sin 3\theta = 3\cos^2\theta\sin\theta - \sin^3\theta$, $\cos 3\theta = \cos^3\theta - 3\cos\theta\sin^2\theta$,
$\tan 3\theta = \dfrac{(3\tan\theta - \tan^3\theta)}{(1 - 3\tan^2\theta)}$.
3. $e^{-3x}\dfrac{(-3\sin 4x - 4\cos 4x)}{25}$; $e^{-4x}\dfrac{(-4\cos 3x + 3\sin 3x)}{25}$.
4. $r = 2$, $\theta = 60°$; $2^{20}(\cos 120 + j\sin 120) = 2^{19}(-1 + j\sqrt{3})$.

Exercise 75.

1. $\cos 4\theta = \cos^4\theta - 6\cos^2\theta\sin^2\theta + \sin^4\theta$, $\sin 4\theta = 4\cos^3\theta\sin\theta - 4\cos\theta\sin^3\theta$,
$\tan 4\theta = \dfrac{(4\tan\theta - 4\tan^3\theta)}{(1 - 6\tan^2\theta + \tan^4\theta)}$.
3. 3125 ($\cos 94^\circ 20' - j\sin 94^\circ 20'$).
4. $\pm(\cos 3\theta + j\sin 3\theta)$; $\cos\frac{\theta}{2} - j\sin\frac{\theta}{2}$, $-\cos\frac{\theta}{2} + j\sin\frac{\theta}{2}$; $\pm\left(\cos\frac{\pi}{4} + j\sin\frac{\pi}{4}\right)$;
$\pm\sqrt[4]{2}\left(\cos\frac{\pi}{8} + j\sin\frac{\pi}{8}\right)$.
5. $\cos 3\theta + j\sin 3\theta$, $\cos\left(\frac{2\pi}{3} + 3\theta\right) + j\sin\left(\frac{2\pi}{3} + 3\theta\right)$,
$-\cos\left(\frac{\pi}{3} + 3\theta\right) - j\sin\left(\frac{\pi}{3} + 3\theta\right)$; $\cos\frac{\pi}{6} - j\sin\frac{\pi}{6}$, $\cos\frac{\pi}{2} + j\sin\frac{\pi}{2}$,
$-\cos\frac{\pi}{6} - j\sin\frac{\pi}{6}$.
6. $1{\cdot}18 + 0{\cdot}33j$, $-0{\cdot}33 + 1{\cdot}18j$, $-1{\cdot}18 - 0{\cdot}33j$, $0{\cdot}33 - 1{\cdot}18j$.
7. (*a*) $x = \cos\left(\frac{2n+1}{6}\pi\right) + j\sin\left(\frac{2n+1}{6}\pi\right)$, $n = 0$—5;
(*b*) $x = \cos\left(\frac{2n+1}{5}\pi\right) + j\sin\left(\frac{2n+1}{5}\pi\right)$, $n = 0$—4
and $x = \cos\frac{n\pi}{2} + j\sin\frac{n\pi}{2}$, $n = 0$—3;
(*c*) $x = \cos\left(\frac{2n+1}{3}\pi\right) + j\sin\left(\frac{2n+1}{3}\pi\right)$, $n = 0$—2
and $x = \cos\left(\frac{2n+1}{4}\pi\right) + j\sin\left(\frac{2n+1}{4}\pi\right)$, $n = 0$—3.

Exercise 76.

1. $\frac{5}{4}$. 2. $\pm 2\sqrt{2}$. 3. $\frac{2}{3}\sqrt{2}$. 4. $\dfrac{2}{\sqrt{5}}$. 5. $\dfrac{2}{\sqrt{3}}$.
7. A = 7, B = − 1. 8. $\dfrac{x^2}{a^2} - \dfrac{y^2}{b^2} = 1$. 10. A = 3, B = − 1.
12. 17·36 knots. 13. $\frac{1}{2}\left(x - \frac{1}{x}\right)$, $\frac{1}{2}\left(x + \frac{1}{x}\right)$. 14. $\frac{3}{2}$; $x = \frac{1}{2}\log 5$.
15. $\sec\theta + \tan\theta$; $\sec\theta - \tan\theta$.

Exercise 77.

8. $(x - ye^{a})(x - ye^{-a})$. 9. $x = e^{a}$ or e^{-a}.

Exercise 78.

1. (*a*) $\frac{1}{3}\operatorname{ch}\frac{x}{3}$; (*b*) $15\operatorname{sh}5x$; (*c*) $6\operatorname{sech}^2 3x$; (*d*) $6\operatorname{ch}^2 2x\operatorname{sh}2x$; (*e*) $6\operatorname{sh}3x\operatorname{ch}3x$;
(*f*) $2\operatorname{ch}4x$; (*g*) $-\dfrac{4\operatorname{ch}4x}{\operatorname{sh}^2 4x}$; (*h*) $-\dfrac{1}{2}\dfrac{\operatorname{sh}\left(\frac{x}{2}\right)}{\operatorname{ch}^2\left(\frac{x}{2}\right)}$; (*i*) $\frac{1}{2}\operatorname{th}\frac{x}{4}\operatorname{sech}^2\frac{x}{4}$; (*j*) $3\operatorname{th}3x$;
(*k*) $\operatorname{cosech}x$; (*l*) $1 - \operatorname{cosech}^2 x$; (*m*) $3\sin 2x\operatorname{sh}3x + 2\cos 2x\operatorname{ch}3x$;
(*n*) $x^{\operatorname{sh}x}\left(\log x\operatorname{ch}x + \frac{1}{x}\operatorname{sh}x\right)$; (*o*) $e^{ax}(b\operatorname{sh}bx + a\operatorname{ch}bx)$;
(*p*) $\dfrac{\operatorname{th}x\sec^2 x - \tan x\operatorname{sech}^2 x}{\operatorname{th}^2 x}$; (*q*) $\operatorname{sech}x(1 - x\operatorname{th}x)$;
(*r*) $\dfrac{1}{x^3}(2x\operatorname{ch}2x - 2\operatorname{sh}2x)$; (*s*) $(\operatorname{ch}x)^x[x\operatorname{th}x + \log\operatorname{ch}x]$.
2. 4. 6. $x = 1$ or 6. 7. (*b*) 1; (*c*) 1; (*c*) $-\frac{2}{3}$; (*d*) $\frac{1}{3}$.
10. $4ay\operatorname{sh}\theta - bx = ab(2\operatorname{sh}^2\theta - 1)$. 11. 0·345. 12. 0·931.

Exercise 79.

The constant of integration is omitted.

1. (*a*) $\frac{4}{3}$ sh $3x$; (*b*) $\frac{10}{3}$ ch $\frac{3x}{2}$; (*c*) 2 log ch $\frac{x}{2}$; (*d*) $\frac{1}{12}$ sh $6x - \frac{1}{2}x$; (*e*) $\frac{2}{5}$ th $5x$; (*f*) $\frac{1}{7}$ sh $14x + 2x$.
2. (*a*) $\frac{1}{2}x$ ch $2x - \frac{1}{4}$ sh $2x$; (*b*) x^2 sh $x - 2x$ ch $x + 2$ sh x; (*c*) x th x − log ch x.
3. (*a*) sh 2 = 3·627; (*b*) 0·813.
4. 2.
5. $A = 4 \log (2 + \sqrt{3}) - 2\sqrt{3} = 1{\cdot}804$; $V = \pi[7 \log (2 + \sqrt{3}) - 2\sqrt{3}] = 5{\cdot}76\pi$.
6. $\frac{1}{3}$ log 5.
7. log (ch $\frac{4}{5}$).

Exercise 81.

1. $\dfrac{2}{\sqrt{(4x^2 + 9)}}$.
2. $\dfrac{3}{\sqrt{(9x^2 - 16)}}$.
3. $\dfrac{6}{4 - 9x^2}$.
4. $\dfrac{1}{\sqrt{(x^2 + 3x + 2)}}$.
5. $\frac{1}{2}$ sec x.
6. $\dfrac{1}{\sqrt{(x^2 - 1)}}$.
7. sec x.
8. sec x.
9. sec x.

Exercise 82.

The constant of integration is omitted.

1. $\text{sh}^{-1}\left(\frac{x}{2}\right)$.
2. $\text{ch}^{-1}\left(\frac{x}{3}\right)$.
3. $\frac{1}{2}\,\text{ch}^{-1}\left(\frac{2x}{5}\right)$.
4. $\frac{1}{3}\,\text{sh}^{-1}(3x)$.
5. $\frac{1}{a}\,\text{sh}^{-1}\left(\frac{ax}{b}\right)$.
6. $\frac{1}{b}\sin^{-1}\left(\frac{bx}{a}\right)$.
7. $\frac{1}{3}\sin^{-1}\left(\frac{3x}{4}\right)$.
8. $\text{sh}^{-1}(x^2)$.
9. $\text{ch}^{-1}\left(\frac{x^2}{a}\right)$.
10. log (4 − $\sqrt{7}$).
11. 0·284.
12. log 3.
13. $\frac{3}{2}x\sqrt{x^2 + \frac{16}{9}} + \frac{8}{3}\,\text{sh}^{-1}\left(\frac{3x}{4}\right)$.
14. $\frac{1}{2}x\sqrt{x^2 - 9} - \frac{9}{2}\,\text{ch}^{-1}\left(\frac{x}{3}\right)$.
15. $10 + \frac{9}{2}\log 3$.
16. $\frac{15}{2} - 8\log 2$.
17. $a(2\sqrt{3} + \text{sh}^{-1}\sqrt{3})$.

Exercise 83.

1. $\frac{1}{2}Mh^2$.
2. $\frac{1}{2}Mh^2$.
3. $\frac{1}{6}Mh^2$.
4. $\frac{3}{10}M\dfrac{r_1^5 - r_2^5}{r_1^3 - r_2^3}$.
5. $\frac{4}{5}Mab$.
6. $\frac{1}{3}Mr^2$.
7. $177\frac{1}{3}$M lb. in.².
8. 160 in.⁴.
9. $K^2 = \dfrac{1}{2}\dfrac{b(R^4 - r^4) + ar^4}{b(R^2 - r^2) + ar^2}$.

Exercise 84.

1. $M\left[\frac{a^2}{12} + d^2\right]$.
2. $\frac{5}{4}Ma^2$; $\frac{3}{2}Ma^2$.
3. $M\frac{b^2}{3}$; $M\frac{a^2}{3}$.
4. $\frac{1}{18}Mh^2$.
5. $\frac{2}{5}Ma^2$; $M\frac{83}{320}a^2$.
6. $\frac{M}{20}(3r^2 + 2h^2)$; $M\frac{3}{80}(4r^2 + h^2)$.
7. $Ak^2 = 924\frac{1}{3}$ in.⁴.
8. 2944 in.⁴.
9. 42·15 in.⁴.
11. $m_1 = 40{\cdot}6$ lb., $m_2 = 159{\cdot}4$ lb.; 0·714 ft.

Exercise 85.

1. $\frac{1}{2}wab^2$.
2. $\frac{1}{2}wab(2c + b)$.
3. $\frac{1}{2}wab(2c + b\sin\theta)$.
4. 628·75π lb. wt.
5. 162·8 lb. wt.
6. 25·3 ft.

Exercise 86.

5. $\frac{5d}{7}$.

Exercise 87.

2. Upper = 466·5 lb. wt. Lower = 515·6 lb. wt.
3. 23,676 lb. wt. 4·1 ft. above bottom.
5. (i) 1·5 ft.; (ii) 5·8 ft.

Exercise 88.

1. $\frac{1}{2}a$. 2. $\frac{1}{4}\left(2+\frac{x}{4}\right)$. 4. $(2Ax + B)^{-1}$.
5. x (max.) $= 8$, x (min.) $= 4$; v (min.) $= -3$; acc. (min.) $= -12$ at $t = 0$.
8. $\frac{9}{16}\pi$ ft./min.; 3·75 ft.
10. (*a*) $\frac{1}{45}h^{\frac{1}{2}}$ ft./sec.; (*b*) $90\sqrt{6}$ sec.; (*c*) 64·6 sec. 11. $\frac{8}{15}kH^{\frac{5}{2}}$ cu. ft./min.

Exercise 89.

1. 24 log 2 ml.; 3·1 hr. 3. 2500 log 2 ft. 6. 1·29 sec.
7. $\frac{\log(2)}{2au^2}$. 8. 24,942 m.p.h.

Exercise 90.

3. 60 m.p.h. 10. $x = 3·3$. 12. 223·5 ft.

Exercise 91.

1. (1) $\omega = 3$ always, $\alpha = 0$ always;
(2) $\omega = 4t + 7$, $\alpha = 4$. When $t = 3$, $\omega = 19$, $\alpha = 4$;
(3) 462.
2. 300. 3. 5%. 4. 11·8 lb. ft.
5. 11·9 ft./sec. 6. 18 lb. ft. 8. 10 rad./sec.
9. 1·4 ft. 10. 3·4 revs.; 8·2 sec. 11. 2·49 ft.
12. $\omega^2 = \frac{Pr}{k}(1 - e^{-ax})$, where $a = \frac{2kg}{r(I + Pr^2)}$. 13. 5·01 lb. in.
14. $a\sqrt{\frac{23}{12}}$; $2\pi\sqrt{\left(\frac{131a}{36g}\right)}$.
15. $x = \frac{l}{2n}\left\{\sqrt{\left(1+\frac{4n}{3}\right)} - 1\right\}$; $n = 0$, $T = 2\pi\sqrt{\frac{2l}{3g}}$; $n \to \infty$, $T = 2\pi\sqrt{\frac{x}{g}}$.

Exercise 92.

1. $y = -\frac{2}{x} - \frac{3}{2x^2} + C$. 2. $y = \frac{1}{a}\log(ax + b) + C$.
3. $y = 3 \log \sin x + C$. 4. $a = 3$. 5. $y = x^2 + 1$.
6. $x = \frac{1}{2}\log(3y^2 + 2y) + C$.
7. $x = \frac{1}{2}\log(3y^2 + 2) + \frac{1}{\sqrt{6}}\tan^{-1}\left(y\sqrt{\frac{3}{2}}\right) + C$. 8. $i = i_0e^{-Rt/L}$.
9. $q = ECe^{-t/RC}$. 12. $3y^2 = x^3 + 11$. 13. $y = \frac{1}{2}x^2 + \frac{8}{x} + 1$.
14. $y = 2x^2 + \frac{3}{4}x^4 + 2$. 15. $s = -2\log t - \frac{5}{t} + \frac{3}{2}t^2 + At + B$.
16. $s = \frac{1}{20}t^5 + \frac{7}{12}t^4 - \frac{7}{12}t$. 17. $\theta = 2 - 2\frac{1}{4}t + t^2 - \frac{1}{12}t^3$.
18. $y = \frac{1}{6x^2} + \frac{9}{8}x + \frac{65}{24}$. 19. $6EIy = W(3lx^2 - x^3)$.
20. $24EIy = w(6l^2x^2 - 4lx^3 + x^4)$.

Exercise 93.

1. $2y^2 + \frac{1}{2}\cos 2x = C$. 2. $\cos y = K \cos x$.
3. $\sqrt{1 + x^2} + \sqrt{1 + y^2} = C$. 4. $\sqrt{1 + y^2} = Ax$.
5. $q = EC(1 - e^{-t/RC})$. 6. $y = Axe^x$.
7. $\sin^{-1} y = \sin^{-1} x + C$. 9. $Q = \frac{1}{2}k\pi a^4$.

Exercise 94.

1. $y = Ae^{3x} + Be^{-3x}$. 2. $y = Ae^{5x} + Be^{-4x}$. 3. $y = Ae^{-2x} + Be^{-3x}$.
4. $x = Ae^{3t} + Be^{-t}$. 5. $10x = 7e^{5t} + 3e^{-5t}$. 6. $2r = 9e^{-\theta} - 5e^{-3\theta}$.

Exercise 95.

1. $y = e^{-\frac{1}{2}x}\left[A\cos\frac{\sqrt{3}}{2}x + B\sin\frac{\sqrt{3}}{2}x\right]$. 2. $y = A\cos 2x + B\sin 2x$.
3. $x = e^t(L\cos 2t + M\sin 2t)$. 4. $y = (A + Bx)e^{-2x}$.

5. $x = e^{at}(\mathrm{A} \cos bt + \mathrm{B} \sin bt)$.

6. $\mathrm{Q} = \mathrm{A} \cos \frac{t}{\sqrt{\mathrm{LC}}} + \mathrm{B} \sin \frac{t}{\sqrt{\mathrm{LC}}}$.

7. $y = 3e^{-2x} \sin 5x$.

8. $x = 2e^{-2t} \sin t$.

9. $x = 2 \cos 4t + \frac{5}{2} \sin 4t$.

10. $a = 10$ ft. $\mathrm{T} = \frac{2\pi}{5}$ sec.

11. $\mathrm{T} = \frac{2\pi}{3}$ sec. $a = \frac{1}{3}\sqrt{65}$ ft.

13. $e^{-\mathrm{R}t/2\mathrm{L}}(\mathrm{A} + \mathrm{B}t)$; $2e^{-\mathrm{R}t/2\mathrm{L}}\left(1 + \frac{\mathrm{R}t}{\mathrm{L}}\right)$.

Exercise 96.

4. $\frac{1}{4}l$ and $\frac{3}{4}l$; $\frac{\mathrm{W}l^3}{192\mathrm{EI}}$.

5. $\frac{3}{8}wl$; $x = 0, \frac{3}{4}l$. (Origin at supported end.)

6. $\frac{19wa^4}{24\mathrm{EI}}$.

7. $\frac{7wl^4}{1152\mathrm{EI}}$.

9. $\frac{1}{\mathrm{EI}}\left\{\frac{\mathrm{W}l^3}{48} + \frac{5wl^4}{384}\right\}$.

10. $\frac{3wl}{8} - \frac{3\mathrm{EI}d}{l^3}$.

11. 23·75 tons.

Exercise 97.

2. $\mathrm{A} = -6, \mathrm{B} = 1$.

3. $\frac{6}{7}$.

4. $\frac{2}{3}x + \frac{5}{9}$.

5. $-\frac{1}{5}e^{3x}$.

6. $\frac{4}{5} \cos 2x$.

7. $y = \mathrm{A}e^{-2x} + \mathrm{B}e^{-x} + \frac{1}{6}e^{-4x}$.

8. $x = \mathrm{A}e^{-2t} + \mathrm{B}e^{-3t} - \frac{2}{234}(15 \cos 3t + 3 \sin 3t)$.

9. $x = e^{-2t}(\mathrm{A} \cos 5t + \mathrm{B} \sin 5t) - \frac{3}{425}(16 \cos 4t - 13 \sin 4t)$.

10. $y = e^{4t}(\mathrm{A} \cos 3t + \mathrm{B} \sin 3t) - \frac{7}{40} \sin 5t + 2$.

11. $x = \mathrm{A}e^{-5t} + \mathrm{B}e^{t} - \frac{1}{5}t^2 - \frac{23}{25}t - \frac{227}{125}$.

12. $y = e^{3x}(\mathrm{A} \cos x + \mathrm{B} \sin x) + 2 - \frac{1}{2}e^{2x}$.

13. $y = \frac{2}{3}e^{-x} - \frac{3}{4}e^{-2x} + \frac{1}{12}e^{2x}$.

14. $y = -\frac{2}{3} \cos x + \sin x + 1 - \frac{1}{3} \cos 2x$.

15. $y = \frac{61}{50}e^{4x} + \frac{36}{50}e^{-x} + \frac{1}{50}(3 \cos 2x - 4 \sin 2x)$.

16. $x = -\frac{3}{2}e^{-\frac{1}{3}t} + \frac{7}{2}e^{t} - 2t + 5$.

17. $y = -2e^{\frac{3\pi}{4}}e^{-3x} \sin 4x + 2e^{3x}$.

18. (ii) $x = e^{-2t}(\frac{3}{4} \cos t + \frac{5}{4} \sin t) + \frac{1}{4}(\sin t + \cos t)$.

(iii) $x = \frac{1}{2\sqrt{2}} \sin \left(t + \frac{\pi}{4}\right)$.

19. $x = 3e^{-t} - \frac{7}{4}e^{-2t} + \frac{3}{2}t - \frac{5}{4}$.

$\dot{x} = -3e^{-2} + \frac{7}{2}e^{-4} + \frac{3}{2} = 1{\cdot}16$ ft./sec.

$\ddot{x} = 3e^{-2} - 7e^{-4} = 0{\cdot}28$ ft./sec.^{2}

20. $y = \frac{w\mathrm{EI}}{\mathrm{P}^2}\left[\cos nx + \tan\left(\frac{nl}{2}\right) \sin nx\right] + \frac{w}{2\mathrm{P}}\left[x^2 - lx - \frac{2\mathrm{EI}}{\mathrm{P}}\right]$;

$\frac{w\mathrm{EI}}{\mathrm{P}^2}\left[\sec\left(\frac{nl}{2}\right) - 1\right] - \frac{wl^2}{8\mathrm{P}}$.

Exercise 98.

1. $y = \mathrm{A} + \mathrm{B}e^{-4x} + \frac{3}{2}x$.

2. $y = \mathrm{A}e^{2x} + \mathrm{B}e^{-x} + xe^{2x}$.

3. $x = \mathrm{A} \cos 3t + \mathrm{M} \sin 3t + \frac{2}{3}t \sin 3t$.

4. $y = 3\left(\frac{\pi}{4} - 1\right) \cos x + 2 \sin x - \frac{2}{3}x \cos x$.

5. $x = e^{-2t}(t + \frac{1}{2}t^2)$.

6. $x = a \cos wt + \frac{b}{w} \sin wt + \frac{\mathrm{A}}{2w}t \sin wt$.

7. $\mathrm{V} = \mathrm{A} \cos nt + \mathrm{B} \sin nt + \frac{\mathrm{E}_0}{2n\mathrm{LC}}t \sin nt$.

9. $x = \mathrm{A}e^{-2t} + \mathrm{B}e^{-t}$.

10. $x = (\mathrm{A} + \mathrm{B}t)e^{-t} + \frac{1}{2} \sin t$.

Exercise 99.

1. (*a*) 68·88; (*b*) 93·1.

2. (*a*) $x = 76$, $\sigma = 3{\cdot}227$; (*b*) $\bar{x} = 84$, $\sigma = 3{\cdot}416$.

3. (i) 33·9; (ii) 1·51.

4. 3·24; 0·24.

5. 1380 hours; 120·3.

10. (*a*) 50, 20; (*b*) 21, 43, 61, 74.

11. $\bar{x} = 2$, $\sigma^2 = 0{\cdot}8$.

12. $\bar{x} = 0{\cdot}1$, $\sigma^2 = 0{\cdot}01$.

Exercise 100.

1. (*a*) 1/6; (*b*) 1/2; (*c*) 1/3; (*d*) 1/3. 2. (*a*) 1/4; (*b*) 1/2.
3. (*a*) 2/5; (*b*) 3/5; (*c*) 1/5. 4. (*a*) 1/8; (*b*) 3/8; (*c*) 7/8.
5. 25/216. 6. (*a*) 6; (*b*) 5; (*c*) 1/6; (*d*) 5/36; (*e*) 11/36.
7. (*a*) 25; (*b*) 13; (*c*) 13/25. 8. (*a*) 1/210; (*b*) 3/7; (*c*) 37/42.
9. (*a*) 0·128; (*b*) 0·48; (*c*) 0·384. 10. (*a*) 1140; (*b*) 171; (*c*) 57/380.
11. 117/495. 12. 216/625.
13. (*a*) 1/15; (*b*) 7/15. 14. 18/35; 144/343. 15. 45/91.
16. 91/228; 35/76; 5/38; 1/114.
Sum is unity, since one of these events is certain to occur.
17. (*a*) 323/1827; (*b*) 760/1827; (*c*) 744/1827.
18. 0·362. 19. (*a*) 0·08208; (*b*) 0·41.

Exercise 101.

1. (*a*) $p_1(1 - p_2)$; (*b*) $p_2(1 - p_1)$; (*c*) p_1p_2.
Chance is (*a*) + (*b*) + (*c*) $= p_1 + p_2 - p_1p_2$.
The given form is 1 − (chance problem is not solved).
2. (*a*) p_1p_2; (*b*) $p_1(1 - p_2)$; (*c*) $(1 - p_1)p_2$; (*d*) $(1 - p_1)(1 - p_2)$;
(*e*) 1 = chance of a certain event.
3. $1 - (0{\cdot}96)^4 = 0{\cdot}151$. 4. $7!\,4!/11! = 1/330$.
5. (*a*) 1/4; (*b*) 1/2; (*c*) 21/50. 6. (*a*) $1/(6)^3$; (*b*) 25/72; (*c*) 91/216.
7. (*a*) $(1 - p)^{14}$; (*b*) $2[1 - (1 - p)^7](1 - p)^7$; (*c*) $[1 - (1 - p)^7]^2$.
8. (*a*) 5/12; (*b*) 7/12. 9. 23/60. 10. 207/625.
11. 1/4. 12. 4. 13. (*a*) 1/7; (*b*) 4/7.
14. (*a*) 0·000125; (*b*) 0·007125; (*c*) 0·135375; (*d*) 0·857375.
15. ${}_nC_rp^rq^{n-r}$; 0·196. 16. exp (− 1). 17. 0·94. 18. 0·3634.
19. (*a*) $1 - p^2$; (*b*) $1 - 4p^3 + 3p^4$; (*c*) $0 < p < \frac{1}{3}$; (*d*) $\frac{1}{3} < p < 1$.

Exercise 102.

1. (*a*) 3·5; (*b*) 120/49. 2. 0·867P. 3. No; $3\frac{1}{3}$%.
4. £1/6. 5. (*a*) 3·37; (*b*) £9·558. 6. £6.

Exercise 103.

1. (*a*) 0·9606; (*b*) 0·0388; (*c*) 0·9994. 2. 200; 100. 3. 270; 15.
4. (*a*) 0·0083; (*b*) 0·2803. 5. 1. 6. 1.
7. (*a*) 0·349; (*b*) 0·387; (*c*) 0·194; (*d*) 0·07; (*e*) 1. 8. 323.
10. $n = 180$, $p = 1/3$, $q = 2/3$. 11. $p = 0{\cdot}2575$; 61, 84, 44, 10, 1.
12. 0·298. 13. ${}_{10}C_2p^8q^2 + {}_{10}C_1p^9q + p^{10}$. 14. $(0{\cdot}90)^{10} = 0{\cdot}349$; 44.
15. 0·604; No. 40% of product is rejected although exactly to specification.
16. (*a*) 0·814; (*b*) 0·663. 17. 0·7198.

Exercise 104.

1. $1/\pi$; 1/2. 2. $1/c$; $1/c^2$.
3. A = 15/1024; $\bar{x} = 16/7$; $\sigma = 2\sqrt{6}/7$.
4. A = 2·314; $\bar{x} = 0{\cdot}343$; $\sigma = 0{\cdot}418$. 5. $\pi/10$.
6. $a = 1/6$, $b = 1/18$, $c = -1/72$. 8. 105. 9. $a = 1/3$, $b = 2$.
11. (*a*) 0·1093; (*b*) 0·1150; (*c*) 0·9565.
12. $\bar{x} = 21{\cdot}6$, $\sigma = 1{\cdot}8$; $y = 11{\cdot}08 \exp\left[-\dfrac{(x - 21{\cdot}6)^2}{6{\cdot}48}\right]$.
13. 0, 2, 4, 9, 14, 19, 19, 15, 10, 5, 2, 1.
14. $\bar{x} = 165{\cdot}50$, $\sigma = 14{\cdot}98$. 1, 3·5, 10·5, 20·5, 26·5, 21·5, 11·5, 4, 1.
15. 0·1, 1·2, 12·0, 55·1, 114·2, 108·4, 45·4, 8·7, 0·8. 16. 1·423; 114·34.
17. (*a*) 0·242; (*b*) 0·8413; (*c*) 0·5328. 18. $\bar{x} = 5{\cdot}182$, $\sigma = 4{\cdot}124$ mm.; 73·7%.
19. $\bar{x} = 32{\cdot}093$, $\sigma = 0{\cdot}0839$; 13·35%; 32·138 oz.
21. 0·50202 in.; 9·988*d*. 22. 10·038 oz. 23. 100·6.

Exercise 105.

1. (*a*) 0·226; (*b*) 0·528. 2. 0·0154. 3. 0·097 (·0955 exactly).
4. 0·40 (0·3712 exactly). 5. 0·964. 8. (*a*) 231; (*b*) 243.

Exercise 106.

1. 3 min. 43·8 sec.; 2·48 sec.; 0·063. 2. $50 \pm 6{\cdot}62$; $100 \pm 9{\cdot}36$.
3. 6·5%; 0·0012. 5. 472,400 oz.; 38,158 oz.; $13{\cdot}18 \pm 2{\cdot}09$ tons.
6. 29,588 ohms. 7. 13%. 9. 20·8225 oz. 11. 79·6–80·4%.

MISCELLANEOUS EXERCISES

Section A

A1. 6645 years.
2. 2·4400, 0·4098; 1·0151, 1·4249; $x = 0{\cdot}5999$.
3. 9·999. 4. (*a*) 1·5464; (*b*) 463·8.
5. 54·6°. 6. $a = 5{\cdot}62$, $n = 1{\cdot}16$.
7. (*a*) $\dfrac{(1 + 2x - x^2)}{(1 - x)^2}$. 8. (*a*) -2ω; (*b*) $v = 2{\cdot}94$.
9. (i) $2x^3e^{-2x}(2 - x)$; (ii) $\dfrac{14x}{(x^2 + 1)^2}$; (iii) $2 \operatorname{sh} x \operatorname{ch} x$; $-\dfrac{1}{2\sqrt{2}}t^{-\frac{3}{2}}$.
A10. (*a*) $61 \sin (100t + 0{\cdot}61)$; (*b*) 27.
11. (i) $x(1 + 2 \log x)$; (ii) $\dfrac{(1 + x)}{2\sqrt{x}(1 - x)^2}$; (iii) $6x^3(2x^4 + 1)^{-\frac{1}{4}}$;
(iv) $-4 \cos^3 x \sin x$.
12. (*a*) $\frac{4}{3}$, $\frac{1}{3} \log_e 5$; (*b*) $\frac{3}{2}\pi$; (*c*) $y = 100 \operatorname{ch}\left(\dfrac{x}{100}\right)$.
13. (i, -7; (ii) $\frac{1}{2}$; (iii) $-x \cos x + \sin x + C$; (iv) 0·001.
14. (i) $\frac{1}{6}$; (ii) $\frac{1}{6} \log_e 10$; (iii) $xe^x + C$. 15. $\dfrac{2}{\pi}$; $\dfrac{1}{2} : \dfrac{1}{\sqrt{2}}$.
16. (*a*) 0·180; (*b*) $\left(\dfrac{2k}{b}\right)^{\frac{1}{2}}$. 17. 6·8 lb.
18. $\frac{7}{9}$ in.; 29π cu. in. 19. (*a*) 3·3 in.; (*b*) 299·3 in.^{4}.
A20. (i) $s = \sin 2t$; (ii) $-\dfrac{1}{y} = \log (1 + \theta)$; (iii) $v = \pm\sqrt{\mu(a^2 - x^2)}$.
21. (i) $\omega = \pm 2\sqrt{\theta + 4}$; (ii) $y = e^{3x}$; $y = \dfrac{wx^2}{48EI}(3l^2 - 2x^2)$.
22. $y = A \cos ux + B \sin ux \left(u^2 = \dfrac{P}{EI}\right)$.
23. (i) $2\frac{2}{3}$ sq. in.; (ii) $\frac{7}{8}$ in.; (iii) $\dfrac{26\pi}{3}$ cu. in.

Section B

B1. (*a*) $\dfrac{4 \sin 2x}{(1 + \cos 2x)^2}$; (*b*) $-\dfrac{(y^2 + 4xy)}{2(xy + x^2)}$.
2. (*a*) (i) $\dfrac{x^2(3a^2 - 4x^2)}{(a^2 - x^2)^{\frac{1}{2}}}$; (ii) $\dfrac{1}{(x^2 + 3x + 2)^{\frac{1}{2}}}$; (iii) $\dfrac{308}{243}$.
3. (*a*) (i) $-e^{-3x}(2 \sin 2x + 3 \cos 2x)$;
(ii) $6x^2 \log \dfrac{(3x - 2)}{(7 - 4x)} + \dfrac{26x^3}{(3x - 2)(7 - 4x)}$.
4. (*a*) (i) $-\dfrac{(2 \sin 2x + 2x^2 \sin 2x + 2x \cos 2x)}{(1 + x^2)^2}$; (ii) $\dfrac{5}{2(2 + 3x)(3 + 2x)}$;
(iii) $\dfrac{b}{\sqrt{(a + bx)^2 + 1}}$.
(*b*) $A = -\frac{24}{2257}$, $B = \frac{41}{2257}$.

5. 0·77.

7. $h = \frac{1}{2}r\sqrt{\frac{k}{l}}$, $g = p\sqrt{kl}$; 38·58.

8. (i) $\frac{1}{2}x \sin 2x + \frac{1}{4}\cos 2x + C$; (ii) $\frac{1}{2}\sin^{-1}\left(\frac{2x}{7}\right) + C$;

(iii) $\frac{1}{3}\tan^{-1}\left(\frac{x+2}{3}\right) + C$; (iv) $\frac{3}{5}\log(x+1) + \frac{2}{5}\log(x-4) + C$.

9. (a) (i) $\frac{1}{2}\text{ch}^{-1}\left(\frac{2x}{5}\right) + C$; (ii) $\log_e\left(\frac{4}{3}\right)$.

(b) 0·4 tons.

B10. $\ddot{x} = -\omega^2 r\cos\omega t - \frac{\omega^2 r^2}{l}\cos 2\omega t$.

11. $x = 0{\cdot}578$.

13. $A = D^2(\sin 2\theta - \cos^2\theta)$.

14. $\frac{8}{3}a^2$; $\frac{32}{3}\pi a^3$.

16. $y^2 = 500x$; 51·2 ft.; 8000/3 sq. ft.

17. π; 3π.

18. $x = 2$ (max.), $x = 5$ (min.), $x = 3\frac{1}{2}$ (inflex^n), area = 31.

19. $95{\cdot}1\pi$; $\bar{x} = 2{\cdot}5$, $\bar{y} = 0$.

B20. 1·77.

21. $814{\cdot}9\pi$.

22. (a) $\frac{wl^5}{720EI}$. (b) (i) $x = \frac{l}{2}$; (ii) $\frac{l(3 \pm \sqrt{3})}{6}$.

23. 357π cu. in.; 1·44 in.

24. 2·13; $8{\cdot}71\pi$.

25. $\bar{x} = 2{\cdot}1$, $\bar{y} = 2{\cdot}4$.

26. (b) 580·4 lb. in.^{2}.

27. 9 ft.; 375 lb./ft.

28. 128 lb./cu. ft.

29. (a) $\frac{V_0 I_0}{2\pi}[3\pi + 8]$; (b) $30\sqrt{2}$.

B30. $\frac{3\pi}{2\sqrt{2}}\frac{\sqrt{E_1^2 + E_3^2}}{(3E_1 + E_3)}$.

31. (a) R^2; (b) $\sqrt{13}(\cos 56{\cdot}3° - j\sin 56{\cdot}3°)$; (c) $0{\cdot}174 + j0{\cdot}168$;
(d) $\cos^4\theta - 6\cos^2\theta\sin^2\theta + \sin^4\theta$.

32. (a) $2{\cdot}55e^{j(0{\cdot}88)}$; (b) $25\{\cos(106°\,16') - j\sin(106°\,16')\}$.

33. (a) $y = Ae^{-2x} + Be^{-3x}$; (b) $y = \frac{Wx^2}{48EI}(2x - 3l)(x - l)$.

34. $i = i_0 e^{-Rt/L}$; 0·55 sec.

35. (a) $y = 6e^{-x} - 3e^{-2x}$; (b) $x = 4(\cos 2t + \sin 2t)$.

Section C

C1. $-6\sin 3x$; $xe^{-3x}(2 - 3x)$; $\frac{4x}{(x^2+1)^2}$; cosec x.

2. $-\omega^2 s$.

3. $2xe^{-2x}(1 - x)$; $-\frac{2}{(x^2 - 1)}$; $-\frac{\sin 2x}{\sqrt{\cos 2x}}$; $x\frac{d^2v}{dx^2} + 2\frac{dv}{dx}$.

4. $\sec x\tan x$; $-\frac{2}{(1 - x^2)}$; $\frac{1}{x\sqrt{x^2 - 1}}$; $\sqrt{1 - z^2}\frac{d\omega}{dz}$; $-z\frac{d\omega}{dz} + (1 - z^2)\frac{d^2\omega}{dz^2}$

5. Depth 2·5 ft.; length 5 ft.

6. $\pi\sqrt{\frac{8}{3}}$.

7. 24° 28′.

8. 0·58R; $0{\cdot}128\pi R^3$.

9. (i) Min. at 0° and 180°. Max. at $180° \pm \cos^{-1}(\frac{3}{5})$; (ii) 114·59°.

C10. 2·18.

11. 0·860.

12. 0·567.

13. (a) $\frac{1}{2}x^2 - x + 3\log(x + 2) + C$;

(b) $\frac{1}{2}\log(x^2 + x + 1) + \sqrt{3}\tan^{-1}\left(\frac{2x+1}{\sqrt{3}}\right) + D$;

(c) $\sqrt{(x^2 + x + 1)} + \frac{3}{2}\text{sh}^{-1}\left(\frac{2x+1}{\sqrt{3}}\right) + E$; 1·142.

14. (i) $\sin\theta - \frac{2}{3}\sin^3\theta + \frac{1}{5}\sin^5\theta + D$; (ii) $\frac{2}{5}(1 + x)^{\frac{5}{2}} - \frac{2}{3}(1 + x)^{\frac{3}{2}} + E$;

(iii) $-2e^{-\frac{1}{2}x}(x^2 + 4x + 8) + C$; (iv) $\log\left(\tanh\frac{u}{2}\right) + F$.

15. (i) 0·347; (ii) 0·119; (iii) 0·574.

16. $\cot^{-1}\left[\frac{\cos x}{B + A\sin x}\right] + C$. [$A = \sec\alpha$, $B = \tan\alpha$.]

17. $\frac{1}{6}$; $\bar{x} = 6{\cdot}4$, $\bar{y} = 2{\cdot}5$.

18. $x = -2, \frac{1}{2}, 2$; 0·386.

19. (i) $\frac{x}{a} - \frac{x^3}{3a^3} + \frac{x^5}{5a^5} \ldots, \left|\frac{x}{a}\right| < 1$; (ii) $\frac{\pi}{2} - \frac{a}{x} + \frac{a^3}{3x^3} - \frac{a^5}{5x^5} \ldots, \left|\frac{a}{x}\right| < 1.$

C20. $\frac{dy}{dx} = \frac{1}{2+2x+x^2}$. $y = \frac{\pi}{4} + \frac{1}{2}\left[x - \frac{1}{2}x^2 + \frac{1}{6}x^3 - \frac{1}{20}x^5\right]$; 0·8330.

21. $\frac{Ax}{6l}(l^2 - x^2)$. 22. 0·201. 23. $\frac{3(b^2 - x^2)}{2b^2}$.

24. $1 + \frac{1}{2}\theta^2 + \frac{5}{24}\theta^4 + \ldots$ 25. 0·6932. 26. 1·0538.

27. $\rho = 0{\cdot}279$; (0·33, 0·85).

28. $\frac{e^{-at}(-a \cos bt + b \sin bt)}{(a^2 + b^2)}$; $\frac{mp^3V^2(1 - e^{-2k\pi/p})}{8\pi k(k^2 + p^2)}$.

C30. $y = 2x^3 - 8x^2 + 8x + 1$.

32. $\frac{a \sin a}{a}$; $\frac{4a}{3\pi}$; (i) $2\pi a(b\pi + 2a) + 4\pi ab$; (ii) $\frac{\pi a^2(3b\pi + 4a)}{3}$.

33. $152{\cdot}6\pi$ cu. in.

34. Centre $x = -\frac{\beta}{a^2}$; period $\frac{2\pi}{a}$; amp. $\frac{(\beta^2 - a^2\gamma)^{\frac{1}{2}}}{a^2}$.

35. 27·5 ft./sec., 605 ft./sec.². 38. $\bar{x} = 3{\cdot}57$; $\sigma = 1{\cdot}84$.

INDEX

(The numbers refer to pages)

TABLES

THE AREA UNDER THE NORMAL CURVE

(to the left of the ordinate at Z)

$$\phi(Z) = \frac{1}{\sqrt{(2\pi)}} \int_{-\infty}^{Z} e^{-\frac{x^2}{2}}\, dx, \text{ where } Z = \frac{x - \bar{x}}{\sigma}, (x \geqslant \bar{x})$$

[For negative values, $\phi(-Z) = 1 - \phi(Z)$]

Z	0·00	0·01	0·02	0·03	0·04	0·05	0·06	0·07	0·08	0·09
0·0	0·5000	0·5040	0·5080	0·5120	0·5160	0·5199	0·5239	0·5279	0·5319	0·5359
0·1	0·5398	0·5438	0·5478	0·5517	0·5557	0·5596	0·5636	0·5675	0·5714	0·5753
0·2	0·5793	0·5832	0·5871	0·5910	0·5948	0·5987	0·6026	0·6064	0·6103	0·6141
0·3	0·6179	0·6217	0·6255	0·6293	0·6331	0·6368	0·6406	0·6443	0·6480	0·6517
0·4	0·6554	0·6591	0·6628	0·6664	0·6700	0·6736	0·6772	0·6808	0·6844	0·6879
0·5	0·6915	0·6950	0·6985	0·7019	0·7054	0·7088	0·7123	0·7157	0·7190	0·7224
0·6	0·7257	0·7291	0·7324	0·7357	0·7389	0·7422	0·7454	0·7486	0·7517	0·7549
0·7	0·7580	0·7611	0·7642	0·7673	0·7703	0·7734	0·7764	0·7794	0·7823	0·7852
0·8	0·7881	0·7910	0·7939	0·7967	0·7995	0·8023	0·8051	0·8078	0·8106	0·8133
0·9	0·8159	0·8186	0·8212	0·8238	0·8264	0·8289	0·8315	0·8340	0·8365	0·8389
1·0	0·8413	0·8438	0·8461	0·8485	0·8508	0·8531	0·8554	0·8577	0·8599	0·8621
1·1	0·8643	0·8665	0·8686	0·8708	0·8729	0·8749	0·8770	0·8790	0·8810	0·8830
1·2	0·8849	0·8869	0·8888	0·8907	0·8925	0·8944	0·8962	0·8980	0·8997	0·90147
1·3	0·90320	0·90490	0·90658	0·90824	0·90988	0·91149	0·91309	0·91466	0·91621	0·91774
1·4	0·91924	0·92073	0·92220	0·92364	0·92507	0·92647	0·92785	0·92922	0·93056	0·93189
1·5	0·93319	0·93448	0·93574	0·93699	0·93822	0·93943	0·94062	0·94179	0·94295	0·94408
1·6	0·94520	0·94630	0·94738	0·94845	0·94950	0·95053	0·95154	0·95254	0·95352	0·95449
1·7	0·95543	0·95637	0·95728	0·95818	0·95907	0·95994	0·96080	0·96164	0·96246	0·96327
1·8	0·96407	0·96485	0·96562	0·96638	0·96712	0·96784	0·96856	0·96926	0·96995	0·97062
1·9	0·97128	0·97193	0·97257	0·97320	0·97381	0·97441	0·97500	0·97558	0·97615	0·97670

2·0	0·97725	0·97778	0·97831	0·97882	0·97932	0·97982	0·98030	0·98077	0·98124	0·98169
2·1	0·98214	0·98257	0·98300	0·98341	0·98382	0·98422	0·98461	0·98500	0·98537	0·98574
2·2	0·98610	0·98645	0·98679	0·98713	0·98745	0·98778	0·98809	0·98840	0·98870	0·98899
2·3	0·98928	0·98956	0·98983	0·9^{2}0097	0·9^{2}0358	0·9^{2}0613	0·9^{2}0863	0·9^{2}1106	0·9^{2}1344	0·9^{2}1576
2·4	0·9^{2}1802	0·9^{2}2024	0·9^{2}2240	0·9^{2}2451	0·9^{2}2656	0·9^{2}2857	0·9^{2}3053	0·9^{2}3244	0·9^{2}3431	0·9^{2}3613
2·5	0·9^{2}3790	0·9^{2}3963	0·9^{2}4132	0·9^{2}4297	0·9^{2}4457	0·9^{2}4614	0·9^{2}4766	0·9^{2}4915	0·9^{2}5060	0·9^{2}5201
2·6	0·9^{2}5339	0·9^{2}5473	0·9^{2}5604	0·9^{2}5731	0·9^{2}5855	0·9^{2}5975	0·9^{2}6093	0·9^{2}6207	0·9^{2}6319	0·9^{2}6427
2·7	0·9^{2}6533	0·9^{2}6636	0·9^{2}6736	0·9^{2}6833	0·9^{2}6928	0·9^{2}7020	0·9^{2}7110	0·9^{2}7197	0·9^{2}7282	0·9^{2}7365
2·8	0·9^{2}7445	0·9^{2}7523	0·9^{2}7599	0·9^{2}7673	0·9^{2}7744	0·9^{2}7814	0·9^{2}7882	0·9^{2}7948	0·9^{2}8012	0·9^{2}8074
2·9	0·9^{2}8134	0·9^{2}8193	0·9^{2}8250	0·9^{2}8305	0·9^{2}8359	0·9^{2}8411	0·9^{2}8462	0·9^{2}8511	0·9^{2}8559	0·9^{2}8605
3·0	0·9^{2}8650	0·9^{2}8694	0·9^{2}8736	0·9^{2}8777	0·9^{2}8817	0·9^{2}8856	0·9^{2}8893	0·9^{2}8930	0·9^{2}8965	0·9^{2}8999
3·1	0·9^{3}0324	0·9^{3}0646	0·9^{3}0957	0·9^{3}1260	0·9^{3}1553	0·9^{3}1836	0·9^{3}2112	0·9^{3}2378	0·9^{3}2636	0·9^{3}2886
3·2	0·9^{3}3129	0·9^{3}3363	0·9^{3}3590	0·9^{3}3810	0·9^{3}4024	0·9^{3}4230	0·9^{3}4429	0·9^{3}4623	0·9^{3}4810	0·9^{3}4991
3·3	0·9^{3}5166	0·9^{3}5335	0·9^{3}5499	0·9^{3}5658	0·8^{3}5811	0·9^{3}5959	0·9^{3}6103	0·9^{3}6242	0·9^{3}6376	0·9^{3}6505
3·4	0·9^{3}6631	0·9^{3}6752	0·9^{3}6869	0·9^{3}6982	0·9^{3}7091	0·9^{3}7197	0·9^{3}7299	0·9^{3}7398	0·9^{3}7493	0·9^{3}7585

Percentage points

$100\phi(Z)$	50	75	90	95	97·5	99·0	99·5	99·9	99·95
Z	0·0000	0·6745	1·2816	1·6449	1·9600	2·3263	2·5758	3·0902	3·2905

Based on Fisher and Yates, *Statistical Tables*, by kind permission of the authors and the publishers Oliver and Boyd.

LOGARITHMS OF FACTORIALS

n	$\text{Log}_{10} n\,!$	n	$\text{Log}_{10} n\,!$	n	$\text{Log}_{10} n\,!$	n	$\text{Log}_{10} n\,!$	n	$\text{Log}_{10} n\,!$
		20	18·38612	**40**	47·91165	**60**	81·92017	**80**	118·85473
1	0·00000	**21**	19·70834	**41**	49·52443	**61**	83·70550	**81**	120·76321
2	0·30103	**22**	21·05077	**42**	51·14768	**62**	85·49790	**82**	122·67703
3	0·77815	**23**	22·41249	**43**	52·78115	**63**	87·29724	**83**	124·59610
4	1·38021	**24**	23·79271	**44**	54·42460	**64**	89·10342	**84**	126·52038
5	2·07918	**25**	25·19065	**45**	56·07781	**65**	90·91633	**85**	128·44980
6	2·85733	**26**	26·60562	**46**	57·74057	**66**	92·73587	**86**	130·38430
7	3·70243	**27**	28·03698	**47**	59·41267	**67**	94·56195	**87**	132·32382
8	4·60552	**28**	29·48414	**48**	61·09391	**68**	96·39446	**88**	134·26830
9	5·55976	**29**	30·94654	**49**	62·78410	**69**	98·23331	**89**	136·21769
10	6·55976	**30**	32·42366	**50**	64·48307	**70**	100·07841	**90**	138·17194
11	7·60116	**31**	33·91502	**51**	66·19065	**71**	101·92966	**91**	140·13098
12	8·68034	**32**	35·42017	**52**	67·90665	**72**	103·78700	**92**	142·09477
13	9·79428	**33**	36·93869	**53**	69·63092	**73**	105·65032	**93**	144·06325
14	10·94041	**34**	38·47016	**54**	71·36332	**74**	107·51955	**94**	146·03638
15	12·11650	**35**	40·01423	**55**	73·10368	**75**	109·39461	**95**	148·01410
16	13·32062	**36**	41·57054	**56**	74·85187	**76**	111·27543	**96**	149·99637
17	14·55107	**37**	43·13874	**57**	76·60774	**77**	113·16192	**97**	151·98314
18	15·80634	**38**	44·71852	**58**	78·37117	**78**	115·05401	**98**	153·97437
19	17·08509	**39**	46·30959	**59**	80·14202	**79**	116·95164	**99**	155·97000
20	18·38612							**100**	157·97000

For larger values of n use Stirling's formula

$$n\,! \simeq \sqrt{(2\pi n)}\,.\left(\frac{n}{e}\right)^n$$

The student will find the following sets of tables useful.

(1) *Practical Five-Figure Tables.* Attwood (gives the values of $n\,!$ in addition to those of $e^{-x}\,.\,\log_e x$ and the usual tables).

(2) *Advanced Five-Figure Tables.* Attwood. (Gives the Normal curve areas and ordinate values amongst many others.)

[Both the above are published by Macmillan.]

(3) *Statistical Tables.* Fisher and Yates. (The standard work for the statistician. Published by Oliver and Boyd. Edinburgh.)